The East India Company at Home, 1757–1857

The East India Company at Home, 1757–1857

Edited by

Margot Finn and Kate Smith

UCLPRESS

First published in 2018 by
UCL Press
University College London
Gower Street
London WC1E 6BT

Available to download free: www.ucl.ac.uk/ucl-press

A CIP catalogue record for this book is available from The British Library.

ISBN: 978–1–78735–028–1 (Hbk.)
ISBN: 978–1–78735–029–8 (Pbk.)
ISBN: 978–1–78735–027–4 (PDF)
ISBN: 978–1–78735–026–7 (epub)
ISBN: 978–1–78735–025–0 (mobi)
ISBN: 978–1–78735–024–3 (html)
DOI: https://doi.org/10.14324/111.9781787350274

Acknowledgements

Any edited volume is a collaborative venture, but this one is perhaps more collaborative in character than is typical. This book is the product of a three-year research project funded (first at Warwick University and then at UCL) by the Leverhulme Trust (grant number RPG-174). Our first thanks are to the Trust for its generosity in supporting *The East India Company at Home, 1757–1857* from September 2011 through August 2014. Drs Helen Clifford and Ellen Filor, fellow members of the project's core team for its duration, were acute, enthusiastic and rollicking interlocutors; Helen not only played a formative role in shaping the original funding application but also connected the project to a capacious spectrum of material culture experts and enthusiasts both inside and outside the academic community. Paul May designed the website, which played a central role in recruiting researchers to our programme: http://blogs.ucl.ac.uk/eicah/. Drs Chris Jeppesen and Yuthika Sharma, who joined *The East India Company at Home* as short-term fellows funded at UCL by the Arts and Humanities Research Council, added new dimensions to both the project's research base and its public engagement work, and were also great fun to have on board. Small awards from the National Association of Decorative & Fine Arts Societies (NADFAS) and the Royal Historical Society allowed us to provide bursaries for our final conference, for which we are most grateful.

From the outset, throughout the project and beyond its period of Leverhulme funding, we enjoyed the support and generosity of a proactive – at times provocative (in the nicest sort of way) – advisory board. Viccy Coltman (Edinburgh University), Marion Moverley (independent historian), Margaret Makepeace (British Library), Lowri Ann Rees (Bangor University), Sue Stronge (V&A), and Keith Sweetmore (then at the North Yorkshire Record Office and now at The National Archives) were sage advisors and good companions on our investigative forays through the archives, collections and built environments of the imperial past.

During the Leverhulme-funded stage of our research, over three hundred researchers – archivists, curators, family and local historians, genealogists, staff and volunteers at stately homes and other heritage sites, as well as academics – joined us as project associates. Both literally and figuratively, they brought to the table a rich spectrum of expertise, manuscript evidence and material objects from their own collections. They asked us questions and offered us answers that significantly changed how we approached the East India Company's history and legacy. Several are represented as authors in this volume. Others to whom we owe particular thanks include Hannah Armstrong, Alison Bennett, Huw Bowen, Deborah Cohen, Oliver Cox, Marietta Crichton Stuart, Brian Crossley, Francesca D'Antonio, Joanna De Groot, Lucy Dow, Stuart Howat, Ruth Larsen, Elizabeth Lenckos, Rosie Llewellyn-Jones, John McAleer, Stephen McDowell, George McGilvary, Andrew MacKillop, Joe Mason, Angela Nutting, Kevin Rogers, Jan Sibthorpe, Doreen Skala, Blair Southerden, Jon Stobart and Spike Sweeting. Jane Wainwright's warmth and hospitality have been appreciated by the core team throughout the project. We have benefitted from comments, suggestions and questions from seminar, lecture and workshop audiences at (among many other places), the British Library, Edinburgh University, Institute of Historical Research, North Yorkshire County Record Office, Southampton University, National Museums Wales, Queen Mary University London, Sheffield Hallam University, Sheffield University and UCL.

Staff at several archives, businesses, heritage sites, museums, private homes and universities that hold Company or cognate collections have been generous in providing us with access and expert knowledge. We are especially grateful to Mr Andan and the late Mr Mand (Gurdwara Sri Guru Singh Sabha, Hounslow), Liesl Barber (Shugborough House), David Beevers (Brighton Pavilion), Penny Brook, Phil Hatfield, Antonia Moon and Richard Morel (British Library), Andrew Bush and Emile de Bruijn (National Trust), Ainsley Cameron and Rosemary Crill (V&A), Judith Quiney (NADFAS), Patrick Conner (Martyn Gregory Gallery), Andrea Davies, Angela Pierce and Margaret Woodall (Belmont House), Judith Evans and Claire Reed (Osterley House, National Trust), Martin Fiennes and Lady Saye and Sele (Broughton Castle), Andrew Grout (Edinburgh University Special Collections), Andrew Renton and Oliver Fairclough (National Museums Wales) Helen Dorey (Soane Museum), Lord Ronaldshay (Aske Hall), the Tamil Community Centre of Hounslow and Dawn Webster (Kiplin Hall).

At Warwick University, where this project was conceived, we derived much support from the History Department, History of Art Department and the Global History & Culture Centre, especially David Arnold, Maxine Berg, Rosie Dias, Anne Gerritsen, Felicia Gottmann, Hanna Hodacs, Maria Luddy, Chris Nierstraz, Liese Perrin and Giorgio Riello. At UCL, we benefitted in particular by support and engagement with Stephen Conway, Laura Cream, Kate Donnington, Nick Draper, Catherine Hall, Rachel Lang, Keith McClelland, Claire Morley and Kristy Warren. An Octagon Gallery exhibition we co-curated at UCL with Claire Dwyer, Ulrich Tiedau and Stephanie van Gemert gave us new perspectives on the challenges of exhibiting the material past. At UCL Press, Lara Speicher's early enthusiasm for the project and Chris Penfold's patient assistance with a volume that has proven complex to produce have been warmly appreciated. After completing her work as Research Fellow on The East India Company at Home project, Kate Smith moved to the History Department at Birmingham University and has benefitted from support and suggestions generously offered by Chris Moores, Sabine Lee, Matt Houlbrook, Tara Hamling, Marga Small, Nick Funke, Richard Cust, Matthew Hilton, Jonathan Willis, Dan Whittingham, Matthew Francis and Manu Sehgal. This book benefits from the work of many hands; responsibility for any errors that have emerged from (or survived the scrutiny of) this collaborative teamwork remains our own.

Margot Finn (UCL)
Kate Smith (Birmingham University)

Contents

Figures and tables xii
Abbreviations xxii
Contributors xxiii

Introduction 1
Margot Finn and Kate Smith

Section 1 The social life of things

1. Prize possession: the 'silver coffer' of Tipu Sultan and the Fraser family 25
Sarah Longair and Cam Sharp Jones

2. Chinese wallpaper: from Canton to country house 39
Helen Clifford

3. Production, purchase, dispossession, recirculation: Anglo-Indian ivory furniture in the British country house 68
Kate Smith

4. 'A jaghire without a crime': the East India Company and the Indian Ocean material world at Osterley, 1700–1800 88
Yuthika Sharma and Pauline Davies

Section 2 Objects, houses, homes and the construction of identities

5. Manly objects? Gendering armorial porcelain wares 113
Kate Smith

6. Fanny Parkes (1794–1875): female collecting and curiosity in India and Britain 131
Joanna Goldsworthy

7. Refashioning house, home and family: Montreal Park, Kent and Touch House, Stirlingshire 153
Margot Finn and Kate Smith

Section 3 The Home Counties: clusters and connections

8. Warfield Park, Berkshire: longing, belonging and the British country house 175
Kate Smith

9. Englefield House, Berkshire: processes, practices and the making of a Company house 191
Kate Smith

10. Swallowfield Park, Berkshire: from royalist bastion to empire home 205
Margot Finn

11. Valentines, the Raymonds and Company material culture 231
Georgina Green

12. Growing up in a Company town: the East India Company presence in South Hertfordshire 251
Chris Jeppesen

Section 4 On the borders: region, nation, globe

13. A fairy palace in Devon: Redcliffe Towers, built by Colonel Robert Smith (1787–1873), Bengal Engineers 277
Diane James

14. Partly after the Chinese manner: 'Chinese' staircases in north-west Wales 298
Rachael Barnwell

15. The intimate trade of Alexander Hall: salmon and slaves in Scotland and Sumatra, c.1745–1765 318
Ellen Filor

16. Connecting Britain and India: General Patrick Duff and Madeira 333
Alistair Mutch

Section 5 Company families and identities: writing history today

17. The career of William Gamul Farmer (1746–1797) in India, 1763–1795 355
Penelope Farmer

18. The Melvill family and India 389
David Williams

19. The Indian seal of Sir Francis Sykes: a tale of two families 412
Sir John Sykes

Conclusion 429
Margot Finn and Kate Smith

Notes 433
Bibliography 486
Index 505

Figures and tables

Figure 1.1	Openwork silver and silver gilt filigree casket, H: 9 cm; W: 12 cm; D: 8.5 cm. 1904,1006.1.a. © The Trustees of the British Museum.	27
Figure 1.2	Family tree of the Fraser family showing casket's passage between family members, designed by C. Sharp Jones.	35
Figure 2.1	Detail of Chinese wallpaper at Felbrigg, Norfolk supplied by the architect James Paine (1717–89) in 1751, as part of the 1749–1761 refurbishment carried out by the owner William Windham II (1717–61). Printed and painted on paper. © National Trust.	43
Figure 2.2	Detail from one of the Chinese wallpapers at Erdigg, Wrexham on the front cover of *Chinese Wallpapers in National Trust Houses* (2014).This paper is in the State Bedroom, named as such in the 1770s, when this paper was hung. © National Trust Images/John Hammond.	44
Figure 2.3	Detail from one of the Chinese wallpapers at Saltram, Devon showing scenes from everyday life, moved from a bedroom on the north east side of the first floor, to the current site in the 1930s. Painted on silk. © National Trust Images/Andreas von Einsiedel.	45
Figure 2.4	One of the Chinese wallpapers at Belton House, Lincolnshire hanging in the Chinese bedroom, painted on paper. Framed by a later European border on machine-made paper (therefore 1830 or later). © National Trust Images.	46
Figure 2.5	Chinese Room, Erdigg, Wrexham. © National Trust/Andreas von Einsiedel.	47

Figure 2.6	Detail of a Chinese wallpaper at Ickworth, Norfolk, hung in the Chinese dressing room, according to family tradition purchased 'at one of the great exhibitions'. The butterfly has been cut out and pasted onto the paper. Photograph courtesy of Andrew Bush.	48
Figure 3.1	Detail of ivory and ebony inlay from early eighteenth-century Vizagapatam Anglo-Indian ebony and padoukwood games table. Tyntesfield, Somerset. 1207460. © National Trust Images/John Hammond.	72
Figure 3.2	Oval work table, wood with ivory veneer and lacquer detail, 1770–1800, Vizagapatam. Powis Castle and Garden, Powys. 1180670. © National Trust Images/Erik Pelham.	73
Figure 3.3	'Warren Hastings (1732–1818), Governor General of Fort William, Bengal, 1774–85', George Romney, 1795. © British Library Board, F1.	79
Figure 3.4	West Front of Basildon Park, Berkshire. © National Trust Images/Andrew Butler.	85
Figure 4.1	Francis Child the Elder (1642–1713). Attributed to Sir Godfrey Kneller (1646–1723). Reproduced by kind permission of Christ's Hospital.	92
Table 4.1	The Child Family as Directors of the EIC	91
Figure 4.2	Ceramic Parade Jar, c.1700–1770 Osterley House. Image courtesy of Stuart Howat.	99
Table 4.2	*Osterley* Ships	97
Figure 4.3	Chinese lacquer chest, Osterley House. Image courtesy of Stuart Howat.	101
Figure 4.4	Chinese lacquer secretaire, Osterley House. Image courtesy of Stuart Howat.	102
Figure 4.5	Child family armorial porcelain plate, c. 1700–1725, Osterley House. Image courtesy of Stuart Howat.	104
Figure 4.6	Detail of Mrs Child's silk bed canopy, Osterley House. Image courtesy of Stuart Howat.	105
Figure 5.1	Chinese porcelain plate decorated with the arms of Charles Raymond and his wife, Sarah Webster. c.1760. Private collection. Image courtesy of Georgina Green and Heirloom & Howard Ltd.	114

Figure 5.2	Tureen from armorial Chinese porcelain service, Qianlong reign (1736–96), c.1765–70. NT 266484.3. Basildon Park, National Trust Collections. © National Trust/Thomas Boggis.	116
Figure 5.3	Scalloped-edge plate from armorial Chinese porcelain service, Qianlong reign (1736–96), c.1765–70. NT 266484.12.6. Basildon Park, National Trust Collections. © National Trust/ Thomas Boggis.	122
Figure 5.4	Plate with cut edges from armorial Chinese porcelain service, Qianlong reign (1736–96), c.1765–70. NT 266484.10. Basildon Park, National Trust. © National Trust/Thomas Boggis.	123
Figure 5.5	Detail of coat of arms from original grant of arms. 1763. Image courtesy of Sir John Sykes.	125
Figure 5.6	Plate from armorial Chinese porcelain service, Qianlong reign (1736–96), c.1743. NT 1271545. Shugborough, Staffordshire. © National Trust Images/Robert Morris.	129
Figure 6.1	Frontispiece and title pages of *Wanderings of a Pilgrim in Search of the Picturesque*, vol. 1. British Library digital copy p.13; print copy facing i and i. © The British Library Board, 1947.b 170 vol. 1 frontispiece.	132
Figure 6.2	Fanny and Charles Parkes' grave, The General Cemetery of All Souls, Kensal Green. Image courtesy of Joanna Goldsworthy.	138
Figure 6.3	*Wanderings*, vol. 1, digital edition p.20: *'The Camels were being branded for the Public Service and the Spider came to be marked also'. Fanny represents herself as a large spider holding a book titled* The Pilgrim*; books hanging from three camels' necks are titled* Luard, Princes and People *and, interestingly,* Afghanistan. © The British Library Board, 1947. B 170 vol. 1 p. 20.	139
Figure 6.4	*Wanderings*, vol. 1, digital edition p.84: *The Churuk Puja, or Hook Swinging*. © The British Library Board, 1947. B. 170 vol. 1 p. 84.	147
Figure 6.5	Lower sections of an image-frame of Visnu in two parts showing attendant figures. Carved in dark	

	grey sandstone. Twelfth century. 1880.35.39.a–b. © Trustees of the British Museum.	149
Figure 6.6	*Wanderings*, vol. 2, digital p.472: *'Three Satis and a Mandap near Ghazipur',* © The British Library Board, 1947. B. 170 vol. 1 p.472.	150
Figure 6.7	*Wanderings*, vol. 2, digital p.476: *'Kulsas',* © The British Library Board, 1947. B. 170 vol. 1 p. 476.	151
Figure 7.1	Postcard featuring Montreal Park, Kent. Courtesy of Kent History & Library Centre, Maidstone.	165
Figure 7.2	'South Elevation Montreal showing a proposed addition' (November 1828). Kent History & Library Centre, Amherst Papers, 'Detailed Plans of Alterations at Montreal by Mr. Atkinson (1829–31)', U1350 P21. Courtesy of Kent History & Library Centre, Maidstone.	166
Figure 7.3	'Ground floor plan showing additions and alterations to Montreal Place' (November 1828). Kent History & Library Centre, Amherst Papers, 'Detailed Plans of Alterations at Montreal by Mr. Atkinson (1829–31)', U1350 P21. Courtesy of Kent History & Library Centre, Maidstone.	167
Figure 7.4	'Ground Plan for Additions Montreal' (February 1829). Kent History & Library Centre, Amherst Papers, 'Detailed Plans of Alterations at Montreal by Mr. Atkinson (1829–31)', U1350 P21. Courtesy of Kent History & Library Centre, Maidstone.	168
Figure 8.1	Photographs of Warfield Park, Berkshire (lot 1), 'Sale Catalogue of Warfield Park' (1933), D/ENS/B13/26. Image courtesy of Berkshire Record Office.	179
Figure 9.1	Englefield House, Berkshire. Image courtesy of Georgina Green.	192
Figure 9.2	Portrait of Margaret Maskelyne, Lady Clive by Nathaniel Dance. Powis Castle, Powys, Wales. © National Trust Images.	199
Figure 10.1	Swallowfield Park. © Brian Steptoe, FRPS. Source: Historic England Archive.	206
Figure 10.2	Sir Henry Russell, 2nd Baronet, by Sir Francis Leggatt Chantry. © National Portrait Gallery, London.	221

Figure 11.1	Valentines Mansion and Gardens, Ilford. Image courtesy of Georgina Green.	231
Figure 11.2	Porcelain plate decorated with the arms of Charles Raymond and his wife, Sarah Webster. China, c.1760. Private collection. Image courtesy of Georgina Green and Heirloom & Howard Ltd.	234
Figure 11.3	*A New and Complete History of Essex by a Gentleman,* vol. 4 (1771), 276–79. This image shows the orangery, situated to the left of the house.	235
Figure 11.4	Illustration from the journal of the East Indiaman *Suffolk 1755/6* (L/MAR/B/397D) British Library. © The British Library Board, 1755/6 (IOR/L/MAR/B/397D).	240
Figure 11.5	Diver Richard Keen preparing to dive near Guernsey. Image courtesy of Georgina Green.	244
Figure 11.6	Map of wreck location. Courtesy of Georgina Green.	245
Figure 11.7	Porcelain shards from the *Valentine*. Image courtesy of Georgina Green.	246
Figure 11.8	Agate pieces from the *Valentine*. Image courtesy of Georgina Green.	247
Figure 11.9	Metal handles and bottle stoppers from the *Valentine*. Image courtesy of Georgina Green.	248
Figure 11.10	*Stain* by Kathy Taylor. Indian cotton, stained with tea, indigo and dye extracted from red dyewood/ red sander's dust from the Valentine cargo. The flag design is based on the British East India Company Flag of 1707–1801. Image courtesy of Kathy Taylor.	249
Figure 12.1	John Cary, Map of Hertfordshire, in *Cary's new and correct English atlas: being a new set of county maps from actual surveys* (London, 1787), not paginated https: //commons.wikimedia.org/wiki/ File:Hertfordshire-Maps-Cary-1787-49.jpg	255
Figure 12.2	Close-up of North Mimms [sic], in *Cary's new and correct atlas: being a new set of county maps from actual surveys* (London, 1787), not paginated https: //commons.wikimedia.org/wiki/File:Hertfordshire-Maps-Cary-1787-49.jpg	259
Figure 12.3	Portrait of John Hunter of Gobions, by Sir Thomas Lawrence (1789/90). Reproduced by kind permission of Musée des Beaux-Arts, ville de	

	Bordeaux. Image courtesy of L. Gauthier, F. Deval.	261
Figure 12.4	Memorial to John and Ann Hunter, and her daughter Ann Hornby in St Mary's church, North Mymms. Image courtesy of Chris Jeppesen.	268
Figure 13.1	The Hotel Redcliffe (Redcliffe Towers), Paignton, Devon, early twentieth-century. © The Redcliffe Hotel.	277
Figure 13.2	Jivan Ram, Raja (Raja Jirvan Raja), *Portrait of Robert Smith, Bengal Engineers*, c.1830, oil painting. © British Library Board, Foster 870.	279
Figure 13.3	Robert Smith (1787–1873), *Sketches of the Line of March with Elephants, Camels, Hackeries* [bullock drawn carriages]*, horsemen and coolies*, 1814, pencil on paper. © British Library Board, WD 312 f.25v.	280
Figure 13.4	Robert Smith, *Barrackpore House*, 1815–19, Oil on canvas, 13 x 20.5 cm (estimated). © British Library Board, F864.	281
Figure 13.5	The Red Fort, Delhi, India. Photograph by Diane James © 2014.	282
Figure 13.6	Robert Smith's bungalow (known as William Fraser bungalow), Delhi, India. Photograph by Diane James © 2014.	283
Figure 13.7	The Eastern Gate of the Jama Masjid, Delhi, India. Photograph by Diane James © 2014.	285
Figure 13.8	Postcard: Villa Mills on the Palatino, Rome. © akpool GmbH – www.akpool.de.	286
Figure 13.9	Le Château de l'Anglais, Mont Boron, Nice. Photograph by Diane James © 2013.	289
Figure 13.10	The old lookout tower on the edge of the cliff. After J. W. Tucker, *Paignton*. Coloured steel vignette, published by H.Besley, Exeter 12.5 x 17 cm. By permission of www.rareoldprints.com.	291
Figure 13.11	Early drawing of Redcliffe Towers, n.d. © Redcliffe Hotel, Paignton.	291
Figure 13.12	*Plan of Mansion and Grounds, Redcliffe Towers*, n.d. © Redcliffe Hotel, Paignton.	292
Figure 13.13	The Central Rotunda, Redcliffe Towers, Paignton, Devon, with the door of the plunge-pool tunnel	

opening above the beach. Photograph by Diane James © 2013. 293
Figure 13.14 Fountain in the hotel car park, framed by holm oak trees, remnants of the Redcliffe garden. Photograph by Diane James © 2013. 294
Figure 13.15 The remains of one of the flagstaff towers. Once a prominent feature it stands half-buried in the undergrowth. Photograph by Diane James © 2013. 295
Figure 13.16 No longer isolated on a headland, Redcliffe Towers is now surrounded by the town of Paignton. Photograph by Diane James © 2013. 297
Figure 14.1 The main staircase from the entrance hall at Tan-Yr-Allt, showing the ascent to the first floor and hinting at fluted window reveals. D12013_0674, NPRN 16895. © Crown copyright: Royal Commission on the Ancient and Historical Monuments of Wales. 300
Figure 14.2 The 'Chinese' staircase at Bishopsgate House, showing the first floor landing. The stylized wave design carved into the tread ends is just visible in the bottom centre of this image. D12011_1011, NPRN 15946. © Crown copyright: Royal Commission on the Ancient and Historical Monuments of Wales. 301
Figure 14.3 The 'Chinese' staircase at Trefeilir, probably photographed in the 1930s, showing the main balustrade of the staircase with its latticework. D12011_1010, NPRN 15898. © Crown copyright: Royal Commission on the Ancient and Historical Monuments of Wales. 303
Figure 14.4 Illustration from Nieuhof's *Embassy*, showing a Chinese pagoda. 309
Figure 14.5 Railing designs as depicted in Thomas Chippendale's *The Gentleman and Cabinet Maker's Director*, 206. 311
Figure 14.6 Railing designs as depicted in Thomas Chippendale's *The Gentleman and Cabinet Maker's Director*, 208. 313
Figure 14.7 Railing design from William Halfpenny's *Rural Architecture in the Chinese Taste*, showing

	similarities with staircase designs at Tan-yr-Allt, Bishopsgate House and Trefeilir.	314
Figure 14.8	'Chinese' staircase design from William Halfpenny's *Rural Architecture in the Chinese Taste*.	314
Figure 16.1	Colonel Patrick Duff, of the Honourable East India Company's Artillery by Romney, 1790. Image courtesy of Alistair Mutch.	333
Figure 16.2	Gatehouse, Mains of Carnousie, 1797. Image courtesy of Alistair Mutch.	335
Figure 16.3	Cart arches, Mains of Carnousie. Image courtesy of Alistair Mutch.	336
Figure 16.4	Gatehouse, Harthil Castle, Oyne, Aberdeenshire. Image courtesy of Alistair Mutch.	337
Figure 16.5	Old House of Carnousie. Image courtesy of Alistair Mutch.	338
Figure 16.6	Delgaty Home Farm entrance, Turriff, Aberdeenshire. Image courtesy of Alistair Mutch.	339
Figure 17.1	Nonsuch Park, Surrey. Image courtesy of Penelope Farmer.	357
Figure 17.2	The Farmer family tree. Image courtesy of Penelope Farmer.	361
Figure 17.3	Penelope Farmer and Margot Finn with the manuscripts. Image courtesy of Penelope Farmer.	376
Figure 17.4	Samuel Farmer's will. Image courtesy of Penelope Farmer.	386
Figure 18.1	Philip and his father at Presmennen (Frontispiece of *Memoirs*). Image courtesy of David Williams.	390
Figure 18.2	The mural at the Summer Palace, Srirangapatna, depicting the Battle of Pollilur. Note the defensive British square, the ammunition cart exploding, Colonel Baillie's palanquin and, somewhere in the centre, Philip Melvill fighting. Image courtesy of David Williams.	391
Figure 18.3	Philip and Elizabeth Melvill from *The Melvill Family, Roll of honour.* Image courtesy of David Williams.	393
Figure 18.4	The memorial to Philip Melvill in Falmouth Church (with an incorrect age). Image courtesy of David Williams.	394
Figure 18.5	Philip I's four sons who had careers in the EIC. From a–d, James Cosmo, Philip, Henry and Peter.	

	From *The Melvill Family, Roll of honour.* Images courtesy of David Williams.	397
Figure 18.6	Sir James Cosmo Melvill by Eton Upton Ellis c.1853. © The British Library Board, Foster 667.	399
Figure 18.7	Lady Hester Melvill by John James Napier c.1858. © The British Library Board, Foster 668.	399
Figure 18.8	Tandridge Court today. Image courtesy of David Williams.	401
Figure 18.9	Haileybury College, designed by William Wilkins, unknown artist, c.1855. © The British Library Board, WD 541.	402
Figure 19.1	Image of coat of arms of the Cossimbazar Raj. Image courtesy of Dr S.C. Nandy.	412
Figure 19.2	Image of coat of arms of Sykes of Basildon. Image courtesy of Sir John Sykes.	413
Figure 19.3	Seal, engraved steel and gunmetal holder. Image courtesy of Sir John Sykes.	414
Figure 19.4	Two miniature portraits of Francis Sykes. On the left, as an older man, possibly by Thomas Richmond and on the right as a younger man by Henry Bone, 1804, copied from an earlier portrait by Thomas Gainsborough destroyed by fire in 1874. Images courtesy of Sir John Sykes.	415
Figure 19.5	Detail of Sykes crest. Image courtesy of Sir John Sykes.	416
Figure 19.6	Detail from map of 'The Countries of Indostan East of Delhi' by James Rennell published in Robert Orme, *A History of the Military Transactions of the British Nation in Indostan* (London, 1778). Muxadabad was the former name of the Nawab of Bengal's capital of Murshidabad. Image courtesy of Sir John Sykes.	417
Figure 19.7	Frans Balthazar Solvyns, 'Banian', 1790. The image included here is thought to be of Cantoo Baboo. Image courtesy of Victoria Memorial Hall, Kolkata.	420
Figure 19.8	Page from Francis Sykes's bank account at Goslings Bank (1770/1771), showing purchases of East India stock. Image courtesy of Barclays Group Archives.	424

Figure 19.9 Sir Francis Sykes 9th Baronet in Bengal Mounted Rifles uniform, c.1931. Image courtesy of Sir John Sykes. 425

Figure 19.10 Photograph featuring from left to right, Sir John Sykes 10th Baronet, Dr Nandy, Charles Sykes, Lady Susan Sykes and Sir Francis Sykes 9th Baronet at Basildon Park, 1978. Image courtesy of Sir John Sykes. 426

Figure 19.11 Photograph featuring Sripur Palace, Cossimbazar, 2012. Image courtesy of Dr S.C. Nandy. 427

Figure 19.12 Photograph featuring the wedding of Dr Nandy's son Samit Chandra, 1988. Image courtesy of Sir John Sykes. 427

Abbreviations

AULSC	Aberdeen University Special Libraries and Collections
BL	British Library
BRO	Berkshire Record Office
EIC	East India Company
HRO	Hertfordshire County Record Office
IOR	India Office Records
LMA	London Metropolitan Archives
NLS	National Library of Scotland
NMRW	National Monument Record of Wales
NRS	National Records of Scotland
PRO	Pembrokeshire Record Office
RAS	Royal Astronomical Society
RCAHMW	The Royal Commission on the Ancient and Historical Monuments of Wales
TNA	The National Archives
TP	Tasker Papers
V&A	Victoria & Albert Museum
WGF	William Gamul Farmer

Contributors

Rachael Barnwell is a graduate of the University of Leicester, with an MA in Interpretation, Representation and Heritage. She currently works at Durham University as part of their Research and Innovation Services team. Prior to joining the university, she spent five years at the Royal Commission on the Ancient and Historical Monuments of Wales in Aberystwyth. She has previously published *Inside Welsh Homes*, investigating domestic interiors in Wales, and curated touring exhibitions of material from the National Monuments Record of Wales.

Helen Clifford read History at Cambridge before completing her PhD from the joint Victoria and Albert Museum/Royal College of Art Design History course. She was Senior Research Fellow on *The East India Company at Home, 1757–1857* team, and museum consultant to the Trading Eurasia: Europe's Asian Centuries project at Warwick University (2010–14). She runs the Swaledale Museum in Reeth, North Yorkshire and is a freelance writer and curator specializing in early modern luxury trades. She is currently writing the history of the Worshipful Company of Grocers.

Pauline Davies OBE trained and worked as a librarian before joining the Department of Trade's policy staff. A volunteer at the National Trust's Osterley Park and House (https://www.nationaltrust.org.uk/osterley-park-and-house) for over 10 years, she is fascinated by both the corporate and maritime history of the East India Company and continues her research into the Child family's connection with both.

Penelope Farmer is a writer and editor. Her best known book, *Charlotte Sometimes*, set during the First World War, has been in print for nearly 50 years. After reading history at Oxford she published her first book at the age of 21. Following Oxford with a diploma in social studies at

Bedford College, London, she alleviated family life by writing a succession of novels, for both children and adults, in some of which her interest in social and anthropological issues appeared (she edited a collection of creation myths *Beginnings* and later based one novel, *Snakes and Ladders*, on a medical and anthropological study of treating epilepsy in rural third world settings). Finding the collection of family letters between India and England led her back to history – and to this chapter on the East India Company career of her great-great-great grandfather's elder brother, William Gamul Farmer. She is currently attempting a family memoir based around the same letters.

Ellen Filor was the PhD student on *The East India Company at Home, 1757–1857* project. She received her PhD from University College London in 2014. Since graduating, she has held research fellowships at the University of Michigan, University College London and the University of Edinburgh.

Margot Finn is Professor of Modern British History at University College London. A former editor of the *Journal of British Studies*, she is the author of two monographs, *After Chartism: Class and Nation in England Radical Politics, 1848–1874* (Cambridge University Press, 1993) and *The Character of Credit: Personal Debt in English Culture, 1740–1914* (Cambridge University Press, 2003). Her previous co-edited volumes are (with Michael Lobban and Jenny Bourne Taylor), *Legitimacy and Illegitimacy in Nineteenth-Century Law, Literature and History* (2010) and (with Kate Smith), *New Paths to Public Histories* (2015), both published by Palgrave. Finn was the Principal Investigator of the Leverhulme Trust grant from which the current volume developed. She is currently completing a monograph on the family and the East India Company and is President of the Royal Historical Society.

Joanna Goldsworthy worked in general trade publishing for many years, becoming publishing director of Victor Gollancz Ltd and associate editor of Doubleday (London) before leaving the industry to study history at University College London, taking a BA and MA as a mature student. It was there that she became interested in the British in India in the early nineteenth century, specifically in the life and writings of Fanny Parkes, continuing her research after graduating, including archival and location research trips to India. Her publications include, as editor and contributor, two collections of essays, *A Certain Age: Reflecting on the Menopause* (London, 1993) and *Mothers by Daughters* (London, 1995), and, more recently, several academic papers including 'A Pilgrim in Search of the

Picturesque: Fanny Parkes and Colonial Modernity' in Pradip Basu (ed.), *Colonial Modernity: Indian Perspectives* (Kolkata, 2011). Her current research is into the hidden past of her Prussian grandfather who died in unexplained circumstances in 1941 in The Hague, Netherlands.

Georgina Green has been involved with local history in Epping Forest, Redbridge and Waltham Forest for over 35 years and has written several books. In 1999 she was asked to investigate the history of Valentines Mansion, owned by the London Borough of Redbridge. Her research contributed to the successful bid for a Heritage Lottery Fund grant towards restoring the building, which opened to the public on 14 February 2009. When Georgina retired from her post as Local Government Officer in neighbouring Barking she focused her research onto Sir Charles Raymond who owned Valentines in the eighteenth century. Using her skills with spreadsheets she compiled statistics to show he was of major importance with the East India Company as a leading Managing Owner of their ships. This also showed that a number of other residents of Redbridge were connected with the East India Company. In 2015 Georgina published *Sir Charles Raymond of Valentines and the East India Company*.

Diane James is a PhD student in the History of Art at the University of Warwick. She submitted her thesis 'An endless variety of forms and proportions': Indian Influence on British Architecture and Gardens, 1740–1850', in November 2017. Her dissertation examines the development of Indian design in Britain from the end of the eighteenth century to the mid-nineteenth century, coinciding with the height of the trading of the British East India Company and the return of military officers and administrators from India. She has previously co-authored *Historic Gardens of Warwickshire*, with Timothy Mowl, Emeritus Professor, Bristol University.

Chris Jeppesen is an historian of Britain and the British empire in the nineteenth and twentieth centuries. He completed his PhD at the University of Cambridge in 2013 and subsequently worked as an AHRC Cultural Engagement Fellow and Research Associate on a collaborative project based between UCL and the British Library – *East Meets West: Caribbean and Asian Colonial Cultures in British Domestic Contexts*. The project offered a preliminary exploration of the connections between the East India Company, Britain and the Caribbean slave economy, which he has developed in subsequent research for the *East India Company at Home* and *Legacies of British Slave-ownership* projects. From 2013 to

2017, he was a Teaching Fellow at UCL and is currently a postdoctoral researcher at the University of Cambridge.

Sarah Longair is Senior Lecturer in the History of Empire at the University of Lincoln and previously worked at the British Museum for 11 years. Her research examines British colonial history in East Africa and the Indian Ocean world through material and visual culture. Her first monograph, *Cracks in the Dome: Fractured Histories of Empire in the Zanzibar Museum* (2015), examined the history of the museum and colonial culture in Zanzibar. She is currently working on an oral history project with former colonial officers about objects in their homes, sponsored by a British Academy-Leverhulme Trust small grant, and a study of Indian Ocean islands and material culture in the nineteenth and twentieth centuries, supported by a Leverhulme Trust research fellowship in 2015–16.

Alistair Mutch is Professor of Information and Learning at Nottingham Business School. He writes on the history of management, amongst other things. His book *Religion and National Identity: Governing Scottish Presbyterianism in the Eighteenth Century,* was published in 2015 by Edinburgh University Press. Alistair's fascination with General Duff started because his uncle farmed the land Duff's estate buildings stood on. Many family members still live and farm in the area, which he visits as often as he can. Alistair has a particular interest in farm buildings, especially those of the late eighteenth century, of which Aberdeenshire possesses some particularly fine specimens. The story of General Duff also connects with the work Alistair has done on the distinctive nature of Scottish religious practices and the influence they have had on secular activities. His book on *Tiger Duff: India, Madeira and Empire in Eighteenth Century Scotland* was published by Aberdeen University Press in 2017.

Yuthika Sharma has been Lecturer in Indian/South Asian Art in the History of Art at University of Edinburgh since 2015. She was previously a research fellow in the Department of Asia at the British Museum. Her recent research has looked at cross-cultural exchanges in Mughal India in the eighteenth and nineteenth centuries. She is the curator of *Highlands to Hindustan* (July–Nov 2017), which is the first exploration of the University's South Asian collections through the lens of Scottish engagement in colonial India. Her recent essays deal with the conceptual framework of visual culture in late Mughal India (Flood and Necipoglu, eds. *Companion to Islamic Art*, Wiley Blackwell, 2017) and the diplomatic and material culture of portraits on ivory (Sunder Rajan and Mc Donagh et al., *Commodities and Culture in the Colonial World*, Routledge, 2017).

Cam Sharp Jones is a PhD student at the Centre for the History of Science, Technology and Medicine, University of Manchester researching nineteenth-century colonial ethnography with specific reference to India. She currently works for the Archives department of the Royal Botanic Gardens, Kew on the Joseph Hooker Correspondence Project, which aims to make Joseph Dalton Hooker's correspondence freely available through digitization and transcription. Cam has previously worked on the South Asian collections at the British Museum and the British Library on projects researching Company School paintings and Gupta era coinage.

Kate Smith is Senior Lecturer in Eighteenth-Century History at the University of Birmingham. Prior to joining Birmingham in 2014, Kate worked as Research Fellow on the Leverhulme Trust-funded project *The East India Company at Home, 1757–1857*. Kate is a cultural historian of eighteenth- and nineteenth-century Britain and empire with particular interests in the production, consumption, use and possession of objects and the built environment in the past. Her first monograph, *Material Goods, Moving Hands: Perceiving Production in England, 1700–1830* (2014), explored the changing ways in which consumers, makers and manufacturers related to and perceived the manufacture of consumer goods. Kate is currently working on her second monograph project, which examines the history of lost property practices and the ways in which people learned to maintain possession of their things in urban spaces.

Sir John Sykes (10th Baronet) is the direct descendant of Sir Francis Sykes (1st Baronet) and a retired solicitor. After reading law at Oxford in the early 1960s, he learned the practical side with a firm of Lincoln's Inn solicitors and then moved to Wiltshire where he was a partner in a firm of Swindon solicitors for some 30 years. Over time he accumulated a great amount of information about his forebear, helped along the way by many fortunate events. Chief amongst these was the gift of Basildon Park to the National Trust by Lord and Lady Iliffe in 1977 and meeting Dr. Somen Nandy, Maharajkumar of Cossimbazar, in 1978, the first time the two families had met in over 250 years, a friendly relationship which has continued ever since.

Sir John is married to Susan, an art historian. They married in 1966, have three sons and six grandchildren and have lived in Marlborough for over 40 years. In 1991 he co-founded a charitable trust to restore the outstanding seventeenth-century Merchant's House in Marlborough, in 2009 co-founded the Marlborough Literature Festival and has enjoyed Venetian-style rowing in Venice and on the Thames.

David Williams was educated at Sevenoaks School and Cambridge University, where he read history. He qualified as a Chartered Accountant with Coopers & Lybrand and was with them for 12 years before working in various financial and administrative roles, principally with the French investment bank Paribas, in London and overseas. After retiring in 2003 he has been a Trustee for a number of charities and acted as Treasurer for other organisations, and pursued his interest in family and local history. He discovered that his wife was descended from Cosmo Melvill, the last secretary of the EIC, which led to his involvement in the EIC at Home project. He has co-authored two books on local history; *Seal: The History of a Parish* (2007) and *Ightham: At the Crossroads* (2015). He and his wife have travelled extensively including visiting, in 2014, the site of the Battle of Pollilur and other places associated with Philip Melvill, Cosmo's father, in Southern India.

Introduction

Margot Finn and Kate Smith

The imprint of imperialism looms large in the built environments of postcolonial Britain. To walk the streets of London, Leamington Spa and Liverpool; to explore the elegant Georgian mansions of Aberglasney, Hertfordshire and the Scottish Borders; or to ramble across agrarian estates in Banffshire, Berkshire and Caernarvonshire is to inhabit a landscape shaped by the British empire. Material monuments to Georgian and Victorian imperial endeavour punctuate urban, suburban and rural historic sites – so common and so familiar that they occasion only episodic comment, much less analysis.[1] Public archives, heritage sites, libraries, museum collections and stately homes likewise display and embody the spoils of imperial warfare, trade and bureaucratic service. Here the material traces of African conquest, Caribbean slavery and the Indian Raj have come 'home' to rest on British soil.[2] In London, an East End warehouse built in 1802 to store sugar produced by enslaved labourers on West Indian plantations now houses the Docklands Museum, while the former collections of the East India Company Museum underpin the South Asian galleries at the Victoria and Albert (V&A) Museum. Across Britain, the close imbrication of colonial history and postcolonial heritage extends far beyond the metropolitan ports that served as nodal points of imperial commerce. In Derbyshire, the Palladian exterior and neoclassical interiors of Kedleston Hall, designed in the 1760s for the Curzon family by the celebrated Robert Adam (1728–92), are connected to Britain's Indian empire by a dense reticulation of material ties. Constructed by Adam to exemplify 'Rome reborn' in Britain, this stately home provided the architectural model for Government House, Calcutta (now Raj Bhavan, Kolkata), the official residence of successive nineteenth-century British Governor Generals. Built for Marquis Wellesley in 1799–1803 and serving as the seat of British rule in India until 1912, Government House was home from 1899–1905 to Lord Curzon of Kedleston (1859–1925), in his capacity as Viceroy of India. An avid collector of Asian artefacts, Curzon exploited his political position on the subcontinent to acquire ornately decorated brass teapots, silver boxes, ivory miniatures, wooden shrines to Hindu goddesses, swords and scabbards – decorative objects that constitute the 'Eastern Museum' at Kedleston today.[3]

Country houses such as Kedleston functioned as vital sites of imperial power in the Georgian and Victorian era and continue to play a central role in global, national and local representations of Britishness in contemporary tourism, on television and at the cinema.[4] The imperial dimensions of Britain's stately homes however, have only recently begun to be explored by historians. For despite their obvious physical presence and material traces, the objects, persons and furnishings of the Georgian and Victorian empire have often been hidden in plain sight in the country house and its cultural representations. The domestic scenes that animate Jane Austen's *Mansfield Park* (1814), as Edward Said observed in 1993, reflect a national idiom intent to mask its imperial taproots. Daily life at Austen's fictional country seat was underpinned by Caribbean slavery, yet she relegated this colonial source of wealth and exploitation to the margins of her text.[5] In the past decade, historians have begun to recover this hidden imperial history by excavating the material legacies of Caribbean slavery in modern and contemporary Britain. Tracing the translation of plantation wealth into Britain's country houses and systematically scrutinizing the wider material impact of Parliamentary compensation for the 1833 abolition of British slave-owners' property in enslaved persons, their research informs lively – often heated – disputes about the salience of imperialism and its legacies in and beyond colonial and postcolonial Britain.[6]

This volume of essays contributes to these ongoing debates by exploring the domestic impact of empire on British country houses, their residents and their interiors. It focuses on the propertied families of the East India Company (EIC) in the heyday of Company rule. From the Battle of Plassey in 1757 to the outbreak of the Indian Uprising in 1857, objects, persons and wealth flowed to Britain from Asia. Gifted or purchased, inherited or looted, Indian material culture was both a prime source of wealthy Britons' desire for trade with India and a conspicuous consequence of their imperial exploits on the subcontinent. Whereas agricultural produce and its byproducts (notably Caribbean sugar and rum) dominated Britain's Atlantic commerce, Indian Ocean trade extended from raw goods and comestibles to a cornucopia of 'Oriental' luxuries manufactured by skilled craftsmen. Access to commodities that spanned from spices and saltpeter to fine textiles and Chinese porcelain motivated the Company's merchants from the EIC's charter as a trading monopoly in 1600 until the loss of its remaining commercial privileges in 1833. Exceptionally high levels of risk bedeviled this Asian trade, and swingeing mortality rates cut swathes through the EIC's ranks, but Company men who survived and flourished could (and demonstrably did) gain vast wealth.[7] Channelled back to Britain, Company profits provided abundant funds for country house purchases, refurbishment and interior display, figuring British, continental European and Asian wealth, craftsmanship and design in exotic new domestic combinations. Already in the early eighteenth century, Indian profits had begun to leave conspicuous marks on British interiors. The Madras fortune of Elihu Yale (1649–1721) was displayed prominently at Yale's London residence and at Plas Grono, his ancestral home in Wales: together, Golconda diamonds, a 'Blackamoor's head', Dutch and Flemish paintings, as well as portraits of 'six *Indian* Kings', an '*Indian* Queen' and 16 'Chinese Noblemen' lent the profits of his lucrative Company career domestic material form.[8]

As men in the EIC service increasingly shifted their activities from trade to military expansion and political administration – a transition that accelerated sharply after the Battle of Plassey – a new population of civil servants, army officers, surveyors and surgeons journeyed to India to make their fortunes.[9] Here they lived in variegated household units which, in aggregate, comprised Indian spouses, concubines and domestic slaves, legitimate and illegitimate children, British and European wives, and a diverse array of siblings, cousins and friends.[10] Often resident on the subcontinent from adolescence until mature adulthood, the most successful of these Company men built, purchased or rented ornately furnished Indian residences in keeping with their place within the Company's hierarchy, developing a connoisseurial eye for both European luxuries and the 'Oriental' textiles and objects with which the Indian princes (whom they sought to supplant) marked their own social and political power over subject populations.[11] These Company men, and the family members from Britain with whom they resided, acquired wealth, tastes and identities in India which – if they survived the perils of the tropical climate – travelled home with them to Britain. Their stories, the biographies of their Indian possessions and the narratives of the stately homes in Britain that came to house them frame our explorations of imperial culture and its British legacies in *The East India Company at Home*.

In publishing this volume, our goals are four-fold. First, building on new research that highlights the extra-European histories of British country houses and their interiors, we showcase the contributions made by Asian wealth, material culture and politics to elite domestic aesthetic traditions too often viewed from an insular 'island-history' optic. Precisely because the country house now occupies a central place in heritage and tourism, its dynamic history as a site of transnational and trans-imperial socioeconomic and political contestation, rather than a stable repository of fixed British identities, is often obscured. Second (and relatedly), by situating British country houses within a wider world of eighteenth- and nineteenth-century trade and empire, we contribute to ongoing debates about global history and its relation to conceptions and practices of nation, region and locality. Much Company history is written from the two-fold perspective of London and Calcutta; our studies explore as well a range of provincial hinterlands – in Britain and India – that provided distinctive contexts for engagement in trans-imperial domesticity and self-fashioning. Our third aim is methodological. Borrowing approaches from the study of material history inspired by anthropology and cognate disciplines, the chapters in this volume interrogate the objects acquired by Company men and women in India to explore the ways in which these ostensibly inert artefacts animated both the actions of EIC personnel and the narratives they deployed to record and justify their Indian lives. Like our third goal, our fourth aim is also methodological. The essays in this volume evolved in the context of a collaborative project that united researchers from a wide spectrum of domains – local and national archives and libraries, heritage organisations, the buoyant community of independent family historians, the museum sector and universities. By drawing from expertise, manuscripts and artefacts dispersed across these varied sectors of the research community, that project – like this volume – was calculated to enrich conventional academic narratives of empire and its domestic impact with knowledge co-produced across the artificial boundaries that typically demarcate university-based and public history.[12]

Nation and empire in country house histories

The Englishness of the English country house is an axiomatic theme of the many authors who, in the aftermath of World War II and decolonization, sought to assess the place of stately homes in Britain's changing historical landscape. Simultaneously fuelled by mounting fears that historic homes in private hands were in a state of terminal decline and inspired by rising visitor numbers at properties managed by heritage organizations such as the National Trust, a burgeoning secondary literature celebrating the country house as a national icon emerged in these years.[13] The V&A's provocative *Destruction of the Country House* exhibition of 1974 galvanized this strand of analysis, depicting stately homes as the precious, indigenous and endangered jewel in a beleaguered English heritage crown. For Roy Strong (the V&A's newly appointed Director) and his co-curators, country houses captured the very essence of national identity and national culture: as their exhibition catalogue proclaimed, 'English country houses, whether palaces or manors, epitomize English history.'[14] In this interpretation, a distinctive, national material culture – of furnishings, decorative ornaments, textiles, portraiture and wallpapers – marked the country house as quintessentially English (an ascription that typically either ignored or subsumed Scottish, Welsh and Irish identities). 'It has repeatedly been stated that the country house is England's unique contribution to the visual arts', they concluded, with obvious satisfaction.[15]

Attention to the European dimensions of country house architecture and furnishing exposes the limitations of this nationalist frame of analysis. Constructed in Palladian, Baronial, Neo-classical, Baroque and Gothic architectural forms, eighteenth- and nineteenth-century English, Scottish and Welsh country house exteriors derived their characteristic structures and styles from French and Italian architectural traditions.[16] Through the avid collecting practices associated with the Grand Tour, moreover, the men – and women – of Britain's propertied elite developed transnational cultural tastes and amassed a wealth of continental European objects and artwork for their stately homes in Britain.[17] From the outset, the processes of building, renovating and furnishing eighteenth-century 'English' country houses were firmly embedded in European material conventions. The stately homes styled and decorated by fashionable designers such as William Kent (1685–1748), Julius Bryant argues, 'can be understood as the result of a need to create a Grand Tour ambience in England, one where guests would be reminded of their heady days out hunting for masterpieces, outmanoeuvering Papal controls over exports, and now enjoying the trophies of their cultural safaris'.[18]

Just as the Grand Tour encouraged the owners of Britain's stately homes to embrace European tastes and designs, so too the rapid expansion of Britain's empire promoted new, hybrid forms of domestic aesthetics. At the apex of the Company service, men who lived on the subcontinent from late adolescence to middle age in the enjoyment of fortunes swelled by high salaries, mercantile profits and political corruption both honed their appreciation of European fine and decorative arts and acquired a new taste for the 'Oriental' luxury goods to which their employment gave them privileged access. As Joanna Goldsworthy's chapter on Fanny Parkes (1794–1875) attests, Company women joined eagerly and avidly in the collection both of these prized material objects and of curios that recalled their lives in India.

The co-residence of British, French, Dutch, Portuguese, Swedish and other European mercantile and military men in India – at times at war with each other, at times working in each other's service – ensured that 'English' engagement with Asian material culture often merged with and was complemented by Britons' participation in wider European aesthetic traditions.[19] The development of armorial porcelain – elaborate services of chinaware produced by skilled artisans in Jingdezhen and decorated both with European heraldic devices and Chinese decorative motifs – for example, linked British, Dutch, Portuguese, Spanish and Swedish merchants and consumers through transnational networks of both trade and self-fashioning.[20] Regional differences flourished within this global context, rather than being obliterated by transnational and trans-imperial trends. Scots composed perhaps 12 per cent of the British population but owned 21 per cent of documented armorial porcelain services. Their disproportionate possession of Chinese porcelain reflected both the conspicuous presence of Scottish men in the Company's service (including its trading hub in Canton) and the flight of Scots from Britain to the Swedish East India Company in the aftermath of the eighteenth-century Jacobite rebellions.[21]

Like porcelain, the carpets, wallpapers, lacquerware and textiles that journeyed through Company commerce from Asia to Britain's stately homes were doubly domesticated upon their arrival. Helen Clifford's chapter on Chinese wallpaper emphasizes the extent to which these Company imports combined Asian and British styles and tastes. As Oliver Impey has argued, such exotic luxury goods exerted a powerful impact on elite homes 'both by their own presence and by the imitations and pastiches they engendered'.[22] Far from representing unmediated examples of extra-European craftsmanship and design, Asian luxury items reflected the global character of Company trade and material culture. 'Almost all these imports from the East were heavily influenced by Western demand, and are thus often barely representative of the true arts of their origin', Impey reminds us. 'The carpets with coats of arms, the lacquer in Western shapes, the porcelain…and above all the wallpaper, that splendid amalgam of European, Chinese, and Indian styles, were all demanded in styles and shapes useful in a Western setting'.[23] Yuthika Sharma and Pauline Davies's chapter in this volume explores the accumulation of goods such as those by the Child family, prosperous bankers whose eighteenth-century Company connections filled Osterley House with Chinese and Indian luxuries that remain on display in this National Trust property today.

Studies of British landed estates and of the construction and design of stately homes have conventionally discounted imperial wealth as a source of country house culture, or have collapsed imperial fortunes into the generic category of 'new' money.[24] As global historians have traced the traffic of persons, goods and fashions from Asian centres of production and exchange to an entangled nexus of European consumer markets, the image of the country house and its interiors as a uniquely English or British contribution to material culture has however become increasingly problematic.[25] Stephanie Barczewski's recent survey of country houses built or purchased with imperial wealth identifies over a thousand landed estates in the British Isles acquired through imperial service between 1700 and 1930, suggesting that 6–16 per cent of stately homes were owned at some time in this interval by empire families. Barczewski estimates that 'men who made their fortunes either as employees of the East India Company or as "free traders" (i.e., independent merchants) in India', purchased 229 landed estates between 1700 and 1850 – figures that Chris Jeppesen's chapter in this volume suggest are an underestimate. The most substantial period of Company purchasing occurred between the 1750s and 1790s, the two generations that followed Clive's victory at Plassey.[26] Arguably the zenith of opportunity for private trade and political corruption by Company men, this period left an enduring mark on contemporary perceptions of Company wealth and material culture in the stereotype of the nabob.

As image and icon, the nabob dominates historians' efforts to assess the impact of Company trade, politics and culture at home in Britain.[27] The term first occurred in the English language in the early seventeenth-century as a derivation of the Persian 'nawab', denoting powerful officials in the Mughal court.[28] Deployed in Britain as a term of abuse, 'nabob' described an EIC official who had lived on the subcontinent, amassing a large fortune as well as a taste for Asian luxuries, practices and women. As Company officials gained new wealth and power after victory at Plassey in 1757, these men, their families and their fortunes were increasingly caricatured in the popular imagination, through news reporting, theatrical performances and novels. Plays such as Samuel Foote's *The Nabob* (first performed in 1772), Richard Sheridan's *The School for Scandal* (1777) and Fanny Burney's *A Busy Day; or, An Arrival from India* (1801) used the figure of the nabob to highlight issues of individual and nation-wide transformation in response to imperial wealth and power.[29] Visual representations drew attention to nabobs' two-fold acquisition (with their excessive Company fortunes) of country houses and Parliamentary seats, a depiction that both reinforced the traditional function of British stately homes as 'power-houses' and underscored the tendency of imperial wealth and politics to threaten established British hierarchies. James Gillray's 1797 caricature of the Madras merchant and MP Paul Benfield (1741–1810), who bankrolled both his Parliamentary seat and the purchase of Woodhall Park, Hertfordshire with his Indian profits, derided this nabob as 'Count Roupee'. A dark-complexioned horseman riding in Hyde Park, Gillray's retired Company servant flaunted the cultural attributes of a country gentleman even as he figured as nouveau riche and racially 'other'.[30]

Print culture, performance and the visual arts all represented Company men and women as problematic upstarts.[31] One of the central ways in which nabobs and their ilk mounted this challenge to traditional British identities was through the purchase, building, renovation and furnishing of country houses and estates. Tillman Nechtman argues that country house acquisition by EIC families caused alarm not only because these men and women encroached on the British establishment, but also for fear they might turn rural landscapes into 'micro-Indias'.[32] Such concerns were typically unfounded. To be sure, a small number of Company men (such as Charles Cockerell at Sezincote, Gloucestershire) designed stately homes calculated to remind visitors of their Asiatic lives and fortunes.[33] Far more common however was the encasement of Indian wealth in Palladian, Gothic, mock Tudor or Scottish Baronial architecture. A particularly vivid example of resistance to referencing Indian motifs in the fabric of country houses is seen in Kate Smith's chapter on Englefield House, Berkshire. Englefield's exterior projects a history of stability and lineage from the Elizabethan era onwards, rather than the labile narrative of global trade and politics chronicled in the archives of the interconnected Company families that inhabited and refashioned it in the eighteenth century.

As several of the chapters in this volume demonstrate, once in possession of a country house, Company men and women often worked sedulously to erase or obscure the provenance of their wealth. In doing so, they followed an example set by families whose fortunes were enriched by the slave trade and plantation slavery. Sheryllynne Haggerty and Susanne Seymour's research on Bolsover Castle and Brodsworth Hall has highlighted the tendency of country house owners to efface the traces of Caribbean commerce and plantations from their stately homes in Britain. They find, for example, 'no explicit evidence of Charles Thellusson's links to slavery, beyond the extensive use of mahogany, in the fabric and contents of the current Brodsworth Hall'.[34] Moral revulsion for Britain's central role in slavery and the slave trade encouraged propertied and powerful families to remove both material and text-based evidence of Caribbean colonialism from the historical record.[35] Margot Finn's chapter on the Russells of Swallowfield Park, Berkshire, suggests that Company men and women deployed analogous strategies of colonial amnesia in purchasing, furnishing and populating their stately homes. Asian wealth, moreover, repeatedly faded from memory and view through the strategic marriages of Company daughters – provided by their fathers with generous dowries funded by Company service. The marriage portion of Henrietta Russell, the daughter of a retired Chief Justice of Bengal, was Indian in origin. But the Lancashire marital home her fortune helped to build and furnish, Whittington Hall, figured in contemporary representations as quintessentially 'English'.[36]

While the caricature of the nabob was and remains important in understanding how the broader British public saw and understood the domestic impact of Company imperialism, this volume also works to locate Company men in wider social and cultural perspectives. Pushing beyond stereotypes to explore imperial practices that include erasure, evasion and reconfiguration, the chapters recognize the essential roles played by family members and networks (rather than focusing alone on the heroic individuals and villains who dominate Company hagiography and caricature). They acknowledge ways other than conspicuous consumption in which Indian fortunes were expended (such as agricultural improvement). And they underline the failure of many Company men to gain wealth, status or domestic comfort from their imperial careers. For, as Ellen Filor's chapter on the struggles of Alexander Hall (c.1731/2–64) and Penelope Farmer's chapter on her hapless ancestor William Gamul Farmer (1746–97) attest, access to the Company's privileged markets and sites of power did not invariably create pathways to the stately home and its elite interiors.

Understanding the multiplicity of motivations for purchasing or building a country house allows us to see a broader range of motivations at stake within both Company circles and the British country house tradition more generally. In his influential history of the stately home, Mark Girouard argued that 'people did not live in country houses unless they either possessed power, or, by setting up in a country house, were making a bid to possess it'.[37] Scrutiny of Company men's investment of their Indian fortunes reveals a wider range of country residences that embodied English, British and imperial knowledge and power. Alistair Mutch's chapter on General Patrick Duff (1742–1803) thus describes a Company man keen to purchase his Scottish estate not for the opportunities it offered to establish a 'power house' in which to display wealth and accumulate status, but rather to realize a long-held agrarian ambition to deploy at home skills and knowledge first learned in India.

Exploring Company families across their lifecycle, and including the experiences of Company women and children, also extends the range of practices and processes entailed by EIC investment beyond the stereotypical behaviours of nabobs. Focused on construction and purchase, the extant secondary literature on country houses takes little account of the vibrant rental market. Renting allowed the nouveau riche to experiment with and sample country life and to develop or test regional preferences prior to purchasing a country estate. For Company women, this intermediate stage of stately home possession was especially important, for many wives returned to Britain (often accompanied by gaggles of Indian-born progeny and attended by Indian servants) years before their husbands. The seeming permanence attached to country houses as family seats, an image conventionally cultivated in histories written by their owners, belies the fact that Company kin often occupied a succession of temporary homes – ranging from cottages to townhouses and stately homes – for significant periods before or after their acquisition of a family seat. Margot Finn's chapter on Swallowfield Park follows Lady Russell upon her return to England from Calcutta. Decades before her husband and eldest sons purchased the family seat, Lady Russell established a succession of itinerant households for her younger children and her remaining Indian servants in rented homes in London, Somerset and Kent. Similarly, Kate Smith's chapter on Warfield Park follows Company widow Margaret Benn Walsh from this Berkshire stately home – which she vacated to make space for her married son and his family – through a succession of rented houses in its vicinity. Wealthy Company widows such as Walsh were key figures in the country house landscape: Smith's chapter on Englefield House includes among its many Company residents Lady Margaret Clive (the widow of Clive of Plassey). Margaret Clive's occupation of Englefield in the 1780s allowed her to be near the concentrated cluster of Company families whose residence led contemporaries to dub

Berkshire the 'English Hindoostan', even as she enjoyed ready access to London's marriage market.

If the salience in Company women's biographies of temporary residence in a succession of rented stately homes counters dominant stereotypes of lavish nabob expenditure on country house ownership, the theme of failure that runs through many of our chapters likewise reminds us that the vast fortunes amassed by later eighteenth-century nabobs were the exception rather than the rule. Failure took many forms in Company families and Company homes: failure to accumulate wealth, failure to marry, failure to provide support for Indian concubines and their children, failure to return home or to reside in the imagined domestic comfort about which so many Company men wrote so poignantly in their private letters. All are leitmotifs of this volume. Ellen Filor's chapter on Alexander Hall chronicles this hapless Company servant's persistent failure to build a fortune in Sumatra, notwithstanding Hall's frantic efforts to capitalize on his entrepreneurial talents. Penelope Farmer's chapter likewise details William Gamul Farmer's chequered financial success during lengthy Company employment in the Bombay Presidency, only to die before he could enjoy an affluent retirement in Britain. (In contrast, Farmer's brother Sam, who remained in England and ran a successful dye manufactory, purchased Nonsuch Park in Surrey, possibly with inherited wealth derived from William's imperial endeavours). Like William Gamul Farmer, Archibald Seton failed to return home to Britain. Entering the Company service in a desperate effort to preserve his Perthshire family seat, Touch House, from creditors, Seton remitted tens of thousands of pounds from India to pay his father's debts and to refurbish Touch's interiors, but died on board ship on his final voyage home. His sister and her daughter inherited the historic Highland house, rehabilitated by Seton's protracted Company employment. Familial collaborations such as this, centred on country house preservation and refashioning, are also the focus of Margot Finn and Kate Smith's chapter on Touch House and Montreal Park.

While the failures experienced by some British families reframe our understanding of the nabob's place in the Company's social landscape, they also provide forceful reminders of the extent to which imperial success was won at the expense of others. If Company men figured in their own and their contemporaries' imaginations as acquisitive individuals, they relied heavily in practice upon the resources of subaltern and subjugated men and women to expand their activities and ambitions. Sven Beckert's *Empire of Cotton* emphasizes that the European East India Companies entered seventeenth- and eighteenth-century Asian trading networks through violent means, a conjoint commercial and military process he denominates 'war capitalism'.[38] Similarly, appropriation and exploitation fundamentally shaped Company men's personal lives on the subcontinent. Company domesticity was sustained by emotionally and sexually intimate relationships with Indian women, liaisons characterized by unequal power relations that have now been explored in considerable detail by historians of colonialism.[39] We know much less about the histories of those among the 'mixed-race' children born to these relationships who were sent 'home' to Britain by their fathers. Ellen Filor's chapter on Alexander Hall and Margot Finn's chapter on Swallowfield Park both note the marginal place occupied in Britain by children removed from their Indian mothers. As the episode of Philip Melvill (recounted in David Williams' chapter) also demonstrates, by the nineteenth century Company officials deemed such relationships controversial and destabilizing, and accordingly stepped into the supposedly private realm of the family to disrupt and displace them.

Understanding the importance of imperial wealth and artefacts to the purchase, building and furnishing of eighteenth- and nineteenth-century country houses underscores how these built environments – far from being exclusively British or English – were shaped by long histories of global interaction. Moving beyond the nabob as the key exemplar of EIC wealth also reveals longer and more complex genealogies of empire within the country house tradition. While the nabob heyday of the late eighteenth century significantly increased the numbers of country houses purchased through imperial wealth, early nineteenth-century perspectives provide glimpses of the longer-term impacts of imperial projects and connections. Diane James's chapter on Redcliffe Towers, Devon, explores the history of a new-built stately home constructed as late as the 1850s by Colonel Robert Smith (1787–1873), who had honed his skills as an architect and builder decades earlier on the subcontinent, in the service of the Bengal Engineers.

Global histories, local & national tastes

The studies in this volume link the received island-story of Britain's country houses to new histories of the global. Building on the work of earlier 'California School' scholars such as R. Bin Wong and Kenneth Pomeranz, Maxine Berg's research has argued that commerce with Asia deeply affected how Europeans traded, manufactured and consumed material goods in the eighteenth century.[40] Taking a pan-European approach, her research team has demonstrated the highly competitive relationships that existed between the European East India Companies and how their trade with Asian merchants – and with each other – multiplied the range of goods available in European markets.[41] Berg's work demonstrates the importance of examining both the circulation and the material qualities of commodities, and the extent to which high demand for these goods prompted European manufactures to imitation – forging new technologies and material cultures in Britain.[42] As Giorgio Riello and Robert Duplessis remind us, however, the popularity of these Asian commodities in Europe and the Atlantic World was not inevitable. Rather, their domestication required processes of appropriation and embedding. Consumers needed to learn to desire and deploy goods such as cotton, integrating them into sartorial and furnishing practice and using them as their own before their wider popularity was able to grow. Space mattered in this process of acculturation. Global lives are lived locally, and life in empire did not obliterate regional tastes and practices.[43] Understanding how the global worked at a local level is vital, and the 'glocal' is repeatedly at issue in this volume.[44]

Houses and households provide ideal sites for exploring the intersection of global processes and local lives. In the eighteenth and nineteenth centuries, British households increasingly purchased 'exotic' groceries and other global goods.[45] Propertied men and women used different global and imperial commodities, such as porcelain and tea, in tandem, mutually reinforcing their importance. The creation of stable demand gave room for the development of predictable, ever-increasing forms of supply. At the high end of the luxury market, country houses were key to the creation of this demand. As Jon Stobart and Mark Rothery's recent work demonstrates, rather than following 'taste leaders' such as globally connected merchants, country house owners were at the centre of new fashions, purchasing and commissioning goods from Asia and the Atlantic World.[46] The ostensible division between merchants and country house owners is however less distinct than it might appear. As this volume demonstrates, many country house owners were merchants or had connections to global trade in the eighteenth and nineteenth centuries. Research on country house consumption expands our understanding of the complex 'global' provisioning and furnishing of stately homes and underlines the country house as dynamic process, not fixed 'thing'. Through processes such as consumption, country houses were continually coming into being.[47]

The specific make-up of global commodities consumed within particular country houses was shaped not only by the tastes of their individual owners, but also by local and regional British tastes. The chapters in this volume identify distinct consumer preferences across the English regions, Highland and Lowland Scotland and Wales.[48] Regional difference is also important in considering the consumption of country houses themselves. Barczewski has shown that Company families were particularly conspicuous purchasers in the counties around London and in distinct areas of Scotland. Several contributions to this volume amplify this point. Finn and Smith's chapters on Berkshire, like Chris Jeppesen's chapter on Hertfordshire and Georgina Green's chapter on Essex, explore local clusters of Company kin that, once formed in the eighteenth century, shaped modes of living, marriage patterns and social networks into the Victorian era. Architectural features within country houses were also configured by engagement with Asian styles and tastes – a practice that included, but was not confined to, families with close Company connections. Rachael Barnwell's chapter identifies a trend for Chinese-style staircases in elite homes in North-West Wales in the 1750s and 1760s, a development which may reflect the material traces of Welsh service in the EIC or instead testify to the cosmopolitan tastes of a local Welsh builder alive to the contemporary rage for chinoiserie. Far from stretching uniformly across the country, the influence of Britain's trade with Asia displayed regional distinctions. Global connections are rooted and expressed in the particularity of local contexts.

Object stories

Ensconced in stately homes at the end of their long journeys in Company ships, objects of Asian provenance did not figure as inert backdrops to country house life. Rather, they were active players, shaping human behaviours and actions in Company homes. In this interpretation, more than merely reflecting society and its relations of power, objects work to constitute both power relations and society itself.[49] The formative – at times intractable or resistant – roles played by the Company's material objects have been under-developed, for much existing historical literature examines country house material culture through an art historical lens that renders imperial goods primarily as aesthetic objects.[50] More recent work however has begun to reveal these objects' shifting cultural meanings. Stacey Sloboda's analysis of chinoiserie, for example, argues that certain styles of Chinese porcelain imported by the EIC had the capacity 'not only to reflect – but also to shape – taste, identity, and political opinion'.[51] Stephen McDowall's study of the eighteenth-century armorial porcelain dinner service still displayed by the National Trust at Shugborough House, Staffordshire attests to the longevity and tenacity of Asian luxuries' purchase on narratives of empire, demonstrating their use in contemporary interpretations of Britain's imperial past in stately homes.[52] These lines of argument inform and resonate with the approach taken in the chapters of *The East India Company at Home*. Here the trans-imperial lives of 'objects' that included attar caskets, Persian seals, tinned salmon and Sumatran slaves figure actively in Company men and women's lives, working to build, and sometimes disrupt, political power and personal identities in India, China and Europe, and between the Indian Ocean World and Britain.

Understanding objects' mobility, impact and instability requires removing 'things' from the static environments in which they are placed in museum cases and stately homes. Displacement from the studied curatorial order of the museum reveals both these objects' potential utility as instruments for manufacturing memories and meanings, and the liability for such strategies to fall prey to alternative counter-narratives. Like the Company's broader claims to exert paramount power on the subcontinent, the ability of Company relics to impose orderly interpretations of the imperial past was partial and contested. Removed from its display case at the British Museum, the attar casket of Tipu Sultan, now held in the British Museum's collections, which provides the focal point of Sarah Longair and Cam Sharp Jones's chapter, proves to have an extended genealogy entangled with the extended family history of a Highland Company clan. Tracing the biographies of objects across time and space allows us to examine cross-cultural exchange and the formation of individual and group identities more closely. Throughout (and beyond) the Company era, European families deployed selected objects in projects of self-fashioning, but the multiplicity of meanings their imperial possessions were capable of evoking or channelling repeatedly subverted these familial agendas. Far from ordered and controllable, objects' meanings always threatened to spill over into unexpected territories. Kate Smith's chapter on the design, acquisition, use and display of armorial porcelain services by Company families within British country houses, demonstrates how objects were key to animating specific identities, such as elite masculinity. In Sir John Sykes's chapter, a seal used to complete business transactions on the subcontinent by his ancestor, Sir Francis Sykes (1730–1804), moves backwards and forwards between his own family and that of Sykes's banian (man of business), Krishna Kanta Nandy (c.1720–94). A mobile marker of Sykes's power which allowed business to happen, the seal was also a sign of trust, given to Indian 'others' to enact business on his behalf. Left in Nandy's safe hands when Sykes returned to Britain to establish himself as the owner of landed estates and a Berkshire stately home, the seal made both Sykes and Nandy powerful, and in the case of Nandy enabled multi-generational prosperity. Its biography illuminates the often-hidden Indian side of the Company story, albeit by focusing on Indian elites rather than the much more elusive subaltern men and women whose labours underpinned Company sociability, wealth and politics at home and on the subcontinent.[53]

Exploring the social life of these objects in a trans-imperial frame over time allows us to distinguish, through a material lens, between eighteenth- and nineteenth-century caricature and prescription, on the one hand, and social and economic practice, on the other. These Company objects continue to animate the stories that twenty-first-century contemporaries and heritage institutions tell about the past.[54] Postcolonial historians have rightly underlined the limitations of the textual archives that record past European empires, and the extent to which these archives distort our understanding even of imperial elites.[55] The object archive is likewise skewed and selective, privileging elites over subaltern historical agents and British over Indian voices and narratives. But its selectivity often reflects different processes of remembering and forgetting than the 'official' written archives of the Company and the state, and its use can thus help to reveal alternative narrative lines. Material objects, propertied Company families and country houses offer an imperfect, elite window onto the past. But precisely because exclusivity was central to their operation, they also reveal vital (albeit often fleeting and partial) glimpses of the excluded.

Research communities

This volume is a collaborative exercise, benefitting from the proliferation and integration of numerous research communities. Alongside curators, heritage professionals, archivists, antiques dealers, research consultants and academics, increasing numbers of independent researchers now investigate local and family histories, and in so doing discover their connection to global stories. Genealogical research is a particularly buoyant area of activity, attracting growing commercial interest and leading to the establishment of online search tools such as Findmypast and Ancestry. Projections suggest that the family history market will be worth $4.3 billion by 2018.[56] *The East India Company at Home* project and this ensuing volume are premised on the belief that engaging with the full spectrum of research communities and their methodologies is mutually enriching. Working closely with a range of archivists, heritage sector professionals, curators, dealers, research consultants, local historians and family historians across Britain and beyond to co-produce open-access publications – initially on the project website and now in this volume – has invited different conversations, material objects and interlocutors to our discussions of the East India Company's impact on British society and culture. Family and local historians in particular brought manuscripts and objects not available in the public domain quite literally to the table. Penelope Farmer's chapter on her ancestor William Gamul Farmer uses a collection of letters that remains within the family's possession; Georgina Green's chapter on Valentines Mansion benefits from porcelain shards not housed by any museum; Sir John Sykes's chapter is illuminated by family photographs absent from the public archive. A key purpose of this volume is to show that recovering histories of now defunct empires and their legacies for our own time requires greater acknowledgement of research produced not only outside universities, but also outside of public museums and archives.

This volume is organized into five sections. The sections move from a focus on the lives of objects purchased, looted, traded, gifted and collected by Company families, to Company families themselves and how they cultivated their identities and power over ever-expanding imperial distances and over the generations. The EIC's creation in 1600 gave British merchants and consumers new access to the wealth of objects and commodities on offer in Asia. Accordingly, the first section, 'The social life of things', includes chapters which focus on the transnational and highly mobile lives of commodities acquired and traded by Company men and women. It explores both the distances these things travelled and the changing purposes to which they were put. Following these objects and their place in British homes and institutions up to the present day demonstrates the complex locations and roles they have occupied as country houses have become heritage sites, and as private family collections have moved into public museums. The second section, 'Objects, houses, homes and the construction of identities', builds on earlier chapters by looking more closely at the uses to which Company families originally put Asian luxury objects. Whether by animating a gendered and imperial identity or by serving as sites through which to explore the impacts of imperialism, objects played active roles in the lives of Company men and women. Section three, 'The Home Counties: clusters and connections', begins to interrogate the importance that Company families placed on being located near to other Company families and their domesticated collections of material goods. It examines the lives and homes of families in Berkshire, Essex and Hertfordshire during the later eighteenth and early nineteenth century, seeking to understand the political, social, emotional and cultural benefits that accrued from proximity. These chapters track families or their stately homes over time to show how specific locales became marked as Company spaces or domestic nodes. Section four, 'On the borders: region, nation, globe', similarly examines issues of connection, proximity and distance at play in Britain more broadly. These chapters track local families with global connections to the Company and Asia, and also assess 'glocal' styles and interior architectural features. Section four pays particular attention to regions conventionally treated as peripheral to English identities, areas distant from London and the Home Counties such as the Scottish Borders and Highlands which played central parts in Company imperialism. Finally, section five, 'Company families and identities: writing history today', highlights individual Company men and women and their place within familial and wider kinship networks. These chapters ask how such networks were sustained over time and space and for what purpose. They also explore the ways in which networks were reconstituted when families returned to Britain and examine how Company connections persisted over multiple generations.

Country houses and the material objects they contained played pivotal roles in processes of imperial fashioning and refashioning. They continue to shape our perceptions and misperceptions of the East India Company today. Their history and its myriad entanglements attest to the persistent presence of empire in modern British culture.

Conclusion

Country houses, their elite occupants and luxurious furnishings conventionally figure in twenty-first-century British media as icons of an insular national identity. In Julian Fellowes's film *Gosford Park* (2001), as in his wildly successful *Downton Abbey* (2010–15), stately homes appear to radiate timeless convention, depicting power in material form as tradition and continuity even as their occupants' lives reflect fundamental changes in British society, culture, economics and politics. By treating stately homes and their material culture as active historical agents rather than as passive backdrops against which human agency occurs, the chapters in *The East India Company at Home* have sought to suggest both alternative genealogies of country house power and alternative definitions of

British identity. New imperial wealth – an exogenous force in pervasive present-day media representations of the eighteenth-, nineteenth- and twentieth-century country house – emerges from these studies as a vital cog in the machinery that maintained traditional 'British' structures of power and identity. To be sure, the threat of nabob wealth loomed large in Georgian caricature, where its conspicuous presence in elite stately homes represented an affront to established systems of property, privilege and Englishness. By the Victorian era however, this critique and its accompanying stereotype had long lost their force: Berkshire, Essex and Hertfordshire – like myriad British regions outside the Home Counties – proved more than capable of absorbing the material spoils of empire and of accommodating Company men, women and children into the propertied governing elite. Far from undermining the British country house as a bastion of power, East India Company fortunes helped to underpin the 'power house' tradition in these decades.

The East India Company at Home has demonstrated the importance not only of imperial wealth, but also of imperial objects and their meanings to Britain's country houses in the eighteenth and nineteenth century. As Jan de Vries has shown, the significance in Europe of Asian luxury goods lay less in the sheer volume of goods traded than in the impacts they exerted on culture and society.[57] By studying the interlinked material histories of 'objects' across a range of scales – in and between country houses, in different types of furniture and fine art and among different family groupings – we have sought to locate local and regional identities into a more productive dialogue with global and cosmopolitan histories of material culture. Adopting this approach helps to illuminate both the interconnections and the differences that marked Georgian and Victorian mobilizations of wealth and goods from Asia in British 'power houses'. Shared cultural systems such as the stereotype of the nabob afforded a common language for contemporary critiques of imperial endeavour in public discourse, but in the private settings of family and home a wider spectrum of interpretation – and validation – was available and repeatedly exploited. Meanings varied across time and space; they were activated by contexts, by individuals and by relationships with other objects. Global material culture studies must give greater credence to how local contexts produced meanings and power relations through imperial goods. More exploration is required of how such understandings then shaped the very systems of political control, exploitation, manufacturing, trade and consumption that produced these material items.

Ultimately, the chapters in this volume scratch only the surface of the EIC's material legacy on Georgian and Victorian stately homes, and the stately home itself affords only a partial view of the wider impact of empire on wealth and power in Britain in this period. While this volume has actively sought to bring into view the women, children and extended family members involved in EIC activities, the Indian servants who toiled in Company country houses are largely absent from our chapters, although archival traces of their journeys from the subcontinent to the country house – charged with the care of Company wives, children and animals – provide fleeting glances of their residence and labour.[58] Further research is needed to locate their lives, and the biographies of Company fathers' mixed-race children, more securely within the histories of the British country house and its material cultures.[59] By identifying EIC wealth, personnel and objects as integral components of Georgian and Victorian stately homes, however, we hope to prompt other family historians (and historians of the family) to uncover these hidden histories, and to encourage heritage sites to incorporate these imperial stories fully into their displays and narratives. Gaining and voicing a clearer understanding of the relationship between the local and the global will prompt historians and the wider public to move beyond the false dichotomy of the imperial 'here and there'. At the same time it will allow for a fuller investigation of the processes of silencing and evasion that have long been underway, hiding histories of empire in plain sight.

Empire fundamentally shaped elite British country houses in the eighteenth and nineteenth century, adding to the constellation of dynamic processes by which British built environments absorbed and reflected global material cultures. Situating EIC objects and their owners within specific country houses and locales and focusing in depth on the practices and identities they animated, the chapters in this volume demonstrate how global tastes and practices were embedded in local contexts. Entangled with fortunes built with Caribbean slave labour, stately homes are domestic sites that embody Britain's global histories. These histories, often painful and often effaced, deserve to be recovered more fully.

Section 1
The social life of things

In his introduction to *The Social Life of Things: Commodities in Cultural Perspective* (1986), Arjun Appadurai argued that 'we have to follow the things themselves, for their meanings are inscribed in their forms, their uses, their trajectories'.[1] Following the material objects that animated Britain's eighteenth- and nineteenth-century imperial project can prove taxing, however, for even the most seemingly immobile of things – animals, monuments, perishable foodstuffs – became highly portable in the Company era.[2] Trade, smuggling, gifting, looting, collecting, migration, decay and loss made objects both mobile and labile. Carried by merchants, mariners, family, friends, patrons, clients and their outright owners, Company things journeyed on sea and land routes, from port to retailer to recipient. Once on British soil, they moved between and among, moving between houses and household members. As Appadurai asserts, movement and change shape what commodities, things and objects are, how they function and what they mean. To understand material objects in imperial contexts at home in Britain, we must track their social lives, their entangled relationships with people, other objects and places and explore how such embodied material networks affected their values and meanings.

The four chapters in this section explore the acquisition, display and interpretation of Asian and Company material objects in domestic British contexts, heritage sites and museums. Sarah Longair and Cam Sharp Jones's chapter analyses an intricately decorated filigree casket now in the British Museum's collections. Documentary evidence suggests that the casket once belonged to Tipu Sultan (c.1750–99) but was removed – perhaps looted – from Seringapatam (present day Siringapatna) in 1799 after Tipu's defeat by the British in the Fourth Anglo-Mysore War. The casket's subsequent history in private hands demonstrates how Company men and women fostered and perpetuated the Indian genealogies of their Asian objects long after these items had been relocated to Britain. Yet, even as they used mobile material things to document, celebrate and justify their lives on the subcontinent, the casket's successive owners also deployed this meaningful thing to knit together a shared family identity for the far-flung kin of the Fraser of Lovat clan. Enmeshed in family stories that stretched from Karnataka and Tamil Nadu to the Scottish Highlands, the casket came to rest in London's Bloomsbury. Here, its donation to and exhibition in the British Museum have worked at multiple levels to domesticate an exceptionally violent episode in the East India Company's protracted campaigns to assert territorial and mercantile hegemony on the subcontinent.

Helen Clifford's chapter on Chinese wallpaper also examines questions of provenance, origin and connection. Focusing on the processes and routes by which Chinese wallpaper came to adorn so many stately homes in Britain, it explores both how Company connections provided access to 'Oriental' furnishings and why elite men and women – living in an age most often associated with neo-classical tastes – invested time, money and social capital to acquire, install and elaborate these exotic Company goods. Like Longair and Sharp Jones's chapter, Clifford's contribution benefits from engagements with a diverse range of expertise, stretching from the heritage sector through the museum to the academy. Her analysis of Chinese wallpaper, researched in collaboration with National Trust staff, demonstrates how the interpretation of complex imperial objects benefits from interdisciplinary methodologies that work to unpick both material conditions of production and the meanings things can embody and express.

Kate Smith's chapter on ivory furniture looks both at the making of these imperial objects and the meanings attached to their presence in British country houses in the eighteenth, nineteenth and twentieth centuries. Now subject to global export bans inspired by conservationists, ivory furniture was among the most luxurious of Asian commodities to which Company commerce and connection gave elite Georgian men and women privileged access. At moments of purchase, dismantling and recirculation, ivory furniture provided a matrix for the construction, display or perpetuation of families' connection to the East India Company. The aesthetic and material particularities of ivory furniture represented the craft cultures of specific areas of the subcontinent, such as Vizagapatam and Murshidabad. Ivory furniture crafted in these sites allowed Company men (and their descendants) to signify the specificity of their imperial experiences in different regions of the subcontinent. As potent symbols of the imperial project these objects continue to act as signifiers of imperial histories within families and museums today.

Yuthika Sharma and Pauline Davies's chapter on Osterley Park and House, Hounslow reminds us that not all Company men and women obtained Asian luxury objects during periods of residence on the subcontinent. Three generations of the Child family, which owned and furnished Osterley, were involved at a distance in administering the late seventeenth- and eighteenth-century East India Company. Although none of the house's denizens are known to have travelled to Asia, the Childs obtained a wealth of lacquer furniture, textiles and armorial porcelain through their Company connections. These objects still reside in Osterley today, yet their conspicuous presence has historically figured as an anomalous backdrop in a National Trust site more typically presented to the public in its guise as a neoclassical stately home fashioned by the celebrated Robert Adam (1728–92). It is precisely by exploring the intersection of material histories such as these – the entangled British, European, Indian and Chinese biographies of things – that this section aims to illuminate the domestic lives of Company society and culture.

1
Prize possession

The 'silver coffer' of Tipu Sultan and the Fraser family

Sarah Longair and Cam Sharp Jones [1]

Amongst the myriad treasures in the British Museum is an intricately decorated filigree casket, displayed for many years in the museum's Addis Gallery of Islamic Art (see Figure 1.1).[2] Inside are six small bottles, a ladle and a funnel bearing a minute Persian inscription on the rim. Two documents written by one-time owners of the casket – one an undated letter, the other an incomplete note – give tantalizing details about the casket's provenance.[3] These fragments of evidence describe how General Hastings Fraser (1771–1852) obtained the object from the palace of Tipu Sultan (1750–99), the celebrated ruler of the Kingdom of Mysore, after the dramatic defeat of Tipu's army and his death at Seringapatam (present-day Srirangapatna) on 4 May 1799. As we learn from the second letter, the Frasers believed the Persian inscription on the funnel referred to Haider Ali (d. 1782), father of Tipu Sultan.[4]

These documents contain further intriguing references to the casket's subsequent journey until its donation by Colonel Henry Fraser to the British Museum in 1904. The first letter, dated 11 August 1846, is from an unspecified correspondent:

> At the taking of Seringapatam in 1799 my Uncle Mr Fraser was present and afterwards appointed Prize Agent to the treasures, jewels, etc there found. This silver coffer was in Tipoo's own room and with a silken carpet and coral chaplet was sent by HF to his mother at Mt Capper and were by her given to her youngest daughter Charlotte Catherine, From whom the boxe was given to her son J M Heath who

wished his youngest cousin H Fraser to have it as a family relic. His surviving sister Isabella A Heath now transfers it to HF as d...

The second, subsequent letter dates from c.1876 and was composed by Isabella A. Heath:

> Dear Henry I believe you are the discoverer of Hyder's name on the casket, & of course to an outsider who did not know its history it increases its value as a genuine historic relic. There was an article in a recent no. of 'The World' on Mr Lowe, there they spoke of two of the few relics of Tipoo's time preserved at his house, got by someone who had them at the siege of Seringapatam, one was a small drinking horn or flask of Rhinocerous horn found in his private apartments and both highly valued by their possessors. With love ever your affect. cousin Isabella A Heath

In this chapter we untangle the history of this object and the associated individuals to shed light on several wider questions about how material culture from India operated within the homes of East India Company (EIC) families, of which the Frasers – a Scottish Highland family and branch of Clan Fraser of Lovat – represent a useful example. These questions include: how does the domestication of spoils of war represent family identities, dynastic legitimacy and imperial legacies over generations across the empire?[5] When was the association with Tipu Sultan mobilized and to what end? How did this connection shift in and out of view as the casket's meaning and value changed in different contexts? The enduring significance of Tipu Sultan in nineteenth-century Britain and the particular attention paid by family members to transferring the casket between generations both in India and England make this object's biography particularly revealing.[6] It was not an explicitly martial object, offering possibilities for domestic reinterpretation.[7] We remain mindful of the risks associated with isolating a specific object for investigation to draw wider conclusions, as it was likely to be one of many produced.[8] However, the associations embodied within this particular object merit further scrutiny.

While the documentary evidence connected to the casket remains minimal, we can usefully situate it within different historical and material contexts to establish the significance of its history. Large numbers of objects from Seringapatam remain in the private collections of the descendants of army officers present at the battle.[9] For this reason their changing locations, uses and meanings remain concealed. Evidence of the casket's treatment therefore offers a window into these hidden histories. The chronology of the

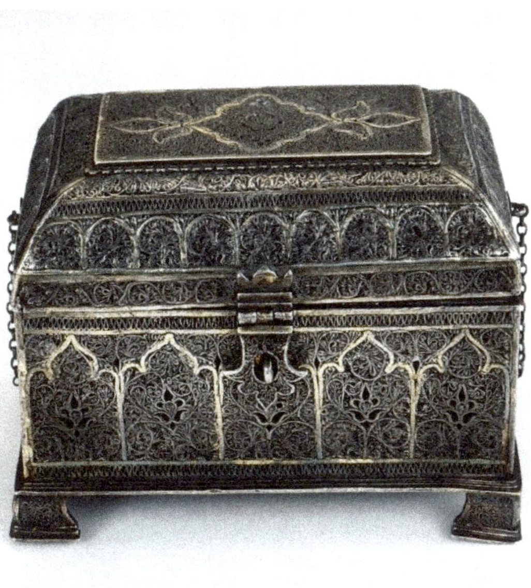

Figure 1.1 Openwork silver and silver gilt filigree casket, H: 9 cm; W: 12 cm; D: 8.5 cm. 1904,1006.1.a. © The Trustees of the British Museum.

Frasers' entanglement with India is also notable. In contrast to the Scottish elite 'sojourners' of the late eighteenth century whose relatively short periods in India were devoted to the rapid acquisition of fortunes leading to accusations of 'nabobery', families like the Frasers established a form of family 'seat' in Cuddalore. Subsequent generations lived mobile lives maintaining connections across the empire and in the metropole.[10] This case study indicates that for this group, material culture was and remained a source of pride, and a symbol of imperial identity and status. The timing of this object's donation to the Museum and the scant but illuminating documentary and material evidence therefore offer a view into the domestication of Tipu's legacy in Company family homes across time and space.

The casket's origins in eighteenth-century India

The casket, measuring 12cm long, 9cm high and 8.5cm deep, is made entirely of fine, openwork filigree. The filigree consists of silver wire in the form of florets and volute-like patterns imitating scrolling foliage, contained within frames of flattened silver gilt wire that creates a panelled effect across the sides of the casket. The scrolling foliage design continues across the hinged bevelled lid in smaller panels and bands whilst the top of the lid is decorated with a central six-petal flower surrounded by a scalloped diamond in gilded, flattened wire which develops into a trefoil design. The base is decorated with a radiating rosette motif surrounded by volute curls that is raised up on four feet and can be closed using the loop and palmette-shaped hinged hasp. Interestingly, no evidence is visible (wear or scratching) on the casket or hasp, suggesting it was not repeatedly locked shut. Both the feet and the hinged lock are decorated with the same scrolling foliage pattern found on the rest of the casket. Inside the casket is an inserted silver panel with eight circular holes that separate and hold six 7cm-high silver bottles.[11] The two smaller holes in the panel hold a small silver funnel and ladle. The bottles, ladle and funnel are made of highly polished silver, whilst the inserted panel is decorated with the same scrolling foliage seen on the exterior of the casket, indicating that the interior insert was made at the same time as the casket and was not a later addition.

Dated to the eighteenth century, the casket's decoration and form combine both European and Indian motifs and designs. As with many examples of early filigree, it contains no maker's marks to identify the locality of production. The shape of the casket is found in European examples of filigree and silver work as well as Mughal and Iranian examples of this period, whilst the tightly scrolling decoration is common to Indian and South-East Asian-made articles of this type.[12] During the eighteenth century, growing global engagement resulted in increasing levels of artistic exchange, not just in metal work but also painting, sculpture and architecture. Filigree production flourished in various centres in South Asia during the eighteenth century, including cities such as Goa and those in the Deccan as well as South East Asian centres such as Batavia and Macau.[13] Increasing trade links and mobility between such localities created an environment in which artistic styles were transmitted from place to place, making the attribution to a specific centre problematic. Susan Stronge suggests that the casket was possibly produced in the Deccan, although the shape bears a strong resemblance to boxes and caskets known to have been produced in Goa. A recently acquired and stylistically similar casket in the Victoria and Albert Museum's collection is attributed to Karimnagar, India.[14] The donor of the V&A casket intriguingly also stated that it was said to come from Tipu Sultan's palace. Other examples of silver filigree work attributed to the collections of Tipu Sultan are found in the Clive collection at Powis Castle and are ascribed an East Asian origin – highlighting the influence expanding trade routes had on the ability to collect material goods from wide-ranging localities.[15]

The use of silver filigree throughout the construction of the casket, including the base, makes the casket lightweight and easy to handle and as such to transport. Whilst in many examples the function of such caskets or 'dans' (meaning box) is unknown, in this case the presence of the funnel and ladle indicates that the casket was an 'attardan' or scent holder for storing perfumed oils and waters. These fluids, such as rosewater, were typically used during festivals, dinners and social events to create a luxurious and fragrant atmosphere as well as having specific social functions such as the sprinkling of rosewater to indicate the end of formal gatherings.[16] Perfumes also had a more intimate use for both men and women through the perfuming of the body and clothes. Although the use of perfumes was not limited to the elite, the combination of the silver filigree casket with such liquids, indicates that the casket was most likely regarded as a luxury item both within the Mysorean court and European society.

We know from the transcribed letters which accompany the casket that Henry Fraser identified a minute stamp on the silver funnel, translating the Persian inscription as 'Hyder' which he read as a reference to Haider Ali, Tipu Sultan's father. This reading reinforced the Frasers' belief in the connection between the casket and the family of Tipu Sultan. Interestingly a reappraisal of the inscription has highlighted that what Fraser read as 'Hyder' can also be transliterated as 'Haider' or 'Haydar'.[17] Haider can be both a personal name, meaning lion, or as Stronge states, is the title given to the Prophet's son-in-law 'Ali (the first Shi'ite Imam).[18] Stronge argues that the writing, stamping or inlaying of 'Haider' (ردیح) or more simply a 'H' (ح) onto items from Tipu Sultan's court, provided a multi-layered association to both the Prophet's son-in-law as well as Tipu's father.[19] This association was further enhanced by the 'Haider' being surrounded by a stylized tiger stripe which appeared on numerous objects associated with Tipu, including guns, textiles, swords, painting and architectural decoration.[20]

The tiger motif became so closely associated with Tipu Sultan that he was often referred to as the 'Tiger of Mysore' within contemporary literature.[21] This use of the tiger as a symbol was not only a reference to the Islamic and Iranian belief in the tiger and lion being interchangeable symbols of power and religion, for these creatures also had spiritual significance for Hindu communities.[22] Although Tipu Sultan and Haider Ali were Muslim, the kingdom they ruled was predominantly Hindu. The use of the tiger was open to multiple interpretations and may have produced a positive association with the local populace towards these new rulers. Richard Davis argues that the use of the tiger motif created a visual connection between earlier dynastic rulers of the region, such as the Colas who had also used the tiger stripe as an official insignia.[23] In this regard, the use of 'Haider' within the tiger stripe produced multiple allusions and associations on both a local and global level.

These varied meanings not only allied Tipu Sultan and his kingdom to the local population and so helped to maintain a stable populace, but also demonstrated his religious devotion. This is also mirrored in the 'Haider' stamp. When transliterated by Henry Fraser, he took it to mean 'Hyder 'Ali' and so confirmed a dynastic connection, through Tipu's inheritance of the casket from his father. Although Henry Fraser most probably missed the religious association that Stronge argues was one of the meanings behind the stamp, the fact that he was researching and studying this casket shows an attempt to understand the object in his possession, not just as a decorative item but also its history and the significance of its inscription.

Material culture from Seringapatam

Tipu Sultan, born on 20 November 1750 to Haider Ali's second wife, Fatima, or Fakr-un-Nissa, was well-known during his lifetime as one of the most formidable opponents of the East India Company, and his reputation endured throughout the nineteenth century.[24] Both his and his father's resistance to European expansion effectively kept the Company at bay for decades through their command of large and well-resourced armed forces in battle. The fall of Mysore and Tipu's death at the battle of Seringapatam in 1799 became symbolic of EIC domination in the subcontinent, all the more potent as Tipu was a respected leader who had resisted for so long and died heroically defending his city. According to Denys Forrest, while politicians' pride in the success was tempered by their suspicion about the ambitions of Lord Wellesley who led the attack, it was a time for celebration for the wider population: 'on the demotic level, among the ordinary John Bull patriots of market place and farm and tavern, there was a robust and enduring sense of triumph over the terrible Tiger of Mysore. Beating Tipu might not be quite the same thing as beating Boney, but it was a step in the right direction!'[25] This sentiment is entangled with a sense of admiration and awe. Walter Scott remarked in 1814 that Tipu possessed greater resolve and 'dogged spirit of resolution' than Napoleon, dying 'manfully upon the breach of his capital city with his sabre clenched in his hand', an assessment written at the time of Napoleon's abdication.[26] Comparison between these enemies brought home the serious threat that Tipu had posed to Britain's empire in India and the nobility of his death.

Beyond the inevitable political shifts which occurred in the wake of the defeat of Tipu Sultan, the impact of the battle was transmitted tangibly to Britain by the dissemination of images and the material legacy of the encounter. Artists in Britain were inspired by the dramatic events, imagining key moments in the battle in paintings. Prints of such images were popular and circulated widely.[27] Robert Ker Porter created one of the most spectacular renditions of Seringapatam in the form of a 21-foot high and 120-foot long semi-circular painted panorama, first displayed in the Lyceum in London, which then toured Britain and the United States.[28]

The seizure of material from the palace and city by the East India Company army had an even wider resonance. The extent of the looting and plunder of the palace was vast and unprecedented. As Moienuddin writes, 'The manner in which Tipu's palace was pillaged for his priceless possessions, handkerchiefs and footwear included, has no parallel in Indian history.'[29] The Prize Committee, officially charged with the task of allocating Tipu's possessions and the contents of his treasury, noted that: 'There was everything that power could command or money could purchase.'[30] General Hastings Fraser, acquirer of the casket, was a member of this Prize Committee. The most celebrated of such objects is of course the so-called Tipu's Tiger – the mechanical organ which when wound creates a roaring sound as the wooden tiger mauls an English soldier, which went on public display at the EIC's India Museum in London.[31] The vast majority of the material from the siege and the Prize sales, however, was not presented to the Company but remained in private hands, as with the casket.[32] As Anne Buddle notes, 'Any Seringapatam souvenir was carefully preserved.'[33]

A large number and wide variety of pieces were taken. Manuscripts, jewellery, armour, cabinets, silverware, porcelain and weaponry were amassed in Britain, many of which were described as the personal property of Tipu Sultan.[34] Jasanoff vividly assesses the quantity of objects said to come from Tipu's body: were these attributions genuine, 'the king had staggered into battle swaddled in turbans, padded jackets, helmets and sashes; slung around with pistols, muskets, daggers, and sabres; and packed up with a baffling assortment of trinkets and bibelots – from a folding wooden telescope to a gold European pocket watch'.[35] She highlights the importance of direct connection to Tipu's body to objects gaining specific value as relics. In the second letter above, Heath specifically notes the Haider stamp as proof of its being a 'genuine historical relic'.

The careful preservation of these objects in many families, evidence of which can be seen in the exhaustive work of Moienuddin, indicates how attachment to Tipu Sultan remains significant to this day.[36] 'Hero relics' – such as those associated with Nelson – similarly captured the imagination of Victorians.[37] The element of nobility in battle associated with these objects serves as a contrast to the criticisms surrounding the material culture of nabobs in the late eighteenth century, whose finery and conspicuously 'eastern' possessions represented their new wealth and suspicious exotic lifestyles.[38] The connection with Tipu Sultan trumped such negative connotations.

Myths establishing the pieces as personal possessions of Tipu Sultan, whether asserted by the soldiers who seized them or later embellished within family folklore, indicate the particular significance of proximity to the great ruler and the family's direct involvement in the iconic battle. Such objects authenticated these narratives. Interestingly, Moienuddin notes that Wellesley ordered all Tipu's personal belongings to be returned to England to prevent them 'from being distributed as "sacred relics of Tipu Sultan the Martyr" lest they be used to mobilize the people against the expansionist policy of the British'.[39] In Britain, Tipu's possessions ensured that his legendary status endured: it was vital that he was seen as a powerful foe in order to maintain the significance of the British victory and justify an expansionist policy in India. At the level of individual objects, their return to Britain transformed them into relics of a different kind: moving from a Mysorean palace to British domestic settings, they embodied ancestral service to the expanding empire.

Such objects and the memory of Tipu remained significant throughout the nineteenth century, a phenomenon which prompted Isabella Heath to write her letter to Henry Fraser.[40] She was inspired by 'an article in a recent no. of "The World" on Mr Lowe' which referred to 'two of the few relics of Tipoo's time preserved at his house'. This refers to a 'through the keyhole' style article about the home of the Chancellor of the Exchequer, Robert Lowe (1811–92), later Viscount Sherbrooke.[41] Articles such as this underline the interest in possessions, display and domesticity of the Victorian era.[42] Lowe's distant cousin, Sir John Sherbrooke (1764–1830), who rose to become Governor General of British North America in 1816, had earlier in his career led one of the battalions at Seringapatam. Throughout his life he retained 'the curved sword of Tippoo Sultaun, with its blade inlaid with mother-of-pearl; and his rhinoceros-horn drinking-cup, known as the "poison cup", a short, flat bottle, which he exclusively used to avert being poisoned. Also Tippoo's bridle, saddle, and holsters'.[43] These items evidently passed to Lowe, who, as a boy had referred to Sir

John as 'Uncle'.[44] Reading this description impelled Isabella Heath to put pen to paper and proclaim the 'genuine' history of the casket stamped upon its surface and assert her family's similarly distinguished global history.

The Fraser family and the casket: between Britain and India

Colonel Henry Fraser donated the casket to the British Museum in 1904, and the references in the letters allow us to trace its journey from Seringapatam to the Museum via various members of the Fraser family. The history of the family is worth exploring in full as it reflects the complex nature of imperial families from the late eighteenth to the early twentieth centuries (see Figure 1.2). The 'Uncle Fraser' to whom the first letter refers and who acquired the casket is General Hastings Fraser (1771–1852), mentioned by Major Alexander Allan in his account of the battle.[45] Fraser was one of 10 children of General Charles Fraser (c.1737–95) and Isabella Hook (1755–1821). The Frasers of Ardachy were members of the Scottish elite, descended from a branch of Clan Fraser of Lovat on Charles's father's side, while his mother was daughter of the ninth Earl of Argyll.[46] Charles Fraser had previously served in the Marines and joined the East India Company in 1762 taking his first post in Madras.[47] He returned on leave in 1768 when he and Hook married and they returned together to Madras the following year for 10 years residence in India, thereby establishing themselves as an expatriate family rather than the more typical individual male 'sojourners'.[48] Their eldest child, born in 1771 at Vellore, was named Hastings 'in acknowledgement of several acts of kindness rendered to the father by Warren Hastings', then member of the Council at Madras.[49] The future Governor General wrote to the parents thanking them for this honour, offering the gift of a shawl. The whole family moved back to Britain around 1779. Charles returned to India without his family, dying in 1795 as General of Division of the Company Army. His widow Isabella lived for a further 26 years, returning herself to India and dying at Mount Capper, Cuddalore, in 1821.[50]

Of their ten children, three died before reaching adulthood – one, Pasley Weir, drowning on the way to join his father as a cadet in India. Their eighth child, Elizabeth Fraser, aged only 15, married Colonel Francis Capper in 1791. Although Elizabeth died without issue in 1795 the families appear to have remained closely connected. Mount Capper in Cuddalore (just over 100 miles south of Madras) seems to have been the centre of family activity. Evidence indicates that the villa was built by a member of the Capper family in 1798 and passed to Hastings Fraser in 1805.[51] The first letter suggests that Isabella Fraser moved into the house during her widowhood as she was resident there when Hastings presented the casket to her. The weddings of Charles and Isabella's ninth daughter, also named Isabella, to Charles Carpenter in 1805, and of their youngest daughter, Charlotte Catherine, to Josiah Marshall Heath in 1816 both took place at Mount Capper.[52]

We return now to the original acquirer of the casket, Hastings Fraser, who joined the army in 1788, serving in several campaigns in the East Indies, and rose to a high rank by the late 1790s. He was only 28 when he led his regiment against Tipu Sultan in 1799. He was nominated as one of the Prize Agents who were tasked with distributing the treasury of Tipu Sultan. The first letter records that of the items he himself received, he sent this 'silver coffer ... from Tipoo's own room', a silk carpet and a string of coral beads (the 'chaplet') to his mother at Mount Capper. Later in his career, Hastings Fraser's fine leadership at the taking of the Island of Bourbon (Réunion Island) in 1810 was recognized by his own corps, who presented him with a valuable sword, and by the 'native' regiments, who gave him a silver plate. These were the first items mentioned in his will, in which Hastings Fraser bequeathed them to his brother James (see below) with instructions that they were to be passed on to his nephew and namesake.[53] He died unmarried in London in 1852, aged 83, after receiving several military offices.[54] It is clear, therefore, that objects associated with military victories held particular significance to the family.

Charles and Isabella Fraser's fifth son, James Stuart Fraser (1783–1869), who inherited the estate on Hastings's death, was also a distinguished East India Company officer, who at one stage was responsible for transporting the Princes of Mysore, the descendants of Haider Ali and Tipu Sultan, to Bengal in 1807. Rising to the position of British Resident at the Court of the Nizam of Hyderabad in 1839, he remained in India until 1853 after resigning the previous year due to a disagreement with the Marquis of Dalhousie over the Company policy of expansion into Berar. His marriage to Henrietta Stevenson (1809–60), daughter of another significant Company family, had also taken place at Cuddalore. Of their eight children, Hastings was the eldest son, named after his uncle. Their third son Henry (c.1833–1906) was the final family member to possess the casket before he gave it to the British Museum.[55] Their eldest child Harriet (1827–82) had 13 children – several of whom served in imperial territories. In maintaining and benefitting from a close connection to the Company over generations, the Fraser family mirrored the

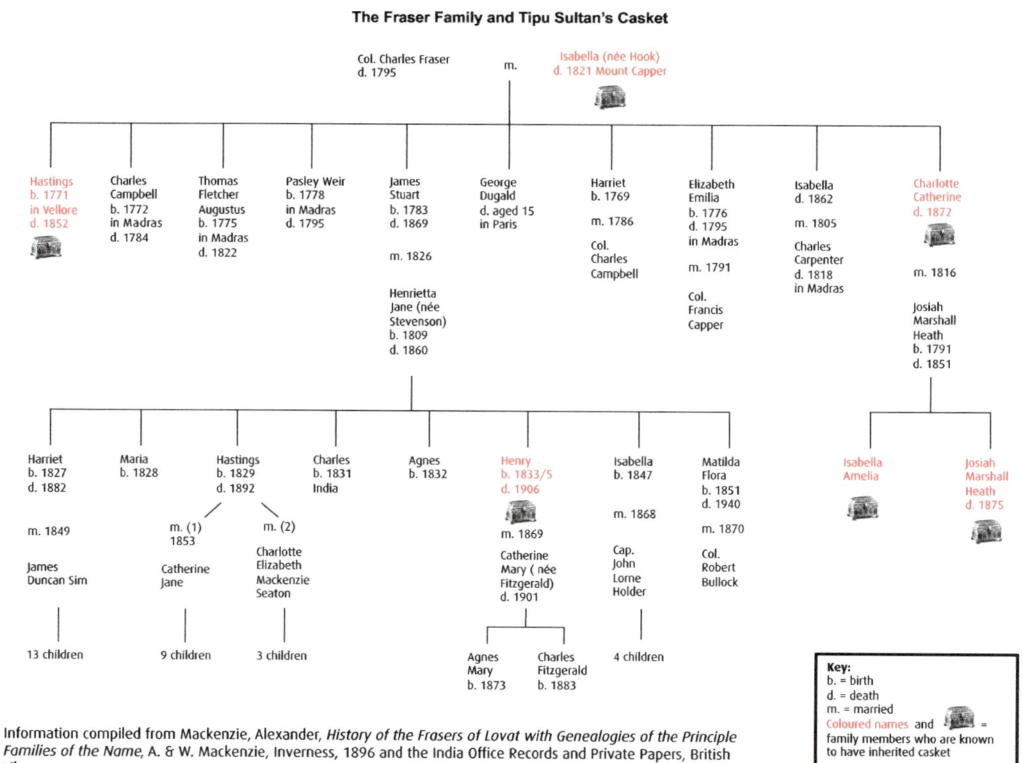

Information compiled from Mackenzie, Alexander, *History of the Frasers of Lovat with Genealogies of the Principle Families of the Name*, A. & W. Mackenzie, Inverness, 1896 and the India Office Records and Private Papers, British Library.

Figure 1.2 Family tree of the Fraser family showing casket's passage between family members, designed by C. Sharp Jones.

experiences of other imperial families, such as the Melvill family (discussed in Section 5 of this volume).

Before the casket came into Henry Fraser's hands, the first letter indicates that Josiah and Charlotte Heath's son, also named Josiah Marshall Heath (1827–75), received it from his mother.[56] It was Josiah who felt it appropriate that Henry Fraser, his cousin, receive the casket, an act, we learn from the letter, undertaken by his sister Isabella Heath. This Isabella was the author of the second letter, which reveals the intriguing detail that Henry Fraser translated the Haider Ali inscription. As discussed earlier, this stamp is minute and would have required a magnifying glass and expertise in reading Persian script to decipher. We can then infer that the object was not only a 'family relic' with anecdotal history but also one which was subject to close scrutiny by its new owner, a source of fascination and perhaps pride, beyond being an exquisite piece of craftsmanship. Heath specifically noted the significance of the Haider Ali stamp. While clearly of eastern origin, its particular direct link to Tipu Sultan was not evident to the naked eye. This allowed the violence surrounding its acquisition to be silenced or disclosed at the will of the owners. While it is an undeniably aesthetically impressive artwork, Heath in this letter underlined the wider value of such items and their provenance, reinforcing its meaning to the next generation. Its enduring association with the celebrated Indian rulers and its particular passage between different family members – both male and female – suggest that it came to symbolise the family's lengthy connections with the empire in India.

Henry Fraser did not donate any other objects to the British Museum, and within the scope of this research, we have found no other references to donations to other institutions. We cannot therefore draw conclusions about his motivations. Within the longer history of the casket, however, certain elements stand out. This treasured possession was not simply passed down from one generation to another but presented specifically to relatives to whom it was deemed of interest or relevance – indicating that it had heightened importance.[57] Unlike a sword which might have automatically been passed between male relatives, this object was given first from son to mother, then mother to daughter, to her son, to his sister and finally to their male cousin. The enthusiasm by Lady Clive to acquire objects after Seringapatam suggests that collecting this material was taken up by men and women alike. The casket seems not to have acquired a specifically gendered meaning – a delicate and exquisite piece of craftsmanship designed to hold scented oils, it was also bound up with a narrative of battle, bloodshed and empire-building.[58]

The casket in the British Museum

Whilst it is not possible to determine how the casket was displayed or used by the Fraser family either in India or in Britain, we can explore aspects of the casket's history as a 'social' and 'exhibited' object in the British Museum. As already mentioned, it was donated to the Museum by Henry Fraser in 1904, and the register records that on 6 October 1904 Colonel Henry Fraser gave an 'attar khana, taken at siege of Seringapatam 1799, the native forces being under Tipoo Sultan, whose father's name (Hyder 'Ali) is on the silver funnel'.[59] Although brief, this record highlights that even when the casket was donated, its intended use, as a holder of perfumes and, most importantly, its historical connection to Tipu Sultan and his father, were intrinsic elements of its value to the Museum and possibly the reason for its donation. The casket was initially deposited in the collection of the British and Mediaeval Antiquities and Ethnography department and then transferred to the new Oriental Antiquities and Ethnography department in 1933. This department was renamed the Asia department in 2003.[60]

When put on display in 2002, the casket was housed in a cabinet containing Mughal-era objects in the Addis Gallery of Islamic Art as a fine example of South Asian artistry. As with other material goods taken from Tipu Sultan's palace on display in public collections around the country, the casket's accompanying label refers to its link to Tipu Sultan and the siege of Seringapatam.[61] In the limited word-count of museum labels, only one aspect of the casket's history can be highlighted. The brevity of the label veils the casket's position as a colonial 'prize' and its symbolism of the dynastic connections between the Fraser family and the East India Company. The familial connections that the Fraser family wove around the casket exposed in this essay offer perspectives on the 'colonial moment' in the lives of objects, elements of the continuing history and social life of the object from its creation to the modern day, which are rarely given space in museum labels.[62] The casket is soon to be moved from the British Museum's gallery devoted to Islamic art to a newly-curated case in the South Asia gallery exploring colonial India, a recontextualization which brings the object's connections to imperial expansion to the fore.

Conclusion: shifting meanings

Different aspects of the casket's history continue to be mobilized. In this paper we have traced the earlier relocations of the casket and discussed the changing and simultaneous meanings it held. To augment the fragmentary evidence about the casket's history, we have located it within three contexts: its production and connection to the dynasty of Tipu Sultan, its role as one of spoils of Seringapatam, and its place within the Fraser family. While the casket's story fits within the broader pattern of South Asian material culture coming to Britain in the Company era and during Crown rule, we have revealed several remarkable elements about this particular object. In the first instance, the presence of the Haider Ali stamp gives a direct link to Tipu Sultan's palace, which other similar caskets do not have. As we have shown, however, the meaning of this stamp is not only of interest for asserting provenance. As Moienuddin states, all objects from Tipu's palace 'define very clearly the personality of Tipu and his tolerant religious perceptions and practices'.[63] The multiple interpretations of the stamp support this view of Tipu and his possessions.

The casket is notable in the dispersal of material from Seringapatam for its retention in India for several decades. The Frasers are significant in the late eighteenth century-history of the Company for establishing a family home in India. Characteristics such as large numbers of children, some of whom perished young, others who led transient lives between Britain and the subcontinent, and relocating for education, marriage and career prospects, would become more common throughout the nineteenth century. Perceptions of imperial service had shifted by the mid-nineteenth century when the casket came to Britain. Members of the Fraser family were evidently proud of their involvement in the early history of the Company, as made clear by the naming of one of their children as Hastings in 1829. This name not only honoured the boy's uncle but also recalled the family's connections to the late eighteenth-century grandees of the EIC. The casket was a material representation of such personal and political tributes. No longer did Indian material culture prompt accusations of 'nabobery', and therefore this object could unequivocally celebrate the long and distinguished history of the Frasers as early participants in the subjugation of the subcontinent and establishment of the empire.

2
Chinese wallpaper

From Canton to country house

Helen Clifford

Made from bast fibres (material made from the inner bark of trees, such as paper mulberry and blue sandalwood) and backed with a thicker paper made of bamboo fibres, laminated together with starch, Chinese wallpaper was (and still is) hand painted in vivid colours, sometimes with the aid of block-printed outlines, with flowers, foliage and birds, and more rarely with scenes from Chinese life.[1] The history of Chinese wallpaper is inextricably linked to that of the East India Company (EIC) in whose ships it travelled from Canton (modern Guangzhou) to London. It remains a distinct and luxury product to this day. Chinese wallpaper was rarely closely imitated by competing European manufactures (unlike porcelain or the lacquer that spawned 'japanned' wares); it did not accommodate Western fashion cycles like cotton; it remained a small scale private trade, retaining its elite status, distinct identity, and high price over time.[2] Its acquisition was as likely to come through gifting as through purchase, and Chinese wallpaper thus avoided becoming a 'new consumer commodity'. Although associated, like porcelain, with feminine desire and female spaces, it appears in drawing and billiard rooms as well as ladies' bedrooms, in public as well as private arenas. These very problems of positioning create opportunities for reconsidering the contemporary experience, and later evaluation, of Asian goods in domestic contexts.

In his exploration of design and the domestic interior in England, Charles Saumarez Smith observed that, in the late seventeenth century 'the most visible sign of new wealth, and an obvious target for social criticism, was the import of luxury goods from the Far East' and instanced as examples the impact of lightweight Indian chintzes, translucent porcelain and glossy lacquered furniture.[3] The curator Oliver Impey added Chinese wallpaper and carpets to the porcelain and lacquer, considering them the four most prominently displayed categories of goods imported from the East.[4] It would be a mistake however to assume that these goods followed similar pathways from point of manufacture to country house, moving over time from collectors' rarities to commonplace commodities, and eventually overtaken by their imitators. The case of Chinese wallpaper challenges any overarching or simplistic model of production, export and consumption.

The aim of this contribution is to examine the impact that Chinese wallpaper made on the British country house, where its presence has been seen by many as its defining feature. Although we know that it was hung in homes that were not country houses, like that of the actor Samuel Foote (1720–77), who had bought it for the private rooms of his London residence, surviving evidence connects most Chinese wallpaper in Britain with the country house.[5] Examples have been located across the British Isles, from Blair Castle in Pitlochry, Scotland to Penrhyn Castle in North Wales, from Clyne Castle in South Wales to Tregothan deep in Cornwall.[6] In the east of England there are fine examples including those at Ickworth in Suffolk and Houghton Hall in Norfolk, while Ireland boasts papers in both the north and south.[7] In the sheer surface area it covers within the home, it can claim to be the dominating decorative element of a room, setting the style and acting as a backdrop for the country house interior as stage. It is frequently mentioned in diaries, letters and guidebooks both past and present, indicating its high visibility and distinctiveness, and appears in widely differing and often surprising sources and contexts. Yet its high profile within the consumer context is not matched by records of its manufacture, export and sale on its route from Chinese workshop to country house within the legendary detail and scale of East India Company archives. Neither is there any comprehensive study of these wallpapers, although this will soon be remedied with the publication of the proceedings of the *Chinese Wallpaper: Trade, Technique and Taste* conference, which brought together curators, conservators, country house owners and scholars to consider European, American and Chinese perspectives in London in 2016.

In the following contribution the evolution of Chinese wallpaper will be mapped, reflecting this luxury good's birth as a subtle hybrid born of ancient Chinese manufacturing skills and a Western desire for the exotic. Its key characteristics compared with its European counterparts will then be considered, in order to understand its unique qualities. The rest of the paper will explore the pivotal role that the East India Company played in the dissemination of Chinese wallpaper through the country houses of Britain. This role is best understood through an examination not of hard, quantifiable trade facts but of the soft, flexible and opaque web of associations that defined the influence and networks of East India Company employees, whose connections spread far and wide.

The evolution of Chinese wallpaper: the story from east and west

Exotic wall coverings were used to decorate the homes of the wealthy in Europe, long before the invention of wallpaper. Available to a select few, these precursors of wallpaper included embossed leathers, tapestries and woven damasks. The earliest European papers were printed on single sheets of paper. A fragment found in Christ's College, Cambridge was printed on the reverse of a recycled proclamation issued by Henry VII. It is the earliest known example of English wallpaper, and was probably hung after 1550.[8] In the later seventeenth century individual black and white wooden block printed papers became popular.[9] Later, sheets of rag paper were glued along the edges to form a roll, ground colour was applied by hand before printing on designs with wood blocks and/or stencils using distemper pigments. This became the formula for English wallpaper production until the mid-nineteenth century.[10]

The Chinese of course also used paper in their homes, but it was quite different in size, format and design to that made for the West. We know surprisingly little about the use of the plain, coloured and patterned paper that furnished Southern Chinese interiors, where it was customary to paste the windows of houses with plain paper and sometimes to paint this decoratively. Perhaps these were the papers that John Evelyn noted in 1664 when he admired 'a sort of paper ... with such lively colours, that for splendour and vividness we have nothing in Europe that approaches it ... [it is], exceeding glorious to look on', that had accompanied goods brought back from China by a Jesuit.[11] It is thought by some that the appreciation of such ornament by European visitors might have prompted the Chinese to produce similar work for export. It is more likely however that the Chinese wallpapers we know in the West originated from the less familiar wall decorations on paper created in China especially for export to Europe.[12]

Chinese pictures and prints were imported in small quantities first by the Portuguese in the sixteenth century, and then into France by Dutch traders, towards the end of the seventeenth century.[13] The earliest precise reference to the import of graphic art from China to England is 1727.[14]

There is a later but very informative description of these pictures by Robert Fortune (1812–80) the plant hunter, who took the tea plant from China to India. Fortune observed in the house of a mandarin 'a nicely furnished room according to Chinese ideas, that is, its walls were hung with pictures of flowers, birds, and scenes of Chinese life. ... I observed a series of pictures which told a long tale as distinctly as if it had been written in Roman characters'.[15] These pictures continued to be popular in Britain and were used alongside Chinese wallpaper. For example Lady Cardigan bought 88 'Indian pictures' in 1742, which were pasted over the walls of her dining room.[16] Nearly 30 years later there is a description of a dressing room at Fawley Court, Henley-on-Thames decorated with 'the most curious India paper as birds, flowers etc., put up as different pictures in frames of the same'.[17]

Contesting a deceptively simple and linear trajectory of development, Emile de Bruijn has persuasively suggested that the Western taste for Chinese pictures and prints which developed in the late seventeenth century stimulated European designers and craftsmen to produce wallpapers with imitation Asian motifs at the beginning of the eighteenth century. It was *only then*, he suggests, that Chinese painting workshops responded to that demand by producing pictorial wallpapers from the 1730s–1740s, like those at Felbrigg in Norfolk and Dalemain in Cumbria (see Figure 2.1).[18]

This may explain why, although one of the first mentions of Chinese wallpaper appears in 1693 in an advertisement in the *London Gazette* for the sale of 'paper hangings of Indian and Japan figures', it is only from the mid-eighteenth century that any of these Chinese papers survive in Europe.[19] The heavy weight, rough surface, crude and repetitive printing and limited palette of the early European wallpaper formed a rather drab contrast to the light, soft, flexible and smooth Chinese wallpapers, colourfully painted with endlessly varied scenes, which began to appear in the West. The wallpaper was made using ancient techniques pioneered in China in the eighth century BCE, in production-line workshops in Guangzho (Canton) and involved many specialized hands, responsible for block printing outlines to hand painting, using the same methods, and probably the same skilled workforce, that worked on silk.[20]

This paper was more widely known in Britain, until the mid-nineteenth century, as 'India hangings' in recognition of the power and influence of the EIC which held the monopoly on its importation, and on whose ships it travelled to Europe. The name also reflected the older European custom of covering walls in textile hangings, and the wider attraction of all things exotic, which did not include an interest in their precise place of origin. Although the techniques of manufacture were ancient, the product was new and created specifically for export to Europe.

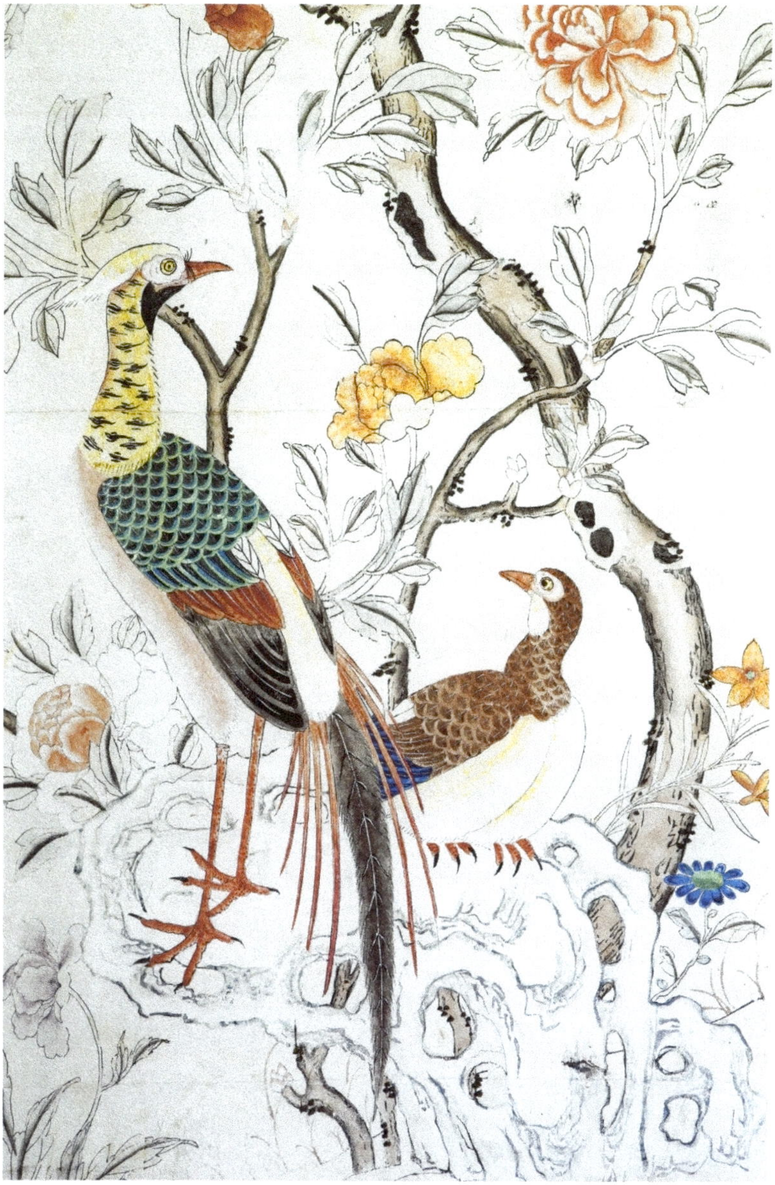

Figure 2.1 Detail of Chinese wallpaper at Felbrigg, Norfolk supplied by the architect James Paine (1717–89) in 1751, as part of the 1749–61 refurbishment carried out by the owner William Windham II (1717–61). Printed and painted on paper. © National Trust.

The number and range of sources mentioning Chinese wallpaper increased over the first half of the eighteenth century. John Macky's description of his visit to the Palace of Wanstead, built by Sir Richard Child in 1720, is typical of the growing awareness of this new type of furnishing. He includes a reference to the parlour 'finely adorned with China paper, the figures of men, women, birds and flowers the liveliest I ever saw come from that country'.[21]

Through an analysis of 149 Chinese wallpapers located across Britain, gathered by Emile de Bruijn and Andrew Bush as part of the Chinese Wallpaper Study Group, it has been possible to divide these papers into three types.[22]

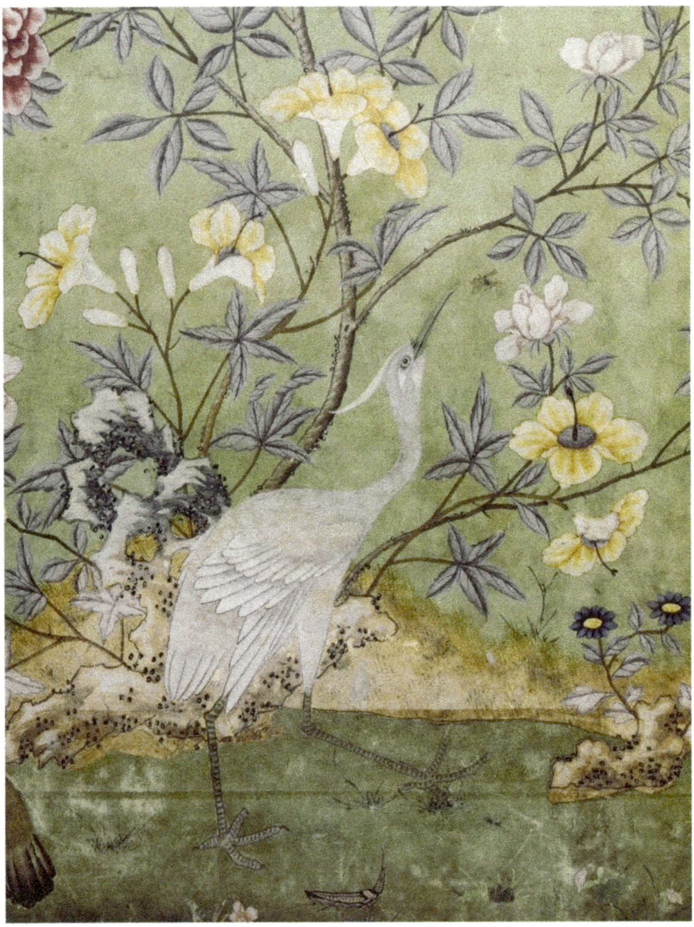

Figure 2.2 Detail from one of the Chinese wallpapers at Erdigg, Wrexham on the front cover of *Chinese Wallpapers in National Trust Houses* (2014). This paper is in the State Bedroom, named as such in the 1770s, when this paper was hung. © National Trust Images/John Hammond.

The following analysis relies heavily on this pioneering attempt to discern patterns of change and preference. Papers decorated with flowering trees and plants, birds, insects and rocks, representing idealized gardens were more popular (and more affordable), accounting for 95 papers, that is 60 per cent of all examples collated (see Figure 2.2). These kind of papers appeared from the mid-eighteenth century, and have continued in popularity ever since. Much more unusual were the papers decorated with figures in landscapes engaged in agriculture and industry, showing buildings and gardens and festivals, which account for 15 per cent of the 149 listed, which appeared at the same time as the 'idealized garden' papers described above (see Figure 2.3).

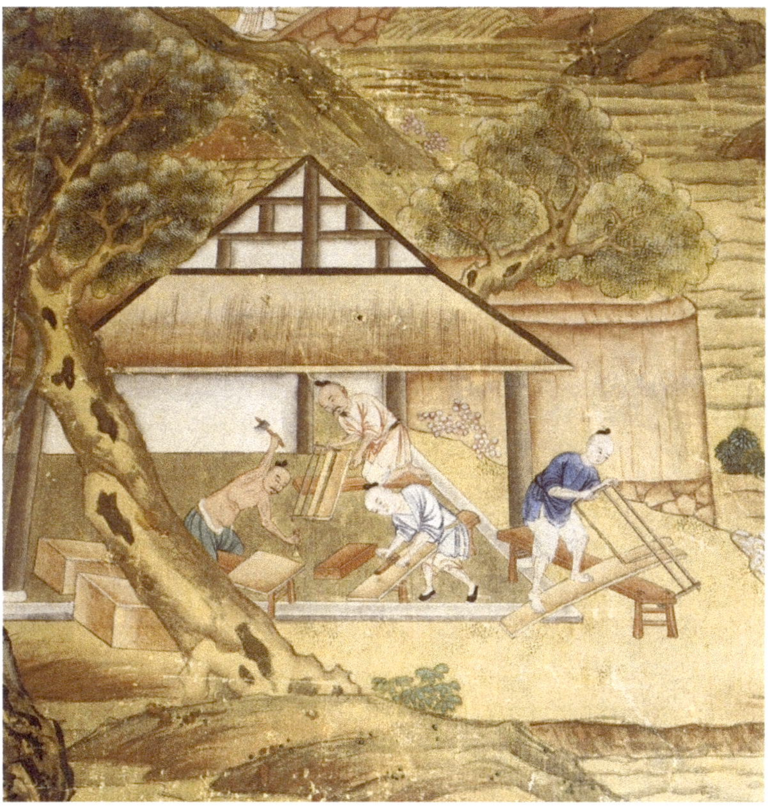

Figure 2.3 Detail from one of the Chinese wallpapers at Saltram, Devon showing scenes from everyday life, moved from a bedroom on the north east side of the first floor, to the current site in the 1930s. Painted on silk. © National Trust Images/Andreas von Einsiedel.

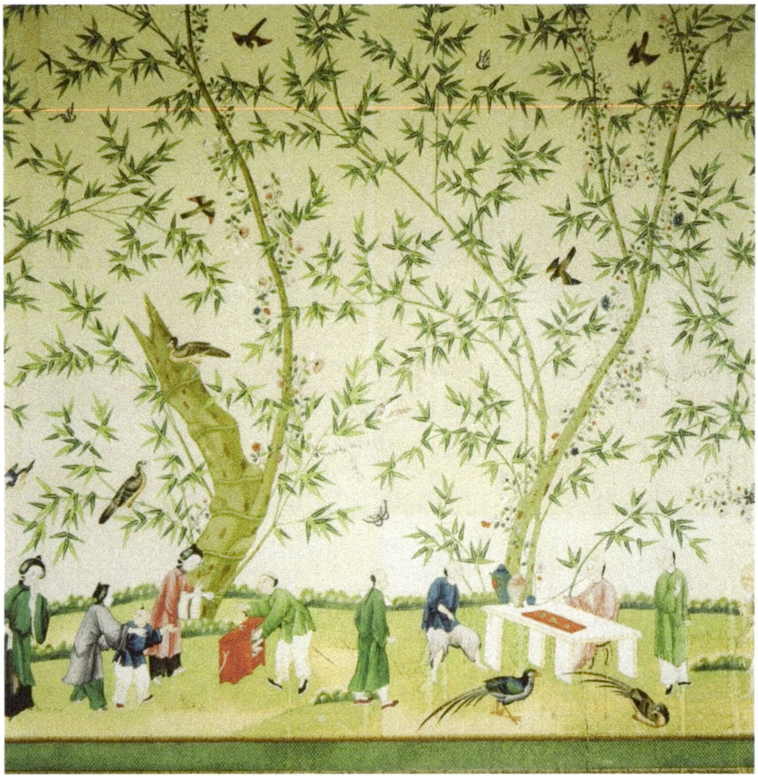

Figure 2.4 One of the Chinese wallpapers at Belton House, Lincolnshire hanging in the Chinese bedroom, painted on paper. Framed by a later European border on machine-made paper (therefore 1830 or later). © National Trust Images.

Another distinctive and identifiable group are those papers which incorporate figures at the bottom edge, with trees and bamboo, which appear from the 1790s (see Figure 2.4). The remaining 15 per cent relate to Chinese pictures used as paper, either separately or deployed in groups as collage and which are found up until 1800.

Since the publication of this study in 2014, another 20 Chinese wallpapers have been discovered in Britain.[23] The British fascination with Chinese wallpaper ebbed and flowed over the centuries, but has never disappeared. Although it reached the height of its popularity between the 1750s and the 1770s, it was revived in the 1820s–1850s, and was rediscovered in the 1920s. Although there are signs of changes in style, for example the introduction of paper that created a 'print room'

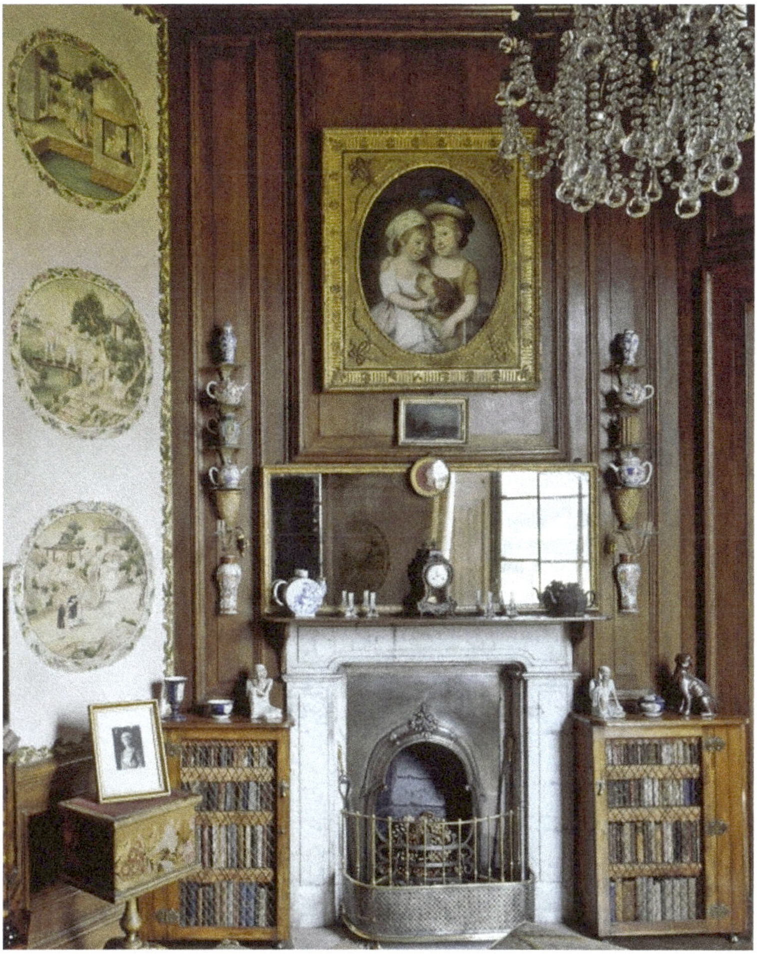

Figure 2.5 Chinese Room, Erdigg, Wrexham. © National Trust/ Andreas von Einsiedel.

effect in the 1780s, Chinese wallpaper – to Western eyes – seems to have remained timeless, complementing interiors that were successively rococo, neoclassical, empire and even antiquarian (see Figure 2.5). Today old Chinese wallpapers make good prices at auction, and new ones are being made to satisfy the demand for the exotic, expensive and unusual in the interior.[24]

What were the distinctive characteristics of Chinese wallpaper, the features that set it apart from its European counterparts, ultimately protecting it from widespread import substitution? It was unmatched for its colour and texture. It came in non-European dimensions, accommodating non-repeat mural-like and diverse designs, which appealed to an enlightened audience seeking an idea of what China was really like, as well as satisfying the unquenchable thirst for exotic fantasy, while retaining its cachet of rarity and expense.

Malachy Postlethwayt (1707(?)–67) in his *Universal Dictionary of Trade and Commerce* (1757) ascribed the popularity of Chinese export paintings to their colours, diversity and fantasy. 'The pictures', he wrote 'are valued for the liveliness and briskness of the colours and variety of figures'.[25] The same criteria could also be applied to Chinese wallpaper, which as we have seen, was so closely associated with these export paintings. Like the textiles with which they were associated, including Indian-made chintz, Chinese wallpaper was admired in the West for its colour. We know that many interiors combined the two materials, for example at Harewood House, near Leeds the room with the 'Chints [bed] Hanging lined with silk', was hung with Chinese wallpaper. This was a European-wide phenomenon. In Italy the casinos were 'neatly fitted up with India paper, and furnished with chintz'.[26] Hargrove and Bewick described the best bedchamber at Newby Hall, near Ripon in 1789 as 'hung with India paper, on which the flowers and foliage, birds and other figures, are represented in the most lively and beautiful colours'.[27] Here the word 'lively' indicates vibrancy of colour. Admiration for this attribute did

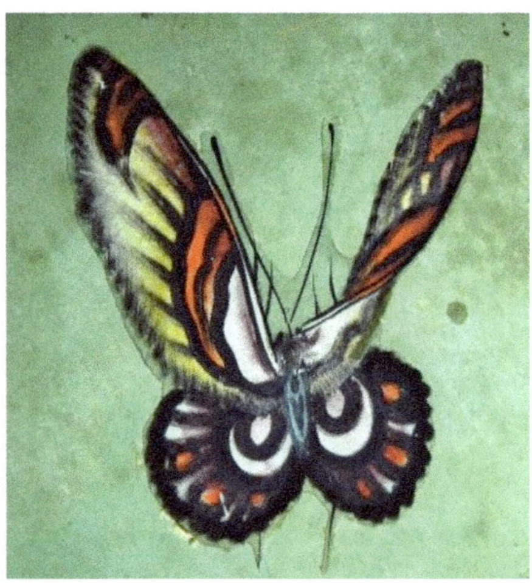

Figure 2.6 Detail of a Chinese wallpaper at Ickworth, Norfolk, hung in the Chinese dressing room, according to family tradition purchased 'at one of the great exhibitions'. The butterfly has been cut out and pasted onto the paper. Photograph courtesy of Andrew Bush.

not wane over time. In 1825 these papers were still described as 'glowing and brilliant'.[28] Even though many surviving wallpapers have suffered from deterioration by light, some still glow with bright blues, greens and reds (see Figure 2.6).

For example the figural and floral paper now in the sitting room at Powis Castle, near Welshpool retains its green background, while bright red berries look ready to pick.[29] Unable to match this brightness of colour on such a scale, European wallpaper makers like John Baptist Jackson (1695–1777) cast doubt on its virtues, dismissing 'the gay glaring colours in broad patches of red, green yellow blue etc which are to pass for flowers and other objects' because, although they delighted the eye, they had no 'true judgment', that is good taste.[30] In 1810 R. Phillips's most damning criticism of a flower painting was to liken it to 'Chinese paper hangings … striking to the vulgar eye, that always delights in gaudy tints'.[31]

It was not, however, only the colour of Chinese wallpaper that seduced westerners, but also its smoothness, opacity and uniformity, akin to the European fascination with porcelain and silk.[32] Thanks to the work of expert paper conservators we know that these admired characteristics were achieved by coating the support paper onto which the design was executed with a white pigment bound in animal glue dusted with alum or mixed with mica, giving it a shimmering appearance like silk. This type of paper coating was developed in China in the fourth century CE which not only had an aesthetic purpose but also a practical one, in that it aided the absorption of the inks, which were used to form painted and block printed outlines, that were filled in with colour.[33]

Chinese wallpaper usually came in up to 40 lengths, each roll measuring 3.5m by 1m, sometimes with discernible numbers that indicated the sequence in which it should be hung. Although Chinese wallpaper was made for the European market, it never seems to have been manufactured to European dimensions, not even for special commissions. The problems that resulted demanded inventive solutions, as extensive modifications made to Chinese wallpapers at the point of installation prove. Additions were made to top and base, as at Felbrigg, where the bottom was cut in a wavy line to obscure the join; and cutouts pasted on to hide joins, as at Erdigg in Wrexham where 3cm flies have been applied, or at Ickworth where butterflies have been pasted onto the paper (see Fig. 2.6). Some examples show evidence of skies painted in, as well as strips added at the base, like the paper at Milton Manor, in Oxfordshire. At Blickling in Norfolk individual paper lengths were reduced in width and height, the original sky was cut away and a replacement with the addition of a mountain and trees painted in on an additional layer of western-made paper. At Ightham Mote in Kent, when the supply of Chinese paper ran out, sections of Indian printed silk were added. In some cases European printed borders were supplied to frame the Chinese wallpaper, as at Woburn in Bedfordshire and Belton in Lincolnshire.[34] Postlethwayt, it will be remembered, admired the 'diversity' of Chinese wallpaper, compared with its European counterparts. This can be interpreted in two ways, in relation to the design of single papers (that is the lack of repeats), and across papers (that is, the scarcity of duplicates).[35] Although the use of wood block outlines in earlier papers meant that the same motifs can be identified on Chinese wallpapers now hung across the country, the individual hand-colouring of them ensured they were never exactly the same. These techniques of production created an impression of uniqueness, the admiration of which may explain why the Chinese moved from block-printed outlines to hand-painting, which enabled even more flexible production.

For the European consumer Chinese wallpaper satisfied two seemingly contradictory attributes. It was admired both for the accuracy of its depiction of Chinese life – its people, activities, and flora and fauna – as well as for its fantasy. The distinguished botanist, Sir Joseph Banks (1743–1820), observed in his journal in 1770: 'A man need go no further to study the Chinese ... than the China paper, the better sorts of which represent their persons and such of their customs, dresses, etc., as I have seen, most strikingly like, though a little in the *caricatura* style. Indeed, some of the plants which are common to China and Java, as bamboo, are better figured there than in the best botanical authors that I have seen'.[36] Yet while some 'read' Chinese wallpaper as an accurate narrative, others like Postlethwayt noted that it satisfied the desire for 'Odd fancies [that] commonly hit the general taste, and the Chinese do not seem to have any fancy for pieces of gravity'.[37] There is only one known surviving example of a Chinese wallpaper made to a European design, from engravings by the French designer of ornament Gabriel Huquier (1695–1772) after the French painter Jean-Antoine Watteau (1684–1721), made for Hampden House in Buckinghamshire, and hung around 1756.[38] The practice of supplying models and patterns from Europe, for production in China, (as in the case of Chinese armorial porcelain), never seems to have been adopted for wallpaper.

Part of the attraction of these papers was their rarity. As Lady Mary Coke commented in 1772, 'I have taken down the Indian paper, put up another upon a blue ground with white birds & flowers: 'tis very pretty & has the additional recommendation of being quite new. There are but eight sets come to England'.[39] Her note 'come to England' refers to the annual arrival of the EIC ships in London, which took advantage of the north-east monsoons, arriving home between November and March. A return expedition from London to Canton took an average of eighteen months, and in the 1700s the Company was making 20 to 30 sailings to East Asia each year. Supplies of Chinese wallpaper were therefore limited, which added to their desirability, and expense. Lady Anna Miller noted in 1776 that 'India paper is more expensive in England than damask here [in Italy]'.[40] At Croome Court in Worcestershire the bills for the '29 fine India landscapes' of 1763 sent to Lord Coventry reveal each landscape cost £2 2s, making a total of £60 18s. This would have bought a smart new coach.[41] It was so expensive, offcuts were kept, as at Penryhn Castle, Gwynedd, and old papers removed and put into storage.[42] Its cost and rarity meant that it was more likely to be left on a wall, than stripped off when fashions changed. While middle-class home owners were exhorted to change their wallpaper every few years, these expensive papers tended to survive, their appeal seemingly eternal, shielding them against the relentless cycles of changes in fashion.[43] While novelty might have been part of their original appeal, when old they acquired a value of their own, and like the scenes they depicted evoked a timelessness that made a satisfying counterpoint to a Western world that was perceived to be increasingly governed by change.[44]

East India Company connections

Although imported by EIC ships, Chinese wallpaper, like hand-painted silk (and rosewood furniture, mirror paintings and armorial porcelain) was solely part of the privilege trade, and never undertaken by the Company, at least for the English EIC.[45] This trade was instead part of the allowance given to employees, such the captains and supercargoes (the merchants who were responsible for the cargo, its purchase and sale, and the commercial concerns of the voyage) who although paid modest salaries, were permitted to trade on their own account to specified levels, enabling the most successful to increase their income thirty-fold.[46] As Meike von Brescius has noted 'The size and scope of the private trade in Chinese export wares during the first half of the eighteenth century has been greatly underestimated', and the official documentation that does survive is fragmentary.[47] The Company derived income from every private trade good that passed through its public sales, as it accrued warehouse fees, handling charges and commission paid by the importer.[48] Although we know that some Chinese wallpaper arrived through this privilege route – it bears auction house marks – much bypassed it, being declared 'gifts' or objects 'of personal use', thus sidestepping documentation.[49] As the Chinese export porcelain historian David Howard reminds us 'These private traders were socially and financially in touch with wealthy private clients, who might often be related by blood, and it was they who elected the most fashionable products available at Canton by carrying special commissions. They gained a much wider understanding of what was available, which knowledge was in turn, at the disposal of the Company'.[50] In some cases, although not with Chinese wallpaper, the Company, seeing the success of privately traded goods at auction, might decide to add them to the EIC trade, prohibiting or limiting them from private trade.

Yet we need to put this private trade in context. It accounted for a small percentage of the whole trade with China, and Chinese wallpaper made up only a small proportion of this. Furthermore as Jan de Vries has demonstrated, even the official Company trade (which focused on tea and textiles) only equated, by the later eighteenth century, to around 50,000 tons per year (equivalent to the capacity of one modern container tanker).[51] What was important about these goods was not their volume, but the impact they made, which was quite disproportionate to their number. These distinctive luxury goods were undoubtedly part of wider fashion whereby 'persons of quality and distinction, who had Taste and all that', were advised to 'have something foreign and superb'.[52] Of the 149 Chinese wallpapers located in Britain for the Chinese Wallpaper in National Trust Houses project, it is clear that a significant number, at current calculation 20 per cent, were connected with individuals and families boasting traceable links with the EIC.[53] It is more than likely that many more from this survey had such associations, as yet unidentified.

It is rare to be able to connect the arrival of a Chinese wallpaper in a country house with a specific person. One of the exceptions relates to James Drummond, 8th Viscount Strathallan (1767–1851) who brought his Chinese wallpaper back with him from Canton. Drummond was a nephew of the London banker Robert Drummond of Cadland, Hampshire, and prospered in the service of the EIC in China. He began his EIC career as a supercargo, and became assistant to the Head of the Committee at

Canton in 1792, and by 1800 he was a member of the Select Committee there. The following year he became President, a post he held until 1807 when he returned to Scotland. The 18 rolls of 12-foot by 4-foot mulberry bark and bamboo paper are hand-painted with a scene of the 'hongs', or foreign factories at Canton (Guangzhou), which enable its dating to c.1790. These 'factories' were not places of manufacture, but mercantile warehouses, where the foreign merchants were allowed to operate. The paper would thus have had a very personal meaning to Drummond, who would have resided in the British 'factory' on the waterfront at Canton. However when it arrived at Strathallan Castle in Perthshire it was not put up in his private rooms, but on the walls of the Ladies' Salon, where it stayed for almost 200 years, before it was acquired by the Peabody Essex Museum in Salem, Massachusetts.[54]

A significant proportion of the Chinese wallpapers that survive, and which can be connected with the EIC, relate to its Directors. On its foundation in 1600 the Company was led by one Governor and 24 Company Directors who sat on its Court. While the Company ruled millions of people, and employed a vast army of officials abroad, it operated from tiny headquarters in London, staffed by only 159 men in 1785 and 241 in 1813. Unlike Drummond, few of the Directors had actually worked in or even visited China. However due to their position of power and influence they had privileged access to the luxuries imported by the Company, via their enviable and often complex network of contacts. Henry Lascelles Senior (1690–1753), Collector of Customs in Bridgetown, Barbados, for example served as a Director of the East India Company between 1742 and 1746. Henry's youngest son, also called Henry, became a Captain for the EIC and by 1741 was in command of a ship called the *York*. Over the next seven years Henry made three trips to the port of Canton. However it has not been possible to make a direct link with these trips and the Chinese wallpaper that hung in the East Bedroom at Harewood House in 1769, which belonged to Henry's brother Edwin, 1st Baron Harewood, who built the house between 1759 and 1771. At Harewood it was more the wealth gained from West Indian sugar plantations than profits from the East India trade that contributed to its creation. However the two sources of income, and access to goods, were inextricably entwined in the formation of this and many other country houses across Britain.[55]

At Erdigg in Wrexham the Chinese wallpaper in the State bedroom, may have been installed during the modernization of the house in the 1770s by Philip Yorke (1743–1804) and his wife Elizabeth

(1750–79), daughter of Sir John Cust of Belton. It is possible that the Chinese wallpaper was supplied by Elizabeth's uncle, Peregrine Cust (1723–85) who was deeply involved in East India Company affairs, becoming a Director in 1767. When Agneta York wrote in 1772 that the bedrooms and dressing rooms at Osterley were furnished 'with the finest chintzes, painted taffetys, india paper and decker work and such a profusion of rich China and Japan that I could almost fancy myself in Pekin', she was acknowledging the fruits of three generations of owners who had close connections with the Company, as attested by the chapter in this volume on Osterley House and Park.[56] The Chinese wallpaper at Broughton Castle, c.1850 which bears similarities to those at Belton, Burton Constable, Ickworth, Penrhyn, and Woburn, may have been introduced by Frederick Twistleton, 16th Lord Saye and Sele (1799–1887), as he refurbished the Castle in the 1860s.[57] The family had close connections with the EIC via the 13th Lord Saye and Sele (c.1735–88). His wife, Elizabeth Turner was the heiress of Sir Edward Turner whose Company wealth funded the restoration of Broughton. Edward Turner's mother, Mary, was the daughter of Sir Gregory Page (c.1669–1720) a London merchant whose wealth partly stemmed from the EIC, of which he was a Director.[58] As can be seen from these examples it was often the connections of the women of a family, as much as that of the men, who were responsible for making available Asian privilege trade goods for the British interior.

Another level of association with the EIC came via its investors. Some owners of Chinese wallpaper, like Edward Howard, 9th Duke of Norfolk (1686–1777) can be identified as EIC shareholders, although it has not been possible to link the wallpaper which decorated the principal bedrooms of his properties of Norfolk House, St James's Square, and at Worksop Manor, with specific ships. So despite this wealth of potential connections between the Company and Chinese wallpaper it is frustratingly difficult to link surviving papers with East Indiamen and Company personnel, and the houses which they graced. To do this we need to turn to the Russells, Dukes of Bedford, whose family archive supplies a wealth of EIC related material, and whose major country house, Woburn, retains much of its original furnishings. (The Bedford Russells are not related to the Russells of Swallowfield Park featured elsewhere in this volume, notwithstanding the two families shared surnames and Company connections).

The associations of the Russells and the EIC covering six generations from the 1st to the 6th Dukes of Bedford, are revealed in successive waves of Asian influence on their patterns of collecting and decorating.[59] The wealth of Chinese wallpapers (and other Asian decorative goods) relating to Bedford property combined with the survival of household accounts and letters documenting their shipping, purchase and installation are a uniquely rich source of information.[60] Study of the Bedfords' patronage of the arts (both fine and decorative) has until recently been restricted to European sources, revealing the hierarchy of interest that has dominated decorative arts research.[61] When there are 21 paintings by Canaletto at Woburn why bother with the Chinese wallpaper? Yet when the close connections of the Bedford family with the East are drawn out, it is clear that their Chinese wallpapers were intimately bound up with their fortunes, and valued across generations.

The Dukes of Bedford used their position as owners of East Indiamen hired to the Company, and as investors to gain privileged access to these Asian goods. The marriage of the 1st Duke of Bedford's grandson Wriothsey Russell, Lord Tavistock (1680–1711) to Elizabeth Howland (1682–1724) in 1695 brought a spectacularly large dowry of near £100,000 (roughly equivalent to £9 million today) into the family whose estates included Thames-side property at Rotherhithe. The marriage also connected the Russells with the Childs of Wanstead House, as Elizabeth was the granddaughter of Sir Josiah Child (1630–99) whose advocacy of the EIC's monopoly led directly to his appointment as a Director in 1677, rising to Deputy-Governor and Governor of the Company in 1681.[62] At Rotherhithe the 1st Duke of Bedford (1613–1700) built the first docks, whose rental brought in a useful income, first from the Greenland, and then the South Sea Companies. At these docks he built the *Streatham* which was presented by his grandson to the EIC. *The Bedford*, *Tavistock*, *Russell* and *Howland* followed, all commissioned before 1700, to which were added the *Tonqueen,* and later the *Houghton* and *Denham*.[63] The Bedfords invested between one-sixteenth to one-eighth part in the voyages these vessels took, and thereby had considerable holdings in the East India Company.

When John Russell, 4th Duke of Bedford (1710–71) began remodelling and redecorating Woburn Abbey in Bedfordshire and Bedford House in London in 1748, he combined Chinese wallpaper and ceramics with new Louis XV-style furniture and portraits by British artists. Tracking their purchase reveals the ways these exotic commodities, including wallpaper, entered the British home. The Green Drawing Room at Woburn, now known as the Ballroom, is hung with a hand-painted Chinese wallpaper of c.1800–20. When this wallpaper was conserved in 1998 two separate inked inscriptions were found on the back of the wallpaper. 'Royal George' refers to the ship that transported the wallpaper from China to England, and 'No 48' may refer to the package and '46 sheets' to its contents.[64] 'Lot 25' is written in a different hand and confirms it was consigned to auction at East India House, and comprised '24 sheets'. This shows that the original consignment was divided, which suggests that another set was made from the remaining 22 sheets.[65] There were five ships named the *Royal George* which made voyages between 1737 and 1822; the one conveying the wallpaper was a 1,333-ton ship that made seven voyages between 1802 and 1817.[66] This wallpaper relates to the 6th Duke's (1766–1839) campaign of re-decoration.

Another route via which Chinese wallpaper entered the Bedford homes, was purchase from a range of specialist shops, not confined to, but predominantly in London. The paper in 'His Grace's Bedchamber' at Woburn was bought from the London wallpaper suppliers Crompton and Spinnage in 1751–52, at a cost of £60 13s 10d (a similar price to that purchased for Croome Court), part of a larger bill for hanging Chinese wallpapers at Woburn of £253 13s 10 ½ d. It is one of the earliest known Chinese wallpapers to survive, contemporary and similar to those at Felbrigg Hall in Norfolk, Ightam Mote in Kent and Uppark in West Sussex. It was still there in 1771 when it was described in an inventory of that year as 'Hung with India Paper'.[67]

The Russells clearly liked their Chinese wallpaper, as it was also used at Oakley House, in Bedfordshire, not far from Woburn and at Endsleigh Cottage in Devon. After the purchase of Oakley House (built between 1748 and 1750) by the 4th Duke in 1757, the old house was demolished and a new one was built on the site, serving as a hunting box for successive Dukes. The 1935 sale catalogue lists three rooms clad with Chinese wallpaper, on the ground floor smoking room, the staircase hall and in the first floor bedroom. One of c.1790, survives. They were probably related to the 5th Duke's influence, who employed Henry Holland to modify Oakley for him. The paper for Endsleigh Cottage, which was hung in the main guest bedroom, may have been bought at the same time as that for the Green Drawing Room at Woburn. This was one of a number of Chinese wallpapers at Endsleigh. The house was built between 1810 and 1816 by John Russell, 6th Duke of Bedford as a private family residence, to the designs of Sir Jeffry Wyattville, as a grand form of the cottage orné, where house and landscape were designed as one. It was usefully positioned to serve as a residence whilst the Duke, normally residing at Woburn Abbey, was inspecting his extensive Bedford estates in Devon and Cornwall. It was the Duke and Duchess's favourite residence and was used for entertaining intimate friends.[68]

The Chinese wallpaper in the Russell residences was part of a wider strategy of furnishing which included Chinese porcelain and silk, and Indian furniture (all either acquired before the 4th Duke's time, or made in the style of this period). These interiors were a constant reminder of the family's links with the EIC, which dated back, as we have seen earlier, to the 1st Duke, and through it, to the wider world. Chinese wallpapers appeared in their grand country house at Woburn, as well as in their smaller retreats. These furnishings demonstrated the family's power to access these goods over several generations. As Lucy Johnson has noted, this engagement with Asian goods, via their EIC connections, was underpinned by a deeper fascination with the culture of China, evidenced by the 4th Duke's purchase 'from 1735 onwards [of books] which covered virtually every aspect of Chinese history, life and culture'.[69] The 5th Duke went on to build a Chinese Dairy at Woburn, designed by Henry Holland in 1787, decorated by John Crace, and completed in 1794. Humphrey Repton supplied designs for a Chinese garden at Woburn in 1804–5. The 6th Duke employed Sir Joseph Banks to advise and acquire Chinese plants for his gardens, and bought as many Chinese wallpapers as the 4th Duke.

Gifts and gifting

There was another route which Chinese wallpaper took from the workshops of Canton to the country houses of Britain. The gifting of Chinese wallpaper dominates their history, although it is difficult to verify any of the stories connected with their presentation. It has been suggested, although not substantiated with evidence, that 'sets of painted wallpaper were specially created by Chinese merchants to give as gifts to finalize deals with their European trading partners'.[70] Within a culture that placed great emphasis on ritualized gift-giving, this strategy appears plausible. Perhaps having started life as gifts, there was a stronger likelihood that these wallpapers should then continue their life as gifts once they reached the West. It gave them a special status, embedded them in a narrative that was told and retold through the generations. Through gifting, these expensive commodities slipped their economic context, and gained a separate and higher level of existence. The reciprocity of a business transaction, for example the purchase of Chinese wallpaper from a London shop, was both immediate and specific, a self-enclosed episode, while acquisition by gift was more complex. The latter enhanced and complicated their value, influenced the site of installation and attitudes of reception. The last part of this contribution examines some of these gifting episodes.

Although it has been impossible to verify any of these gifting 'stories', whatever their truth, they indicate that they were given a high status, especially when the gifting was connected with royal favour. It is from the 1780s that the narratives of 'imperial' and 'royal' gifts of Chinese wallpaper begin to appear, perhaps as a reaction to the increasing availability of wallpaper from the 1750s, in an attempt to make some papers more distinct than others. Charlotte Abrams reporting in a recent fashion magazine warns readers 'that the trend [of hanging expensive wallpapers] is so ubiquitous it is becoming increasingly tricky to keep ahead of one's paper-buying friends'.[71] Surely the same such worries also engaged wealthy house owners of the eighteenth century? How much greater was the value of a set of papers that came with its own story and unique connections? It helped set it apart from others.

The earliest record of the gift of Chinese wallpaper found so far is connected with the royal physician Dr John Turton (1736–1806).[72] A man of ample fortune even before he was appointed in 1771 as George III's doctor, Turton had duties that included the delivery of numerous royal babies. His role made him a great favourite of Queen Charlotte. On his retirement in 1786, Turton left Adam Street, in the Adelphi, where he had been a neighbour of the actor David Garrick, and bought Brasted Place in Kent, which he immediately demolished and began rebuilding and decorating with the assistance of Robert Adam.[73] Of the several royal favours he received, one included 'a wallpaper which had originally been sent by the Emperor of China as a present to King George III and was bestowed on Dr Turton by the Queen'.[74] This paper therefore had a doubly inflated status. Some accounts say the paper was put up in the billiard room, others in the drawing room, although the latter was more likely. The paper was recorded *in situ* at Brasted by English Heritage, where it is described as '2 panels of Chinese wallpaper depicting scenes of everyday life', some removed to Kent Museum.[75] Papers depicting this type of scene, and those illustrating Chinese manufactures, were more expensive than other types of Chinese wallpaper, such as those with trees and birds. It has been shown earlier, using data from *Chinese Wallpaper in National Trust Houses,* that these papers accounted for only 15 per cent of the total of known wallpapers.[76] Hence this royal gift was distinguished further by the rarity of its design.

A gift of Chinese wallpaper is said to have been the impetus for the creation of Brighton Pavilion between 1787 and 1826. Whether or not it is true that the paper was a gift to the Prince Regent, the story itself suggests a desire to root this fantastical construction in a response to 'real' Chinese sources.[77] Other decorative goods like Chinese porcelain, furniture and other decorative objects, were acquired via John and Frederick Crace who were responsible for negotiating with the Custom House for their importation. Gordon Lang reminds us that Frederick Crace took an 'almost slavish adherence to original Chinese sources, using motifs from eighteenth century 'famille-rose' export ware porcelain, Canton enamel and even Mandarin robes'; and asks if in his scheme whether he was following the wishes of the Prince of Wales?[78] There are three different Chinese wallpapers at the Pavilion, none of which is early enough to be the paper that supposedly inspired the project: one c.1790, acquired in 1815, and hung in 1820 in the Adelaide corridor; one c.1815 part of Frederick Crace's scheme for the Saloon;[79] and one hung in Queen Victoria's bedroom when she resided there between 1835 and 1845. (The wallpaper currently in this bedroom is a recent facsimile).

Perhaps it was from the earliest cache of Chinese wallpaper that the Prince Regent made his gift in 1806 to the feisty Frances Ingram, Lady Irwin (1734(?)–1807) of Temple Newsam in Leeds, as an indication of his affection for her eldest daughter Isabella, Marchioness of Hertford (1759–1834), who became his mistress the following year. It was she who had the paper hung, 20 years later, in 1827, creating the Blue Drawing Room (also known as the Chinese Drawing Room) out of what had been the best dining room at Temple Newsam. She embellished its design with 28 hand-watercoloured exotic birds cut from 10 loose prints from John James Audubon's *The Birds of America* whose first volume appeared in the same year that the wallpaper was hung.[80]

It was the popularity of Brighton Pavilion that was responsible for a second wave of interest in Chinese wallpaper which began in the 1820s. After visiting the Pavilion Marianne, Lady Clifford Constable and her sister Eliza were inspired to create their own Chinese Room at Burton Constable, in East Yorkshire. The walls were hung with new Chinese wallpaper (originally a powdered pink colour), while stencilled designs were added to doors and walls, and silvered bells hung from the cornice and doorway.[81] During the removal of the wallpaper in 1992 as part of a conservation project, an earlier Chinese wallpaper of the 1780s was discovered underneath. This paper can be related to bills paid to Thomas Chippendale's foreman, William Reid in 1783, revealing a predisposition for Chinese wallpaper that perhaps laid the foundation for the later decoration.

These narratives of multiple gifting lie at the heart of the reception and employment of these Chinese wallpapers, which like their patterns distract and entertain, blending veracity and fantasy to create a magical world of make-believe. The Chinese wallpaper that can be seen in the Board Room at Coutts Bank on the Strand in London today is said to have been a gift to Thomas Coutts (1735–1822) from George Macartney (1737–1806).[82] It originally hung in Coutts's private rooms 'above the shop', at 59 the Strand.[83] Coutts was an 'old friend' of Macartney's, who organized remittances for him from India, when he was appointed Governor of Madras in 1781.[84] This was a position of trust: Macartney relied on Coutts to advise his wife, discharge his debts and dispose of any surplus money to his advantage 'always taking care it be in such a manner as that I may command it at a moment's warning'.[85] Macartney had been appointed first Ambassador to China, responsible for the trade mission to the Qianlong Emperor in 1793, the total costs (calculated at £95,000) of which were defrayed by the EIC. This was not simply a commercial mission. Facilitating and extending trade were key priorities of both the East India Company and the government, which instructed Macartney to cultivate the friendship of China in order to increase 'the sale of our manufactured articles and of the products of our territories in India'.[86] Yet as one of the advisors to the mission, the Birmingham manufacturer Matthew Boulton explained 'Our knowledge of China is so imperfect that it will be difficult to point out the most necessary articles to send thither. The women are kept so confined that we know nothing of them but from pictures'.[87] As a result they were not sure what to send from Britain to tempt Chinese interest.

On arrival in Peking, Macartney and his entourage were given accommodation in the only building large enough to house the whole embassy, the Palace of Eleven Courtyards. This was the home of a Collector of Customs who was in jail awaiting execution for misappropriating the profits of European trade.[88] The historian Paul Gillingham states that it was here that Macartney saw the paper that he was to take home to Coutts. From the published journals and diaries of those who were part of the embassy, it is possible to gain some idea of their impressions of the decoration. The pavilions where they were lodged were described by the official recorder of the embassy George Staunton. He noted that they were decorated with paintings, and while some from the mission appreciated them, the general attitude was critical: 'If a lake is surrounded by houses and trees, the painter does not show the reflection on the water', and the 'Distant landscapes seem larger than a house in the foreground and they do not touch the ground'.[89] They were not to stay here long however, as the imperial audience was to take place in the emperor's summer residence 120 miles to the north, at Jehol in Manchuria. In Peking they left behind a team to set up the display of the 'presents' and make arrangements for transforming the Palace of Eleven Courtyards into the British embassy.

Although the embassy was a failure in terms of establishing trade relations, Maxine Berg argues that it was a success in terms of the gathering of 'useful knowledge' about China.[90] The Chinese wallpaper that Macartney brought home depicts different Chinese manufactures. Their source was Song Yingxing's (1587–1666) *Tiangongkaiwu* published in 1637, an encyclopaedic work which examines numerous aspects of technology and manufacture practiced in China at the time including porcelain production accompanied by detailed woodblock illustrations.[91] These illustrations were themselves 'useful knowledge'. An example of how Chinese wallpaper could convey such useful information is given by William Marshall, in his *The Rural Economy of Yorkshire* (1788), in which he discusses the origins of the winnowing machine. He notes that 'We are probably indebted to the Chinese or other Eastern nation, for the invention of this machine. I have seen it upon an India paper drawn with sufficient accuracy, to shew that the draughtsman was intimately acquainted with the uses of it. The Dutch, to whom the invention has been ascribed, imported it, in all probability, from the East Indies'.[92] The connection between the scenes of Chinese labour and that of a nation undergoing an agricultural and industrial revolution was drawn upon by Viscount Torrington when he visited Cromford in 1789, the site of Arkwright's new textile 'factory', where 'There is so much water, so much rock, so much population and so much wood that it looks like a Chinese town'.[93] As Clive Aslet has commented 'it was a whimsical picture' evoking the contrast made between the busy cotton spinners and the wild Derbyshire scenery amid which their industry took place'.[94] Yet as Craig Clunas has reminded us, in relation to Chinese export watercolours, the reading of such information is not so simple. 'Whatever the customer may have thought, he was not buying a piece of reportage, an accurate picture … Nor was he buying a product of Chinese imagination. Rather he was receiving his own preconceptions of the mysterious inland provinces as a land of grotesque and fantastic landscapes, inhabited by ingenious and curious people living an idyllic life of harmony with nature, reflected back at him by an artist whose sole concern was to please'.[95]

Macartney's wallpaper depicted an idyllic picture of manufacture at a time when Britain was launching into its own system of factory production. Perhaps there was some irony too in the fact that this paper showed Chinese goods such as porcelain, tea and silk which Europeans were desperately keen to imitate, acquired by an ambassador who had failed to entice the Chinese into buying European goods. The Emperor dismissed the embassy and its gifts explaining that 'we have never valued ingenious articles, nor do we have the slightest need of your Country's manufactures'.[96]

When Thomas Coutts sat in this room above the 'shop', the wallpaper that Macartney had given him must have reinforced the global image and ambition of his business. Coutts kept closely in touch with public affairs at home and throughout the world, through leading politicians and by maintaining a close network of Scottish friends and relatives abroad. As Macartney brought him wallpaper from China, so Lord Minto (1751–1814) who was Governor General of India between 1807 and 1813, brought him news from India.[97] Coutts had interests in a number of East India Company vessels, two of which were named after him.[98]

A second failed mission to the Emperor of China, led by William Pitt Amherst (1773–1857) while Ambassador Extraordinary to China in 1816–17, led to the gift of another Chinese wallpaper. It was sent by Amherst to fellow diplomat Henry Chamberlain (1773–1829), who he had visited in Brazil, where Chamberlain was Consul-General. Amherst, writing at sea to Chamberlain in 1817, remembered 'that at one of your hospitable dinners ... the conversation turned upon hanging your dining room with Chinese paper. It will give me the greatest pleasure if the accompanying parcel should be found useful for that purpose. At all events I beg you to do me the favour to consider it as proof that your friendly reception of myself and my companions at Rio Janeiro [sic] was not forgotten by me while I resided at Canton'.[99] The value of the gift was enhanced by the miracle of its journey, as Amherst noted in the same letter: 'I hope the paper will not be found to have suffered any injury from the misfortune which befell the *Alceste* in the Straits of Gaspar. She was one of the few articles which I was enabled to save from the wreck'.[100] The ship which had been chosen to carry Lord Amherst on his 1816 diplomatic mission to China had foundered on its return journey on a reef in the Java Sea where, after the evacuation of passengers and crew, it was plundered and burned by Malayan pirates.[101]

The gift of Chinese wallpaper from one diplomat to another perhaps helped convey a shared sense of risk that their appointments involved. Amherst's gift was even more poignant given that the Embassy which he headed, financed by the East India Company and sent to redress interference with trade by the Viceroy of Canton, was a complete failure.[102] Amherst never did see the Emperor as the mission was dismissed.[103] The Chinese wallpapers that lay at the heart of these missions, as material evidence of superior manufacturing, were witness to both the failure of gift-giving from West to East, and of successful gifting and commerce from East to West.

As noted at the beginning of this chapter the impact of Chinese wallpaper was nationwide, and reached at least as far as Blair Castle in Perthshire and Eglinton Castle on the north-west coast of Scotland. There are a cluster of Chinese wallpapers in the east, below the Firth of Forth found at Newhailes, Newbyth, Dunglass, Arniston and Bowhill. Perhaps the most well known in this area is at Abbotsford, not because of its rarity, but because it hangs in the home of the celebrated author Sir Walter Scott (1771–1832).[104] This was not an aristocratic country house, but a home that was the culmination of Scott's creative ambitions as a writer and the source of his inspiration for his novels and poems.

The vivid green Chinese wallpaper that hangs in the Drawing Room at Abbotsford in the Scottish Borders might strike the modern visitor as incongruous in a baronial antiquarian interior, created by Scott between 1812 and his death. However its presence not only illustrates the power of the gift, but also how intimately Asian goods and Scottish history could be intertwined. We know that Scott 'direct[ed] everything personally, connected with the building and decorating of his mansion', transforming what the locals called Clarty Hole farmhouse into a 'rambling, whimsical and picturesque' country house.[105] Scott was advised by a close group of male friends: James Skene of Rubislaw (1775–1864), Daniel Terry (1780(?)–1829), Edward Blore (1787–1879), William Atkinson (1773–1839), William Stark (1770–1813) and George Bullock (1782/3–1818).[106] Scott's wife, Margaret Charlotte Charpentier (d.1826) seems to have had little say in the project. As a result we know a great deal about the furnishing of Abbotsford through Scott's correspondence with his advisors; because of Scott's fame, we also have the published comments of his workmen and visitors. It is in a letter dated 10 November 1822 to Daniel Terry, that the origin of Abbotsford's Chinese wallpaper is revealed: 'Hawl the second is twenty-four pieces of the most splendid Chinese paper … a present from my cousin Hugh Scott, enough to finish the drawing room and two bedrooms'.[107]

Captain Hugh Scott (1777–1852) was the second son of Walter Scott, Laird of Raeburn (1744–c.1830), Sir Walter Scott's uncle, who at the time was in the Naval Service of the East India Company. He had been made Captain of the East Indiaman, *Ceres,* which made several voyages to China, until it was relegated to hulk in 1816. The painting of the ship, in its original frame, remained in the possession of Hugh Scott's family at Draycott until recently.

This was not the only Chinese wallpaper to hang on the walls at Abbotsford however. Scott's painter and decorator, Mr Hay, refers in his *Laws of Harmonious Colouring adapted to Interior Decoration,* (published in 1847) to 'an Indian paper of a crimson colour with a small gilded pattern upon it' to complete the decoration of the Dining Room walls at Abbotsford, for which the final plans had been made in 1818.[108] This paper may also have come from Scott's cousin Hugh. Hay remarks that Scott 'said he did not altogether approve of' this paper 'for a dining room, but as he had it in a present expressly for that purpose, and as he believed it to be rare, he would have it put upon the room, thither than hurt the feelings of the donor'.[109] This Chinese wallpaper reveals two important points. First, it highlights the presence of a type of wallpaper that is rarely commented upon. It was the floral and figural papers that caught contemporary attention, and we know little about these plainer papers. Scott himself remarked that it was 'rare'. Secondly, the presence of the wallpaper demonstrates that the power of the gift-giver overrode convention in the hanging of the paper in an 'inappropriate space'. The National Trust Chinese Wallpaper Project has confirmed the dominance of private spaces such as bedrooms, dressing rooms and drawing rooms (often, but not only, feminine spaces) for such paper, with only very few examples of a paper hung in a dining room, at Abbotsford, and a twentieth-century reproduction made for Avebury Manor. Hay observed to Sir Walter that there would scarcely be enough to cover the whole remainder of the wall after the pictures were fixed up, to which he replied, that if that was the case I might paint the recess of the sideboard 'in imitation oak'. He noted that 'Scott abominated the common-place daubing of walls, panels, doors and window-boards, with coats of white, blue, or grey. ... He desired to have about him, wherever he could manage it, rich, though not gaudy hangings, or substantial old-fashioned wainscot work, with no ornament but that of carving, and where the wood was to be painted at all, it was done in strict imitation of oak or cedar.... He ordered me to paint the dining-room ceiling, cornice, niches &c in imitation of oak to match the doors, window shutters and wainscoting which were made of that wood'.[110] These instructions suggest that Scott was making the most of his limited supply of this wallpaper, and that he felt that it needed to be used, not put in store, in recognition of the value of the gift, and the status of the donor in the recipient's eyes.

The Abbotsford Chinese wallpapers may seem an odd addition to Scott's antiquarian interior to modern eyes. However it is clear that Asian connections and influences percolated throughout the house, and indeed through Scott's own family and friends, as well as through his work, most notably in *The Surgeon's Daughter* (1827). Sir Walter resided for many years at Ashestiel, near Selkirk, the home of his cousin General Sir James Russell who was then in India. It was not only Scott's cousin Hugh who had ties with the East India Company. His brother Robert died young while serving with the EIC in India. Sir Walters's nephew, Walter Scott (1807–76), the only son of Thomas Scott, spent a considerable portion of his youth under the immediate care of his uncle. At the age of 17 he entered the service of the East India Company as a lieutenant in the Engineers. He attained distinction in the Mooltan campaign (1848–9), and was, in 1861, promoted as Major-General, and in 1875 as General.[111] His brother-in-law Charles Charpentier (later Carpenter) was also a Company servant, finally taking up residence in the Madras estates in Salem, where he died in 1818. Scott's eldest son Walter (b.1801) became a Lieutenant General in the 15th Dragoons, and served in Bangalore until his death in 1847.[112] Scott's younger son Charles (b.1805) died in Tehran, in 1841, while part of a Foreign Office mission to the Court of Persia.

Abbotsford boasted an armoury, adjoining the dining room, which was described in 1818 as including 'the armour of true celebrated Jalabad Sing Son of Nadior Shah (1688–1747)' as well as 'pretty complete suits of armour – one Indian ... and the clubs and creases of Indian tribes', alongside those of Highlanders' accoutrements.[113] The 'curious antique ebony chairs' in the Drawing Room, were Indo-Portuguese, c.1800 and were combined with furniture from the Palace of Falkirk. Sir Walter Scott also had a connection, if remote, with Thomas Coutts. In his *Life of Scott,* Lockhart (Scott's son-in-law and biographer) remarks that 'Sir Walter's grandmother, Barbara Haliburton, wife of Robert Scott of Sandyknowe, was the banker's first cousin'.[114] The story of Walter Scott and his Chinese wallpaper emphasizes the crucial importance of how complex relations with the East India Company could be. Mediated through the agency of friends and relatives, the exotic could be drawn into the fabric of the interior, overcoming what appear to us contradictions in taste to create richly nuanced spaces, where ancient oak furniture shared space with Mughal armour and Chinese wallpaper.

Concluding remarks: afterlife

Chinese wallpaper illustrates the myriad ways in which East India Company trade pervaded British social and cultural life, shaping the domestic interior in fundamental ways. Although the papers themselves were (and still are) conspicuous in their colouring, patterns and design, their pivotal roles in globalizing the British home have received little systematic attention. The impact of Chinese wallpaper was not restricted to those who had houses decorated with it, or had access to these houses as visitors and servants. Despite the success of British-made wallpapers, the allure of Chinese wallpaper continued beyond the nineteenth century. Its high value ensured that this exotic and fashionable luxury item survived beyond redecoration. Offcuts and scraps were framed as pictures, used to ornament chimney boards (at Osterley, a Chinese print was used with an applied border), or deployed to back embroidered pole screens and craft work. Chinese wallpaper was used to cover boxes, and larger sections were turned into screens.[115]

In the 1920s and 1930s Nancy Lancaster invented the 'English Country House Style', and one of its crucial components was Chinese wallpaper, which was 'sold both as rooms and panels' and spawned 'a cottage industry of talented copyists' whose handiwork has deceived many a country house visitor.[116] The fascination with Chinese wallpaper continues into the twenty-first century. The firms of de Gournay and Fromental create handmade papers in Wuxi, the latter supplying 22 panels for Avebury Manor based upon the Coutts and Drummond papers, which took 12 Chinese artists 4,000 hours to make. Meanwhile Lord Macartney's gift of paper to Thomas Coutts, has become a symbol of the bank's distinguished heritage, parts of which have been copied to furnish key rooms in each of their offices around the world. The paper is a key marketing tool that conveys both the stability of its eighteenth-century foundations and the reach of its global connections.

Acknowledgments

I would like to thank Margot Finn, Emile de Bruijn, Andrew Bush and Lucy Johnson for reading drafts of this case study, and Kate Smith for her support and idea sharing. As a member of the National Trust Chinese

Wallpaper study group I have also benefitted immensely from the lively comments on the subject from which I have learnt much. Thank you Emile de Bruijn for organizing permission for images of Chinese wallpaper from National Trust houses, and generous sharing of knowledge which will be made known to more via his *Chinese Wallpapers in Britain and Ireland* which was published when this volume was in press; Andrew Bush for permission to use his exceptionally detailed close-up pictures reflecting his keen conservator's eye; and Stuart Howat for his photograph taken at Osterley.

3
Production, purchase, dispossession, recirculation

Anglo-Indian ivory furniture in the British country house

Kate Smith

The term 'ivory' describes the teeth or tusks of elephants and other mammals, including the Asiatic and African boar, the Arctic walrus, hippopotamus, warthog and whale. Ivory is a dense material that can be carved, engraved, turned, pierced and painted, and it has the strength and elasticity required for use both as a solid material and a veneer. In the Indian context, hunters removed ivory from the upper front tusks of the elephants found across the subcontinent, from the foothills of the Himalayas to the southern tip of Ceylon.[1] This chapter explores the objects made from these tusks. It particularly focuses on the furniture pieces, made by skilled craftsmen in the subcontinent during the eighteenth century. Although Europe had a long tradition of ivory goods, often made from African and Asian elephant ivory (which was imported to Europe in greater quantities from the 1500s onwards), skilled Indian craftsmen made ivory furniture which presented European consumers with new and desirable aesthetic options.[2] Ivory furniture thus acts as a lens through which to examine how individuals in the modern period related to objects from the subcontinent.

More particularly, ivory furniture is useful in considering a question central to *The East India Company at Home*: were objects purchased, transported, gifted and retained by East India Company (EIC) families understood as distinct from commodities traded more generally by the EIC? If so, how? Despite greater scholarly interest in commodities traded between Europe and Asia by companies such as the EIC, less is known about what objects that were imported through other, more exclusive, routes came to mean in Britain. Tillman Nechtman has argued that these objects were understood as deeply imperial: 'a means of narrating an imperial identity, of spanning the distance between empire and nation'.[3] While it is possible to make this argument for remarkable objects such as diamonds and dress, which were worn, gifted and scrutinized in public spaces such as the court, it becomes more difficult to track reactions to objects in domestic spaces.[4] Yet, as this volume seeks to show, elite domestic objects and spaces were and are important in understanding how contemporaries confronted empire.

The range of Indian ivory furniture found in the collections of British museums, such as the V&A, as well as private collections, reflects eighteenth- and nineteenth-century Britons' desire to possess these exotic luxury goods. Yet as Anne Gerritsen and Stephen McDowall warn in the case of porcelain, the survival of many items in museum collections should be treated with caution and should not be understood as unproblematic evidence of historical popularity.[5] Compared to better-known large-scale imports of domestic goods such as porcelain and textiles, however, ivory furniture's presence in British collections is noteworthy precisely because the Company did not trade in it. In contrast to widely traded commodities like tea, textiles and porcelain, ivory furniture generally came to Britain through individual purchases made by EIC servants while in India. Moreover, whereas men and women in Britain could commission armorial porcelains or Chinese wallpaper at a distance, families or individuals tended to purchase items of ivory furniture while in India or when trading on the Indian coast. While these purchases could be acquired from Company individuals on the secondary market, their initial acquisition meant that they were firmly associated with families involved in trading. Furthermore, ivory wares proved difficult for European manufacturers to imitate. Given the limitations imposed by modes of purchase and manufacture, ivory furniture provides a particularly clear lens through which to ask, did British men and women understand specific types of imperial luxury goods as distinctly different from widely traded Asian commodities?

This chapter shows that although ivory furniture was increasingly made to European forms, contemporaries in Britain continued to understand it as representing a family's link to the subcontinent. Although those lower down the social scale may have encountered ivory in small items such as snuffboxes, fans or ivory-handled cutlery, substantial furniture items were rare and valuable and thus marked elite status.[6] Furthermore, ivory furniture continued to act as a prompt for retelling

EIC family narratives long after the family members with links to the Company had died. Like the men and women who bought, collected and retained them, Company objects had complicated and global biographies, which shaped British material cultures long after the initial point of exchange. To understand the history and significance of these imperial objects then, we need to study their meaning both at the point of initial purchase and after it, as they moved on into other families, houses and institutions.

To capture the meanings that such objects held in wider British culture, this chapter examines ivory furniture both *in situ* in particular houses and at moments in which these goods moved and circulated. For it is often in moments of movement that objects emerge onto the historical record with their greatest force. In the eighteenth and nineteenth centuries, when people advertised objects for sale, singled them out for inheritance, or valued them, they tended to describe and arrange them, privileging certain components for inclusion or note. The texts created to record exchange and circulation offer historians important evidence through which to understand the meanings affixed to objects. These texts are steeped in particular conventions (the inventory, the sales catalogue), which need to be fully understood and accounted for as shaping forces, altering how descriptions and notes are written. Nevertheless, these texts provide important sources for the question at hand, and therefore this chapter uses newspapers, sale catalogues, inventories, wills and correspondence, to examine three different types of movement chronologically. After considering the production of these objects in India, the first part of the chapter examines the initial purchase of ivory furniture by members of the EIC elite, such as Edward Harrison (1674–1732), in the early eighteenth century. It investigates why EIC officials bought ivory furniture by asking what the visual and material qualities of such pieces might represent. The second section of the chapter explores how collections purchased in the eighteenth century came to be dismantled and re-circulated in the nineteenth century, focusing on Warren Hastings and the sale of parts of his ivory furniture collection in the mid-nineteenth century. It examines the ways in which these goods were presented to interested parties and questions how and why newspaper writers used the sale of his country house Daylesford's contents to embark on further retellings of the Hastings myth. The chapter ends by looking at non-EIC families, such as the Morrisons and the Kleinworts, who purchased Indian ivory furniture in the nineteenth and twentieth centuries and asks what ivory objects might have meant when circulated outside EIC networks.

In following these avenues this chapter explores British public understandings of empire through ivory objects across the eighteenth, nineteenth, twentieth and twenty-first centuries. It finds that when exchanged between family members, gifted to other families or advertised on the open market after the death of the initial purchaser, ivory objects retained biographies that explicitly linked them to imperial geographies and narratives. As such, they played important roles in consolidating the narratives of empire constructed by and about particular families. At the same time, claims to origin were aided by the materiality of the objects, referring as they did to particular regions, through the veneering techniques of Vizagapatam or the solid ivory turning technologies of Murshidabad. These objects thus enjoyed very different biographies and meanings to those commodities traded in large numbers by the EIC; as holders of particular meanings and narratives they also significantly shaped the places and people to which they became attached.

Production

Before the Battle of Plassey in 1757, Murshidabad was an important centre of ivory carving, primarily producing solid ivory pieces of furniture and decorative items.[7] After the Treaty of Allahabad in 1765, as the British began to administer the diwani (tax collection and revenue administration) in the Bengal region, ivory carvers in Murshidabad increasingly sought to make goods that were desirable to Anglo-Indian consumers by producing furniture that more readily conformed to European styles. The circulation of print sources, such as Thomas Chippendale's *The Gentleman and Cabinet Maker's Director* (1754) and George Heppelwhite's *The Cabinet Maker and Upholsterer's Guide* (1788), containing European designs, facilitated this process.[8] Information about European designs was also transmitted to Indian workshops through the arrival of skilled furniture makers from Europe. Amin Jaffer gives particular credit to the presence of Charles Rose, a British furniture maker who was recorded as being in Bengal from 1772 and was registered as an inhabitant in Murshidabad in 1793.[9] In the later eighteenth century, Murshidabad workshops began to produce chairs, candle stands and worktables. Particular skills in solid ivory carving allowed these workshops to produce items with distinctive arms and legs made of turned solid ivory. Jaffer has argued that Murshidabad 'can now be recognised as most probably the source of most surviving Anglo-Indian solid-ivory furniture'.[10]

Much further south from Murshidabad, Vizagapatam on the Coromandel Coast was also a key production site for ivory furniture. From the late seventeenth century until the mid-eighteenth century, Vizagapatam was especially known for furniture that featured inlaid ivory work (see Figure 3.1). As in Murshidabad, artisans in this area increasingly used their ivory carving skills to produce furniture in Western forms.[11] Between 1760 and 1780, Kamsali-caste ivory carvers in Vizagapatam began to use new techniques involving ivory veneer (see Figure 3.2). During this period ivory veneer gradually replaced ivory inlay as the main form of production. It was constructed by attaching a thin layer of ivory, by means of fixatives and rivets, to a wooden carcass. Decorative schemes appeared on these veneers through engraving the ivory and then filling the spaces with a type of black lacquer to create a monochrome design. While visiting Vizagapatam in 1801 with her mother and sister, Henrietta Clive witnessed the production of these ivory furniture pieces. On 4 April 1801 she described to her father (the Governor of Madras) watching monochrome ivory veneers being manufactured. She described how 'We have seen the people inlaying the Ivory [with lac]' and that 'it appears very simple'. Henrietta observed that 'they draw the pattern … they intend with a pencil and then cut it out slightly with a small piece of Iron, they afterwards put hot Lac upon it, and when it is dry scrape it off and polish it, the Lac remains in the marks made with the piece of Iron'.[12]

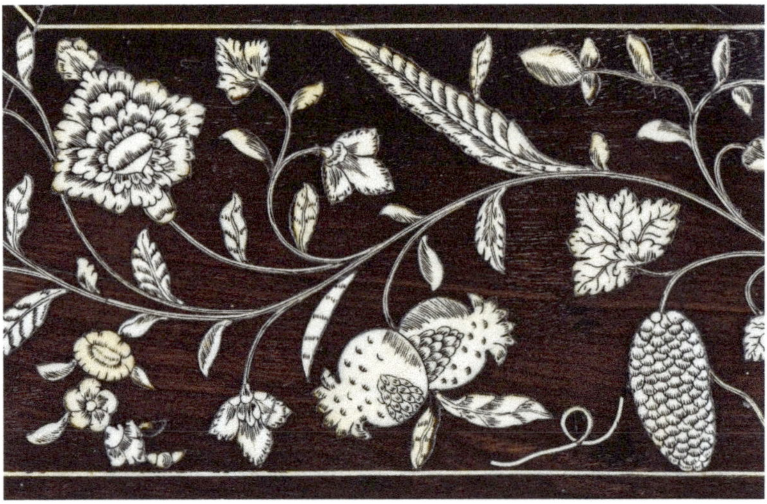

Figure 3.1 Detail of ivory and ebony inlay from early eighteenth-century Vizagapatam Anglo-Indian ebony and padoukwood games table. Tyntesfield, Somerset. 1207460 © National Trust Images/John Hammond.

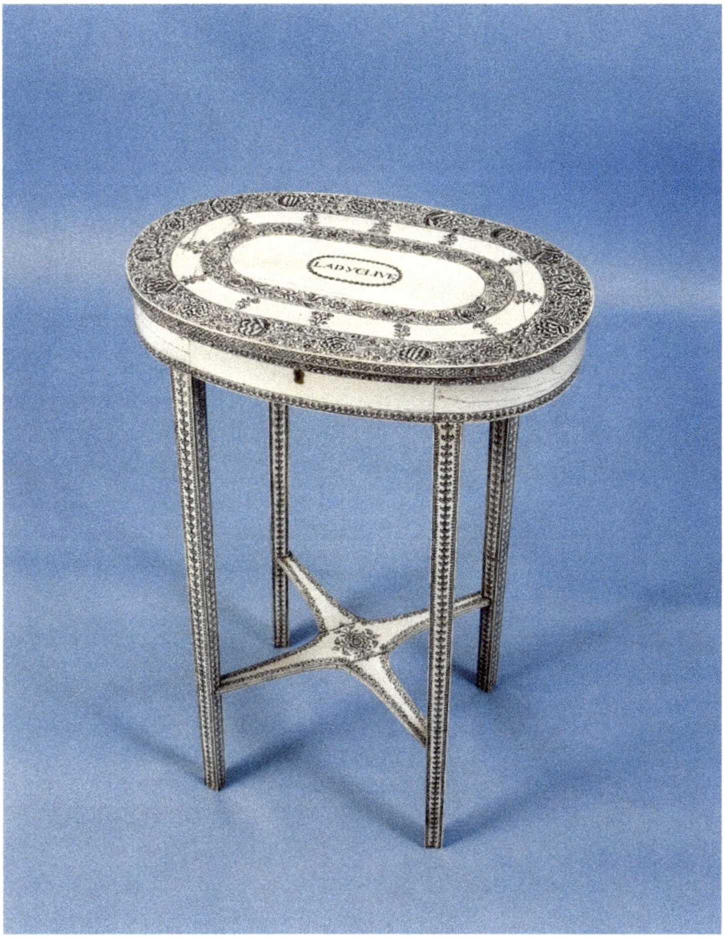

Figure 3.2 Oval work table, wood with ivory veneer and lacquer detail, 1770–1800, Vizagapatam. Powis Castle and Garden, Powys. 1180670. © National Trust Images/Erik Pelham.

Switching to ivory veneer was an important change in aesthetic terms as it allowed makers a greater degree of flexibility when designing decorative schemes for furniture. Being able to implement a range of decorative schemes became important in the later eighteenth century as carvers began to incorporate increasingly elaborate figurative and architectural scenes into their furniture. Decorative ivory veneers proved a popular innovation with consumers. The circulation of European prints was important to the construction of these wares. Many of the veneer panels included scenes inspired by European prints, which became widely available on the subcontinent in this period.

As Henrietta Clive's written description of ivory engraving for her father demonstrates, elite British consumers became increasingly curious about ivory's material properties and the production techniques involved in making ivory furniture, workboxes, chairs and cabinets.[13] For EIC women, imperial employments offered opportunities for observing production and gaining further material literacy. Some elite women who remained in Britain also became curious to further their knowledge; Margaret, second Duchess of Portland (1715–85) and Mary Delany (1700–88) took up ivory turning themselves.[14] Alongside genteel and feminine interests in learning japanning techniques to produce objects in imitation of Chinese and Japanese lacquer wares, such forms of making provide a genteel and domestic variation on narratives of Asian import substitution, which, Maxine Berg argues, shaped British manufacturing distinctly in the eighteenth century.[15] While a wider interest in ivory had emerged by the mid-eighteenth century, in the early decades of the century elite EIC families, such as the Harrisons, were collectors of ivory furniture pieces.

Purchase

Edward Harrison (1674–1732) inherited Balls Park in Hertfordshire after the death of his father Richard Harrison in 1726.[16] Prior to establishing himself at the estate during the 1720s, Edward had worked in different capacities in the service of the EIC. It is possible that he began his EIC career as purser upon the *London* in the early 1690s.[17] He certainly went on to captain EIC ships including the *Powderham Castle*, which sailed to Borneo in the late 1690s and the *Kent*, which he commanded on voyages to China in 1704–5 and 1706–10.[18] Towards the end of 1710, after completing his final voyage on the *Kent*, Harrison was appointed Governor of Fort St George, Madras.[19] After completing his tenure as Governor in 1717 Harrison returned to England, where he continued to be involved with the EIC and simultaneously established a career in Parliament. Between 1717 and 1722 he acted as MP for Weymouth and Melcombe Regis before going on to represent Hertford between 1722 and 1726. After moving to Balls Park in 1726, Harrison re-established himself once again within the Company by becoming Deputy Chairman of the Court of Directors in 1728, Chairman in 1729 and Deputy Chairman for a second time in 1731.[20] By the time of his death in 1732 Edward Harrison was deeply embedded in EIC life – he had travelled to places as diverse as Macao and Batavia on Company business, he had led Company operations in Madras and had worked to govern the Company in London.

Edward Harrison's EIC career is visible not only through Company records that list orders from the Directors for copper, tea, green ginger, rhubarb, wrought silks, raw silk and china.[21] Harrison's experiences of Asia and Eurasian trade were (and are) also made materially manifest through the objects he returned with and the wealth he acquired.[22] Of particular interest here is the ivory furniture he purchased while in India, most likely as Governor of Fort St George between 1711 and 1717. Ivory furniture acts as an important signifier of Company connections for historians because once acquired by an individual it is one of the few Asian goods that can be identified in inventories.[23] As a distinctive material, appraisers writing up probate records often included the descriptor 'ivory' when itemizing these objects.[24] On Edward Harrison's death in 1732 appraisers compiled an inventory of movable goods at Balls Park estate. Although Harrison had served as an MP in the later years of his life, in constructing the inventory the unnamed appraiser identified Harrison through his EIC career, as 'the Honourable Edward Harrison Esq deceased late-Governor of Fort St George at his seat Balls in the County of Hertford'.[25] The inventory demonstrates that the Harrisons were keen collectors of Indian (or Indian-inspired) textiles as well as of ivory furniture. Calico quilts appear in many rooms, including the Nursery, Drawing Rooms, Mrs Harrison's Room, the House Keeper's Room and Brown Room. The presence of calico in these rooms and not others marks both the rooms and the calicos as of less social importance. In contrast, those rooms specifically linked to Edward Harrison and his wife, contained more valuable Indian textiles such as chintz (spelt 'Chince' in the inventory).[26] Similarly the ivory objects owned by the Harrisons appear in some of the house's most important rooms. 'The Governors Bed Chamber', contained 'a very curious India Book case inlaid with Ivory', while 'The Long Galery [sic]' included twelve ebony 'China' chairs inlaid with ivory, as well as two similar elbow chairs and two couches.[27] It is probable that Harrison bequeathed some of his movable household goods, including the bookcase, to his only child Etheldreda (commonly known as Audrey) (c.1708–1788). A 1737 inventory for her London home in Grosvenor Street notes that her personal room contained 'A Desk and book case inlay'd with Ivory'.[28]

In 1723 Etheldreda married Charles Townshend (1700–64) afterwards third Viscount Townshend.[29] While the relationship between Etheldreda and Charles remained turbulent, the alliance instituted an important link between the EIC and the Townshend family. Such links were further consolidated when Charles's brother Augustus captained the East Indiaman *Augusta*.[30] On his final voyage, destined for China, another Townshend, Roger (d.1759), the fifth son of Etheldreda and Charles, joined Augustus and further consolidated the family's links to global trade. Before preparations to sail on the *Augusta* began, Charles and Augustus worriedly wrote numerous letters, assuring each other that Roger was sufficiently prepared for the voyage. Augustus advised that around £200 would be required to see Roger set up on ship and during the journey.[31] After setting sail in February 1745, Roger finally returned to Britain in November 1749. He returned without his uncle who had died on board ship and despite the *Augusta* being captured by the French as it tried to return home.[32]

The difficulties Roger experienced might explain why on returning he was distinctly keen to switch profession, hoping instead to join the army or navy. Charles wanted Roger to remain in the Company, but remarked to his brother that at least a change would mean that the family were no longer dependent on the solicitations of the Court of Directors.[33] While the Townshend family's growing range of connections to the Company is made visible through these professional concerns, Etheldreda's earlier connections to the Company through her father and his links to the Coromandel Coast were manifest through material possessions that were recognizably Indian and more specifically, recognizably from Vizagapatam in the Madras Presidency of which Harrison was Governor.

Placed on the market in 2011 and attributed as one of Edward Harrison's pieces, an ivory-inlaid teak, ebony and tortoiseshell bureau-cabinet continues to act as a material manifestation of Harrison's particular links to the subcontinent.[34] The bureau-cabinet is likely the 'Desk and book case inlay'd with Ivory' that belonged to Etheldreda, which she had inherited from her father. Moreover, the Harrison bureau is aesthetically similar to one purchased by Richard Benyon (1698–1774) who worked as Governor of Fort St George, Madras after Harrison, between 1735 and 1744.[35] As pieces featuring ivory inlay work, these bureau-cabinets linked Harrison, Benyon and their families to Madras and the Coromandel Coast. Unlike more perishable goods such as textiles, these valuable and highly valued cabinets remain as testimony to such connections. They have been passed down through generations and retain a strong sense of provenance.[36]

Not all ivory furniture pieces, however, stayed within EIC families. Company servants also purchased them to be later gifted or sold. Moreover, while it was the EIC elite who predominantly purchased ivory furniture in the early eighteenth century, in the later decades of the period, those (slightly) lower down the social ladder were also able to acquire such pieces. Evidence for the consumption of ivory furniture by those below the Governor rank can be seen through the example of Captain James Monro (1756–1806) who purchased a miniature cabinet with ivory veneers, made in Vizagapatam in the second half of the eighteenth century. As it displays such an elaborate collection of ivory veneer sections, the piece can be dated to the post-1760 period when the majority of Vizagapatam ivory production shifted focus from ivory inlay work to ivory veneer.

In researching the miniature cabinet, furniture historian Elizabeth Jamieson demonstrated how objects themselves are sometimes able to allude to their histories.[37] Hidden on the sandalwood top of the lower section of the cabinet Jamieson found an inscription that read 'Out of No. 201 Houghton/Capt Monro'. The inscription connects the cabinet to the East Indiaman, the *Houghton*. Between 1766 and 1789 James Monro was a member of the crew on every voyage that the *Houghton* took. Monro, the third son of physician John Monro,[38] began his seafaring career at the age of 10 when he worked as a captain's servant on the *Houghton* as it travelled out to trade at Whampoa near Canton. After this early engagement with shipping, Monro went on to work as midshipman and fifth mate on the *Houghton* before completing a further voyage as fourth mate on the *Osterley II*.[39] At the age of 20, Monro returned to the *Houghton* as second mate, a role he also performed on the *York* before finally gaining command of the *Houghton* for the first time in 1782. After this, Monro captained the *Houghton* on three further journeys to Asia.[40] Most significantly for this chapter, on his voyage to Bengal, as second mate on the *Houghton,* between 1777 and 1778, Monro stopped at Vizagapatam. The port had acted as an important English trading post or 'factory' since 1668. After 1768, however, when the Northern Circars came under the control of the English East India Company, Vizagapatam increased in importance as a place of settlement and a lucrative port for conducting Coromandel Coast trade in textiles.[41] Here Monro would have been able to see a range of ivory furniture pieces at first hand, perhaps encouraging him to purchase a piece later on when he had risen to the position of captain and was able to afford it. As captain, Monro would have been well placed to purchase pieces such as this and to transport them back to Britain as part of his privilege allowance.

James Monro's letters demonstrate that he purchased smaller items such as ceramics and furniture while on voyage, for gifting and sale once he returned to England. Writing to his elder brother Charles as he sailed from China to St Helena in November 1785, James described how he had managed to purchase some Chinese tables and tea sets, as well as some small chairs.[42] He generously offered Charles and his new wife first refusal on his bountiful supplies. Like other Company men, James Monro appears to have depended upon his brother for support and information.[43] Even when in England, but away from the centre of news and markets in London, James requested Charles to complete payments and order clothes on his behalf.[44] After James's death in 1806, Charles continued to play an important role in the life of his family. James's wife Caroline (d. 1848) outlived him and Charles took responsibility for her and the remaining children. For instance, a letter from 1811 suggests that Charles was actively involved in managing the family's financial affairs, particularly those of James's daughters. He ensured that household goods such as furniture were turned into investments such as an 'Old South Sea Ann'ty' and kept distinct from the 'Estate'. After Caroline's death it was these items and not the 'Estate' that would have been allotted to her daughters and Charles realized that they would 'not be generally divisible' or financially useful.[45] If the Vizagapatam cabinet remained in the family rather than being sold when James returned from India, it may well have been unsentimentally sent to market to provide for his daughters and their future life.[46] These ivory objects, bearing materials from the subcontinent and Africa, produced through the enactment of highly skilled Indian craftsmanship to European designs, remained valuable and desirable commodities. Their links to the subcontinent through the EIC were part of their allure. Moreover, they often experienced an afterlife linked to, but independent of, their Company history.

Dispossession

Throughout the late eighteenth century Warren Hastings (1732–1818) (see Figure 3.3) and his wife Marian (1744–1837) held an important place in Britons' imaginings of empire. The press and the public used the Hastings as an important conduit through which to understand empire broadly and Britain's relationship to the subcontinent more particularly. They did so in three key ways: first, through Hastings's career, second, through his marriage to Marian and finally, through his estate – Daylesford.

Warren Hastings's career path mirrored Britain's increasingly imperial role in the subcontinent. Hastings joined the EIC in 1750 after his guardian Joseph Creswicke secured him a writership in Calcutta. Twenty-two years later in 1772, Hastings rose to the position of Governor General. Although Hastings fulfilled many objectives, his long tenure as Governor (13 years in total) was also marked by war and accusations of

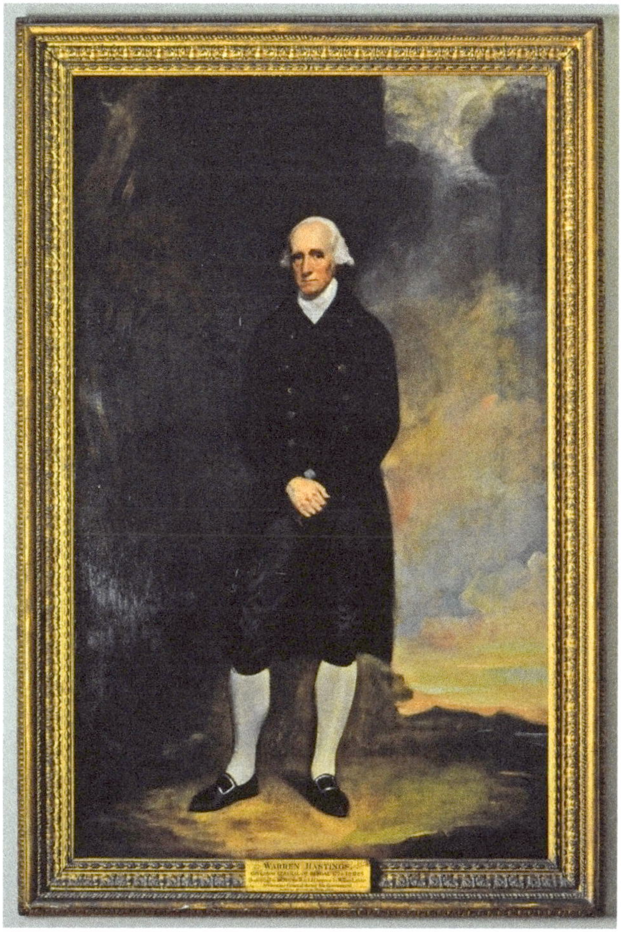

Figure 3.3 'Warren Hastings (1732–1818), Governor General of Fort William, Bengal, 1774–85', George Romney, 1795. © British Library Board, F1.

corruption.[47] As Britain's control of the American colonies became weaker during the course of the Wars of Independence, the British public's interest in India increased. When Hastings resigned in 1785 and returned to Britain, his impeachment and trial (1787–95) had a ready audience.

As Tillman Nechtman has shown, interest in Hastings's personal life further consolidated and shaped the public's desire to understand the nature of Britain's empire.[48] Warren Hastings first met Marian von Imhoff (née Anna Maria Apollonia Chapuset) while sailing to India in 1769. At the end of the journey Marian went with her husband to Calcutta, while

Hastings went to Madras to take up the post of second-in-council at Fort St George. Once appointed Governor in 1772, Hastings moved to Calcutta, the seat of the Company's government, where Marian and her husband Baron Carl von Imhoff were resident. In 1773 Marian remained in India when the Baron returned to Europe. Her husband divorced Marian in 1776, and a year later she married Hastings. Their marriage underlined how the social rules structuring life in the metropole often became blurred once abroad.[49] When the couple returned to Britain in 1785, Marian was subject to further criticism because she both wore and distributed the fruits of empire. She supposedly appeared at court decked out in diamonds and offered up rich and elaborate gifts to the Royal family – including ivory armchairs from Murshidabad. Critics, such as Fanny Burney, feared that Marian would undermine the morality of court, bringing it under the influence of empire and imperial riches.[50]

The couple's country house, Daylesford, also acted as an important part of the family's myth. During his trial, for example, the press used Hastings's purchase of Daylesford variously as a means to reaffirm his morality and immorality. The Hastings family had been linked to the Daylesford estate since the thirteenth century, but when they experienced reduced circumstances in the early years of the eighteenth century, the lands were sold off. Both Hastings's father and grandfather continued to live near the estate and Warren Hastings's desire to re-acquire it and re-establish the family fortune acted as a compelling part of his life narrative. As the trial wound on, writers explored Hastings's desire and motives for different ends. For example, articles in both the *St James's Chronicle or the British Evening Post* and the *World* discussed his purchase of Daylesford in terms of his family's long attachment to the estate. An anonymous letter published in the *St James's Chronicle or the British Evening Post* on 29 September 1785 (after Hastings had returned to England) noted that although Hastings had been linked to several houses, he never had any intention of purchasing anything other than Daylesford.[51] The writer went on to note that Daylesford had been in the possession of his family from '1281 to 1715' and that in reacquiring it Hastings sought to return to the status of 'respectable Country Gentleman'.[52] Similarly a biographical sketch published in the *World* at the height of his trial in 1792 noted that Hastings's grandfather had been forced to sell the Daylesford estate, 'which had been possessed by the family of Mr Hastings from 1280 to 1715'.[53] In contrast to using Daylesford to make claims regarding the respectability and longevity of the Hastings family, other publications used Daylesford (and more particularly its rebuilding) to suggest Hastings's duplicity. On 6 October 1795 (after the final acquittal), for example, rather than take pity on Hastings and the high costs he incurred as a result of the lengthy trial, *The Morning Post and Fashionable World* took umbrage at the Indian profits he was seen to retain. They particularly noted the money Hastings had spent on ornamenting his gardens. The writer quipped that 'To throw away [£]50,000 in making Shrubberies and Gravel Walks is an unquestionable proof of poverty.' It further asked 'When a man throws away [£]90,000 in merely ornamenting the grounds about his Country House, what may we calculate his whole fortune to be?'[54]

By examining how the Hastings family were described in the press and other print forms, it is possible to understand the role that objects, such as ivory furniture, played in consolidating links between individuals and empire. That Daylesford was an important site through which the public could discuss Hastings (and by implication empire) became doubly apparent during its sale in the 1850s. In this instance, ivory furniture was of particular importance in providing signifiers that linked Hastings to empire. The sale of Daylesford in the early 1850s and the subsequent sale of its contents in August 1853 attracted the attention of newspapers across Britain. Such was the perceived public interest in these events that following the sale, on 10 September 1853 the *Oxford Journal* republished an article that had appeared in *The Times*, which proposed that:

> It is scarcely possible to read this announcement of the sale of Daylesford without emotion – so much of hope and feeling had been bound up with the trees and pastures of that pleasant spot ... Well did he [Hastings] keep his word [to reclaim Daylesford] ... He did purchase the estate – he did build upon it a mansion suitable for the Inhabitants of an English country gentleman.[55]

Why was the Daylesford sale such an important event? Cynthia Wall has drawn our attention to the importance of understanding auctions and house sales as 'dismantlings'. For Wall 'The auction is the site for the disassembling of one instance of the existing world and the promise of the reconstruction of a new one.'[56] As *The Times* article reprinted in the *Oxford Journal* demonstrates, the attention that the sale of Daylesford and its contents attracted, focused specifically on the house's relationship to Warren and Marian Hastings rather than its most recent owner (Marian's son by her first marriage) Charles von Imhoff, or its purchaser, a financier called Mr Grisewood.[57] The catalogue, and its later dissemination, constructed and consolidated this focus. It too primarily understood Daylesford House as 'The Seat of the late Right Hon. Warren Hastings', while the sale itself was framed as occurring 'By orders of the Executors of the late Mrs Hastings'.[58] Playing to the connection between Warren and Marian Hastings and Daylesford, the frontispiece of the sale catalogue hints at the end of such connections and the dismantling of their lives.

Even in the 1850s, as his house and contents were sold, Warren Hastings' connection to empire remained the key frame through which he was understood. Such connections were significantly underlined through material manifestations of empire – such as ivory furniture. In its first few lines, the frontispiece to the Daylesford sale catalogue highlighted the ivory furniture belonging to the Hastings. It described itself as 'A catalogue of the valuable contents of the mansion embracing a unique & costly drawing room suite of solid ivory, finely carved and gilt, and finished in the Richest Style of Oriental Magnificence, comprising Two beautifully formed Sofas, Nine Chairs, Two Ottomans, a Table, and a pair of Screens'.[59] Ivory furniture, brought from the subcontinent, was the first type of object that any potential purchaser was asked to consider. Rather than 'Indian', however, in this part of the catalogue its geographical origin is unclear. It is marked as 'Oriental Magnificence' in style, simultaneously suggesting at its perceived exuberance and that of Asian goods more generally. Inside the catalogue ivory furniture was further highlighted, this time through the use of typographical techniques, rather than hierarchical positioning. Other pieces of furniture in the Daylesford collection were described through a standardized font of the same point size. In contrast, bolding, capitalizing and italicizing marked out the ivory furniture pieces as distinctive, important and (it could be assumed) valuable – here there were important things to see that required special billing. In employing typographical strategies to emphasize certain goods, the catalogue reimagined the sale as spectacle and show.[60] For instance the catalogue listed the drawing room contents as:

> **A SOFA OF SOLID IVORY,** *in the richest style of Oriental magnificence, superbly carved and richly gilt, the elbows finished with tiger heads, stuff seat and two bolsters,* covered en-suite with curtains, and extra Indian dimity cases – 6 ft. 6 long
>
> THE COMPANION COUCH
>
> A PAIR OF ELBOW CHAIRS, **IN SOLID IVORY,** *of corresponding style, and of equal magnificence with sofas*
>
> A PAIR OF DITTO
>
> A PAIR OF DITTO
>
> ONE DITTO
>
> ONE DITTO
>
> ONE DITTO (damaged)

> **A SOLID IVORY TABLE,** *of elegant form, on shaped legs, beautifully carved and gilt, fitted with two drawers with silver locks and handles, and covered with fine green cloth, edged with silver lace*
>
> A SQUARE FOOT OTTOMAN, **OF SOLID IVORY**, gilt, stuffed and covered en-suite with sofas
>
> A DITTO
>
> A PAIR OF CARVED IVORY ORIENTAL OFFICIAL STAFFS (5ft. long), ornamented with silver gilt bands and wire, mounted in ebonized and gilt frames and silk mounts to form fire screens, and white Indian dimity covers

Whereas the catalogue placed little significance on the material qualities of other items, in promoting the ivory objects its author was at pains to highlight the importance of 'solid ivory' furniture. In nineteenth-century Britain, as understandings of 'veneer' shifted from skilled practice to false and cheap rendering, claims of 'solid ivory' would have been quickly understood as holding higher value.[61] As noted earlier, underlining this quality might have also made certain purchasers aware that these items likely came from a particular part of the subcontinent – Murshidabad. For those with an understanding of the subcontinent, the catalogue provided grounds on which to establish a connoisseurial engagement with the auctioned items.

While the catalogue imagined the ivory furniture within the expected space of the drawing room, it also destabilized the idea of a domestic setting by itemizing the pieces. As with other auction catalogues, such lists create a productive tension between the idea of plenty (something for everyone) and exclusivity (particular objects are of special import). At the same time, by using the convention of newspaper advertisements, which appeared to artlessly itemize many goods, auction catalogues underlined that these objects were for sale and could sell themselves.[62] Rearranging the items for sale both by randomizing their location in the lists and giving importance to some over others, the Daylesford catalogue reordered the Hastings' possessions and allowed them to be reimagined within other homes and lives.[63]

Alongside dismantling Hastings's home, articles appearing in newspapers across Britain in 1853 used the event to re-examine Hastings's life and legacy. Central to these re-examinations was (perhaps inevitably) his imperial career. The importance of imperial connections in shaping what Daylesford (and Hastings) was and meant, was further confirmed through the way in which the objects were arranged for sale. The subcontinent loomed large in the contents sale, through the presence of a collection of ivory furniture. It was this and not the mahogany and satinwood furniture that received top billing. As such this example reminds us of the important role furniture played in representing the subcontinent and Britain's imperial ambitions there. The sale of the contents of Daylesford also reminds us that by the nineteenth century an active market arose that enabled the recirculation of goods originally linked to EIC families in the eighteenth century. The dispossession of collections, such as that belonging to the Hastings family, also offered up an occasion upon which to dismantle their family narrative. Yet as the Hastings example shows, it also reified the Hastings drama, allowing others to purchase pieces understood as important to the imperial story. Chief amongst these, as the sale catalogue promised, was the ivory furniture largely bought from skilled craftsmen in Murshidabad. What happened to pieces such as these as they entered new settings and new narratives? How were they presented and understood? What position did they hold?

Recirculation

By studying examples of ivory furniture situated in British country houses in the nineteenth, twentieth and twenty-first centuries, we can begin to understand the changing positions that objects such as these held for contemporaries. This section of the chapter examines ivory furniture pieces held in two specific collections – Basildon Park, Berkshire in the nineteenth and early twentieth century and Sezincote, Gloucestershire in the mid-twentieth century. Both these collections were (and *are,* in the case of Sezincote) situated in country houses that were significantly rebuilt in the late-eighteenth and early-nineteenth centuries as a result of Company money. Both sites have EIC narratives to reclaim and explore, making them productive examples of the recirculation of meaning through Indian ivory furniture. I will first explore a pair of ivory chairs owned by the Morrison family in the nineteenth century and then briefly contrast these purchases with those made by Sir Cyril and Lady Kleinwort in the 1940s. Is it possible to recover the intention of these individuals in purchasing these items? What were the narratives told by these pieces? What did they mean and what purposes did their purchase enable or allow? What histories are revealed by the long afterlives of imperial objects?

James Morrison purchased Basildon Park (see Figure 3.4) in the late 1830s. Originally built by EIC servant Francis Sykes in 1776, the mansion

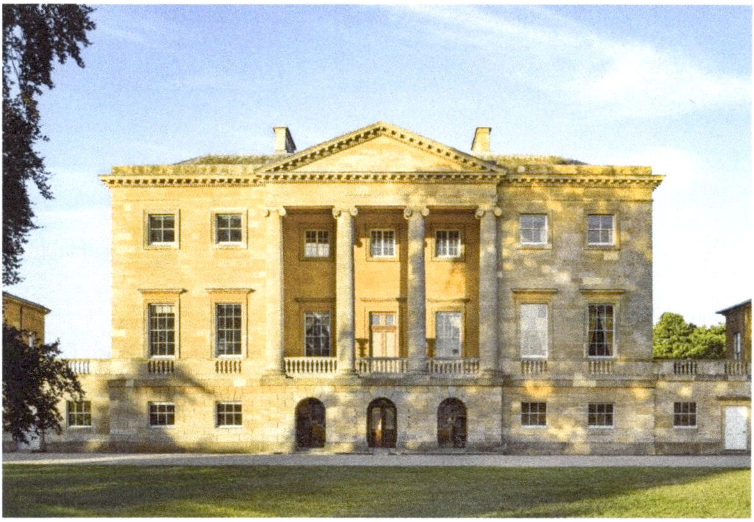

Figure 3.4 West Front of Basildon Park, Berkshire. © National Trust Images/Andrew Butler.

and estate at Basildon passed to Sykes's son and then soon after his grandson Sir Francis (3rd Baronet), who was just four years of age when he inherited. Mismanagement during his minority and the fulfillment of the expensive tastes of the 3rd Baronet and his wife meant that the family fell into serious financial difficulties. The estate was put up for sale in 1829 and after much negotiation was finally sold to James Morrison in 1838. Morrison made his wealth not through the EIC, but rather through a textile trading business based in London. His financial successes allowed him to also establish a career as a Member of Parliament and accumulate a large and prestigious art collection, which he housed at Basildon Park.[64]

On James Morrison's death in 1857 the house passed to his eldest son Charles and was inhabited by Charles's sister Ellen. On Charles's death in 1909 the house passed to his son Archie. In straitened circumstances the house was sold in 1929 and was purchased and restored by Lord and Lady Iliffe in the 1950s. Before the sale of the estate itself, Archie Morrison sold its furniture collection in 1920. Amongst other items, the furniture sale catalogue demonstrates that the Morrison family owned a pair of ivory chairs.[65] The chairs do not appear in the 1859 inventory of Basildon Park or the Morrison's London house in Harley Street.[66] Rather than acquiring them from Basildon's previous residents, the Sykes family, it seems likely that Charles or Archie purchased them on the English or European market. Their intention in purchasing them is unclear – did they buy them to reference the earlier connections of Basildon to the EIC through the Sykes family? Did they purchase them because they had become a *de rigueur* piece within British country houses? Did they purchase them because in the late-nineteenth century they once again became fashionable?

The Morrison family's intention in purchasing these intricately designed goods appears opaque in the historical record. In contrast the Kleinwort's intention is perhaps more readily discerned. As Jan Sibthorpe's research on Sezincote, Gloucestershire has shown, in the mid-twentieth century the Kleinwort family worked to restore Sezincote to its early-nineteenth-century splendour, reinvigorating Indian elements and features that had originally been designed by Samuel Pepys Cockerell (1753–1827) and installed for his elder brother Charles Cockerell (1755–1837).[67] Situated just a few miles from Warren Hastings's Daylesford, Sezincote came to be partially inherited by EIC official and private trader Charles in 1798. He then fully purchased it from his siblings in 1801. He worked with his brother Samuel to design and build one of the few Indian-inspired country houses of the period. Sezincote fell out of the possession of later Cockerell family members and was purchased by James Dugdale in 1884. It remained in the Dugdale family until the Kleinworts purchased it, in a somewhat dilapidated condition, in 1944. As part of this renovation, Lady Kleinwort purchased at auction in the 1940s, a set of six sandalwood chairs, veneered with ivory, highlighted with black lac and gilt, with cane seats.[68] As with the Morrison pieces, the veneering on the chairs suggests that they were made in Vizagapatam in the 1770s. Displayed in the house they act to visually reaffirm Sezincote's connections to India.[69]

The Sezincote chairs underline how ivory furniture continued to hold its EIC connections long after the Company's demise. In recent years when ivory furniture pieces have come onto the market, their provenance and thus their links to an EIC past through reference to a particular individual, have been underscored. As such then, these objects have acted as relatively stable markers of Britain's involvement in and relationship to the subcontinent.

Conclusion

Exploring the production, purchase, dispossession and recirculation of ivory furniture reveals the different kinds of value at play within imperial material cultures – emotional, monetary, political and historical – and the ways in which these values have changed over time. Purchasing these objects while in Company service and engaging with the often difficult process of bringing them home intact, early EIC families recognized their emotional value as pieces which could mark their imperial service and experiences on the subcontinent. Bequeathed to family members, as in the cases of Edward Harrison, these pieces continued to act as important affective objects as they came to be possessed and used by younger generations. Later in the eighteenth century, their purchase by EIC servants not only for familial use but also for possible resale on the open market, suggests that as European audiences became aware of these pieces (and more particularly their increasingly European forms and styles), they gained market value and could be easily resold. Recognizing, and simultaneously adding to, their status, these items were also considered worthy gifts within the court. Given to Queen Charlotte by Warren Hastings, ivory furniture pieces obtained political value in the later eighteenth century. Nevertheless, after what might be understood as their high point in the late-eighteenth century, in the nineteenth century these same pieces of ivory furniture were understood to retain their links to the previous century and in recirculation became principally valued for their historic connections. In the postcolonial era, they offered compelling instruments for the reconstruction of a particular imperial British past.

Uncovering the changing values embedded within ivory furniture pieces is important in demonstrating the ways in which objects from the subcontinent acted as sites upon which and through which contemporaries recognized links to the EIC and empire. Despite being increasingly made to European designs, these pieces often resisted naturalization and remained connected to the narratives of empire that families and other individuals constructed – a process encouraged by appraisers, auctioneers and country house owners. Becoming entangled in different forms of meaning making, these objects came to embody empire and even in the twentieth century could be called upon to represent imperial links.[70] Easy to recognize and difficult to imitate, their material form marked these wares out as distinct. Such recognition was reproduced in the historical record by appraisers constructing inventories, auctioneers writing catalogues, and historic house staff producing guidebooks. Reproduced and replicated over time, the distinction of ivory furniture marked these pieces, making them distinct from the more ubiquitous porcelain and textile goods. In consequence, this chapter demonstrates that what might be regarded as a domestic object – ivory furniture – exists as an important route through which to understand the ways in which EIC families, but also British culture more broadly, understood and recognized Britain's imperial projects.

4
'A jaghire without a crime'

The East India Company and the Indian Ocean material world at Osterley, 1700–1800

Yuthika Sharma and Pauline Davies

> On Friday we went to see – oh! the palaces of palaces! and yet a palace sans crown, sans coronet – but such expense! such taste! such profusion! and yet half an acre produces all the rents that furnish such magnificence. It is a jaghire got without a crime. In short, a shop is the estate, and Osterley Park is the spot. The old house I have often seen, which was built by Thomas Gresham; but it so improved and enriched, that all the Percies and Seymours must die of envy. …[1]

The words of Horace Walpole (1717–97), writer, connoisseur, antiquarian and intellectual underline the change of status of Osterley's owners resulting from their wide-ranging involvement in global maritime trade. Walpole's observations highlight the elevated status of the Child family, and their multi-generational link with East India Company (EIC) trade and shipping networks in the Indian Ocean. They were neither aristocrats nor members of the circle of newly enriched nabobs, whose acquisition of wealth contemporaries linked to corrupt practices in the colonies.[2] In contrast, the family's rise as technocrats and their association with the corporate arm of the British Empire were fostered through a long-standing career in precious stones, prior to their rise in EIC circuits of trade and governance.

The Osterley estate contained a simple farmhouse when it was first acquired in 1562 by Sir Thomas Gresham (1519–79), financial adviser to Queen Elizabeth I.[3] He built a fine manor house there, and it is known that the Queen paid 10 visits to Osterley Park. Nearly two centuries later, it was fitting that City money should fund Osterley Park's architectural and interior redesign as a classical home by Robert Adam (1728–92), one of the most important British architects working in the neoclassical style, bringing it into line with current fashion once again. Osterley Park is distinguished by its wealth of original eighteenth-century furnishings made in accordance with Adam's drawings and by the range of his evolving styles visible under one roof. It is this quintessentially English eighteenth-century style that dominates the National Trust's presentation and interpretation of the House today. The oriental objects in the House are shown as typical of the period; their use alongside the neoclassical style is a recognised norm of interior decoration at that time. But if we look beyond this to the acquisition of the wealth that enabled Adam's re-styling, a different story emerges.

In this chapter, we analyse the Childs' engagement with the EIC to consider how these growing connections with maritime trade bore a material imprint on Osterley's domestic interior. The impact of global trade on the visual culture of Osterley House illuminates the Child family's personal and professional aspirations. The decorative arts of Osterley were part of a fashion for the oriental in the eighteenth century, at a time when the category of the orient was being actively crafted in the European imagination. Rather than fixating on the 'unfamiliarity' of the orient that is often used as a modality of postcolonial writing on the East, this chapter will highlight the formative importance of maritime commerce on the perceived 'social value' of decorative arts at Osterley. It was the range of 'oriental' objects at Osterley that impressed Walpole. Among them was a book of illustrations of birds brought in from various parts of the world through EIC trade displayed alongside paintings by European masters, with the birds themselves visible in the imposing menagerie in the grounds. Walpole wrote:

> Mrs Child's dressing room is full of pictures, gold filigree, china and japan. So is all the house – there are Salvators, Gaspar Poussins, and to a beautiful staircase, a ceiling by Rubens.[4] Not to mention a kitchen garden that costs £1400 a year, a menagerie full of birds that comes from a thousand islands which Mr. Banks has not yet discovered ...[5]

We query the role of such objects sourced from the East as mediators of a social identity in that they displayed a personal connection with the Childs while also broadly referencing the complex interactions of European and Asian trade and artistic exchange. The first section of this chapter examines the career of three generations of the Child family focusing on their imbrication with the leadership and governance of the EIC. The second section provides greater context about the family's maritime operations through their commercial ventures in shipping. The final section on material goods brings together a selection of objects that embody the tangible links of the Child family with East India Company trade to highlight the role of these 'oriental' objects as markers of a desirable yet niche market for globally sourced luxury goods,[6] prior to their widespread appeal and dispersal as consumer goods in nineteenth-century Britain. Rather than focusing on the period of Adam's interventions in Osterley Park (and their European orientation), we focus on the arrival of furnishings and objects from the East prior to the 1760s. We suggest that it is through the acquisition of these objects – Chinese armorial porcelain, lacquerware and Indian textiles – that the Childs created a distinctive visual identity and enduring status for their family in London society. Moreover, as this study elaborates, the inflow of luxury objects may have been a result of personal choice as well as current fashion.

Family commerce

The family's fortune was founded by Sir Francis Child (1642–1713), initially through his skill and business acumen as a goldsmith, and later by the bank he founded and his and its relationship with the EIC (see Figure 4.1). By the early eighteenth century, the Child family had successfully navigated the connected worlds of finance, global trade and politics and had amassed both wealth and influence. Of the senior partners in the renowned Child & Co. bank, two served as Lord Mayor of London,[7] three were knighted and at least one member of the family sat as an MP for all but one of the years from 1722–82. The family-owned bank both financed and profited from the EIC. Shares in the Company remained an important source of their wealth throughout this period. We know that the third Francis Child (1735–63) had EIC annuities worth £32,000 when he employed Robert Adam in 1760.[8] By the time this generation began working with Robert Adam on the designs for Osterley Park, the family had been close to the centre of the often-overlooked global networks that supported the English financial revolution for nearly 100 years (see Table 4.1).

Their connection to, and influence within, the Company was significant. For over 30 years one of the immediate family was a Director,[9] while two were investors in ships that carried the goods for a wide and growing consumer market.[10] They thus sat, and had influence, at the centre of the political, financial and commercial world at a time when the Company was in its formative phase of growth. The family profited from these connections, both financially and as elite consumers who could access the finest luxuries, and importantly, specially commissioned goods. By the time they began working with Robert Adam on the designs for Osterley Park, the global networks that supported the English financial revolution could not but affect the choices they made.

Although his life falls outside the main date range for this study, Francis Child the Elder (1642–1713) provides the most compelling case for including Osterley Park within this project. His success was fuelled by the mutually supportive global and national networks that

Table 4.1: The Child family as Directors of the EIC

1630–1700	1701–1720	1721–1732
Sir Francis Child the elder was a substantial stockholder in the Old East India Company with the Company account in Child & Co. bank. He was appointed to the committee set up to finalize negotiations for a merger with the new Company The United Company of Merchants of England trading to the East Indies 'provided that it can be done on safe, just and reasonable grounds'.[11] And a parliamentary list of early 1700 classed him in the 'interest' of the Old East India Company.[12] He served on the EIC Court of Directors between 1698 and 1701.	Sir Robert Child served on the court of Directors between 1710–12 and sat on a number of committees. Sir Francis the elder was also a Director 1711–12. Sir Robert was elected Deputy Chairman between 1714–15 after a struggle with supporters of the Bank of England candidate. Sir Robert was elected Chairman 1715–16[13] and his influence with the Treasury is apparent in the Court Minutes.[14] Sir Robert was re-elected as Director in 1720.	Sir Francis Child the younger served as Director in the years 1721–22, 1724, 1726, 1728 and 1732.[15] He was variously a member of the Warehouses, Accounts and Private Trade Committees.

underpinned the growth of the City of London. He acquired Osterley Park in 1712, shortly before his death. The son of a cloth merchant, Francis Child moved to London in 1656 as an apprentice, and eventually became a Freeman of the Company of Goldsmiths in 1665.[16] Around this time, it is known that he went to work for Blanchard and Wheeler, one of the pioneering banker/goldsmiths who had premises in the Strand. Blanchard's widow had married William Wheeler and when in 1671 he married her daughter, he inherited their combined fortunes rapidly raising Francis Child's status in London society. Blanchard and Wheeler, and its successor business, Child & Co. survived the many pitfalls that befell other banker/goldsmiths at this time, and when he died in 1713 Sir Francis Child was a very wealthy man, with assets of £250,000 – assessed by Philip Beresford to be equivalent to £3.8 billion today.[17]

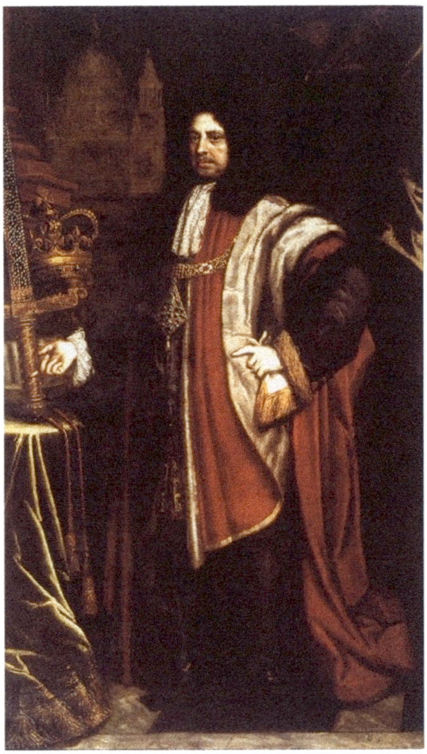

Figure 4.1 Francis Child the Elder (1642–1713). Attributed to Sir Godfrey Kneller (1646–1723). Reproduced by kind permission of Christ's Hospital.

Child & Co. was a favourite bank for the landed groups and clients included not only the landed gentry such as the Earl of Dorset, a friend and patron, but such notables as Nell Gwyn and Isaac Newton.[18] The firm heavily invested in East India securities, underlining the close connections of the family with the politics and finance of the EIC.[19] In 1698 Francis Child was Lord Mayor of London and was elected to the EIC Court of Directors later in the same year.[20] In 1709 the old and the new EIC merger became a reality and the United Company was to be run by a Court of 24 annually elected Directors, each of whom was a major stockholder in the Company.[21]

Francis Child's jewellery business was also one of the largest in London.[22] In 1690 his stock of loose diamonds was valued at over £5,000, equivalent to at least £750,000 today.[23] The previous year he had been made an Alderman, was knighted by William III and became 'jeweller in ordinary' to the King.[24] Child was one of the largest importers of precious stones in London at a time when stockholders in the EIC could buy privately traded diamonds at half the rate of duty paid by other merchants. It may have been this business that first ignited his interest in the Company, as a source of precious stones.

Success in the diamond business depended on cross cultural cooperation and the building of personal and commercial connections and trust.[25] As a successful importer and warden of the Goldsmiths' Company, Sir Francis would have been familiar with these networks. Diamonds bought from EIC men, such as Captain Chamblett, captain of the ship *Samson* in 1670, would be polished and remounted for sale. His partner, John East (1613–88) had bought rough diamonds from an EIC Director John Joliffe (1613–80) and a number of Portuguese *Marrones* (new Christians) who had settled across Europe such as Isaac Alvares and Antonio Rodrigues Marques. Sir Francis continued to invest, often using Abraham Pluymer, a Dutch diamond cutter to do the buying, but later also using a Daniel Chardin in Madras.[26] Sir Dudley North (1641–91) is recorded as buying 2,000 pieces of eight from Sir Francis Child at 5s 4 ½d for export to Aleppo.[27] This international experience, allied to his standing in the City and his political clout, meant he was well placed to accompany the Earl of Pembroke, part of the English delegation negotiating the Treaty of Ryswick that ended the Nine Years War with France and Spain in 1697.

'A short account by way of Journal of 10th I observed most remarkable in my travels thro' some part of the Low Country, Flanders, & some part of Germany whilst on the Rhine' – a journal kept by Francis Child during a momentous visit to the Netherlands in 1697, survives in the collection of the London Metropolitan Archives in two copies in bound notebooks.[28] This journal conveys how significantly Child's travel to the Netherlands shaped his aesthetic sensibilities, at a time when he was about to begin his substantial engagement with the EIC. Francis Child's impressions provide a vivid account of the décor and furnishings of grand mansions in the region and of the display of 'exotic' objects from the Americas and Asia. In Delft, Child made a special mention of the quality of porcelain manufactured in the town. His many visits to country mansions and palaces highlight his specialist interest in Asian objects and furnishings – painted screens, porcelain, and lacquerware to name only a few exotic commodities associated with the EIC. Child was keenly aware of decorative art from Asia, its status as a rarefied privilege, and the all-important channels of maritime trade that brought decorative objects from Asia into Europe. For example, in the King's house in the Bosc, he noted 'a curious closet made of the best sort of Indian Screens, the floor inlaid'.[29] Likewise, in Honselersdijk, south of The Hague, 'are closetts of choice pieces, especially one very large of Japan [lacquer], the ceiling of lookin glasse with flowers painted on it'.[30] The town of Middleburgh, 'a rich, populous and beautifull town, has many merchants which trade to all parts of the world, has a share in the East India Company and have during this war sent out many capers whereof some have carried 30 guns'.[31] He went on to detail the topographical qualities of Rotterdam that affected sea trade between England and the Netherlands.

Child's visit resulted in the purchase of over 60 paintings by great masters, at a cost of £4,850, a sum equivalent to millions today. He listed these paintings in the journal under the heading 'A catalogue of my pictures in my house in Lincoln Inn's Fields taken March 9, 1706 and of my drawings in frames with glass'. His son Robert purchased 42 Lincoln's Inn Fields (now the Royal College of Surgeons) in 1702, where Francis the Elder lived from 1704. Thus, this entry was made into the journal a few years later.[32] It is possible that the list was entered into the journal around the time of the Child family's relocation to Osterley Park after 1713.

Francis's son Robert (1674–1721) was the first of the family to live at Osterley. Knighted by King George I in April 1714, he continued and enhanced the family's global and political connections. Like his father he was the senior partner in the family bank and a diligent Director of the EIC, identified by Abel Boyer as one of the 'High Church' candidates standing at the elections for the East India Company.[33] During his time as Director the Spitalfields riots led to a ban on imported cotton textiles, the Treaty of Utrecht was signed and the Company had to help the government pick up the financial pieces following the demise of the South Sea Company. But in Daniel Defoe's anonymously authored pamphlet, *The Secret History of the White Staff* (1714) Sir R Ch. is referenced as one of the 'jobbers and monied men' who had grown rich at the nation's expense.[34]

Not just a businessman, Sir Robert displayed a personal interest in connoisseurship and critical appreciation of art which can be ascertained at the very early stages of the acquisition of Osterley House. In the appendices of the list of paintings that documented the move from Lincoln's Inn Fields to Osterley, is Robert's portrait by the Swedish painter Michael Dahl (1656–1743), who had served as the figurative head of an exclusive debating society called the Society of the Virtuosi of St Luke (active c.1689–1743), also known as St Luke's Club or Vandyke's Club.[35] The Society's records show that in the first decade of its activities in the eighteenth century, Robert Child was one of an exclusive group of 20 members along with Christopher Wren the younger (1632–1723), the surgeon and anatomist William Cowper (1666–1709), and the painter Hugh Howard (1675–1737). This mixing of artists, art lovers and collectors formed an influential group of intellectuals who drove the discussions on taste and aesthetic judgment. These ideas and trends were likely consequential to the early stages of the design and furnishings for Osterley House.

Sir Robert died in 1721, and was succeeded by his brother Francis (1684–1740). Knighted on 28 September 1732, Francis Child II consolidated the family's status in the City, following his father as Alderman (from 1721–40), Sheriff of London (1722–3), and Lord Mayor (1731–2). He held senior positions in the influential Goldsmith's company. An MP from 1722, he represented the City of London for the first five years and served as an EIC Director over a 10-year period, attending EIC Court meetings regularly and the Company auctions every week. 1722 saw the establishment of the Company's Council of China, in recognition of the growth of trade with that empire. Under his Chairmanship the banking side of the business continued to thrive. Important advances were made to City dealers secured upon parcels of stock and heavy investments in East India securities.[36] A partner in the Bank, John Morse, left £10,000 each to Francis and Samuel Child in his will of 1736.[37] Child rented out most of the large property portfolio he had inherited, moved to live at Osterley and seems to have been responsible for major alterations there, probably including laying out the formal gardens. His estate passed to his youngest brother Samuel (1693–1752) in 1740.[38]

Sir Francis's youngest surviving son, Samuel was the only Child of his generation to marry. Although he did not follow the family tradition into the EIC Court he maintained an interest in the Company's affairs by joining a group of investors which owned and chartered the *Northampton* to the EIC. This ship was unfortunately lost in a violent storm in 1744 on its way back from China and India. He played a significant part in the making of Osterley Park as it remains today. He brought his family to live at Osterley, left them the wealth to continue to furnish the house with the finest things and introduced his sons into the society where they found their wives. Samuel Child took on responsibility as head of the family banking firm in 1740, having been a partner for a number of years. He held substantial EIC stock, and in his will left his wife £45,000 in Company stock and £3,000 of the same to his son Francis (1735–63).[39]

His two sons, Francis III (1735–63) and Robert (1739–82), inherited the Child family fortune. Both were educated at Oxford, and were partners in Child & Co., and were responsible for transforming Osterley into the house it is today. On 31 December 1760 Francis III held nearly £33,000 worth of East India stock.[40] He left his fiancée £50,000 when he died in 1763, days before his impending marriage. The bulk of his estate went to his brother Robert, though he does not seem to have passed on his interest in the ship *Osterley*, which was also chartered to the EIC.

Robert married Sarah Jodrell (1741–93) of Ankerwyke in Buckinghamshire in 1763. She brought more EIC associations to Osterley. Robert and Sarah are credited with working with Robert Adam to change Osterley House into the neoclassical house it is still today. Robert Child died 28 July 1782, aged 43. The Jodrell family had longstanding links to the Company. Both her grandparents had an EIC heritage: Richard Craddock had been an EIC factor in India and Persia in the seventeenth century and Daniel Sheldon was a factor in India. In 1659, Sheldon wrote to another factor for the company at Bandel, urgently requesting a sample of tea to send home to his uncle Dr Gilbert Sheldon, Archbishop of Canterbury: 'for God's sake, good or badd, buy the chaw if it is to be sold. Pray favour me likewise with advise what 'tis good for, and how it is to be used'.[41] It seems, however, that Child's interest in the EIC, which had always been commercial, passed to those partners who had an active role in running the bank. Thomas Devon, a partner in 1752, was a significant supporter and backer of Laurence Sulivan (1713–86) in the highly charged fight between him and Robert Clive (1725–74), the first Governor of India, over control of the Company.[42]

Winds of trade

In the second half of the eighteenth century, there were three Company ships called *Osterley*, each of which bore a connection with the Child family (see Table 4.2). The ships in which the Child family invested are representative of the larger networks of Company trade in Asia at this time. They carried the goods that met the demand of the burgeoning consumer market at home. All of the Child family who served as Directors also served on the Committees that commissioned them. They were well placed to understand and benefit from this trade, not least from the private trade, a form of regulated corruption whereby East India Company's Committees placed bulk orders with the ships' captains and supercargoes.

Sanctioned through indulgences in Company policy, ship's captains could earn up to 10 times their actual salary by taking on such commissions. The most popular privately traded commodities from India and China were porcelain, lacquerware, silk and cotton textiles, and ivory. The lacquer furniture and armorial porcelain on display at Osterley would almost certainly have resulted from special commissions.

Table 4.2: *Osterley* Ships

Osterley I[43]	Osterley II	Osterley III
Investor/owner: Francis Child III Launched 1758 Principal Managing Owner: Charles Raymond Voyages: 1) 1757/8 China 2) 1760/1 Benkulen, Madras and Bengal 3) 1765/6 Bombay and China 4) 1768/9 Madras and China	Principal Managing Owner: William Dent, Brother of Robert Dent, a partner at Childs Bank. Launched 1771 Voyages: 1) 1771/2 Benkulen and China 2) 1774/5 St Helena and Benkulen 3) 1777/8 Madras and Bengal	Launched 1780 Principal Managing Owners: William Dent, Robert Dent and (later) John Atkins Voyages: 1) 1780/81 Bombay and China 2) 1784/5 Madras and China 3) 1786/7 Madras and China 4) 1789/90 Bombay and China 5) 1792/3 China 6) 1794/5 China 7) 1797/8 Madras and Bengal

Examining in detail a sample journey of the *Osterley I* when Francis Child III was an investor illustrates the commodities traded on it, and the challenges encountered. Osterley I's final voyage from Madras to China provides a good example of the Company's dealings in Asia. Harbour logs from Captain Francis Fortescue's journal for the voyage indicate that like most East Indiamen, it sailed along with other companion ships (the *Pigott*, *Thames*, *Ankerwick*, *Lincoln*, *Triton*, *Nottingham*, *Havannah*, *Hector*, and *Ashburnham*) as well as country vessels (ships that sailed Asian but not European waters). *Osterley I* sailed for Madras on 31 January 1769. In June, while on its journey from the Goan port of Cabo de Rama (Cape Rama) in northwest India to Cape Comorin in the southernmost tip of India, the ship picked up an important consignment of elephant bone (ivory). On 12 July 1769 while docked close to Madras, the ship received redwood and cotton on behalf of the Company. These goods were usually brought to the main ship on smaller country ships, which did the rounds from ports and factories. The ship then sailed towards Bengal and stowed additional loads of 500 bales of cotton and 30 tons of redwood. It was only in October that the ship reached Whampoa, after passing through the Malacca Straits. Once near Canton, much of the cotton and redwood and the ship's cargo of lead were unloaded and the ship 'received on board 90 chests of china of the Hon'ble comps [Honorable Company's], and 62 Private trade'.[44] This suggests that Fortescue was acting on behalf of several private clients, one of whom may have been Robert Child II, under whom many restorations and refurbishments occurred at Osterley Park. *Osterley*'s journey back in January 1770 was its last, as in its next incarnation the ship changed owners.

The EIC ships *Osterley II* & *Osterley III* retained a connection with the Child family through indirect means. Robert Dent, a partner in Child & Co. from 1763, was a member of the charter party on a number of his brother William Dent's ships including *Osterley II* and *Osterley III*. Both ships made regular voyages to India and China. But these ships, like others, also played an important part supporting the expansionist ambitions of the Company through serving in battles. Towards the end of its third voyage, *Osterley II* was captured by the French following an attack by two frigates *Purvoyeuse* and *Elizabeth* in February 1779.[45] A similar fate befell *Osterley III*, which had one of the longest runs out of the three ships. After many successful voyages to India and China, *Osterley III* was embroiled in the rising Anglo-French rivalry at the end of the eighteenth century, while towards the end of its seventh run, *Osterley III* was captured by the French ship *La Forte* (on 13 February 1799) but later rescued.[46]

The 'oriental' interiors at Osterley

The presentation of the surviving interiors of Osterley House privileges its neoclassical ethos, honed under Robert Adam.[47] Within this explicit neoclassical programme are embedded 'oriental' objects that were sourced through EIC maritime trade in material and luxury goods. The display of objects that travelled on the Company's ships alongside the fashionable neoclassical interiors created by Robert Adam raises an important conceptual question about their place in the narrative of neoclassical design (see Figure 4.2). Would this juxtaposition have created a perception of incongruity of style and décor in the eighteenth century? Given the burgeoning globalization of the period, especially in the way precious goods were valued for their place associations as well as their artistic merit, it is worth re-thinking how these seemingly out of place objects became an important

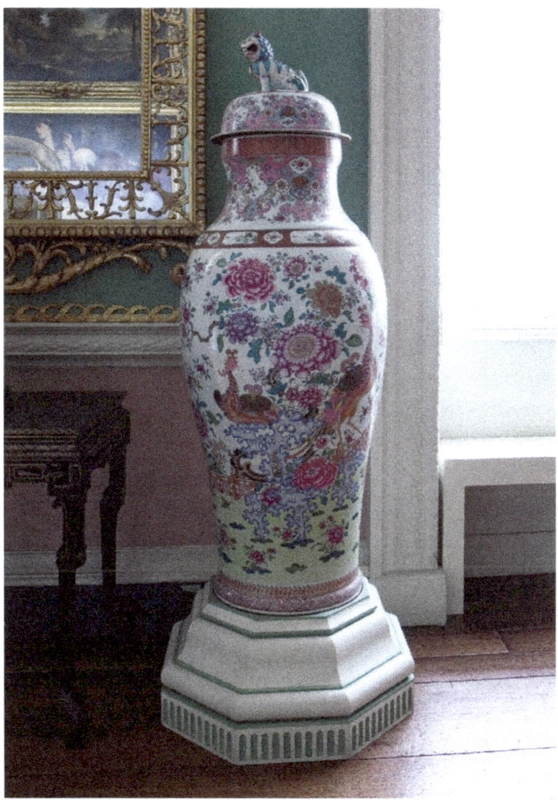

Figure 4.2 Ceramic Parade Jar, c.1700–1770, Osterley House. Image courtesy of Stuart Howat.

part of the emotional economy of global maritime trade. In this section, we examine examples of 'oriental' goods that were made, circulated and acquired for the personal pleasure of the Child family.

A decorative art in Japan, Korea and China, lacquerware held a particular exotic appeal for its European collectors as a luxury craft especially popular for its polished finish and vibrant lustre. The process of lacquering in itself was labour-intensive – successive coats of lacquer could at times be built up into a pile of over 100 layers.[48] A large private trade of lacquered goods flourished in the eighteenth century, and lacquered furniture became an especially popular import into English country houses as the Chinese imperial court relaxed its trade barrier in 1672. The armorial lacquer furniture at Osterley House includes a brilliantly finished wooden lacquer chest, wooden hall chairs, and a stunning eight-part folding screen made of leather, brass, and wood. The lacquer collections at Osterley highlight the popularity of a particularly delicate technique of gold engraving on lacquer, a Chinese variant of the Japanese style that combined gold and silver inlay with surface painting on lacquer.

Company records show that in 1730, the period in which Francis Child II was deeply involved in the EIC, an order for two large lacquered screens was completed.[49] There is every possibility that Francis the younger had knowledge of this commission, which would have made for a memorable addition to the courtroom. It is possible that the screens' arrival spurred the private commission of a large eight-panelled lacquer screen completed with the Child family coat-of-arms. The screen features a landscape scene with a palace complex fronting an enclosed landscaped garden with its rivulets, bridges, and fenced gardens. The scene is populated with figures shown engaging in their daily activities. The bottom section is complemented with a floral design enclosed within a rectangular cartouche; the decoration is picked up in gold, silver, and red and both the design and technique pay homage to the Japanese aesthetics. Other notable lacquer objects include a rectangular dome top beech-wood coffer, sourced in India and traded in Canton, with brass fixtures finished in black lacquer bearing the Child family crest on its front panel that was brought into Osterley in the second quarter of the eighteenth century. The utilitarian design of the coffer and the minimalist geometric diamond decorative border in gold suggest its use as a travelling sea chest. Such coffers would have been ideal containers to store personal items or to pack specialist buys of armorial porcelain and tea acquired on behalf of the Child family in Canton (see Figure 4.3).

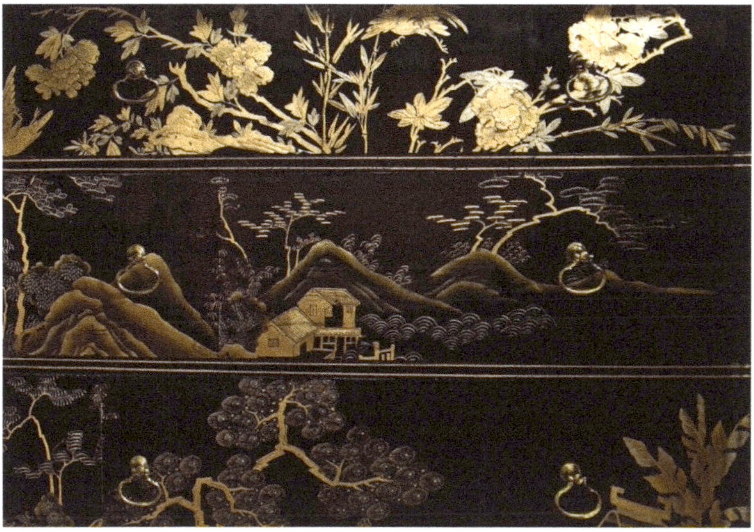

Figure 4.3 Chinese lacquer chest, Osterley House. Image courtesy of Stuart Howat.

The lacquerware furnishings sourced from China are in contrast to the planned placement of the lacquer secretaire (c.1773) and commode in the now-famous Etruscan Dressing Room (1775), the ante-chamber in the State Apartment at Osterley Park (see Figure 4.4). Adam's designs for this room were inspired by his four-year study tour of Europe in 1754–8. The discoveries at Pompeii and Herculaneum inspired the decoration of the Etruscan Room at Osterley Park, demonstrating how past values could influence the present. The most complete remaining example of Adam's Etruscan interiors, the designs on all four walls are believed to be painted by Pietro Maria Borgnis (1739–1810) and were repeated on both doors, the ceiling and a set of eight chairs. The visually contiguous design of the Etruscan Room, the hallmark of the integrated style championed by Adam and emulated in interior design for decades afterwards, was considered experimental for its time. The intellectual impact of Adam's mentor Piranesi on his work is well documented, and the Etruscan Room's sensibility owes much to the engraved wall scheme published in Piranesi's book of chimney-piece and furniture designs, *Diverse maniere d'adornare I cammini* ... (1769), which was much used by Adam and his contemporaries.[50]

The lacquerware placed within the room would have provided a distinct counterpoint to the 'relentless patterning' effect of the neoclassical interior of the room,[51] where the 'chair rails are both the same dimensions and painted as the same manner as the room's dado' in essence 'doubling the painted surface [that] blurs and confuses the chair's relation to the wall'.[52] Thomas Chippendale's (1718–79) *The Gentleman and Cabinet Maker's Director* ... (1756) made clear that English designers were happy to mix Chinese-influenced styles with Gothic, Palladian and French. This is evident in the Osterley secretaire attributed to Chippendale that incorporates panels of Chinese lacquer as well as English 'japanning,' the common term for the Western imitation of the lacquer technique. However,

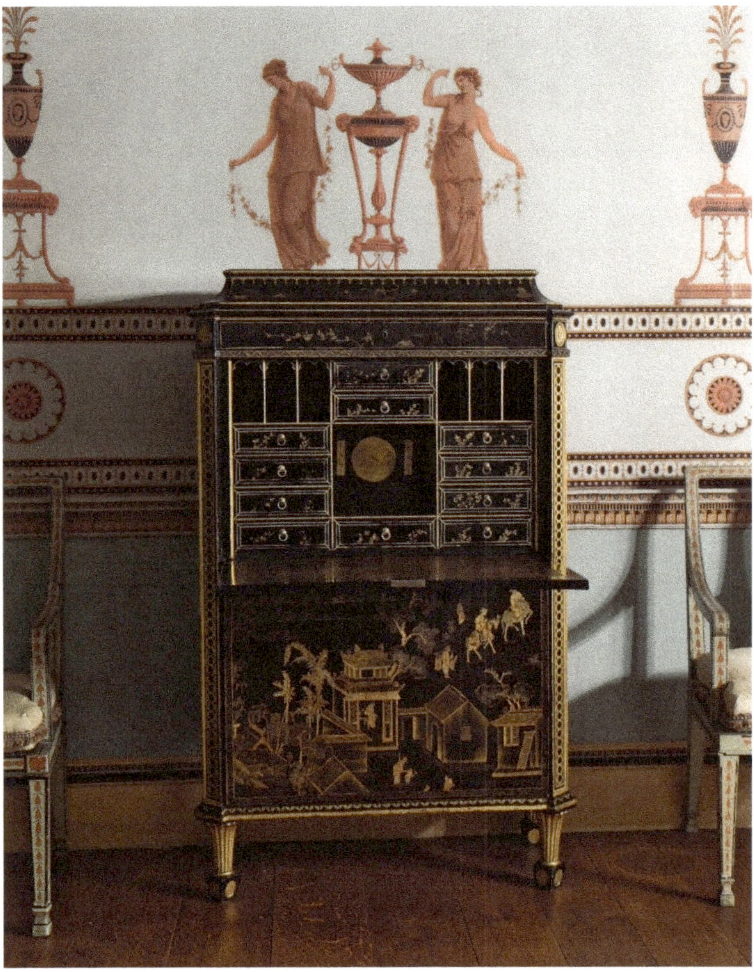

Figure 4.4 Chinese lacquer secretaire, Osterley House. Image courtesy of Stuart Howat.

it has been pointed out that the core style of the commode and the secretaire remained distinctly French in character while echoing the overall design of the Etruscan Room through the use of *paterae* and *guilloche* motifs on the furniture.[53]

An investigation into the commission of the lacquerware featuring Chinese craftsmanship and Robert Adam's oeuvre lies outside the scope of this chapter. However, the co-existence of 'oriental', Chinese lacquer screens in a French design, alongside 'neoclassical' furnishings raises the possibility that Adam's original design plan for the Etruscan Room included the addition of lacquered furniture. It is equally likely that Chippendale's designs at Osterley were bespoke commissions inspired by the armorial lacquerware sourced by older generations of the Child family. The lacquerware would have served as an appropriate reference to the legacy of the family's connections with the EIC and global trade networks. For an eighteenth-century audience, embedding objects seen to belong to the exotic East – the source of precious spices, diamonds, fine porcelain – within the calm grandeur of this room, would have decidedly challenged notions of the familiar.

The rapid expansion of the English market for porcelain from about 1720 to 1770 saw nearly 25–35 million pieces of porcelain entering the country making it one of the largest importers in Europe. East India Company officials, ship captains and supercargoes discovered that there was a market in England for unusual, large or colourful porcelain such as the ceramic parade jars commissioned to sit alongside the fashionable neoclassical interior being created at Osterley Park by Robert Adam. Fired to perfection in the kilns of Jingdezhen, in south China, porcelain objects travelled nearly 500 miles south to the port town of Guangzhou (Canton) where they were sold in shops and warehouses managed by Chinese merchants who, as members of a guild, or co-hong, regulated the terms of their trade.[54]

The decorative appeal of personalized bespoke tea sets, dinner services and other tableware led to armorial porcelain becoming a central marker of taste and dynastic prestige.[55] Among the earliest armorial services for the English market is the stellar service at Osterley, made for a member of the Child family. The Child crest repeated on the rim depicts an eagle holding an adder in its beak. Their coat-of-arms in the centre was granted in 1700 to Sir Francis Child, the Elder. On the basis of style, it has been suggested that the service was ordered by Francis the elder's son and EIC Chairman Sir Robert Child, since his brother Francis Child the younger only succeeded him in 1721.[56]

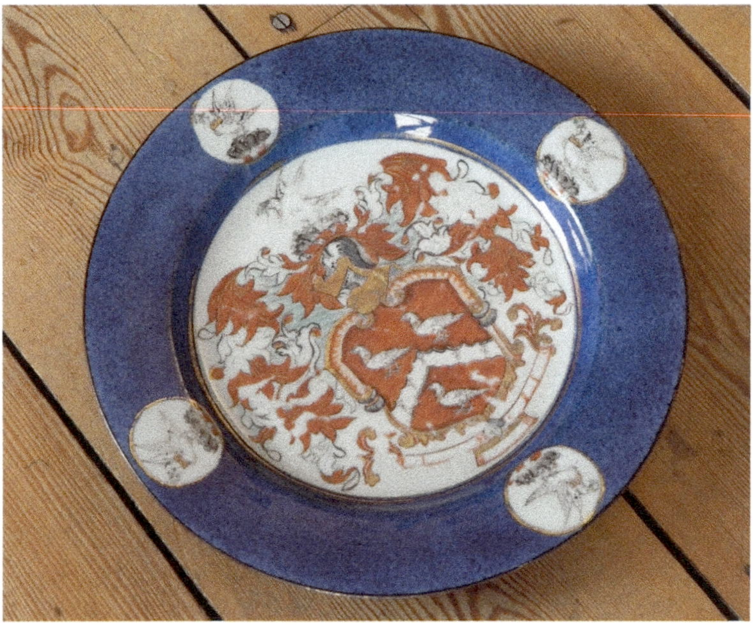

Figure 4.5 Child family armorial porcelain plate, c.1700–1725, Osterley House. Image courtesty of Stuart Howat.

Figure 4.5 depicts the armorial service ordered between 1700 and 1725. It is the only known example decorated with a 'powder blue' ground associated with luxury ornamental wares. The powdered cobalt, suspended in water, was blown through a bamboo tube with a gauze cloth at the end onto unglazed porcelain. This evenly distributed the ground colour. White panels designed to be painted with coloured enamels after a glaze firing, were protected from the sprayed cobalt with paper panels. The porcelain was then glazed and fired. It was then painted with translucent enamels over the glaze, in primarily red and green, known as the 'famille-verte' or green family palette.[57]

The textiles at Osterley encompass complex creative processes that were shaped through networks of Company trade in Asia. They highlight the central role of EIC sea trade in creating a global economy of artistic exchange that shaped the domestic interior in England. During Francis Child the Elder's tenure as EIC committee member and later as a Director, the Company was responsible for augmenting the trade in cotton textiles from India, with calicos accounting for nearly three-quarters of Company trade. The enhanced supply of cotton fabrics and prints into Britain not only upset social hierarchies of elite and everyday use of printed fabrics, but also posed a threat to the livelihoods of wool and silk weavers.[58] In 1721, imported cotton textiles of every description from India, whether pure cotton or mixed composition, were banned and restrictions were placed on the sale of most cotton textiles through what were known as the Calico Acts (1690–1721), and this prohibition was not lifted until the 1770s.[59] However, the prohibition was not so successful in curbing the demand for cotton prints and fabrics, the supply of which was picked up by the English EIC.[60] Some of the best Indian embroideries to enter Osterley date from the period of turmoil and prohibition.

At Osterley, the opulent silk embroidered bed pelmet cover and canopy in Mrs Child's bedchamber was likely bought at Surat around 1700–30, during the height of the popularity of Cambay embroideries in Europe (see Figure 4.6). The textile features a plain cream background, which is contrasted with brightly embroidered patterns of thin branches and leaves in a dark green colour and red and yellow flowers. It is now understood that these embroideries were created by the artisans of the Mochi (cobbler) caste of Gujarat who originally worked the delicate chain-stitch hook and needlework on leather and later adapted this technique on to cloth.[61] The weaving process itself was quite seasonal with the best weaving done during the rains since the moist air was less brittle for the threads. Thus most agreements and orders were usually placed before the monsoons set in and the raw cloth dyed and cured in the autumn sun.[62] The Mughal court also actively patronized embroidered textiles, but after the rise of European trade in the subcontinent their designs were adapted to suit the demands of Company trade. By the first quarter of the eighteenth century, the monopoly of the English EIC in Gujarat had significantly declined, though it retained the factory in the port town of Surat on the western coast of Gujarat.

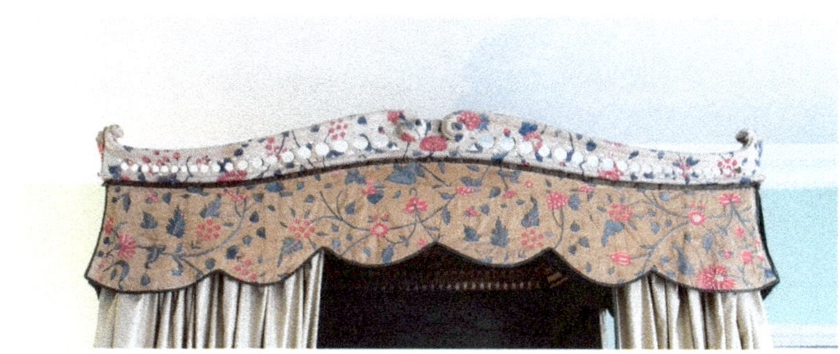

Figure 4.6 Detail of Mrs Child's silk bed canopy, Osterley House. Image courtesy of Stuart Howat.

China too was the primary exporter of silk to the EIC in the eighteenth century, supplying both raw silk for English weavers as well as bulk silk textiles for retailers with the finer pieces reserved for private trade. Popular designs on silks included a combination of painted patterns and embroidered motifs of flowers, leaves, birds and animals which were part of the craze for a decorative style broadly known as 'chinaworke' or chinoiserie in Europe. This 'oriental' style could be copied in India or China from European pattern books brought through sea trade.[63]

The Canton Factory records for the year 1732 give a particularly vivid account of the commission of painted silks by EIC supercargoes: 'We gave each merchant [at Canton] a particular charge that their skills be made of the best Nankeen silk, that the flowered silks be all new patterns & collours as near as possible to the patterns we delivered them, that the taffaties & gorgorons have a good gloss on them'.[64] In the backdrop of political warring and unrest between the Company and the Mughal ruler Shah Alam II (r. 1759–1806) the EIC experienced a decline in silver that consequently weakened their power to purchase raw silk. In December 1760, it was ordered that the Committee of Treasury be desired to ship five chests of foreign silver for China to the ship *Osterley* (and other similar ships) for Bencoolan.[65] The impact of the trade impasse is addressed in a letter to Thomas Hodges Esq., Governor of the Council of Bombay. Captain Payne reported that they:

> are sorry to find that you Gentlemen are much in the same situation as those at Madras and Bengal but as Peace is restored we hope that Trade will flourish. Our being disappointed of silver from Bengal and Madras has obliged us to fill our sixteen ships with China ware and tea and not an ounce of Raw silk, which we find bears a good price in Europe.[66]

Thus, Company trade in India and China was closely connected and political fluctuations at either end impacted the nature of commodities that could be shipped back to Europe.

Conclusion

> They brew very good beer, but are perticularly famous for their Porcellane or earthern ware, which they paint better than the Chinese, make more large, and as beautifull everyway, could they

> but make their small ware transparent in which the Chinese have the advantage of them.[67]

This record of Delft earthenware recorded in Francis Child the Elder's diary evokes the growing fervour for objects from the East in Europe in the backdrop of the ever-widening channels of global maritime trade. Francis Child's observation about the unique transparency of Chinese porcelain compared to Delft earthenware was astute. Tin-glazed pottery had been produced in Holland since the first quarter of the sixteenth century, and Delft had emerged as one of the main centres for its production in the seventeenth century. With the rise in imports of Chinese porcelain by the Dutch East India Company (VOC) after 1602, the fashion for blue and white porcelain put traditional Delft ceramic wares into competition with their exotic counterparts. As a result, from the first quarter of the seventeenth century, Delft potters had begun to imitate the transparent finish of Chinese blue and white porcelain ware by using Chinese style decorations in cobalt blue over a white-tin glazed background.[68]

The fashion for objects in the manner of Chinese blue and white porcelain rose to epic proportions in the decades to follow, a prime example of the re-casting of oriental designs and objects as exotic goods in the European marketplace. Yet, for the Child family who were at the very forefront of East India Company operations, the 'orient' was familiar ground, and its objects well within reach. Their ability to imprint their own identity on these luxury goods through bespoke commissions of armorials meant that they could have access not only to objects but also to the narratives that shaped them. The continued pre-eminence of these 'oriental' luxuries alongside and often embedded within the neoclassical interior of Osterley speaks to the Child family's desire to foster a global identity.

Section 2
Objects, houses, homes and the construction of identities

Rather than understanding objects as inert and inanimate entities, historians are increasingly attentive to the ways in which 'things' animate practices, behaviours and identity formation.[1] In keeping with this thinking, these chapters underline the dynamic character of engagements between East India Company (EIC) families and the material world, through the manufacturing, consuming, trading, using, displaying and destruction of objects. The processes and practices at stake in their interactions with material culture created active spaces in which identities were forged, maintained and re-constructed. Company men and women were materially literate and unsurprisingly used material practices to express their sense of self.[2] Their projections of identity through things were prolific, but also often problematic: the material world enabled but also resisted and subverted self-fashioning, often creating anomalies and unexpected effects. The armorial porcelain featured in Kate Smith's chapter provides a window onto gendered identity formation in the Company era. Armorial porcelain services were popular amongst Company families and particularly Company men, who commissioned wares bearing their family arms to be manufactured and decorated in China. Families required wealth, connections and patience to embark on the commissioning process, and to witness its successful completion. Once the lengthy processes of commission, manufacture, acquisition and transportation were complete, the expression of family identities required the use and display of armorial porcelain services in particular ways. Smith's chapter argues that the acquisition of armorial porcelain offered material manifestations of patience, sociability and connections, characteristics important to understandings of elite masculinity in eighteenth- and nineteenth-century Britain. Armorial services were often acquired by men to demonstrate their elite masculinity through use and display in the dining rooms of country houses. When in use, porcelain services allowed large groups to socialise: the sound, sight and feel of these Chinese porcelain wares animated social interactions, creating the means by which masculine family identities could be asserted.

Joanna Goldsworthy's chapter also focuses on processes of acquisition, use and display. She explores the purchase by Fanny Parkes (1794–1875) of a series of objects while on the subcontinent with her husband, EIC official Charles Crawford Parkes (1798–1854). Acquired between 1822 and 1845, these objects became the basis of a collection which was exhibited in print through illustrations in Parkes' *Wanderings of a Pilgrim in Search of the Picturesque* (1850) and in three-dimensional form as part of her 'Grand Moving Diorama of Hindostan', shown in London (1851) and Hull (1853). Through her writing and the display of her collection, Parkes made claims about her knowledge of the subcontinent, thereby gaining a degree of power and prestige notwithstanding her exclusion from formal Company employment. Through objects, she refashioned herself as a woman of some distinction, whose adventurous spirit had allowed her to visit and extract knowledge from 'unknown' sites and spaces on the subcontinent, including the zenana (the site within the house within which women were secluded). At the same time, these projects enabled Parkes to make money, an important consideration (particularly during Charles's ill health and after his death in 1854). Using the objects she had collected for illustrative purposes in her publication failed to satisfy her ambitions: public demand or curiosity allowed Parkes to find subscribers to support the physical display of her collection and the creation of a form of 'context' in the shape of the Diorama. As with Smith's chapter, Goldsworthy's research demonstrates how engaging with objects allowed Company men and women to construct and consolidate identities that lent them power. As her chapter reminds us, however, not all objects completed the journey home. The material world could thwart as much as aid projects of Company self-fashioning.

Kate Smith and Margot Finn's chapter on Montreal Park, Kent and Touch House, Stirlingshire explores material objects within the wider context of the house building projects underpinned by wealth accrued on the subcontinent. Rather than focusing upon heroic individuals associated with specific collections of objects, their chapter underlines the extent to which collection, display and house design were collaborative projects in which women often played important roles. Houses were important sites through which collective identities could be formulated and exhibited. The re-creation of Montreal Park and Touch House shows both the importance of empire in shaping country houses and the key labour elite women contributed to this domestic work. For families, refashioning of country houses did not simply allow for the production of new identities reflecting higher wealth or status. Producing the house itself prompted families to collaborate on a shared task and thus renew a collective identity, often after intervals of separation dictated by Company service.

5
Manly objects? Gendering armorial porcelain wares

Kate Smith

Research by historians and literary scholars has shown that Chinese porcelain was understood as distinctly gendered in seventeenth- and eighteenth-century Britain.[1] It quickly acquired a reputation as a 'female' good and contributed to the creation of an understanding of the 'Orient' as feminine and effeminizing. This chapter focuses upon a distinct subset within the wide range of Chinese porcelain available in eighteenth-century Britain, examining whether armorial wares shared the feminine gender connotations and understandings that marked other Chinese ceramics. Chinese armorial ware, porcelain services specially commissioned by families to include their coats of arms within the decorative scheme, were fashionable items in eighteenth-century Europe and Britain, particularly among those with East India Company (EIC) connections (see Figure 5.1).[2] David Sanctuary Howard has argued that throughout the century employees of the EIC were especially prolific buyers.[3] Armorial porcelain services feature in a number of *East India Company at Home* chapters, including those on Osterley Park and Valentines Mansion. Often acquired by men and bearing coats of arms, these wares suggest that certain forms of porcelain may have been perceived as male and 'manly'. As such, their presence challenges our understanding of porcelain as a homogenous 'feminine' good and instead illuminates the differences that came to be established within the category of porcelain over the eighteenth century.

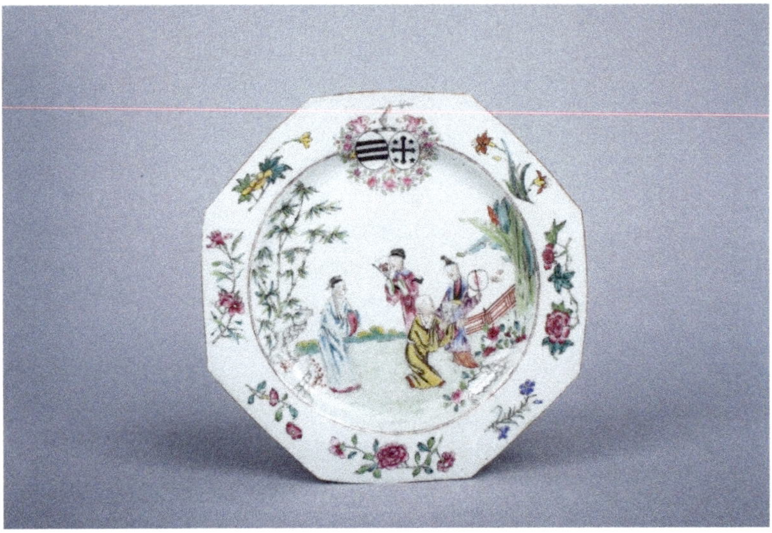

Figure 5.1 Chinese porcelain plate decorated with the arms of Charles Raymond and his wife, Sarah Webster. c.1760. Private collection. Image courtesy of Georgina Green and Heirloom & Howard Ltd.

Introduction

British houses first included Chinese armorial porcelain services at the turn of the eighteenth century.[4] Obtaining these wares was notoriously difficult as ordering, production and transportation required knowledge of different people, practices and spaces. The only means of acquiring armorial services were by placing a commission through a supercargo officer involved in trade with China, working with a dealer who had connections to a supercargo, or (for those based on the subcontinent) through engaging with country trade between India and China.[5] Supercargoes were particularly important to armorial porcelain commissions. As individuals who worked for the EIC, they were responsible for dealing with Chinese merchants in Canton (Guangzhou). They oversaw the purchase of bulk commodities for the Company, such as tea. Alongside negotiating purchases and supplies, supercargoes also executed private trade and were well placed to fulfill commissions for particular objects, such as armorial porcelain services. In placing a commission, the supercargo would pass on written instructions and sketches to Chinese decorators (often based in Canton), who would then paint the necessary armorial design onto a series of porcelain forms obtained from the ceramic factories in Jingdezhen, which, by the early eighteenth century, had long produced forms to European tastes.[6]

Armorials were used throughout Europe to demarcate elite status, but were not part of the Chinese decorative lexicon prior to the arrival of the European EIC merchants. Working from written instructions and sketches in an unknown idiom, Chinese decorators unsurprisingly made mistakes (a point perhaps overly noted by historians). Dolphins replaced birds and bear claws transmuted into clumps of grass, reworking the coat of arms and creating entirely new meanings.[7] Nevertheless, these services proved particularly popular with EIC directors, captains and supercargoes, who had the connections and wealth necessary to commission them. Robert Finlay estimates that in the eighteenth century more than half of all EIC directors, captains and supercargoes purchased armorial dinner and tea services.[8] In total, English buyers commissioned around 6,000 armorial sets, with some going to regiments and societies.[9] After 1745 armorial services also became popular with Scottish and Irish families. David Sanctuary Howard estimates that 'nearly twenty per cent of all services were ordered by families north of the Border' in the second half of the eighteenth century.[10] Families such as the Lascelles and the Beckfords, who gained fortunes through their involvement in Caribbean slavery and the slave trade, also commissioned these wares, but were far less conspicuous among commissioners of Chinese porcelain than Company families.[11]

Surviving examples inform us that these armorial services were extraordinarily elaborate, with some containing more than 500 pieces.[12] Services included not only dining ware such as plates, dishes, hot-water plates, soup tureens and sauce boats, but also items for large entertainments (such as punch bowls), decoration (pierced baskets and vases) and the tea table (coffee and chocolate pots, teapots, teapoys, caddies, milk jugs, spoon trays and sweetmeat dishes, cups and saucers).[13] Commissioning a complete service thus involved a substantial outlay of money. A service (including shipping and custom duties) cost around £100 (roughly £11,000 today) in the early eighteenth century and was around 'ten times as expensive as other porcelain'.[14] Although it took around three years (from order to delivery) for these services to arrive, the difficulties undertaken in obtaining them heightened their desirability. At the same time, bearing coats of arms, these exclusive objects allowed families to proclaim their elite identities and lineage.

This chapter examines the identity politics that Britons embedded in armorial porcelain services during the long eighteenth century. It considers how family names were displayed and bolstered as a result of owning dinner plates and other armorial porcelain bearing a particular coat of arms. It also asks whether the plates, dishes and sauceboats that made up lavish armorial dinner services actively shaped other identities.

Principally, it asks, were armorial services gendered? If so, how and why? While many scholars have explored the relationship between women and porcelain in the eighteenth century, this chapter uses armorial porcelain to consider the relationships that contemporaries conceived as existing between men and this highly prized translucent material.[15] In exploring these questions, this chapter investigates the place Chinese porcelain held within British culture and the ways in which Britons used Chinese porcelain to perform specific cultural work.

While the arguments explored below could be examined through the armorial porcelain services found at Osterley Park, Shugborough or Valentines Mansion, this chapter focuses on a different set of wares – those purchased by Francis Sykes of Basildon Park, Berkshire in the 1760s (see Figure 5.2).[16] Sykes worked at the EIC's Cossimbazar factory in Bengal between 1751 and 1761 (rising to chief of the factory in 1760) and then served between 1764 and 1769 as Resident at Murshidabad and also as chief of the Cossimbazar factory from 1766 onwards.[17] From the scant documentary sources left by Sykes, it is difficult to interpret exactly why and how he purchased his armorial service. By situating his acquisition within the wider context of porcelain consumption and use, however, this chapter suggests that EIC men were keen to purchase armorial porcelain services for their country houses and town houses because Chinese porcelain acted as an important emblem of elite masculinity, while also signalling their place within the EIC hierarchy to their associates and the world at large.

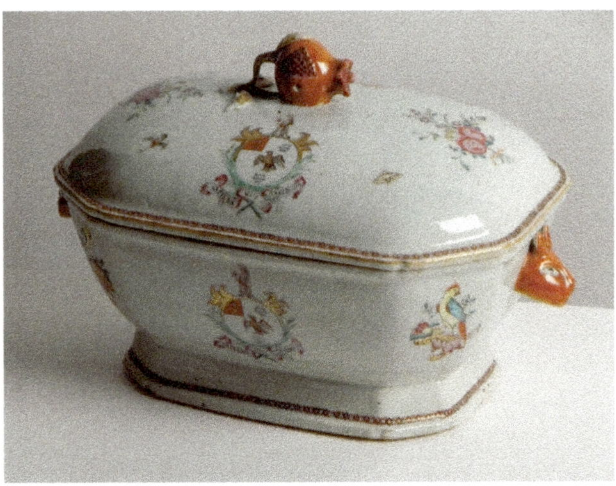

Figure 5.2 Tureen from armorial Chinese porcelain service, Qianlong reign (1736–96), c.1765–70. NT 266484.3. Basildon Park, National Trust Collections. © National Trust/Thomas Boggis.

As Henry French and Mark Rothery remind us, gender identities were never absolute. Nevertheless, in eighteenth-century Britain, contemporaries 'believed in the existence of such all-embracing behaviourial norms – even though they could not agree precisely on what these might be'.[18] Like women, men also constructed gendered identities and operated within specific understandings of behaviourial norms. Elite men 'conceived their gender identity by reference to a number of competing stereotypes, rather than in relation to a single, "hegemonic" form'.[19] French and Rothery's study suggests that certain attributes remained constantly significant for elite men throughout the period from 1660 to 1900, namely autonomy, honour, reputation and self-control.[20] For EIC officials keen to join, re-join or consolidate their position within Britain's elites, armorial porcelain allowed them to enact and signify many of these attributes. The design of armorial wares, the modes by which they were acquired and their practices of use all allowed Company men to display and maintain their reputation, autonomy and honour. Armorial wares showed their lineage, as well as their relationship to networks of influence in spaces (such as the dining room) of male sociability. Is it possible then to understand Chinese armorial wares as distinctly male? If so, how did these wares shape British material cultures and does this change our understandings of Chinese porcelain and its role in British material cultures more generally?

Women, porcelain and pleasure

Scholars argue that during the eighteenth century porcelain was consistently gendered female. As Elizabeth Kowaleski-Wallace asserts, throughout the period a variety of authors deployed references to fine china or porcelain to denote women and their weaknesses.[21] China and porcelain 'made it possible for people to talk about women and their qualities in a particular way'.[22] Scholars such as David Porter note that porcelain was significant in providing a space in which different ideas about women, desire, sensuality, novelty, temptation and exchange could come together, 'giving form through its very materiality to fears and pleasures which, in the absence of a suitable substitute, might otherwise have remained hauntingly inchoate'.[23] In contrast to work that has focused on the relationship between women and porcelain, this chapter seeks to show how men utilized and related to porcelain goods in important ways.

In the early decades of the eighteenth century, writers such as Alexander Pope and Joseph Addison used 'china' as a means through which to discuss female sexuality, desire and subjectivity. In these texts, authors frequently conflated women's bodies with the material qualities of porcelain. Delicate, translucent, fragile and breakable – porcelain could be equated with characteristics that increasingly came to define a specific view of femininity. Here women came under the male and female gaze as objects of desire. Kowaleski-Wallace argues, however, that what was principally at stake in these discussions was not women as objects of desire, but rather the issue of female desire itself.[24] Chinese porcelain provided an acceptable space in which to discuss concerns that women possessed and expressed tangible desires of their own. More worryingly still they engaged with the market in order to satisfy those desires, supposedly buying up porcelain in their droves.

Elizabeth Chang notes that discussions regarding women and porcelain must also be understood in class terms. As particular axes of identity formation, gender and class have long been understood to intersect in important ways. She asserts that 'only wealthier kinds of women were held to possess the leisure necessary to build an impressive collection of imported porcelain'.[25] Nevertheless, women from the genteel and middling classes also actively engaged in and took pleasure from purchases of china.[26] In representations depicting the relationship between women and Chinese porcelain then, commentators gestured towards the threatening nature of class mobility implied by middling women purchasing and owning these wares.[27] Importantly, it must also be remembered that over the course of the eighteenth century, renderings of women and their relationship to and with porcelain steadily shifted. Porter understands these shifts as undergoing three stages. First, in the early decades of the eighteenth century, women were particularly linked to porcelain in terms of commoditized desire.[28] Women were frequently portrayed as entering the marketplace to purchase or view porcelain goods at all costs, and such representations often eroticized these desires, understanding them as uncontrollable passions and lusts. Second, porcelain came to be increasingly portrayed within domestic settings. Here, porcelain was often linked to subversive female agency. While painters such as Hogarth used broken jars to signify illicit liaisons and sexual acts, painters could also highlight female resistance and subversion by including thrown and broken ceramics.[29] Finally at the turn of the nineteenth century, ceramics brokered women's submersion in domestic and maternal roles. Here, women were shown lovingly pouring tea from teapots to signify both matriarchal control and love.[30]

If then, as scholars such as David Porter and Elizabeth Kowaleski-Wallace suggest, Chinese porcelain (and other forms of ceramic ware) were consistently linked to women in the eighteenth century, how can we begin to understand the relationship between men and porcelain wares? Have British understandings of porcelain been distorted by a lack of attention to male consumption of Asian goods *and* a predominant focus on rich extant sources outlining connections between porcelain, women, desire and femininity?[31] This chapter examines the cultural work armorial Chinese porcelain performed within eighteenth-century English society and questions how that work was understood within elite culture. Three key avenues of enquiry can be used to consider these questions – acquisition, design and use. By examining the modes by which armorial porcelains were purchased, the designs with which they were decorated and the way in which they were used, this study suggests that armorial wares were distinctly male – carrying a different set of connotations and meanings to other porcelain pieces.

The Basildon Park service

This chapter probes these themes by focusing on a single service, which belonged to Francis Sykes in the late eighteenth century and was probably used at his country estate, Basildon Park in Berkshire.[32] The son of a prosperous and well-established yeoman farmer, Francis Sykes rose to become an important EIC official. While in India he maintained a substantial household, which (like Henry Russell, featured in the chapter on Swallowfield Park) shaped his later experiences of British country house living. Writing to his mother from Murshidabad in September 1767, Gerard Gustavus Duccarel (1745–1800) described how he was working in the service of Francis Sykes and had found that his employer had little patience for the hot climate. Sykes and his party had thus 'removed for the summer to a pleasant country house about 7 miles from the City in the middle of a beautiful plain'. A fine grove of tall trees meant that these Company men were able to participate in English country pursuits whilst employed as merchants on the Indian subcontinent. As Duccarel reported, they could 'play at bowles there in the middle of the day without the least inconvenience, and spread our tables either there, or in the house, as the variety is more or less agreeable'.[33]

Having accumulated a vast fortune through Company trade, Francis Sykes first came to practice country living in Britain on his return to England in 1761. On this visit Francis took two years to purchase Ackworth Park, near Pontefract in Yorkshire. Originally from Yorkshire, Sykes used his residence there to reconnect with family and acquaintances in the West Riding area, particularly the powerful Monckton family with whom he forged a closer alliance when he married the Hon. Elizabeth Monckton (1754–1835), eldest daughter of the 2nd Viscount Galway (d.1772), in 1774. After his second return to England in 1768, Sykes consolidated his place as a member of the landed elite in 1771, when he purchased Gillingham Manor Estate in Dorset (primarily to acquire political influence) and Basildon Park in Berkshire. In June of that year, Sykes wrote to Harry Verelst from Basildon about his 'delightful situation in a large house with many servants and no one to keep me company at present but my two dear little boys'.[34] Despite his seeming contentment in 1771, by 1776 Sykes had begun to employ the nationally acclaimed and hugely fashionable architect John Carr (1723–1807) to oversee the rebuilding of Basildon. The Palladian villa that Carr designed still stands today (refer to Chapter 3, Figure 3.4).

Sykes's rapid accumulation of wealth in India enabled him to purchase and then rebuild Basildon Park. Having worked for the EIC in Bengal between 1751 and 1761 and then again between 1764 and 1769, he had returned to England with a fortune that was large even by EIC standards for the period and has been estimated as between £250,000 and £500,000.[35] Current catalogues for Basildon's collection suggest that it was during his second stint on the subcontinent that Francis Sykes commissioned and purchased an armorial porcelain service.[36] That he commissioned the service between 1764 and 1769 seems likely as on his return to India, Sykes would have had the necessary contacts, wealth and position to order an armorial service, the commission probably being carried out through country trade. Such timing is also made more plausible by his being granted arms in 1763. His purchase followed the grant (1763) but preceded his baronetcy (1781).

Acquisition

How did Francis Sykes originally acquire this service and did his modes of acquisition mark these objects out as distinctly different from more feminized goods? In conflating women and porcelain, eighteenth-century British commentators often made much of the modes of acquisition – the worryingly public act of shopping. Entering the marketplace to purchase ceramic objects meant engaging in increasingly complex shopping practices staged in specialized, enclosed spaces. Ceramic and glassware dealers invited shoppers to enter their shops (rather than haggle at a window), browse their displays, and socialize with shop assistants who would readily produce a further selection of wares for their perusal.[37] Nevertheless it must be remembered that it was not women alone who enacted these practices in these public retail environments. Both women and men participated in shopping practices, suggesting that both women and men were skillful shoppers and perhaps enjoyed shopping as a particular pursuit. Men certainly took advantage of new practices of browsing, which allowed shoppers to peruse certain goods, often with no purchase. For example, in his 1796 *Scarborough Guide* James Schofield described how 'Shopping, especially for articles of foreign elegance, is a very usual amusement among the ladies, who are not unfrequently [sic] attended by the gentlemen'.[38] In 1791, Charles Bowden Topham also delighted in the experiences of shopping and noted that Mr Kennedy's shop in London 'entertained me for an hour'.[39] Yet despite men's enjoyment in shopping and browsing, it was women out a-shopping on whom commentators focused. Troublingly present in city streets and ceramic shops, women engaged with and interrupted the 'real' (male) business of the marketplace.[40]

In contrast to purchasing through retailers, individuals acquired armorial porcelains through commissioning processes that required contacts, influence and patience. Armorial porcelain services could be commissioned in England through connections to supercargoes involved in trade with China or in India by EIC officials with access to country trade vessels and thus access to merchants in Canton. In placing a commission the supercargo or merchant would pass on instructions (often including a book-plate depicting the family's heraldic device) to Chinese decorators usually based in Canton, who would then paint the necessary armorial design onto a series of porcelain forms obtained from the ceramic factories in Jingdezhen. The commissioning process marked armorial wares as distinctly different to those purchased in shops. Even individuals who placed elaborate commissions with British manufacturers such as Wedgwood did not have to engage in the extended processes demanded for armorial wares.[41] Rather than the instant gratification of a shop purchase or the delayed delight of a Staffordshire commission, families who wanted to purchase Chinese armorial wares had to meet elite masculine ideals by displaying sustained self-control, patiently waiting for up to three years. In commissioning such wares it was also necessary to possess the correct reputation and be able to call on business and political contacts.

The material record of the Sykes service – the pieces now situated at Basildon Park – reminds us that the commissioning of these items was likely more complex than most. For instance, while some of the plates have scalloped edges possibly created through press-moulding (see Figure 5.3), others have cut octagonal edges (see Figure 5.4). These

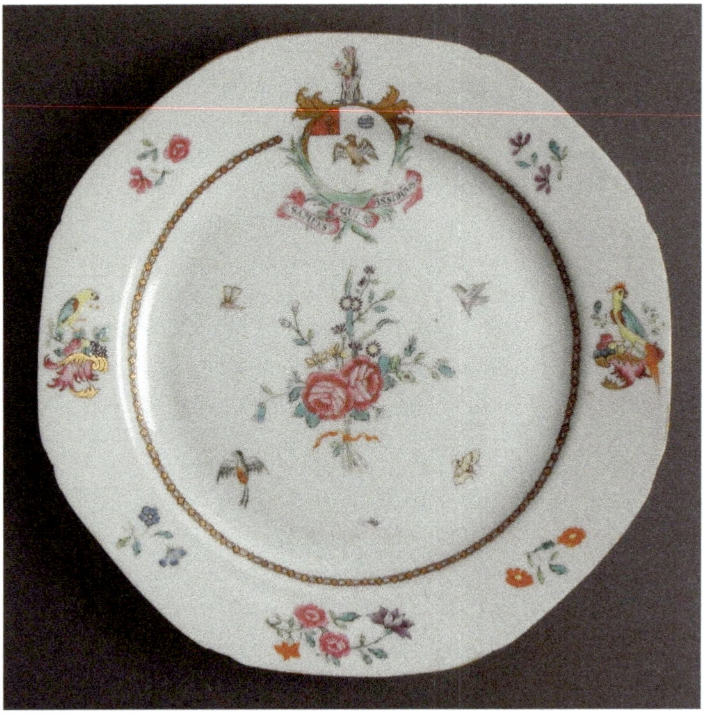

Figure 5.3 Scalloped-edge plate from armorial Chinese porcelain service, Qianlong reign (1736–96), c.1765–70. NT 266484.12.6. Basildon Park, National Trust Collections. © National Trust/Thomas Boggis.

material differences suggest that Sykes commissioned the service in two stages. It is possible that while he commissioned the first part of the service during his time in India, he completed the second commission once returned to Britain. If Francis Sykes commissioned the first part of the service through country trade, he would have used one of the two ships that traded between Bengal and China each year.[42] Alternatively he might have used a contact well connected with the China trade. During his later period in Bengal (1764–9) Francis Sykes had men in his employ, such as Thomas Pattle Jr., who had such connections.[43] Thomas Pattle Sr. had worked on board East India Company ships as third and second mate during the 1730s and by the 1760s was wealthy enough to act as Principal Managing Owner to the *Speke*, which travelled to both China and India in the late 1760s.[44] Sykes may have ordered the services through Thomas Pattle. It is difficult to identify how exactly Sykes acquired these wares as his bank records, which might highlight payments to particular individuals, only

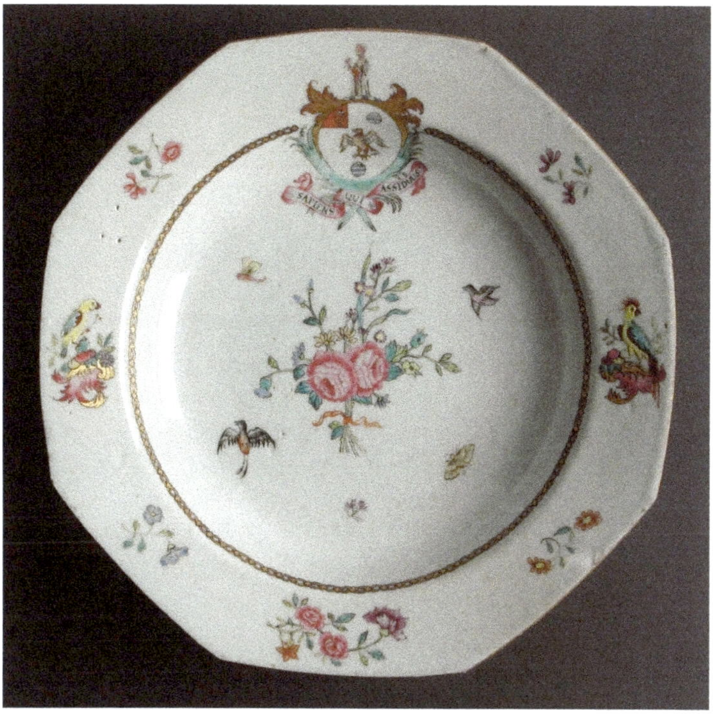

Figure 5.4 Plate with cut edges from armorial Chinese porcelain service, Qianlong reign (1736–96), c.1765–70. NT 266484.10. Basildon Park, National Trust. © National Trust/Thomas Boggis.

begin on 11 November 1769 when he began to bank with Goslings and do not include payments for the service. Nevertheless, despite such ambiguity in the historical record, the modes of acquisition required to purchase armorial wares marked these pieces out to contemporaries as distinct from other porcelain wares on the market and marked them as distinctly male. Commissioned by men from men, these wares embodied the homosocial ideals of the EIC and eighteenth-century trade.

Designing the service

It was not only a question of the processes through which individuals purchased ceramics, but also what they bought. The Basildon porcelain service, manufactured in the mid-1760s, features decorative motifs rendered in the famille rose palette and combines flowers and butterflies with colourful birds. As the name suggests, famille rose enamel colours contained hues of pink and allowed for more intricate designs to be painted. Famille rose enamel colours came into common use in the early 1720s and from the 1730s onwards remained the dominant palette for armorial wares through the eighteenth century.[45] As such the Basildon service is similar in layout and colour scheme to other services of the mid to late eighteenth century, though decorative motifs could vary widely (see for example the Shugborough service c.1743, featured in Figure 5.6, or the Valentine service c.1760, featured in Figure 5.1).

Although men who enjoyed purchasing porcelain may have 'regarded it as a slightly female, perhaps even deliciously feminine pre-occupation', the question of how and what was purchased is important.[46] Examples exist of men *and* women purchasing dynastic items, yet it was largely men who involved themselves in the purchase of large dynastic and/or expensive items, such as dinner services.[47] Hence purchasing certain *types* of ceramics, such as dinner services, may not have been regarded as 'deliciously feminine' but rather as a distinctly masculine pursuit. Armorial services were particularly dynastic items, not only due to their expense and size but also because they bore coats of arms and thus familial identities. At the top of the plate the Sykes coat of arms is included (see Figure 5.3). The College of Arms granted Francis Sykes his arms in 1763, 18 years prior to his being created baronet in 1781.

The tradition of arms originated on the battlefields of medieval Europe as men in full armour sought to challenge their enemies. Unable to recognize friend from foe amidst the legions of plated metal, men took to wearing distinctive coats over their armour to ease identification. The colours and patterns that made up these 'coats of arms' then came to be displayed in other ways, both on the battlefield in flags and shields and away from the battlefield upon the clothes and accessories of civil life.[48] Coats of arms bred their own distinctive heraldic language, communicating lineage and affiliations. These symbols came to include a shield often adorned with a helmet and crest above. While predominantly concerned with the promotion of the male line, arms could gesture towards the importance of the female line through impaling or the inclusion of a wife's family arms on marriage (see for example Figure 5.1).

The arms displayed on the Sykes armorial service can be deciphered through the rules of arms and heraldry (the design of the arms can be understood more clearly from viewing the original grant of arms, featured in Figure 5.5). The centre of the arms is occupied by a 'shield', which features an argent (an eagle with wings outstretched – possibly an allusion to Sykes's meritocratic rise) between two 'sykes' (the heraldic form of fountain), which are the blue and white circles. On the left the 'canton gules'

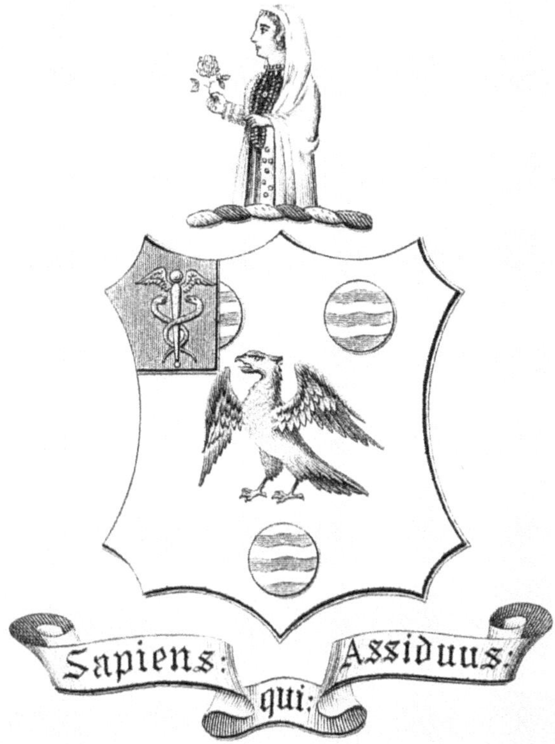

Figure 5.5 Detail of coat of arms from original grant of arms. 1763. Image courtesy of Sir John Sykes.

(the red-coloured square) features a caduceus (Mercury's wand with two serpents and wings, emblem of merchants among others). Above the 'shield' sits a helmet (not depicted in the service) and above that a mantling (represented by the wreath of silk), which is adorned with a 'crest', in this case a woman dressed in head scarf, robes and beads and holding a rose. Significantly this female figure was described as 'A demy lady of Bengal in the compleat dress of that kingdom, holding in the dexter hand a rose'.[49] The motto included on a ribbon banner beneath the shield reads 'He is wise who is industrious', suggesting a desire to gentrify Sykes's mercantile activity in an era concerned with nabob excess.

The armorial service commissioned by Francis Sykes affirmed (as did Basildon Park itself) his newfound social status on returning to England. It did so through embodying Sykes's recently granted arms and thus the Sykes family's legitimate place within the established elite. Asserting a family name was a powerful act, but it was not a solely male act. In her studies of eighteenth-century New England material culture, Laurel Thatcher Ulrich reminds us of the often complex ways in which names, objects and property came to be inherited in the eighteenth-century Atlantic world.[50] In this context women, such as Hannah Barnard and her descendants, were able to establish matrilineal descent through bequeathing a cupboard bearing Hannah's maiden name.[51] Similarly, while coats of arms may be understood solely as a male preserve, marriages to women who carried the family name could be and were represented upon arms, and armorial services could be commissioned to celebrate a union and mark the joining of family lines. Despite these strategies, however, coats of arms were (and are) primarily considered a male preserve, highlighting as they do the ideal of patrimony. For Sykes, the armorial service he commissioned played a key role marking *his* coat of arms and thus forwarding *his* name and line. The designs decorated onto armorial wares marked them as distinctly masculine, an identity that was further reaffirmed through use.

Using the service

Armorial services did not only include dining wares. These elaborate ensembles often contained dining, decorative and tea table wares. While dining wares might have been more recognizably masculine, tea wares were distinctly feminine.[52] Women became linked to tea drinking practices and the ceramic accoutrement that accompanied them.[53] Women's engagement with the display of objects and practices at the centre of tea drinking, allowed for further conflations of women and porcelain.[54] Amanda Vickery takes issue with this reading, however, and warns that 'The tea table has received disproportionate attention in the history of consumerism, though the focus has been narrow and often unquestioning'.[55] Vickery argues that the tea table has primarily come to be understood as a site of female control, in which women encountered the regulating force of the female and male gaze. In contrast, Vickery has sought to clarify the social reach of tea drinking practices (a 'universal habit' by 1760), as well as the importance of the tea table, which she highlights as a key site of female sociability during this period.[56] For Vickery the tea table simultaneously acted as a sign of female gentility and 'the very headquarters of female opinion, a byword for feminine confederacy, gossip and slander',[57] at the same time it was also 'a forum for business dealings in the widest possible sense'.[58] In contrast to the drawing room and its focus on female sociability and tea drinking, during the eighteenth century families living in country houses increasingly came to define dining rooms as masculine spaces and significantly it was dining rooms in which armorial services were put to conspicuous use.

Employing armorial services in increasingly 'masculine' spaces such as dining rooms encouraged these objects to be understood as an important part of male, mercantile culture. At the turn of the eighteenth century saloons started being used principally for dancing, rather than gathering and eating, and substantial houses started to contain grand dining rooms. Mark Girouard argues that in the middle decades of the eighteenth century the 'dining room was always one of the best and biggest rooms in the house'.[59] After dinner women would enter the drawing room to brew coffee and tea, before the men joined them later. As the century progressed, the period of 'withdrawing' became longer and longer as men wished to spend more time in homo-social conversation and drinking at the dinner table. In consequence, 'the dining room began to be thought of as a mainly masculine, and the drawing room as a mainly feminine room'.[60] By the end of the eighteenth century, these separate spaces were further demarcated by the inclusion of a room in between the dining room and drawing room, which acted as a buffer, allowing greater aural privacy for homo-social practices.[61] While Mark Girouard notes how gendered spaces became increasingly important in country houses during the eighteenth and (to a certain extent) the nineteenth centuries, by the end of the nineteenth century such demarcations had begun to dissolve.[62]

As dining services made up the greatest number of pieces within porcelain services it is often dinner plates – the mainstay of dining room activities – rather than tea services that survive in armorial ware collections. The long survival of these particular pieces might also suggest that they were highly valued by the families who owned and inherited them. When in use, armorial porcelain services played an important role by asserting an elite masculine identity to other men that joined them and then lingered around the dining table.[63] Their presence (and acquisition) represented the owners' sociability and connections, as well as their honourable reputation within the world of the EIC. In sitting there within such spaces men were not only able to claim the status of a separate dining room, but also the status begot through symbols of lineage marked on the wares. These objects came to play important roles in the performance of gender identities that valued autonomy, honour, reputation and self-control, spanning across the established elite and the East India Company set.

Conclusion

Recent research on the 208-piece Qianlong-period porcelain dinner service brought to England by Commodore George, later Lord Anson (1697–1762) in 1744 and now housed at the Shugborough Estate in Staffordshire, challenges the different ways in which previous historians have envisaged armorial services (see Figure 5.6).[64] Traditionally the Shugborough dinner service has been understood as having been presented to George Anson by European merchants in Canton in recognition for his and his crew's courageous involvement in extinguishing a fire that threatened to engulf the city in 1743. In this interpretation the dinner service has come to represent 'the ultimate triumph of this level-headed, courageous and determined commodore over the dithering, deceitful and obstructive Chinese mandarins, as well as the gratitude of the European merchants towards their champion'.[65] Recent research demonstrates the inaccuracy of this depiction of Anson's time at Canton, recognizing it as a partial reading of what was 'in reality, a highly contested episode'.[66] Contemporary accounts also call into question the idea that Anson acquired the service while in Canton, as a gift from European merchants. It seems more likely that, like other British officers, Anson commissioned and purchased the service while at Whampoa between July and September 1743.[67] Rather than emerging from accounts penned by eighteenth-century writers, it seems that the incorrect link between the Canton episode and the dinner service first emerged in a series of articles published in *Country Life* in 1954.[68]

While such research challenges traditional interpretations of the Shugborough service particularly, and Sino-British relations in the mid-eighteenth century more generally, what is of more interest here is that the story of the service as a gift given by oppressed European merchants to their champion was compelling to twentieth-century audiences and has remained so. In the traditional account of the Shugborough service the object became intrinsically associated with a tale of imperial masculinity. That audiences were willing to invest in an interpretation that recounted men gifting an armorial dinner service to a man as a marker of his seeming courage, fortitude and resourceful nature, tells us much about what twentieth- and twenty-first-century audiences expected armorial wares

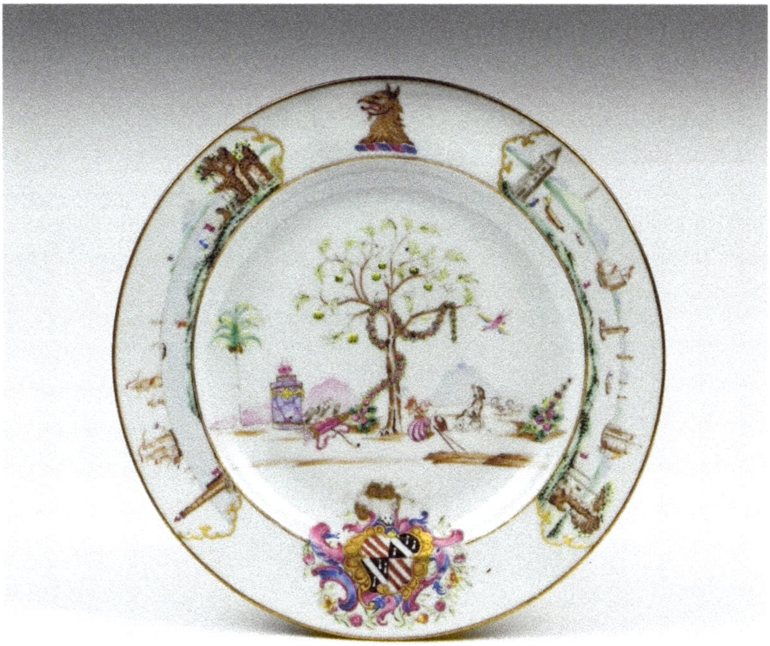

Figure 5.6 Plate from armorial Chinese porcelain service, Qianlong reign (1736–96), c.1743. NT 1271545. Shugborough, Staffordshire. © National Trust Images/Robert Morris.

might have been and done in the eighteenth century. In this rendering, armorial porcelain is introduced as an object intimately tied to undertakings that reinforced conceptions of masculinity and domination, as well as homo-sociability in the eighteenth century. In this story armorial porcelain appears as the male-object par excellence.

In considering the meaning of armorial porcelain services to eighteenth-century British society, this chapter has also understood these global luxury goods in distinctly masculine terms. While the material – porcelain – was primarily conflated with women and the feminine during this period, this chapter has suggested that by examining the modes by which individuals acquired armorial wares, their design and their use, it becomes clear that certain porcelain wares may have been associated with other gender identities. Acquired through EIC networks, maintained through rigorous adherence to certain codes of reputation, honour and connection, these wares provided contemporaries with evidence of an individual's ability to call on others and demand service and respect. The inclusion of designs (armorials), which demonstrated a family's name and lineage was also important in establishing elite identities that required a sense of history and evidence of status. Finally their use in spaces primarily understood as masculine – dining rooms – further served to mark these wares as specifically gendered. While women were continually conflated with the fragile and delicate qualities of porcelain, not all porcelain wares were understood as feminine. Men acquired expensive and exclusive armorial porcelain services to perform and mark a particularly elite form of masculinity.

6
Fanny Parkes (1794–1875)

Female collecting and curiosity in India and Britain

Joanna Goldsworthy

On 9 December 1834 an exuberant, rather plump, Englishwoman who had celebrated her fortieth birthday the day before set off up the Jumna river from Allahabad in the Northern Provinces in India in a two-masted pinnace (sailing boat), the *Seagull*, her only companions the 22-strong Indian male crew. Her husband, the Collector of Customs in Allahabad, would join her for a few days if he could get leave from his employer, the East India Company (EIC). Following the *Seagull* was the cook boat containing goods for the voyage: live sheep, goats and chickens; wine and other provisions; servants included a dhobi (washer-man); and the crew of nine. They travelled from six o'clock in the morning to seven in the evening, anchoring at night and with armed watchmen on shore. The frequent storms, the contrary current, the treacherous rocks in the river, the uncharted sandbanks, the risk of being plundered by robbers – all combined to make this a hazardous but thrilling journey for a woman who craved excitement to counter the boredom of life for a childless Englishwoman in the Indian mofussil (countryside). Who cared what colonial society thought of this enterprise? Certainly not the indefatigable wanderer: Fanny Parkes.

Following Fanny's death in 1875, on 17 February 1876, Fanny's first cousin, Clement Robert Archer Esq, presented a copy of Fanny's account of her travels in India, entitled *Wanderings of a Pilgrim in Search of the Picturesque* (see Figure 6.1), to the India Museum in London.[1] One month later another relative, J. Coutts Antrobus Esq of Eaton Hall,

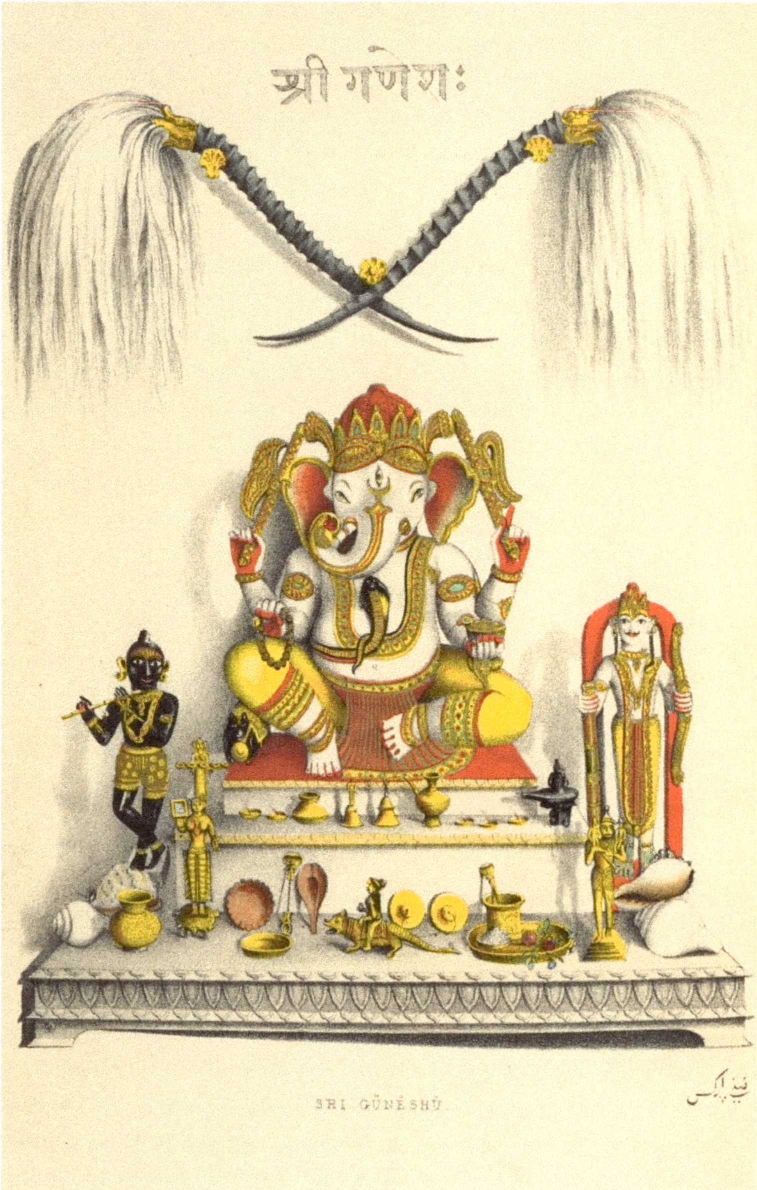

Figure 6.1 Frontispiece *Wanderings of a Pilgrim in Search of the Picturesque*, vol. 1 British Library digital copy p.13; print copy facing i and i. © The British Library Board, 1947.b 170 vol.1 frontispiece.

Congleton, presented three sculptures to the same museum: two pieces of carved dark grey sandstone, now in the British Museum collection, which Fanny had obtained from a fisherman living on the banks of the Ganges, and a piece of white carved stone acquired by Fanny in Pooree (now Puri) in 1844.[2] These three sculptures, together with a large and disparate collection of other artefacts gathered together by Fanny and Charles Parkes during their 23 years' residence in India, were brought back to England in the *Essex,* which left Calcutta in September 1845, and arrived at Folkestone in January 1846.

The collection and Fanny Parkes' published recollections of her travels in India appear to have given her a public legitimacy and authority lacking before she went to the subcontinent. As a young woman she was a typical product of her background and upbringing in a military family, 'eminent in beauty as in talent … wounding many a heart', before finding a role for herself: that of traveller, collector and ethnographer.[3] India and her experiences there changed her and enabled her to construct a new identity for herself. 'Whatever the wandering traveller says, he does so from having seen that of which he speaks' was the oriental proverb she quoted in the opening pages of *Wanderings of a Pilgrim*, emphasizing the veracity of her enterprise.[4] 'Knowing India first-hand' was a claim frequently made by travel writers of the period when attempting to add authority and authenticity to this literary aspect of the imperial project.[5] Fanny's sense of 'knowing' was enhanced by gathering objects from the subcontinent and by sharing her acquired knowledge with a public eager to see the 'curiosities, the monsters and the idols' that she took with her when she left India forever.[6]

Historian Maya Jasanoff argues that collectors 'shared one crucial characteristic: all of them used objects to advertise, hone or shape their social personae. Collecting was a means of self-fashioning'.[7] Fanny's enthusiasms appear in her own account so unfeignedly artless as she gathers people, customs and curiosities on her travels through India, that it is hard to see a conscious self-fashioning in her actions, certainly while she was living in India.[8] Yet in writing of her collecting as artless enthusiasm, *Wanderings* suggests that Fanny distinctly wished to be understood as someone who had formed knowledge and expertise through 'authentic' experience. With little means of corroborating the events that Parkes described in *Wanderings*, it is difficult to ascertain the exact nature of her experiences in India and the gaps between those experiences and the stories she told about them. Rather than work towards ascertaining such knowledge, this chapter instead focuses on analyzing the stories Parkes did tell and seeks to understand their meanings and effect. This chapter principally uses Fanny Parkes' published work *Wanderings of a Pilgrim*, to analyze the ways in which she sought to present herself to the public on her return to Britain. Alongside *Wanderings*, it looks to the objects she collected and how she in turn curated these for audiences in Britain in the mid-nineteenth century. When she returned to the metropole, this chapter argues, her writings and collection lent her authority in an almost exclusively masculine society of Indian 'experts'. She gained entrée to a social world to which she might not otherwise have been admitted and formed 'a life independent of her own life'.[9] On returning to Britain then, she publicly utilized her collection to validate and enhance her experiences. In analyzing these writings and practices of exhibition, this chapter seeks to show how a woman linked to the EIC was able to use her experiences of the subcontinent to effect on her return. While other chapters in this volume are largely concerned with the material and social gains (or losses) derived by male service to the EIC, this chapter underlines the particular advantages that women could garner.

Alongside contributing to studies of EIC officials and imperial service, this chapter also seeks to engage with histories of collecting. Building on the work of other scholars, it underlines the importance of female practice of collecting in particular. The chapter finds that previous studies of collecting as a phenomenon, from the age of the 'cabinet of curiosity' to the present, have focussed overwhelmingly on male collectors – men whose professional lives and wealth often gave them privileged access to exotic plants, animals, artwork and objects. In consequence, we have a much more detailed understanding of the Company men whose collecting helped to furnish the British country house and later many British museums.[10] This chapter, however, illustrates the way in which one Company woman took advantage of her colonial experiences to collect, describe and display Indian material culture. At the same time, it demonstrates how her collections, their display and description, generated a perception of 'expertise', which gave her legitimacy in the male-dominated world of collecting, as well as status and independence in metropolitan society.

Who was Fanny Parkes?

Frances Susanna Archer was born on 8 December 1794 in Conwy, North Wales, and baptized there on 22 January 1795. Her father was

Captain William Archer, formerly of the 16th Lancers, her mother Ann Archer, née Goodhew. She had an older sister, Anne Augustine, who, like Fanny, lived in India. On 25 March 1822, Fanny, 27 years old, talented and beautiful, married 23-year-old Charles Crawford Parkes (1798–1854), a Writer in the East India Company.[11] Arriving in Calcutta later that same year, Fanny and Charles rented a house in Chowringhee. Charles attended Fort William College and worked as assistant to the Collector of Sea Customs, Calcutta while waiting for a more permanent and better-paid position up country. Fanny learnt how to run a house with a multitude of servants, enjoyed riding her Arab horse on the Maidan at dusk after the heat of the day, took lessons in Hindi and Sanskrit, and started to explore the intricacies of Indian culture. In particular, she also became 'very anxious to visit a *zenāna* [harem]', and to witness the lives of the high-class Indian women kept in seclusion behind its closed doors.[12]

Fanny was 35 years old in 1830 when she and Charles moved to Cawnpore, where Charles had the post of Acting Collector of Customs. Childless, with servants aplenty (in 1831 Fanny calculated that they had 57, and needed an additional 14 in the hot months), there was little to occupy such a spirited and adventurous woman in Cawnpore's limited social setting.[13] Restless and underemployed, Fanny looked for and found a temporary cure in travel, preferably on horseback: 'Roaming about with a good tent and a good Arab [horse], one might be happy for ever in India,' she wrote in her journal in 1838. 'Oh! the pleasure of vagabondizing over India!'[14] Fanny Eden, sister of Governor General Lord Auckland, commented acidly that '[Mrs Parkes] has a husband who always goes mad in the cold season, so she says it is due to herself to leave him and travel about … she informed us she was an independent woman and was going to travel to Simla by herself – which sounded very independent indeed.'[15] Fanny herself never mentioned Charles's reaction to the weather, hot or cold; from remarks in her journal, it is clear that it was Fanny who suffered most from the heat – and boredom.[16]

Finally, in September 1832, Charles was appointed Collector of Customs at Allahabad, a permanent posting. Fanny, temporarily back from her travels, enthused about the place which was an enormous improvement on Cawnpore. There were 'dinner-parties more than enough; balls occasionally; a book society; some five or six billiard-tables, a pack of dogs … and (how could I have forgotten!) fourteen spinsters!'[17] What's more, there were officers aplenty to ride with, even if she and her horse ended up in quicksand or she was inadvertently dunked in the river, adventures she related with great gusto in her journal.[18] She was clearly a woman whose company young officers sought, in spite of Fanny Eden's barbed opinion that she had 'once been a beauty' but was now 'abundantly fat and lively'.[19] Despite such excitements, however, the dinner parties of Allahabad were not enough for Fanny and for the rest of her time in India she travelled frequently and extensively.

In August 1835 she went to Fatighar where she met – and became friends with – the Baiza Bai, ex-Queen of Gwalior. She returned to Allahabad in October. By July 1836 once again she was finding life 'weary and heavy … one's mind and body feel equally enervated'.[20] In September 1836 she was invited to accompany Sir Henry Fane's party and to act as interpreter for the Baiza Bai in Benares, then carried on to Calcutta and did not return to Allahabad until March 1837. By August 1837 she was bored again ('nothing to relate in the monotony of an Indian life at home … I … must go to the hills to recruit my weary frame') and in September she started preparing for a march 'up the country', leaving in December 1837.[21] Lord Auckland and his sisters, Emily and Fanny Eden, were en route up country too, stopping in Allahabad in early December. Fanny was introduced to the sisters, then became something of a camp follower, shadowing the Auckland camp wherever it went on its leisurely progress, her presence irritating the Edens and prompting a satirical account by (the very thin) Fanny Eden in one of her letters home:

> How odd of me not to have told you that the very first person I saw at the very first ball at Meerut was Mrs Parkes. How she got there nobody knows and nobody will ever know. The day after we got here they got up a morning review for us – blew up mines and took a fort, and not only a fort but Mrs Parkes, for as the smoke blew off she was discovered riding. If she were not so fat I should say she was something supernatural. My spirit is broke about her. I dare say we shall find her settled in our home at Simla and shall not have strength to turn her out.[22]

Fanny Eden's comments may have been underpinned by a certain amount of envy of her namesake's apparent freedom from the claustrophobic demands that were her lot as the Governor General's sister as well as the frustrations of the provincialism of the British in India with whom she was obliged to socialize.[23] Her sister Emily Eden's sharp comment that up-country Europeans had had their civilized manners 'jungled out of them', echoed Fanny's opinions.[24] Clearly Fanny Parkes was perceived to have gone beyond the bounds of respectability. As David Arnold argues, the jungle, with its dangerous wild animals and bandits, symbolized the ruination of India in many contemporary travel writers' accounts.[25] Fanny Parkes was, by association, herself ruined.

In September 1838, while Fanny was travelling in the Himalayan foothills, she received word from Charles that her father had died the previous May.[26] She returned to Allahabad immediately and sailed by the next available ship from Calcutta, arriving in England in May 1839. England, to Fanny, 'looked so wretchedly mean, especially the houses', while Fanny, to her mother – who had not seen her daughter for 17 years – had changed completely: 'My child, I should never have known you, – you look so anxious, so careworn.'[27] Another sign of how different England was from India – and how much India had changed Fanny – was revealed to her when she visited a horticultural show in Plymouth: 'I went to the place alone, and the people expressed their surprise at my having done so – how absurd! as if I were to be a prisoner unless some lady should accompany me – wah! wah! I shall never be tamed, I trust, to the ideas of propriety of civilized Lady *Log*.'[28] It is ironic that it was precisely by travelling to India, where Britons believed women to enjoy few rights, that Fanny was to enjoy exceptional freedom of movement.

Her mother died in December 1841 and Fanny remained in Europe until early 1843 when she heard that Charles was ill in Cape Town and went to look after him; they had been apart for four years. They returned to India, and finally to Allahabad, in December 1844. As Charles' health did not improve, he applied to go to England on furlough and they left India nine months later, in September 1845. They would never return. Charles did not recover from the illness that brought him back to England. He died in 1854 while Fanny lived on for another 20 years. She died, aged 81, in 1875 of 'shingles and exhaustion' at her home in Cornwall Terrace, Regent's Park.[29] She was buried in Kensal Green cemetery where she shares a grave with her husband (see Figure 6.2).[30]

Wanderings of a Pilgrim in Search of the Picturesque

Fanny and Charles settled first in St Leonards-on-Sea in Sussex on their return from India in 1846. In the 1820s, James Burton had developed the town into a seaside resort and it seems that Fanny and Charles were living in a seaside villa.[31] Fanny constructed her account of her travels

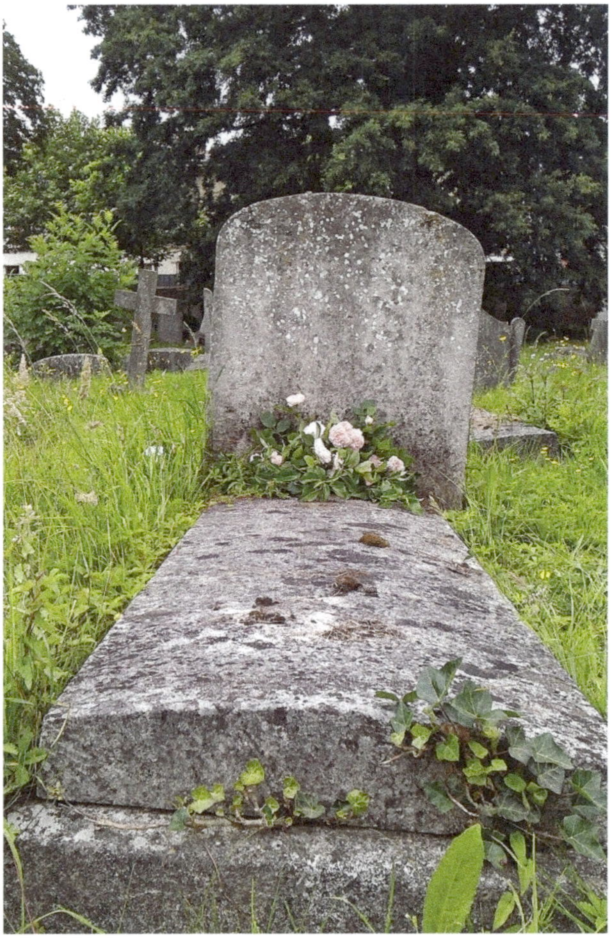

Figure 6.2 Fanny and Charles Parkes' grave, The General Cemetery of All Souls, Kensal Green. Image courtesy of Joanna Goldsworthy.

in India by using her journals and the long letters she had written to her mother, finishing her tale with a revealing 'Farewell':

> And now the pilgrim resigns her staff and plucks the scallop-shell from her hat, – her wanderings are ended – she has quitted the East, perhaps for ever: – surrounded… by the curiosities, the monsters, and the idols that accompanied her from India… the pleasure she derives from her sketches, and the sad sea waves, her constant companions, form for her a life independent of *her own* life.[32]

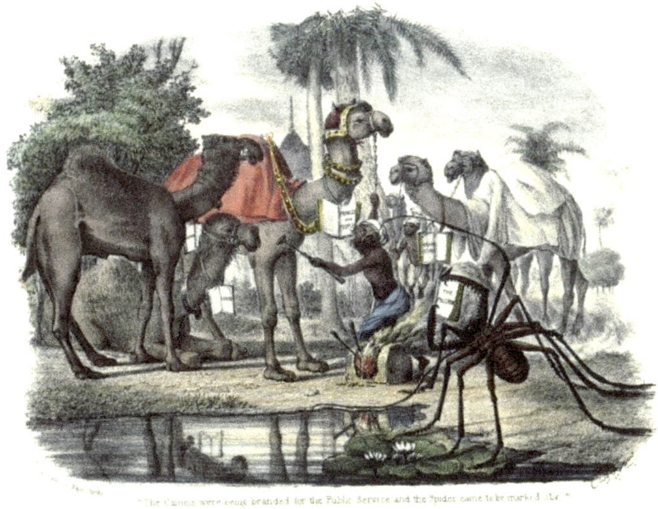

Figure 6.3 *Wanderings*, vol. 1, digital, p.20: *"The Camels were being branded for the Public Service and the Spider came to be marked also". Fanny represents herself as a large spider holding a book titled* The Pilgrim*; books hanging from three camels' necks are titled* Luard, Princes and People *and, interestingly,* Afghanistan. © The British Library Board, 1947. B 170 vol. 1 p. 20.

Fanny had 'collected an empire' for herself that liberated her from the constraints of life in the metropole and through the exotic objects she had acquired she gained an independence – 'a life independent of her own life' – that opened a new world for her.[33] Her detailed and valuable knowledge of another culture and her understanding of its social world – particularly that of the zenana, a world closed to men – gave her status in a metropolitan, masculine society. Her collection, initially a jumble of 'the curiosities, the monsters, and the idols' as she described it, had been acquired haphazardly, as the fancy took her. It now assumed an importance as a discrete entity, allowing those British men and women who saw it to visualize their empire.[34]

Wanderings of a Pilgrim was published in a handsome two-volume edition in 1850, priced £2 12s 6d and illustrated throughout with Fanny's own sketches and paintings (see Figure 6.3). Many of the contemporary reviews of the book were generous, indeed waxed ecstatic: 'Fresh, intelligent, and minutely interesting' (*The Court Journal*)[35]; 'This … is a very splendid, very attractive work' (*The Asiatic and Colonial Quarterly Journal*);[36] 'The tone of bold and careless frankness in which this interesting and instructive work is written, is singularly attractive' (*The English Review*)[37] and finally, '... one of the most beautiful monuments of genius, taste, feeling ... without parade, ostentation, or intrusive aims at vulgar popularity ... ' (*Blackwood's Lady's Magazine*).[38] Others, however, were violently critical: 'The flippancy and levity ... with which she refers to her own faith, savour more of the cock-pit than the boudoir...in future editions...we trust to see every thing undeniable indecent or profane carefully expunged from the work' (*Calcutta Review*).[39] The extreme reactions to Fanny Parkes' 'authentic' depiction of life in the colonies expressed in these reviews is interesting and point to a fracture in attitude by writers in two very different locations, towards what was acceptable in the metropole and in an outpost of Empire.

Just as critics in the 1850s proved both generously receptive and unstintingly appalled by Parkes' writings, her work today continues to attract a range of responses. Often understood as deeply problematic by historians and literary scholars for its homogenizing depictions of colonial subjects, *Wanderings of a Pilgrim in Search of the Picturesque* continues to fuel debate.[40] Nevertheless, focusing on Fanny Parkes as an avid collector of Indian material culture allows us to see how men and women within the Company's ambit often engaged with multiple aspects of Indian society, seeking out meaningful ways of communicating with indigenous peoples and entering with enthusiasm into the Indian Ocean World. While created for public audiences, her writings and collection also served private purposes. The objects she purchased and returned with served to act as 'traces of authentic experience', incorporating memories of a more adventurous and independent life in India, unimaginable had she stayed in England.[41] Fanny shared her love for India with others through the journals and letters, which were published as *Wanderings of a Pilgrim*; she painted and drew vivid scenes, which were reproduced in her book; and she created a visual journey for the public with her 'Grand Moving Diorama of Hindostan'. In publishing her writings and making them available to a wider audience and in creating exhibitions from her writings and collection, Parkes self-consciously sought to use her experiences to greater effect. They provided a space in which her experiences of India and the stories she wished to tell of them could shape a broader conception of who she was and what she had achieved.

The 'Grand Moving Diorama of Hindostan'

In 1851, the year of The Great Exhibition of the Works of Industry of All Nations, Fanny instigated and funded the construction of a 'Grand

Moving Diorama of Hindostan', which was staged at the Asiatic Gallery in the Baker Street Bazaar.[42] India, Britain's 'jewel in the crown', featured centre-stage at the Great Exhibition, the EIC itself having been one of the most enthusiastic supporters of the enterprise from its inception. The Company's Directors saw the Exhibition as an opportunity to astonish visitors with exquisitely crafted riches from Britain's Eastern Empire.[43] They also saw it as a way of promoting a new self-image through the display of objects from the subcontinent.[44] The Exhibition constituted an important means of recreating India as spectacle and justifying further imperial endeavours on the subcontinent.

In contrast, the Grand Moving Diorama of Hindostan offered not objects but vistas, visual evocations of the landscapes of India, specifically those seen from India's most sacred river, the Ganges. As such, it provided an important source of context to the Great Exhibition's display of astonishing objects made in India. In fact, the description that survives makes it clear that Fanny's diorama was no run-of-the-mill affair and was modelled on the moving dioramas invented by Daguerre. Panoramas and dioramas were a popular attraction in the first half of the nineteenth century. While panoramas were essentially very large, realistic, paintings of a scene, dioramas, which also used painted backdrops, introduced a three-dimensional element to the viewing experience.

Daguerre's diorama, first shown in Paris in 1822, was brought to London in 1823 and erected in a special building constructed in Regent's Park at a cost of £10,000.[45] The Daguerre diorama depended on clever lighting effects and a revolving auditorium that moved the sizeable audience (the Regent's Park diorama accommodated 200 people; the original diorama in Paris could hold an audience of 350) from one scene to another. The enormous painted scenes (22 metres wide by 14 metres high), ingeniously lit with a system of screens and shutters and worked with pulleys and counterweights, were so convincing that few in the audience thought they were looking at a painting. Some dioramas had sound effects and songs, some a piano accompaniment, but the strongest impression was that of brilliant illusion caused by the subtly changing lighting.[46] Much was made of the fact that this was a form of armchair travel, the *Journal de Paris* of 22 July 1822 urging Parisians 'who like pleasure without fatigue to make the journey to Switzerland and to England without leaving the capital'.[47]

The success of Daguerre's diorama led to a mass of imitators and variations on the original idea (amongst them inventions with names such as Hydrorama and Uranorama[48]), but even as late as 1851 a

London guide book was still of the opinion that the original diorama was 'decidedly superior, both to the Panorama and the Cosmorana, in the fidelity with which the objects are depicted, and in the completeness of the illusion … and it is difficult for the spectator to persuade himself that he is only contemplating a work of art'.[49] Constructed in 1851, Fanny's 'Grand Moving Diorama' came in on the tail end of the craze caused by Daguerre, but was nevertheless a success, in part due to astute marketing and publicity by Fanny and her collaborators. In a move that would endear her to philanthropic societies and educational reformers, *Blackwood's Lady's Magazine* reported that 'In the spirit of true liberality, Mrs. Parkes admits daily fifty or sixty children (gratis) from the National and Parochial schools of London; for the enlightenment of these young students in religion and useful learning'.[50] This largesse by Fanny may account for the florid prose of the same magazine's appreciation of Fanny's diorama:

> The DIORAMA OF HINDOSTAN (where its immortalised originator is herself a frequent visitor), constructed in the splendid galleries recently annexed, at her own proper cost, to the Baker Street Bazaar, is confessedly the most extraordinary exhibition that has appeared in the present century... The painting is in the highest finish of body colour, realising the most exquisite atmospherical effects, and frequently affecting the senses by its sublime and almost incomprehensible truthfulness... In the course of less than two delightful hours, the spectator traces the river Ganges from Fort William, Calcutta, through Barrackpore, Benares, Mirzapur, Allahabad, and Hurdwar, to its source in the Himalaya mountains... There, at length... the mystical fount is seen to flow; the spirit of solitude fills the dread eminence, and a mysterious, unaccountable dread steals over the mind of the audience, in the presence of night descending on a scene, whose awful features may best be conceived from their effect on the nerves, as the curtain terminates the exhibition, and the breathless silence of intense and gazing admiration.... The spectacle, now within reach of even the humbler classes, is, in fact, a boon to our population... we may now set foot on the banks of the Hooghly... through the instrumentality of one single, high-born, highly-gifted, persevering, and amiable woman, whose labours, *'non sibi sed aliis,'* have provided one of the more purely intellectual and heart-touching gratifications ever yet offered for the enlightenment, the entertainment, and, we might add, the honour of her nation.[51]

The 'Grand Moving Diorama of Hindostan' was sufficiently popular for it to be exhibited in Hull in 1853, although the transport of the equipment from London to Hull would have been a challenging exercise. If able to catch the Diorama before its move north, London visitors would have enjoyed the additional attraction of being 'allowed to inspect THE MUSEUM' – in other words, Fanny's cabinet of curiosities.[52]

The cabinet of curiosities

The cabinet of curiosities first appeared in continental Europe in the mid-sixteenth century, largely collected by the nobility. Frances Bacon wrote that they were 'in a small compass, a model of universal nature made private'.[53] They were essentially collections of artefacts, of anything that took the collector's fancy, in what Tony Bennett has described as the 'jumbled incongruity' that was in time supplanted and surpassed by the museum.[54] In Germany they were called *wunderkammer*, in Italy *stanzino*, and there were collections in Russia. Britain was 'notably absent' from early lists of universal cabinets, although the royal gardeners, father and son John and John Tradescant, gathered together a collection of objects in the first half of the seventeenth century that was to become the Ashmolean Museum in Oxford.[55] The first cabinets were literally that – a cabinet, in which small objects could be displayed. Later, as collections grew, the display space was a specially designed room, until a collection became so big that it was impossible to show it in a single space. Sir Hans Sloane (1660–1753), for instance, collected over 100,000 objects, which were to eventually form the basis of the British Museum collection.[56]

Tony Bennett extends Michel Foucault's exploration of power and knowledge relations seen in the spaces of the asylum, the clinic and the prison to include the cabinets of curiosity that were essentially under private ownership and had restricted access to the privileged few. With public displays such as that of the Great Exhibition of 1851, collections of objects were opened up to the public and created spaces in which people were increasingly taught how to act and be, creating self-regulating citizens in their wake.[57] Similarly, Fanny's own 'Cabinet of Curiosities' (or her 'Museum' as she now termed it) was made available to visitors to the Grand Moving Diorama of Hindostan and seen by many. It thereby became part of a metropolitan process of education in empire and imperial culture, providing a space in which Britons living far from imperial dominions learned to look and engage with others through imperial eyes.

In writing about her collecting practices in *Wanderings of a Pilgrim*, Fanny Parks's approach to collecting curiosities can be seen as distinctly unsystematic and driven more by an eclectic inquisitiveness, an enthusiastic grasping of the moment, than by the wish to build a well-organized group of objects illustrating defined aspects of Indian culture. In marking out her collecting practices as eclectic and curious, Fanny connected them to earlier (often male) traditions. Gavin Lucas has noted that, 'One of the most striking aspects of much early collecting is the lack of distinction among objects; curiosities formed a generic group, where items such as fossils, butterflies, tribal weapons, and antiquities might all jostle side by side in a collector's cabinet' but adds that, 'In a sense, the "fieldwork", if one can use the term, of early modern collectors largely involved visiting other collections and dealers, rather than travelling to the source of such curiosities', which was not true of Fanny who was usually to be found 'travelling to the source'.[58]

These souvenirs of her time in India became more important to Fanny on her return to England. They represented a lived experience and could be organized for her private satisfaction or public view. Susan Stewart, in exploring the meaning of the souvenir, points to the way in which it 'speaks to a context of origin through a language of longing … it is not an object arising out of need or use value; [but] … out of the necessarily insatiable demands of nostalgia'.[59] Fanny's nostalgic needs were met not only by her curiosities, but by her writing about them, by sharing her longing through the medium of her published journals, and reliving the events through her 'Grand Moving Diorama of Hindostan'. In addition, these actions gave her agency in a society where once she would have been largely invisible, enabling her to construct a new identity for herself from the experiences of a life lived to the full in India, notwithstanding her exclusion (as a woman) from formal Company employment.

Fanny Parkes appears to have begun collecting her curiosities in 1830, eight years after her arrival in India. She and Charles were by then living in the mofussil, in Cawnpore, a large station 'on a bleak, dreary, sandy, dusty, treeless plain, cut into ravines by torrents of rain' and unbearably hot.[60] The first item she acquired was a lathi, a large, heavy weapon made from bamboo and banded with iron, which had been confiscated from a man who had killed two others with it. Fanny reported that she took it 'as a curiosity', an impulse that seems to have fuelled many of her moves when acquiring objects.[61] Not long afterwards, in October 1830, she was given a set of Thugs' dice by the acting magistrate in Cawnpore, the Thugs having been arrested and executed for the murder of 35 travellers.[62] Her last purchase, bought in Cape Town in 1845 when she and Charles were on their way back to England, having left India for good, was a 'kaross [cloak] of eighteen heads' for which she paid four pounds. 'It is very large and handsome,' Fanny wrote, adding that: 'With the exception of the kaross the Kafir is entirely unincumbered with clothing.'[63]

Most of her acquisitions, however, were made in Allahabad between the years 1831 and 1845. She largely purchased these wares at the great fair (now called the Kumbh Mela, although Fanny's term for it is Bura Mela) held annually on the banks of the Ganges at its confluence with the Jumna, being the site of enthusiastic commercial activity as well as intense religious worship. This location, which even today is to Hindus one of the most sacred sites of their most sacred river, reaches a peak of religious significance every 12 years and is celebrated with a Maha Kumbh Mela which millions of pilgrims attend.[64]

On 2 February 1832 Fanny wrote that she 'went to the Bura Mela, the great annual fair on the sands of the Ganges, and purchased bows and arrows, some curious Indian ornaments, and a few fine pearls'.[65] But her ethnographic interest lay more broadly than curious objects, writing in the same paragraph about one of the *fakirs* (holy men) at the fair:

> On the sands were a number of devotees, of whom the most holy person had made a vow, that for fourteen years he would spend every night up to his neck in the Ganges; nine years he has kept his vow: at sunset he enters the river, is taken out at sunrise, rubbed into warmth, and placed by a fire; he... is apparently about thirty years of age, very fat and jovial, and does not appear to suffer in the slightest degree from his penance.[66]

One year later, in January 1833, Fanny visited the fair once again. In *Wanderings*, she noted that the area had been filled with commercial and sacred booths, and that it had attracted 'merchants from all parts of India'. At the booths 'Very good diamonds, pearls, coral, shawls, cloth, woollens, China, furs, &c., are to be purchased.'[67] She also chose to relate an amusing story against herself, of how she bought a 'remarkably fine' pink coral necklace at this fair; and how some years later a friend of hers, a Mahratta lady, seeing her wearing the beads, exclaimed: 'I am astonished a mem sahiba should wear coral; we only decorate our horses with it.' Fanny immediately gave her necklace to her horse.[68]

The fair took place over a period of two months, offering many opportunities for finding curiosities. Amongst other things, she bought 'a Persian writing-case, and a book beautifully illuminated, and written in Persian and Arabic: the Moguls beguile me of my rupees' as well as two musical instruments and other 'curious things; Hindoo ornaments, idols, china', she reflected.[69] It was at this fair that Fanny bought her most splendid and beloved curiosity, a huge white marble statue of Guneshu weighing some three hundredweight, painted and gilded. Growing wise to the ways of the merchants, she 'sent a Rajput to the owner, and, after much delay and bargaining, became the possessor. ... The man had scruples with regard to allowing me to purchase the idol, but sold it willingly to the Rajput.'[70] Fanny related that (see Figure 6.1) 'Although a *pukka Hindu*, Ganesh has crossed the *Kala Pani* or Black Waters, as they call the ocean, and has accompanied me to England. There he sits before me in all his Hindu state and peculiar style of beauty – my inspiration – my penates.'[71]

Fanny clearly gained a reputation for collecting curiosities and frequently described objects she had been given. In May 1832 she wrote that a friend gave her 'a pair of the most magnificent cow-tails, of the yak or cow of Thibet', adding that 'They are great curiosities, and shall go with my collection to England'.[72] These cow-tails feature in the frontispiece illustration to *Wanderings of a Pilgrim*, at its centre the huge marble Ganesh, and featuring the rarest and most interesting items from her museum – from the white marble statue of Ram to the 'brazen image of Gunga' represented by a woman sitting on an alligator (see Figure 6.1). This idol was, according to Fanny, rare and valuable. 'Victory to Gunga-jee!'[73]

Another 'great curiosity' sent to her by a friend was 'a common dark brown-red shawl, worn by low caste women at Hissar. It is worked all over in large flowers, in orange silk; the centre of the flower contains a circular bit of looking-glass about an inch and a half in diameter. ... The appearance of the dress as the light falls on the looking-glass is most strange and odd ... in what an extraordinary manner the light must be caught on all those reflecting circles of glass!'[74] Including this 'low caste' item in her collection allowed Fanny to show that her interest in textiles extended beyond luxury items, demonstrating her wide-ranging interest in Indian culture. One can only imagine how astonished she would have been to see skirts of this mirrored material being worn by young European women in the 1960s.

In March 1832 the Parkes' close friend Colonel Gardner stayed with the couple in Allahabad, much to their delight. While there, he taught them how to use an Indian bow and arrow. Fanny described how 'Archery, as practised in India, is very different from that in England'. Fanny tells us, 'The arm is raised over the head, and the bow drawn in that manner: native bowmen throw up the elbow and depress the right hand in a most extraordinary style'. While learning of the skills of archery, Fanny was also the recipient of a bow. She described how, 'A very fine bow has been given to me, which was one of the presents made by Runjeet Singh to Lord Wm. Bentinck ... when strung, it resembles the outline of a well-formed upper lip, Cupid's bow.' Fanny added that she 'could not resist going continually into the verandah, to take a shot at the targets, in spite of the heat.'[75] The bow was undoubtedly one of the curiosities brought back to England, the story of its origins adding lustre to the gift. Ownership of the bow, the narrative discourse of its acquisition, and the nostalgic memories it evoked, were more important to her than the object itself.[76]

Fanny's reputation as a collector brought visitors to her door, one being a German-Jewish convert to Christianity, Mr Wolff, who was keen to see her collection of Hindu idols.[77] Fanny had by this time been in India for 11 years and her knowledge of Hindu culture, the language and the rituals, had increased enormously since her arrival in the country. She would no longer feel, as she had earlier in her residence in Calcutta, that she was 'much disgusted' by rituals such as the Churuk Pooja in which men swung from hooks pierced through their skin – even if she admitted that she was also 'greatly interested' by the sight (see Figure 6.4).[78]

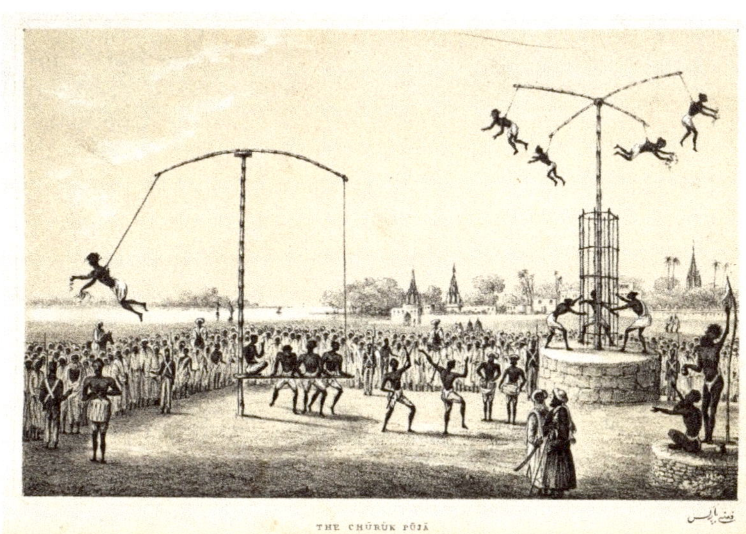

Figure 6.4 *Wanderings,* vol. 1, digital edition p.84: *The Churuk Puja, or Hook Swinging.* © The British Library Board, 1947. B 170 vol. 1 p. 84.

Her energetic pursuit of information had led her to be able to fashion herself as an expert – albeit an undisciplined (and thus perhaps a more 'authentic') one – in anything that took her interest. Her perceived expertise would give her cultural leverage when she returned to the metropole, and is an example of one of the ways in which British women came to benefit from empire.

One of the sculptures given to the India Museum on Fanny's death was a piece of white stone on which a figure had been carved.[79] Fanny's account of the circumstances in which she acquired it is very typical of her all-embracing enthusiasm. In March 1844 she and Charles were on their way back to India from Cape Town where Charles had been recuperating from an unspecified illness. The ship had dropped anchor off Pooree (now Puri) and Fanny had, as always, grasped the opportunity to go ashore.

> A carved stone was presented to me, brought from the ruins of a city of great extent, about forty miles from Pooree; its name has escaped my memory, but it appeared from the account I received to be full of curiosities; few persons, however, had ventured to visit the ruined city, deterred by the probability of taking a fever, in consequence of the malaria produced by the thick jangal by which it is surrounded. The stone is white, and upon it is carved the figure of some remarkable personage, above which is an emblem of Mahadēo.[80]

She added, demonstrating the jackdaw tendencies in her collecting, that 'A very fine tiger's skin was also added to my collection. I carried off my prizes with great delight, and they now adorn my museum.'[81] It was this museum of curious objects that visitors entered after viewing the diorama.

The palimpsest of all these objects is clear, and even though their whereabouts today is unknown, Fanny's brilliantly evoked images bring them vividly to the mind's eye. But it is the curiosities that have a known resting place in today's metropole, albeit on the confined shelves of a museum's basement, that are freighted with particular meaning. These are the two pieces of carved black stone that were presented to the India Museum on Fanny's death and which are now in the British Museum collection (see Figure 6.5).

Fanny's description of these objects lacks hard information, but her account of how she acquired them and her comments on the place, the people, and the culture in which she found them are especially revealing about the ways in which colonial material culture mediated relations between the colonizer and the colonized. Fanny and Charles were taking

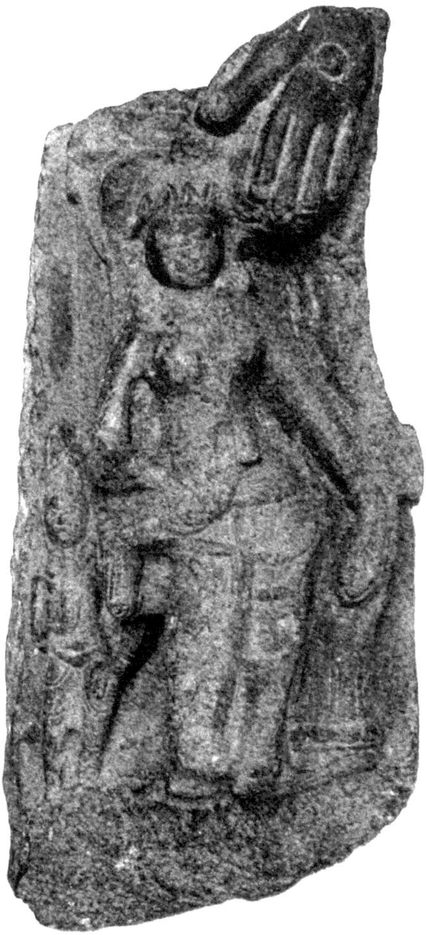

Figure 6.5 Lower sections of an image-frame of Visnu in two parts showing attendant figures. Carved in dark grey sandstone. Twelfth century. 1880.35.39.a-b. © Trustees of the British Museum.

the slow boat upriver to Allahabad from Calcutta in November 1844 rather than travelling the more rigorous overland dak route. The journey gave them ample opportunity for exploration. Fanny wrote (see also Figure 6.6 and 6.7):

> Lugaoed at Barragh, a small village on the right bank: climbed the cliff in the evening; a fisherman who resided there showed me two sati mounds on the top of it, – the one built of stone sacred to a

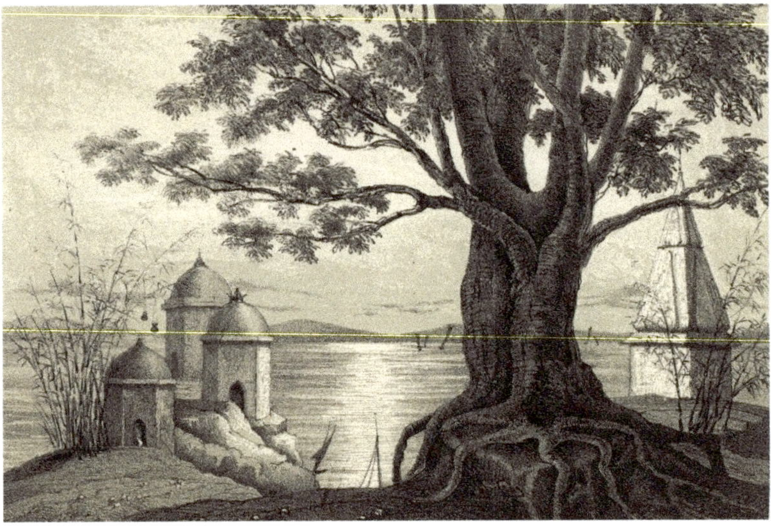

Figure 6.6 *Wanderings* vol. 2, digital edition p.472: *'Three Satis and a Mandap near Ghazipur'.* © The British Library Board, 1947. B. 170 vol. 2 p. 472.

Brahmān, the other of mud in honour of a Kyiatt. A *kalsā* is the ornament on top of a dome; there were two of stone, without any points on the satī mound of the Brahmān; and two of mud, decorated with points, and one small image, on that of the Kyiatt.

I gave a small present to the people, and took away one of the kalsās of mud as a curiosity: a number of broken idols in black stone had been dug up, and placed on the satī mound of the Brahmān, – I was anxious to have two of them, and determined to ask the fisherman to give them to me. The old man told me with great pride that one of his family had been a satī, and that the Brahmāns complained greatly they were not allowed to burn the widows, as such disconsolate damsels were ready and willing to be grilled.....

The Brahmānī ducks are calling to one another from the opposite banks of the river... The wind is down, there is a soft and brilliant moonlight, – the weather is really charming, and the moonlight nights delicious; from the high bank by the satīs one can see the stream of the Ganges below, glittering in its beams....

Ten P.M.; I have just returned from the satī mound, accompanied by the old fisherman, who brought with him two of the idols of black stone from the Brahmān's mound... the old man gave them to me the moment I asked for them; I gave him a present afterwards, therefore he did not sell his gods; but he requested to be allowed to bring them to the boats during the darkness of the night. He and his family are now the sole inhabitants of a little hamlet of five houses... his four brothers... are dead, and their houses, which are in ruins, are close to the mounds; the old man lives in the centre, with one young son and two daughters, and keeps his dwelling of mud in comfortable condition. They tell me fowls and *chakor* (the red-legged partridge) are abundant there; I was unable to procure the latter.[82]

Fanny's actions and her assumption that it was acceptable to buy objects of religious significance from this native subject echo the collecting practices of the time. But what she was conveying here in this intimate

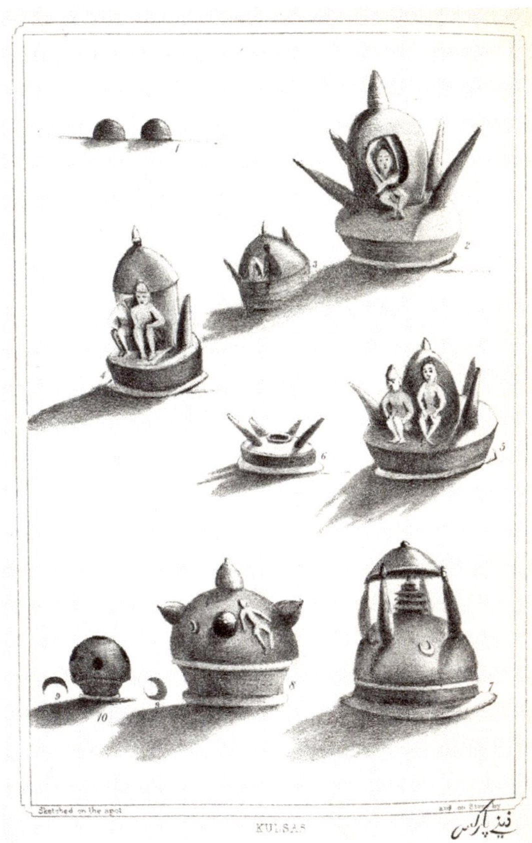

Figure 6.7 *Wanderings* vol. 2, digital edition p.476: *'Kulsas'.* © The British Library Board, 1947. B. 170 vol. 2 p. 476.

encounter was the assertion of 'knowing first-hand' the country and culture that she was about to leave.[83] The 'authenticity' of this experience rings true, even if it is underpinned by a sense of patronage and dominance, displaying as it does the supposed superiority of the colonial ruler.

Conclusion

Ten months later, in September 1845, Fanny and Charles left India forever. She was 51 years old and in good health. Charles, four years younger and unwell, would die in 1854 of kidney disease. During the eight years before his death, Fanny arranged the publication in 1850 of her account of her life in India, based on her journals and letters to her mother and lavishly illustrated with her own drawings and paintings; in 1851 she organized a display at considerable expense to herself, the 'Grand Moving Diorama of Hindostan'; and exhibited her 'Cabinet of Curiosities'. Fanny's impulse to bring her memories of India and the objects she collected there to the attention of the public demonstrates not only her urge to forge a new persona for herself shaped by her life in India, as Jasanoff would suggest, but also satisfied what Susan Stewart describes as the 'insatiable demands of nostalgia'.[84] Her experiences and her accumulated knowledge, shared with the British public, gave her authority and status in a largely masculine area of activity. Her access to the intimate world of the exclusively female harem of high-caste Indian women and her descriptions of this offered a rare insight into an exotic world and enhanced the picture of the colonized for a fascinated metropolitan public. She turned what she had gained in India – independence, knowledge, experience – into a new life for herself in the metropole. Her expertise brought her status and legitimacy in this imperial metropolitan world.

Her engagement with India may have been limited and partial in its investigations, her 'travelling gaze' to some extent blinkered by a sense of imperial entitlement and prejudice, the arrangement of objects in her Cabinet of Curiosities lacking coherence and organization, the picture she drew revealing more about colonial beliefs and behaviour than those of the subject race. But it is the energy and enthusiasm fuelling her project that now brings colonial British India in all its failings and insecurities vividly to life.

7
Refashioning house, home and family

Montreal Park, Kent and Touch House, Stirlingshire

Margot Finn and Kate Smith

This chapter explores the collaborative processes used by East India Company (EIC) families to retain and refashion stately homes in Britain, creating country houses that befitted the new wealth, status and power their inhabitants had accrued through imperial service in Asia. Since the Victorian period, much imperial history-writing has highlighted the agency of heroic (or deeply flawed) individual men, ensuring that figures such as Robert Clive (1725–74), Warren Hastings (1732–1818), Charles Cornwallis (1738–1805) and Arthur Wellesley (1769–1852), for example, loom large in narratives of Company politics and statecraft.[1] More recently, attention to the Indian and British networks of family and friends that not only sustained these powerful men on the subcontinent but also promoted and protected their political interests in the metropole has illuminated the inherently collaborative character of imperial endeavour, underlining the extent to which power and wealth creation in Company circles demanded the exploitation of social ties, kinship relations and patronage obligations.[2] Shifting the focus from individual imperialists to empire families and their associates, this vantage point replaces historians' earlier emphasis on material culture as a prime site of self-fashioning with new recognition of the pivotal roles played by material processes in establishing, maintaining and expressing collective social identities.[3] By studying families' collaborative efforts to refashion existing country seats as imperial homes with the proceeds of their Indian service, this chapter argues, we can better understand not only the entangled histories of Company politics and the country house but also the salient part played by kinship groups (including elite women denied official employment in the Company by their sex) in constructing a materially-embodied imperial culture at home in Britain.[4]

As Mark Girouard reminds us in the opening pages of *Life in the English Country House,* from an early date British stately homes 'were power houses', acting as markers of status and wealth.[5] Historians have conventionally characterized the purchase, building and renovation of country houses by returned EIC men as assertions of individual wealth and status and a means through which these men integrated themselves into the structures of power constituted by the existing elite. Building on James Holzman's earlier work, Tillman Nechtman argues that by purchasing an estate or a parliamentary seat, EIC 'nabobs' – the elite Company officials who accrued vast fortunes in India – sought to domesticate wealth and power gained on the subcontinent by converting them into material and institutional forms recognized and valued in Britain.[6] This chapter expands upon this received interpretation by examining imperial domestication as a collaborative process that entailed complex negotiations both within the family circle and between family and friends. The refashioning of Touch House, Stirlingshire and Montreal Park, Kent illuminates both the role of empire in shaping Britain's iconic 'power houses' and the function of collaborative family strategies – including strategizing by and on behalf of women – in country house material culture.

Alan Mackley and Richard Wilson's research has shown that British men embarked on house building not only to demonstrate their status and wealth, but also to accrue benefits manifest in the process of building itself. Through their decisions and close management of domestic construction or refurbishment, propertied men displayed taste and discernment, thereby consolidating their social and political position.[7] Judith Lewis has augmented and challenged this reading of masculine self-fashioning by demonstrating that women were often actively involved in managing and directing elite house building projects: Sarah, Duchess of Marlborough (1660–1744), for example, took direct control of the building project at Blenheim when her husband, the Duke, suffered a stroke in 1716. Seizing the initiative, Sarah promptly fired Sir John Vanbrugh (1664–1726) and hired the cabinetmaker James Moore (c.1670–1726) in the hope of completing the project before the Duke died.[8] In this instance, and in Lewis's other examples, although women were consulted over house building projects embarked on by husbands, they became most directly involved as widows rather than wives. The refashioning of the country seats discussed in this chapter reveals additional levels of female participation in the construction of country power houses. Building on Lewis's insights, we demonstrate how prominently women often figured (whether as active agents or as intended recipients) in collaborative building projects designed to accommodate not only heroic individuals but also broader family circles over the generations.

As the examples of the Seton of Touch siblings and in-laws and the Amherst family of Montreal Park both demonstrate, design decisions for Company homes were often made collaboratively. House building was an endeavour shared across a broad network of family and friends, a negotiated process that invoked, mobilized, strengthened and taxed ties of affection and kinship. Fashioning and refashioning country houses allowed imperial families as a whole to signal their new wealth and status and to integrate imperial fortunes into established systems of culture and politics. These processes were also instrumental in allowing families whose imperial lives entailed extended periods of separation across great distances to reintegrate and to reconstruct shared familial identities. Architectural plans, journals, and private correspondence reveal the country house as a prime site of collective, collaborative identities in the far-flung imperial families whose administrative and military labour sustained the Company's power on the Indian subcontinent.

Touch House, empire and identity

Touch House, located three miles to the west of Stirling, forms the architectural centrepiece of a country estate now comprising 3,750 acres of cultivated fields, parkland and forest. A corporate and commercial hub contained within a graceful Georgian exterior and providing office facilities, event venues and historic film locations, this stately home was the seat of the first lairds of Touch, the Frasers. Passing in the fifteenth century to the Seton family, Touch House was extended by successive generations. Originally fortified and dominated by the tower that marked its strategic function on the route that served as the gateway from Glasgow to the Highlands, Touch gradually gained the hallmarks of a genteel British country residence: a dining room, drawing room, library and private bedrooms marked its early modern transition from a medieval military stronghold to a site of social and political power securely located within the Scottish state.[9] Hereditary Armour Bearers of the Scottish kings, the Setons retained fierce loyalties to the Stuart monarchy. James Seton of Touch (d. 1742) rejected William of Orange's elevation to sovereignty in the Glorious Revolution, and his sons Archibald and George were imprisoned in 1708 for supporting the Old Pretender. James's sister Elizabeth (d. 1775) succeeded him in 1742; she continued the family's tradition of Jacobite activism by entertaining Prince Charles Edward (the Young Pretender) at Touch on 13 September 1745, during the Rebellion. The Prince gifted her a ring, a quaich (drinking cup) and miniature portrait by way of thanks for her hospitality. The Setons thereby acquired Jacobite memorabilia treasured by their descendants for generations: together with the sheets and counterpane from the Prince's bed, the relics were preserved at Touch until 1928.[10]

The careful preservation of treasured Stuart artefacts and the canny use of domestic space to conceal or display Jacobite objects were key strategies in the political armoury of landed eighteenth-century Stuart sympathizers.[11] Stuart allegiance, however, had significant consequences for the maintenance of Highland lairds' landed estates, curtailing their access to government appointments in an agrarian context in which profits increasingly rested on costly improvements.[12] At Touch, Hugh Seton's grandiose schemes for agrarian improvement and domestic refurbishment after the '45, increasingly compromised not only the security of their treasured Jacobite memorabilia but (more fundamentally) the Setons' continued ownership of their family seat. Married to Elizabeth a few weeks after she had entertained the Young Pretender, the Jacobite Hugh Seton (born Hugh Smith) had taken the family name, and promptly entered into the two-fold project of estate improvement and 'power house' building at Touch.[13] Expensive drainage systems created new acres of fertile arable from bog-land on the estate; Touch House itself was in the hands of the builders from 1757 to 1770, acquiring an elegant 'Georgian' façade and plasterwork in the drawing room, dining room and music room undertaken by the celebrated Thomas Clayton (b. c.1710).[14] Hugh Seton however had little time to enjoy his new home. Although his improvements had reputedly increased the rents at Touch from £500 to £2,000 per annum, his debts dwarfed the estate's income. Forced to meet his creditors in 1785, he sold property in Argyleshire, his family's wine business and his own life interest in the estate, but debts of £31,000 nonetheless remained.[15] His finances exhausted, he reportedly suffered imprisonment for debt before fleeing in disguise from Dover to the Middle East and ultimately India.[16]

Denied access to official patronage and employment in Britain by the representatives of the Hanoverian state, Jacobite landowners determined to maintain their family homes after the '45 turned increasingly to imperial ventures.[17] Hugh and Elizabeth's eldest surviving son, Archibald Seton (1758–1818), like many an impecunious Highlander before and after him, entered the service of the EIC in an effort to save the family home and support his siblings. Appointed to the Company civil service in 1779, he arrived at Madras in 1781 and thereafter rose through a succession of junior offices to become Resident of Delhi in 1806, Governor of Prince of Wales Island (Penang) in 1811 and member of the Bengal Supreme Council in 1812.[18]

Although the surviving Seton family correspondence is fragmentary, the letters that remain amply illustrate the role Touch House played in driving two generations of Seton men to the subcontinent. Hugh Seton's letters to Archibald chronicle an itinerant life of cadging from friends based at foreign embassies, occasional commercial interloping and episodic military service, all retold to his son in histrionic tones that combined complaint, lament and perpetual longing for his Scottish marital home. Reporting an unsuccessful speculative investment from Mocha before proceeding to Bombay in 1791, Hugh Seton justified his earlier financial mismanagement by claiming that his exertions were all intended to save Touch for his descendants. 'I was ... urged on by a Strong Desire to leave you a noble addition to Touch ... but Alas! Alas! In place of that, I have involved you, my dearest Archie, cruelly involved you; if Touch be safe I may still drag on with more Comfort the few Days which God permits to me, but I can never again be happy', he lamented. 'All I desire, my ever dear Archie, is to have two Lines from you, to tell me first, that you are well & that Touch is safe'.[19] Preservation of Touch from his creditors was the impetus that propelled Hugh Seton to the Company's domains, where he shuttled between Bombay, Malacca and Penang, sought refuge at the Poona (Pune) Residency of Charles Warre Malet (1752–1815), and joined Cornwallis's forces in the Third Anglo-Mysore War (1790–92). Homelessness abroad was an integral component of Hugh Seton's campaign to preserve his country seat in Scotland.

Archibald Seton's letters to his father reveal an alternative strategy of imperial domestication marked not only by disciplined saving and regular remittances to Scotland but also by a settled life in India. Although he was not one of the 'white Mughals' described by William Dalrymple, who embraced Indian styles of dress, family life and cultural preferences,[20] Archibald Seton enjoyed a life of genteel domesticity on the subcontinent – and repeatedly sought to fix his peripatetic father in his successive Indian homes. Safely ensconced at Gaya as Collector of Bihar province and rapidly accumulating savings with which to repay the debts that encumbered Touch, Archibald pleaded with Hugh Seton to live at home with him in India. He protested that his father's decision to bypass Gaya when he left the Maratha campaigns for Bombay had 'cruelly ... mortified and disappointed' him, contrasting the 'constant terrors' of Hugh's 'unsettled life' to the imagined joys of their renewed co-residence, in an Indian home that promised to restore their Scottish estate to their family. 'Here your situation would be comfortable—at least, it shd be the study and delight of my life to endeavor to render it such', he reasoned. 'Come, then, my Dearest and most Revered Sir, come (and O! come speedily) to the arms of duty, love and gratitude.' Promising 'the help of society, books, and the unremitting attentions of one who lives but for your sake', Archibald Seton was careful to depict his Bengal residence and its well-appointed library as a material means toward the end of preserving Touch within the family. 'I entreat you … to consider, that our family estate remains safe tho burdened, and that the burden is daily diminishing by means of the exertions I am enabled to make by my present situation; a situation which I owe solely to your active efforts at the time of my appointment', he urged, calculating that his salary and emoluments would both liberate the estate from debt and afford 'an ample provision for all our wants and wishes' once the Setons of Touch were 'restored to the actual enjoyment of it'.[21]

Hugh Seton, rumoured dead from autumn 1795,[22] was only one member of the extended family circle acknowledged as his dependents by Archibald, and was hardly the most troublesome kinsman with whom Archibald navigated the treacherous shoals of Company domesticity at a distance. A younger brother James travelled to India without first obtaining an EIC appointment – very much against Archibald's advice – and rapidly replaced their father as a perpetual charge on his older brother's pocket. Established in trade with money borrowed from Archibald in 1798, James proved no more financially adept than their father, and failed spectacularly as a merchant in India. Leaving Archibald to repay massive debts, he agreed to return to Europe in 1807 only when his brother promised him an annual pension of £500, and died by shipwreck on the voyage home.[23]

Repeated payments to support his feckless father and brother impeded Archibald Seton's efforts to pay the Scottish creditors who held a lien on Touch House and the surrounding estate and figured in his letters to family in Scotland as the chief obstacle to his return. Writing to his brother-in-law Henry Stewart (1759–1836) – the husband of his younger sister, Lally – in 1807, Archibald was at pains to underline the intensity of his desire to return to Touch. 'I can swear by the sacred memory of my loved parents that my desire to return is eager and feverish, and some part of every day is passed in fond anticipation of the happy time when I shall be restored to my family and home', he insisted. Eschewing ownership of a carriage or even a cabriolet notwithstanding he was now the Company's chief diplomatic representative at the Mughal court at Delhi, Seton confined himself to ownership of a single riding horse.[24] Fiscal prudence in India, he hoped, would ensure an ample retirement among kin at Touch House.

Although Archibald Seton bore the principal burden of redeeming Touch through Company service, his conception of the estate's ownership, past and future was emphatically collective and female, rather than individualistic and male. The death of his brother James and his own unmarried state placed his sisters next in line in the succession to Touch – a pattern of inheritance already prefigured in his mother's generation. Instructing his agents in Calcutta to remit £6,500 to his Edinburgh banker in 1808, Seton noted that £500 was to be paid to his eldest sister, the widowed Mrs Brotherton, and the remainder used to pay down the debt on Touch. Uneasy with his brother-in-law's suggestion that four acres of the estate should be sold to a neighbour and several trees felled, Seton articulated a vision of proprietorship that discounted primogeniture and instead traced the estate's family identity through the female line. 'I do not, I cannot consider myself as sole proprietor of the estate of our adored, blessed mother I call heaven to witness that, whatever little superiority or advantage the law may assign to the adventitious unmeritorious circumstance of being an eldest son, I consider the estate not as a possession of my own, but as a property belonging to all of us, and held by me in trust for all my mothers [sic] children', he asserted. Distant from home, he personified the estate's assets to underscore his continued emotional identification with Touch. 'They are well known to me', he urged in resisting Stewart's suggestion that the estate's trees could profitably be sold for timber. 'I should feel as if I had lost so many of my friends.'[25]

A bachelor, Seton worked to preserve Touch House and its estate not for children of his own but for his female siblings and their descendants. Drafting his will in c.1809, he noted two surviving siblings, his sister Barbara, a childless widow, and Lillias (known as Lally), married to Henry Stewart of Allanton, Lanarkshire.[26] The Stewarts had one surviving daughter, Elizabeth, who by 1812 was married to the Scottish landowner Reginald McDonald and was the mother of several sons and daughters. Writing to his brother-in-law to detail his plans for new investment at Touch, Archibald Seton envisioned the estate's continued inheritance through the female line. 'If indeed you had no children I should in that case, most certainly have married', he acknowledged, to 'do so would then have been a duty, which I would have fulfilled'.[27] His niece

Elizabeth's fecund marriage, however, liberated Seton from the burdens of matrimony and tied him in turn to an extended kinship network which stretched through sisters and daughters from his immediate family to the Stewarts and the McDonalds. Citing payment of his brother James' Indian debts as the reason for his continued residence in India, Seton promised to return to Touch in 1813. 'The Estate as estimated by you will be more than sufficient for our purpose', he observed to his brother-in-law. 'I say for our purpose because I consider the two families as one.'[28] Henry Stewart was at pains to ensure that his daughter Elizabeth – born years after Seton's departure for India and personally unknown to him – featured in her uncle's estate planning as a worthy recipient of his inheritance, despite her female gender. In 1814 he reported that new leases had, under Elizabeth's keen eye, been successfully negotiated with the Touch tenants. Crediting his daughter with the diplomatic skills of a prime minister, Stewart noted that she 'shows a talent for business and a knowledge of country affairs, which, I trust, will prove hereafter not less useful to herself, than they are foreign and superior to the frivolous recreations, and the wretched pursuits of the greater part of her sex'.[29]

Plans for the large-scale refurbishment of Touch with his Indian savings, notwithstanding the debt with which the estate remained encumbered, figured prominently in Archibald Seton's correspondence with Henry Stewart, allowing Seton, his sister and brother-in-law to imagine a shared family home notwithstanding the great distances – of space, culture and experience – that divided them. Seton, whose salary as Resident of Delhi was £4,000 per annum plus allowances, remitted tens of thousands of pounds to his agents in Scotland, and begged Stewart anxiously for advice on improvements that could be made to the estate before his return home. From his own Lanarkshire home of Allanton House, Stewart dispatched the architect Gillespie to Touch in 1809, reporting to Seton that the house and tower could fall within a few years, 'being in a very crazy and infirm state'. Propping the existing structure, Stewart suggested, should form only the first phase of Seton's refurbishments. A mere 3,000 guineas, he estimated, would add two new wings to the house. Creating a home with five public rooms, 12 bedchambers and 11 dressing rooms, these renovations would render Touch a fitting residence for a high-ranking Company official's Scottish retirement.[30] Archibald Seton welcomed these suggestions, linking his in-law to the family cause by deploying a dynastic architectural metaphor. Thanking Stewart for his care of the estate, Seton warmly declared that 'my dear father was the Peter the Great of Touch, you are the Catherine the Second'.[31]

Letters such as these attest to the power exerted by country houses and country estates in Company family sociability, to the vital role played by imagined homes in Britain purchased or refurbished with Indian fortunes in creating and maintaining kinship ties in global and imperial contexts. But Archibald Seton's letters also remind us of the fragility of these domestic ties in Company circles. Seton's reiterated claim that only paternal and fraternal debts precluded his return to Touch appear in his letters alongside his repudiation of rumours that he had fallen prey to the allure of Indian life and was reluctant to repatriate.[32] His repeated assertion that only prudential saving of his Company salary would allow him to preserve Touch for his own retirement, for his siblings and for his sister's daughter allowed Seton to evade his brother-in-law's constant badgering for loans to improve his own and his children's estates. But Seton's reasoning on this head was exposed as a fiction in 1812, when (to the horror of his sister and brother-in-law) he announced that his return would be delayed until at least 1814 due to a loan of £6,000 now offered to William Fraser (1784–1835).[33] Fraser, formerly Seton's assistant at the Delhi Residency, was the scion of a Highland landed family whose estate near Inverness, Moniack, was encumbered by debt as a result of his family's mismanagement of its Guiana investments. Like Seton, Fraser had been driven to Company employment in India by a desire to save his Scottish family seat.[34] Inexplicable to his family at home, Seton's willingness at this juncture to assist a young man to whom – by his own admission – he had neither ties of blood nor kinship undercut his earlier pronouncements of deep family feeling. Henry Stewart, no stranger to the epistolary economy of emotional blackmail, wrote in response to report his wife's rapidly deteriorating health. 'She bore up wonderfully well, till we received the intelligence of the loan to Mr. Frazer [sic.]; and that seemed quite to overpower her spirits', he observed. 'Though struck with admiration (as indeed we all were) of your unequalled generosity to that gentleman, the idea (she said) that her beloved brother, in whom her whole heart and soul are wrapped up, should, on any consideration, now delay his return, after an absence of more than three and thirty years, was more than she could support.'[35]

Mutual recriminations on this subject continued – alongside reiterations of shared family interest and love – until Seton set sail for Britain on the *William Pitt* in 1817. To be sure, discussion of strategies for furnishing Touch with objects from Seton's Indian home provided a continued context for collaboration with his brother-in-law. Seton's assertion that 'Among the many sources of Rational delight [to] which I look forward at home, none is contemplated by me with greater satisfaction than being able to Devote some part of my day to study and reading' elicited helpful advice from Stewart on the need to write his name in each volume from his Indian library sent back to Britain, so as to avoid payment of Customs duties.[36] But the money lent to Fraser continued to rankle. In a letter of 1816, Stewart accompanied his own request for a loan of £20,000 with the comment that, should Seton delay his return any longer, his family with regret would conclude that his public employments in India had bred 'an indifference to those truly domestic and Scottish feelings, which breathe through your Letters'.[37] Stung by reports that malicious gossip about his loan to William Fraser had been heard and indeed circulated by his elder sister at Bath, Seton on the eve of his departure for Britain complained to Stewart that:

> the impression of dissatisfaction & disgust which the whole has made upon my mind, is not to be eradicated. It gives me, by anticipation, a melancholy picture of the sentiments & manners of those with whom it will shortly be my misfortune to live. Accustomed, as I have long been, to a society of liberal, enlightened men, who are wont to put the fairest & most favourable construction on the conduct of others, it will be quite insupportable to me to live among people who are in the habit of drawing narrow-minded ungenerous conclusions.[38]

His long-cherished plan to live with the Stewarts at Allanton House while Touch was refurbished now filled Seton with dread. Already ailing when he set sail from Calcutta, he was spared a painful family homecoming by death at sea before the *William Pitt* docked in Britain.

It is easy to dismiss the Setons' story as exceptional. Hugh Seton's extravagant expenditure on the estate and his picaresque progress from the Highlands to the Middle East and India were, like the man himself, extreme examples of Jacobite excess in the aftermath of the '45; Archibald's persistent refusal to return home to the country house for which he laboured so sedulously, although not exceptional among Company men, was hardly characteristic of them. Nonetheless, their family story shares key characteristics with many Scottish families – Highlanders and Lowlanders alike – and with English and Welsh Company men and women. Collaborative to the core, orientated toward securing the inheritance of daughters as well as sons, and often spanning imperial careers in both the Atlantic and the Indian Ocean Worlds, retaining and refashioning extant country houses – as the case of Montreal Park also illustrates – mobilized a wide spectrum of family members, rather than senior male proprietors alone.

The Amhersts and familial belonging

Like the history of Touch House, the history of Montreal Park was marked by lapses of succession, imperial disappointments and collaborative family endeavor. Jeffrey Amherst, 1st Baron Amherst (1717–97) originally built Montreal Park in the 1760s, to mark both his return from America and his Canadian successes as commander-in-chief of British forces. This home passed to Amherst's nephew, William Pitt Amherst (1773–1857), in 1797. Like his uncle, William Pitt played a variety of important (yet often unsuccessful) roles in global affairs.[39] Despite his lack of success on the international stage, however, in 1823 Amherst was appointed to the role of Governor General of India. Accompanied by his wife Sarah (1761–1838) and their eldest son Jeffrey (1802–26) and daughter Sarah Elizabeth (1806–76), Amherst travelled to India and began what would become a highly problematic tenure as a colonial governor. He declared war with Burma in early 1824, and mounted an attack on Rangoon. Two expensive years of fighting only yielded the territories of Arakan, Tenasserim and Assam. In 1828, Amherst returned home to Britain with his wife and daughter, his son having died in India.[40] Soon after returning to England, the Amherst family began rebuilding their country house, Montreal Park in Riverhead, Kent.

Maintaining a shared identity across imperial space was an important but endless task for the Amhersts. As several historians have observed, imperial families keenly felt the distances placed between different members and developed a range of strategies to traverse spaces of absence.[41] Correspondence and gift-giving, for instance, went some way to mediating a sense of family belonging over time and space. William Pitt Amherst's daughter Sarah Elizabeth was an active correspondent, who sent sketches as well as letters while in India between 1823 and 1828. In 1824, for example, she wrote to her brother Frederick (1807–29) – who had remained in England – and included a detailed set of five sketches showing their primary residence from several different angles in the hope that he would 'better to understand the local situation of Government House'. These sketches were accompanied by written notes, which further described details represented in the drawings. Sarah Elizabeth asked that Frederick not keep the sketches to himself, but rather share them with their half-sisters Maria and Harriet to show 'how the flower garden is laid out'.[42] She thus encouraged her brother to respond to the sketches as he would do letters, as a form of communication that could be shared and read communally.[43]

The Amherst family also developed other techniques through which they could create and recreate a sense of family across distance. They employed journals to recount experiences and events, which other family members then read at a later point. On her younger brother Frederick's return from Italy in 1829, Sarah Elizabeth recalled how she 'read with the greatest pleasure & admiration his journal in Italy – it was so neatly kept & his account of every thing he saw so good & clear'.[44] While scholars have long understood letter reading as a shared and communal practice, less attention has been given to similar practices of journal reading, but this remained an important strategy for the Amhersts and others, such as the Clives.[45] When in India between 1823 and 1828, Sarah Amherst and her daughter Sarah Elizabeth both used journals to record their journeys to and experiences of India. Sarah wrote a total of seven journals beginning in 1823 with their journey to India and ending with their return to England in 1828, while Sarah Elizabeth wrote four journals covering the years 1820 to 1842. Sarah Elizabeth's reading of Frederick's journal suggests that her own (and her mother's) journals were produced with a particular audience in mind and actively participated in reaffirming a sense of familial belonging when read by others on their return from India. Significantly, through the emphasis placed on reading journals in Britain, these practices suggest at the importance the Amherst family placed on reconstituting a sense of familial belonging once physically present and returned home.

After returning to England in 1828, the Amhersts initiated other projects to restore their sense of familial identity, most notably by refashioning their country house, Montreal Park in Kent. At one level, domestic refashioning can simply be understood as an attempt to render in material terms the new wealth and status they had acquired in India. Certainly on making the decision to go to India in the winter of 1822–23, the economic benefits that might accrue from service featured highly in their discussions. They asked their acquaintances and friends for advice on whether the post would be economically and emotionally worthwhile, and their advisers suggested that although the emotional costs might be high, the economic gains justified this dislocation. More particularly, acquaintances suggested that the Indian post would ultimately allow their male children to prosper – 'only consider what an advantage a few score thousand pounds will be in setting up these Lads'.[46] In addition to wealth, moreover, while in India, Amherst also managed to acquire new status. In 1826 William Pitt had been created 1st Earl Amherst of Arracan and Viscount Holmesdale, honours that moved the family up a rank within in the peerage. Yet, despite having reasons to embark on the materialization of power and wealth through house building, the new house created by the Amhersts remained relatively modest. Significantly, in the 1970s, the 5th Earl Amherst simply described Montreal as 'a comfortable Georgian house' (see Figure 7.1).[47] It is important then to look beyond the architectural outcomes of building and to instead focus upon the building process itself to understand why the Amhersts embarked on their renovation of Montreal in the late 1820s. In reconstructing their country house, they sought primarily to reconstitute a family identity and sense of belonging, which had been dispersed by imperial distance.

In 1829 the Amhersts commissioned the architect Atkinson to draw up plans for a substantial extension to accommodate a billiard room and new bedrooms and dressing rooms for Lord and Lady Amherst.[48] Notwithstanding their employment of Atkinson, the Amhersts actively involved themselves with the design process and conceived it as a collaborative act. In her journal, William Pitt Amherst's daughter Sarah Elizabeth, described how before they hired Atkinson, they spent much time working with a scale model of the house and its proposed extension. She described how they 'had a model of it in wood, with a moveable

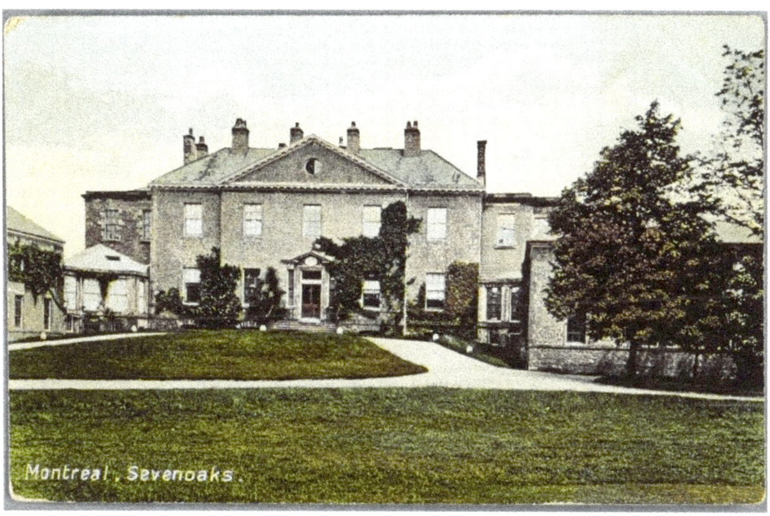

Figure 7.1 Postcard featuring Montreal Park, Kent. Courtesy of Kent History & Library Centre, Maidstone.

additional form, to be placed where one chose, but on every side it looked like an excrescence & deformity'.[49] The family took the unusual step of providing themselves with specialized tools through which they could consider different solutions to the problem of creating an extension at Montreal Park. The construction of a scale model of the house and the proposed extension suggest at the time and effort they invested in the building process.

Moving the model into different places, the family's first solution to the problem of an acceptable extension was to build a two-storey section in front of the house, which could be connected by an arcade to the wings at either side of it (see Figure 7.2). Atkinson, however, soon drew the family's attention to the difficulty of creating an adequate chimney system and began to introduce the alternative idea of extending to the east of the house. He suggested that a substantial addition, which included both extra service rooms on the basement floor and an impressive dining room on the ground floor, could be built on the east side of the house (see Figure 7.3). Such a substantial extension, he argued, would create enough space within the central building of the house to include a billiard room.

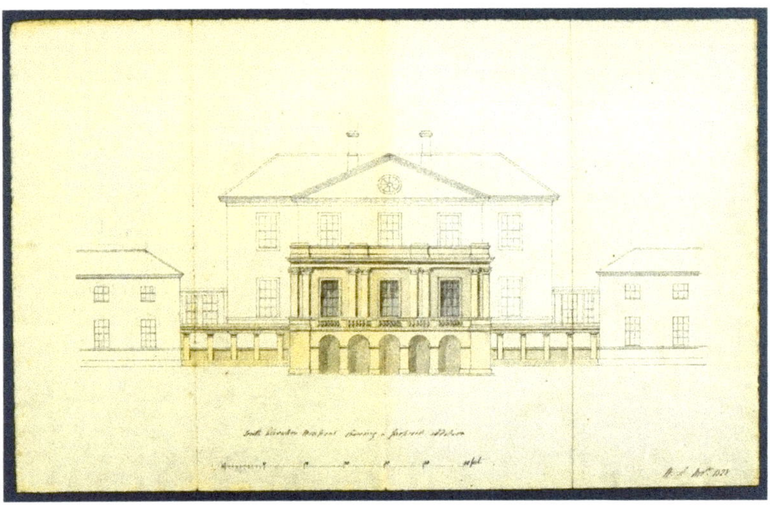

Figure 7.2 'South Elevation Montreal showing a proposed addition' (November 1828). Kent History & Library Centre, Amherst Papers, 'Detailed Plans of Alterations at Montreal by Mr. Atkinson (1829–31)', U1350 P21. Courtesy of Kent History & Library Centre, Maidstone.

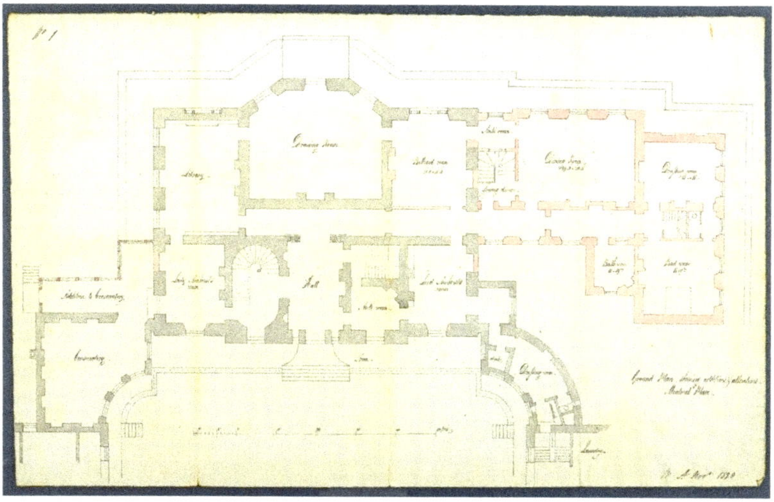

Figure 7.3 'Ground floor plan showing additions and alterations to Montreal Place' (November 1828). Kent History & Library Centre, Amherst Papers, 'Detailed Plans of Alterations at Montreal by Mr. Atkinson (1829–31)', U1350 P21. Courtesy of Kent History & Library Centre, Maidstone.

As Sarah Elizabeth explained in her journal, however, the family greeted Atkinson's plan with much disapproval because it disturbed the symmetry of the original house. What he was suggesting was an extension that would align the form of the house more closely with contemporary fashions. In the 1790s asymmetric houses began to appear in great numbers. Joseph Bonomi's (1739–1808) work on Longford Hall in Shropshire and James Wyatt's (1746–1813) work on Dodington in Gloucestershire in this decade encouraged further asymmetrical houses to emerge in the early years of the 1800s.[50] In the same period the emergence of the Gothic Revival further disrupted the dominance of symmetry, leading to new conceptions of the country house form during the nineteenth century. Although at odds with prevailing trends, the Amhersts' desire for a symmetrical house remained unchanged.

That the family saw their building project as an endeavour that could benefit from (and provide benefits to) their wider circle becomes clearer at this point in the design process. As described by Sarah Elizabeth, William Pitt actively encouraged other family members and friends, not resident at Montreal Park, to engage in the project. His wife's daughter by an earlier marriage, Lady Maria Windsor (1790–1855), was called upon and as Sarah Elizabeth notes, she 'was of great use'. Concerned by Atkinson's suggestion to build an asymmetrical house, the family 'pondered a long time over this plan'. At last a certain Mr Addington found a solution: extending the house on both sides. Building two extensions allowed for a less obtrusive addition, retained symmetry and created much needed space. Sarah Elizabeth describes how her sister 'immediately reduced the idea to a scale on paper'.[51] After some adjustment, it was this idea that came to be completed at Montreal (see Atkinson's rendering of the design in Figure 7.4 below).

Significantly, the design work for the extension at Montreal Park was configured as a collaborative endeavour, which utilized the opinions and skills of a range of people, including women. Lady Maria Windsor's drafting skills – rather than the services of the architect – were particularly useful in allowing the family to move quickly from idea to drawing. Sarah Elizabeth's description of this act – 'reduced the idea to a scale on paper' – suggests that Lady Maria had some experience of drafting and working to scale. Such evidence gestures towards her previous experience of design work, suggesting that she may have been actively involved in other projects. At the same time, the engagement of daughters in the design process reveals how broad collaborations between family members were enacted to achieve house building schemes.

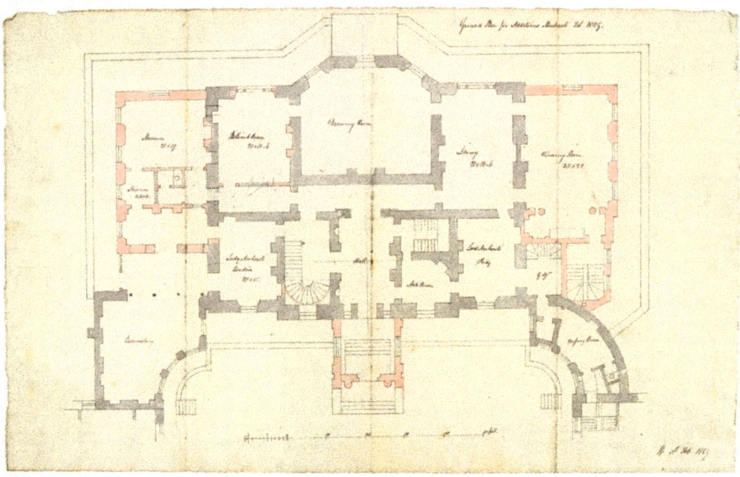

Figure 7.4 'Ground Plan for Additions Montreal' (February 1829). Kent History & Library Centre, Amherst Papers, 'Detailed Plans of Alterations at Montreal by Mr. Atkinson (1829–31)', U1350 P21. Courtesy of Kent History & Library Centre, Maidstone.

In early February 1829 the Amherst family left 'Mr Atkinson the architect in possession of the house to begin operations immediately' and moved to their London abode.[52] Eight months later they returned to Montreal, and Sarah Elizabeth recalled how 'every thing was so changed, in consequence of the alterations in the house, & the enclosure of the new garden that we hardly knew the place again'.[53] Despite creating a new space that seemed unrecognizable at first, the process of creating that newness spoke more of consolidation than change. In working together as a family, the Amhersts created a solution acceptable to all. Montreal Park became an important and meaningful place again because family members invested time and expertise in its reconstruction. Country house building allowed imperial families to integrate not only with elites, but also (and perhaps more importantly) with each other.

Conclusion

Touch House, Stirlingshire and Montreal Park, Kent illuminate the multiple motivations that drove families to embark on imperial projects connected to the purchase, re-building or re-establishment of country houses. They demonstrate the ways in which country house projects acted not simply as a means to stabilize the wealth and power of an individual, but rather acted as part of more complex attempts to establish financial security for families and broader kin networks over generations. Such attempts were not solely focused on sons, but also included and benefitted female members of the family. The refashioning of country houses was also important in creating a space in which families could come together (even across global distances) and make decisions as a collective group. The collaborative rebuilding and refashioning of country houses allowed families to re-establish their relationships and familial identities. These examples underline the role played by material processes in establishing, maintaining and expressing collective social identities. Families, and the projects they embarked on across time and space, need to be understood as no less significant than 'nabobs' in the domestic imperial projects of the eighteenth and nineteenth centuries.

Section 3
The Home Counties
Clusters and connections

East India Company (EIC) employment typically required Company men – and any kin who accompanied them to the subcontinent – to establish long-term homes far distant from Britain. Retirement at the end of imperial service thus required both the de-location and re-location of Company homes, processes that offered both challenges and opportunities to Company families' senses of self, community and belonging. What choices confronted these Company families that returned home? For a small minority enriched with Indian wealth, purchasing a country house afforded a means of establishing new status and power: Stephanie Barczewski has identified 229 landed estates purchased by EIC employees or independent merchants who had traded in India, between 1700 and 1850.[1] Power gained in Company service was manifest in these country homes in myriad forms, encompassing knowledge, formal political engagement, marriage, inheritance and sociability. Some Company men created substantial residences to deploy skills acquired in Company military service; others used country estates to fulfil long-held ambitions in domestic husbandry and agriculture. For others, country estates gave access to parliamentary seats, or allowed consolidation of family wealth and its safe passage between the generations. Residence in country houses also enabled Company men and women to remain close to each other, simultaneously consolidating their British identities and reinforcing their Company connections. A key area in which multiple Company families settled was the Home Counties adjacent to London. Eighteenth-century Berkshire, indeed, was so replete with EIC families, that contemporaries dubbed the county 'the English Hindoostan'.[2]

The Home Counties' appeal to returned EIC men and women is unsurprising. Proximity to London allowed families to benefit from easy access to Company news from Leadenhall Street, investment opportunities in trade and infrastructure projects, potential positions in Parliament and regular contact both with each other and the metropolitan marriage market. Owning a country estate also provided the benefits of established status and power, country pursuits and leisure activities. Kate Smith's chapter on Warfield Park illustrates how the Walsh (and later the Benn Walsh) family sustained a Company country house in Berkshire over generations. The initial purchase of Warfield Park by John Walsh (1726–95) in the 1760s provided his niece, nephew and friends with an English home; when these kin were in India, Warfield also served as a site upon which to focus their longings for return. Walsh's niece Margaret (1758–1836) and her husband John Benn (1759–1825) inherited the Park in 1795 and held it in safekeeping until their first son came of age in 1819. During this time, possession of Warfield allowed them to maintain regular contact with other Company families in the area while socializing with new networks. Warfield Park also provided Margaret and John with a shared domestic project: the continual improvement of the house required time, effort and money. Investing in the Park enlarged its importance in the family's image of itself, and it slowly became the centre of their kinship network. When Margaret and John's son Sir John Benn Walsh, 1st Baron Ormathwaite (1798–1881) inherited the house in 1825, Margaret Walsh ensured that she rented a house nearby, a situation that involved regularly moving. Her peripatetic later years underline the importance of the country house as a chief nodal point within Company families and show how maintaining familial relationships was often pivotal in the creation of residential clusters as access points to wealth and status.

Kate Smith's second chapter in this section focuses on another Berkshire home, Englefield House. Englefield's architecture gestures to its Elizabethan history and thus suggests a stable and consistent lineage of influences and occupants. Smith's chapter however reveals the constant movement of people and objects which marked Englefield's eighteenth-century history. Company men and women (and their Indian wealth) moved in and out of Englefield, maintaining and improving the house with infusions of Indian wealth. Richard Benyon (1698–1774), who ended his service for the Company as Governor of Fort St George, Madras between 1735 and 1744, entered Englefield by marrying the widow Mary Wrighte (d.1776) in 1745. Lady Margaret Clive (1735–1817), wife of Robert Clive (1725–1774), rented Englefield in the 1780s, maintaining the house, while its owner Nathaniel Wrighte (d. 1789) struggled financially with its maintenance. Finally Elizabeth

Sykes (d. 1814), only daughter of Company servant Sir Francis Sykes (1732–1804) of Basildon Park, Berkshire, became connected to Englefield's networks when she married Richard Benyon (1770–1854) of Englefield in 1797. Although Elizabeth did not live long enough to witness the changes Richard made to their home, her marriage and residence ensured that the house's history became increasingly intertwined with the EIC. Charting the changing occupants of Englefield House suggests that estimates of country house purchases by Company men and women may well underplay the extent of the Company's impact. Rather than a simple narrative of house purchase or building, Smith's chapter demonstrates how Company families and connections shaped 'English' country houses over time and in multiple ways.

Margot Finn's chapter on Swallowfield Park, Berkshire also underlines the reticulation of imperial ties that sustained the fabric and furnished the interiors of an ostensibly 'English' country house over extended periods of time. From Thomas 'Diamond' Pitt (1653–1726) in the early eighteenth century to the Russell family in the nineteenth century, Swallowfield served as an important nodal point within the Berkshire EIC network. Finn's chapter, like Diane James's contribution to this volume, demonstrates that material skills and knowledge first acquired on the subcontinent were later successfully invoked in the creation of Company country houses. The Russell brothers Henry (1783–1852) and Charles (1786–1856), learned how to furnish elite interiors while Henry was the diplomatic Resident at Hyderabad in the 1810s. In retirement, they consolidated and supplemented their expertise as elite consumers through continental European tours in the 1820s and 1830s, creating a fashionable country house interior at Swallowfield calculated to sustain their new claims to a venerable lineage. While the two brothers were central to the purchasing and decorating of Swallowfield, other family members also played key roles. Their father provided Indian wealth for the purchase of Swallowfield, but their mother had laid crucial groundwork for country life prior to the Russell men's retirement from Indian employment by renting a succession of English family homes on her own return from the subcontinent. Finn's chapter emphasizes the collaborative nature of country house purchases and furnishing. Country houses functioned as important family projects, which allowed different members to re-establish connections and a sense of belonging. Carefully crafted, this cohesive sense of belonging demanded the exclusion of both perceived outsiders and their alternative family narratives: across successive generations of Russell residence, Swallowfield's entanglement in the history of slavery, race and illegitimacy was repeatedly effaced.

Georgina Green's chapter on Valentines Mansion also reflects the importance of regional residential clusters in the Home Counties. As a retired EIC captain, Charles Raymond (1713–88) purchased Valentines Mansion in Essex from Robert Surnam (founder of the Surnam, Dineley and Cliffe bank) in 1754. The house provided Raymond with easy access to the City, where he invested his Indian fortune, and to the EIC docks, where he managed and financed multiple Company voyages. In Essex, Raymond operated at the heart of an EIC network that included William Webber (1713–79), John Williams (c.1723–74), Pinsom Bonham (1724–91), Andrew Moffat (c.1730-80), Henry Fletcher (c.1727–1807), Donald Cameron (c.1740–97) and Richard Benyon (1698–1774). These men purchased houses near each other and consolidated their links through marriage and shared investments. Green highlights how this group of men and women continued to bear risks together, long after their active service for the Company, and by doing so exemplified and consolidated the trust they shared through domestic life, intermarriage and financial innovation.

Finally, Chris Jeppesen's chapter on North Mymms, moves to Hertfordshire. His chapter on North Mymms in South Hertfordshire shows how empire configured both a county and a parish. Like earlier chapters in this section, however, Jeppesen also explores longer narratives of adaptation, integration and transformation that Company families experienced over time. He suggests that earlier estimations of the numbers of country houses purchased or built by EIC men and women in Hertfordshire may be too low – an underestimate that has contributed to wider erasures of the imperial imprint from public memories of English built environments. Jeppesen reveals the extent to which families in South Hertfordshire were linked to the EIC as investors, directors or servants, demonstrating the important ways in which Company people and wealth shaped the history of the parish. In doing so, he highlights the necessity of revising our understanding of local histories as stable and grounded, urging instead that we pay greater heed to the movement of people, objects and wealth to Britain from empire and beyond. Together these chapters emphasize how studying the global within a local context prompts new understandings of global goods and lives (and their integration within specific sites), as well as revised conceptions of the 'local' as it existed in eighteenth- and nineteenth-century Britain.

8
Warfield Park, Berkshire

Longing, belonging and the British country house

Kate Smith

In the 1850s, Sir John Benn Walsh, 1st Baron Ormathwaite (1798–1881) used letters and diaries from his family's collection, as well as his own memories, to write a memoir of the life of his mother, Margaret Benn Walsh (née Fowke) (1758–1836).[1] To structure this lengthy piece, he used the different houses she had inhabited to organize her life story. Central within these homes was a relatively modest country house, Warfield Park in Berkshire. The structure that Benn Walsh employed underlines the importance the family placed on houses, and their roles as central nodes within family networks. Rather than the family's London town house, it was country abodes that Benn Walsh assumed to be the important sites that marked milestones in his mother's life. Often lived in by different generations of the family, it was country houses that mattered most and to which his family gave meaning. Towards the middle of the memoir Benn Walsh further extended the significance of Warfield Park by using it as a frame through which to distinguish between his parents' characters. He described how the 'difference in their characters was perceptible in the manner each followed what was a favourite object with both, the improvement of Warfield'.[2] He felt that his mother wanted to create a 'handsome park like residence' full of beauty, while his father fostered a different approach, 'always endeavouring to improve the soil, to enclose & reclaim the commons, to add to the productive value of the property.'[3] Margaret Benn Walsh's own writings confirm the importance of houses, and particularly Warfield

Park in Berkshire, in the maintenance of a familial dynamic and sense of belonging over generations. For the Walsh family, houses, and particularly their country house, became the central means by which different generations could construct an understanding of who they were and where they belonged.

This chapter acts as a complement to the earlier chapter on Montreal Park, Kent and Touch House, Stirlingshire, by exploring the ways in which elite East India Company (EIC) families constructed and reconstructed country houses when they returned home from the subcontinent. As with that chapter, this approach moves beyond questions of wealth and status, to examine how EIC families used country houses as important places within which to cultivate a sense of familial belonging. While the Montreal Park and Touch House chapter examines the specific point of return and the role played by the country house in initially embedding families back within broader kinship networks and alliances, this chapter follows the country house as it was utilized by families both immediately upon their return and then over multiple generations. It tracks the changing significance of Warfield Park to the Walsh and later the Benn Walsh family to demonstrate how different understandings of belonging were manifest over several generations.

Recent studies have underlined the importance of families and kinship networks to imperial enterprises.[4] Sustaining and cultivating these relationships across distance and over time was an essential component of the work of empire, and the failure to maintain kinship networks posed an ever-present threat to the familial imperial project. Material culture afforded family members with multiple mechanisms for bolstering kinship networks in this context. Letters and gifts provided families with important means by which to remain connected and aware of each other's different trajectories across ever-expanding imperial domains.[5] Within letters families shared news about the Company, family members and family homes to keep each other informed of and invested in developments.[6] As David Williams' chapter in this volume shows, families with connections to the Company often retained those links over multiple generations. The work of building and maintaining a particular and recognizable family identity needed to take place not only over distance, therefore, but also over time. Families often completed such work, this chapter argues, through the employment of material spaces, as much as material objects and letters.

This chapter takes a multi-generational approach to explore how one imperial family attempted to instantiate a sense of familial identity. It argues that a key means of sustaining a shared familial identity over time was through creating and maintaining a particular space and place, namely a country house which could act as the family's central site in Britain. While London townhouses were adopted and well-used by East India Company families, particularly as sites that kept them close to Leadenhall Street and thus abreast with Company news, it was often country houses that proved important in shoring family belonging across space and time.[7] Previously dominated by aristocratic and landed gentry families, the British country house tradition provided an important model for generational projects of alliance and shared identity elaborated by the Company's mercantile and military men and women. Outside of the metropolis, within a distinct locale and often with particular aesthetic features, parklands and estates, the country house had long worked to symbolize and embody the identities of elite families. Particularly in the second half of the eighteenth century, wealth achieved through EIC service provided a number of families with the resources necessary to buy, build or rent a country house.[8] If families wished to then retain a house beyond the lifetime of a particular generation, however, they required a financial and emotional investment from multiple family members and different generations. In order for such investments to take place, the house needed to be highly valued and closely associated with the family and thus central to their continued prosperity. In EIC families, members could contribute to the centrality of a country house within the family network through practices such as writing and imagining, as well as directing and completing material practices such as cleaning, design, decoration, building and expansion. Recognized as vital to identity formation both by those outside the family and within it, the country house proved an important emotional, material and social investment. Hence, by privileging a country house as *the* central node within their family's understanding of itself, Company families consolidated an understanding of even modest country houses as dynastic items and thus bolstered the British country house tradition in new ways.

A country house of one's own

Following John Walsh's (1726–95) initial purchase of Warfield Park in Berkshire in 1764, a series of family members contributed to the project of highlighting the house's central role within the family network. First, there were periods when members of the wider family, such as his niece and nephew, joined John Walsh in living at Warfield. Second, the house was visited by the family's wider social circle, often to pursue leisure activities, which marked it as an important and valuable site of domestic comfort. Third, a range of family members also wrote about the house in their correspondence and thus marked the house as a shared project, in which different individuals were invested. Finally, building and rebuilding at the site ensured that the house could respond to the specific needs of the family at different moments, marking its possession by a succession of distinctive individuals. Together these social and cultural ways of inhabiting the house constructed Warfield as the Walsh's primary family residence from an early stage.

After completing his role as Robert Clive's secretary and agent, John Walsh returned to England in 1759, determined to establish himself as a Member of Parliament and give time to his scientific interests.[9] In late 1764 he bought Warfield Park in Berkshire (see Figure 8.1), which allowed him to enjoy country pursuits, accommodate his nephew and niece and be near to Parliament and sources of EIC news in London. Writing to Robert Clive from his London house on Chesterfield Street in January 1765, Walsh apologized for his late response, noting that he had intended to write earlier, but had been prevented 'by a troublesome Purchase I have lately made of a House & some Land in Berkshire'.[10] For Walsh, purchasing Warfield was not simple. In his opinion, the house at point of purchase was incomplete and he was compelled to make 'several other Purchases as well as enclosing some Common Land'. By acquiring additional land Walsh felt that he had created a 'compleat Place'.[11] Completing his project at Warfield proved important as it allowed Walsh to create a space in which Clive and he could enjoy the homo-social comforts of male friendship and sport. Walsh hoped that Warfield would offer Clive 'a convenient place for you to run down to [from London] and hunt and spend what vacant time you had for the Country, when Shropshire was at too great a Distance'.[12] He presented Warfield as a place where Clive could come and hunt with him. Yet, his vision of domestic comfort in England was entangled with his identification with the Company's expanding empire in India: when describing Warfield Park in his 1813 *The History of Windsor and its Neighbourhood*, James Hakewill suggested that Walsh had named Warfield 'Plassey House' in commemoration of Clive's victory at Plassey.[13] Similarly, John Walsh's grandson John Benn Walsh recalled how his grandfather had been known to describe the house as his 'Tent', underlining his and its associations with Clive's military campaign.[14] Walsh successfully cast Warfield as a country house able to perform the traditionally important role of providing country pursuits, hospitality and patronage and simultaneously recast it as a space shaped by his newly acquired imperial comforts of escape and mobility.

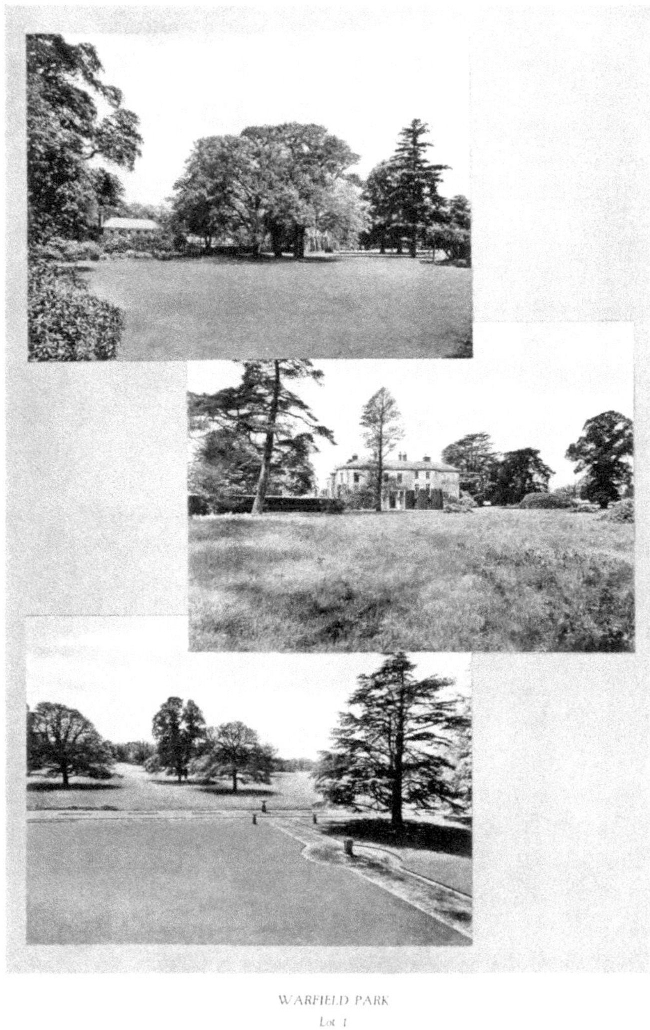

Figure 8.1 Photographs of Warfield Park, Berkshire (lot 1), 'Sale Catalogue of Warfield Park' (1933), D/ENS/B13/26. Image courtesy of Berkshire Record Office.

In February 1766, just two years after Walsh's purchase, a fire afflicted Warfield and large portions of the house burned down, leaving only the offices standing. Rather than demolishing the remaining house and building a new house in its stead, Walsh rebuilt the house, incorporating what was left in the new structure. In doing so Walsh affirmed his attachment to Warfield. Writing to Clive about the destruction of the house, he seemed unperturbed by the financial loss he had sustained. He also appeared relatively unconcerned by the loss of his furniture and books although he did acknowledge it was 'something' to lose such material possessions. What really affected Walsh, however, was the 'Loss of Time'. His comments to Clive underline Walsh's investment of time and money in making Warfield a comfortable and 'compleat' place, a significant and important site.[15]

In rebuilding the house Walsh benefitted from its being 'insured for two thousand pounds'. Wilson and Mackley have calculated that the average cost of house building ranged from £7,000 to £22,000 between 1770 and 1800, depending on estate size.[16] They estimate that, on average, building a new house on an estate of around 3,000 to 5,000 acres cost £7,000, while the cost of an estate of 5,000 to 10,000 acres was £12,500 and that of a large estate of greater than 10,000 acres entailed building costs of £22,000. That Walsh was pleased to have insured his house for £2,000 suggests that Warfield was a small property to begin with and that any rebuilding was likely to be modest. Nevertheless, his grandson John Benn Walsh, 1st Baron Ormathwaite later described how Walsh had employed James 'Athenian' Stuart (1713–88) to complete the rebuilding.[17] He observed that 'Stuart of Athens did his Work at Warfield judiciously, converting the house into a pretty modest residence according to the wants of that day, which was much less luxurious than ours.'[18] Stuart had recently completed work on townhouses such as Spencer House (begun about 1759) and other country houses such as Hagley Hall, Worcestershire (1758) and Wimbledon Park, Surrey (1758) and continued to be in demand during the 1770s. It seems unlikely then, even in the late 1760s as Stuart moved into the later part of his career, that Walsh's employment of him indicated modesty, rather than investment.[19] Similarly, any calculation regarding the rebuilding of Warfield Park in 1766 must also acknowledge that Walsh is likely to have had large sums of money at his disposal after returning from India.

Whether or not Warfield Park was materially and aesthetically compelling, we do know that multiple kin developed strong emotional attachments to it. Warfield became important for more than material reasons and Walsh seems to have actively encouraged others to form a relationship to the house. He shared it not only with his friends, such as Robert Clive, but also with his extended family. After his sister Elizabeth's death in 1760, Walsh accommodated his nephew Francis (1753–1819) and his niece Margaret (1758–1836).[20] Although Francis Fowke went to be educated at Dr Gilpin's in Cheam, Surrey and then travelled to Bengal to become a Writer with the East India Company in 1773, Margaret spent much of her youth at Warfield.[21] As a result, she developed a life-long attachment to the house. The first record of her relationship to the house can be seen in 1776, when, at the age of 18, Margaret journeyed out to India. She embarked on this journey to join her father and brother, but also ostensibly to search for a husband. While in India she also wrote about Warfield in order to reflect on her place in the family and its Anglo-Indian domestic life.

Although Margaret seems to have found her first few years in India difficult, she came to live there happily and engaged in different aspects of Indian culture, including its music.[22] Yet, in letters back to family members, Margaret expressed her longing for England. Writing to her uncle John Walsh from Calcutta on 20 April 1781, for example, Margaret noted that 'I have heard so much of the improvements of Warfield that I shall expect to see it quite changed by the time we return to England. I was very fond of it in the form I left it but I am persuaded you have increased its beauties.'[23] Although Margaret may have included these statements as a means of flattering her uncle, who may well have supplied her with ready details of the changes he had made, the tone of the letter suggests their shared warmth for the place and her excitement in its improvements. Similarly, in a letter written to her uncle five years later on 3 February 1786, just before embarking on her return journey to Europe, we learn what an important a reference point Warfield remains. Margaret described how, 'The Residents [sic] house is just on the skirts of the town, and is an exceedingly good one, but my Brother resigned it to the officers who were stationed there, and lived entirely in Bungalows, a few miles from Benares, and so delightfully situated that they might almost lie in that particular, with your house at Warfield.'[24] Rather than the splendour of the Residency, a 'rural' situation is valuable to both her and her brother, suggesting at his particular suitability as potential heir to Warfield. In the same letter she went on to note that 'I reflect with singular pleasure on the new beauties & improvements I shall discover at Warfield.'[25] Warfield, rather than his London house in Chesterfield Street, was an important place for Margaret and a significant shared reference point between her and her uncle.

Much later, after her return to Britain, Margaret continued to place great value in country houses. In the summer of 1811, Margaret journeyed north to visit her relation Lady Clive at Oakly Park in Shropshire. She found her 'dear Lady Clive in excellent health & spirits. Her figure much bent, but with the same sweetness of countenance & vivacity of manner.'[26] While she greeted Lady Clive calmly, being in Oakly Park led Margaret to feel 'many various emotions'. She had not been to the house since the summer she had spent there prior to 'embarking for India' in 1776. She had not returned to the house after she came back from India because Lady Clive had been living at Englefield House in Berkshire. She was pleased to finally return and described how 'The many, many years which have rolled over my head since I inhabited that sweet spot seemed compressed into a small space, which fancy easily leaped over & restored the long lost scene'.[27] For Margaret then, houses stored memories of previous times, which could be re-entered by visiting. They allowed her to collapse the time between her departure for India and her return home to England, providing an immediate connection with a familiar 'English' domestic past.

As the second and then the third generation of the Walsh family grew they became attached to Warfield as a particular place upon which they focused their notions of familial belonging and shared history. After buying Warfield in 1764, John Walsh demonstrated his own increasing attachment to the house through continual rebuilding. Even after the majority of the house was burned down in 1766, Walsh decided to rebuild rather than begin again. In his writings to others, we see that Walsh often represented Warfield as a place of comfort to which he could invite and entertain others. His niece Margaret greatly benefitted from his generosity and lived there for most of her childhood and teenage years. During this time she also constructed a ready attachment to the house, which, when she lived in India in her early adult years, she referred to as her reference point. It was her uncle's country house rather than his town house that she invested with notions of home and belonging. In her later life Margaret continued her connection to Warfield, investing in it anew. While in the early period Warfield had been marked by the distant longings of other family members, as the second Walsh generation came to take possession of the house, they distinctly marked it through material practices which extended its reach and significance.

Rebuilding Warfield together

As John Walsh had no legitimate children of his own, the inheritance of his estates, including Warfield was entirely at his own behest. Although Walsh had earlier considered bequeathing his estates to his good friend Sir Henry Strachey (1736–1810), it seems that an argument between the men meant that Warfield did not pass to him.[28] Walsh also overlooked his nephew Francis (Margaret's older brother). A relationship with the actress Mary Lowe (c.1769–1847) from 1788 onwards, with whom he had 15 children but who he did not marry until 1813, appears to have stopped Walsh from bequeathing the estate to him.[29] Rather, Warfield was left in trust to his nephew-in-law, Margaret's husband, John Benn (1759–1825) when Walsh died in 1795, with the hope that it would eventually pass to their first son (John Benn Walsh, 1st Baron Ormathwaite b. 1798).

John Benn was, like Walsh, an East India Company man. Like his uncle-in-law he had started working for the Company as a writer, but quickly rose up the ranks. In 1781, just four years after his initial appointment to the Company service, he became Assistant to the Resident at Benares.[30] Margaret's brother Francis Fowke had acted as Resident at Benares for eighteen months beginning in 1775 and was briefly reinstated in this position in 1780 and then again in 1783.[31] During his time in Benares, John Benn must have become acquainted with Francis and possibly with his sister, who moved there in 1782. In that year Benn became Factor, before being promoted again in 1785 to Junior Merchant.[32] Crucially for the Benn-Walsh alliance, John Benn returned to England in 1786 on the *Dublin* with Margaret and soon after disembarking, they married in 1787. The wedding would have taken place at Lady Margaret Clive's abode Englefield House, if it had not been for Margaret petitioning her uncle for a much smaller and more intimate affair at her brother's house in London.[33] Nevertheless, as the chapter on Englefield House in this volume shows, while on their wedding journey, the newly married couple visited Englefield House and Lady Clive.[34]

John Benn had made a reputed £80,000 trading in diamonds and opium while Assistant Resident at Benares. When John Walsh died Benn significantly enlarged his fortune by inheriting Warfield (including all the household goods, linen, furniture, china and glass ware, books and paintings contained within it) as well as his other property and land in Berkshire, Radnorshire, Cork and Kerry.[35] Under the terms of the inheritance Benn assumed the Walsh name. As their son described it, 'On the death of Mr Walsh, & their succeeding to his property, in March 1795, their pretty cheerful Villa at Leatherhead was given up, & they established themselves at Warfield.'[36] He went on to detail how the move to Warfield was 'a source of great pleasure & happiness to both of them'. For his mother, Warfield had been a place of happiness in her childhood, but she also possessed 'a strong taste for the country & the establishment of a country place'.[37] At the same time, for his father, 'it furnished a pursuit, and occupation, which became the principal business, and amusement of the rest of his life. The improvement of this place, & the management of his farm, objects which he pursued with his characteristic … frugality, & economy, engrossed his whole time & thoughts.'[38] The dominant stereotype of the returned Company man was the nabob, a man addicted to luxury and metropolitan pursuits.[39] Benn Walsh's son countered this negative image, depicting his father – notwithstanding his vast Indian fortune – as a man of modest tastes and a love of rural pursuits, character traits epitomized by his country house life at Warfield.

Warfield undoubtedly enjoyed the benefits of Margaret and John's efforts to improve and manage the estate. They invested both time and money in the house over a sustained period. Sixteen years after her husband inherited the property, Margaret noted in her memorandum book how in March 1811 she had been 'much engaged in opening a road thro' the shrubbery in the North-East, which is to be the approach to the new entrance in the house'.[40] Her husband had relinquished 'this amusing employment' to Margaret because he was 'so much engaged in building'.[41] The division of labour, which this comment suggests, with Margaret improving the garden and John working on the house, however, is not consistently reflected in other sources. According to the memoir written by her son, Margaret was involved with the building work, allowing as it did a practical outlet for her mathematical interests. As her son described it, if he wished to 'ascertain the quantities of roofing, & Brickwork in the erection of a range of Buildings, she was prepared to furnish me with them'.[42] Nevertheless when describing the changes in full in the memoir, Margaret and John's son gave full credit to his father.[43] It seems likely, however, that the extent of the building works which Margaret and John embarked on, from around 1809 onwards, necessitated the active involvement of both.[44] On inheriting Warfield they took on a house, which had primarily housed a bachelor and his visitors rather than a more extensive family. The rooms were deemed too small and low for the newly incumbent Benn Walsh family. In the memoir, John Benn Walsh Jr described how he remembered the house 'perfectly' and thought that his 'fathers additions made it more commodious within'.[45]

John Benn Walsh, 1st Baron Ormathwaite presents his father as leading the changes that took place at Warfield in the early decades of the nineteenth century. Benn Walsh fancied himself as an architect and set to, creating detailed plans and drawings to guide the work. As his son noted, 'Such a task was more feasible perhaps then, as the prevailing fashion required so little ornament.'[46] A man known as Lewis 'a remarkably intelligent practical Builder, Joiner & working Carpenter', significantly aided Benn Walsh in his work.[47] Assisted by his two sons, Lewis based himself on site in the old offices at Warfield for several years while the changes gradually took shape. Benn Walsh decided to affix a new house onto the old one. Lewis was primarily responsible for carrying out the joinery, carpentry and finish on the new part of the house and although Lewis's joinery work may have provided a frame for the house it is not clear who completed the other aspects of the building work.[48] Bricklaying must have taken place, however, as John Benn Walsh had spent the majority of 1808 preparing for the changes at Warfield by ordering bricks. Sustained brick working, joinery and carpentry resulted in substantial changes, such as raising a new floor on the North Front, and expanding Warfield's layout. By the end of 1811 it was possible to dine in the dining room, although the rest of the house took at least another year to complete.[49]

The exact nature of what Margaret and John sought to create at Warfield remains unknown, however, they clearly used the house as a social space allowing them to extend their reach with the Company. Their son describes how it was 'often filled by a succession of old friends & relations for weeks together'.[50] The Benn Walsh's social circle was made up of East India Company connections – the Hollands, Stracheys, Plowdens, Metcalfes, Casamajors, Dallas's and Cummings.[51] After they moved to Warfield they slowly expanded their social circle by including families in the local area, some of which also had Indian connections such as the Russells, who purchased the nearby Swallowfield Park in the 1820s.[52] The focus placed on the dining room, as the first complete room and the extent of the changes, suggests Margaret and John invested in the fabric of Warfield in order to create a house that could accommodate and entertain an increasingly wide circle of family and friends. The time and money they spent on the house and its use as a site for entertaining and hospitality suggest that Margaret and John wanted Warfield to remain and be recognized in both the family and their ever-extending network as a significant place, their principle country seat. Warfield was no longer simply a sanctuary then; it had ambitions of its own. Rebuilding Warfield also acted as a shared project in the family, something to improve and work on, and in investing time, care and money Margaret and John made the house their possession and more meaningful to them and their family. Such investments played dividends, as the house remained an important focus point and the central site of familial belonging.

A new generation

After a period of sustained investment by Margaret and John in the early 1800s, in 1819 the house was inherited by the next generation.

Once Warfield had passed to the third generation, the question of how it could continue to act as a central point of focus for the extended family emerged again. Although now living at a distance from Warfield, Margaret continued to contribute to its importance in different ways. As had been the case when she lived in India, Margaret expressed her longing for Warfield and thereby consolidated the value of the house. Her efforts to place herself in closer proximity to the house explicitly demonstrate its continued importance within the family. Moreover, Margaret's continued emotional investment in the house further shows how the house had emerged as an intergenerational project of familial belonging.

In 1819, when John and Margaret Benn Walsh's son John Benn Walsh came of age, John Walsh's original will ensured that he inherited all the properties that John and Margaret had inherited in 1795. Nevertheless, Margaret and John continued to live at Warfield until 1825. In that year Margaret's husband John Benn Walsh died after suffering a series of strokes. Six months later Margaret's son John married and she began to look for a new country house. In his memoir John Benn Walsh, 1st Baron Ormathwaite described how it was his wish that his mother should continue to live at Warfield as 'its Mistress' and that he and his wife should live at the London house on Upper Harley Street. His mother, however, 'would not hear of such an arrangement' and resolved to find another house. Significantly, Margaret sought a house within the vicinity of Warfield.[53]

Finding a suitable country house near Warfield, however, was not easy and Margaret increasingly found herself travelling at speed across the country in order to secure first refusal on a particular house. In a letter written in August 1826, Margaret recounted how she had spent her summer poring over newspapers for house advertisements. At length she was surprised to see an advertisement for Cooper's Hill – 'ready furnished in capital letters!'[54] Although situated out of the immediate range of Warfield, Margaret decided that Cooper's Hill was an ideal house and so she 'instantly determined to set off & endeavour to obtain it'. Accompanied by her maid, she took the post from Malvern, slept at Tewkesbury and finally arrived in Upper Harley Street. Before ten the next morning she presented herself at the house agent for Cooper's Hill and found that three applications had already been made for the property.[55] Seeing that she had no time to lose, she travelled directly to Cooper's Hill, again with her maid in tow. The house was offered for £600 per year and could only be rented until February 1828. After seeing the property, Margaret considered its advantages and disadvantages at length. As she did not require the house for six months and because the price of the lease was so high she was reluctant to agree. Nevertheless, she felt that by living at Cooper's Hill she would be well placed to find another property in the area without 'scampering 150 miles to catch a place'.[56] At the same time although the rooms were 'low', she liked the location of Cooper's Hill, describing it as 'high', 'dry', 'healthy' and 'shady'. For Margaret it was 'a most pleasing residence'.[57] In the end, however, her negotiations for Cooper's Hill fell through and she resorted again to poring over advertisements, which she then neatly noted down in the back of her diary.[58] Eventually Margaret secured the residence of Hurst Lodge from a Mr Elliott. She planned to lease Hurst Lodge for a short time until the tenants of Binfield died, at which point she would lease Binfield from Elliott.[59]

Around six miles from Warfield, a certain Robert Palmer had purchased Hurst Lodge in 1742. By 1796 the Palmer family's main residence became Holme Park in Sonning and it seems likely that the house was then rented out, possibly to the Elliott family. Margaret recorded some of her responses to the experience of renting Hurst Lodge in her diary. These brief notes suggest some of the anxieties endured by widows on removal from the main family home. She described how in early October 1827 her servants had worked hard to clean and tidy Hurst Lodge, removing 'the immense confusion occasioned by Mr Elliott's long continuance' there.[60] By Friday 11 October when Margaret finally took up residence in the house, 'everything was put in its place'. Nevertheless, despite the servants' hard work, despite everything being 'put in its place', when Margaret ventured into the new home she could not 'conquer the melancholy that seized' her on 'taking possession of a new home!'[61] She experienced grief for all that she had lost. For Margaret that past was 'still so vivid' in her remembrance 'it seemed like reality'.[62] The next day Margaret continued to feel downcast by her new surroundings. Although she conceded that 'the pleasure ground is pretty & the house comfortable' it gave her 'very little pleasure'. She described how she 'regretted that [she] had taken it, & yet condemned [her]self for any discontent'.[63] Margaret's wealth protected her from the trials of dependence that many women experienced.[64] Nevertheless, the independence that her wealth bought her also guaranteed her removal from a home that contained multiple meanings and pleasures.

Margaret continued to live at Hurst Lodge until the summer 1831 when she finally took up the lease of Binfield. It seems likely that she rented Binfield Park from a descendant of the original builder of the property – Onesiphorus Elliot – who constructed the house in 1775. Her move to Binfield was a happy one. Her son John believed that his mother was much happier at Binfield because her happiness was so dependent on her proximity to him. After his father's death in 1825, John felt that, 'the interest, the consolation, the enjoyment' of his mother's remaining years, 'were all centred' on him.[65] Nevertheless, in the memoir he also writes at length about the interiors of Binfield and the time and money that Margaret invested in improving them. His lengthy descriptions of her improvement projects suggest that while Margaret may well have sought primarily to find comfort in living near to her son, she also worked hard to secure her own *material* comfort at Binfield and that of her fellow inhabitants.

Her daughter Elizabeth, grandchildren, their governess and the servants all lived in Binfield with Margaret. John described how 'Binfield Park was a large, Handsome, commodious, well built mansion' with 'ample accommodation'.[66] The rooms were large and several showrooms were included in the layout. The drawing room and dining parlour were both 'handsome moderate sized rooms, about thirty feet long'. On the first floor of the house, Margaret created a suite of rooms for herself, which included a spacious sitting room. As with the country house libraries built by elite gentlemen, Margaret's sitting room lined with bookcases, existed as both a representation of her erudition and as a space in which her learning could be extended.[67] Here she benefitted from having her 'Books, papers and all her little personal belongings' surrounding her, providing a space in which she could read and further her mathematical studies.[68]

Before Margaret began to inhabit the house with her family she had the whole property repainted and papered. Like Warfield before it, Binfield benefitted from the skills of a particular carpenter – this time a certain 'Morris' who worked closely with Margaret to enact the various repairs and improvements she wanted to take place.[69] In the memoir John, as ever, uses his description of the project to emphasize his mother's superiority and skill. In this case he describes her success by stressing how she implemented change at relatively little expense through tight management of the process. He describes how she 'managed all this with so much calculation, & economy'. Here Margaret embodies the female ideal of genteel prudence and neatness explored by Amanda Vickery.[70] Yet the economy employed by Margaret and commended by her son also suggests at Margaret's vulnerable financial position and her awareness of it. Moved out of her home – *the* home – Margaret remained mobile until she was able to rent a house on the periphery of the grounds. John's claim that improving Binfield was 'a great amusement & occupation to her' needs to be treated sceptically. His assertion that 'Warfield was to her another home always in reach' is perhaps more telling.[71]

Conclusion

Finally, it might be assumed that John Benn Walsh, 1st Baron Ormathwaite's intimate relationship with his mother ('The word reserve was unknown between us') assured that he would also assume a deep attachment to Warfield.[72] Throughout the memoir Benn Walsh reaffirms the importance his mother placed on Warfield – '[Margaret] loved Warfield, she had known it all her life, it had been the home in such measure, of her childhood'.[73] Yet before Margaret's death on 29 September 1836, John expressed very little attachment to the house. Rather it was after her death that he established a much stronger relationship to the house and all that it represented about his mother. On her death John wanted to be at Warfield. In his own diary he described how 'During my whole life I never was more disposed to remain quietly at Warfield.' While there he began to enter into activities which he had previously enjoyed with his mother. He set to pruning and thinning the trees in the grounds and tried to complete little improvements that he felt his mother 'would have liked, or such as she had planned'.[74] These activities related to his earlier experiences, such as when he returned from school one Easter vacation and helped his mother to thin the trees in the shrubbery. He describes how he 'was then about eleven or twelve, tall & strong enough to wield my Hatchet with very … desirable effect'.[75] On Margaret's death her son John imbued the house with new meaning. Rather than his childhood home, Warfield became important for its connection to his mother and the sense of belonging he associated with her. Unlike for earlier generations who were displaced from the house and thus linked it to broader narratives of home and belonging, for John the house was established in the family, meaning that it could be appropriated for much more particular and personal associations.

As different generations took possession of Warfield Park, they each invested money, time and effort on the house and gardens. Whether away from Warfield and expressing feelings and longings for it, or resident at the house and planning changes and expansions, different members of the family and kinship network contributed to the project of making Warfield an important and meaningful place. By engaging in an intergenerational project focused on one site, the Walsh and Benn Walsh family simultaneously worked to instantiate the importance of their own family and its position within broader Company networks. Giving a geographical and material location to their sense of belonging strengthened and clarified their familial identity.

While the purchase, building and rebuilding of country houses by East India Company families was clearly linked to the establishment of their status within elite groups in Britain, it must also be recognized that embarking on such projects allowed families to fashion other needs. Often globally mobile due to imperial service, EIC families were often adept at maintaining the necessary familial belonging over space. Once returned, locating themselves and their families at a particular country house and investing time, money and effort in its maintenance and expansion allowed families to create a sense of belonging over time. If they were to benefit from the wealth raised by Company service (a particular feature of the second half of the eighteenth century) embarking on an intergenerational project would prove significant. Moreover, if other family members were to benefit from imperial contacts formed by the first generation, retaining a sense of familial identity and coherence was also important. Nevertheless, in conclusion it is necessary to note that while Margaret prospered at and from Warfield, her brother Francis did not – the house was hers, not his. Building a coherent identity thus relied as much on exclusion as inclusion.[76] It was through building, longing, editing and erasing that the Benn Walsh family managed to create and recreate Warfield and in turn maintain their family as a recognizable and significant unit over multiple generations.

9
Englefield House, Berkshire

Processes, practices and the making of a Company house

Kate Smith

When W. Fletcher and Edmund J. Niemann toured Reading in the 1830s they noticed a 'splendid mansion', 'seated on the declivity of a hill', which remained sheltered from the north-east winds 'by the verdant summit'.[1] Englefield House was the 'splendid mansion' in question. Fletcher and Niemann depicted Englefield as a solid, constant entity 'bounded by swelling hills, adorned with elegant seats, woods, and cultivated grounds'.[2] In referring to Englefield's surrounding land, Fletcher and Niemann stressed the importance of Englefield as a landed estate and thus a receptacle and symbol of power and wealth. In case readers were in any doubt of the historical longevity of the house, Fletcher and Niemann set out further to reassure them. The house, they claimed, corresponded 'in its style with those erected about the time of Elizabeth, with handsome bay windows, battlements, and towers'. Englefield's appearance was 'noble', possessing as it did 'all that uniformity of design characteristic of fine architecture'. A present day image of Englefield (see Figure 9.1) confirms and reiterates Fletcher and Niemann's earlier depiction. Although perhaps 'superficially mid-Victorian', its Elizabethan architecture continues to remain imposingly solid today.[3]

Surviving as it has for so many centuries, the architecture of the house represents continuity and longevity. As a result, in looking to the house's material form, certain elements of its history are obscured. On first sight, for example, its eighteenth- and early nineteenth-century history and its connections with the East India Company (EIC) in this period, are largely

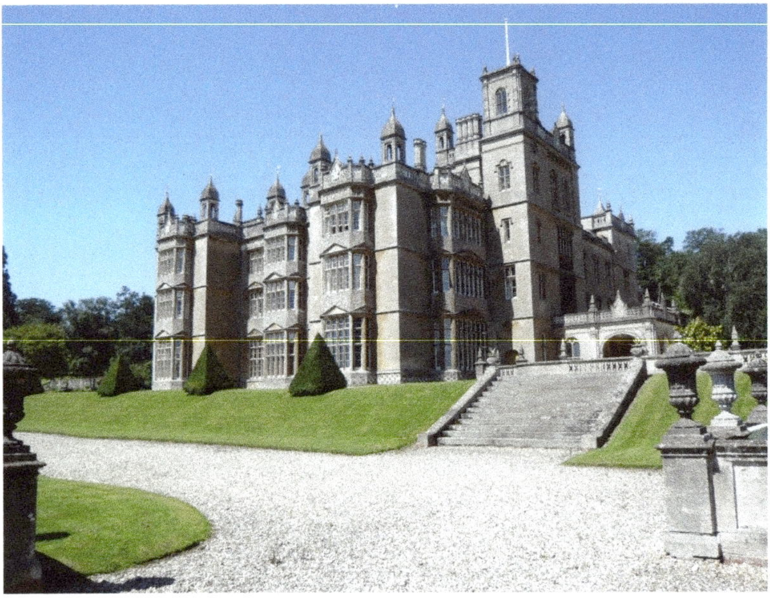

Figure 9.1 Englefield House, Berkshire. Image courtesy of Georgina Green.

hidden. Unlike country houses such as Sezincote in Gloucestershire, there is no sign at Englefield of the East India Company and its Indian ventures marked on the exterior of the building. Nevertheless objects, people and money all linked Englefield House to the EIC in the eighteenth and early nineteenth century and these links shaped Englefield in its turn. In that certain elements of its history do not appear to be represented by its material form and aesthetic motifs, Englefield might be likened to houses such as Bolsover Castle, Brodsworth Hall, Marble Hill, Northington Grange, Kenwood House and Osborne House, which can be linked to the slave trade but upon which few material reminders can be found.[4] To contribute to the broader project of uncovering the often hidden histories of empire in Britain's country houses, this chapter moves past Englefield's architecture to instead focus on the flows of people and possessions into and out of the house. In doing so it reveals Englefield's imperial history and demonstrates how constant change rather than continuity shaped the house in the eighteenth and early nineteenth century.

Rather than treating Englefield as an inert object then, this chapter understands this country house by examining its dynamic use. Marriage, inheritance, purchase and renting ensured that successive waves of inhabitants entered and occupied Englefield in the eighteenth and early nineteenth century.[5] The EIC encouraged individuals connected with the Company to form and constantly renew their social networks. Often established on the subcontinent in unfamiliar circumstances in the eighteenth century, connections flourished as officials helped each other to transport personal goods and family members to and from India, pass on news of kin, facilitate the movement of wealth or private trade and circulate letters and gifts. EIC officials also relied on their networks to provide opportunities for advancement.[6] Once home, individuals continued to cultivate their connections in order to hear news of the Company and fellow officials, as well as connected families. It was these links that often provided opportunities after return to Britain and, if necessary, allowed family members to return to empire. While patronage, wealth, gifts and letters could pass through EIC networks, this chapter argues that, so too could houses. In Berkshire particularly, the proximity of certain estates and homes to each other meant that once an EIC family possessed a country house in a specific location, that area often became attractive to other EIC men and women. Richard Benyon, Lady Margaret Clive and Elizabeth Sykes were all connected to the East India Company and came to reside at Englefield House at different points and for different reasons during the eighteenth century. Richard Benyon (1698–1774) worked for the Company, ending his service as Governor of Fort St George, Madras between 1735 and 1744; Lady Margaret Clive (1735–1817) was effectively married to the Company, once she had become bethrothed to Robert Clive (1725–74) in 1753, and continued to be involved in Company politics after his death; and Elizabeth Sykes (d.1814) was daughter to Company official, Sir Francis Sykes (1732–1804) of Basildon Park. By focusing on the house, rather than a particular family, by including Company women, as well as Company men and by privileging moments of change, loss and discontinuity a fuller picture of country house living and the East India Company emerges – one that is significantly closer to a narrative of change and disruption than continuity and consistency. In sum, this chapter explores how, during the eighteenth and early nineteenth century, the movement of people into and out of Englefield ensured that this 'English' house became a node within the Company's Asian empire. In this period, Berkshire became known as the 'English Hindoostan', and Englefield was at its centre.

The East India Company arrives

Englefield's imposing structure stands within rolling grounds near the village of Englefield in Berkshire, on the site of an earlier house, which belonged to the Englefield family. The Englefields surrendered most of the estate in 1585 and the house then remained in varying degrees of splendour until Anne Wrighte (née Paulet) inherited it from her brother Lord Francis Paulet in 1712. At the time, Anne was married to Reverend Nathaniel Wrighte. During their marriage the Wrightes had three sons, the eldest of whom (Powlett Wrighte) inherited Englefield in 1729. Powlett Wrighte (d.1741) augmented his inheritance by marrying well. He tied his own estate to that of the Beauvoirs by marrying the heiress to the Beauvoirs' fortune – Mary Tyssen (d.1776), daughter of Francis Tyssen (d.1712) and Rachel Beauvoir from Hackney in Surrey.[7] Powlett Wrighte and Mary Tyssen had one son, Powlett Wrighte the Younger. Following Wrighte's death in 1741, Mary remained at Englefield with their son. John Wilder and Daniel May held the estates and lands in trust for Mary and her son Powlett, until he came of age in his twenty-first year.[8] In 1745 Mary remarried, to Richard Benyon and it is at this point that Englefield's history became intertwined with that of the EIC.

Richard Benyon was born in 1698, and in 1712 he began his career with the East India Company.[9] Little is known of Benyon's early life or family connections. In *Swallowfield and its Owners* (1925), Lady Constance Russell suggests that the Mr Benyon who witnessed Thomas Pitt's (1653–1726) acquisition of his famous diamond in 1702 was Daniel Benyon (1664–c.1709), who she asserted to be Richard Benyon's father (a claim supported by Bernard Burke's A *Genealogical and Heraldic Dictionary of the Landed Gentry of Great Britain and Ireland*).[10] In contrast, in *The Nabobs of Berkshire*, Clive Williams argues that the Benyon who witnessed Pitt's purchase might have been Bernard Benyon (d.1715) who was then a member of the Madras council.[11] Henry Dawson Love, writing his *Vestiges of Old Madras* (1913), noted that Bernard Benyon might be Richard Benyon's brother.[12] Bernard Benyon of the Madras council had a daughter (Grace) with his wife Grace in 1713, but then died and was buried in Madras on 7 February 1715.[13] It is likely therefore that he would have been established in Madras in 1712 when Richard Benyon arrived there, suggesting that he was older than Richard and was possibly his uncle. Whether brother or uncle to Richard, Bernard Benyon was certainly well connected elsewhere: when Thomas Pitt (of diamond fame, Governor of Madras from 1698 to 1709 and later the first 'Indian' owner of Swallowfield Park) found out that Benyon was dead he described how he had experienced 'a great loss, which delays my leaving town till Monday'.[14] With such connections, Bernard and

Daniel Benyon were well placed to ensure their family's rise through the Company and indeed Richard Benyon rose swiftly within its service. In 1718, just six years after his appointment to the civil service, he had become a member of the Madras Council, and he later went on to become the Governor of Madras in 1735.

On 17 October 1724, at the age of 26, Richard Benyon married Mary Fleetwood.[15] Mary was the granddaughter of Robert Fleetwood, who had arrived in Madras in 1662 and became the Chief at the Company's Factory at Madpollam in Golcanda (Hyderabad). Robert Fleetwood survived for 14 years in India before dying in 1676 in Madras.[16] Mary Fleetwood was possibly the daughter of the supercargo Edward Fleetwood.[17] Clive Williams infers that Mary Fleetwood was related to Elizabeth Fleetwood (b.1700) who married Richard Shelley in 1726. This couple later became grandparents to Anne Barbara Whitworth (d.1814), who married Henry Russell Sr (1751–1836) in 1782, who purchased Swallowfield Park in 1820.[18] These relationships remind us that the Company's increasing grip on the Indian subcontinent was sustained by a cohesive elite, which maintained its identity (notwithstanding the many challenges of trans-imperial domestic life) through intermarriage and domestic life in a nexus of connected domestic sites. An eighteenth-century conversation piece further confirms the link between the Benyons and the Shelleys. The information listed for the painting in the catalogue to the 1906 Whitechapel Gallery exhibition 'The Georgians', attributed the piece to William Hogarth and noted that it featured Lady Shelley, Mr and Mrs Richard Shelley, Misses Fanny and Martha Rose Shelley, Capt The Hon. W. Fitzwilliam, Mr. Benyon, and Miss Beard.[19] As the provenance of the painting is uncertain, it is difficult to tell to which Benyon the painting refers. Nevertheless, it shows that Richard Benyon may well have had multiple links to Berkshire and to Swallowfield Park from an early stage: first through Thomas Pitt's connection to Bernard and Daniel Benyon and second through his first wife Mary, who was possibly great-aunt to Anne Barbara Whitworth. Like many other East India Company officials Richard Benyon soon became connected to multiple Company persons and sites.

After only one year of marriage the Benyons returned home to England, in 1725. At this juncture, Benyon made full use of his newfound wealth and bought the Manor of Coptfold Hall in Margaretting, Essex, in 1728.[20] Despite the purchase of his new home, he soon returned to India. In 1732 he was reappointed to Fort St George, Madras as Second-in-Council; he arrived in Madras in 1733. On 20 January 1735 the Company appointed Benyon Governor of Madras. While in this role,

Benyon (now a widower) married for the second time, on 14 October 1738 to Frances Davis.[21] Just over two years later, on 24 January 1741, Frances gave birth to their daughter (also Frances), who died shortly thereafter, leaving the couple to bury her the next day.[22] A year later, Benyon's wife Frances died in childbirth, on 21 October 1742.[23] Shortly after this, in January 1744, Benyon boarded the *Duke* and returned to England for the final time. In 1745 he bought Gidea Hall near Romford (now a boys' school), which had recently been rebuilt as a mansion. In the same year, Benyon acquired another property through marriage. In 1745 he married the widow Mary Wrighte of Englefield House.

Richard and Mary Benyon lived together in Englefield for 29 years before Richard died in 1774. Despite the affective value that they placed on objects, little is known of the changes the couple made to the interior of Englefield House.[24] Alongside Englefield and Gidea Hall, the Benyons also owned Great Newbury in Ilford, which they had purchased from Thomas Webster in 1747, after Benyon had moved to Englefield. In 1758 they purchased yet another property, North Ockendon in Essex from Hugh Meynell.[25] Like other returned Company men, Benyon's conspicuous consumption of multiple properties contributed to ensuring that the figure of the 'nabob' became a powerful image in the second half of the eighteenth century. The proximity of these properties to each other in particular locales consolidated an understanding of such purchases as conspicuous. Gidea Hall, Great Newbury and North Ockenden, for example, all lay along a 15-mile route, which stretched around present day Romford and finished in Ilford. North Ockenden, like Gidea Hall, descended through the Benyon side of the family with Newbury until 1891. The *Victoria County History* records that 'North Ockenden Hall lay within a moated enclosure immediately south of the churchyard. The redbrick house was of sixteenth-century origin with additions of the early eighteenth and the nineteenth centuries. It was damaged by bombing in 1944 and later demolished.'[26] Unlike North Ockenden, Gidea Hall and Newbury, Englefield descended through the Powlett Wrighte side of the family, and when Mary Benyon died in 1776, Englefield passed to Powlett Wrighte the Younger (d.1779), her son by her first marriage.

The Wrightes return

During the 1770s Powlett Wrighte the Younger made many changes to Englefield. He added a neoclassical frieze featuring a repeating lotus and anthemion pattern (which originated in Ancient Egypt and profoundly influenced the arts of Eurasia) to the drawing room. At the same time, Wrighte also picked out a matching white marble chimney-piece and Corinthian pilasters for the dining room.[27] Such opulence was matched in other areas of the house. Powlett Wrighte's executor accounts list payments of over £1,400 to the upholsterers Ince and Mayhew for two sets of chairs and settees.[28] At the same time, it also seems that Powlett Wrighte made substantial changes to the fabric of the house. A few clues remain as to whom he might have employed as an architect. In January 1781, Powlett Wrighte's executors paid 10 guineas to a certain 'Mr Woods Surveyor'. Jackson-Stops argues that Mr Woods was 'most certainly' the landscape gardener Richard Woods, who came from Essex and who laid out the park at Gidea for Wrighte's half-brother Richard Benyon the Younger (1746–97).[29] Another surveyor, Clement Read, was paid £60 in November 1781. Yet, in employing surveyors, possibly making changes to the exterior, and definitely altering the interior, Powlett Wrighte accumulated many debts upon the estate. As John Habakkuk has argued, such house building often arose from motives of comfort, aesthetics, prestige or taste and was generally paid for not by capital or an enlarged income but by a landowner's current income. In paying for house building using this method many families accumulated debt as costs became uncontrollable.[30] The debts incurred on the estate by Powlett Wrighte the Younger ultimately became a problem that the next owner of Englefield would have to solve.[31] Although Powlett Wrighte the Younger married in 1777, he died childless in 1779 and left Englefield to his uncle Nathaniel Wrighte, in accordance with his father's will.[32]

At this point, according to Nathaniel Wrighte an 'Inventory and Appraisements of the Household goods & Furniture of Englefield House' was carried out by Higgs, while a 'Catalogue of & Valuation of the Books in the Library' was completed by Fletcher.[33] As a result of the appraisement the 'Goods' were valued at £160 and the books at £144. After having the books 'clean'd and properly arranged', Wrighte offered to send them to Richard Benyon the Younger, 'if you would chuse to have them sent to you, please to let me know where and I will send them immediately'.[34] Just one year later, in 1780, Nathaniel Wrighte wrote to Benyon expressing his concerns about the amount of debt carried by the Englefield estate.[35] By the summer of 1781, Nathaniel Wrighte had begun to take action – he was keen to let Englefield. Although renting-out remains understudied in country house literature, it was an important strategy for retaining country houses within families. As this chapter shows, however, renting simultaneously stabilized and destabilized the country house. Although in the long term it allowed Englefield to remain within the wider structure of the Wrighte and Benyon families, in the short term, leasing resulted in a change of character for the house as a new occupier inhabited it. Nathaniel Wrighte and Richard Benyon the Younger were alert to the possibility of destabilization, which renting prompted, and worked hard to find a 'suitable' tenant.

Initially Wrighte courteously offered Richard Benyon the Younger first refusal on the estate, but Benyon turned this offer down, despite his hopes that the estate would remain in the family. In a letter to Wrighte, Benyon described how he felt 'much obliged to you for your attention in giving me the first offer, which numberless reasons tender it absolutely impossible for me to accept. I hope however that your resolution is not unalterably fixed & that you will still pass many happy years there.'[36] Wrighte was determined, however, and after careful consideration felt that 'I am to find myself obliged to make a temporary resignation of it, but so it must be, for after having been now all most two years in possession of this Estate, I am fully convinced, that the unavoidable outgoings and deductions are greater than any Income can support'.[37] Almost three weeks later, Wrighte wrote to Benyon again. He valued Englefield highly and estimated that the rent should be 400 guineas per annum, 'for the use of nearly two thousand Pounds worth of furniture & Books, a hundred acres of exceeding rich lands, a Park well stocked with Deer a Pond or rather Lake abounding with the most excellent Fish, the sporting Liberties of three good Manors, cannot be thought one farthing too much'.[38] Wrighte hoped that Benyon would be able to recommend some potential tenants, 'such a one as you yourself may approve of'.[39]

It is difficult to know whom Richard Benyon would have recommended to Wrighte – perhaps one of his mother's family or one of his father's East India Company connections. Wrighte though clearly felt that Benyon was well connected enough (particularly perhaps to EIC connections with ready money) to recommend someone suitable. From Benyon's correspondence it seems that he was keen for a certain Mr D'Oyly to take Englefield.[40] But after making enquiries through Mr Southouse, he found that D'Oyly had already taken Ware Park in Hertfordshire.[41] By December 1781, Mr Wrighte had found a tenant and negotiated a rent of 300 rather than 400 guineas.[42] The new tenant of Englefield House was the widow of Lord Robert Clive – Lady Margaret Clive (1735–1817).

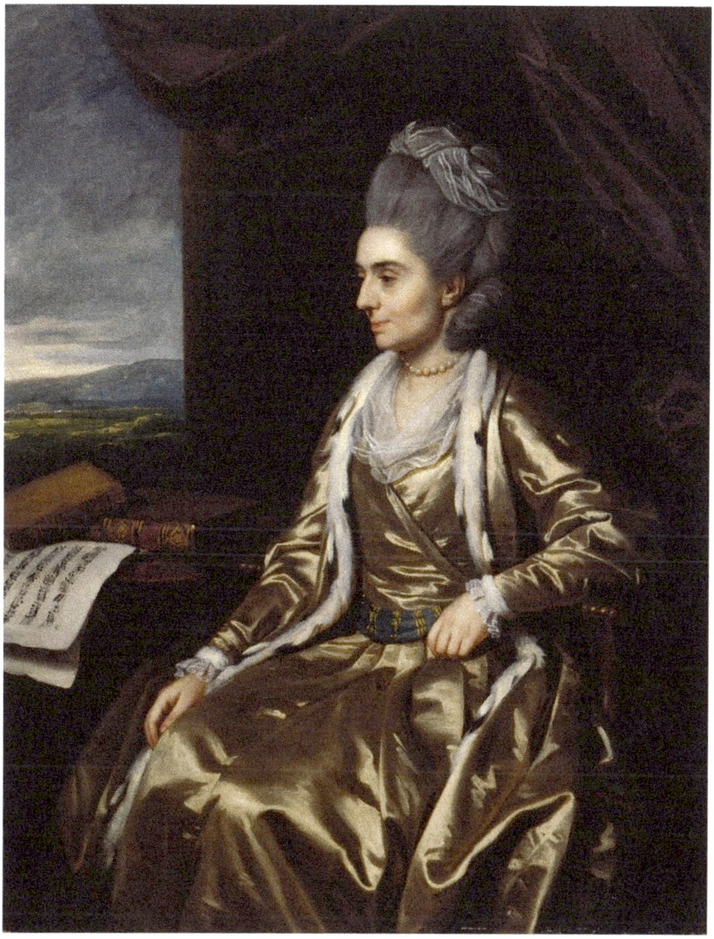

Figure 9.2 Portrait of Margaret Maskelyne, Lady Clive by Nathaniel Dance. Powis Castle, Powys, Wales. © National Trust Images.

Lady Margaret Clive at Englefield House

It seems that Richard Benyon did not recommend Lady Clive (see Figure 9.2), but rather that she came under recommendation from others. Nathaniel Wrighte described to Benyon how he had been 'informed by many who had the honour of being acquainted with Lady Clive, that her Ladyship was possessed of many excellent Qualities, and that there was no room for doubt but that she would take all possible care of the Books, Furniture etc left in the house and of the Premises in general', therefore he 'prevailed … to give her Ladyship the preferences to all others who had before made or were then making applications for that most delightful place'.[43] Wrighte chose Lady Clive to be tenant at Englefield in part because he believed that she would give due attention to the material objects and interiors belonging to the house. He clearly valued Englefield's interiors and objects highly and was prepared to accept a lower rent in order to secure a tenant whom he believed would do the same. At the same time, he must have recognized the importance of a link with a 'nabobina' such as Lady Clive who was wealthy and well connected.[44]

Lady Clive was a significant and well-known figure within the Company's networks, and her tenancy of Englefield saw the house's links with the EIC progressively enlarge. As a figure connected to wider public conceptions of the Company, Lady Clive's presence consolidated Englefield's place within the 'English Hindoostan'. At the same time, she welcomed other Company visitors to the house, marking this home still further with Company connections. In 1787, for instance, Margaret Fowke, niece of the East India Company official John Walsh who lived at nearby Warfield Park, planned to marry John Benn of Ormathwaite, Cumbria (who had been in the Company's civil service in Calcutta from 1778 to 1786) at Englefield House. Lady Clive was cousin to John Walsh and retained close connections with the family and Margaret in particular. Although Margaret ultimately decided to have the ceremony at her brother Francis's house in London and the reception at Richmond on Saturday 30 June 1787, she visited Englefield with her new husband in July. Writing to John Walsh in 1787, Margaret explained that 'I should be happy to follow your advice in having the ceremony performed at Englefield & should receive a most [?] pleasure from the presence of Lady Clive. The only reason why I prefer London & my brother's house is that it is infinitely more private – a circumstance to my feeling of the utmost moment in a marriage.'[45] Country houses could be used to host marriage ceremonies, but they also acted as important sites from which East India Company families could launch young daughters onto the marriage market.

Lady Clive moved to Englefield in the 1780s in order to place her youngest daughter in a suitable location for entry into society. Outside of London, but close enough to visit out of season and near to other East India Company connections in the area, Englefield was an ideal location at this moment in Lady Clive's life cycle. When that moment ended in the late 1780s, she moved to another location. As demonstrated in the chapter on Swallowfield Park in this volume, women connected to the East India Company often returned from India with young children and led peripatetic lives, moving from country house to country house. Similarly, as the chapter on Warfield Park in this volume demonstrates, as widows Company women were also often required to become mobile in order to fulfill the needs of their families. Lady Clive's experience further illustrates how peripatetic living continued into later life for widows. Just before her youngest daughter married a certain Mr Walpole, as her maternal duties ended, others in the Englefield household assumed that Lady Clive would leave for a smaller residence.[46] In 1788 as she began to look for another house and considered renting Dunston Park, located around nine miles away from Englefield House in Thatcham, Berkshire, but decided against it. She also looked at some houses in Essex. Her efforts to change residence could not have come too soon. In 1789 Nathaniel Wrighte died and Richard Benyon the Younger inherited Englefield.

The Benyon legacy (1789–1854)

Richard Benyon the Younger's possession of Englefield was short-lived. He died in 1796, leaving his son Richard Benyon (1770–1854) to inherit. On 27 September 1797, a year after his father's death and his own inheritance of Englefield, Richard Benyon married Elizabeth Sykes, only daughter of Sir Francis Sykes of Basildon Park. Upon this marriage Englefield's connection with the East India Company grew stronger still. At the same time, Benyon's connections to Berkshire and the English establishment likewise increased.

In *An Open Elite?*, Lawrence and Jeanne C. Fawtier Stone argued that between 1540 and 1880 the English elite was not as open as has previously been assumed by historians. They asserted that 'Only a very small handful of very rich merchants succeeded in buying their way into the elite, and by the second generation they were fully assimilated'.[47] In contrast, this chapter reminds us that 'rich merchants' could both buy *and* marry into the elite. However, it took a third generation for this family to become assimilated, and even then assimilation was not necessarily 'full'. Richard Benyon joined the elite by focusing on parliament, local civic responsibilities and house building. In 1802, he became MP for Pontefract, remaining in this seat until 1806.[48] In the same year, Benyon sold Gidea Hall to Alexander Black and Englefield became the principal family seat.[49] In the following two parliaments, from 1806 to 1812, Benyon acted as

MP for Wallingford. He continued to focus his attentions on Berkshire by becoming Justice of the Peace, Deputy Lieutenant of Berkshire and High Sheriff of Berkshire. Benyon's marriage revealed the coexistence of these local connections with wider Company networks: he and his 'English' country house simultaneously figured in local, national and global worlds.

From 1806 onwards, Benyon began improving Englefield and employed the celebrated architect Sir John Soane (1753–1837) to complete the designs.[50] As part of his alterations, Benyon added an elevation to the east front. Gervase Jackson-Stops argues that this change suggests that they intended to remove the eighteenth-century Venetian windows on the south side and the cupolas to the towers and insert a new door and windows.[51] He also suggests that the construction of the elevation might have been connected with the removal of 'Paulet Wrighte's offices' on the east front. In 1814 Benyon was in the fortunate position of acquiring an extensive inheritance through his connections to the Powlett Wrighte family and rapidly adopted the Powlett Wrighte name. Eight years later, Richard Benyon Powlett Wrighte's wife Elizabeth died. In that same year 1822, he gained another fortune, from his de Beauvoir cousin who owned land in Hackney and became Richard Benyon de Beauvoir. With his identity (as signified by his surname) in a state of constant flux, Benyon turned to bricks and mortar to fix his family in Berkshire and the traditions signified by the English country house. He used his newfound wealth to begin another improvement campaign at Englefield.[52]

Initially Benyon de Beauvoir approached architect Thomas Hopper, who had previously worked on Penrhyn Castle and Leigh Court and restyled Purley Hall between 1818 and 1820. In the earliest surviving letter to Hopper, Benyon de Beauvoir included a pencil sketch of the south-east corner of the house, outlining the addition of two bay windows, which would light the room and rooms above it.[53] In response to his client's desire for more light, Hopper added windows to the dining room side that replicated the proportions and decorations of the central porch bay. He also changed the silhouette of the house by adding a series of tall, square turrets, many of which disguised chimneystacks and made some internal alterations, for instance the ceilings of the library and dining room even though the latter incorporated earlier plasterwork. These alterations continued for a decade, and Benyon de Beauvoir finally made his last payment to Hopper in 1829.[54]

In an 1832 watercolour, John Constable portrayed the changes Benyon de Beauvoir had made to Englefield. Constable described Englefield as a house still marked by its original construction in the Elizabethan period, and it is interesting to conjecture whether Benyon himself sought to use this image to project a suppositious Elizabethan family history with this home. For Constable's vision for Englefield as an Elizabethan house was reflected not only in the exterior character of the house but also in its interior decoration. Very few of the furnishings bought by Richard Benyon de Beauvoir survive, but when Jackson-Stops researched the house in 1981 he found a battlemented state bed supplied in 1833 by the upholsterers Allaway and Davis. It was originally hung with blue and silver brocade, the tester 'trimmed with 52 Blue silk Gothic shape ornaments.'[55] By using the 'Gothic shape', Benyon de Beauvoir showed both his engagement with the fashionable Gothic revival movement, which looked to the architecture and arts of the twelfth to sixteenth centuries, but also the house's original Elizabethan history. In this manner, Benyon de Beauvoir aesthetically closed the space between its original building and the contemporary moment of his residence at Englefield.

Conclusion

In 1849 Richard Benyon de Beauvoir purchased South Ockenden Hall in Essex. The property remained in the family until 1937 when it was sold along with the family's other Essex properties to pay for death duties.[56] Englefield, however, remained in the Benyon family and does so today. Within the Benyon family, therefore, Englefield continued to be relied upon as a marker of history, lineage and thus power. Nevertheless, as this chapter has shown, rather than an apparently 'timeless' continuity of ownership, in the eighteenth century it was colonial sources of wealth that allowed the Benyon family to slowly take possession of Englefield. Moreover, Company money was important in allowing the family to maintain and reconfigure the house in ways that asserted its Elizabethan roots, roots that predated the family's wealth and association with the house. Rather than 'timeless' continuity, processes such as inheritance, marriage and renting constantly brought new occupiers to Englefield's door in the eighteenth century. Amongst those new occupiers Richard Benyon, Lady Clive and Elizabeth Sykes brought their East India Company connections and wealth and political power with them. Hence, Englefield took its due part in the 'English

Hindoostan' not necessarily because its exterior or interior changed but rather because the people connected to it changed its character. Englefield continued to act as a 'power house' from the sixteenth century onwards, but as with many other 'English' powerhouses, did so as a result of Indian wealth.

10
Swallowfield Park, Berkshire

From royalist bastion to empire home

Margot Finn

In *Swallowfield and Its Owners*, published in 1901, Lady Constance Russell (wife of the 4th baronet) presented her marital family home to readers as a quintessentially 'English' country house. Tracing Swallowfield's history seamlessly from the Norman Conquest to the Victorian era, her volume embedded this Berkshire country house into a continuous narrative of English state formation by underlining its connection to a succession of medieval and Renaissance kings, queens and statesmen. Granted as dowry to Elizabeth of York by Henry VII, Lady Russell noted, Swallowfield was held in succession by five of Henry VIII's six wives. The present-day house, built by the Tory earl Clarendon in the seventeenth century, was later improved by the king's own architect, and served as a royalist bastion into the eighteenth century, a persistent association with the English monarchy which Lady Russell repeatedly underlined. Like her chapter on 'Swallowfield and the Dowry of Tudor Queens', her concluding chapter on 'Some Old Customs and Antiquities of Swallowfield' suggested that the home's biography exemplified the history of merry England.[1] This insular, 'island' history of Swallowfield persists to the present day. Marketing materials for the luxury flats carved out of the estate in the twentieth century continue to advertise Swallowfield as a 'classic', 'historic' and 'traditional' oasis of English country life.[2] Described by managing agents Sunley Heritage (itself an evocative name) as 'A Home with a History', Swallowfield in the twenty-first century presents a simulacrum of establishment England, a house whose emphatically national heritage is constituted by 'Politics and Nobility' (see Figure 10.1).[3]

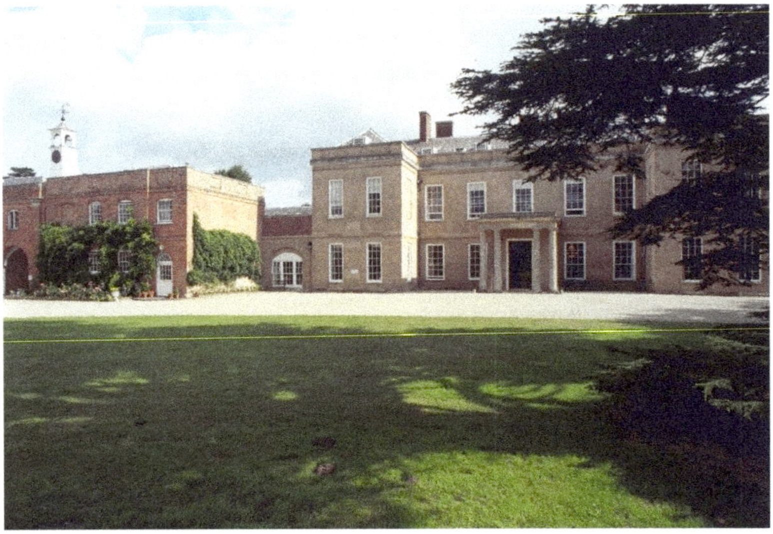

Figure 10.1 Swallowfield Park. © Brian Steptoe, FRPS. Source: Historic England Archive.

This imagined island history, shorn of both European and imperial referents, effaces global connections that have shaped this stately home for generations. For, as Lady Russell was well aware, Swallowfield's English history had been closely intertwined with British imperial expansion since the early eighteenth century. In 1719, Thomas 'Diamond' Pitt (1653–1726) purchased the estate. He had secured a vast private fortune by illegal trade in India, and sought to launder this Indian wealth through judicious investment in English landed estates.[4] Pitt's acquisition set an imperial precedent at Swallowfield that persisted into the nineteenth century. The estate passed from East Indian to West Indian hands in 1788, when Timothy Hare Earle (1737–1816) acquired Swallowfield for his family. In her 1901 history, Lady Russell passed discretely over the source of Earle's wealth, noting only that he had inherited property on St Kitts and that his son later sold Swallowfield 'in consequence of the depreciation of West India property'.[5] We know, however, from the UCL *Legacies of British Slave-ownership* project database that Earle was a substantial slave-owner: when emancipation was enacted in 1834, he received over £3,600 from Parliament – or, just under £3 million in current money – as compensation for his loss of his property in 187 enslaved persons.[6] The 'depreciation of West India property' to which Lady Russell so delicately alluded followed directly on from Parliament's abolition of the British slave trade in 1807. The excision of slavery from

Swallowfield's history in her text reflects much wider patterns of selective amnesia that have shaped British history writing, and British historical consciousness more broadly, since the abolition of Caribbean slavery in the 1830s.[7]

The Russell family's purchase of Swallowfield from Earle in 1820 ensured that this 'English' home would remain tightly bound to empire throughout the Victorian era. Men and women whose two-fold investment in English and global domestic life spanned three generations, the Russells of Swallowfield illustrate many of the key themes and questions that shape this volume. Henry (later Sir Henry) Russell (1751–1836) was the son of a middling Kentish merchant. He rose – through imperial service in India – to great wealth and status, shedding his mercantile origins to secure (for himself and his sons) positions within both the British state apparatus and English country-house society. Russell's appointment to the Supreme Court of Calcutta in 1797 allowed him to amass a prodigious private fortune, and to establish three of his sons in the lucrative service of the East India Company (EIC). Sir Henry Russell's eldest son, also named Henry (1783–1852), served in the civil and political service of the Company from 1797 until 1820, assisted at Hyderabad for many years by his brother Charles (1786–1856). A younger brother Frank Russell (1790–1852) joined his siblings in the Company's employment in 1806 as a Bengal civil servant, and died at Chittagong; his son and namesake Francis Whitworth Russell (1829–72) died at Jubbulpore, a Major in the Bengal army. The 1st baronet's wife, Lady Russell (1764–1814), also participated actively in the family's imperial project, bearing the last two of Sir Henry's ten children in Calcutta, before returning to England to begin the couple's search for an appropriate home, a country house in which the family intended their new private fortune (and the power it conferred) to be made publically manifest.[8]

In all this, Swallowfield Park is an archetypal English country estate. Now converted from a single-family residence into luxury flats, Swallowfield Park's stately home illustrates a longstanding country house tradition that has adapted in successive centuries to major changes in Britain's economic, social, cultural and political landscape. Its architecture and history are caught up in the events that saw England emerge from the seventeenth century as a parliamentary democracy. Yet the evolving biography of this family seat was also fundamentally shaped by its entanglement with a wider British colonial world in which – contemporary Britons alleged – 'Oriental' exoticism and despotism held sway. In what follows, I situate Swallowfield within this broad imperial context by tracing the estate's acquisition and transformation in the late Georgian and early Victorian periods. Purchased by Sir Henry Russell, 1st baronet, in 1820, Swallowfield was remodelled, redecorated and recreated in the following decades by its new proprietor's eldest son, Henry (later the 2nd baronet). The Russells' purchase of Swallowfield attests to the crucial role played by Britain's empire in underpinning country house society, culture and politics in late Georgian England.[9] The strategic refurbishment of Swallowfield by the 2nd baronet in the 1830s and 1840s highlights the role of men in fashioning the imperial domestic interior and reminds us of the salience of European art and design in the construction of 'English' interiors.[10] The aesthetic and social histories of the house attest to the use of Indian capital, material culture and built environments by Company men and women to entrench their status and privilege as white Europeans within the imperial order. They also forcefully illustrate the stratagems deployed by Company families to conceal selected aspects of their Indian histories, and to police the racialized boundaries of the family circle. Viewed alongside our new understanding of the entwined histories of Caribbean slavery and the country house,[11] a global and colonial analysis of Swallowfield allows this stately home's 'Englishness' to be seen both as a material manifestation of imperial wealth and as the product of an ongoing process marked by the sublimation and erasure of imperial power.[12]

Swallowfield before the Russells

The royal associations so lovingly detailed by Lady Russell in the first chapters of *Swallowfield and Its Owners* persisted beyond the Tudor era, growing entangled in the eighteenth century with the biographies of statesmen whose wealth and power extended beyond England and Europe to imperial theatres of war and empire. Present-day Swallowfield house was built in 1689–91 by Henry Hyde, the second earl of Clarendon (1638–1709), replacing the Tudor mansion of the alchemist and antiquary William Backhouse (1593–1662). In these early decades, the home's history lay largely within the confines of an English narrative of English history. Clarendon had taken as his second wife William Backhouse's daughter, the heiress Flower Backhouse (1641–1700). Owing debts of over £19,000, the second earl sold lands (eventually including the Hyde family seat, Cornbury) to stave off his creditors, and retreated to his wife's estate at Swallowfield to reduce his expenditure. Through its connection with Clarendon, seventeenth-century Swallowfield was associated with both the Court party and the Stuart cause. As an infant, Henry Hyde had been taken into continental exile by his parents after the royalist defeat in the Civil War. His subsequent political career, with only a few short-lived departures, was staunchly royalist. Having declined to accept the new regime imposed by the Glorious Revolution of 1689, Clarendon was imprisoned in the Tower by William III in 1690 and 1691.[13]

Denied a place in parliamentary politics by his continued allegiance to the Stuart cause, Clarendon turned to the consolations of domestic architecture. In replacing the existing Tudor mansion at Swallowfield with a new country house, he chose William Talman (c.1650–1719) as his architect. Talman, who as comptroller of the king's works undertook Hampton Court Palace's interior decoration, has been described as 'the leading country house architect of the late seventeenth century, responsible for some of the most innovative and influential designs of the period'. He is now known for producing 'a group of relatively plain Renaissance-style houses' that includes Swallowfield. Talman was also the architect of Holywell House, St Albans (which he built for John and Sarah Churchill in c.1686), of Richard Lumley's Stanstead Park, Sussex (built from 1686 to 1690) and of Uppark, also in Sussex (built for Ford Grey in c.1690). A small vestibule at Swallowfield is now the only surviving Talman interior. Other country houses that bear the impress of Talman's hand include Burghley House, Northamptonshire and Chatsworth House, Derbyshire.[14]

If its association with the Hyde family connected Swallowfield to England's tumultuous transition from Stuart absolutism to constitutional monarchy, the eighteenth century initiated its protracted association with British rule in India. In 1719 Swallowfield passed from Tory into emphatically Whig hands with its purchase by the politician and nouveau riche Indian merchant Thomas Pitt (1653–1726).[15] Born in Dorset, Pitt gained notoriety for his opposition to the EIC's trade monopoly in Asia. He first set sail for India in 1673, and rapidly became a successful interloper in the Company's developing commercial empire – much to the chagrin of the Court of Directors. Having returned to England in the 1680s, Pitt was elected MP for Old Sarum, and lambasted the Company's monopoly over Indian trade from the safety of his seat in the House of Commons. He journeyed back to India as an interloping merchant in 1693, forcing the Company's directors to reconcile themselves to his commercial presence on the subcontinent. Although Pitt remained estranged from many senior EIC figures, he secured appointment by the Company in the late 1690s as Governor of Fort St George at Madras (present-day Chennai).[16]

From his base in Madras, Pitt accumulated a vast fortune, a process of enrichment perhaps best exemplified by his purchase from an Indian merchant in 1702 of a 410-carat diamond.[17] Acquired for £20,400 and shipped to England to be cut and sold for profit, this gem initially proved a vexing investment. Warfare had disrupted the European diamond market, and Pitt (who sailed from India for Europe in 1709) succeeded in selling his Indian jewel only in 1717. The Pitt diamond, purchased for £125,000 by the Regent of France, came to adorn the French crown, was worn by Marie Antoinette and later decorated Napoleon I's sword. In the meantime, profits from his lucrative Indian commercial dealings and the sale of his diamond had allowed Pitt, the son of a Dorset rector, to purchase extensive estates that stretched from Cornwall to Westminster. Shortly after the sale of his Indian gemstone, Thomas 'Diamond' Pitt established himself as a Berkshire country gentleman at Swallowfield. He died there in 1726, leaving this new country seat to his son Robert (c.1680–1727), who like his father had traded as a free merchant in Madras before settling in the Berkshire countryside. Intrepid trader and Whig politician, Pitt in India had laid the foundations of a political dynasty that was to include two Georgian prime ministers: his grandson William Pitt, first earl Chatham (1708–78) and his great-grandson William Pitt the Younger (1759–1806).[18] This was a lineage – at once domestic and imperial, and marked by the Pitt family's successful transition from mercantile interlopers to revered statesmen – which Lady Russell in 1901 was happy to own for her home. Her history of Swallowfield devotes four chapters to Governor Pitt and his progeny – including one chapter dedicated to the Pitt Diamond – notwithstanding Lady Russell acknowledged that Pitt's business dealings for the Company lacked a scrupulous regard for honour.[19]

The Russells in India: Anglo-Indian tastes

Swallowfield changed hands several times in the Georgian era, and its link to Britain's expanding Indian empire was temporarily broken. The Pitt family sold the estate in 1737, reportedly for £20,770; in 1783, Sylvanus Bevan purchased Swallowfield from Colonel John Dodd. It was Bevan who sold the estate in 1788, to the Caribbean plantation owner Timothy Hare Earle, reconnecting Swallowfield to Britain's imperial networks. His son, Timothy Hare Altabon Earle (1779–1836), inherited Swallowfield in 1816. Earle's fortune declined as West Indian wealth depreciated in the early nineteenth-century. Swallowfield's lands were enclosed in 1817, an agrarian strategy calculated to drive up its landlord's profits.[20] But in 1820 – when Earle, a staunch royalist, served as sheriff of Berkshire – the combination of a declining fortune and an extravagant lifestyle forced Swallowfield's sale. Earle retired to a dower-house near Wokingham, where he died in 1836, shortly after Parliament awarded him compensation of over £3,600 for loss of his property in 187 enslaved persons on St Kitts.[21]

With its sale by Timothy Hare Altabon Earle to the Russell family, Swallowfield's imperial associations reverted from the West to the East Indies, a development that exemplifies the broader 'swing to the East' within the British empire in the aftermath of the loss of the American colonies.[22] Sir Henry Russell, 1st baronet (1751–1836) had been born in Dover, the son of a merchant. Educated at Charterhouse and Cambridge, Russell trained in the law at Lincoln's Inn. His legal ability and a strategic marriage combined to raise his social aspirations and economic prospects. In 1782, as a widower, Russell took as his second wife Anne Barbara Whitworth (d. 1814), the youngest daughter of Sir Charles Whitworth (c.1721–78) and sister to Charles, Earl Whitworth (1752–1825). In 1797 Russell was knighted and appointed a judge of the Bengal Supreme Court, launching his family into an imperial sphere they would continue to occupy for generations.[23]

India was the making of the Russell family. The judge reached Bengal in 1798, where his eldest son Henry (1783–1852) took up an appointment in the Company's civil service. The younger Russell children remained in England, but Lady Russell (having given birth to her eighth child in December 1797) set sail for Bengal with her nieces Mary Lloyd and Rose Aylmer (1779–1800) in tow – both joining the so-called 'fishing fleet' of nubile British daughters who tried their fortunes on the colonial marriage market.[24] The reunited Russells now settled in Calcutta (present-day Kolkata), where the street on which they lived continues to bear their name.[25] The couple's two youngest children were born in India. Rose Aylmer (1800–89) was named to commemorate her cousin, who had died of a tropical fever before she could secure a husband, and George Lake (b. 1802) was named for the first Viscount Lake of Delhi (1744–1808), commander-in-chief of the army in India and a distant relation.[26] Two further sons later joined their father in Bengal. Charles Russell (1786–1856) had arrived at his parents' Calcutta home by 1802, a cadet in the Company's Bengal army. Their third son, the feckless Francis Whitworth Russell (1790–1852), was appointed to the Bengal civil service in 1808, and remained in India, with only short sojourns home, until his death.[27]

The processes by which the Russells' Indian careers shaped their engagement with English country house culture are complex and multi-layered. By the time they returned to Britain, Sir Henry and his eldest sons were so-called 'nabobs', officials whose access to Asian wealth allowed them to construct new identities through the acquisition and use of new built environments and a global array of material goods.[28] High salaries, gifts from 'Oriental' potentates and opportunities for commercial profit swelled the family's coffers in India, laying the financial foundations upon which Swallowfield's purchase and refurbishment would later rest. From 1798 until his departure for England in 1813, Sir Henry presided over his often-distant family from his home in Chowringhee, Calcutta. His eldest son, Henry, was appointed assistant to the Resident of Hyderabad in 1800. (The Resident was the Company's political agent to the Hyderabad court, whose ruler was the Nizam of Hyderabad). Henry's career later took him to Madras (Chennai), where he married his first wife, Jane Casamaijor (1789–1808) and furnished his first marital home in 1808.[29] After a brief interval in Poona (Pune), he was appointed Resident at Hyderabad, where his brother Charles served as his assistant until 1819. Their mother's return to England with the two youngest Russell children in 1804 connected Henry and Charles closely to London's metropolitan consumer markets during their prolonged residence in India, as did the in-laws acquired through Henry's first marriage. At home in England, Lady Russell travelled between a succession of rented English country homes, spa towns and London dwellings with her younger children while awaiting Sir Henry's return. This peripatetic life allowed the family to sample a wide array of rural retreats and town houses prior to the purchase of Swallowfield in 1820, notwithstanding the Russell men's residence in India.

Colonial Calcutta was a vast emporium of luxury goods in this period. Ships' captains purchased fashionable items in London for resale to Europeans in Calcutta, while skilled Indian craftsmen manufactured not only 'native' textiles and furnishings but also imitations of European luxuries and products in which European and 'Oriental' components were melded.[30] Auction houses plied a lively trade in both new items of fashion and second-hand goods – left behind by Company servants returning home, or released for sale by less fortunate men and women, who succumbed each year to the tropical climate.[31] In this burgeoning consumer culture, the Russells developed sophisticated and demanding consumer tastes, which they would later elaborate at Swallowfield. The family's domestic life in India centred around three urban hubs: Calcutta, Hyderabad and Madras. Employment in Madras, Poona and Hyderabad exposed the brothers to south Indian craftsmanship and familiarized them with the consumer markets of Bombay (Mumbai). The return of first Sir Henry and then his two eldest sons to England between 1814 and 1820, moreover, was swiftly followed by their departure for Europe on shopping expeditions to Paris, Rome, Venice, Florence and other European centres of fine art, trade and industry. Recorded in exceptional detail in the letters that passed between the far-flung family members, Swallowfield's formation as the Russells' English family seat was a global, not a national, collective family enterprise.

Sir Henry's house in Calcutta functioned as a clearinghouse for goods sent to and from his sons in south India. It was through this channel that Henry and Charles received fashionable goods from their kinfolk in England, and through this conduit too that the brothers sent gifts of Asian luxuries to their political patrons at home. When Charles first arrived in Calcutta in 1802, Henry promptly wrote from Hyderabad to discover whether his sibling had brought him any fashionable European goods, and to enquire whether their aunt, Lady Aylmer, had received his gift of Oriental fans.[32] Equipping his sons with appropriate domestic goods as they established their imperial careers was a task that Sir Henry took seriously. When Charles was appointed to a junior post in Hyderabad in 1804, his father sent him household items by sea from Calcutta. The list of these goods underlines the Russells' ambitions to genteel status: it included a writing table, a chest of drawers, a stand for a *chillumchee* (basin for washing hands), a looking glass, book shelves and language and history books. Alive to the tendency of young Company men to succumb to the allure of the Indian marketplace and fall into debt, Sir Henry admonished Charles that from this time he must financially 'be on your own bottom'.[33]

Henry Russell's brief interval of employment in Madras saw furniture and matrimony come to the forefront of his sensibilities.[34] By the early nineteenth century, colonial Madras had both a flourishing marriage market and a thriving consumer culture inspired by conceptions of fashionable gentility.[35] Charles suspected his brother of harbouring matrimonial intentions when Henry wrote requesting him to send 'the large Bed, with the Bedding, [and] the net Counterpane' which he had left behind in Hyderabad. Henry acknowledged that 'The Precision of my Orders about the Bedding and Irish Net was certainly very suspicious', but hastened to deny that these instructions were a token of his intentions toward 'the charming Jane' Casamaijor, the daughter of a senior Company civil servant.[36] In the event, in October Jane and Henry indeed married, and settled into a home that Henry had furnished with lavish abandon. Jane's agonizing death a few weeks later led to Henry's dispersal of these marital goods, which reminded him too painfully of her. In January 1809 he wrote to Charles announcing the imminent sale of his furniture and plate. Subsequent letters detailed his sale of items that were the height of Madras fashion at the time, blending European motifs with the current craze for all things Egyptian. The list of goods Henry disposed of underscores the importance of colonial consumption in shaping Company men's domestic tastes. Items sold by Henry included 12 black varnished chairs with a red Etruscan border, a 12-foot long ottoman covered in chintz, a bookcase with Egyptian bronze figures, two couches in the Egyptian style and 'a pair of the newest fashioned Sofa Tables on Pillar Legs inlaid with Brass and fitted up with Brass Ornaments'.[37] These items, combining goods crafted from Indian and African materials with new fashions current in Europe, illustrate the cosmopolitan markets in which Company men's concepts of the domestic interior were formed, far from their English homes, and yet enmeshed in intimate, familial households which boasted close ties to European markets.[38]

Hyderabad, where Charles and Henry resided together for nearly a decade after Henry's appointment as Resident in 1810, afforded the brothers a rich canvas for interior design. A princely state renowned for its wealth, exceptionally rich material culture, craftsmanship and political intrigue, Hyderabad state was a key cog in the Company's subsidiary alliance system, its autonomy increasingly under the Company's sway in Russell's day.[39] It was here that the brothers developed a dynamic and enduring partnership, carefully calculated to deploy material culture to establish their family's social status and political power. Although Hyderabad's fortunes were on the wane, the city and its surrounding state remained a vital centre of wealth, luxury and Company diplomacy. Its opulence fed in part by the diamond trade, Hyderabad was known for its rich bazaars and elegant pleasure gardens. The British Residency was located opposite the old city, across the river Musi. Both Henry and Charles had first served at Hyderabad during the Residency of James Achilles Kirkpatrick (1764–1805; Resident 1797–1805). At the outset of Kirkpatrick's tenure, the Residency complex was a disorderly assemblage of buildings. Poorly constructed and rapidly deteriorating, the Resident's two-storey house was surrounded by the many bungalows of his staff, each including a *zenana* wing to house the men's Indian wives, concubines, children, servants and slaves. Kirkpatrick himself, scandalously, had not only settled with but married a Hyderabadi Muslim noblewoman, Begum Khair un-Nissa (1786–1813), with whom he had two children.[40]

In 1800, Kirkpatrick conceived an ambitious building campaign which, within a few years, transformed the Residency into a Palladian palace notable for its combination of European and Indian stylistic elements. Gardens laid out along conventional Mughal lines surrounded a capacious *zenana*; a veranda surrounded the Resident's new house, which boasted a durbar hall for which Kirkpatrick ordered a carpet measuring 60 by 30 feet. But the Residency's new structures, ornamentation and furnishings also emphatically pronounced the Britishness of the Company's waxing power in Hyderabad. Its classical Palladian exterior commanded a deer park overlooked by a pediment carved with the East India Company's arms. The house itself boasted a grand salon, a gallery with a painted ceiling and an elaborate chandelier reputedly sold to the Company by the Prince of Wales.[41]

Delayed by business at Poona, Henry Russell took up residence at Hyderabad only in 1811. In the intervening months Charles assumed oversight of the Residency's refurbishment. The question of whether to amplify or repress the Residency's Mughal stylistic motifs occupied them both in these months. Kirkpatrick's immediate successor as Resident had sought to reduce the Residency's close links with Hyderabadi culture – earlier enhanced by Kirkpatrick's liaison with Khair un-Nissa – in keeping with Company pressure to expunge visible evidence of this scandalous alliance.[42] Henry Russell was awkwardly placed in this context. After Kirkpatrick's death and prior to his own first marriage, he had begun an intimate relationship with Khair himself. He remained in contact with her and her female relatives for years thereafter, but – intent to conceal this relationship from his superiors in the Company service – used Charles as his intermediary.[43] At Hyderabad, Henry (like Kirkpatrick before him) insisted on adherence to strict Indian caste rules in the Residency kitchens.[44] But Russell, newly rich and immensely ambitious, was keen to stamp the Residency with an elite European impress. He wrote to Charles that he was willing to pay his predecessor a thousand pounds for his library, and was also happy to purchase his sporting prints. He also ordered vast quantities of new furnishings from Calcutta's select emporia. On 29 August 1810, Henry informed Charles that as the Residency's alterations reached completion he had resolved to purchase 'an entirely new Set of Furniture adapted to it from Calcutta' and wished to have Charles's advice on its selection. The acquisition of fashionable European goods threw Henry upon the mercy of his Casamaijor in-laws. He remitted £3,500 to Elizabeth Casamaijor (his late wife's mother, herself enmeshed in the Company's metropolitan patronage networks) in London, and reported happily in 1812 that she had despatched busts, glassware and china to him on the *William Beasley* and *City of London*. The goods were shipped to Madras, to be forwarded to Henry in Hyderabad by his deceased wife's father, yet another example of the key roles played by family and in-laws in mediating colonial consumer and patronage relations.[45]

The furnishings selected by Henry were not uniformly European. His prints of fox-hunting, for example, were complemented in the Residency by pictures depicting scenes from the *Arabian Nights*. But European styles and motifs increasingly supplanted Kirkpatrick's more cosmopolitan furnishings. Notwithstanding his privileged access through his Company connections to the luxury products of Jingdezhen, Henry commissioned his mother-in-law to send him British chinaware, a shift from Chinese to domestic porcelain that reflected new trends in English taste.[46] Henry's new Hyderabad furniture included gilt chairs, 'splendid beyond anything I could conceive', as he wrote to Charles, while 'Wilton's Vases are very elegant, and exquisitely worked'. The Residency's library projected with particular force Henry's determination to be numbered among the empire's gentlemanly elite. Forty feet long, it included busts of the 'Ancients' on one side and the 'Moderns' on another. Here the knowledge systems that underpinned colonial power were encapsulated not in the Islamic and Hindu texts revered by earlier Company men such as William 'Oriental' Jones (1746–94), but instead in sculptures that depicted Aristotle, Homer, Cicero, Shakespeare, Milton, Newton, Locke, Burke, Fox and Pitt.[47]

Family portraits were an integral part of the furnishing of Georgian country houses, items of material culture that allowed men and women of new wealth to inscribe the walls of their homes with venerable family lineages, of varying degrees of fiction or veracity.[48] Portraits specifically commissioned by Henry for the Residency both enhanced its European emphasis and reminded visitors that the Russells were now a powerful and well-connected imperial clan. In 1812 Henry commissioned George Chinnery (1774–1852), the premier society artist of colonial Calcutta in this period, to paint a portrait of Sir Henry for the Residency – an image that remains at Swallowfield today. He supplemented memorial portraits of Jane Casamaijor with images of her surviving female kinfolk, commissioned together with portraits of Henry's mother and sisters.[49]

By the time that Henry (in considerable disgrace) left Hyderabad for England in 1820, the Residency had gained international renown for its magnificence. Its splendour was celebrated in many engravings, lithographs and watercolours in the following years, a reputation that Henry was keen to burnish.[50] Life in Calcutta and at the Hyderabad Residency set a high bar for the Russell family in England: Sir Henry's letters to his wife during his visit to his sons in Hyderabad, immediately prior to his return to England in 1813, exulted in the opulence, status and power exemplified in their Residency life. His reception at Hyderabad had reduced him to tears. Mounted on an elephant, Sir Henry was greeted solemnly at the Residency gate by a band playing 'God Save the King'. Describing the Residency as 'a most magnificent palace', he observed rhetorically: 'Who could have believed that I, who started from such an humble origin, should ever witness such a scene; that I should ever be of Rank enough to be received with such Honors, [sic] & that my own Son should pay them.'[51] Establishing an English country seat that could match their lavish Indian homes would tax the Russell men's financial and cultural capital heavily in the next quarter of a century.

Testing the English market

Until recently, historians have paid little attention to women's role in shaping country house culture in England, but it was Lady Russell who led the first stage of the family's protracted migration from their elite residences on the subcontinent to the stately home.[52] She sailed from India in the *Preston* in 1804, taking with her the two youngest children and two female Indian servants (known in the family as 'Black Mary' and Anne Ayah, albeit the latter was re-named Mrs Williams when she began to serve as a lady's maid in England).[53] In the decade before Sir Henry joined her, Lady Russell established a succession of transient households for her five daughters and three youngest sons in London, Bath, Tunbridge Wells, Dover, Walmer (a convenient spot for smuggling goods from India ashore) and the countryside. By spring 1806, assisted by her brother Whitworth, she had taken an extended lease on a house at Hookwood, Surrey, surrounded by several acres of garden.[54] A few months later, she and her family were residing in town, occupying a small rented house in Park Lane opposite the Grosvenor Gate and adjacent to the residence of a Whitworth aunt. The Park Lane house had been taken to allow the Russells' eldest daughter, Anne (d. 1808) to be presented at Court, an essential step in the family's campaign to secure their status within the upper classes. Her younger sons' fortunes were cultivated by ensuring that they enjoyed privileged access to her brother Whitworth, by being placed in schools near his stately home in Kent, Knole.[55]

Complaints from Sir Henry in India about the excessive cost of Lady Russell's peripatetic lifestyle in England were a leitmotif in the couple's correspondence. She wrote to Charles in 1809 about her chronic worry regarding 'money concerns: they so much vex and hurt me that at times I feel entirely wretched'.[56] A month later, she took her children to visit their uncle Whitworth at Buckhurst Park, his East Sussex estate. Here her younger sons enjoyed their uncle's largesse, prompting their mother to write to India to petition her second eldest son for Indian shawls, luxury items that figured prominently in the family's patronage networks.[57] In 1811, she took a house near Knole at Riverhead, Kent, but this proved only a temporary settlement. By 1813 Lady Russell was based in London at Baker Street, but informed Sir Henry that she had taken a lease on a house and stables at Clifton for £350 per annum. It was from the Clifton residence that she reported to her husband how much her London friends had admired the family portraits she had sent to Henry in Hyderabad. Clifton too, however, proved only a temporary way-station. Caroline Russell wrote to her brother Charles in 1814, shortly before their mother's death, that she had taken a three-year lease on Cannon Hill, a large villa with a park five miles from Windsor Castle.[58] This was the family's first step into the 'English Hindoostan' of Berkshire, home to so many returned Company nabobs.[59]

Sir Henry sailed for England in the *Metcalfe*, which departed Calcutta on 13 December 1813. His reunion with his wife, who died on 1 August 1814, was only brief. For the next several years he headed a household at 62, Wimpole Street, London that – until their marriages – included his four surviving daughters, Caroline (1792–1869), Kate (1795–1845), Henrietta (b. 1797) and Rose (1800–89). His two youngest sons, the clergyman William Whitworth Russell (1795–1847) and the lawyer George Lake Russell (b. 1802), visited at Wimpole Street when not absent at school or university. Sir Henry, who had critiqued his wife's apparent extravagance in England from his base in Calcutta, was shocked to learn at firsthand about the cost of genteel English life. In January 1816, he wrote to Charles that 'the expense of living in England is not to be conceived: the furnishing my House, which I have done elegantly; & the portioning [that is, the allocation of a marriage settlement to] Kate, which I must do liberally, have reduced my Finances very much: but by keeping as much of my property as can be prudently kept, at Hyderabad, at 12 [%] … Interest, I hope in a short time to be recruited'.[60] His descriptions of the furnishing of the house at Wimpole Street help to explain Sir Henry's perceptions of the high cost of living in London. Returned to England after years of service on the subcontinent, Sir Henry promptly took his daughters to the continent to shop.[61] The house at Wimpole Street, he wrote to Charles, 'is magnificently furnished; the clocks, candelabras, & vases, which we brought from Paris, added to the Ebony Chairs, crimson & gold curtains … large Mirrors, & several beautiful cabinets, make it really very superb & the taste of Caroline has preserved aptness & uniformity in the colouring'.[62] Eschewing Asiatic commodities for French furnishings was a sensible strategy for Sir Henry's re-immersion in Georgian culture and society. Caricatures of the tastelessness and effeminacy of 'Oriental' excess were widely pervasive in English literature and culture.[63] Significantly however, it was his Indian investments – Hyderabad's 12 per cent interest rate far outpaced returns of 3–4 per cent on the London markets – that funded Russell's European expenditure.

Although Sir Henry settled in London, neither he nor his eldest sons had abandoned their collective intention to translate their Indian fortunes into English landed estates. To the contrary, Sir Henry's elevation to a Baronetcy and appointment to the Privy Council expanded their ambitions to join the governing elite. In 1813 he had written to his wife that he intended to combine his wealth with that of his sons: Sir Henry proposed to pay £100,000, his son Henry £60,000 and Charles £40,000, with the rents divided proportionately.[64] Henry Russell was reluctant to return to England from Hyderabad until he could ensure an annual income of £3,000, which he estimated would require an investment in land of £80,000. Desire for wealth vied with social ambition in Henry's investment calculations. The yield on government bonds was greater than that on land, but gentility held sway over mere profits as he contemplated his return to England: 'I had rather have 3,000 a Year in Landed Property, than 5,000 in the Funds', he wrote to Sir Henry in 1815.[65]

Henry Russell's second marriage, to a Catholic woman from the French royalist enclave of colonial Pondicherry, significantly complicated these plans. Solemnized in Hyderabad in 1816, this was the second marriage Henry had undertaken precipitously and without his father's consent. As a union with a French Catholic, it presented obstacles to his establishment as an English gentleman of the governing elite at home, where the campaigns for the inclusion of Catholics within the political nation were to generate internecine political conflict in the 1820s and 1830s. Henry broke the news of his second marriage to his father with a characteristic combination of bravado and emotional blackmail. 'My Marriage will hardly affect the Amount of my Fortune, or require me, on that Account, to stay longer in India than I otherwise should have done', he wrote to Sir Henry in October 1816. 'But when I find that you are estranged, and that your Door will be shut against me, I shall have lost one of the strongest inducements I had to return to England, and shall probably therefore remain more years at Hyderabad, and amass a greater Fortune, than I have hitherto intended.'[66]

Clotilde Mottet (c.1795–1872) bore Henry four children in rapid succession in India, of whom two (Henry and Anne) survived to sail with the couple for England in 1820. Notwithstanding his initial shock at this union, Sir Henry was readily reconciled to his new daughter-in-law (not least because she bore him several grandsons), and the purchase of country seats again moved to the forefront of the Russells' ambitions. Sir Henry had contemplated the acquisition of Summer Hill estate (near Tunbridge Wells, one of his wife's many resting-places on her transit through town and countryside upon returning to England) for £125,000 in 1815, but ultimately decided against the purchase.[67] He also sought to negotiate the purchase of Gosfield Hall in Essex for £120,000, but the Duke of Buckingham had insisted on 150,000 guineas, and this sale too was unsuccessful.[68]

While his father debated the merits of properties such as these, Henry Russell and his wife plunged into fashionable European consumer markets (see Figure 10.2). Throughout the revolutionary and Napoleonic wars, aristocratic collectors had continued to acquire French furniture for their country houses, with bronze statuary and boulle veneer marquetry – often embellished with 'Oriental' motifs – especially prominent among their purchases.[69] January 1822 saw Henry write to Charles from Paris, where he and Clotilde had already begun to purchase furnishings for their prospective home. Here Henry acquired bronze horses for 1,500 francs and a chest of drawers for 500 francs, holding back from other purchases only because he lacked a house in which to put them. As in Hyderabad, he relied on Charles for aesthetic advice. 'I wait for your Opinion before I decide whether to buy some pieces of very fine Bowle [*sic*: boulle] Furniture which are for sale here', he wrote to Charles, concluding with instructions for a vase, adorned with an elephant's head, that he had commissioned to be made in London.[70]

Back in England, Henry and Clotilde joined the landed gentry, if only vicariously, when they took a lease on Sutton Park, Bedfordshire in 1822. The family seat of the Burgoyne family, Sutton Park was connected to both the North American and the Indian empire through its proprietors' military service. The 7th baronet, Sir John Burgoyne (1739–85), had been a cavalry officer in India in the 1780s, marrying and dying in the Madras Presidency.[71] Sutton Park's material culture provided Henry with an object lesson in the successful assimilation of imperial wealth

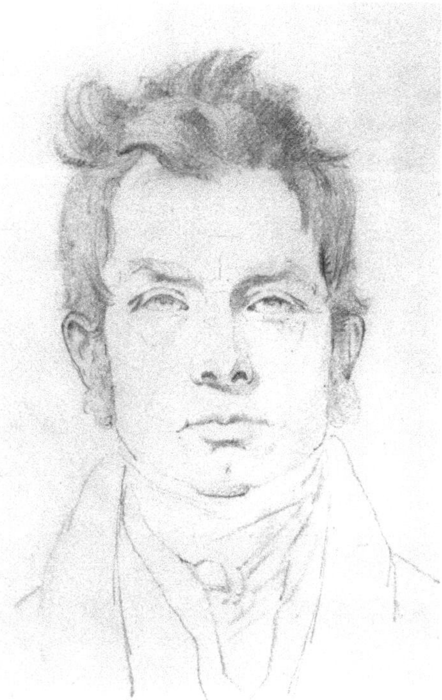

Figure 10.2 Sir Henry Russell, 2nd Baronet, by Sir Francis Leggatt Chantry. © National Portrait Gallery, London.

into a genteel English landed lineage. 'The place that we have taken belongs to the family of the Burgoynes, and has … for generations', he wrote to a friend in Hyderabad. 'They are one of the oldest Families in England: the Hall is lined with the Pictures of their Ancestors.' Costing Henry only £300 per annum, the house was also ideally placed to preserve his links with the families that had provided him with powerful political patronage in India. Its location near the Great Northern Road made Sutton Park a convenient staging post for the family of the late Gilbert Elliot, first Earl Minto (1751–1814) – who as Governor General had promoted Henry to the Hyderabad Residency, and whose son John Elliott had married Jane Casamaijor's sister, Amelia – as they travelled between London and their family seat in the Scottish Borders, Minto. 'The Dowager Lady Minto, when she was coming here, actually drove past the Park, not thinking it possible such a place to be had for so low a rent as she knew I paid', Henry observed. 'The habits of Country life too are much more like those of India, and I do not like them a bit the less on that Account', he concluded with satisfaction.[72]

Swallowfield and its reformation

If Sutton Park served to whet Henry Russell's appetite for settled life as an English country gentleman, the purchase of Swallowfield in 1820 finally brought this aspiration to fruition.[73] He moved his family to Reading and then to Brighton while extensive renovations were undertaken at Swallowfield.[74] Yet again, Charles stepped in to supervise renovations and furnishing in Henry's absence. In October 1826 he wrote to Henry to describe designs for Swallowfield's mantelpieces and statuary prepared by the London tradesman Atkinson, and debated the relative merits of Sienna and black and gold marble for the dining room.[75] Soft furnishings for Swallowfield preoccupied Charles a month later. Cotton fabrics that a century before had been exotic luxury handicrafts imported from India to England were now available at short notice from domestic British manufactories. Charles wrote that their supplier had sent Henry 'a parcel of patterns of chintz for bed furniture. If you like them, but would prefer them in other colours, they can be printed in any colour you please, in the course of three weeks', he marvelled.[76]

Although new British manufactures were often appealing, his increasingly cosmopolitan knowledge of the luxury market often caused Charles concern. As the family increasingly familiarized itself with French fashions – a development assisted by visits to Clotilde's Parisian relations – a preference for continental material culture increasingly challenged the brothers' British and colonial tastes.[77] Upon returning from a French excursion in 1827, Charles fretted about the quality of the new wallpaper at Swallowfield. 'Where the pattern of the paper is pretty & full, the rooms look handsome, but in two or three of them the paper looks rather common; perhaps more so from my having just seen such rich papers in France', he observed.[78] Their London supplier had shown Charles patterns for Swallowfield's silk furnishings, but again Charles was concerned that silks from Lyons that he and Henry had seen in France were superior.[79] March 1828 saw Charles recommend Belgian carpets – available in London at a shop at 145 Leadenhall Street or directly from the Belgian warehouses – to Henry both for Swallowfield and to send to his Mottet in-laws in Hyderabad. In May, the brothers travelled to Tournai to visit the factory itself, and selected a carpet with a pink ground for Swallowfield's dining room.[80] By November 1828, the brothers had spent a small fortune of their father's money on Swallowfield's embellishment. 'My Father last night got Atkinsons [sic] account of outstanding bills amounting in London & Swallowfield to £5276', Charles wrote on 26 November. 'He takes it astonishingly well.'[81] Expenditure on this scale, decades after the classic age of eighteenth-century nabob excess, provides a telling reminder both of Company men's keen participation in the design of stately home interiors but also of the extent to which new imperial wealth was recast in new European material possessions.

Although Sir Henry Russell invested substantial sums in Swallowfield's refurbishment, received rents from the estate and was an occasional house guest there, it was Henry and Clotilde Russell – together with their six surviving children – who made this house their home. Charles, who served as a Tory MP for Reading from 1830–37 and 1841–47 and was Chairman of the Great Western Railway from 1839–55,[82] was a constant visitor, and continued to work in harness with Henry both at Swallowfield and from London to make Swallowfield a venerable English family seat. Family portraits, which had featured prominently in Henry's refashioning of the Hyderabad Residency, were likewise central to the brothers' plans for Swallowfield. Retired from the Company service, Henry now enjoyed the wealth, leisure and connections to raise his collection to new heights. Both brothers entered eagerly into genealogical research from the later 1820s onward, intent to familiarize themselves with the biographies as well as the portraits of a family they had left behind as adolescents to seek their fortunes in India.[83]

Commissioning new family portraits, and retouching existing ones, occupied the brothers throughout the 1830s, connecting them with the flourishing English art market.[84] In 1831, Henry Russell paid David Wilkie (1785–1841) to complete a portrait of his uncle, Earl Whitworth, a picture begun by Sir Thomas Lawrence (1769–1830).[85] His mother's family was far more socially exalted than his father's, but Henry was also careful to ensure that his paternal line was well-represented on Swallowfield's walls. He was also eager to continue to use portraits to maintain links with his in-laws. The fashionable society artist George Richmond (1809–96) was a frequent visitor at Swallowfield in the 1830s, welcome as a houseguest, an artist and an art consultant. Portraits of Henry and Clotilde, completed by Richmond in 1834, were sent to Clotilde's sister and brother-in-law, now resettled from Hyderabad to Exeter; another sister, still in India, received a drawing of Clotilde by Richmond in 1836.[86] In 1840, Henry debated with Charles the best way to display his growing collection of family portraits. By October he had decided that the breakfast room would contain his portraits of Mrs Casamaijor (his first wife's mother, a Scot by birth), their paternal uncle, Henshaw Russell of Kent, together with Italian prints, pictures on classical themes and a Madonna. The paintings in the hall, he had decided, would include pictures of St Anne and the child Jesus as well as Chinnery's Indian portrait of Sir Henry. In December, he added to this display a series of images – still extant at Swallowfield – that depicted key figures in England's royal history: Charles II, the Duke of Marlborough, Lord Portland and Queen Anne.[87]

As the inclusion of Italian prints among these family portraits indicates, the death of the 1st baronet in 1836 appears to have given his eldest son new licence to develop his European tastes. Henry and his family spent much of the next few years travelling on the continent, where he discovered a passion for Renaissance Italian art that was to contribute significantly to Swallowfield's interiors. As a young man, Henry had laboured in the Company's civil service to accumulate capital, an occupation that had precluded the cultural education enjoyed by scions of the landed classes on the Grand Tour.[88] The wealth he had accumulated in India now allowed him to remedy the deficiencies of his education. He wrote to Charles from Venice in 1837 to report his enjoyment of paintings by Titian, Veronese and Tintoretto, as well as 'a host of first rate masters whose names even I never heard of before'. He purchased copies of a painting by Titian of the Assumption, and one by Veronese of supper at the house of Levi. The two boxes of purchases he was sending back to Swallowfield, he reported, were filled with a cornucopia of artefacts: books, rolls of prints, old bronze knockers, an ebony writing box, a bust, a sleeping cupid, a marble basin, carved wooden heads, female figures and his Renaissance reproductions.[89] Writing from Naples in 1838, before the family moved on to Rome, Henry told Charles to expect a further eight cases of continental goods – maps, prints, a marble table-top, bronze and Etruscan ware. From Rome, he sent a further 10 cases of goods home to Swallowfield.[90]

It was by refreshing the 1st baronet's Wimpole Street furnishings with continental materials that the 2nd baronet now prepared to integrate these inherited goods from London into his home at Swallowfield. From Paris, Henry wrote to Charles in 1838 asking for the dimensions of their father's ebony couches. 'Clotilde has the dimensions of the seats of the small & circular chairs, and she thinks some of the yellow flowered silk she bought at Genoa, will do to cover them, but we shall want something rich to cover the couch with', he commented. 'If it be not too expensive, Beauvais tapestry would agree admirably with the carpet and curtains, and would be much stronger and more durable than silk.'[91] To bind these new European acquisitions more securely with English traditions, Henry upon his return to Swallowfield immersed himself again in genealogy. 'Now for genealogy', he wrote to Charles in 1839. 'I am making out such an account as I can of our family for the Baronetage, and am, at the same time, preparing notes to be affixed to the backs of the old Dover pictures.'[92] His place in the landed elite now secured by the family's inclusion in Burke's *Peerage and Baronetage*, by Swallowfield's establishment as the Russell family seat and by his ability to identify the paternal lineage from which he had sprung, Henry Russell – nabob and nouveau riche though he had been – had now arrived at home.

Hidden in plain view: Indian legacies

Although English and European material culture dominated Swallowfield's interiors, overt references to the Asian origins of the Russells' wealth remained clearly visible in their home during the 2nd baronet's residence there. A selection of significant Indian subjects and objects was displayed prominently in the house, as the placement of Chinnery's portrait of the 1st baronet, painted in Calcutta, in the main hall attests. When he wrote to Charles with instructions for the painting and framing of family portraits in 1836, Henry also mentioned two pictures of 'Indian subjects' in Wilkie's care.[93] He did not identify these paintings, but we know from William Dalrymple's painstaking research that Henry prominently displayed above the stairs the large portrait painted by Chinnery in 1805 of the two children of James Achilles Kirkpatrick and Khair un-Nissa – the Hyderabadi noblewoman whose lover Henry had become after Kirkpatrick's death. As infants, the children had been raised at Hyderabad within their mother's culture: the first child, a son born in 1801, was named Sahib Allum (Lord of the World) and his sister, born in 1803, was named Sahib Begum. In 1805, to their mother and maternal grandmother's intense distress, their father sent the children to Madras, to embark from there for a new life in England. Chinnery painted them before their departure. They stand together in his large oil portrait in luxurious Indian court dress, adorned with gold and pearls. Christened by Kirkpatrick's relations in England, the children became William George (d. 1828) and Katherine Aurora Kirkpatrick (d. 1889). It was Katherine (Kitty) who in 1841 visited Swallowfield with a friend who was the Russells' neighbour and, immediately recognizing this portrait on the wall, burst into tears.[94]

Russell's acquisition of the portrait speaks to the unequal power relations – sexual, cultural and political – that marked Company rule in India. Unwillingly separated from her children, Khair un-Nissa had struggled unsuccessfully to retain this emotive object within her possession. After Kirkpatrick's death, she brought the portrait from Hyderabad to Calcutta, where Chinnery – keen to use it to advertise his skill as an artist – borrowed it and retained the painting in his possession. First as Khair's lover and later as a married man and widower who corresponded with her only through his brother Charles, Henry Russell made episodic, half-hearted efforts to return the painting to her. It arrived belatedly in Hyderabad – where Henry now presided as Resident – in autumn 1813, several weeks after Khair's premature death.[95] We do not know whether Henry purchased or simply appropriated the portrait of his ex-lover's children (the latter action, based on his family letters, would not have been out of character). Its public display at Swallowfield in the 1840s reflects the confidence with which Henry as a retired Company man now inhabited his home, his place in landed society and his Englishness.

We can see this cultural and political confidence displayed at Swallowfield in other material objects which embodied the violence of empire even as they allowed Henry Russell and his Company contemporaries to celebrate the perceived virtues of British rule in India. The history of a silver-gilt presentation vase, which was commissioned and purchased by Henry Russell for £1,100 in 1822, illustrates the simultaneous ability of material culture to display and to erase the imperial histories of both country house interiors and the Company families who so carefully constructed them. When Henry left his post at Hyderabad to return to England in 1820, the Company men who had served under him at the Residency subscribed funds for the purchase of 'a few Articles of household Plate, which [they hoped] by being in daily use in his family may sometimes remind him of those officers … who … are grateful for the good he has done to the Service'.[96] Executed by Philip Rundell in London from designs to which at least three distinguished Royal Academicians contributed, the 1822 vase was purchased with these subscribed funds. It depicted European officers and soldiers as well as Indian sepoys, and (through devices such as bifurcated snake handles, elephant heads and a tiger) emphatically asserted its Asian imperial origins. Lest these allusions were lost on viewers, a presentation plaque informed them that the vase was 'A TRIBUTE OF GRATEFUL REMEMBRANCE FROM THE OFFICERS OF THE HYDERABAD DIVISION OF H.H. THE NIZAM'S REGULAR TROOPS TO HENRY RUSSELL ESQUIRE'.[97] Unsurprisingly, this presentation vase featured in Lady Constance Russell's *Swallowfield and Its Owners* as an emblem both of Henry Russell's 'distinguished career' in India and his tasteful furnishing in retirement of his English country home.[98] Read through this lens, its imperial provenance adds value to the vase as a material object beyond its precious metals and craftsmanship: Lady Russell's description of the vase's complex commissioning and its place within Swallowfield's interior was cited at length in the 2010 auction catalogue, and the vase – estimated at £20,000–30,000 – sold for £95,000.[99]

An alternative history of Henry's presentation vase, however, emerges from his private letters and from the Company's archives. Directly precipitated by Henry's departure from Hyderabad, the gift of funds for its acquisition appears in these documents to bear witness to the inherent violence of empire, to Henry's active participation in that violence and to the willingness of other Company men in India to close ranks when the right of Englishmen to wield imperial force was challenged.[100] For Henry Russell had left the Company service and returned to England prematurely in 1820, his hasty departure calculated to preempt his official removal from the Residency in disgrace by the Court of Directors. In August 1818, a gang of robbers had attacked the bazaar at the Hyderabad Residency, killing several persons. Two of the men were seized by the Residency's soldiers, and were convinced by Henry to inform on their comrades in return for being spared from capital punishment at the Nizam's hands. The agreement clearly overstepped Henry's civil authority at Hyderabad, and became untenable when the men proved to have perjured themselves. Honouring his promise not to turn them over to the Nizam, Henry ordered each instead a flogging of 1,000 lashes – punishment overseen by his brother-in-law, Lieutenant Holroyd.[101] Both of the robbers had been wounded when captured by the Residency's soldiers; the first (Govinda) died on the morning after the flogging, and the second (Babareea) died shortly thereafter.[102]

A savage and public display of colonial discipline, the floggings and ensuing deaths swiftly mobilized the Company men at Hyderabad in combined support of the surgeon who had monitored the proceedings, Holroyd and Henry Russell. A medical officer who had observed the floggings reported that the men had not fainted during the ordeal and that their backs were so little lacerated 'that I could not help observing to Lieutenant Holroyd how thick their skins were and what little impression the cuts made'.[103] Ten officers stationed at the Residency wrote a memorial to the attending surgeon expressing their concern that the event 'must have deeply afflicted you', observing that the deaths 'could not have been occasioned by either want of humanity in inflicting more lashes than the delinquents could well bear, or want in skill in their after treatment'.[104] To the astonishment and fury of the Directors in London, when they condemned Henry's role in this incident the Governor General in Calcutta accepted his request to leave his post for England rather than dismissing him from the service, as the Directors had demanded. More than this, the Governor General commended Henry for 'the eminent zeal, ability, judgment and address by which your conduct has been distinguished during a long career of public service, and especially in the management of the important interests confided to your charge at the Court of Hyderabad'.[105] For years after their return from India, the time, effort and money Henry and Charles lavished on the refurbishment of Swallowfield as a genteel family seat were matched by their frenetic efforts to protect Henry's reputation by ensuring that this brutal episode remained hidden from public view. The private letters of the 1820s which record the brothers ordering silks and commissioning silver also document their schemes to buy clandestine proof copies of the East India Company's investigative reports into Henry's now notorious tenure at the Hyderabad Residency.[106] Meanwhile, at home at Swallowfield, the display of Henry's presentation vase worked to ensure that this textual record of imperial violence was silenced, and the narrative of its role in Residency politics at Hyderabad was re-inscribed in a conspicuous luxury object of great aesthetic and material value.

Conclusions

Since its development in the 1760s, the image of the nabob has figured in British caricature as a quintessentially possessive individual. Consumed by his individual needs, addicted to Indian tastes and incapable of casting off his commercial origins to acquire gentility, the returned Anglo-Indian was a byword in Georgian England for the failure of social, cultural and national integration. The history of the Russell family suggests many of the ways in which this stereotype falls short of social practice. Whereas the archetypal nabob was a single-minded individualist, the Russell correspondence reveals Sir Henry, his wife and their progeny to have been key collaborators in a collective family enterprise. The flow of material goods – between Calcutta and Hyderabad, between London and Madras, between Paris, Venice, Rome and Berkshire – was an essential agent and marker of this shared endeavour, which was designed to translate a new fortune acquired in India into secure, genteel landed wealth and power in England. Male consumers – too often written out of histories of Georgian consumer culture – were essential players in this familial campaign.[107] Family networks were also vital to the Russells' success in fashioning their place in Georgian society. In-laws as well as blood-kin played key roles in this process of family formation. In India, Henry Russell relied on the family of his first wife, the Casamaijors, not only for emotional support, but also for fine furnishings from the metropolis that would embellish the interiors of the Hyderabad Residency, and for family portraits that would help to underpin his status as Resident. In England, the French in-laws acquired through his second wife later became material assets, connecting him to Parisian fashion and to a wider continental tradition of art and culture that was to transform Swallowfield's interiors.

English and European influences appear increasingly to have displaced Indian motifs in Swallowfield's decor over time, but Company men and women remained central to sociability at Swallowfield through the lifetimes of the first two baronets.[108] Clotilde's French origins and her Catholicism may have been bars to Swallowfield's use as a domestic focal point of parliamentary politics: Charles's electioneering activities were largely confined to nearby Reading, his constituency. But Swallowfield nonetheless emerged as a key gathering place of Company families, and thus as a site of Company politics. The men and women recorded as visitors in the family correspondence include names that recur in the Company's lists of officers over successive generations. The Casamaijors, the Clives, the Elliots of Minto and the Duke of Wellington – who had first risen to military fame in the Madras Presidency and had known the first Sir Henry in India – were all repeated visitors at Swallowfield. The seat's location near Windsor Park helped to solidify these social connections: the region was awash with returned Anglo-Indians who had purchased estates in the surrounding countryside.

If Swallowfield exemplifies a long and English country house tradition, its history as the Russell family seat can only be understood if its Englishness is situated within wider global networks in which both India and continental Europe were conspicuously present. The brothers Henry and Charles laboured for decades to trace their family line backwards through successive English generations, but in constructing the family seat, they drew upon a more cosmopolitan genealogy. Swallowfield's acquisition rested firmly on Indian wealth and was shaped by colonial India's vibrant patterns of consumption; over time, without ever entirely effacing these Asian financial foundations, its material culture increasingly reflected a broadly European style of furnishing that combined English and continental tastes and products. Significantly, this editing of their Indian past was bolstered by the Russells' use of spatial segregation to police the racial borders of their family. Thus Henry's mixed-race illegitimate daughter – born (like the Kirkpatrick children) at Hyderabad but sent 'home' to India by her father – was explicitly excluded from the family seat at Swallowfield. Henry named this daughter Mary Wilson to disguise her paternity, appointed one of his Company friends from

Hyderabad to serve as her guardian and boarded Mary at a school in Croydon, where she was trained up as a governess. He resolutely refused to meet with her in England, to tell her of her parentage or to allow her into his stately home. 'In the first place, I could not tell her who she is, without at the same time receiving her at least occasionally into my house, and I find, what is perhaps not only natural but proper, that Lady R. would object to this, at all counts while her own daughters are unmarried', he wrote to her guardian in 1839.[109]

British country houses, the Russell correspondence repeatedly demonstrates, represent the culmination of ongoing material processes that occur across both time and space, rather than a fixed fabric rooted in a single style, period or locale. The fashioning of Swallowfield reflects a highly mobile confluence of interlocking family histories. Family members' familiarity with Calcutta's exotic emporia, the many mansions through which Lady Russell and her younger children made their peripatetic way while waiting for Sir Henry's return, the two-fold Palladian and Oriental opulence of the Hyderabad Residency during Henry and Charles's residence there and the brothers' discovery (mediated by the French connections of Henry's second wife) of continental European design and fine art all combined in the making of this English home. So too did Henry's exclusion of his daughter Mary Wilson from his family seat, an exclusion that contrasts sharply with his decision to display Chinnery's celebrated portrait of the infant Kirkpatricks prominently on Swallowfield's walls. To understand the Georgian country house as an imperial phenomenon, it is essential to move beyond the individualizing and stereotypical perspective of the nabob, to jettison the notion of English heritage as purely English, and to situate Company homes such as Swallowfield in a dense and dynamic global web of interlinked persons, objects and built environments.

11
Valentines, the Raymonds and Company material culture

Georgina Green

This chapter explores the history of a house (Valentines Mansion, Ilford, see Figure 11.1), a ship (the *Valentine*, in its successive reincarnations) and a network of Georgian maritime investors associated with the East India Company (EIC). More broadly, the chapter examines how wealth from commerce conducted at great risk in Asian outposts and Indian Ocean waters, came to be reinvested in Britain, refurbishing homes and gardens and reshaping the neighbourhoods in which they were located. Grounded in the eighteenth century, this material history extends to the present day. 'Valentines, the Raymonds and Company material culture' illuminates global commerce in the Georgian era, but it also reveals the ways in which the Company's legacy has shaped the built environment of greater London in the twenty-first century.

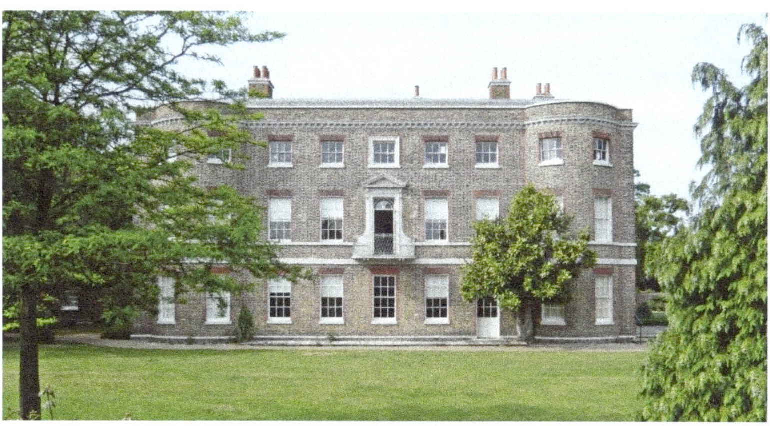

Figure 11.1 Valentines Mansion and Gardens, Ilford. Image courtesy of Georgina Green.

Although the house was originally built in 1696–7, it was in the Georgian period that Valentines saw its greatest luxury, during its ownership by successive men associated with the East India Company. Most prominent among these Company men was Sir Charles Raymond (1713–88) who became wealthy through the EIC's lucrative trade in India and China. Thanks to family connections, Raymond rose rapidly through the ranks and served as captain on four of the six voyages he made, all to India. He was able to accumulate a small fortune through his legitimate private trade. When he retired from the sea at the age of 34, he turned to managing voyages for the EIC. Raymond was never involved as a Director of the EIC but was a Manager of the Sun Fire Office 1756–73, and in 1766 he was elected a Director of the South Sea Company. His charity work included being a Governor of Bridewell and Bethlem Hospitals. He dabbled in politics and became a greatly respected banker before being created a baronet in 1774.[1]

This chapter explores the intertwined histories of the Raymond family and Valentines Mansion and is broad-ranging and interdisciplinary in its methodology. Painstaking research in the Company's archive at the British Library and the text-based practices of family and local history underpin this study. But so too does scuba-diving for shipwrecked Company treasure. The illustrations that accompany the chapter's text seek to capture the highly diverse methods and sources upon which it is based. Like the broader narrative presented here, the illustrations date from the eighteenth to the twenty-first century, ranging from Georgian prints to a contemporary art installation. Together these sources and illustrations reveal the local and global histories lived by East India Company men and women.

Valentines Mansion's EIC owners and their material objects

During the eighteenth century three owners of Valentines were involved with the East India Company: Robert Surman (c.1693–1759), Sir Charles Raymond and Donald Cameron (c.1740–97). Robert Surman, Deputy Cashier of the South Sea Company in 1720, spent a short time in prison when the South Sea 'Bubble' burst but survived with £5,000 and purchased Valentines in 1724. He does not appear to have been unduly tainted by the Bubble and returned to banking, becoming a partner in Martin's Bank and later founding his own bank, Surman, Dineley and Cliffe. He invested in the East India Company, managing the ship

Sandwich. In 1754 he sold the house to Charles Raymond, a retired EIC captain who managed many voyages for the EIC and became a respected figure in the City.[2]

Raymond was a successful captain whose profitable voyages in the Company's service played a key role in his emergence as a man of wealth and fortune. Much of the profit gained by men associated with the Company derived from the private trade goods brought home by the captains and officers of East Indiamen. On his second voyage as captain of the *Wager* 1737/8 (i.e. the ship left England in the winter of 1737/8), for example, Charles Raymond earned £3,100 in this way. However, while his ship was being prepared for the return journey he was free to work with local agents and he deposited rupees with the East India Company's accountant in Bengal for which he was later paid £3,000 in London. Raymond's earnings in trading privately thus earned him at least 30 times the salary paid to him as the captain (approx. £200).[3]

Sir Charles Raymond was Valentines' most important link with the EIC and the material goods from Asia, which so decisively shaped Georgian domestic interiors. Valentines is not a grand house, but it was nonetheless a family home, which boasted many exotic, luxurious objects. It is important as a lonely survivor in East London of the type of home described by Sylas Neville in 1785 as 'the small but neat box of the retired East India captain'.[4] The Sun Fire Office insurance documents illustrate the increase in value of the contents of Valentine House during Raymond's occupancy (1754–78). The value of insured goods rose from £500 in 1755 with the household goods insurance tripling to £1,500 in 1769, with an additional £500 for china and glass.[5]

Domestic luxury goods produced in Britain figured among Sir Charles Raymond's purchases for Valentines: during Raymond's tenure, the original of William Hogarth's *Southwark Fair* was at Valentines, probably one of several works of art in which Raymond invested his fortune. But goods from Asia were especially conspicuous among the material objects recorded as belonging to Valentines during Raymond's day. An extant porcelain plate bearing his arms (see Figure 11.2), demonstrates that, like many other East India Company captains and officials, Raymond commissioned an armorial porcelain dinner service from China.[6] Similarly, Valentines also contained a book presented to Raymond by Captain Josiah Hindman, who served as first mate when Raymond was captain of the *Wager* and went on to captain the ship when Raymond retired and became the principal managing owner (PMO).[7] The book, which is large and bound in leather, was hand painted in China.[8] It contains a series of 814 watercolour illustrations

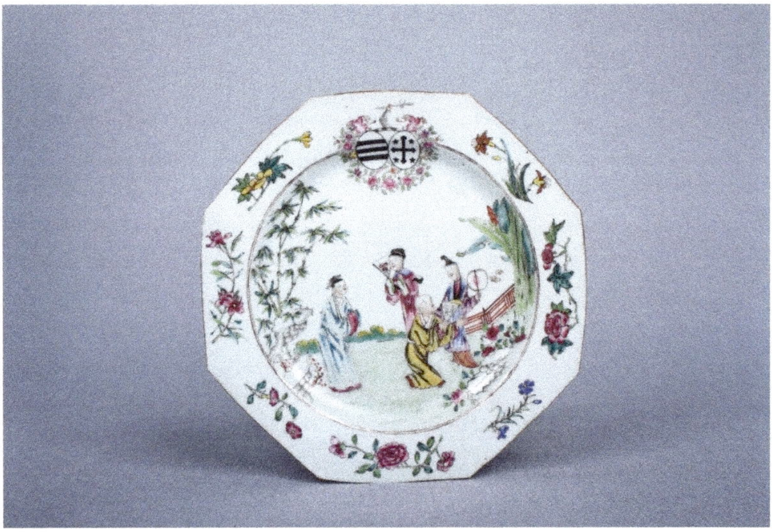

Figure 11.2 Porcelain plate decorated with the arms of Charles Raymond and his wife, Sarah Webster. China, c.1760. Private collection. Image courtesy of Georgina Green and Heirloom & Howard Ltd.

of plants and insects found in China, with Chinese and English captions detailing their medical use. While porcelain and books from Asia may have been regarded as commonplace, especially by the second half of the eighteenth century, other objects received greater attention as particular curiosities. In 1771, for example, the author of a history of Essex claimed that Valentines 'may, with great propriety, be called a Cabinet of Curiosities'.[9] Although it is difficult to know the extent of Raymond's collection, we do know he gave a neighbour a piece of sculpture of a hard, dark marble, which had been brought home from the Island of Elephanta.[10]

As Raymond sought to fill Valentines with Asian objects and curiosities, he also set to work extending the structure of the house. In 1769, he made significant changes to Valentine House, adding a bay and raising the roof. In 1771 the building was described as 'one of the neatest, and best adapted of its size, of any modern one in the county; its ornaments are well chosen, and the grounds belonging to it laid out with great judgement and taste.'[11] The external appearance of Valentines today is much as it was at that time. Raymond enhanced the gardens, which had been created by Robert Surman. In 1758, he planted a black Hamburg vine, which became very prolific, and a cutting was taken to Hampton Court Palace. The cutting has achieved greater fame than the parent plant which died late in the nineteenth century. [12]

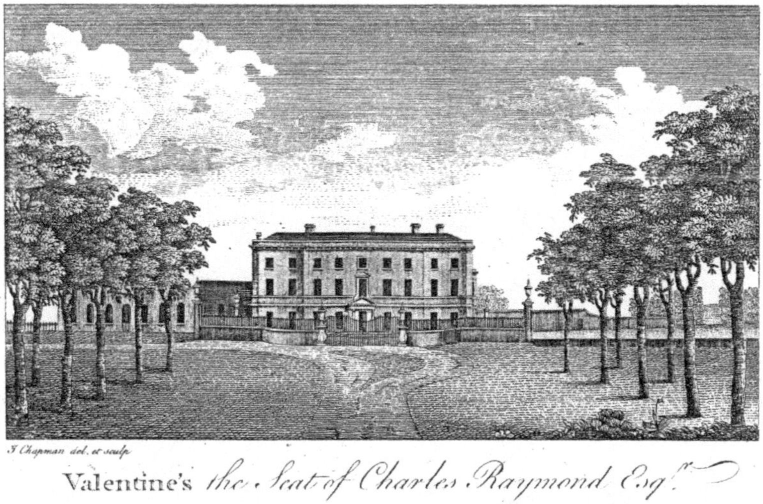

Figure 11.3 *A New and Complete History of Essex by a Gentleman* vol. 4 (1771), 276–79. This image shows the orangery, situated to the left of the house.

Imports from the East adorned not only Valentines' interiors but also its gardens. Both Robert Surman and Charles Raymond came to live at Valentines when they had small daughters, and it is not hard to imagine the girls growing up, playing games and walking in the gardens as they grew older. In Raymond's time there was a conservatory or orangery beside the house, which would have given them an elegant and sheltered place on colder days (see Figure 11.3). The orangery could well have housed plants brought home from Asia. Like the Oriental luxuries with which wealthy Georgians furnished their domestic interiors, gifts of exotic flora and fauna were integral components of the material exchanges that oiled the wheels of the Company's patronage and which helped maintain close ties among members of the Company's far-flung family networks.[13] The orangery and gardens might also have held the 'curious birds and other animals, from the East Indies' that George Edwards, FRS, mentioned seeing in August 1770. Edwards described a new species of bird, which he called a 'snake-eater', known today as a secretary bird. His letter says that a pair of birds was brought home but one died soon after it was landed. From the description given by Raymond's servant, it was thought to be a male of the species. The birds must have been caught when an East Indiaman (possibly the *Granby*) called in at the Cape (South Africa) on the way home.[14]

With Asian imports adorning the house both inside and out, its interior and exterior features stood as testament to Raymond's travels, trades and networks. When Charles Raymond died in 1788, the future of the house and the objects that filled it was decided upon by a lengthy, legalistic will. It ensured his eldest grandson would be provided for, and he left a small amount to his sister-in-law Elizabeth Webber, but otherwise his property was to be divided between his two surviving daughters, Sophia Burrell and Juliana Boulton.[15] By this means, two women who had themselves never voyaged to the Company's territories became custodians of Raymond's Indian collection. Raymond's eldest daughter, Lady Sophia Burrell, became a writer and poetess. She married William Burrell, grandson of Charles Raymond's uncle, Hugh Raymond, who had served as EIC captain and later PMO early in the eighteenth century. It was Hugh Raymond who ensured Charles had a good introduction to the sea and acquired the new ship *Wager* for him in 1734. In default of male issue, William Burrell was named to inherit the baronetcy granted to Charles Raymond on 4 May 1774.[16] Sophia's two younger sisters Anna Maria Newte (who died in 1781) and Juliana Boulton, also married men closely connected with their father through the EIC. The youngest, Anna Maria, married Thomas Newte who was also a second cousin but through Charles Raymond's mother. He had come up through the ranks of the EIC to become captain and later PMO, working in close association with the Raymond family. Sadly Anna Maria died in 1781, two years after they were married.[17] Juliana, the middle daughter, married Henry (Crabb) Boulton, the son of Richard Crabb who had sailed alongside Charles Raymond as a fellow captain and who also became a PMO. Richard's brother Henry Crabb had served as a senior clerk with the EIC and later became a director. Both brothers took the name Boulton from their cousin Richard Boulton who was connected to the EIC for 40 years, and left property to Henry, which later passed to his brother Richard.[18]

After Raymond's death, Sophia and Juliana sold Valentines and many of its contents to the third of its Georgian owners with EIC connections, Donald Cameron. He came from an ancient Scottish family and in 1763 had married Mary Guy, a step-sister of Charles Raymond's wife. By 1778 he was working at the banking house of Sir Charles Raymond and Co. where he later became a partner. He took over the management of several East Indiamen in association with Charles Raymond. Cameron had been living at a property owned by Raymond, immediately to the south of the Valentines estate, later known as Ilford Lodge. In 1791 Cameron served as Sheriff of Essex but by the time he died in 1797 the bank had suffered serious losses due to the French revolution and Valentines and its contents were sold with the other property he owned in Ilford to meet the debts.[19] An advertisement for the auction, featured in the *St James's Chronicle,* lists some of the 'Valuable Effects' that Valentines contained in 1797 and demonstrates its rich interiors.[20] The details of the sale include paintings by eminent masters, prints and drawings, oriental articles and fine ornamental china, a library of books and a considerable quantity of fine wines. As the advertisement attests, by the later eighteenth century, Asian luxuries were fully integrated with English objects d'art in the homes of Company families in Ilford.

The East India Company in Ilford

The East India Company relied on dense networks of kinship, patronage and sociability to maintain its monopolistic control over Asian trade. Charles Raymond had married Sarah Webster in 1743. Her father had died when she was small, leaving her mother, Judith, with Sarah and three little boys. A sister, Elizabeth, was born in 1725, after his death. Soon thereafter Judith married William Guy and had more children. It appears that Ann (born 1734) and Mary (born 1737) were the only daughters of Guy to survive their mother. All three girls married men connected with their older sister's husband.

Unsurprisingly, Company men and women often chose to reside in close proximity to each other. Sir Charles Raymond and his circle were no exception. In 1754 Raymond purchased Valentine House at Ilford, and before long several other retired EIC captains who followed a similar path became neighbours in this area, they included:

William Webber (1713–79) started his EIC career as third mate on the *Wager* when Raymond was the captain. He went on to serve as captain, became a PMO and later a Director of the East India Company. In 1755 he married Elizabeth Webster, a sister of Charles Raymond's wife. They lived at Highlands, a house owned by Raymond on land close to Valentines, to the west.

John Williams (c.1723–74) of Aldborough Hatch in Ilford captained *Hector* on four voyages and then became PMO for EIC. He part-owned a ropeworks at Blackwall in which Raymond had shares. In 1754 he married Ann Guy, a step-sister of Charles Raymond's wife.

Pinson Bonham (1724–91) moved into the house at Aldborough Hatch when Williams' family vacated it. Bonham had served as a captain on ships managed by Charles Raymond after two eventful voyages. As second mate on the *Princess Mary (1)*, the French captured

Bonham as he helped defend Madras on 10 September 1746. On his next voyage, while second mate on the *Duke of Cumberland (2)*, he was shipwrecked off Cape Verde (Senegal) on 16 January 1750. Once he retired from the sea he became PMO for the EIC, working closely with Charles Raymond.

Andrew Moffat (c.1730–80) had not been to sea although two brothers were retired captains, closely involved as PMO or Directors of the EIC. Moffat lived at Cranbrook House in Ilford, opposite Valentines and next to Highlands, and was a ship insurer who often worked in partnership with Raymond as PMO.

Henry Fletcher (c.1727–1807) had worked his way through the ranks to captain ships managed by Charles Raymond and then became PMO of the EIC and later a Director. In the late 1770s a Henry Fletcher was paying rates on a property just south of Valentines, although it has not been possible to confirm that this was the same man. He was created a baronet in 1782.

Donald Cameron (c.1740–97) was the next occupant of Fletcher's house and he later purchased Valentines when Sir Charles Raymond died. As previously stated, he married Mary Guy, a step-sister of Charles Raymond's wife. He had not been to sea and his involvement as PMO was as a result of becoming a business associate of Raymond. In 1771 Charles Raymond, John Williams and Henry Fletcher became founder members of a bank known as Raymond, Williams, Vere, Lowe and Fletcher, with each partner investing £5,000. This eventually became Williams Deacon's Bank and is now part of the Royal Bank of Scotland. William Webber and Donald Cameron became partners in later banks established by Sir Charles Raymond.[21]

Richard Benyon (1698–1774), retired Governor of Fort St George (Madras), also purchased property in the area in the 1740s and 1750s. On his return to England he married a wealthy widow and lived at her home, Englefield House, in Berkshire. He acquired the Great Newbury estate (which at that time adjoined Valentines to the east), Gidea Hall at Romford and land at Ockendon in Essex, as investments for his descendants. They were still living in the area a hundred years later.

Several other close EIC business associates lived nearby at Woodford including Richard Warner (1713–75), Charles Foulis (c.1714–83), Robert Preston (1740–1834) and Pitt Collett (c.1727–80). Identifying these residential nodes – and their connections with other concentrations of Company homes in town and country – adds a new dimension to our understanding of the EIC as a networked monopoly that operated simultaneously at local and global levels.

Significantly, when the Company civil servants who had lived in Asia retired they usually chose to come back to a quiet life in luxurious surroundings (as did Richard Benyon), but the retired captains could not settle in the same way. Having spent years risking their lives and making split second decisions, they chose to continue risking their wealth in the City. The camaraderie built up over the years at sea stood them in good stead in their City work. They knew their colleagues could be relied upon and trusted and were glad to include them in new opportunities as they, in turn, retired from the sea. It is not surprising that Moffat, Foulis and Preston became insurance brokers while Raymond, Williams, Fletcher, Webber and Cameron were banking partners.

The *Valentine*: the EIC's ships at trade and war

Navigating, investing in and managing the vessels that carried the EIC's goods from India to Britain, was a risky business in the eighteenth century. European maritime skills and technologies were severely challenged by the vast distances entailed by trade with China, India and Japan. European death rates in India were horrific: the majority of the Company merchants who traded in eighteenth-century India failed to survive to return home to Britain. Conflict with indigenous military formations (notably the Mughal empire and its successor states on the Indian subcontinent) and competition with the rival East India Companies established by the Dutch and the French raised the costs of trade, and could rapidly annihilate individual traders' profits. War between the British and the French, endemic in the eighteenth century, continually spilled over from European military theatres into the two powers' emerging empires in the Atlantic and Indian Ocean worlds. The maritime trade that allowed Company men such as Sir Charles Raymond to purchase and refurbish homes such as Valentines was fraught with danger, as the history of Raymond's East Indiaman *Valentine* makes emphatically clear.[22]

East Indiamen were designed for carrying cargo, the container ships of their day, and at that time they were built on the banks of the Thames at Blackwall. Each ship was usually owned by a group of investors, with one of them managing the voyage and signing the paperwork on behalf of the group when the ship was chartered for a voyage by the EIC. As East Indiamen were not built for speed they were vulnerable when laden, so were armed and ready to defend themselves. Figure 11.4 shows three ships *Suffolk, Godolphin* and *Houghton*, which fought off two French men-of-war in March 1757.

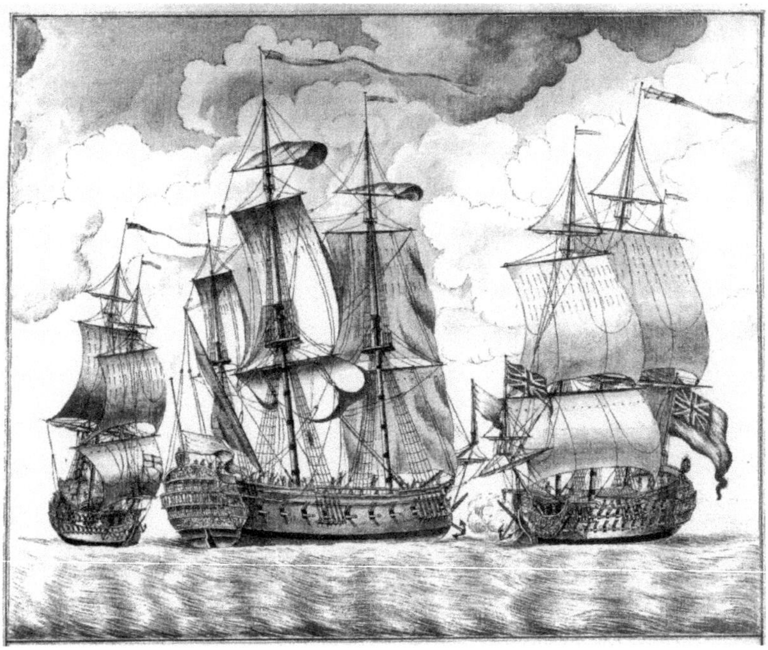

Figure 11.4 Illustration from the journal of the East Indiaman *Suffolk 1755/6* (L/MAR/B/397D) British Library. © The British Library Board, 1755/6 (IOR/L/MAR/B/397D).

One of the East Indiamen which Charles Raymond built was named the *Valentine* after his home in Ilford. The first ship of this name was built by Perry and had three decks, with 3-inch bottom, registered as 655 tons, and was launched in 1758. Its first voyage was to India and China and on the way home in January 1761 the crew witnessed the sinking of Captain Thomas Dethick's *Griffin*, with whom they were in convoy, when it struck a reef off the 'island of Zelo' to the east of the northern tip of Borneo.[23] *Valentine*'s second voyage was to Benkulen and China. The ship was then rebuilt as was customary after deterioration due to weather and the effect of sailing in the warm seas.

Perry also built *Valentine (2),* including three decks and a 3-inch bottom. The length of the ship was 135 ft 11 inches, keel 110 ft 11½ inches, breadth 34 ft 4 inches, hold 14 ft 3 inches, wing transom 20ft 10¾ inches and between decks 5 ft 9¾ inches. It was registered at 690 tons and was launched in 1767. Again the PMO was Charles Raymond. He would have put up a substantial part of the capital for rebuilding the ship, along with several others who relied on Raymond to manage the results of their investment. Others in the consortium may have included his cousin John Raymond and Richard Crabb Boulton who had sailed as a captain at the same time as Raymond (his son Henry married Charles Raymond's daughter Juliana on 3 November 1774) as well as some of the friends and relations previously listed. *Valentine (2)* made four voyages. The first two were under the command of Captain Charles Purvis: the first voyage 1767/8 was to Bengal, and the second 1769/70 to Madras and China. The third and fourth voyages were under Captain James Ogilvie: 1772/3 to China and 1776/7 to Madras, Bengal and Bombay. The last voyage ended in disaster when the ship was wrecked off the island of Sark in the Channel Isles.[24]

James Ogilvie first appears in the EIC records as fourth mate on the *Duke of Richmond* 1763/4. Charles Raymond managed the ship and knew the captain well. Raymond probably selected this voyage as a good introduction to the sea for Ogilvie. Ogilvie then served as second mate on the *Neptune (3)* 1768/9, also managed by Raymond. He was approved by the EIC Directors to be a Captain on 18 August 1772, aged 29, when he took command of the *Valentine (2)*. It seems likely his father was known to Raymond or a close associate to have had such a rapid career progression. Maybe Ogilvie was Scottish and was connected to Andrew Moffatt who was on very friendly terms with the Scottish Earls of Mansfield and Elgin.

Valentine (3) was built by Randall and launched in 1780, but this time the PMO was Donald Cameron who became a partner in the bank of Raymond, Harley, Webber & Co. He purchased Valentine House from Raymond's daughters after Raymond died in 1788. These relationships again illustrate the dense webs of family, residence and business that bound the men and women of the EIC.[25]

Like very many record books of the East India Company, the Captain's journal of the last voyage of *Valentine (2)* can be seen at the British Library. The ship left Portsmouth on 1 January 1777 and arrived at Madras on 25 June. It then visited other ports en route to Calcutta, but from then on had a very unusual voyage. In December, when loaded for the return home, the ship ran aground near Madras due to an error in navigation. It suffered damage to the hull and it was necessary to cut away the masts in an attempt to get the ship afloat. Soon another East Indiaman came to help lighten *Valentine* by off-loading the cargo. Once re-floated, temporary repairs were made at sea so that the ship could make it to the shipyard at Bombay where it spent 10 weeks being repaired and refitted.[26]

However, at this time war was endemic with the French and in August the *Valentine*'s Captain, James Ogilvie, was summoned to the

Select Committee of the East India Company in Madras. After being sworn to secrecy Ogilvie was informed of the Company's orders to besiege Pondicherry (on the coast, south of Madras), and that Sir Edward Vernon was to attack the French Squadron with HM navy ships and had requested the assistance of the *Valentine* along with another East Indiaman, *Seahorse.* On 10 August 1778 the five French and four English ships drew together in two lines, and exchanged fire as they sailed past each other, before the English ships turned to cut through the enemy line and further engage them. Eventually the French withdrew back to Pondicherry, giving an indecisive end to the encounter.[27]

The *Valentine* fought bravely, taking a leading role in the battle. With two dead and 15 injured, it limped back to Madras for repairs. The ship was on its fourth voyage and had been repaired in Bombay earlier in the year. Consequently when it arrived in the English Channel it was struggling to keep up with its companions. At this time a convoy with naval protection was essential due to enemy vessels lurking in the vicinity. But a fierce storm blew up and the convoy was scattered. Evidently Captain Ogilvie must have decided to try and make for shelter at St Peter Port in Guernsey. Sadly *Valentine* was unable to reach this safe haven. As darkness fell on 16 November 1779, with a gale blowing through the remains of the tattered sails, the ship struck the rocks off the little island of Brecqhou, close by Sark. The crew and passengers were able to get ashore safely so thankfully there was no loss of life.[28]

For several weeks the ship was broken up by the waves and its cargo was looted. 4,000 bags of saltpeter had been loaded, along with several hundred bales of raw silk, and 18 boatloads of redwood for the 'Honourable Company' as well as the private trade goods of the officers. Local tradition says the ladies of Sark enjoyed the luxury of silk dresses the following summer! The East India Company were naturally concerned by the loss of the ship but their enquiry exonerated Captain Ogilvie. They reported that 'his behaviour was very commendable, and that he exerted himself to the utmost for the Preservation of the Ship and Cargo, and the Officers on board acquitted themselves properly on the Occasion'.[29]

Shipwrecked East Indiamen provided conspicuous (and common) illustrations of the very high levels of human and financial risk in which the Company's fortunes were grounded in the Georgian era. After Raymond's time the *Abergavenny* East Indiaman was wrecked just outside Weymouth Bay on a dark winter night (5 February 1805), having struck the Shambles sandbank at about 5.00 p.m. As the ship began to sink, perhaps 180 men climbed up the rigging as the main and mizzen masts still remained above water to below their yards. But it slowly settled deeper into the sandy seabed and the men gradually lost their hold in the icy spray and frosty wind. In the morning the topmasts and shrouds could still be seen, while the keel was 10 fathoms below the waves (60 feet or 18 metres) about 1½ miles from shore.[30]

The Captain of the *Abergavenny*, John Wordsworth, was very experienced, but just unable to save his ship. He was the younger brother of the poet William Wordsworth who wrote a poem about his brother, including the lines:

> *All vanished in a single word,*
> *A breath, a sound, and scarcely heard:*
> *Sea – Ship – drowned – Shipwreck – so it came,*
> *The meek, the brave, the good was gone;*
> *He who had been our living John*
> *Was nothing but a name.* [31]

The poet captured the human tragedy in a way that statistics can only hint at. An estimated 6 per cent of Company ships were lost and on those ships which did return home, approximately 12–15 per cent of the crew had either died or jumped ship.[32] Life was cheap, but every loss was a tragedy to those left at home.

Shipwrecks and the EIC's 'immaterial' material culture

As the fate of both the *Valentine* and the *Abergavenny* attests, shipwreck was an ever-present threat in maritime trade of the Georgian era. Of the 980 EIC voyages between 1747–88, and discounting those ships which were to remain abroad, 94 per cent returned home: 39 were wrecked or 'lost', seven were burnt and 12 were captured. By far the worst year was 1779/80 when, out of the 26 that sailed, six ships were captured and two were lost.[33] To bear the possibility and burden of loss, ships were owned by a number of investors, and it seems Raymond had a group of associates who worked together in partnership. Cargos from shipwrecked vessels provide historians with a ghostly counterfoil to pristine collections of Oriental luxuries assembled in many surviving stately homes in Britain, offering a unique, 'immaterial' perspective on the Company's domestic material culture. When divers investigated the wreck of the *Griffin* East Indiaman, which sank in 1761 on her way home from China, they estimated she carried 125,800 pieces of chinaware.[34]

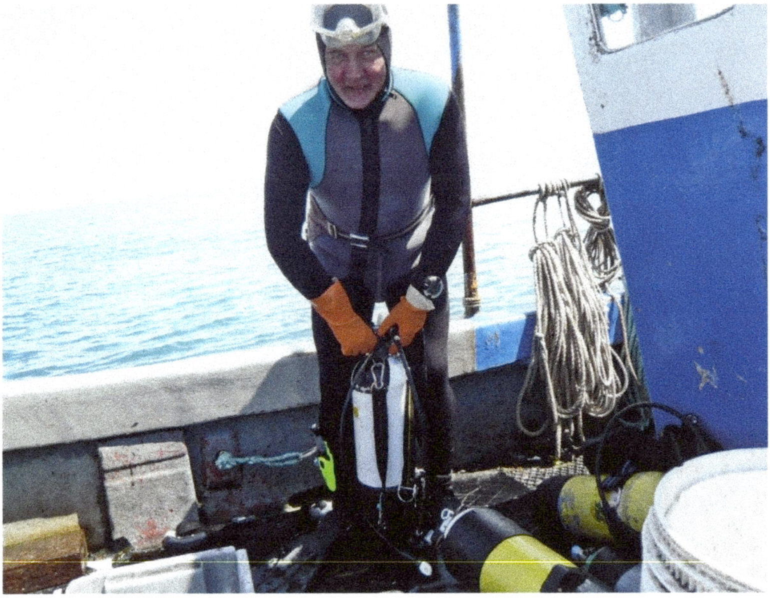

Figure 11.5 Diver Richard Keen preparing to dive near Guernsey. Image courtesy of Georgina Green.

Fragments such as the *Griffin*'s porcelain shards have rarely featured in analyses of the Company's material legacies, but they offer historians a wealth of material for understanding the EIC's contribution to consumer culture. As they remind us, the Asian items displayed in stately homes and country houses today are only a fraction of what arrived in England in the eighteenth century. Indeed, much of the cargo brought home from India and China was of short-term value and use. Tea, spices, fabrics – all were for immediate consumption and almost all are lost to us now. As an example, the cargo carried home from India in 1739 by Captain Charles Raymond on his second voyage of the *Wager* included cotton materials (calico, seersuckers, chints, ginghams, etc.) valued at approximately £85,030; raw silk at £9,780; redwood at £112 (this was dunnage: it was packed between cargo to prevent movement and keep it dry); saltpeter at £1,770; turmerick at £125; and cowries at £1,875. The total value of the cargo was nearly £100,000, which in present day terms would be around £10 million.[35] Unlike Raymond's porcelain plate, books and artwork, these imports have left no traces in domestic interiors. Recovering their histories requires us to step outside the home, and outside the archive, diving instead (quite literally) into the waters in which East Indiamen sailed to trade with the Orient.

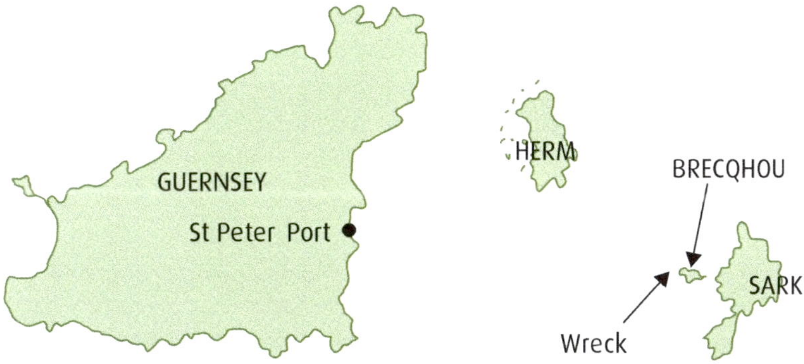

Figure 11.6 Map of wreck location. Image courtesy of Georgina Green.

Nearly 200 years after the *Valentine* was wrecked, a young Guernsey diver, Richard Keen, decided to try and find the wreck (see Figure 11.5). Keen has discovered over 30 wrecks on the rocks and reefs in Guernsey waters, some by accident and others while un-snagging crab pots and trawl nets. He started to research these wrecks, and others, which had been recorded in old newspapers and diaries but had never been located. His most important archaeological find was that of a Roman wreck, known as 'Asterix',[36] which he discovered in the harbour mouth at St Peter Port in 1982.

Some years before this Keen came across a map in the Priaulx Library at St Peter Port which houses some of the island's archives.[37] The map was dated 1816 and showed a rock off the island of Brecqhou (close to Sark) with the words 'Le Neste upon which the Valentine Indiaman was wrecked in 1779'.[38] He became fascinated by the idea of finding the wreck but the very high rise and fall of the tide and the strong currents, with many rocks in the area, made the location outlined a hazardous place in which to dive. However, Keen dived and successfully located the site in 1974 (see Figure 11.6). Others attempted to dive on the wreck the following year but their attempt was aborted. Eventually Keen retrieved some pieces of lead, red dyewood, agate and pottery and they were declared to the Receiver of Wrecks. Two years later the 'Valentines Excavation Group 1976' was established to undertake a coordinated survey of the wreck site, near the rock called 'Le Neste' off the western tip of Brecqhou. Dives were made on 10 days, starting on 10 April with the last on 12 December. The seabed in the area comprised a mass of rocky gullies with gravel in the bottom, and with kelp growing on the rocks. Work on the site was only possible during neap tides and then only close to slack water, due to the strong currents. However the depth of the remains at diving time was between 10 to 18 metres, so the divers did not have any problems with decompression.

The main cargo of the vessel was saltpeter, which was much in demand in eighteenth-century Britain for the manufacture of gun powder. Another significant part of the cargo was red dyewood, which was used for dunnage, as well as being of value for dyeing. As an extremely hard wood, the dyewood (unlike the saltpeter) survived and large logs were retrieved. The timbers of the ship decomposed long ago although some canons remain to mark the site where the *Valentine* foundered. One interesting find was a broken anchor (which had been mentioned in the captain's journal) with a cannon strapped to it. This illustrates the desperate attempts made by the crew to save their ship in 1779.

Since 1976 other dives have been held and a number of local people have retrieved items from the wreck site. Shards of blue and white Chinese porcelain are often found. Manufactured in China, loaded in Canton and either brought directly to England or taken to India by one of the many EIC 'country ships' used by the Company to transport their cargo in Asian waters, porcelain was often packed in boxes with loose tea or pepper for padding. The *Valentine* had only visited India on her last voyage, but her cargo consisted of a range of Chinese porcelain from best quality items for the aristocratic tea party to thicker items for general use. The finer shards illustrated are from a better quality bowl decorated inside (see Figure 11.7). The blue and white china was a popular design in England.

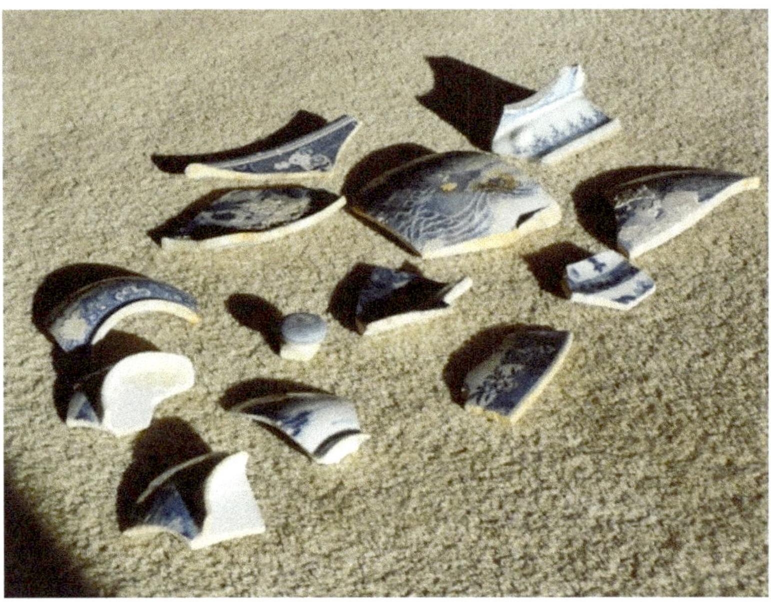

Figure 11.7 Porcelain shards from the *Valentine*. Image courtesy of Georgina Green.

Many small pieces of agate were also discovered, mostly orange or rust in colour (see Figure 11.8). Cut and roughly shaped square or rectangular in India, agate was transported to England to be made into signet rings and broaches. Agate is an extremely hard stone and it is remarkable that these pieces were smoothed and bevelled by India craftsmen without modern technology. Their loading was not noted in the captain's journal so it is likely they were private trade.

Other items retrieved illustrate life on board ship: metal handles from furniture or travelling luggage, and ground glass stoppers for decanters or medical jars (see Figure 11.9). They may have been for items used on the voyage – although there was a significant quantity found, which may suggest they were also part of the private trade. Broken bottles were also found. They may have been loaded in Madeira and would have contained fortified or non-fortified wine. Madeira wine was collected on the outward journey and some of it was required for EIC staff in India.[39] The warmth and movement of the voyage improved the quality, if it was not drunk by officers and passengers before they got back to England![40]

As already stated, quantities of redwood were also salvaged from the wreck. Even after being in the sea for 200 years the red colour remains vibrant when the wood is cut, and it can still be used to dye

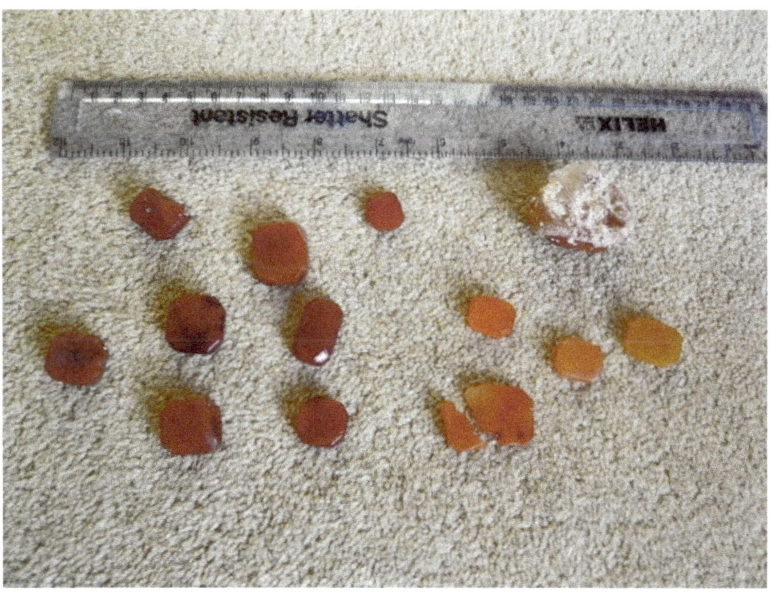

Figure 11.8 Agate pieces from the *Valentine*. Image courtesy of Georgina Green.

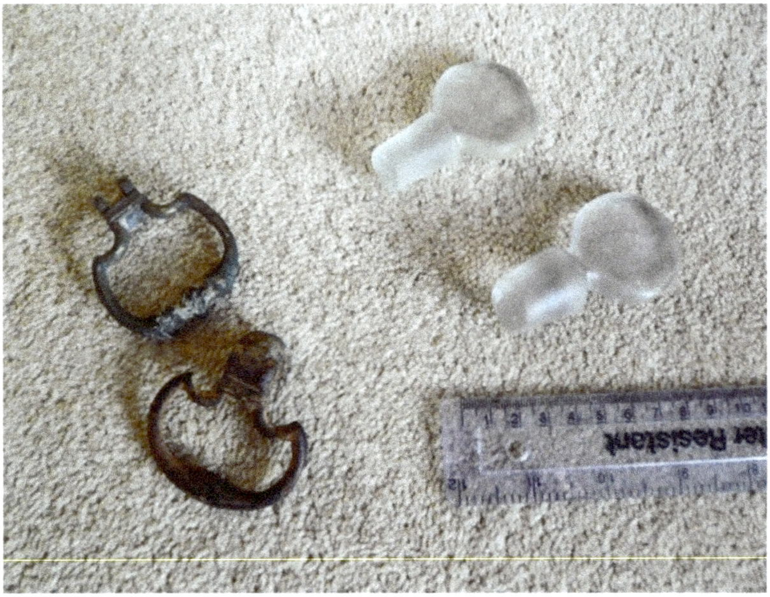

Figure 11.9 Metal handles and bottle stoppers from the *Valentine*. Image courtesy of Georgina Green.

fabric. Georgina Green's research on Valentines and her subsequent lectures and displays contributed to encouraging two local artists, Margaret Duston and Kathy Taylor, to create an installation about the wreck of the *Valentine*. Their artwork interwove different imperial commodities – cotton, tea, indigo, dye from red dyewood – to gesture towards the complex material history of the East India Company. Displayed in the old restored dovecote in the Valentines Gardens in May 2010 and creating considerable interest, the piece embodied the Company's history and mirrored that of the house itself (see Figure 11.10). Long connected to the East India Company through people, objects and wealth it remains in Essex, as a site that is open to the public and a testimony to the ways in which Britain's imperial projects benefitted and shaped British culture.

Conclusion

Only recently brought to light through an innovative combination of historical research and marine exploration, Valentines Mansion's many

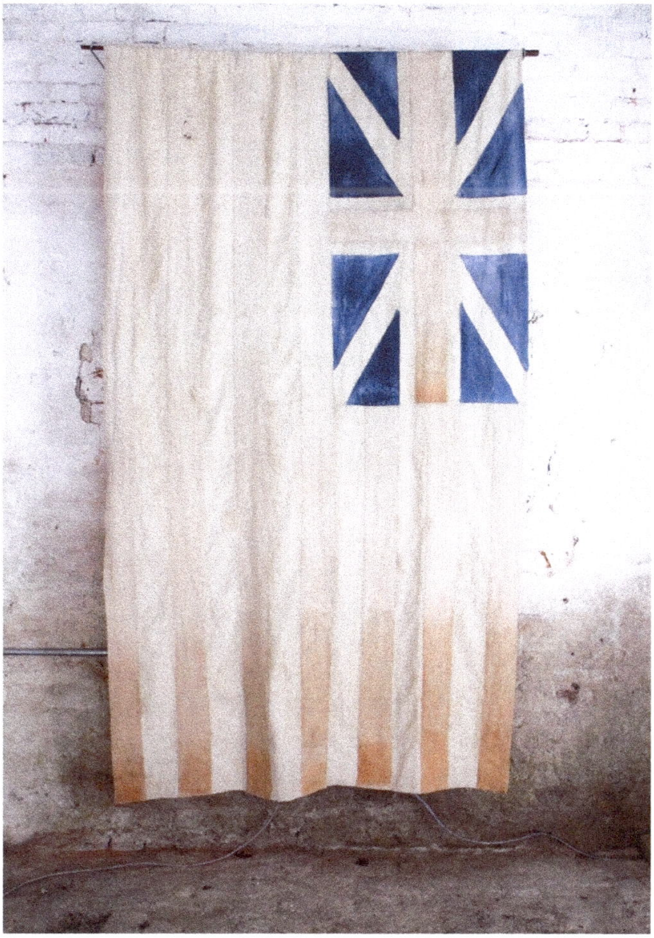

Figure 11.10 *Stain* by Kathy Taylor. Indian cotton, stained with tea, indigo and dye extracted from red dyewood/red sander's dust from the *Valentine* cargo. The flag design is based on the British East India Company Flag of 1707–1801. Image courtesy of Kathy Taylor.

connections to the East India Company in the eighteenth century illustrate many of the characteristic features of Company commerce in the Georgian era.[41] The Raymond family's operation as a collective unit – joined by marriage, patronage, investments, gifts, material objects and residence – testifies to the Company's corporate culture, a culture well calculated to moderate the impact of the enormous risks entailed by trade with China and India in this era. The contrast between the luxury objects with which Valentines Mansion was furnished in Sir Charles Raymond's day, on the one hand, and the fragmentary shards of Chinese porcelain recovered in recent times from the *Valentine*'s wreckage, on the other, nicely captures the threats that challenged Company servants' efforts to extract fortune and status through Asian commerce. By recovering the Company components of Valentines' history, this chapter forcibly reminds us of the global dimensions of eighteenth-century Essex.

12
Growing up in a Company town

The East India Company presence in South Hertfordshire

Chris Jeppesen

Situated just north of the M25 in south Hertfordshire, Brookmans Park is an affluent but otherwise unremarkable commuter village of around 3,500 inhabitants. Perhaps best known today for its assortment of minor celebrities and acclaimed in glossy property magazines for its desirable village living and good transport links, it has always proved attractive to those looking to move beyond, but remain within easy reach of, London's boundaries.[1] The village is centred upon a railway station and small green surrounded by shops and restaurants, its residential streets spreading across the eastern part of the parish of North Mymms.[2] Even as redevelopment proceeds apace, the dominant mix of mock-Tudor detached residences alongside more modest semi-detached housing and bungalows betrays its mid-twentieth-century origins as a middle-class commuter village. Taking advantage of the post First World War building boom, developers began to construct 'a country village with all modern conveniences' on land that formed part of the large Brookmans estate.[3] Over the next four decades the village grew steadily, and by the mid-1960s boasted just over 2,500 residents, served by a golf course, a primary school and secondary school, and large areas of protected park-land.[4] It is here that I grew up in the 1980s and 90s.

In 1800 the area looked very different. Largely agricultural, it was dominated by four grand houses and their estates: Brookmans, Gobions (sometimes spelt Gubbins), Potterells and the smaller Moffats House.[5]

Today only the latter survives intact, albeit in partitioned form, the others having been destroyed by fire or demolished at various points from the 1840s to the 1980s. Much of the local history I learnt whilst attending both village schools recounted an insular past shaped by the rise and fall of these country estates and the coming of the railway. It was a narrative populated with an eclectic cast of characters ranging from Sir Thomas More (1478–1535), whose family owned Gobions in the sixteenth century, to Little Miss Muffet of nursery rhyme fame, purportedly written by an inhabitant of Moffats House.[6] This history has been carefully woven into the village's civic identity: the primary school's crest combines a hart (the area formerly being a royal hunting ground) and a spider's web in testament to the nursery rhyme, whilst the senior school, Chancellors, owes its name and crest (a chancellor's wig) to the connection to Henry VIII's unfortunate counsellor. Growing up, this local history sparked little interest in me, always seeming so mundane compared to the excitement of learning about wider horizons at school: while my village provided a happy place to enjoy childhood, as a teenager it never seemed anything other than parochial.

It thus came as a surprise when research for the *East India Company at Home* project revealed that between 1700 and 1850 all four of these estates were owned, at one time or another, by families with intricate connections to the wider imperial world. Throughout these decades, wealth derived in India and the Caribbean was channelled into the purchasing and redevelopment of the area. Owners and residents included two East India Company (EIC) Directors, three EIC officials, an elite Huguenot family operating at the intersection of trade to Asia and the Caribbean, several West India merchants (including one whose family network spread across three continents), and the son of an early Deputy Chairman of the EIC, whose own fortune came through investments in the South Sea Company. Collectively these families formed a community that exchanged land and property, intermarried, socialized together and, in so doing, remade the landscape upon which my village now stands.

This chapter examines the local world these men and women helped create but also situates this within the entangled web of trade, kinship and patronage that spread from rural Hertfordshire, to the City of London, across Britain and outwards to encompass an expanding global empire. In so doing, it poses questions about how these wider perspectives force us to reconsider entrenched narratives that so often serve to partition the histories of Britain and its empire.[7] Even though wealth from overseas fundamentally changed the area in which I grew up, the empire remained utterly inconsequential to the local history I absorbed. This historical amnesia is partly explained by the fact that these houses no longer remain. Nevertheless, as recent research highlights, the prevailing image of the country house as the most quintessential of English settings frequently belies the legacies of empire embedded in the fabric of buildings and contents.[8] Recovering the forgotten histories of the country estates that now form such a focal point for the heritage and tourism sectors, often within rural settings adamantly resistant to changing cultural realities, forces us to reconsider the dominant narratives associated with these sites and the often exclusionary vision of Englishness they help sustain.[9]

Over the last decade, the process of remembering the empire in Britain has become ever more contested.[10] New voices, often born after formal decolonization into an increasingly multi-cultural society, have disrupted entrenched, self-congratulatory narratives that posit a benign British colonialism as a source of pride and worked to identify a less insular and more diverse national history than 'our island story' permits. At times this battle over memory has erupted around overtly imperial sites, such as the recent Rhodes Must Fall campaign in Oxford, or through former colonized peoples' efforts to gain restorative justice for past crimes.[11] Yet, as the multitude of local history projects undertaken in 2007 to mark the bicentenary of the abolition of the slave trade and the findings of the *East India Company at Home* and *Legacies of British Slave-ownership* projects have laid bare, the impact of slavery, and empire more broadly, permeated the daily lives of groups and individuals across Britain in less obvious but nonetheless profound ways.[12] In challenging the assumption that empire was something that happened elsewhere this work has underscored the contribution made by the new imperial histories over the last thirty years in disrupting the false dichotomy of 'here and over there' that has for so long stood at the heart of many assessments of the empire's impact on British society.[13] It is not, as Catherine Hall has shown, happenchance that a celebratory narrative shaped around abolition and the bringing of modernity to colonial peoples has come to dominate how empire is remembered in Britain. Rather, over the last 200 years this has depended upon a carefully coordinated process of selective remembering and calculated omission.[14]

Recovering this past necessitates a clearer understanding of the relationship between the local and global. As Katie Donington reminds us '[L]ocal areas do not operate in isolation, they were and are places that reach out and connect to different geographic locations. People, capital, goods and ideas constantly circulate, leaving traces of themselves behind.'[15] Empire inflected the daily lives of individuals across Britain in diverse and unpredictable ways. Wealth generated through global trade funded the remaking of local landscapes through the construction of large houses and lavish gardens; exotic items and commodities percolated throughout British society, reconfiguring domestic spaces and individual consumption habits; diverse individuals with experience of life in colonial settings settled across Britain, challenging established social hierarchies and sometimes transgressing entrenched norms of gender and race.[16] By shifting focus from the institutional foundations of imperial authority onto the family as a central structure in the operation of the pre-Victorian empire, scholars have recently opened rich new perspectives on the circuits that enmeshed local and global contexts.[17] In exploring these entanglements within a specific parish, it becomes possible to expose the significance of empire in even the most unlikely of settings and thus escape the illusion that these were insulated bastions of an autochthonous Englishness.[18]

If wealth from overseas and overt connections to empire remained most concentrated amongst the landed elite that dominated local structures of power, country estates also stood at the heart of parish life across rural Britain for much of the eighteenth and nineteenth centuries. Despite the impression of permanence and order they might conjure today, these country estates were never static spaces but rather sites of contestation in which the politics of class, gender, race and empire were negotiated by the families who owned the properties and those who lived and worked on them. These dynamics reveal intimate insights into the economies of labour and community that underpinned the structure of eighteenth-century British society and which helped support an expanding global empire.[19] Tillman Nechtman's recent assessment of the 'Nabob controversy' neatly illuminates how returning wealth and cultural practices from India, personified in the figure of the EIC official-cum-oriental despot, provoked fierce debate around the perceived corrupting effects of empire on core qualities of Englishness. For Nechtman, it exposed the fraught entangling of competing concepts of nation and empire within a febrile late-eighteenth century public sphere. Focusing on this episode as public spectacle, he has less to say about how these individuals reintegrated at a local level or about what happened to their wealth over time, however.[20] This longer narrative of adaptation, integration and transformation starts to emerge with greater clarity when rooted in specific contexts. Examining how parish life intersected with, and was reshaped by global forces, allows us to begin to appreciate more clearly the multifarious ways in which empire entered the daily rhythms of very different people, living in very different places across Britain and, in so doing, integrate them into a conception of British history that situates the enduring connections between empire and metropole at the heart of any national narrative.[21]

The East India Company in Hertfordshire

Within south Hertfordshire's dense belt of country estates, described by Robert Morden in 1704 as running almost as a continual street of beautiful houses from Totteridge in the west to Ware in the east, North Mymms' East India connections were no anomaly.[22] Recent research by Stephanie Barczewski fortifies Lawrence Stone's earlier findings that Hertfordshire was especially popular amongst those looking to reinvest wealth accumulated not just in India but across the empire in English country estates.[23] My own findings indicate that the number of former EIC officials, merchants and directors who lived in the county between 1700 and the 1850s was at least 32 more than previous estimates suggest. As the *Legacies of*

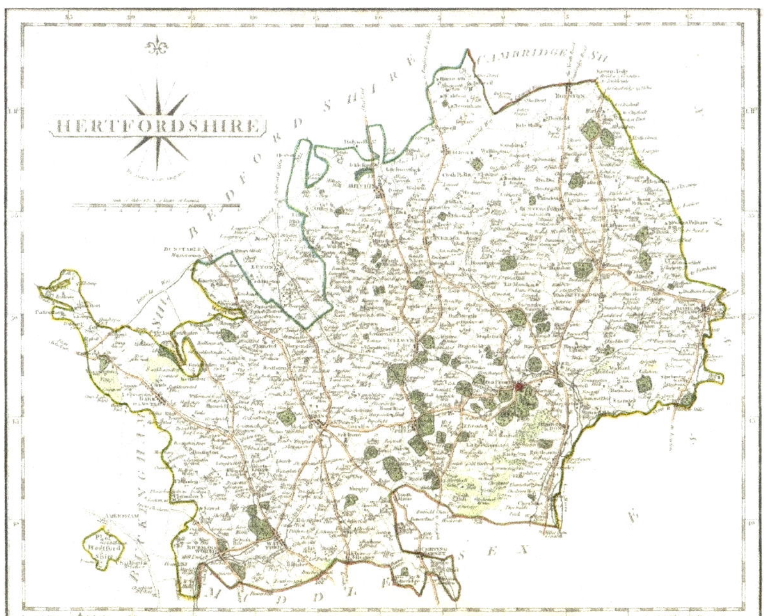

Figure 12.1 John Cary, Map of Hertfordshire, in *Cary's new and correct atlas: being a new set of county maps from actual surveys* (London, 1787), not paginated https://commons.wikimedia.org/wiki/File:Hertfordshire-Maps-Cary-1787-49.jpg

British Slave-ownership project has uncovered, Caribbean derived wealth flowed into the county throughout the eighteenth and early nineteenth centuries, with 26 residents claiming over £624,000 in slavery compensation money in the 1830s (and an additional £100,000 claimed by trustees and unsuccessful claimants).[24] The geographical spread of these associations is also revealing. While those claiming slavery compensation money were distributed across the county, the estates of EIC officials and directors congregated in the south, often proximate to the major roads running north from London.

Unlike the flat, arable landscape of north Herts, the southern half of the county offered picturesque rolling hills, river valleys and woodland, as well as good land for grazing and hunting, which drew especial admiration from mid-eighteenth century writers and landscapers (see Figure 12.1).[25] On a more practical level, south Hertfordshire's proximity to the capital has always ensured its attractiveness to those looking to supplement commercial wealth with country property. Compared to other parts of England, as Stone has shown, the makeup of county society remained in many ways exceptional until the late nineteenth century. From before the English Civil War, Hertfordshire had a higher turnover of property, higher marriage rates outwith the limits of county society and a higher density of estates than almost any other county.[26] Its relatively small size and high land costs meant that, unlike their counterparts in counties with less developed links to London, many Hertfordshire landowners did not derive their incomes from land alone, with most estates not exceeding 1,000 acres.[27] Instead, owners tended to retain close commercial links to the city, whilst developing their country estates in an ostentatious display of wealth and status.[28] For these reasons the county proved especially permeable to new streams of wealth and thus particularly attractive to EIC officials and merchants desirous of remaining close to London in order to participate in Company politics, global trade or to sit as MPs.[29]

East India Company families first appeared in Hertfordshire in the early 1700s and proliferated as British control in India expanded. A century later, Haileybury was selected as the site for the new EIC training college in 1806, both reflecting and further cementing the close associations between Company and county.[30] Before 1759 the Company presence centred on an axis running north along the Hertford road. Notable owners included Edward Harrison (1674–1732) of Balls Park, John Deane (d.1751) and Alexander Hume (1693–1765), successive owners of Wormleybury, Thomas Rolt (c.1631–1710) of Sacombe Park and Joseph Collett (1673–1725) of Hertford Castle, all of whom accumulated wealth and status in – or, in the case of Hume, sailing to – India and remained active in Company politics upon their return. In the aftermath of the Battle of Plassey in 1757 opportunities for personal enrichment proliferated. As Company control solidified in the presidencies of Bengal, Madras and Bombay, its identity transformed from trader to conqueror and occupier. Amongst the generation of 'nabobs' who returned to Britain during the period styled 'the shaking of the pagoda tree' (c.1757–80s), many brought vast fortunes with them, which they reinvested in land, property, luxury commodities and political capital to facilitate entry to the highest echelons of the British elite.[31] Unsurprisingly, it is during the period 1760–90 that the highest number of individuals (10) with a direct personal connection to India purchased estates in Herts.[32] These included such notorious figures as Laurence Sulivan (1713–86) of Ponsbourne Park, Thomas Rumbold (1736–91) of Woodhall and Governor Charles Bourchier (1726–1810) of Colney House. Many spent lavishly on rebuilding older manors, constructing new houses and landscaping gardens. Rumbold, for instance, expended £85,000 of his £200,000 plus fortune purchasing Woodhall and then built a new Palladian mansion designed by Thomas Leverton (c.1743–1824), which he filled with items brought back from Madras.[33] Bourchier outlaid almost £60,000 purchasing and renovating Colney House, bankrupting himself in the process.[34] A further six London-based merchants grown wealthy from the East and West India trades, and often connected to the EIC Court of Directors, also purchased estates during this 30-year period.

In the wake of Warren Hastings's impeachment trial (1788–95) measures were taken to better regulate the Company's activities, thereby making it more difficult to replicate the fortunes of the nabob generation. Nonetheless, the period between 1790 and 1820 still saw notable numbers return from India to purchase Hertfordshire land and property. Amongst them was the controversial Paul Benfield (1741–1810), who not only bought Woodhall from Thomas Rumbold's executors but also became heavily involved in the Hertfordshire property market and West India trade before going bankrupt in 1799.[35] Others included George Sullivan Marten (1763–1826) of Sandridge Lodge, John Fann Timins (1767–1843) of Hilfield Castle, George Shee (1758–1825) of Lockleys and Patrick Haddow (1770–1861) of Colney House. By 1800 the typical profile of purchasers was starting to shift, however. A growing number came from a mercantile and banking background in the City of London, where they were embedded in the East India, China and West India trades and the provision of capital in the expanding banking sector.[36] For instance, in 1799 West India merchant, EIC Director, MP and city banker,

George Woodford Thellusson (1764–1811) purchased Wall Hall (later renamed Aldenham Abbey) for £24,000. Likewise, EIC Director and MP, Robert Williams (1735–1814) used his fortune accumulated through East India shipping to purchase Moor Park in 1801 from the executors of former owner and fellow director, Thomas Bates Rous.

After 1820, ever fewer returning EIC officials could afford to purchase new estates, although several, such as William Raikes Timins (1808–66) of Hilfield (1843) and Thomas Powney Marten (1807–89) of Sandridge (1876), inherited estates originally purchased with wealth accrued in India by their fathers. Others who retired from India without great personal wealth used family networks to transition into careers in the city or banking. Powney Marten offers one such example. He joined his brother as partner in the bank founded by their father, Marten, Call & Arnold, while Augustus Henry Bosanquet (1792–1877) – nephew of EIC Director Jacob Bosanquet (1756–1828) – retired in 1821 after 11 years in Bengal to join the family West India merchant firm. Bosanquet acquired considerable wealth during the mid-Victorian period, purchasing Osidge House near Barnet, and leaving an estate valued at £70,000 in 1877. Although this later period saw fewer new arrivals in the county, many established families remained involved with imperial trade, whilst a growing number of sons from the emerging professional middle classes left the county to take up careers across empire.

It is highly unlikely that the arrival of so many EIC officials in Hertfordshire was a coincidence. The constellations they formed once settled frequently reflected commercial associations, strategic alliances and friendships made in India. For instance, Laurence Sulivan purchased Ponsborne near his friend and business associate Stephen Law (1699–1788), who owned neighbouring Broxbourne House, and with whom he shared an adjoining pew in St Etheldreda's church, Hatfield.[37] Owners competed for county positions, with the post of County High Sheriff being held 19 times between 1730 and 1830 by individuals with an EIC connection. A Hertfordshire estate could also support wider political aspirations. Nineteen became MPs (albeit rarely in local constituencies), a position often used to protect ongoing interests in India. The injection of capital from overseas, combined with rising rents and agricultural production during the late eighteenth century initiated a flurry of building and landscaping activity.[38] The extravagance of scale and style that characterized many renovation projects suggests that these were undertaken with a keen eye on what else was occurring around the county. In hiring leading architects and landscapers, owners showed themselves attuned to the dominant fashions of the day. While nabobs have commonly been associated with the Orientalism most conspicuously displayed at the house of Charles Cockerell (1755–1837), Sezincote, those in Herts tended towards more conventional, neoclassical tastes. This did not mean that the influence of India was rendered invisible in either interior decoration or garden display. Rather, it was carefully integrated amidst European styles.[39]

Nabobs, merchants and planters: networks of empire and North Mymms

In 1801 North Mymms was the largest parish in Hertfordshire (see Figure 12.2). Covering just under 5,000 acres and totalling nearly 16 miles in circumference, it sat astride the southern belt of estates. The parliamentary census of that year recorded a population of 838, living in 150 houses; 170 employed in agriculture, 70 in manufacturing or trade and 598 in other occupations.[40] From the early 1700s this community started to be transformed by wealth from overseas. Confounding the caricature of the nabob, those who purchased land in North Mymms did not conform to an easy stereotype. Their careers were varied and patterns changed over time but all shared and benefitted from an investment in the expanding empire and networks of global trade.[41]

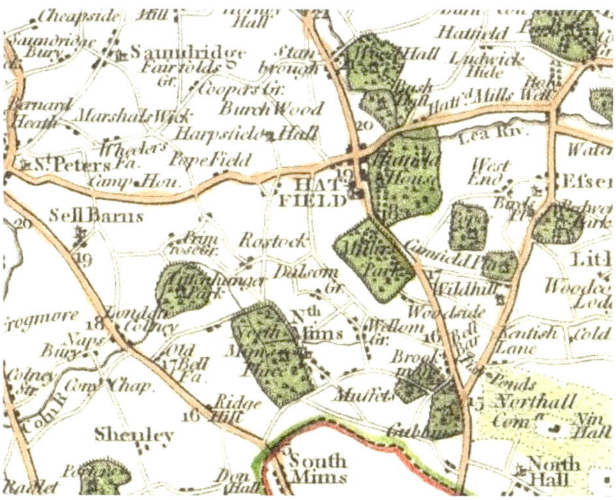

Figure 12.2 Close-up of North Mimms [sic], in *Cary's new and correct atlas: being a new set of county maps from actual surveys* (London, 1787), not paginated https://commons.wikimedia.org/wiki/File:Hertfordshire-Maps-Cary-1787-49.jpg.

Substantial wealth from overseas first arrived in the parish when Jeremy Sambrooke (d.1754) purchased Gobions in 1707. Although lacking a direct career in India himself, Sambrooke came from a family permeated by EIC connections, with his grandfather, father and brother all having been in the Company's service.[42] He inherited a large fortune from his father and capitalized on investments in the South Sea Company shortly before that bubble burst, which allowed him to undertake extensive renovations at Gobions where he resided until his death in 1754. He passed the estate to his sister for life, before settling it on his nephew, John Freeman (c.1722–94), in 1765.[43] Freeman's family had their own extensive empire connections predating the marriage of his father John Cooke Freeman (c.1689–1752) to Susanna Sambrooke (c.1685–1770). John Cooke Freeman had been a merchant in Madras in the early 1700s before inheriting Fawley Court, Buckinghamshire, from his mother's uncle, the Jamaica planter William Freeman (c.1610–1707).[44] John Freeman Jr did not stay long in North Mymms, however. Having built another house in Hampshire, he sold Gobions in 1777 to John Hunter, an exceptionally wealthy nabob who had accumulated a fortune in excess of £100,000 as a free merchant in Bombay (see Figure 12.3).

Little is known of Hunter's life before his arrival in India, beyond that he was born in the mid-1720s and reputedly sailed for Bombay in the late-1750s with no more than £100 to his name; however, over the next 20 years he established himself as a prominent merchant in the city with close links to leading Company officials.[45] Hunter became partner in the firm Hunter, Fell & Ramsay (subsequently Hunter, Fell & Iveson), which was heavily involved in shipping and insurance, and it is likely he had commercial links to Laurence Sulivan. He returned to Britain in the 1770s and was elected to the Directorship in 1781. Despite *The Monthly Magazine's* suggestion that upon purchasing Gobions Hunter settled into the life of a country squire 'fattening oxen' for sale, he by no means retreated into bucolic seclusion.[46] An EIC Director until his death in 1802, Hunter used his position to safeguard his extensive investments in Bombay. Writing from Gobions in the 1790s, he asked his friend John Tasker, then Master Attendant for marine operations at Bombay, to manage his investments in India, look out for new openings and begin to remit his money back to Britain. For all returning officials, this was a complex and risky process that necessitated careful management, and Hunter went to great lengths to instruct Tasker on the best way to proceed. He directed him to invest his cash with Indian agents in Bombay at 9 per cent interest, who would travel to Canton where they would draw bonds of remittance in the name of the Directors at the Company bank,

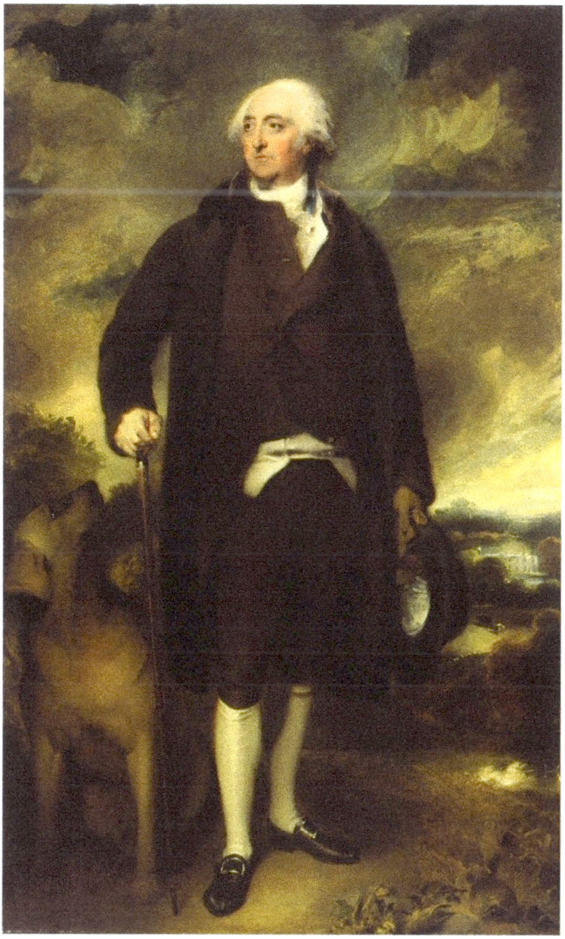

Figure 12.3 Portrait of John Hunter of Gobions, by Sir Thomas Lawrence (1789/90). Reproduced by kind permission of Musée des Beaux-Arts, ville de Bordeaux. Image courtesy of L. Gauthier, F. Deval.

which in turn would be sent to Hunter to deposit them in London.[47] Such networks of information, patronage and trust were utterly crucial to the circulation of goods between Britain and Asia, as well as making possible the remittance of EIC officials and merchants' fortunes.[48]

As well as extending the Gobions estate, Hunter deployed his wealth to support his extended family network. He purchased a farm in the neighbouring parish of South Mimms for Margaret Carpenter, his niece (or illegitimate daughter – it is not clear which) and her husband Daniel, an officer in the EIC Army. Upon his return from India, Daniel Carpenter looked to the Caribbean for investment, purchasing Providence Pen, a Jamaican sugar estate in 1793, which he owned until his death in 1821.[49] Even as his financial interests diversified, Carpenter remained tightly connected to East India networks of patronage and association. During the 1790s and early 1800s, he opened his house to the five sons of his friend and fellow East India Company army officer, General John Bellasis. As Bellasis planned his sons' future careers in India from Bombay, Carpenter was charged with their care in England, a task in which he failed to impress. Once the boys arrived back in India, they complained to their father of mistreatment at Carpenter's hands, which led to a rift between the friends over Carpenter's 'duplicity and mismanagement'.[50] Hunter acquired another property in South Mimms, Oakmere House, which in the 1820s became the home of Carpenter's brother William Leonard, also an EIC army officer, following his marriage to Amelia Chauncy.[51] She was the daughter of the West India planter and Herts resident, Charles Snell of Snell Hall, Grenada, and Theobalds Park, whilst her brothers Nathaniel and Charles Snell Chauncy (owners of neighbouring estates in Little Munden, Herts) claimed a staggering £62,329 in compensation for 3,468 enslaved people in the 1830s.

Hunter's wealth increased rapidly after his arrival in Bombay. In 1763 he married Ann Dick (c.1719–86), a widow whose husband had served in the Bombay Marine. In addition to the 100,000 rupees settled on her by Hunter at the time of their marriage, she inherited property in Bombay from her first husband making her a wealthy woman in her own right.[52] At her death in 1786 at Gobions, her estate totalled £28,000.[53] Her daughter, Ann Atkins (1740–77), married Governor William Hornby (c.1723–1803) thereby sealing a close alliance between the families. Hunter became a keen defender of Hornby during the nabob controversy, and Hornby's children were the principal beneficiaries in Hunter's will.[54] Three younger daughters inherited £20,000 each; Hornby's son John (1764–1832), also an EIC writer, was appointed joint-executor and received £25,000; whilst the eldest daughter Hannah Holmes (1757–1845) received £20,000 and her husband, Thomas Holmes (c.1751–1827), became executor and the new owner of Gobions on condition that he take the name Hunter.[55]

Holmes-Hunter became the fourth successive owner of Gobions to have made his wealth through empire. The son of Worcestershire gentry, he joined the EIC as a Writer in Bombay in 1767, and during his time in India remained a close confidant of his father-in-law and patron Governor Hornby.[56] Nonetheless, Holmes's career ended in disappointment after he was beaten to the position of Governor by Jonathan

Duncan (c.1756–1811) in 1795.[57] His time at Gobions was similarly dispiriting and mired in controversy. In 1801 his 15-year-old daughter eloped and married an Irish soldier about to embark for India. Four years later she left him for another man, which led to Holmes-Hunter being sued for damages.[58] These problems were compounded by family squabbles over John and Ann Hunter's wills, leading to several Chancery cases against Holmes-Hunter as the Hornbys struggled to gain access to legacies they claimed were being withheld.[59] It is not clear why he chose to sell Gobions in 1815, but money troubles certainly seem to have been pressing. By the time of his death in 1827 his effects were sworn at under £450, and his wife and younger daughter do not appear in his will.[60] With Holmes-Hunter's sale of Gobions to a local brewing family its EIC connection disappeared; however, two years later wealth from the Caribbean was flowing back into the estate after it was purchased by West India merchant, Thomas Kemble (1759–1821). In turn, it passed to his son Thomas Nash Kemble (1791–1833), who received over £10,000 in slavery compensation money and left an estate of £120,000 in 1833.[61] Upon his death, the estate was purchased by the owner of Brookmans, Robert William Gaussen, who tore the house down in the early 1840s and amalgamated the grounds into his own.

John Hunter's nearest neighbour was another EIC Director, and coincidentally the uncle of Holmes' victorious rival for the Governorship. Like Hunter, John Michie (1720–88) made his wealth working closely with the Company but not in its direct employ. He initially leased Moffats House in the early 1770s, before purchasing it at the end of the decade. It is not clear how much he initially paid but in 1779 it was insured with the Sun Insurance Company for £7,900.[62] A native of Glenesk, Michie moved south in the early-1750s, taking advantage of the complex trans-imperial networks of Highland Scots to establish himself as a victualler in London.[63] Initial success proved elusive, however, and by 1755 he was imprisoned in the Fleet for debt.[64] After his release from prison, he became a purchasing agent for the Royal Navy in Indian waters, where he acted as secretary to Sir George Pocock (1706–92) and was awarded a share of the prize money for the capture of several enemy ships in 1760.[65] He gained further opportunity in the Caribbean in 1762, where Pocock held a command during the capture of Havana, and subsequently secured the commission to distribute the campaign's prize money, from which he is likely to have derived considerable personal benefit.[66] On returning to Britain, Michie used his wealth and contacts to establish himself within the 'Shipping interest', which provisioned the East India

Company fleet and offered access to powerful patronage networks at the Court of Directors.[67] Based in St Martin-in-the Fields, he did not limit his activities to supply, also entering into partnership with his brother Jonathan as a wine merchant – a role that appears to have combined business and pleasure, with one friend leaving Michie a cask of 40-year-old rum 'because he loves a tiff of punch after supper'.[68] Possessing £2,000 of EIC stock, Michie was first elected to the Directorship in 1770 (the same year he arrived at Moffats) as a nominee on the 'House list', and he remained there until his death in 1788, including serving as Chairman in 1786. He left Moffats to his brother Jonathan Michie (d.1802) and property in St Martin-in-the Fields to be shared between two nieces and his illegitimate daughter.

Tracing individual careers or the ownership trajectory of a single estate provides a sense of how wealth from overseas percolated into Hertfordshire, but to situate North Mymms properly within a wider imperial world it is necessary to map the webs of marriage, wealth and patronage that sustained these families. For the Gaussens of Brookmans and Casamajors of Potterells these liens spread across Britain, India and the Caribbean, incorporating overlapping networks that made viable a variety of commercial and political interests. Prominent Huguenot merchant and governor of the Bank of England, Peter Gaussen (1723–88) purchased Brookmans manor for £16,000 in 1787 as a gift for his son Samuel Robert (1759–1812).[69] The Gaussens first arrived in London from Geneva following the revocation of the Edict of Nantes and quickly established themselves within the influential Huguenot cousinhood.[70] Peter Gaussen's success in the City facilitated his election to the directorship of the Bank of England in 1761 and he became the bank's first foreign-born Governor in 1777, as well as owning £4,500 in EIC stock. Family connections smoothed his rise. In 1755 he had married Anna Maria (1728–1804), daughter of Samuel Bosanquet (1700–65), another prominent Huguenot merchant in the Levant trade and with extensive property in the Caribbean. The marriage agreement underlines both families' prosperity, as well as their confidence that this would continue to flourish. Anna Maria's portion stood at a sizeable £6,000, with Peter promising a further £12,000 for her and their younger children upon his death – a promise far surpassed when he left an estate worth £57,340.[71] Unusually, the marriage ended a decade later in formal separation but, even then, Peter was careful not to sever the relationship with his in-laws who remained close commercial partners, particularly his brother-in-law and fellow Bank of England director Samuel Bosanquet Jr (1744–1806).[72]

The marriages of Peter and Anna's children served to reinforce the connection to the Bosanquets, as well as to other local elites. In 1783, their eldest son and owner of Brookmans, Samuel Robert Gaussen Sr, married into another branch of the Bosanquet family, one involved more in India than the Caribbean. His wife Elizabeth was the daughter of Jacob Bosanquet Sr (1713–67, brother of Samuel Sr), Turkey and East India merchant, and sister of Jacob Bosanquet Jr, East India Company director and leading figure in the London silk trade. This match brought both families considerable financial and commercial benefit.[73] Although it is unclear whether Jacob Jr's decision to purchase the nearby estate of Broxbournebury in 1789, two years after Samuel and Elizabeth settled at Brookmans, was based upon a desire to be close to his sister, his presence nonetheless ensured a strong family network in south Herts, which was augmented further by a third branch of the Bosanquets in the Hadley/Barnet area. Like many of his contemporaries in the City elite, Samuel Robert Gaussen Sr's enthusiasm for commercial life was undiminished by ownership of a country estate. Over the next twenty years he established himself at the centre of overlapping networks that supported the expanding fiscal-military state and empire.[74] He became director of the South Sea Company, an MP and a major EIC shareholder in the 1790s, although he divested himself of his Company shares in the decade before his death. Instead, he bequeathed £10,327 in South Sea Stock and over £100,000 in government securities, leaving each son £30,000 and each daughter £20,000 invested in 3 per cent consuls.[75] Upon his death in 1812, his estate totalled over £175,000, making him the eleventh richest man in the country to die that year.[76] He appointed his Bosanquet cousins as executors, thereby reiterating how important tight-knit family networks were to the transmission of wealth.

Compared to many other merchant and nabob estate owners in Herts, the Gaussens and the Bosanquets at Broxbournebury were unusual in that they kept their estates within the family for more than three generations.[77] As each generation became more established within the local landowning elite, so they shifted how they presented the basis of family wealth. Upon Samuel Robert Sr's death, the estate passed to his eldest surviving son Samuel Robert Jr (1788–1818) who married his cousin Cecilia Franks (1789–1868). His early death in 1818 meant that the estate descended to his infant son, Robert William Gaussen (1814–80). Educated at Eton and Cambridge, Robert served briefly with the British legation at Stockholm, before returning to assume the life of a country gentleman in 1838. He expanded the estate significantly to over 2,000 acres by purchasing both Gobions and Moffats, and despite maintaining a broad stock portfolio and sitting on the board of the Globe Insurance Company displayed none of his grandfather's enthusiasm for commercial life.[78] Instead, he increasingly styled himself a landed gentleman with an interest in stocks, rather than a merchant prince with a country estate to match.

Even as Robert William's horizons narrowed, his marriage to Elizabeth Christian Casamajor (1821–64) of Potterells created yet another filament in an already complicated web. Potterells came into the possession of Elizabeth's cousin Justinian Casamajor (1746–1820) when he inherited it from his friend Charles Delaet in 1792.[79] Before moving to Potterells Justinian lived nearby at High Canons, Shenley and owned land in Northaw. Originally from Spain, the Casamajors settled in Bristol in the 1690s, where they were involved in the Iberian wine trade. By the time Justinian inherited Potterells, the family had spread across Britain's expanding empire as Company officials in India and plantation owners and merchants in the Caribbean.[80] It was to the latter that Justinian owed his wealth, first as a London West India merchant and subsequently through his marriage to Mary, the daughter of Antigua planter Duncan Grant (d.1770), which brought Casamajor property in the Caribbean. Having spent heavily on redeveloping the estate he fell into financial difficulty when profits from his Antiguan investments declined. This left him able to leave only small legacies in his will (although he did stress that his daughters had been amply provided for by his wife's brother). He placed his Caribbean property in trust to be sold. Nonetheless, the terms of Delaet's will ensured Potterells remained in the family, decreeing it should pass to his godson, Justinian's third son, William Charles Casamajor (1779–1847).[81]

Where Justinian Casamajor's activities focused on the Caribbean, the wider family network spread east. His uncle, Noah Casamajor (1700–46), established himself as a merchant at Madras in the mid-1700s, and his son, James Henry Casamajor (1745–1815), joined the EIC as a writer in Madras, rising to the council in 1791. Although his son James Archibald (1787–1864) joined the EIC in turn, it was the marriages of his daughters that really catapulted the Casamajors into the highest echelons of the EIC elite; Jane Amelia (1789–1808) to Henry Russell (1783–1852) son of Sir Henry Russell (1751–1836), Chief Justice of Bengal; Amelia (1791–1872) to the third son of the Governor General Lord Minto (1751–1813); Louisa (c.1801–78) to Charles Farquharson RN (1795–1862), son of William

Farquharson (1758–1813), EIC Bengal; and Elizabeth Rebecca (1788–1866) married John Studholme Brownrigg (1786–1853), MP and partner in the East India merchant firm of Charles Cockerell & Co.[82] This network of patronage and contact helped smooth entry for Justinian's two youngest sons to Company service as writers in Madras, as well as leading to the arrival at Potterells of James Archibald and his daughters following his retirement from the EIC in Madras in 1837. He had also married the daughter of an Antiguan planter, who probably had business links to Justinian, but in the aftermath of emancipation this brought little financial benefit. Unlike the previous generation of officials, James Archibald did not return from India possessed of great wealth and spent a peripatetic retirement moving around the homes of relatives and friends. At his death, his effects were valued as being under £600. Nonetheless, his arrival in North Mymms precipitated the marriage of his daughter Elizabeth to Robert Gaussen in 1841, thus joining two families of global reach in the heart of the home counties.

Like their EIC counterparts across Hertfordshire, those living in North Mymms enthusiastically embraced the opportunity to thrust themselves into parish, county and parliamentary politics. Hunter (1780), Michie (1782), Samuel Robert Gaussen (1790), Justinian Casamajor (1800), Thomas Nash Kemble (1825) and Robert William Gaussen (1841) all won election to county high sheriff, a role the Stones identified as being crucial to the integration of new arrivals into county society and one often assiduously avoided by established families who loathed the inconvenience and expense.[83] Several used their wealth to gain election to Parliament. John Hunter reputedly paid up to £3,000 to gain the seat for Leominster in 1784 but did little once elected.[84] As MP for Warwick (1796–1802), Samuel Robert Gaussen proved similarly inactive in the Commons, although he did work to further the interests of the City for which his brother-in-law Jacob Bosanquet was principal spokesman.[85] Prominence in public life extended to serving on the boards of various philanthropic and charitable institutions. John Michie, for instance, was a steward for the New Lying-in Hospital off Tottenham Court Road and Peter Gaussen a governor of the Foundling Hospital. All assumed similar prominence in parish life. As the surviving memorials in St Mary's church testify, most were closely involved with the parish church where successive generations worshipped, married, baptized their children and were buried (see Figure 12.4). Both Samuel Robert Gaussen and Justinian Casamajor served as church warden at St Mary's, a role that gave them responsibility for allocating pews and handing out charity to the poor.

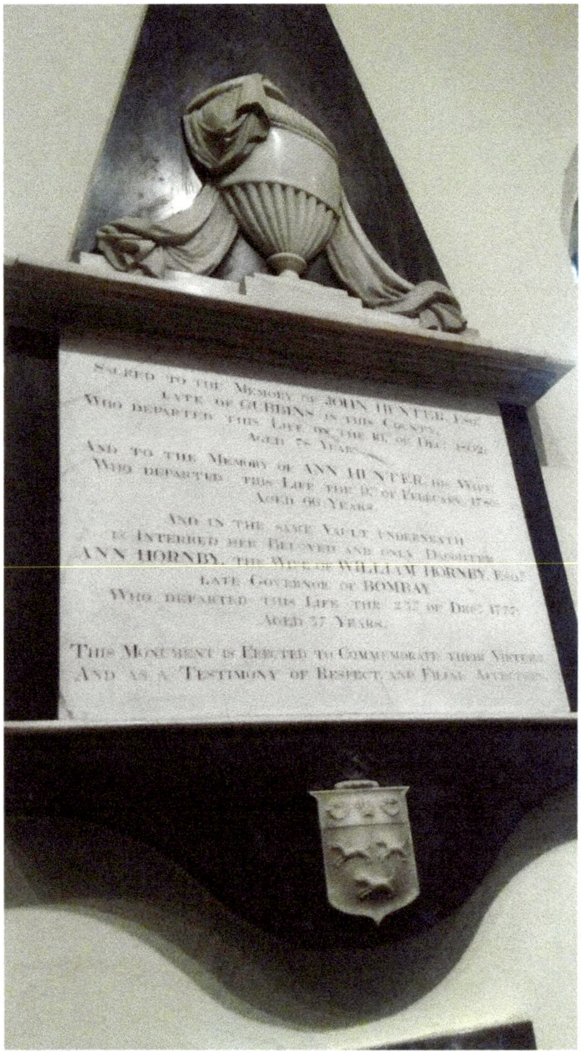

Figure 12.4 Memorial to John and Ann Hunter, and her daughter Ann Hornby, St Mary's Church, North Mymms. Photograph courtesy of Chris Jeppesen.

Gaussen was also a trustee for the Great North Road turnpike, which ran near his estate, and colonel in the county militia.

Although women were barred from holding public office, they were more visible in the parish, revealing their central role in embedding circuits of empire in communities across Britain.[86] A small part of Ann Hunter's wealth from Bombay was left to feed the poor of the parish, whilst her granddaughter, Hannah Holmes-Hunter bequeathed £100 to the church for the benefit of the poor. Justinian Casamajor's daughter Caroline Lydia (1788–1853), at the time of her death leasing Moffats from Robert Gaussen, left £3,000 to endow a school for the children of the parish.[87]

The arrival of wealth from empire initiated profound aesthetic and economic changes to the local landscape as owners redeveloped houses and grounds. Most notable were the changes made by Jeremy Sambrooke to Gobions, where he employed Charles Bridgeman (1690–1738) and James Gibbs (1682–1754). Bridgeman had already worked on several East India Company gardens in Hertfordshire, but it was his efforts at Gobions that elicited a visit from Queen Caroline and her daughters in 1732, as well as drawing rich acclaim from Daniel Defoe a decade later and Horace Walpole in his 1770 essay *On Modern Gardening*. Ornamental gardens, a canal and lake, bowling green and tree lined avenues transformed the park to provide a fitting panorama for the redesigned neoclassical house. To this he added a large mock-Tudor entrance arch, classical statues and hothouse.[88] John Hunter proved less preoccupied with Gobions house, concentrating instead on purchasing local farms and enclosing common land under an act of Parliament in 1778.[89] In 1802 he was awarded a gold medal by the Society of Arts, Manufactures and Commerce in recognition of the 40,000 oaks he had planted.[90] Like Sambrooke, Justinian Casamajor renovated the existing house at Potterells, turning the sixteenth century half H-plan into a neoclassical manor with colonnaded portico. Even so, the house is described by historian John Brushe as resembling 'a beautiful stage set': Casamajor substituted marble and stone for plaster and wood in several places, including in the painted wooden columns sat atop stone bases at the entrance.[91] He also developed the estate, constructing a model farm and experimenting with modern agricultural methods.

In the physical absence of the three houses little detail remains on the objects they contained. Beyond a general impression that these houses were filled with the trappings of genteel life, it remains ambiguous how far empire permeated their interior spaces. For instance, Gobions' advertisement of sale in 1814 gave few particularities other than describing a grand house with spacious cellars, marble chimney pieces and mahogany doors.[92] Nonetheless, hints linger that habits and tastes picked up in India entered quotidian routines. John Hunter wrote to his friend John Tasker asking him to procure him a regular supply of coffee, while in another letter Tasker informed him that he was trying to arrange shipment of the mango tree he had requested.[93] More intriguingly, the wills of John and Ann Hunter reveal that it was not only commodities that returned from India but sometimes people as well. Both left small annuities to Mary Ann Baker 'a black woman' who acted as Ann Hunter's lady's servant and Henry Dick, described by Ann Hunter as 'a gentleman now residing at Gubbins [sic]' and, fifteen years later, by her husband as 'a black man labouring under an imbecility of mind and under the care and custody of Mrs Holmes of Islington'.[94] It is unlikely to be a coincidence that Henry Dick shared his surname with Ann Hunter's first husband. Hunter's obituary in *The Monthly Magazine* asserted that he had remarried to a 'mulatto lady', although no further evidence exists, as well as observing his mindfulness in providing for Baker and Dick who otherwise would have been left destitute. Frustratingly, the archival trace left by these individuals quickly vanishes, giving little sense as to how they experienced life in rural Hertfordshire or interacted with those born locally and working on the estate. Nevertheless, their very presence in the domestic space of Gobions and parish more broadly is important both in terms of how empire was made visible at a local level and also how this shaped the ways nabobs were presented in print.[95]

Conclusion

From the early eighteenth century onwards, wealth from empire flowed into Hertfordshire as returning EIC officials, Caribbean planters and London based merchants purchased land and property across the county. North Mymms illustrates in microcosm how global processes of conquest, trade, enrichment and exploitation that energized Britain's expanding empire became infused with local significance. Growing up, I had no awareness that this layered history lurked within an ever-so familiar horizon. And yet, material markers of the estates endured, incorporated into the fabric of village life that formed the backdrop to my youth: Brookmans' stable block has become the golf course club house; Gobions' ornamental lake and garden forms part of the park in which I walked my dog; Folly Arch, the estate's once imposing entrance gate, now stands forlornly askew on the road entering the village; the gatehouse at Potterells re-appropriated as the village doctors' surgery; Moffats House divided into residential homes that I passed on my way home from school.

In a recent collection of essays, Antoinette Burton and Dane Kennedy asked various historians of empire to reflect upon 'how empire had shaped them'. For Burton and Kennedy, the accounts that emerge offer clues as to how the global and imperial intersect with the national and local in ways that 'reveal the imprint of local space and place on the making of historical sensibilities'.[96] While I cannot claim to have been particularly aware as a child that Britain once had an empire, let alone that it impinged on the world around me, discovering now the significance of empire in the history of Brookmans Park has encouraged me to consider the place I grew up in new ways. David Lowenthal has argued that our sense of proximity to the past is rooted in the familiar surrounds of the present. But in seeking to orient this relationship through surviving material markers, we risk sacrificing complexity in favour of nostalgic, reaffirming narratives.[97] In acknowledging that our local histories may be less rooted than we instinctively assume or that the empire perhaps came closer to home than we ordinarily apprehend, we can start to destabilize narratives that have for so long sustained an insular version of British history. Behind those familiar vestiges that permeate our local landscapes may stand histories of wider entanglements. Rediscovering these not only enrichens our understanding of the past but should also challenge how we think about ourselves in the present.

Section 4
On the borders
Region, nation, globe

Clusters of East India Company persons, objects and wealth appeared not only in the Home Counties during the eighteenth and early nineteenth century, but also at other locations across Britain and on the European continent. Distant from the Company's offices and warehouses in the City of London and from the urban residences of its most powerful men and women, these clusters were nonetheless connected – through fashion, objects, wealth, employment and personnel – both with the metropolis and with the Company's scattered Asian domains. Attending to distant regions that lay outside London and the Home Counties works to connect Britain's peripheries to the metropole, even as it encourages us to look beyond the familiar Company histories focused on the British bridgehead of Bengal.[1]

In this section, Diane James's chapter explores how engineer and artist Colonel Robert Smith (1787–1873) honed skills of drawing and draughtsmanship while working for the Company's Bengal Army in the early nineteenth century. When he returned to Europe in the 1830s Smith continued to consolidate his material knowledge, and when wealth allowed in the 1840s he used his skills to re-design and re-build Villa Mills on the Palatine hill in Rome. Later construction projects in France and then in Devon further exploited his (by now considerable) skills. Rather than passively purchasing elite homes, Smith deployed in Europe material expertise honed on the subcontinent in often-unforgiving terrains. Together with his wife's wealth, his material knowledge gained in imperial service allowed him to produce substantial yet intricate buildings, expressing his cosmopolitan identity in new ways. Smith worked in tandem with the material world, rather than employing it in a 'finished' state. He continually overcame material difficulties or compensated for them through redesign. Far from inert, the material world and its built environments challenged and animated Smith's evolving expressions of identity.

Rachael Barnwell's chapter focuses on regional interiors fashioned in response to Company commerce. She identifies a series of 'Chinese' style staircases that appeared far from Georgian London's metropolitan consumer markets, in north-west Wales. Tan-yr-Allt in Bangor (Caernarvonshire), Bishopsgate House in Beaumaris, Anglesey and Trfeilir in Trefdraeth, Anglesey all acquired 'Chinese' style staircases in the middle decades of the century. No surviving evidence suggests that these staircases were built because the families which inhabited these homes boasted links to Asian trade or the East India Company (EIC). As Barnwell's analysis highlights, however, the period in which they were constructed (c.1755–60) marked the height of British interest in Chinese objects and aesthetics. The middle decades of the eighteenth century witnessed numerous attempts to translate or appropriate 'Chinese' motifs into 'British' design schemes, through publications such as Thomas Chippendale's *The Gentleman and Cabinet Maker's Director* (1754). In north-west Wales we thus see the indirect influence of the Company on British material cultures through its trade in Asian luxury objects. As Barnwell concludes, the 'Chinese' style staircases found in north-west Wales offer evidence of regional and rural desire for 'Chinese' style decoration. They demonstrate how Asian influences came to be embedded into local contexts and tastes, enriching 'British' material culture in turn.

Maintaining clusters of Company sociability often proved more challenging than participating in shared aesthetic tastes inspired by Britain's Asian trade. Distance, evasion, omission and failure marked the experiences of many Company families, with some Company men and women choosing or relegated to life in peripheral sites. Alistair Mutch's chapter on General Patrick Duff (1742–1803) examines a military man whose career, wealth and domestic life were distinguished by the negotiation of vast distances. Much of the Duff family wealth was accrued through connections with empire and the intermediary sites between metropole and empire. Patrick Duff's uncles and brothers were deeply involved in the Madeira wine trade and used Duff's Company connections in Bengal to expand and enrich their commerce. Duff's involvement in the wine trade exemplifies the importance of intermediary sites such as Madeira between Bengal and Britain. These sites made (and make) distinctions between metropole and colony difficult, if not impossible, to sustain. Duff used the wealth gained from Company service and the Madeira trade to purchase a country estate not in the Home Counties, but rather at Carnousie, near Turriff, in the county of Banffshire in north-east Scotland. Here he realised long-held ambitions of domestic husbandry and agricultural improvement. Rather than metropolitan status and national power, Duff longed to cultivate land at a distance from the traditional centres of politics and society.

Alongside intermediary sites used en route to empire, such as Tenerife and Madeira, the Company also maintained several other outposts distant from its Indian seats of power. Often held only briefly or incompletely, these remote spots included Ambon Island, Aden and Sumatra. Ellen Filor's chapter explores how the outpost of Sumatra shaped the Company life of Alexander Hall (c.1731/2–1764). Although other European civil servants based in Sumatra managed to accrue impressive fortunes, Hall conspicuously did not. Indeed, life in Sumatra proved a constant struggle for Hall, distant as he was from the luxury and domestic comfort others experienced – if only in his imagination – in privileged regions such as Bengal. In this beleaguered context, Hall turned to the solace of material things, negotiating the anomie of distance through the objects and letters sent by his family in Scotland. His acquisition and exchange of material goods from afar challenged perceptions of Sumatra's peripheral location, allowing Hall modest comforts from his British home – itself a peripheral site. As Filor demonstrates, the comforts that circulated as 'things' in Hall's world included enslaved persons, underlining both the importance of forced labour to the Company's tenuous grip on Sumatra and the labile boundaries of identity that marked the Company's material world. The presence of enslaved women also provided opportunities for Hall to pursue sexual intimacy, encounters which resulted in the birth of a mixed-race child, Peggy. After Hall's death, his sister Isabella asked his executor Robert Hay to send the child to Scotland. Peggy's story and her journey to Britain with her nurse Betty demonstrate the broader legacies of British lives spent in empire. Like General Duff's negotiation of the Company's distant outposts, Peggy and Betty's journey from Sumatra to the metropole underlines the multiple directions of imperial flows of persons and things, complicating our understanding of empire's impacts.

13
A fairy palace in Devon
Redcliffe Towers, built by Colonel Robert Smith (1787–1873), Bengal Engineers

Diane James

The eccentric building Redcliffe Towers (see Figure 13.1), built on the edge of a cliff in Devon, is now a well-known landmark in the town of Paignton. Colonel Robert Smith constructed the Towers in 1852–64, after his retirement from the East India Company (EIC) and a sojourn

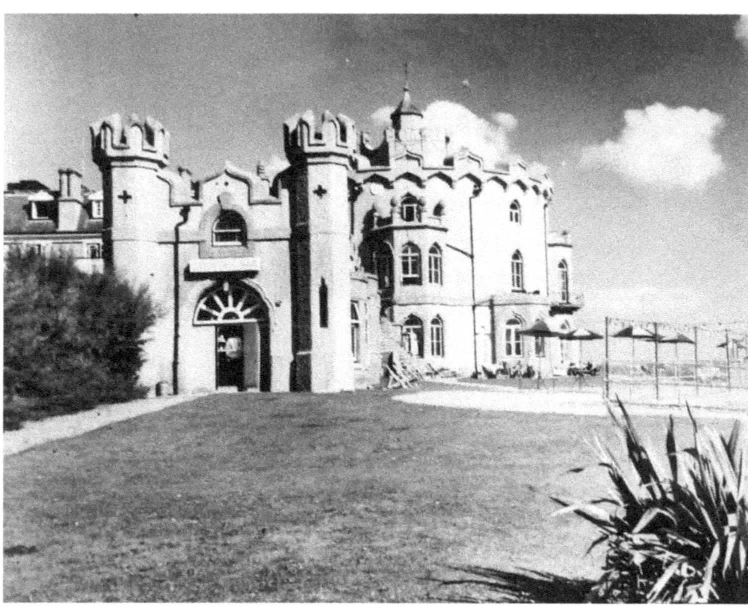

Figure 13.1 The Hotel Redcliffe (Redcliffe Towers), Paignton, Devon, early twentieth-century. © The Redcliffe Hotel.

in Italy where he married a French heiress. Smith, an engineer and artist, was not a member of the landed gentry, however, he used his talents to rise through the ranks of the Bengal Army in India, from Cadet to Colonel. Smith left the Company with just an army pension, and it is likely he would have been unable to build Redcliffe Towers without gaining a considerable inheritance upon the death of his wife. This case study records Robert Smith's journey to India, to Europe and his final days spent in Devon, where he constructed his fairytale fortress, Redcliffe Towers. In doing so it contributes to the *East India Company at Home* volume by demonstrating the ways in which EIC officials' engagements with the subcontinent through practices such as drafting, building, painting and drawing, distinctly shaped the British homes they built on their return.

Background and training

Robert Smith's early family life not only shaped the direction of his later career, but also the locations and houses in which he settled once retired. Although primarily based in the busy, cosmopolitan port of Bideford, Devon, Robert Smith's family frequently journeyed out to Europe and India.[1] In consequence, while two of his brothers were born in India, Smith (see Figure 13.2) – the third son of James and Mary Smith – came to be baptized in Nancy, France, on 13 September 1787.[2] The family enjoyed early connections to the EIC: trained as a lawyer, Smith's father also worked at one time as private secretary to the Marquis of Hastings.[3] Understandably therefore, when the Smith family later moved to an artists' district (Newman Street, off Oxford Street) in London, and financial pressures meant that the sons had to seek employment, the expanding EIC seemed the perfect choice.[4] Robert Smith, aged 16 years, enlisted as a Cadet in 1803, following his older brothers, James and John, to India, while his younger brother, Edward, joined the Company in 1815.[5] Robert Smith became an Ensign in April 1805, soon transferring from the Infantry to the Engineers, which proved a pivotal decision as he was rarely posted to the front-line of hostilities.[6] Tragically, of the four sons who went out to India, joining as Ensigns and rising to at least the rank of Lieutenant-Colonel, all, except Robert died there.[7]

Smith began his military training at the EIC's Great Marlow Academy.[8] As the Company expanded into new territories in India, surveying and accurate mapping skills were imperative to assist revenue

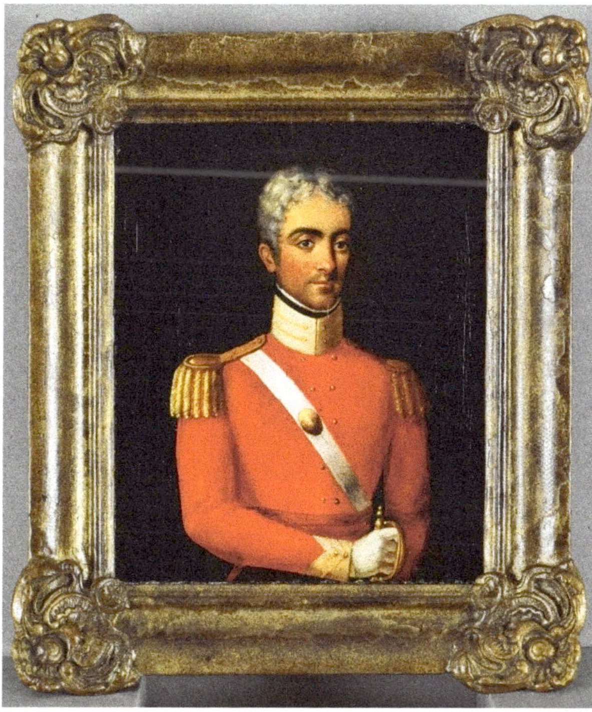

Figure 13.2 Jivan Ram, Raja (Raja Jirvan Raja), *Portrait of Robert Smith, Bengal Engineers*, c.1830, oil painting. © British Library Board, Foster 870.

collection, administrative function, and later military campaigns.[9] The drawing masters at Great Marlow, including William De La Motte (1775–1863) and William Alexander (1767–1816), ensured their pupils became proficient in drafting accurate maps, fortifications, sketching in the field, and painting topographical watercolours and panoramas.[10] Although influenced by the Picturesque paintings of William (1769–1837) and Thomas Daniell (1749–1840) and William Hodges (1744–97), Smith developed his own style and was one of many soldiers in the eighteenth and nineteenth centuries, who took up drawing as part of their leisure activities and showed evidence of accomplished draughtsmanship.[11] Throughout his time in India, Smith was a prodigious artist, both for work and leisure, depicting India's scenery, architecture and culture. As an engineer Smith worked on a variety of projects, but he was also called upon at times to be both an artist and a fighting soldier. These differing strands of his career influenced his later architectural endeavours.

Experiences in India

Having arrived in Calcutta in 1805 and joined the Bengal Engineers, Smith was first employed building infrastructure: bridges and roads, and later a lighthouse at Kijri, Diamond Harbour, near Calcutta.[12] Although promoted to Lieutenant and seeing action with the Bengal force capturing Mauritius from the French in 1810–11, his flair for surveying did not go unnoticed.[13] A report by the Surveyor General suggested Smith was 'by far the best draughtsman I am acquainted with. His masterly rapid pencil particularly qualifies him for survey of the Frontier, as he will be able to delineate the passes and surrounding country with the greatest correctness.'[14] Between 1812 and 1813 Smith joined the camp of the Commander-in-Chief, Sir George Nugent (1757–1849), for his tour of Upper India. At this time, Smith's sketches were commented on by Lady Nugent (1771–1834), who noted in her diary that 'Just as day dawned, we crossed the Jumna … I took the engineer officer, Mr. Smith, with me, and we projected a drawing of the line of march, which will be a treasure to me, if he executes it according to my plan, and I have little doubt of its being quite perfect, by what I have seen of his drawings' (see Figure 13.3).[15]

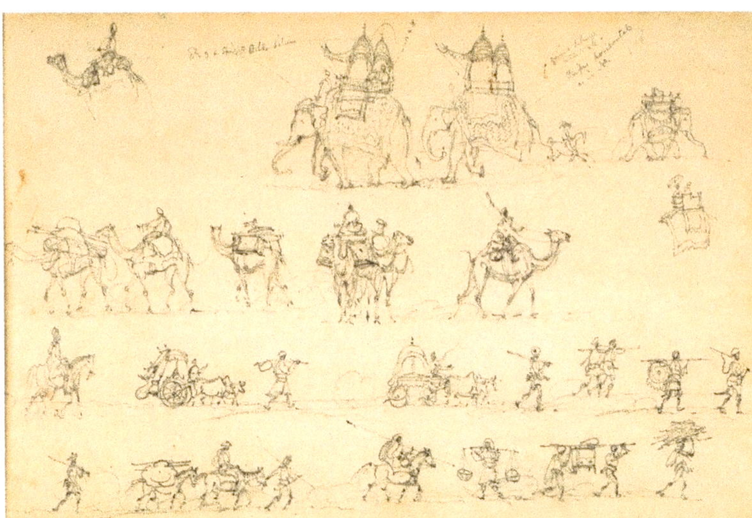

Figure 13.3 Robert Smith (1787–1873), *Sketches of the Line of March with Elephants, Camels, Hackeries* [bullock drawn carriages], *horsemen and coolies*, 1814, pencil on paper. © British Library Board, WD 312 f.25v.

In action again during the Nepal War, 1815–16, Smith gained the India medal. After these arduous tours of duty, however, illness took its toll.[16] He was appointed Superintending Engineer to Prince of Wales Island (Penang) in 1816, a convalescent facility for the personnel of Madras and Bengal, and vital for Smith's recuperation.[17] Smith completed many watercolours of the main places of interest, before leaving on furlough to England from July 1819 until October 1822. While in London he visited William Daniell who agreed to engrave his paintings, making 10 aquatints, which were privately published in 1821 as *Views of Prince of Wales Island*, the only public display of Smith's art.[18]

On his return to India in 1822, Smith continued to paint and sketch the military life around him, for instance the soldiers at the flagstaff and the mansion at Barrackpore (see Figure 13.4). He was appointed Garrison Engineer and Executive Officer at Delhi in December 1822 (and at a later date Major), in order that he might complete work on many of the ancient Mughal monuments (including the Red Fort – see Figure 13.5, Jama Masjid, and Qutub Minar), walls and canals, in need of renovation.[19] Working with red sandstone and Indian topography proved to be defining for Smith's career and inspirational for his painting and later architectural designs in continental Europe and Britain.

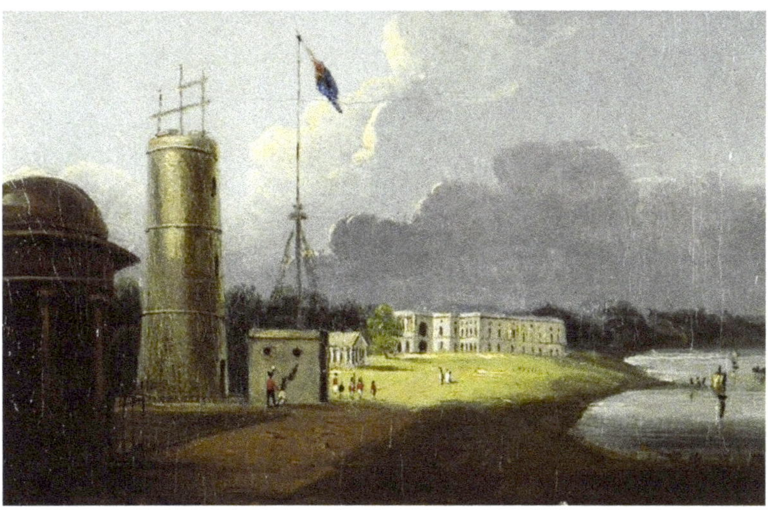

Figure 13.4 Robert Smith, *Barrackpore House*, 1815–19, Oil on canvas, 13 x 20.5 cm (estimated). © British Library Board, F864.

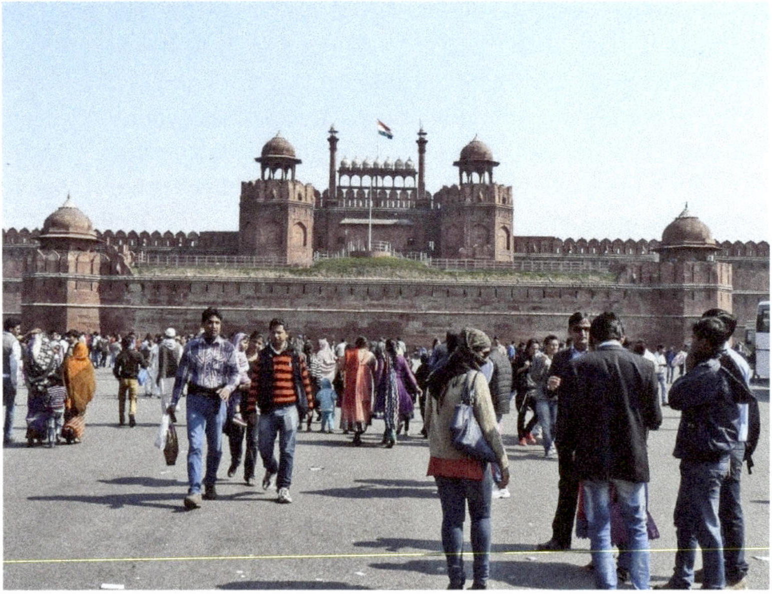

Figure 13.5 The Red Fort, Delhi, India. Photograph by Diane James © 2014.

Building in India

Smith's expertise in the planning and refurbishment of Mughal buildings for the EIC was put to good use when he moved to more permanent lodgings within Delhi's ancient city walls. His previous work on the restoration of local historic structures most likely informed his choice for an architectural fusion of styles when he constructed additional living space and Smith later employed a similar combination of motifs in the creation of his Italian and English mansions and grounds. Smith's restoration work in India was not unusual; old houses or ruins were often adapted for habitation, as many were constructed with tykhanas (underground rooms), which gave respite from the searing summer heat when temperatures typically rose to 40°C. Sir Thomas Metcalfe (1795–1853), the British Resident in Delhi during the 1840s noted that in his Presidential House in Delhi the 'Principal Teh-Khanah or under Ground Apartment [was] occupied during the Hottest Months of the Year'.[20] Smith was put in charge of renovating a house on the city wall between the Kashmir and Calcutta Gates overlooking the River Jumna. The house had been built by 1805 for William Fraser (1784–1835), Assistant British Resident to Delhi, on a site once occupied by the Mughal Palace of Ali Mardan Khan

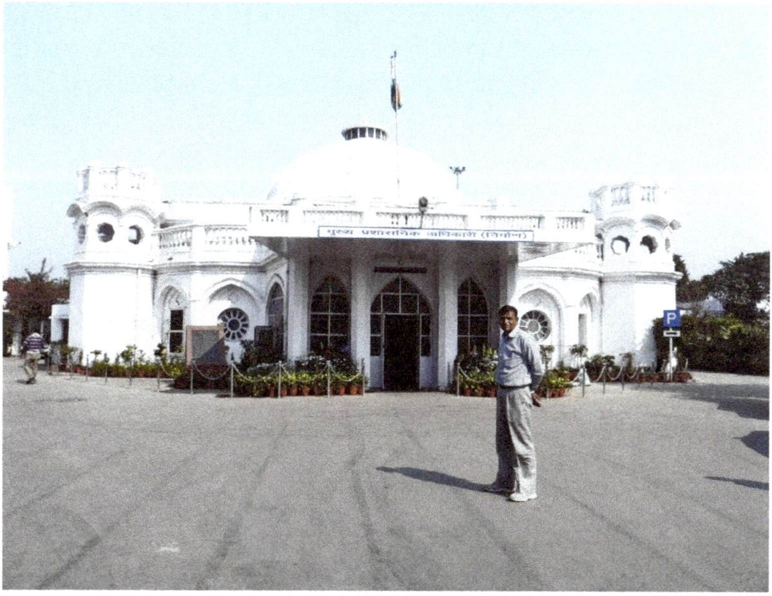

Figure 13.6 Robert Smith's bungalow (known as William Fraser bungalow), Delhi, India. Photograph by Diane James © 2014.

(d.1657), a noble at the Emperor Shah Jahan's court, said to have laid out the gardens of the Taj Mahal and built the Qutub Minar.[21] Fraser, suggested to have 'gone native', gave up eating pork and beef, grew a Rajput beard, and kept a harem of six or seven wives.[22] By 1819 the bungalow-style house was vacant, and during the 1820s Robert Smith took occupation of it. The extant building is an amalgam of British and Indian style architecture; a low central block, with a later domed roof and octagonal corner towers (see Figure 13.6).

Visiting on 2 February 1828, Major Archer observed that 'the view from Major Smith's terrace looking towards the palace and the Selim Gurh, is very beautiful'.[23] Archer was extremely interested in the tykhana of the house:

> We went to see the Ty-Kounahs, or underground houses, forming part of Major Smith's residence … they are formed in the walls of the ramparts, which being of great solidity completely exclude all heat … The one now under mention doubtless belonged at some time in the past to a man of great station or wealth; the descent to the apartment was about thirty feet, and the surprise and pleasure were equal, to find such beautiful rooms and so elegantly

> arranged and furnished. Coloured to resemble marble, the eye is first deceived by the likeness; the deception is countenanced by the coolness, so different from that oppressive sensation always felt above. Long corridors lead to different apartments, embellished with coloured walls, and other decorations, all by the owner's own hands; and it should not be omitted, that many exquisite drawings of places of celebrity in Delhi and its neighbourhood, add to the appearance of this truly fairy palace.[24]

As Sylvia Shorto has noted the extant interior of the tykhana is made up of six rectangular rooms, and another square-shaped room slightly lower beneath, in addition to various other tunnels and rooms now bricked up. One room includes 'a coved bangla ceiling and a deep iwan (seating niche)', with stucco and paint traces.[25] Shorto suggests Smith painted the walls following the Northern Indian tradition of painting interiors, and that he continued this practice in his other houses.[26] It is known from later British sales catalogues that, obsessed by sketching and painting, Smith used wall space to hang his copious paintings of India, and it is possible that these also covered the walls of the tykhana. It is probable that Smith added the two end towers to the bungalow; a central section flanked by octagonal towers with an arcaded gothic loggia (in this case filled in), was emerging as his architectural signature. This design echoed elements of Mughal architecture, the octagonal form often used in towers or bastions on gates or tombs. In the Fraser Bungalow, the upper section of the towers below the balustrading is reminiscent of a cupola Smith designed for the Qutub Minar, exhibiting an experimental mix of styles, which would later become a trademark feature of Smith's building projects.[27]

In March 1823 Smith was selected to survey an ancient Mughal canal, known as the Doab (Jumna) Canal.[28] It had been built in the seventeenth century by Ali Mardan Khan, but due to difficulties with the terrain the canal did not operate fully and had remained unused for many years.[29] In 1825, a new Assistant Lieutenant Proby Cautley (1802–71) joined Smith and became not only his colleague, but also his friend for life.[30] Both officers were withdrawn from their duties, to take part in the siege and capture of Bharatpore, near Agra, 26 December 1825; Smith was wounded, and later mentioned in despatches.[31] In September 1827, elevated to Major for his services at Bharatpore, he returned to take charge of the restoration of the Jama Masjid (see Figure 13.7), the great mosque built in Delhi by the Emperor Shah Jahan (1592–1666).[32] Major Archer, visiting in 1828, observed that 'Major Smith … is particularly well qualified for the charge of restoring such magnificent relics of art,

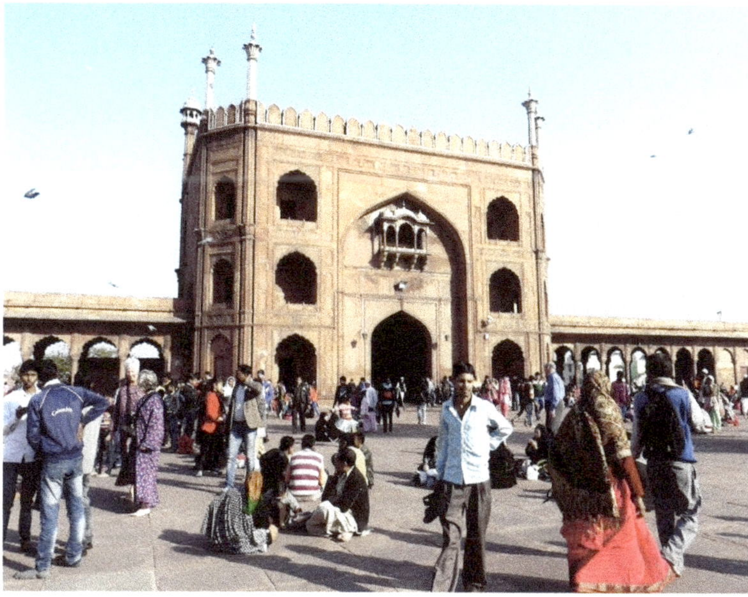

Figure 13.7 The Eastern Gate of the Jama Masjid, Delhi, India. Photograph by Diane James © 2014.

as much as by his exquisite judgement and taste in the style of the works, as his acknowledged professional talents, which place him among the foremost of his compeers'.[33]

Smith was promoted to Lieutenant-Colonel in June 1830, but by this time, his health was poor. He left Delhi for Calcutta on his way to Europe, spending his leisure time during February and March 1830 sailing down the river Ganges sketching and painting watercolours, in the Picturesque style, of the scenes around him.[34] Proby Cautley finally completed the Doab Canal project in 1830, just after Smith had left India.[35] On furlough at the Cape for eight months from 26 November 1830, Smith officially retired from the Bengal Army in July 1832, was created a Companion of the Bath on 26 September 1831, and later given the rank of Honorary Colonel in November 1854 in recognition of his pioneering engineering work.[36] His retirement pension was £1 per day and, unlike the military adventurers or earlier nabobs, no fortune awaited him.[37] Due to the ban on private trading, and the acceptance of gifts, it would have been unusual if he had left the East India Company a wealthy man.

Although his lack of income perhaps at first impeded his ambitions, Smith's love of sketching and painting gained during his surveying and drafting work for the EIC, combined with his acquired knowledge of the construction of Mughal monuments, was instrumental in the choices he made for the next phase of his life. He began to work towards the total design and planning of new mansions, which would enhance his family life and give vast spaces to display larger, more expansive paintings.

Building projects in Europe

Unlike his life in India, the years after Smith left the service of the Company are rather obscure. In the 1830s and 1840s he spent time in Italy and married a French heiress, Julia Adelaide Vitton. Their son, Robert Claude, was born in Venice in 1843.[38] Despite a lack of detail, however, these important events were to have significant consequences for Smith and his architectural projects, which began to take shape quickly after the birth of his child. Soon after 1846, Smith purchased the Villa Mills on the Palatine hill (see Figure 13.8) in Rome.[39] In the sixteenth century the area had consisted of vineyards and gardens, part of the famous Farnese gardens developed by Cardinal Alessandro Farnese.[40] A house was first built on the site by the Stati family, on top of the ruined Domus Augustus, and was later bought in 1818 by Charles Mills (d. 1846), a Scotsman, and the English archaeologist William Gell (1777–1836).[41] In 1824 they restored the villa's small Renaissance open loggia, which featured ceiling frescoes painted by

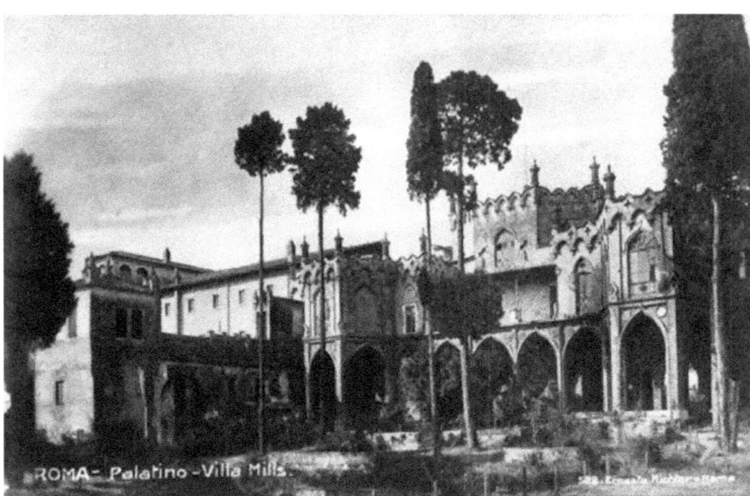

Figure 13.8 Postcard: Villa Mills on the Palatino, Rome. © akpool GmbH – www.akpool.de.

Peruzzi, representing the signs of the zodiac, the muses, and other classical subjects.[42] At a later date medallions containing a rose, a thistle and a shamrock were placed on the spandrels of the first floor painted arches, and the entrance gate piers were emblazoned with thistles.[43]

H. V. Morton suggests that Mills added gothic extensions to the villa, using the services of a 'fashionable English architect' to create 'pinnacles, battlements, casements and cloisters', and two Chinese pagodas, painted in crimson, over the Augustine baths.[44] However, after Charles Mills's death in October 1846, Robert Smith purchased the property and given the lack of evidence concerning Mills's 'alterations', it is possible to make a convincing case that it was Smith rather than Mills, who added these features to the Villa.[45] All articles written on the Villa suggest Charles Mills built it and point out the thistled villa gateposts as a significant link to his Scottish heritage.[46] However, Smith had more claim to Scottish ancestry as his son was later granted a coat-of-arms relating to the arms of Smith of Braco in Scotland.[47] Furthermore, the building has much of Smith's architectural fusion style, with Gothic and Italian elements conjoined with Indian, in a central rotunda flanked by two octagonal towers with an arched loggia beneath. With archaeological remains below of an ancient civilization, and a view from the top of a cliff, the Villa's design clearly echoes the Delhi bungalow. It is also odd that visitors to the Villa while Charles Mills was in residence did not mention the eccentric look of the mansion. For instance Harriet Countess Granville, who was keen to rent the house from Charles Mills, wrote in her journal: 'Drive with us on a glorious summer's day down the Corso, by the ruins of the Temple of Peace, the Coliseum, Arch etc., to Mr Mill's garden, all full of roses, Cape jessamines and heliotropes'.[48] The garden appears to have been the main appeal of the house and not its architecture, so it seems likely that the design of the new additions to the Villa Mills was by Smith, not Mills.

The training Smith had received at the EIC's Great Marlow Academy, and his work for the Bengal army in topographical surveying would have proved extremely helpful with the re-design of the Villa Mills development. However, his drawing and skills were stretched even further with the planning of earth-movements and tunnelling in his next ambitious enterprise when he later created another 'fairy palace' in Europe, on an isolated headland in Nice, on the Cote D'Azur, at first called the Chateau Smith and later Le Château de l'Anglais. A description of the construction of this property gives an impression of the lavish amount of time and money that Smith gave to his building projects. His other house and garden at Redcliffe Towers, Paignton, was developed during this same time scale, and is covered later in this chapter.

Le Château de l'Anglais was constructed near a property belonging to Smith's close friend Proby Cautley, which was left to Smith after Cautley died in 1871.[49] Smith may have found the climate of Nice more agreeable to his health, or conceivably he may have wished for a major project to sharpen his mind and extend his drawing and building skills. He acquired a plot of 20,000 square metres of rocky uncultivated land on Mont Boron, unpatronized by the English gentry, who preferred fashionable Cannes where Lord Brougham (1778–1868) built the first British villa, 'Eléonore Louise', on the Riviera in 1835.[50] With plans drawn up in 1856, Smith was in Nice in 1857, hiring workers for his huge undertaking, which included clearing the rocky terrain, building retaining walls, walkways and tunnels.[51] With his expertise in engineering Smith knew how to gain maximum effect from the slope of the land; Élisée Reclus writing in 1864 observed: 'below the villa, hanging gardens, carved at great expense in the rock, descending terraces by terraces to the sea'.[52]

The exact stone colour used for the Château is unknown, however many painters were inspired to depict the building: Jules Defer's *Le Château de l'Anglais et la grève du Lazaret*, gives the château a rosy glow, while in Vincent Fossat's aquatint, *Nice Le Château de l'Anglais Smith*, the building appears made of buff stone, with red coloured rock in the surrounding countryside; both very different from the pink paint which has covered the building since the 1950s (see Figure 13.9). Perhaps the best judge of the hue is an account in a magazine from the nineteenth century which describes it as 'a red building developed before the road was made to Villefranche.'[53] This unusual colour links with Smith's early work on the Mughal monuments in Delhi.

Returning to Nice in May 1858 Smith stayed at the Hotel Royal, on the Boulevard de l'Impératrice Eugénie; from its elevated site he could oversee the work on the Château from the hotel windows.[54] The next year he returned again to further oversee the work and sketch and paint.[55] By 1862, the main structure of the Château was most likely completed. Described as having a 'perfect spirit of symmetry', the mansion featured Smith's signature, a large central tower with two turrets at each end.[56] A ground-floor arcade (or loggia) along the length of the building was topped by rooms which opened out onto a large terrace, while a long gallery housed one of Smith's huge paintings, a 30-metre mural of Indian life.[57] Above this an outdoor staircase was joined to the central rotunda which was decorated with petal-shaped battlements and onion domes; his architectural style although still displaying echoes of Indian monuments and gates, was becoming more curvilinear and eccentric. Smith built serpentine paths, ornamental lakes, and many other

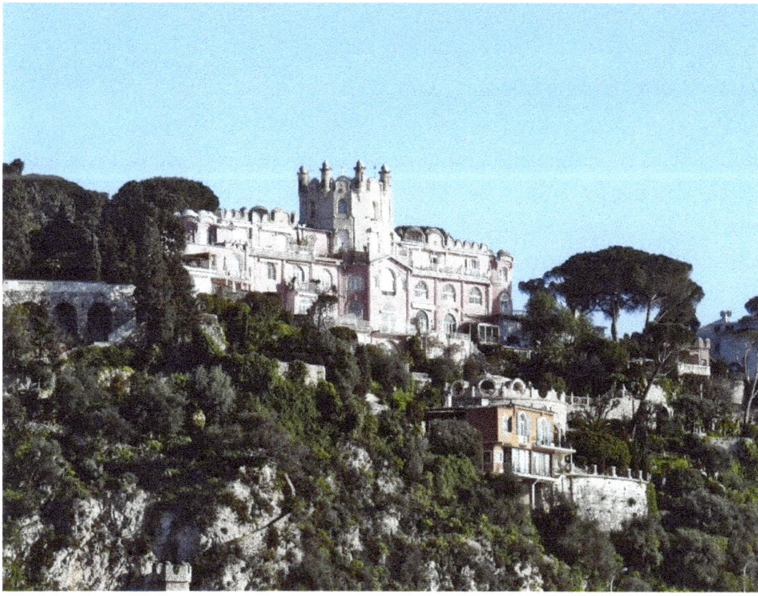

Figure 13.9 Le Château de l'Anglais, Mont Boron, Nice. Photograph by Diane James © 2013.

buildings throughout his property: below the house he constructed a circular gallery to display his paintings; in the south he built a tower or lighthouse; and near the sea a small domed pavilion possibly associated with bathing.[58]

The building drew criticism from local commentators who deemed it unsightly and bizarre, like the décor of an opera, or a wedding cake, yet Robert Smith remained unfazed by the harsh remarks.[59] He lived in the Château, compulsively painting, attending very few local social occasions, receiving only close friends visiting the Riviera and his military colleagues from India. In fact, the building projects in Rome and Nice indicate that Smith had lost little of his artistic skill and well-honed architectural talent that had gained approval and promotion while he was in India. His larger properties allowed experimentation with signature designs, to enlarge the themes and develop them into structures necessary for enjoyment in his solitary life, for instance his picture gallery, exotic plant conservatory, and bathing platform. Scaled down earlier versions of these designs were employed to fit a more domestic style of living at Paignton, whilst continuing to reference his previous military work in India.

Building project in Devon

Smith's wife Julia died some time before 1850 leaving Smith her considerable wealth. While simultaneously building in Nice, Smith also returned to his sister Mary's house, in the fashionable resort of Torquay, selling the family house at Bideford and purchasing five acres of remote headland in nearby Paignton.[60] There, Smith proceeded to build another unusual house, known as Redcliffe Towers. Perhaps Devon with its palm trees and lush vegetation reminded Smith of his time in India – William Daniell visited Devon in 1806 with the architect C. R. Cockerell (1788–1863) who wrote in his notebook: 'At Ilfracombe, Mr.D [aniell] says the foliage approached nearest to India of any he ever saw'.[61] A date of 1852 is suggested by Head for the commencement of building work on Redcliffe Towers, Smith bringing all his experience, and knowledge into the evolution of this extraordinary building.[62] J. R. K. Tozer, the proprietor of a major building company in Paignton, built the mansion in several stages, using drawings by Smith. The size of the building after each stage can be appraised by its rateable value: the first stage progressed in 1855, rated £9 15s 0d; by 1858 it was a considerable building rated £44 16s 8d; the final stage was completed by 1864 and rated £87 10s 0d.[63]

The house was constructed around an earlier look-out tower (see Figure 13.10), possibly with blocks from the red local sandstone, linking English architectural practice with Smith's previous projects when he restored the Red Fort, Jama Masjid and Qutub Minar in Delhi.[64] It was a design which fused Indian, Italian and Gothic motifs together and included the familiar signature of central rotunda and two wings (see Figure 13.11). It is now grey, covered in roughcast with stuccoed detail, which diminishes its impact on the landscape, and conceals all traces of the previous building.

According to an undated plan (see Figure 13.12), Redcliffe was approached by a serpentine carriage drive past a domed hexagonal lodge, which led to the formal garden to the front of the house, where a fountain and arching flower borders enclosed island beds in a floral shape, perhaps the symbolic sacred lotus.[65] Behind was the elliptical billiard room, and Smith's long conservatory housing his collection of rare hothouse plants, leading to the main central rotunda with its master's room, smoking room, and dining room. The two wings were topped by minarets and domes; the West wing accommodated Smith's studio and picture gallery, while the East wing featured service rooms and the kitchen. An octagon with a copper-tented roof and a ball finial topped the rotunda, and its four bay windows faced east towards the sea.

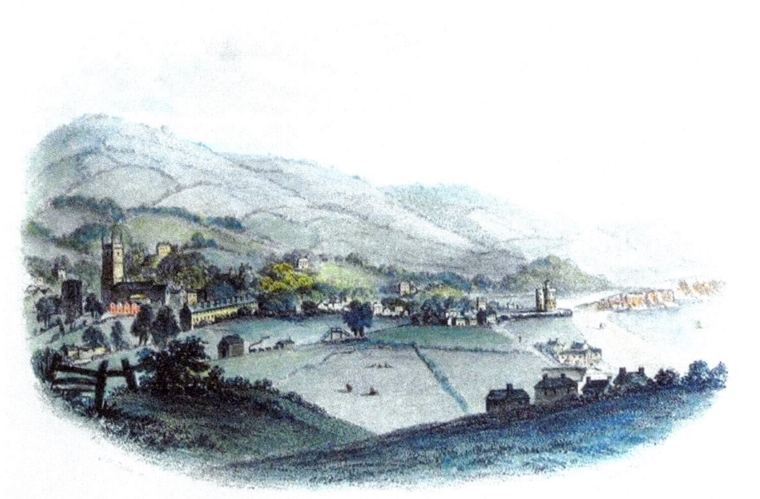

Figure 13.10 The old lookout tower on the edge of the cliff. After J. W. Tucker, *Paignton*. Coloured steel vignette, published by H. Besley, Exeter 12.5 x 17 cm. By permission of www.rareoldprints.com.

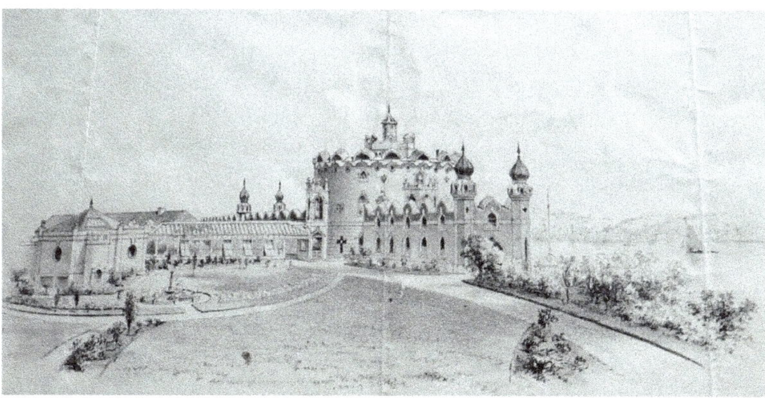

Figure 13.11 Early drawing of Redcliffe Towers, n.d. © Redcliffe Hotel, Paignton.

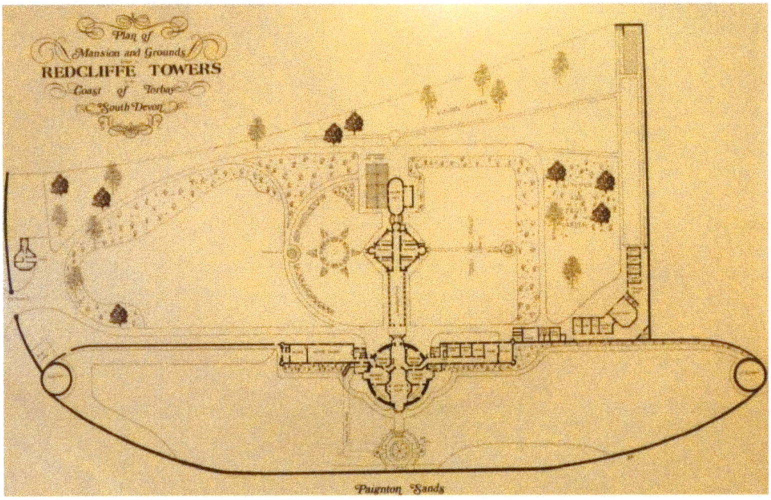

Figure 13.12 *Plan of Mansion and Grounds, Redcliffe Towers*, n.d. © Redcliffe Hotel, Paignton.

Smith's architectural features included ogee-shaped windows with stars at the apex, petal-shaped merlons, and a circular picture gallery.[66] The emblems on the rotunda are reminiscent of the Renaissance frescoes in the loggia on the Palatine, and thistles and apples, roses and shamrocks are used as decorative motifs, alongside Maltese crosses and sea-horses, in wrought-iron and plaster, and on the roundels embellishing the tower.

There were 23 bedrooms and dressing rooms, servants' accommodation, outbuildings and stables.[67] Steps on the eastern side were known as the Mecca steps and the building for a long time was believed to be orientated towards Mecca, undoubtedly myths, which nevertheless added to the mystique of the building. Smith loved to experiment with modern features: gas was piped throughout the house brought from the newly opened Preston Gas Works, and on the first floor the main room was divided into three, but could be made into one room by sliding doors; suggested by Head to be 'a novel feature which allowed a perfect panorama of Torbay to be seen from Redcliffe's clifftop site.'[68] Smith also filled the house with luxurious materials imported from Europe and Asia. Sale catalogues show that the interior of the house included ornate window cornices, and blue silk brocade damask drapes, walnut and mahogany furniture with an expanding Spanish mahogany table in the dining room, Italian marble fireplaces, Florentine marble-topped tables, cut-glass chandeliers and gilded mirror frames, Brussels carpets, antique bronzes, fine Japanese, Dresden, and Wedgwood china, and 300 of Smith's paintings and watercolours mainly of India.[69]

Like many others returning from India, Smith built a bathing complex within his estate. He designed a tunnel (see Figure 13.12 and Figure 13.13) to link his house on the seaward side with an octagonal hydropathic plunge bath, which filled with seawater at high tide.[70] E. M. Collingham suggests that retired Anglo-Indians, on their return from the subcontinent, brought the 'pleasures of personal cleanliness' back to Britain, and that many had adopted the Indian regimes of cold bathing and hair washing to help stave off the onset of tropical disease.[71] Jane Austen in her unfinished novel *Sanditon* (1817) promoted the health values of sea bathing. She remarked that 'The sea air and sea bathing together were nearly infallible, one or the other of them being a match for every disorder of the stomach, the lungs or the blood'.[72] Smith retired from the East India Company on health grounds, so the pool possibly helped with his ailments and war wounds, especially as it was large enough for swimming. Although the pool disappeared in a storm in 1867, the passageway is still in use today as a quick way down to the beach.

Smith also developed the five acres of pleasure gardens at Redcliffe using the space economically, surrounding it with ilex and holm oak

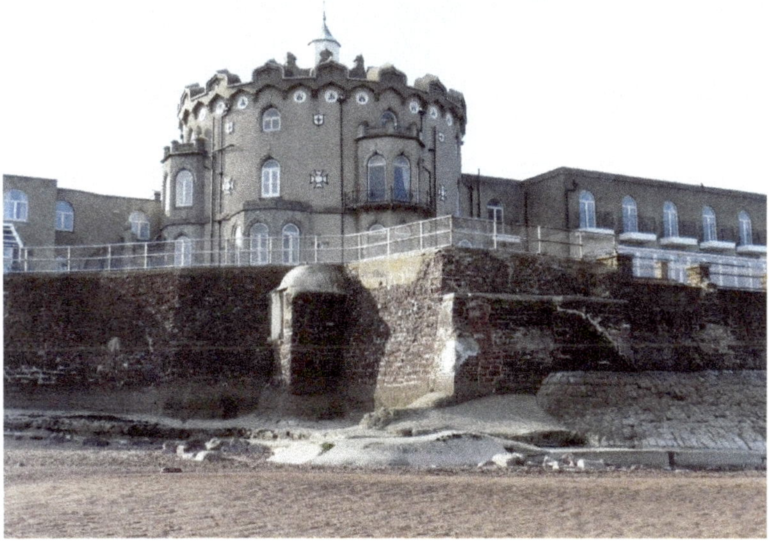

Figure 13.13 The Central Rotunda, Redcliffe Towers, Paignton, Devon, with the door of the plunge-pool tunnel opening above the beach. Photograph by Diane James © 2013.

(see Figure 13.14), with terrace walks and fountains, a kitchen garden, a hot house, a vinery, and a large conservatory containing Indian rare plants.[73] He introduced a military flavour into the garden design with flagstaff towers and bastions overlooking the sea (see Figure 13.15).

Flowerbeds surrounded the property, and the grounds also contained a large collection of valuable antique vases Smith had brought back from Italy.[74] Local reports suggest Robert Smith led a reclusive life at Redcliffe with few visitors apart from his sister and friends returning from India. Considering that as an engineer he would have left the East India Company with only his pension, and as he had built two,

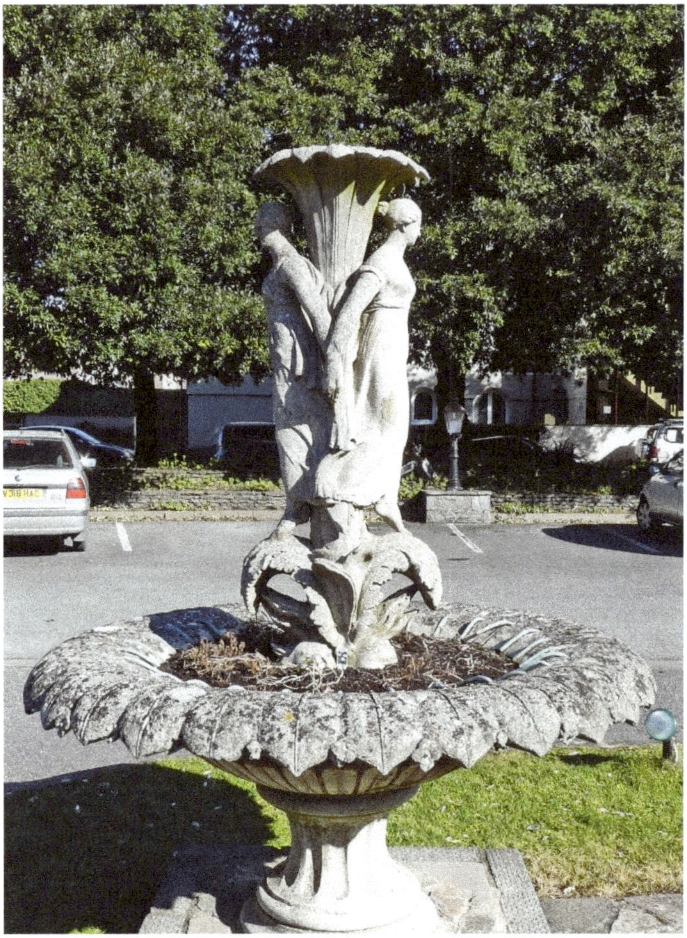

Figure 13.14 Fountain in the hotel car park, framed by holm oak trees, remnants of the Redcliffe garden. Photograph by Diane James © 2013.

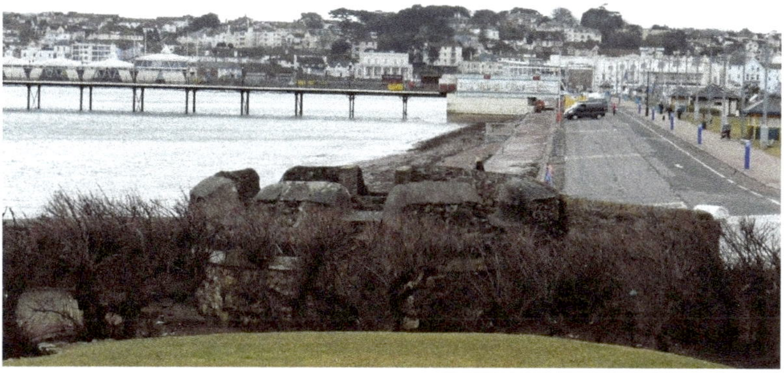

Figure 13.15 The remains of one of the flagstaff towers. Once a prominent feature it stands half-buried in the undergrowth. Photograph by Diane James © 2013.

possibly three large mansions in a synthesis of Indian and western architecture, it is extremely surprising that, after his death on 16 September 1873, the Probate Calendar states he left a sum of £90,000.[75] Whether any investments he had made were exceptionally successful, or his late wife's fortune was immense remains undetermined. Of his 300 oil paintings dispersed in sales after his death, only a tenth have been identified.[76]

Conclusion

Redcliffe Towers is an extremely important building in the story of the Indian influence on British architecture and gardens 1740–1850. It demonstrates such influences can be found not only in the large estates of the aristocracy and landed gentry, but in smaller properties owned by East India Company employees, in Smith's case the eccentric homes of a surveyor and artist.

An amalgam of styles, Indian, British and Italian, was employed in the construction of buildings and gardens using architectural forms far removed from their original functions. Design elements from tombs, temples, towers, gates, walls and villas, were incorporated to develop a new architectural style, a hybrid, part of the British Picturesque. However, the costs of such a building indicate that a retirement pension would not have been enough to build and furnish it. For Robert Smith it took many years after leaving India and the receipt of an inheritance, before it was possible to return to Britain to build a mansion and garden, and also to continue building in Europe on an even more lavish scale.

Smith was highly qualified by both training and experience to design and project-manage his own mansions which all incorporated Indian design alongside classical and gothic features. He was a successful surveyor, with an eye for detail, having survived the wilds of India for many years recording local topography, an important primary aid for the East India Company's expansion. Later restoring the major monuments of Delhi, and developing his experimental fusion style in architecture, he also sketched and painted many hundreds of British troop movements and Company life alongside views of Indian temples, monuments and landscapes, before retiring to Devon. Smith had a unique pioneering spirit, building his mansions on isolated headlands on the periphery of small towns, away from fashionable society. Redcliffe was built in stages over a number of years, and this was repeated at the Château de L'Anglais in Nice; it is not known whether this was due to cash flow problems or the vast quantity of detailed work, which took his builders an inordinate amount of time to complete. The most Indian of Smith's mansions, Redcliffe is testimony to his skills and ingenuity. The Devon site incorporated a domestic garden with military flourishes with a lavish mansion, which provided room for the many artefacts Smith had collected on his world travels, wall space for his hundreds of paintings, and a conservatory for his hothouse plants. Sadly, Redcliffe Towers, which in its heyday stood proud on its red rocky cliff (shocking the local inhabitants with its outlandish style of architecture), has now been subsumed into the town of Paignton, diminishing its scale and obscuring its Indian features (see Figure 13.16). Nevertheless, Robert Smith's Redcliffe Towers illustrates how skills learned in the service of the EIC entered the domestic sphere, and were adapted to cultural changes. Further adjustments in modes of living occurred with the construction of the railways, and the naming of Queen Victoria as Empress of India in 1877, after which Indian design gained fashionable prominence in many sea-side towns. Pleasure piers, band-stands and kiosks echoed the styles and motifs employed by EIC engineers during their

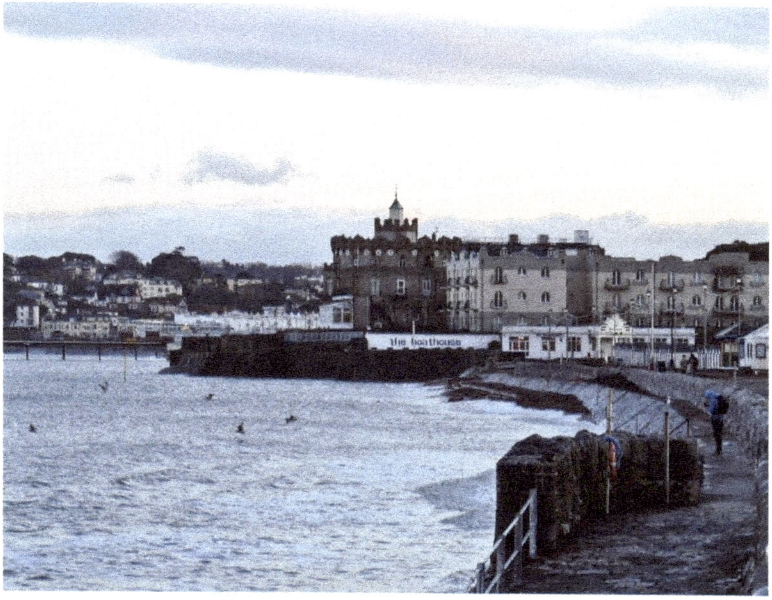

Figure 13.16 No longer isolated on a headland Redcliffe Towers is now surrounded by the town of Paignton. Photograph by Diane James © 2013.

surveying and drafting experiences in India. The unique, Indian-styled Redcliffe Towers, which was originally positioned by Robert Smith on an isolated headland, gradually, over time, became an accepted and well-loved feature of the municipal landscape of Paignton.

14
Partly after the Chinese manner
'Chinese' staircases in north-west Wales

Rachael Barnwell

The Royal Commission on the Ancient and Historical Monuments of Wales (RCAHMW) holds among its extensive collections photographic records of domestic interiors of houses across Wales. In the records of the historic counties of Anglesey and Caernarvonshire in north-west Wales are a series of photographs showing some remarkable staircases.[1] This chapter explores these staircases by working to understand their designs, origins and influences in north-west Wales.

Like many staircases found in homes throughout Wales between the early seventeenth and late eighteenth centuries, the staircases under discussion here feature pierced balusters: flat, thin pieces of wood known as 'splats' that were cut so as to form particular patterns which, when repeated, formed the full balustrade.[2] Splat balusters frequently mimicked popular contemporary designs for more expensive turned balusters that were produced from solid blocks of wood using a lathe. Both splat and turned balusters were typically vasiform, with the woodwork mimicking the curvilinear shape and form of ceramic vessels, particularly vases. By contrast, the unusual staircases in the photographs showed balustrades that sported bold, distinctive geometric designs, formed by repeated sequences of alternating and contrasting latticework patterns (see Figure 14.1). The clean lines and strong angles of these staircases were both surprising and intriguing in their appearance. The notes accompanying the photographs describe them as 'Chinese' or 'Chinese Chippendale' staircases and dated all of them to 1755–c.1760.[3] Unfortunately, the notes gave no indication of the origins of the staircase design.

To date, and with the exception of the continuing work of Huw Bowen and Lowri Ann Rees, there has been a limited assessment of the impact of the East India Company (EIC) on and in Wales, particularly with regards to the domestic environment.[4] This chapter draws primarily on records from the National Monuments Record of Wales (NMRW) held by the Royal Commission, and contributes to the ongoing project of exploring the influences of global trade generally, and EIC trade specifically, on Welsh homes. It will examine each of the staircases photographed as a unique piece of furniture and as a part of each house – as both fixture and fitting. It locates these 'Chinese' staircases within both the wider, global context of 'Asian-inspired' material culture design in the eighteenth century, and within more local, contemporary networks of design exchange. Its aim is to assess if, and to what degree, the EIC's trade network impacted on the interior design in the homes of the propertied classes in north-west Wales in the eighteenth century.

'Chinese' staircases on record in north-west Wales

This chapter focuses on three 'Chinese' staircases in north-west Wales: Tan-yr-Allt in Bangor, Caernarvonshire; Bishopsgate House in Beaumaris, Anglesey; and Trefeilir in Trefdraeth, Anglesey. Tan-yr-Allt and Trefeilir were both originally country houses built or occupied during the eighteenth century, while Bishopsgate House is a townhouse owned and used by the Bulkeley family based at Baron Hill, also in Anglesey. The houses are all within a 17-mile radius of one another, and have 'Chinese' staircases that survive to the present day, though in variable conditions.

First, Tan-yr-Allt (in English 'below the hill') is a two storey, Grade II* house in Bangor, Caernarvonshire, built in 1755 for John Ellis, the Archdeacon of Merionedd. It was built in the Palladian style popularized at the time of its construction by Inigo Jones and his contemporaries, and is believed to have been planned by one Master builder, though there is little remaining evidence to support this supposition.[5] Originally, the house was situated outside Bangor, set within extensive formal gardens sloping downhill to the River Adda, with pathways connecting the property to Bangor Cathedral and Bishop's Palace. However, the house and grounds were purchased by Bangor University in 1928 as part of its post-First World War expansion, along with adjacent land that the university required for its planned development. The house's plot has since been encroached on by university buildings and more recently by the 'PONTIO Arts and Innovation in Bangor' development, obscuring its original rurality.

Royal Commission investigators visited Tan-yr-Allt in the early 1950s while preparing the 'Caernarvonshire Inventories', which were published in three volumes between 1956 and 1964. By that time the building was in use as Bangor University Student's Union. Records at the Commission indicate that at the time of its initial survey the interior features of the building had survived well. They dated the main staircase, windows, fireplaces, cornicing and ground floor panelling to the building's original construction in 1755. Particular attention is given to the main staircase, which the final inventory notes is 'a good example of the local Chinese Chippendale style'.[6]

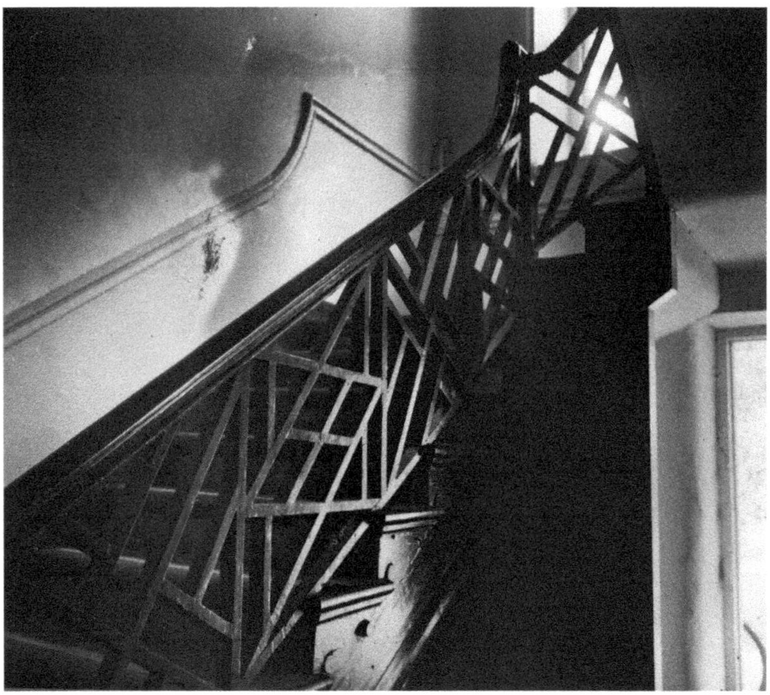

Figure 14.1 The main staircase from the entrance hall at Tan-yr-Allt, showing the ascent to the first floor and hinting at fluted window reveals. DI2013_0674, NPRN 16895. © Crown copyright: Royal Commission on the Ancient and Historical Monuments of Wales.

It ascends from the main entrance of the property to the first floor, with a railing on the landing and fluted reveals to the window at the head of the stairs. It features a latticework design, with two contrasting patterns repeating in sequence to form the balustrade. The stair rail on the landing uses two different but equally contrasting patterns across the span of the landing. In addition, the tread end of each step is carved with a stylized wave design. Although the staircase is now painted white, the photographs from the initial 1950s investigation show the original staircase as being dark wood, though it is not possible to ascertain from the images whether it is made from mahogany or similar, or whether the look of dark wood is the result of wood staining. This staircase is the earliest of all the surviving staircases examined in this chapter, and at the time of writing, the earliest confirmed occurrence of a 'Chinese' staircase in north-west Wales.

Second, Bishopsgate House in Beaumaris, Anglesey: built by the Bulkeley family in the early eighteenth century, it was originally used as a dower house (see Figure 14.2).[7] The family's main residence on Anglesey was at Baron Hill, about a mile from Beaumaris. Commission investigators noted that the house is substantially eighteenth-century in its fabric but with later alterations to the front room and façade of the property,

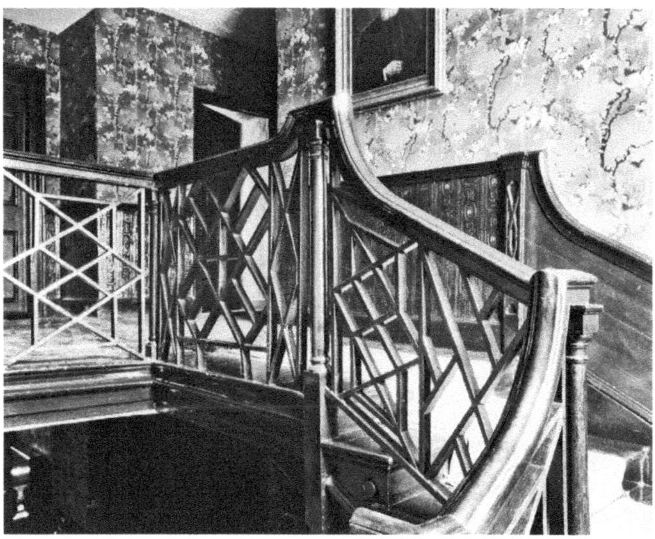

Figure 14.2 The 'Chinese' staircase at Bishopsgate House, showing the first floor landing. The stylized wave design carved into the tread ends is just visible in the bottom centre of this image. DI2011_1011, NPRN 15946. © Crown copyright: Royal Commission on the Ancient and Historical Monuments of Wales.

probably dating to the nineteenth century. Unlike at Tan-yr-Allt, the 'Chinese' staircase in the house is not contemporary with the original construction of the building.

Following a visit to the property in the 1930s, investigators suggested that the staircase was installed in the house in c.1760. It was noted that the panelling in the ground floor rooms and the back stairs of the property are likely contemporary with the installation of the staircase suggesting a broader programme of interior change at the house in the 1760s. This home improvement work occurred following the death of its owner James, 6th Viscount Bulkeley (1717–52) in 1752, and possibly in the same year that the Dowager Lady Bulkeley, née Emma Rowlands (d. 1770) married her second husband, Lt. Col. Hugh Williams (d. 1794) of Nant, Caernarvon and Caerau, Anglesey. The 6th Viscount Bulkeley was succeeded by his son Thomas James Bulkeley (1752–1822) who was born eight months after his father's death, and who therefore had little influence on the interior design of the properties in his ownership at that time.

Just as at Tan-yr-Allt the staircase is the main stairway in the building, and ascends from the ground floor to the first floor in two flights. Again, the Royal Commission records make particular reference to the 'Chinese' staircase at the property.[8] The staircase rail is the same design as at Tan-yr-Allt, and the repeating pattern of alternating and contrasting latticework designs is almost identical with only slight adjustments needed to better fit the space allocated to them, and to accommodate the slightly steeper pitch of the staircase. The pattern for the first flight of stairs is the same as at Tan-yr-Allt, while the second flight and landing also use the same patterns that appear on the landing at Tan- yr-Allt. In addition, the tread ends are decorated with the same carved stylized wave design. The staircase is again constructed from dark wood, though it too has been painted white since the Commission's investigations.

Third, Trefeilir is an eighteenth-century house near Trefdraeth, Anglesey. The majority of the extant structure of the building was constructed in 1735, incorporating the remains of a sixteenth-century house, representing all that remains of an earlier building, into one wing of the property. In a photographic survey of the house, possibly conducted in the 1930s in preparation for the Commission's 'Anglesey Inventories' (published in 1937), the exterior was photographed extensively. Inside, key architectural features were photographed: two sixteenth-century fireplaces and the main staircase (see Figure 14.3).

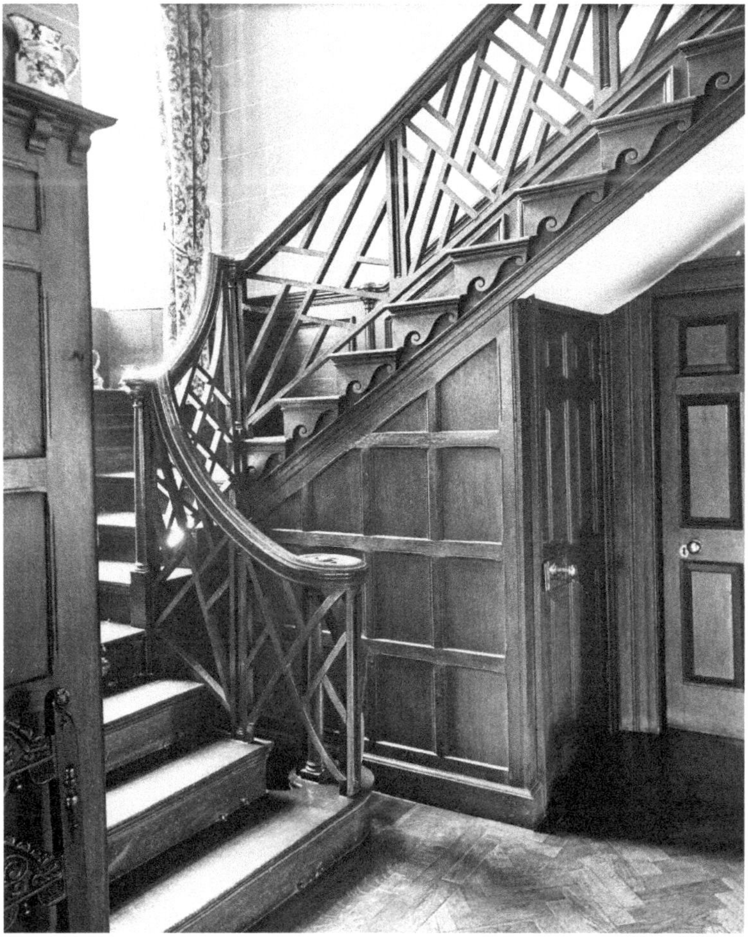

Figure 14.3 The 'Chinese' staircase at Trefeilir, probably photographed in the 1930s, showing the main balustrade of the staircase with its latticework. DI2011_1010, NPRN 15898. © Crown copyright: Royal Commission on the Ancient and Historical Monuments of Wales.

In the notes that accompany the survey the field investigator again describes this as a 'Chinese' staircase, and suggests it was added to the house in c.1760, broadly the same date as the staircase at Bishopsgate House about 17 miles away. It is possible that the new staircase was added to the house in preparation for the marriage of owner Charles Evans (1726–1802) to Elizabeth Lewis (1740–1805) in 1761.

As at both Tan-yr-Allt and Bishopsgate House, the staircase appears to be made from dark wood, and has a reasonably plain handrail, newel and newel cap. The tread ends are also carved with a stylized wave design, though this is slightly more ornate than at the other two properties. The staircase ascends from the central hall to the first floor in two flights, with different sequences of patterns used for each flight and the landing. However, while the latticework patterns utilized at Tan-yr-Allt and Bishopsgate House and their sequence of use are very similar to each other, the designs used at Trefeilir are only broadly similar. Elements of the designs on individual panels are visible though they are configured differently. The designs appear less complex, with the interlocking lozenge shapes of the patterns at Tan-yr-Allt and Bishopsgate House being largely omitted.

A local style

If we accept the observations and conclusions of the Royal Commission's experienced and highly qualified field investigators then all three of these staircases were installed in the properties discussed in the years between 1755 and c.1760. In each example, the staircase is either part of the original interior design of the building or appears to coincide with a change in the marital status of its owner. From the Commission's photographs, the staircases appear to be constructed from materials and feature designs that are extremely similar to one another, as at Tan-yr-Allt and Bishopsgate House, or that share basic, characteristic motifs and patterns that have been arranged differently, as at Trefeilir. All properties share the stylized wave motif carved into their tread ends, though at Trefeilir this is more ornate than at the other properties. It should also be noted that the quality of the craftsmanship exhibited in the construction of each staircase is high. When examined in close detail, the photographs reveal a fine finish to the woodwork, with close, precise joints between component parts. The similarities in both design and materials support the Commission's interpretation of the staircases as part of a 'local' trend. However, despite searches of county archives and a number of documents held at Bangor University and the National Library of Wales, it has not been possible at this time to uncover the identity of the craftsmen that physically installed these staircases.

The geographical and chronological proximity of these staircases relative to one another, as well as their similarities of design and construction, suggests that their appearance in these houses in north-west Wales in the mid-1750s to c.1760 may also be related. Furthermore, the Royal Commission's Caernarvonshire Inventory notes that the staircase at Tan-yr-Allt 'is a good example of the *local* Chinese Chippendale style' (emphasis added).[9] How, then, might a 'Chinese' style become 'local' to north-west Wales in the eighteenth century, and how did the contemporary trade of the EIC affect the appearance of this style of staircase in this area? This chapter seeks to answer these questions by considering the local connections and contexts of the families involved, the broader taste for 'Chinese-style' goods in Britain in the mid eighteenth century, and finally, the particularity of Welsh engagement with the Chinese style.

Possible influence of Plas Newydd

The Commission's *An Inventory of the Ancient Monuments in Anglesey* includes a summary of key or notable architectural features for buildings in the county. The *Inventory* states that '[t]he "Chinese" staircases of c.1760, at Trefeilir (Trefdraeth) and at Bishopsgate House (Beaumaris), are also noteworthy, and an example at Plas Newydd (Llanedwen) has been attributed to James Wyatt'.[10] The note implies that at the time the *Inventory* was being compiled there was a 'Chinese' staircase at Plas Newydd in Llanedwen, Anglesey. Plas Newydd, overlooking the Menai Straits, is one of Anglesey's most iconic buildings, and was home to one of the most influential families in north Wales from the eighteenth century until 1976 when the property passed into the care of the National Trust. The current Plas Newydd was built in the late eighteenth century, incorporating elements of older buildings thought to date back as early as the fourteenth century.[11] However, apart from the reference in the Commission's *Inventory*, no evidence can be found of a 'Chinese' staircase at the property, let alone one that could be attributed to James Wyatt. Without further information about the original source for this information it is difficult to pursue this line of enquiry further. However, it is known that in the early 1750s, Sir Nicholas Bayly (1708–82) undertook a refurbishment of the interior at Plas Newydd, for which he acted as his own architect.[12] Although no known plans relating to this work survive, records of later work at the property show that at the time of Nicholas Bayly's refurbishment, the main staircase of the house was located in what is now the south end of the house. Between 1782 and 1786, Henry Paget (neé Bayly[13], 1744–1812), 1st Earl of Uxbridge, called in local architect and stone mason John Cooper (dates unknown) of Beaumaris to make improvements to the property, which was in use as the family's summer residence. Then, between 1793 and 1799, Lord Uxbridge engaged James Wyatt to undertake further changes, including installing a classical staircase. In 1771, Wyatt had undertaken a refurbishment of the main Bayly residence, Beaudesert in Staffordshire. Wyatt directed the second phase of refurbishment at Plas Newydd, in association with Joseph Potter (1756–1842), a joiner from Lichfield. At this time, the staircase in the south wing of the house was relocated to its current position at the modern main entrance possibly so that the layout of the house would better fit the centrally planned floor plan favoured by the master builders and architects at this time. Wyatt's elegantly ascending cast iron staircase with its stylized anthemion (honeysuckle) motif was more in keeping with the new schema designed for the rest of the house and made good use of cast iron, which had only recently become fashionable in interior design.

Given that by the 1780s and 1790s, 'Chinese' staircase designs were outmoded in Britain, and given the Palladian style of Wyatt's 1790s renovation, it seems unlikely that Wyatt would have chosen to install a 'Chinese' staircase at Plas Newydd as part of his refurbishment.[14] However, it is possible that the staircase installed by Nicholas Bayly in the early 1750s was of 'Chinese' design. If so, it was possibly in situ in the south end of the building for only a few decades between c.1750 and c.1790, when it could have been removed by Cooper, Wyatt or Potter in the course of their work on the house. If so, then Plas Newydd would be the first house in north-west Wales to have a 'Chinese' staircase installed. The political and social power and influence of the Bayly family at Plas Newydd would certainly have had an impact on the local elite, who may have mimicked the Baylys' interior design choices. Sadly, there is no surviving evidence that proves there was a 'Chinese' staircase at the property beyond one unique reference in the Commission's *Inventory*. It should also be noted that the wording of the *Inventory* is ambiguous at best: the paragraph which describes 'Chinese' staircases could also be referring to significant eighteenth-century staircases in Anglesey more widely, reducing the likelihood of a 'Chinese' staircase having ever been installed at Plas Newydd.

Local connections with the East India Company

Despite the ambiguity of the *Inventory's* reference to Plas Newydd, it is nonetheless tempting to attribute the development of a 'local' trend in 'Chinese' staircases to the influential Nicholas Bayly and his possible work on the interior of Plas Newydd in the early 1750s. He certainly had the means to finance a broad programme of renovation work at the house, having married the wealthy heiress Caroline Paget (d. 1766) in 1737. The Pagets also had strong connections to the EIC: Caroline's four times great-grandfather William, 5th Baron Paget (1572–1629) was an investor in the EIC, as well as the Amazon River Company, the Bermudas Company and the Virginia Company, of which he was also a Councillor. The family retained its interest in the EIC for several generations: the 5th Baron's grandson, the Honourable Henry Paget (1663–1743), held numerous political offices throughout his lifetime, and used his influence in Parliament to champion the cause of the Old East India Company. Records show that on the 24 February 1699 he was involved in, and may have championed on the Old Company's behalf, a petition against paying a 5 per cent duty on trade to the New Company.[15] Furthermore by 1800, the copper mines on the Bayly family's lands – most notably Paris Mountain – had agreements with the EIC for the trade of copper trinkets. At the same time, the Bayly and Paget families also had a strong tradition of Naval service, with many of the men taking up posts which allowed them to travel extensively around the world, and would have brought them into contact with the EIC's ships and merchants.

In contrast to Plas Newydd, there are no readily discernible connections between the families or houses at Tan-yr-Allt, Bishopsgate House and Trefeilir, and the EIC. The Archdeacon of Merionedd John Ellis (1720–85), had no appreciable connection to the EIC or to broader contemporary travel and trade to Asia. Prior to his ordination into the Church of England, Ellis is known to have been a chemist and an engineer. However, at the time of writing, little information is available about this period in his life, and nothing to link him specifically to the EIC either as a clergyman or in his engineering or chemistry background. There also is no obvious or direct connection to be found between the families at Bishopsgate House and at Trefeilir and the EIC. Nevertheless, although no direct connections could be found between the properties in this study and the EIC, they all share one characteristic: all three houses were owned or occupied by wealthy and socio-politically influential families. John Ellis, as Archdeacon of Merionedd, was in a position of power both locally and nationally through the Church of England. The Bulkeleys of Baron Hill owned a significant amount of land in north-west Wales and had lived at Baron Hill since its construction in the early seventeenth century. Charles Evans (1726–1802) of Trefeilir was High Sheriff of Anglesey in 1751, then of Caernarvon in 1752. All three families were invested in local politics: the Bulkeley family were even involved in a prolonged political rivalry with none other than the Baylys of Plas Newydd, in which both parties competed to represent Anglesey in Parliament.[16] Likewise, all three families were well-connected in society, both within and beyond Wales, holding numerous political positions and posts. They were well-travelled and possessed property in London; they were well embedded in fashionable, metropolitan culture. It is therefore likely that the decision to install 'Chinese' staircases at the three houses considered in this study was mostly affected by much broader consumer trends for interior design and furnishings across Britain in the mid eighteenth century.

The 'China craze'

From the start of this chapter the staircases under consideration have been identified as having a 'Chinese' or 'Chinese Chippendale' design, primarily because they are identified in the record as such, but also to distinguish between authentic Chinese material culture and design concepts, and a constructed idea of Chinese style known as 'chinoiserie', a mixture of Eastern and Western stylistic elements embedded in European-manufactured objects. To best understand the genesis of the staircases in this chapter, therefore, it is necessary to understand both Chinese and 'Chinese' material culture and design in its historical context.

The eighteenth-century fashion for 'Chinese' material culture in Britain peaked between 1750 and 1760. The staircases at the three properties in this study were built at the height of the trend between 1755 and c.1760, when Britain was consumed by a craze for all things Chinese. The Empire of China had long been an object of curiosity to Europeans. Travel accounts published in the sixteenth to eighteenth centuries, highlighted China's architecture, landscapes, material culture and customs to European audiences.[17] Many of these accounts arose from travel undertaken through business, much of which was on behalf of the EIC. In 1673 an English-language translation of Johan Nieuhof's (1618–72) *An Embassy from the East India Company of the United Provinces* was published (see Figure 14.4). It recounted an account of Nieuhof's travels from Canton (present day Guangzhou) to Peking (present day Beijing) between 1655 and 1657 when he was steward for a 1500-mile mission to China by the Dutch East India Company. His book, dedicated to the contemporary administrators of both the East and West India Companies, featured 150 illustrations and was disseminated widely.

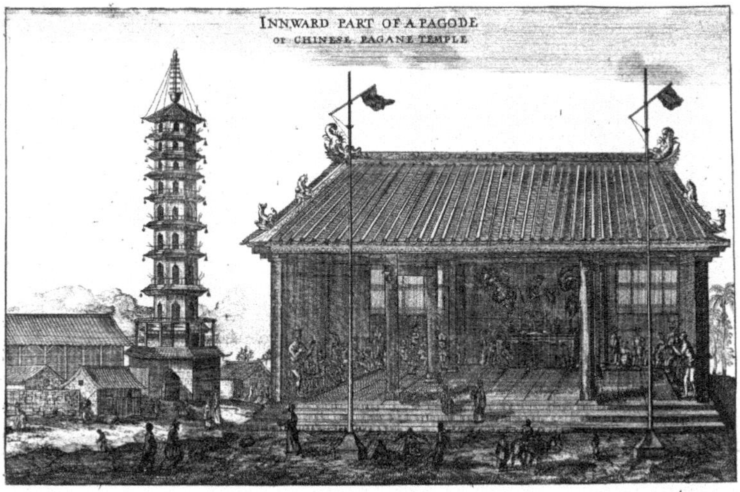

Figure 14.4 Illustration from Nieuhof's *Embassy*, showing a Chinese pagoda. French, German and Latin translations were made available, each of which were published in at least two editions.

By the 1730s other influential works on China were also circulating. The most famous of these is Jean-Baptiste Du Halde's *The General History of China* published in four volumes in France in 1735, with an English translation available from 1741. The extensive and detailed text accompanied by hundreds of illustrations of contemporary Chinese civilization, ignited a deeper curiosity about the country and its culture across European society, and kindled a craze for China in architecture and design.

However, there was more to the trend for Chinese goods and ideas than colourful travel writings and striking drawings. By the mid eighteenth century, the EIC was regularly importing goods from China into Britain. The English East India Company had established a trading post in Taiwan in 1672 and had immediately engaged in frequent, direct trade with the Chinese, making regular voyages to Amoy, Chusan and Canton. By 1700, the Company had transferred its trading base from Taiwan to its 'factory' (trading post) in Canton, and was granted a monopoly on trade with China, which lasted until 1833. While tea fast became the largest trade item in Britain's trading account, the Company also imported Chinese porcelain and silk. Some of the products of this global trade are still on show at Plas Newydd in Anglesey, and illustrate how the EIC's trade with China had a direct effect on the material culture of British homes. The State Bed in Lord Anglesey's bedroom has a flying tester covered with Chinese silk, painted with flowers that match Chinese wallpaper that was at the family's ancestral residence at Beaudesert where the tester was originally displayed until the 1920s. At this time, the 6th Marquess of Anglesey, struggling financially, abandoned his Staffordshire residence and transferred much of its contents to Plas Newydd. Both the tester and the wallpaper are dated to c.1720.

The influx of Chinese material goods, such as the silk tester, and the popularity of illustrated books about the country from the likes of Nieuhof and Du Halde, together provided inspiration for eighteenth-century artisans and architects, who were constantly seeking new aesthetics and designs to tempt the increasingly affluent citizens of a fledgling consumer economy to part with their money.[18] It has also been argued that the growing inventiveness of British interior design was partly a rebellion against the constraints imposed by the strict classical vocabulary utilized on building exteriors; the 'Chinese' style, undisciplined by the five orders that so meticulously structured classical architecture, offered an eclecticism and freedom of form that more conventional designs lacked.[19]

However, such artistic innovation was not always welcome. The 'bluestocking' Elizabeth Montagu, wrote to the Reverend Mr Friend in 1749 in despair of the new Chinese trend: 'thus it has happened in furniture; sick of Grecian elegance and symmetry, or Gothic grandeur and magnificence, we must all seek the barbarous gaudy goût of the Chinese; and fat-headed Pagods, and shaking Mandarins, bear the prize from the finest works of antiquity; and Apollo and Venus must give way to a fat idol with a sconce on his head'.[20] Despite Montagu's disparagement of the style, a report from *The World* in 1753 states that the Chinese was 'the prevailing whim [...] everything ... is Chinese, or in the Chinese taste, or as it is more modestly expressed, "partly after the Chinese manner" [...] chairs, tables, chimney pieces are all reduced to this new-fangled standard'.[21]

Though widely disparaged by contemporary critics as inferior to classical styles, by the 1750s – when the first 'Chinese' staircase appeared in north-west Wales at Tan-yr-Allt, in Bangor – interior decoration "partly after the Chinese manner" was clearly popular with wealthy home owners. Just one year after Elizabeth Montagu wrote her letter, an entrepreneurial designer and cabinet-maker based in London capitalized on the enthusiasm for home decoration by publishing a book of furniture designs, including a set of patterns in the

Chinese taste likely inspired by the publications and goods disseminating among craftsmen and designers, and the vogue for Chinese style. The book was Thomas Chippendale's *The Gentleman and Cabinet Maker's Director* (1754), and it is the most renowned of a series of publications that are likely to have influenced the installation of 'Chinese' staircases in north-west Wales (see Figure 14.5).

'In the Chinese taste'

The Gentleman and Cabinet Maker's Director was published in 1754, and revised in 1755 and 1762. The *Director* was both a pattern book and a concise set of 'how to' instructions or 'Orders' intended for use by cabinet makers, and featured designs in the Gothic, Chinese and contemporary 'modern' taste. Chippendale included designs for dressers, cabinets, chairs, fire screens and railings in the 'Chinese' taste, and though staircases do not feature explicitly, geometric shapes and latticework patterns proliferate throughout his drawings, sharing strong similarities with the staircases at Tan-yr-Allt, Bishopsgate House and Trefeilir.

Indeed, the Commission's own inventories attribute the 'Chinese' staircases at each property to Chippendale, referring to them as

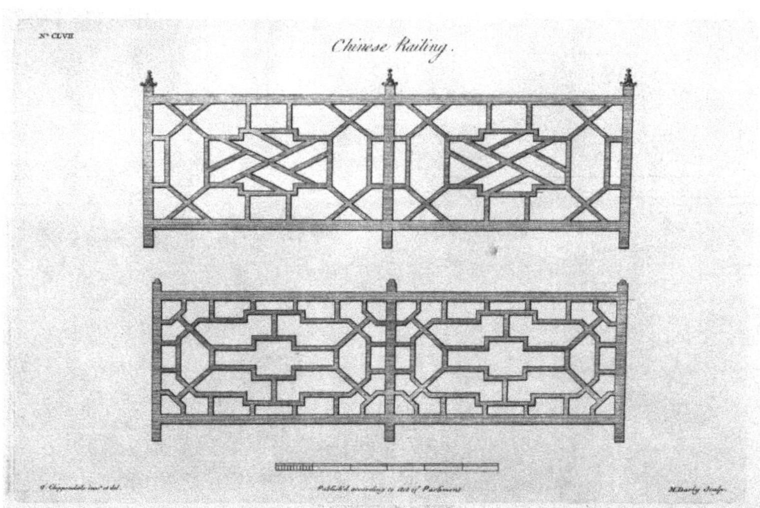

Figure 14.5 Railing designs as depicted in Thomas Chippendale's *The Gentleman and Cabinet Maker's Director*, 206.

'Chinese Chippendale' or 'Chippendale' staircases in both the site files and the official *Inventory* descriptions. Given that the *Director* was the first popular catalogue of its kind with a widespread circulation across Britain, this suggested provenance is perhaps persuasive. However, it is not clear what evidence led investigators to this specific conclusion. It is possible that the *Director's* publication in 1754, which predates the erection of Tan-yr-Allt, and the book's 1755 revision, which is contemporary with Tan-yr-Allt's construction, suggested that the *Director* was the most likely source for the 'Chinese' staircase designs. In addition, the 'Caernarvonshire Inventories' record a number of other items of 'Chippendale' furniture broadly contemporary with the installation of the three staircases in this study. At the Parish Church of St. Mary in Trefriw, near Llanrwst, records show that there was an upholstered Chippendale chair in the chancel.[22] There is also a record of four matching Chippendale chairs in the 'country' style in Bangor Cathedral, which was connected to Tan-yr-Allt by a series of tree-lined pathways: we can only hypothesize that the Commission's investigators envisaged a connection in design between the two properties as well.[23] The appearance of this furniture alongside the 'Chinese' staircases may have hinted further at Chippendale's suspected influence in homeowners' style choices.

The variance between Chippendale's designs and the actual staircases may be accounted for by Chippendale himself: he did not intend the designs in the *Director* to be used rigidly (see Figure 14.6). In his conclusion to the preface he explicitly encourages innovation among his fellow cabinet makers, stating that the publication is 'calculated to assist the one in the choice, the other in the execution of the designs; which are so contrived, that if no one drawing should singly answer the Gentleman's taste, there will yet be found a variety of hints sufficient to construct a new one'.[24] Chippendale was not 'a lone craftsman, turning out fine furniture in a workshop, but a successful entrepreneur', part of a thriving furniture industry which, by 1750, could supply an amazing diversity of types to consumers across Britain who were ravenous for innovation and choice in interior design.[25] Moreover, although the list of subscribers in the *Director* lists no persons or businesses in Wales, there were many located in London or in wealthy English households that Welsh property owners would have been able to access.

While the *Director* was clearly important and influential, it was not the only publication available in 1755 to feature 'Chinese' designs: between 1750 and 1752, William Halfpenny published *Rural Architecture in the Chinese Taste* in four volumes (see Figures 14.7 and 14.8). The book

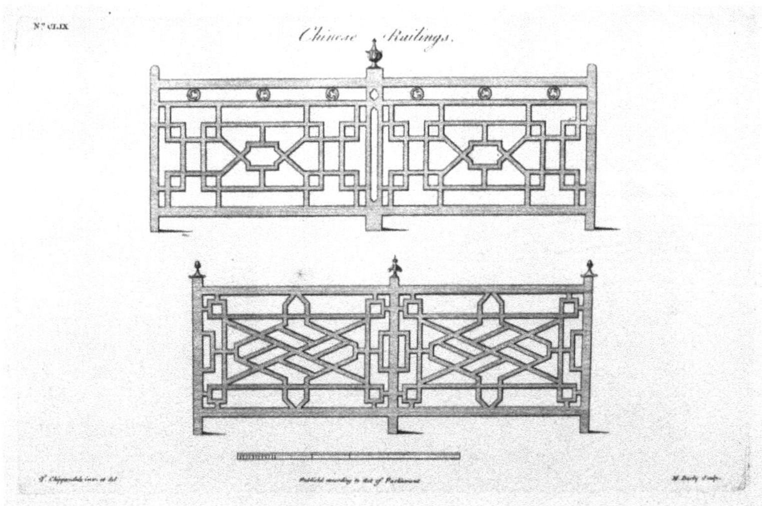

Figure 14.6 Railing designs as depicted in Thomas Chippendale's *The Gentleman and Cabinet Maker's Director*, 208.

featured 60 copperplates of designs 'for the Decoration of Gardens, Parks, Forrests, Insides of Houses & C.', and included crucially – a design for a 'Chinese' staircase. Halfpenny's work is not as renowned today as the work of Thomas Chippendale or his contemporary Sir William Chambers, but arguably his designs had a greater impact on the installation of 'Chinese' staircases in north-west Wales, providing a pattern for staircase designs that bears much greater similarity to all three staircases in this study than anything in the *Director*.

The designs are less complex, with fewer pattern variations and wider frets, and feature the lozenge motif that occurs in all three examples of the staircases in north-west Wales. Importantly, Halfpenny's design also features a stylized wave motif on the risers of each step, which appears on all three staircases in this study. Halfpenny's wave motif features more classical design elements than the ones at Tan-yr-Allt, Bishopsgate House and Trefeilir but is significant nonetheless, as the motif does not appear in any of Chippendale's designs. Halfpenny's inspiration was very likely drawn from the same material as Chippendale: the products of travel and trade enabled through the enterprise of the EIC.

Other works after 1755 only furthered the fashion for Chinese designs among the elite. In 1757, Sir William Chambers published *Designs for Chinese Buildings, furniture, dress etc.* Chambers had served as

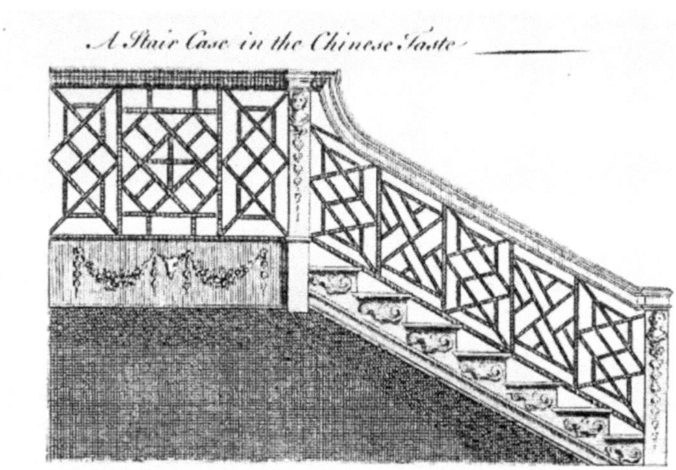

Figure 14.7 Railing design from William Halfpenny's *Rural Architecture in the Chinese Taste*, showing similarities with staircase designs at Tan-yr-Allt, Bishopsgate House and Trefeilir.

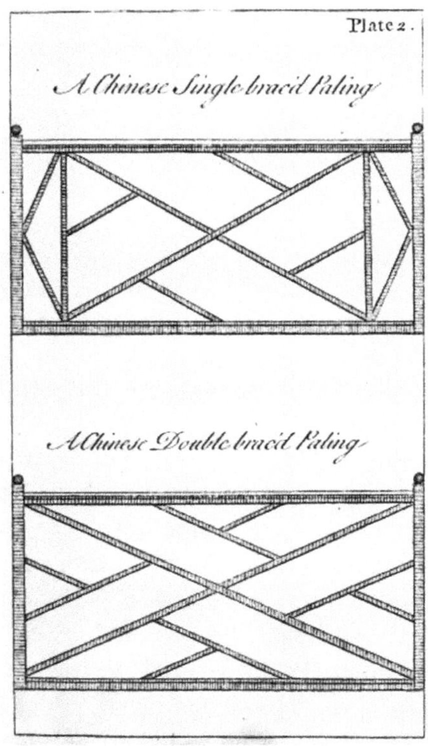

Figure 14.8 'Chinese' staircase design from William Halfpenny's *Rural Architecture in the Chinese Taste*.

a merchant in the Swedish East India Company, twice travelling to Canton in 1743 and 1748 as a 'supercargo' on the ship *Hoppet.* A supercargo was a merchant employed on a vessel by the owner of the cargo it carried, and was responsible for managing the cargo owner's trade throughout a voyage. Four years later in 1761, Chambers started to build the Great Pagoda at Kew for the Princess Augusta. The pagoda was completed in 1762 and has been viewed as the most structurally ambitious chinoiserie building in eighteenth-century Europe. As such, it quickly achieved far-reaching fame. As Aldous Bertram argues, '[t]hat England's most celebrated royal garden should have been a Chinese building serves to remind us that chinoiserie was a fashion of great power and durability'.[26] The erection of the Great Pagoda coincides broadly with the approximate dates of the installation of 'Chinese' staircases at Bishopsgate House and Trefeilir as the trend for Chinese interior decoration was coming to an end, and perhaps lends further credence to Bertram's claim, and weight to the suggestion that wealthy households in Wales were following English trends in fashion at this time.

'Along English lines'

While the current dearth of detailed scholarship on eighteenth-century Welsh interiors may at first suggest that Wales was untouched by these developments, it may be argued that in the 1700s the Welsh elite were modelling their homes along English lines, and following fashions for architecture and interior decoration that were popular with the upper class across Britain rather than being influenced by, or limited to, geographical location and trends. Lord Uxbridge's decision to task well-known architect James Wyatt with the renovation of both his ancestral home in Staffordshire and the family's summer residence in Anglesey may support this interpretation. In addition, at all three properties in this study the installation of a 'Chinese' staircase was part of a scheme to create fashionable houses that could compete with the houses of wealthy contemporaries and peers: Tan-yr-Allt was constructed in the popular Palladian style and was likely designed by a Master Builder, while renovation work was undertaken in the mid-eighteenth century at both Trefeilir and Bishopsgate House to modernize the interiors, including the installation of staircases in the 'Chinese' taste, that were likely influenced by books published in London, and distributed widely across England.

Conclusion: The East India Company and 'Chinese' staircases

Each of the unique staircases examined in this chapter appears in wealthy households in north-west Wales between 1755 and c.1760, when the vogue for interior design "partly after the Chinese manner" was at its peak. Despite the tease of a connection to the Pagets at Plas Newydd, who were early investors in, and continuing supporters of, the EIC, there is no material evidence to connect the appearance of 'Chinese' staircases at Tan-yr-Allt, Bishopsgate House or Trefeilir directly with the EIC either through individuals, families or trade. However, in the mid-eighteenth century all three households were in the possession of wealthy local landowners, who had good connections with the elite of Britain through marriage, politics and social station or occupation. The fashionable and affluent families in Britain at that time were spending money on renovating and refurbishing their homes, fitting out ancestral houses and summer residences alike with the newest and most fashionable goods available in a market that was growing not just in size, but in the types and variety of goods available. Consumer appetites for the novel and unique were inevitably influenced by the influx of goods from around the world, and in this instance, by aesthetics and material goods being imported from China by the EIC.

Sketches of buildings, people and objects by those who had travelled to China on EIC business, alongside painted porcelain, Chinese silk and Chinese art all made their way into Britain and into the consciousness of the British public, through the EIC. Designers such as William Halfpenny, alongside the more celebrated Thomas Chippendale and Sir William Chambers, took these things as inspiration and produced some of the earliest catalogues of furniture, featuring many items 'in the Chinese taste'. Although the 'barbarous gaudy goût of the Chinese' was not received warmly by contemporary cultural critics, it was nonetheless an incredibly popular style that led to many wealthy homeowners purchasing 'Chinese' goods for their homes.[27] In north-west Wales, the British craze for China manifested in particular in the form of the 'Chinese' staircase. As with many local trends, it is likely that the trend started at one house with other local homeowners then mimicking the style in their own houses. While the earliest known surviving occurrence of a 'Chinese' staircase in the region is at Tan-yr-Allt in Bangor, it is not possible to conclude that this was indeed the first to be built: it may simply be the earliest extant example of which we are currently aware.

It is equally possible that a local craftsman sparked the trend for 'Chinese' staircases by adding the design to his repertoire, probably though exposure to works by Halfpenny, Chippendale and Chambers. However, at the time of writing it is not possible to determine who the manufacturer of each of the staircases was, or if the business was a local one.

It must also be noted that the EIC's influence on 'Chinese' staircases across Britain does not end when the trend becomes outmoded, and nor does it end at the British border: 'Chinese' staircases are an interior design phenomenon found across the former British Empire, appearing in wealthy homes in the wider United Kingdom, for example at Wolverton Manor on the Isle of Wight, as well as further afield in places like Bohemia Farm and Sotterley Plantation in Maryland, USA and St. Nicholas Abbey in Barbados.[28] The staircases at these far-flung properties were mostly installed in the late eighteenth or early nineteenth century, and it has been suggested that they were removed from their original settings in British homes when they became unfashionable and transported overseas alongside other items of outmoded furniture. In this way, the EIC's influence on the material culture of the home, and 'Chinese' staircases in particular, reached farther than might be expected and extended beyond the brief decade when the fashion for all things China was at its peak.

15
The intimate trade of Alexander Hall

Salmon and slaves in Scotland and Sumatra, c.1745–1765

Ellen Filor[1]

'I shall follow your Advice in not making haste to get Rich which to my Sorrow is out of my Power', the East India Company (EIC) writer Alexander Hall wrote from Sumatra in 1755 to his sister in Scotland. Hall blamed his misfortune on 'my Losses at Sea, the Heavy Duties laid on by our Masters at Madrass and withall a Dull Trade [which] are very bad circumstances for me and make my Hopes of Reaching an overgrown fortune or even a moderate Competency at a great distance'.[2] Hall's struggle to gain a 'competency' and get 'rich' in a far-flung colony is a useful starting point from which to explore the 'dull trade' East India Company servants took part in during the eighteenth century. Hall's life story, recreated through the letters he sent to and received from his family, details resistance by the indigenous population, warfare between European imperial powers and climatic problems that dogged his attempt to make a 'competency' and return to Scotland rich. His career trajectory from rural Scotland to insecure Sumatra offers further support to the now well-worn narrative of how Scots dominated the East India Company.[3] Hall, however, not only benefitted from these networks of Scottish patronage but also sought to construct a sense of 'Scottishness' in Sumatra through the goods he had sent from home. These goods, ranging from newspapers and salmon to slaves and gold, point to a complex interplay of nostalgic and economic concerns that informed Hall's trading practices. Looking at these practices and Hall's shipping of goods between colony and metropole gives access not only to the economic benefits (or not) of an Indian career but also the emotional baggage of such trade.

The East India Company had outposts (sometimes held only briefly) in places as far apart as the Ambon Island in the east, St Helena in the south and Aden in the west. Among these remote but important outposts of the Company we can count Sumatra. The island was of interest to the English from the very foundation of the EIC. The first voyage of the English East India Company, undertaken by James Lancaster in 1601, stopped at the Sumatran port of Aceh.[4] The island was of strategic importance as a bridge between the Bay of Bengal and the China Sea.[5] In terms of trade, Sumatra was significant primarily for pepper, providing 42 per cent of the 103,908,000 pounds of pepper consumed in Britain between 1711 and 1760.[6] However, as Anne Lindsey Reber has stated, 'From a commercial viewpoint, the Benkulen settlement was never a success.'[7] Nor did this profitability improve in the second half of the eighteenth century, when pepper sales rarely exceeded the massive Company outlay on civil servants, soldiers and slaves.[8] Instead, the British maintained a colony in Sumatra to prevent a Dutch monopoly over the pepper trade, fearing that the profits would allow the Dutch to maintain a Navy that could threaten the power of the British. These concerns of war and trade play out in Hall's letters, demonstrating the domestic impact of global structures on an individual civil servant and the objects he circulated.

The second half of the eighteenth century has long been seen as a period when EIC servants made vast fortunes through private trade. Historians such as P. J. Marshall, George McGilvary and Tillman Nechtman have detailed the hundreds of thousands of pounds that Company men remitted to Britain.[9] Such claims have also been made for Europeans stationed at Sumatra. K. N. Chaudhuri has argued that Bencoolen was 'the inefficient, unprofitable, and corrupt settlement *par excellence*'.[10] Through his reading, it was the individual European civil servants who benefitted from colonial trade in Sumatra. However, if there were fortunes to be made in Sumatra, Hall did not benefit from them. By looking to a distant and (relatively) unprosperous British colony, this chapter will illuminate new ways of looking at Company service and the compromises it required to gain a competency.

Hall's biography and attempts at trade offer insight into how material goods structured imperial service economically and emotionally. Indeed, British life in mainland India has long been seen as shaped by a multitude of servants and luxury objects.[11] However, focusing on mainland India, especially Bengal, threatens to project an unrepresentative picture of luxury and prosperity of the lives led by civil servants in the colonies. In Sumatra, domestic life was far rougher for Company men. Early British buildings in Bencoolen, as A. G. Harfield has demonstrated, were not only highly fortified but with great frequency were attacked by foreign powers and razed by earthquakes.[12] York Fort, for example, was finished in 1685 and abandoned some 35 years after it was established. Fort Marlborough, built between 1709 and 1716, was even shorter lived, burnt to the ground by the indigenous population in 1724, forcing the British to flee. When the British returned a year later, they rebuilt the Fort again. These vicissitudes of climate and revolt meant that Hall's domestic life was defined by the military and lived within military buildings. In the face of this militarized domestic space, Hall sought other means of comfort for his rabid homesickness. Objects were central to the ways he overcame this exile from his homeland. His family sent him objects from Scotland, from necessities like towels and sheets to more indulgent items like wine and salmon. By tracing these more intimate objects between metropole and colony, a more textured picture of Company everyday life and trade can emerge.

The 'things' that the Hall family circulated between Scotland and Sumatra included enslaved people. Sumatra could not have functioned without slave labour. Introduced from Madagascar and St Helena, these slaves were used to harvest pepper, build forts, tend ill Europeans and act as guards. As Frenise A. Logan has detailed, slaves were perceived as a necessity because of the high death rate of the English soldiers who had been previously sent to work on the island.[13] As early as 1687 the Board of Directors refused to commit any more Englishmen to the island: 'For wee cannot be so unkind to our countrymen as to send many more to a place which wee know has prov'd a Grave to so many of them already'.[14] As well as importing African slaves in 1687, convicted thieves were also sent to Sumatra and were to remain there as 'slaves' for the rest of their lives.[15] Indeed, this practice of transporting convicts to Sumatra and making them slaves continued beyond the end of the slave trade in 1807. In 1825, a correspondent to the *Bengal Hukara* wrote to condemn the practice introduced by Stamford Raffles in the 1810s of what was essentially a continence of the slave trade by calling Africans 'debtors' and making them indentured labourers.[16] It is against this long history of trade in people and forced labour in Sumatra that British attempts to colonize such an inhospitable and dangerous island must be read.

Alexander Hall's familiar letters give us access to these intimate histories of slavery and trade. As Kate Teltscher has argued, family letters should be used alongside the official sources in the India Office Records at the British Library.[17] Hall's life and letters offer a more personal, intimate account of life in Sumatra than previous overarching histories of

East India Company involvement with the island afford.[18] Reading Hall's career through his letters explicitly for the 'things' he traded between Scotland and Sumatra gives us access to the primary way Hall sought to maintain intimacy with his family in Europe. From his first letters from London in the 1740s, describing borrowing his brother's coat, to his shipping of Scottish salmon to Sumatra towards the end of his life, material things impacted Hall's life in multifarious and complex ways. Following these letters along the shipping routes Hall used (from his trip out via St Helena to his escape as a prisoner of war via Madras) gives us access to multiple colonies belonging to multiple European nations. Through examining Hall's trading practices, this chapter opens up a discussion about how the (infra)structure of the East India Company was co-opted by its servants for economic gain and emotional sustenance.

Entering the Company service

Alexander Hall (c.1731/2–1764) was the youngest son of James Hall, 2nd Baronet of Dunglass (d.1742) and Margaret Pringle (d.1756), daughter of Sir John Pringle of Stichill (1662–1721). Little is known of Alexander's early life. His father was a substantial landowner and noted 'improver' in the Scottish Lothians.[19] He had four elder brothers whose careers ran the gamut of employments open to Scottish elite men. James (1724–1745) was studying to be a minister when he died, Robert (d.1763) was an officer in the 37th Regiment of Foot, William (d.1800) an officer in the Engineers before inheriting his uncle's lands, and John (d.1776) was trained in the law before inheriting the family estates. Alexander Hall's position in the East India Company was secured through his eldest brother John. With the Jacobite uprising of 1745, large numbers of the Scottish gentry raised an army in support of Charles Edward Stuart's claim to the British throne. In comparison to the rebellious Highlands, however, the Lowlands remained relatively loyal to the British state.[20] Here, the Halls were no exception. In the aftermath of the Jacobite uprising of 1745, Alexander's brother John was one of the Grand Jury for the trial in 1748 of the Jacobite rebels at Edinburgh. Alexander wrote to him, 'I went to Hume-Campbell to whom I propos'd my going to the East Indies he was pretty sure he cou'd find Interest to get me into the Company's'.[21] Hugh Hume-Campbell, third Earl of Marchmont (1708–94), was a great landowner in the Halls' native Berwickshire and a staunch supporter of the Union, helping defend Berwick in 1745 and supporting the actions of the Duke of Cumberland in suppressing the rebellion. Throughout his time in the Company, Hall relied on these local and anti-Jacobite men for patronage: Lord Elibank (1703–78) and Sir Lawrence Dundas (c.1710–81), for example, were applied to for an exchange to Bengal in the 1760s.[22]

While empire, especially Jamaica and India, had long been seen as a place to reform Jacobites and integrate them into the British state,[23] the fact that positions in the East India Company were given out to reward loyal Scots is less widely known. Indeed, while Jacobites often ended up in the Company army, Hall was rewarded with a civil post, offering a lower likelihood of death and greater pay. The superior nature of his post was one way Hall convinced his mother to let him go to India, arguing 'if I don't go there I will inevitably end up in the Army'.[24] In the year before Hall departed for the subcontinent he bought various items of clothing and began to 'learn to speak not only French but English'.[25] This learning of 'English' was a means for Hall to erase his Scottish accent and integrate himself into the 'English' East India Company, especially pertinent in the aftermath of the Jacobite rebellion.

In November 1750, Hall received word that he had been appointed a factor at Sumatra, which he informed his mother was 'as much as I could expect'.[26] During the eighteenth century, Sumatra appears to have gained a reputation for being a dead-end destination for the ambitious Company servant. In 1770, James Swinton wrote of his relative: 'Tommy Swinton is gone out a writer to Bencoolen, & sailed about a Month ago in the Harcort, being all my Brothers Interest exerted to the utmost cou'd procure for him'.[27] The period between Hall's appointment to Sumatra and his departure to the territory from Kent was only three weeks. Hall's letters during this brief juncture worry about his outfitting for India and pester his brothers for money to invest in the East. In the midst of this tumult, Hall wrote to his eldest brother John that 'I never was in such a hurry in my Life. I was last night at Court in one of Willie's Coat's [sic]. Direct my Sheets & c., to Mr Gilbert Eliot's care Searcher at Gravesend & mind some Table napkins. Tell the Captn who carries it to have the parcell [sic] at hand when he passes Gravesend if it be John Fergusson I am sure he'll oblige me much'.[28] This extract suggests how preparations for India were dependent on family and friendship networks: Hall wore his brother William's coat for his interview by the Court of Directors while responsibility for the shipping of his sheets from Scotland to Kent was given to Fergusson, a family friend. This was due to financial necessity as London was too expensive for Hall, and he asked his sister for cheaper towels and sheets to be sent from Scotland.[29] Hall's eldest brother John covered the £170 cost of kitting him out. Nor were all of Hall's goods for himself. The bill Alexander presented to John read, 'Passage £40, Wine

£35, "Wearing Apparel &c. and a 1000 Small things some to sell, some for my own use"'.[30] In exchange for covering his costs, Alexander promised to try to provide John with 'Gay Pyots pink Nutmegs', and black and white pepper from Batavia.[31] This kind of reciprocal trade suggests the role of family and friendship networks in gaining, funding, and kitting out Hall for an Indian career.

Life in Sumatra

Hall set sail for the subcontinent in December 1750, eventually reaching Sumatra over six months after he departed from Kent. His first impressions were favourable. As he wrote to his uncle: 'I was much Surprised on coming ashore here, to see so fine a Country after being told so many bad Accounts of it by the Jack Tars who generaly [sic] do not say any thing Good of any other Country except of Old England'.[32] This positive response was informed by the pleasant weather. He wrote to reassure his mother: 'The Climate here you'll no doubt think, is unspeakably hot, & unhealthy, but I do assure you, it is not warmer, than I wou'd desire, except in the middle of the day, & for Healthiness, it is allowed by all here, to be as good as any place in India'.[33] Despite Hall's reassurances to his mother and the reliance on slaves for manual labour, there was a high death rate of civil servants in Sumatra, mainly due to disease and war. From the beginning of 1760 to April 1762, over a third of the civil servants, military men, surgeons and artificers at the Fort died.[34] One of Hall's contemporaries Robert Hay commented from Fort Marlborough in 1775: 'I shall be glad to quitt [sic] India It becoming Irksome to me being like one who has outlived all his friends and matters begin to wear but a bad aspect'.[35]

Balancing health against his prospects of wealth was one of Hall's primary struggles in Sumatra. As well as being more positive than most observers about Sumatra's climate,[36] Hall's early descriptions of the island itself were similarly favourable: 'It is hereabouts almost quite clear of Woods & fine Champaign Country for about 8 or 10 Miles from the Shore & a perpetual verdure'.[37] However, this enthusiastic response was short lived. By January 1753, he was asking his mother to exert her power to get him removed to Bengal.[38] Hall fluctuated between loathing and love of Sumatra. When he was sent to Natal later in 1753, his mood brightened due to the possibilities available for trading natural resources:

> There us [sic] a great Trade & it is the fountain Head of Gold, Benjamen & Camphire all very fine. The Gold is taken about a days

> Journey up the Country, by navigation & most of it 22 or 23 Carats fine The Benjamen, (I suppose I need not tell you) ouses [sic] out, of a large Tree, the best of it is full of Lumps & Veins as White as Ivory.[39]

While in Hall's description fortune oozes out of the ground, this apparent wealth of natural resources was somewhat illusionary. Madras civil servant Claud Russell (1733–1820) wrote to Hall, 'The Wastage in melting of Gold dust, (particularly the coarse sort from Padang which loses sometimes 9 pr Cent) is so great, that unless the Touch can be very correctly ascertained, it is a precarious Article to deal in'.[40] Such ephemeral economic reward led Hall to renew his call to be sent to Bengal. He wrote to his brother: 'I think on the decayed State of this Coast, where I assure you there are now small Hopes of a Gentleman's picking up a Competency. I must therefore beg of you if its possible, to get me Removed to Bengal & leave you & the rest of my friends to apply for me in the best method they judge proper'.[41]

If Hall's financial fortunes fluctuated, his dislike of the indigenous population was a constant theme in his letters home. He wrote soon after his arrival to his mother: 'the only objection I have to it, is the want of Trade which is owing to the Natives of the Country who although they have all the advantages with regard to Sail &c. yet they are so very indolent as to neglect their own Sustenance in a manner'.[42] This construction of Sumatrans as lazy is a common form of asserting the racial superiority of Europeans in the Georgian period.[43] It also allowed Hall to present himself as an industrious trader in contrast. Even while Hall was positive about the climate and scenery of Sumatra, he cast the indigenous population as lazy and savage, a construction that allowed him to position himself as industrious and civilized.

Hall's thwarted desire to make a 'competency' along with the omnipresent risk of death were made worse by the near constant threat of attack from Dutch, Malay or French forces. In 1755 he joked to his sister: 'So that you have once prophesied true that our penknives are turned to Swords & our Pepper Corns into cannon Balls but however now as we have got the advantage I hope every thing will return to its primitive state'.[44] Any peace was short lived. In 1760, two French ships under the command of Count D'Estaing took Alexander Hall prisoner at Natal before going on to attack Fort Marlborough. Hall and many of his fellow factors were sent to the Dutch settlement at Padang, some 300 miles south-west of Bencoolen, and remained there 'without any means of Subsistence' for five months.[45] While there, the British men tried to get on a Dutch boat to reach the Coromandel Coast but were informed that the Dutch East India Company did not give passage to foreigners.[46] Instead, Hall and William Wyatt, the two most senior civil servants, petitioned the Governors of Padang for 2,800 Spanish Dollars to purchase a boat.[47] They left Padang by this boat on 25 August 1760 and reached Masulipatam on 30 October. They stayed there until the end of the monsoon season before embarking on the short journey to Madras. Before they reached Madras, however, the vessel was wrecked near Nellore, 'where everything was lost but Cloaths [sic] and a Chest of Treasure'. After this misfortune, the nearby Nabob Nasum Boolee Chan gave them palanquins, camels and coolies to carry them to Madras.[48]

Despite his repeated petitioning of George Pigot, the Governor at Madras, Hall could not get exchanged at Madras and freed from the terms of his parole. Instead, finding he could not work, Hall decided to return to Europe. As Linda Colley has suggested in *Captives,* the widespread imperial warfare during this period often saw British individuals 'captured' literally and figuratively in much bigger historical events. Her insight that these British failures represented humiliating stumbling blocks in the wider imperial project allows us to better understand how Hall sought to overcome the indignity of having been captured.[49] For Hall, being captured was yet another failure to be placed alongside his inability to generate a fortune or carve out a successful imperial career. While this incident further interrupted Hall's desire to make a 'competency' it did, however, help reverse his increasing estrangement from his family after an absence of twelve years from Britain. Hall was conflicted about the wisdom of returning to Britain, writing from London: 'Already I have drawn this comfort from my Voyage, that, were it not for the Pleasure of being with you & the rest of my friends in Scotland, I would immediately transport my self again to India, for I am heartily tired of—even London.'[50] This dislike of London was increased by Hall's engagement with the serpentine windings of the Company's bureaucracy. In March 1762, he submitted a minute to the Directors, requesting that they pay off the 2,800 Spanish Dollars he had borrowed from the Dutch at Padang. Eventually, the Directors appear to have grudgingly agreed, even while they refused to pay for Hall's return passage to India.[51] Hall was released from the conditions of his parole in June 1762, but he decided to wait until the following year before returning to India, 'to spare my self the Trouble & Risk of my Health in resettling the West Coast & to be with my friends once more in my Life'.[52]

Before he left London in 1762, Hall petitioned Lord Shelburne (1737–1805), an MP well-connected to the Company, to be transferred to the Bengal Presidency.[53] He was refused on the grounds that his knowledge of Sumatra was too valuable for the Company.[54] Hall did not give up this attempt for an exchange to Bengal and wrote to his brother John from India:

> On account of the great loss of Companies Servants at Bengal lately, I have renewed my request to go there as I daresay they will be send[in]g Gentlemen in pretty high Rank. I have wrote it to (dont be angry) Ld M[archmon]t & Mr Crompton who assisted me before ... I also begg of you to see what you can do, to get me removed from our Cursed Coast. Its true there's Trouble's [sic] at Bengal, but its good fishing in Muddy Water.[55]

His brother replied, stating he would attempt to get him an exchange but expressed his misgivings about Bengal, which he believed 'more unhealthy' and 'more dangerous than any station in all India'.[56]

Before Hall's return, the Company did instigate some changes in the face of the French attack on Sumatra. The council at Madras had written to London in 1761 that 'the Papers delivered in by Govr Carter have been examined, tis thought they put too great a Confidence in the Mallays', continuing 'Slaves will be much wanted at West Coast when the place is resettled'.[57] Duncan Clerk assured Hall from Scotland in 1764: 'I find the Company are resolved to take better care of you, if another war should break out; There will soon be a considerable military force in India'.[58] Hall never succeeded in getting a transfer to Bengal and instead returned to Fort Marlborough in September 1764. Nor did he benefit from the Company's 'reforms' when he returned to Sumatra, dying there just over two months after his arrival.

Tinned salmon and the *Caledonian Mercury*: importing Scotland to Sumatra

While an outline of Hall's career grants insight into the trade (however unsuccessful) and tribulations of a civil servant in Sumatra, this official biography can tell us only part of Hall's imperial life. Throughout Hall's time in Sumatra his fondness for Scotland and his homeland remained. In part, this enduring affiliation reflected the sheer number of Scots entering the Company during this period. Of the journey to India in 1763, he wrote to his brother John that 'we had no less than 28 Messmates, mostly Scots'.[59] In Sumatra, Hall's letters back to his relatives in Scotland were littered with references to other Scottish Company men. In 1755, he listed four other Scots who were in Sumatra in a letter to his sister.[60] These Scottish networks simultaneously maintained Hall's connection to Scotland as well as supporting him in various ways: Charles Stuart offered him accommodation in Calcutta, the Hay brothers from Drumelzier, Peeblesshire executed his will, and Captain Mackleish shipped him claret wine.[61]

Beyond his fellow East India Company servants, the love of his homeland was kept alive by the letters exchanged with his family and friends. He assured his brother at the very beginning of his career: 'You know I cant write you any news, these I shall expect from You, even to the minutest [sic] Article, for you may Sure I shall gape for them.'[62] While epistolary correspondence was the primary means for Hall to maintain connections to his family, it could take six months for a letter to reach Sumatra, meaning the contents often felt out of date. Hall wrote in response to a letter from his mother in 1754: 'You write me a long letter of news, which you may be sure gives me vast pleasure, I can only say I rejoiced at some & sorry for others; Reflections are lost at such a distance of Time & place'.[63] Letters could also get lost. Hall wrote despondently in 1757: 'I should now be more particular was I not almost certain this Bitt [sic] of Paper will be buffetted [sic] about the World and God knows when, come to your Hands'.[64] The weakening of emotional ties over the time he was in Sumatra and the death of his mother in 1756 also led to Hall corresponding with fewer people. In 1764, shortly before his own death, Hall described a dream to his brother John: 'I dreamed of the Two Youngsters last night & don't write to any body now, but you'.[65] The spiritual link of Hall's dreams and more physical one of epistolary correspondence suggest how family networks and intimacy were maintained in empire. These dreams offered an instant connection that could otherwise take over a year to bridge with letters.

Newspapers sent by his relatives from Scotland likewise maintained this link. Hall wrote from Natal four years after his arrival in Sumatra to his brother John: 'My dissappointment [sic] in not having the Caledonian Mercury (by which we call the Scots Magazines) was very great and I believe had I kept a Collections in this Part of the World, my Customers would not all have left me'.[66] Here, his fellow Scots were both his customers and his community. This use of national newspapers attached Hall to an imagined reading (commoditized) community, akin to the nationalist imaginary outlined by Benedict Anderson in *Imagined Communities*. As Anderson argued: 'The date at the top of the newspaper, the single most important emblem on it, provides the essential—the steady onward clocking of homogeneous, empty time'.[67] According to Anderson's analysis, this simultaneous reading of national newspapers created an 'imagined community'. However, for Hall, receiving the newspapers some six months after they had been published, this reading was near-simultaneous only with his fellow Scottish EIC men. Hall's reading of the Scottish newspapers cannot be conceived as 'homogeneous' time, rendering him part of 'a solid community moving steadily through history'.[68] Instead, his position in a precarious British territory, connected to Scotland by a haphazard postal system, meant Hall was outside of this national time. This temporal dissonance demonstrates his insecure connection to Scotland and the instability of the tactics he employed to maintain these swiftly disintegrating relationships.

Food appears to have been another way for Hall to maintain his connection to Britain and sometimes specifically to Scotland. In a letter to his brother William, he indulged in the fantasy of teleportation: 'Had I such a Magicians Rod as you mentiond I would make better use of it than you. You speak of making only one visit here. I would be in England three times a day viz Breakfast dinner & Supper, to eat bread of which we have none on this Coast'.[69] He went on to list the exorbitant price of flour and beer, over three times more expensive in Sumatra than in England.[70] It was perhaps this expense and captive market that encouraged Hall to pioneer his own form of tinning and preserving food. After he was forced to return to London to be exchanged as a prisoner of war, he asked his brother to send eggs, salmon and portable soup from Scotland.[71] The success of these endeavours to package and send Scottish food abroad varied. While portable soup, a powdery substance akin to modern-day stock cubes, was a relatively conventional foodstuff to ship abroad, salmon and eggs were less so. Hall reported from India:

> My Salmon from Cockburn of Berwick, turns out well tho' it had not very fair play, for I told him to put it in Double Cases, its true he did so, but he did not fill up the interstice with a Salt Pickle as I desired him, besides there were some of the Cases which would not hold in some Salt Beef Pickle I poured in, aboard ship during the Voyage. I dare say he may sell many Hundreds Kitts if its done properly. Pray send me out Four 1/2 Kitts every year. Let them also be sent to George Fairholme. The Torwoodlee Eggs would not keep cross the Line, they did not stick much, but they were very much evaporated & of a stinking Straw Taste.[72]

Hall attached a very precise sense of place to his description of the food – both spoilt and unspoilt. Even while economics and monetary returns remain at the forefront of his mind – Cockburn 'may sell many Hundreds Kitts if its done properly' (presumably to Scots in India) – the eggs are 'Torwoodlee' and the salmon 'Berwick'. The sense of place Hall attached to food becomes a means of situating himself in the geography of home: salmon tinned and transported, sometimes unspoilt, relocated his local geography of Scotland to Sumatra.[73] Even so, Hall's importing of Scottish food was scarcely more successful than his previous attempts to export gold or camphire. That his Torwoodlee eggs were 'stinking' and his salmon tasted of beef shows how tenuous a connection these perishable objects could grant him to his homeland. The manner in which economics and sentiment overlapped in Hall's letters and schemes suggests the difficulty of separating out the two. The potential trade in salmon becomes a form of sustenance – literally, figuratively and economically – connecting Hall to the landscape of his birth, even if it was a connection that 'evaporated' all too easily.

Sex and slaves in Sumatra and Scotland

Hall did not only seek intimacy in words, dreams and food while in Sumatra. He also, like many Europeans during this period, had sex with at least one Indian woman.[74] This relationship was detailed in his will, and it was only by reading the document after Alexander's death that his sister found out about his illegitimate, mixed-race daughter. She asked Alexander's executor Robert Hay to send the child to Scotland if thought appropriate.[75] Isabella's brother John harboured more doubts and wrote to Hay inquiring whether Alexander's daughter 'is Tawney Colourd or not'. This concern about skin colour informed whether she should be sent to Scotland. If 'Tawney' she should be kept in India 'where her colour is no detainment', but if 'she is of the ordinary Complexion of this country I dare say my sister would be glad to have her here to exert herself in the care of her Education but if she be of a colour different from our's it would be making her miserable to bring to a place where she would always be particular'.[76] Robert Hay responded, without making reference to skin colour: 'The known regard your Brother had for it put it out of all doubt with me the sending of it'.[77] Hay and Isabella Hall kept up a steady correspondence over the next decade until Hay's return to Peeblesshire in 1777. These letters display real concern for Peggy on both sides while revealing the manifold tensions that sending her to Scotland engendered. Tracing Peggy and her maid's journey from Sumatra to the Borders demonstrates the 'black presence' in rural Scotland during the mid-eighteenth century, suggesting the role that the East India Company had in instigating 'counter-flows to colonialism'.[78]

Peggy was also one of the few material 'things' that Alexander Hall left behind – he made little money in Sumatra. She was born at Madras in November 1761, conceived during Hall's period under parole when he was unable to work, and was christened at Fort Marlborough in 1762.[79] Sending her to Scotland was one of the first difficulties that Hay and Isabella had to negotiate. They sent her in a ship under the care of a man named Braham who was returning to England.[80] By 1770, Isabella could claim Peggy was 'much grown since she came to this Country' and a year later further on that 'she continues to thrive and grow vastly, and is much improved in her colour tho she still speaks like a Foreigner which Im [sic] surprised at as she came here so young'.[81] Here, Scotland is perceived as a country where Peggy can 'thrive and grow vastly' in contrast to her stunted height in Sumatra. Even so, Dunglass could not cure all ills: Peggy continued to speak 'like a Foreigner'. By 1773, Isabella reported that Peggy had outgrown the teaching at the local school and was to be sent to a boarding school in Edinburgh.[82] Isabella perceived education as one means of mitigating Peggy's 'foreignness' in accent, displaying how Peggy's mixed-raceness could be overcome by Scottish climate and education.

If Peggy Hall was an enigma to her Scottish family, then the nurse 'Betty' caused more practical problems. Henry Idell, who brought Peggy from London to Dunglass, listed the following objects 'belonging' to the child:

> One Trunk contg wearing Apparell
> One Pair of Gold Earrings
> One Pair of Gold Sleeve Buttons
> One Gold Ring
> One Slave Woman named Betty
> One chest of Wearing Apparell belg to Betty[83]

The casual listing of 'Betty' as 'belonging' to the young Hall casts the woman as an 'object', even as it acknowledges her ability in turn to own property such as wearing apparel. It suggests that the enslaved could be perceived of as an exotic and valuable object just as a 'gold ring' or clothing from Surat. This translated into Betty being unable to dictate when she could return to Sumatra; Idell wrote 'The Nurse is a Slave & must return to India'.[84] As Margot Finn and Emma Rothschild have demonstrated, slaves and emancipated slaves were a part of Scottish society during the eighteenth century. Both have suggested the dislocations that slaves caused in terms of how slave-ownership conflicted and overlapped with Enlightenment thought, the Scottish legal systems and family life.[85] While the Halls apparently had few qualms about the moral or legal dilemmas surrounding slavery, Betty nonetheless caused problems of a more mundane sort. Namely, the Halls worried about how to ship Betty back to her master in Sumatra. While Idell was supposed to organize Betty's return to Sumatra, by September 1768 the Halls had heard nothing more. Instead, Sir John organized a man called Neilson to carry her by boat to London and then petitioned Braham to get her passage on a ship to India: 'you will have the Satisfaction of doing a charitable action to the Poor Woman who is pining to be home – I believe she belongs to Mr Robert Hay and I suppose he will be glad to have his servant again'.[86]

However, Braham failed to find Betty a passage back to Sumatra, and Isabella wrote that 'I'm affraid [sic] we shall be obliged to bring her back from London again which I shou'd be sorry for, as the poor Woman, wishd much to be home, was of no use here, and probably woud be missed in your service'.[87] Henry Idell resurfaced in the Spring of the next year and finally arranged Betty's passage. She reached Sumatra safely, and in January 1771 Isabella Hall wrote to Robert Hay that 'we were all vastly glade [sic] to Betty the black Maids safe arrival in India and that her being so long away was no unconvenience [sic]'.[88] Some five years later, shortly before Hay was due to leave Sumatra, Isabella stated 'I would wish to make a little present to Betty the black maid that here & beg you will take the trouble to give her two or three Guineas or what you think proper and place it to my account'.[89] Throughout these exchanges, 'Betty' is granted no voice. Indeed, her construction as near object to be shipped to Scotland and back to India is evidence of her relative powerlessness in both colony and metropole. After Hay left Sumatra, Betty disappears from the historical record. Peggy, however, cast a longer shadow over the Hall family papers. As Sally Wilson has detailed, Peggy was mentioned as a regular visitor to Dunglass as late as the 1790s.[90] She died in 1800 and was buried in Greyfriars Churchyard in Edinburgh, leaving property worth £1,400.[91]

Conclusion

The Halls' connection to India did not end with Peggy. When Sir James Hall, 4th Baronet remodelled Dunglass House in 1807, he decorated the drawing room with Chinese wallpaper and lacquered cabinets.[92] Such decorating fits within Nechtman's analysis of objects shipped home by nabobs from India: 'These objects marginalized the comfortable, domestic, and British world, replacing it with luxury objects from imperial India.'[93] Against these 'luxury objects' this chapter has placed the everyday objects and enslaved people who circulated between colony and metropole, a trade which, while not luxurious, was nonetheless equally disruptive to Scottish domestic life. By tracing the official and unofficial life of Alexander Hall in Sumatra, new insights into the difficulty of trade in Sumatra and making it pay (especially in comparison to a far more lucrative position in Bengal) emerge. Alexander Hall offers on one level a compelling example of Scots' dominance of the EIC in the second half of the eighteenth century. Aided by patronage of local Scottish politicians and landowners as well as his family's loyalty to the British state during the Jacobite revolt, he was able to secure a position in the Company civil service. On another level, the warfare that saw Hall made prisoner and the climate that claimed his life demonstrate the high stakes risk these men took, often for meagre reward. The dislocation Hall felt from Scotland while in Sumatra was eased by the exchange of letters, food and newspapers from Europe. In these objects we find Hall's attempt to recreate Scotland in a foreign land, detailing the nostalgic and quotidian trade of goods that sustained Scottish men in the Company on a domestic level. If Europeans faced hardship, however, this was lessened because of their reliance on slave labour. In the case of Hall, this forced labour was most visible in his domestic life, especially in the case of Betty's care of Hall's mixed-race daughter. The history of Hall, Peggy and Betty should suggest the darker histories and forced labour that lurks behind the beautiful, exotic objects that would come to decorate Dunglass in the nineteenth century.

16
Connecting Britain and India
General Patrick Duff and Madeira

Alistair Mutch

General Patrick Duff (1742–1803) gained his 'competency' through military service in Bengal, aided and supplemented by the wealth garnered in the Madeira wine trade by his uncles and brothers (see Figure 16.1). The continuing legacy of his success is the outstanding court of farm buildings built on his estate of Carnousie, near Turriff, in the historic

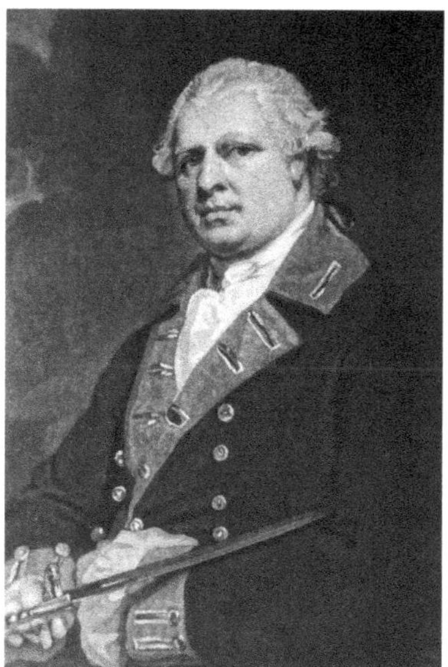

Figure 16.1 Colonel Patrick Duff of the Honourable East India Company's Artillery, by Romney, 1790. Image courtesy of Alistair Mutch.

county of Banffshire in north-east Scotland. His investment in architectural quality, rather than ostentation, and in agricultural buildings, rather than a stately home or urban residence, qualifies the view of 'nabobs' derived from caricatures and fashionable metropolitan society. This chapter examines the agricultural thread which ran through Duff's childhood as the son of a (none too successful) farmer, his deployment of skills in stock management in India, and his participation in the ideology of agricultural improvement back home in Scotland. As well as bringing out this neglected theme of British imperialism in India, Duff's life also illuminates some other aspects of eighteenth-century imperial service. It adds a further example to what we already know about the children born from relationships with Indian women and brought back to Britain. A rather lesser appreciated aspect is the role of the island of Madeira both as an important node in the networks connecting the imperial centre with its outposts and as a source of the wine which was so important in helping the British cope with their Indian sojourns. The chapter starts, however, with a closer look at the farm buildings of Mains of Carnousie.[1]

At the heart of the Mains, or home farm, of Carnousie is a magnificent gatehouse (see Figure 16.2). This structure is dated to 1797, so being firmly in the time of Patrick Duff, who held the estate from 1790 to 1803.[2] What is striking about this building is the quality of the masonry work, its deeply undercut and precisely jointed stones contrasting sharply with the rubble construction of most of the rest of the courtyard of farm buildings. While these were obviously designed to meet agricultural needs, there are aspects of the design which compromise the fulfillment of those needs. For example, it would have been more functional to have placed the openings to the cart sheds which sheltered the implements on the outside of the buildings, as in other examples of courtyard steadings in the region. ('Steadings' was the local term for a range of buildings: good examples of external cart openings are at Manar near Inverurie and, still closer, at Forglen Home Farm two miles away from Carnousie).[3] At Carnousie, however, they are on the inside of the courtyard and are distinguished by the same high quality masonry work that features on the gatehouse (see Figure 16.3). Choices have been made, that is, that prioritize aesthetic and symbolic concerns over purely functional ones.

However, it is noticeable that Duff avoided the temptations open to new money, those of ostentation or eccentricity. His building is elegant and restrained, deriving its impact from the quality of the work and the balance of the composition. It shows no influence of the East, with

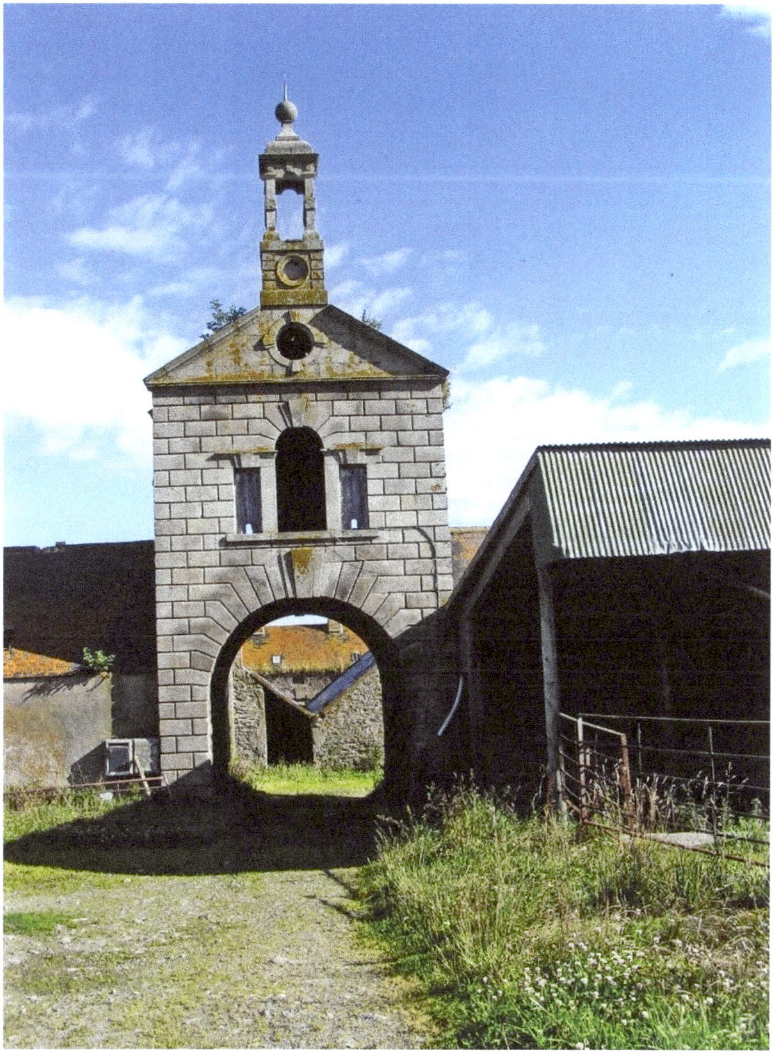

Figure 16.2 Gatehouse, Mains of Carnousie, 1797. Image courtesy of Alistair Mutch.

Duff resisting the temptation, indulged in by other nabobs, to incorporate Indian architectural motifs.[4] This was somebody anxious to display his wealth, but not to shout about it. Indeed, his conservatism can be seen if we place his gatehouse in the local context. Gatehouses with an arched opening and a windowed first floor seem to have been a feature of the entrance to the 'barmkins' or courtyards of service buildings that

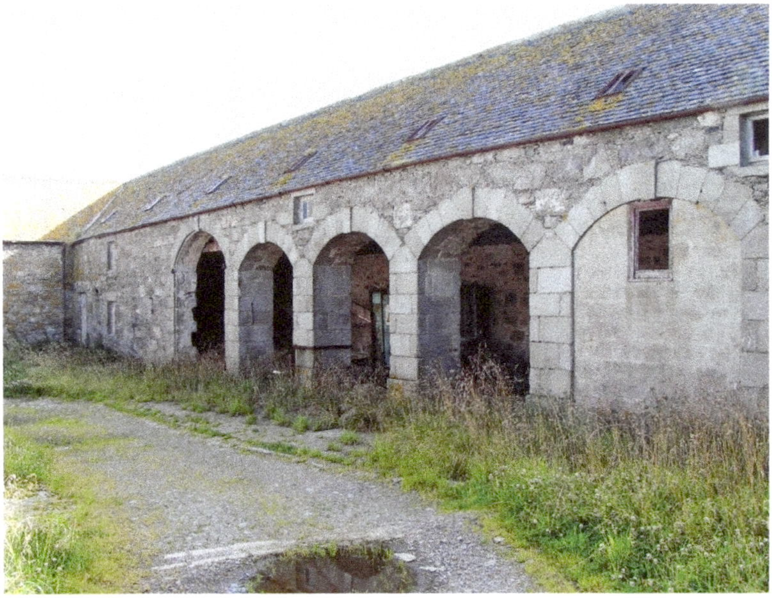

Figure 16.3 Cart arches, Mains of Carnousie. Image courtesy of Alistair Mutch.

surrounded local tower houses. This is certainly the impression one gets from the rare survival of such an entrance at Harthill Castle, near Oyne, Aberdeenshire (see Figure 16.4).[5]

We see here what architectural historians regard as a characteristic Scottish focus on height, something mirrored in the tower house, which was at the centre of Duff's new estate (see Figure 16.5).[6] The tower house's height was coupled with the incorporation of a feature common in the churches of the region, the bellcote. Although having the functional purpose of marking the beginning and end of work periods, this device also connected farm buildings to another dominant local building type.

As agricultural improvement gathered pace in the region in the second half of the eighteenth century, so a model emerged for home farm buildings, one which consisted of a court of buildings entered by a central two-storey gatehouse. The conservatism of Duff's work at Carnousie can be seen if we contrast it with the gatehouse of Delgaty Home Farm (see Figure 16.6), eight miles away and dated by architectural historians at 1768.[7] The remarkable similarities suggest that this was the model for Carnousie, the extra refinement of the latter being given by the wealth available to Duff. How he acquired and repatriated this wealth is detailed in what follows.

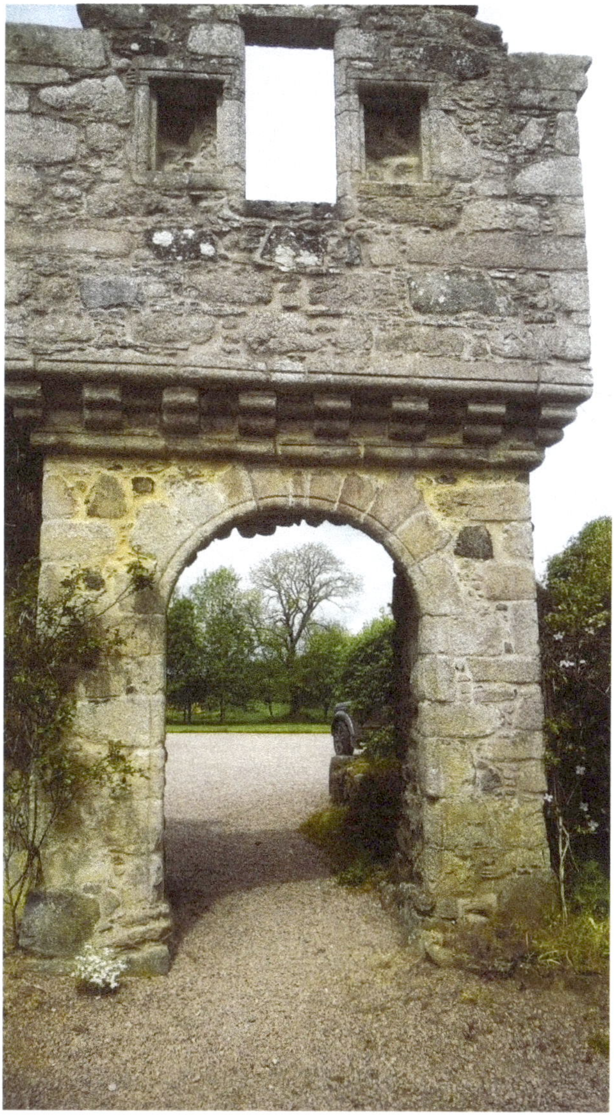

Figure 16.4 Gatehouse, Harthil Castle, Oyne, Aberdeenshire. Image courtesy of Alistair Mutch.

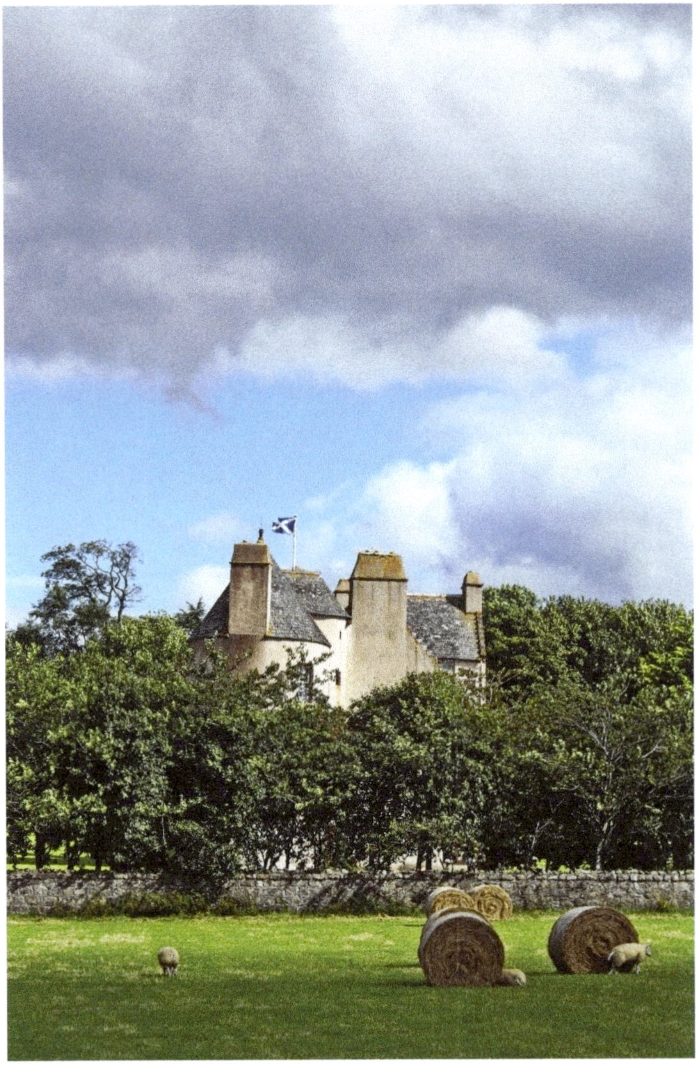

Figure 16.5 Old House of Carnousie. Image courtesy of Alistair Mutch.

Patrick Duff was born in 1742, son of a tenant farmer on unpromising land on the banks of the river Spey in Banffshire.[8] His maternal uncles, James (?1712–90) and Alexander Gordon (1715–97), were successful Madeira wine merchants. James, who was unmarried and childless, provided for the education of his nephews. Two were to enter the service of his Madeira wine business; the remaining three were

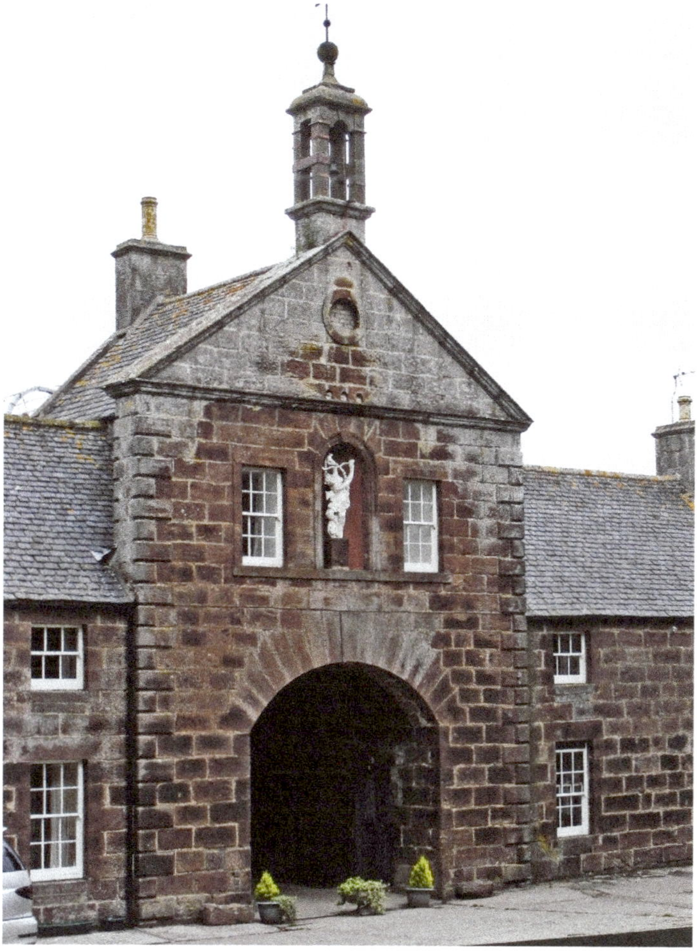

Figure 16.6 Delgaty Home Farm entrance, Turriff, Aberdeenshire. Image courtesy of Alistair Mutch.

destined for military service in India. The eldest was Patrick, who, after initial service in the British Army, transferred to the artillery of the East India Company in 1763. Despite participation in the mutiny of European officers in 1766, Patrick was evidently a competent officer, for he rose through the ranks. His fortune appears to have been made by his command of the Nawab of Oudh's artillery.[9] From the 1780s he was looking to repatriate some of his Indian wealth and invest in a country estate in his native north-east Scotland. He eventually bought the 3,000-acre Carnousie estate near Turriff in 1788. Duff proceeded to invest in works of agricultural improvement, having a magnificent square courtyard steading constructed in 1797. He was involved in local politics, standing unsuccessfully for Parliament in 1795.[10] He had town houses in Banff and Edinburgh and repaired the existing house at Carnousie. Whether Duff would have commissioned a new house (as subsequent owners of the estate did) to be filled with artefacts from India will never be known, as he died in Edinburgh in 1803, aged 61 years.

Rather than concentrating on his military and political exploits, which are recounted elsewhere, this chapter draws on his own letters and other estate papers to focus on Duff's home life in both India and Scotland. His letters were mainly to his brother James and his uncle, also James, and contained a mixture of topics. Material is often duplicated to cover the uncertainty of ships reaching their destinations and was often composed with dates of sailing in mind.[11] Some letters extend to 16 pages, being added to as dates of sailing were put back. 'You are not to expect method or regularity in this letter,' he noted in a letter of 1785, 'I write just what comes uppermost without minding what went before'.[12] While much of their contents are concerned with Duff's prospects of military preferment, they often slip into a more 'domestic' mode, from which we can glean some hints about his memories of home and the material artefacts that he collected.[13] Over time they also give more insight into his important connections with his uncles in Madeira. Although David Hancock has explored in considerable detail the trade of the island especially in the context of colonial America, its key role as a node in the trade and military networks that constituted the relationship between Britain and India has been relatively understated.[14] Duff's letters help bring these networks to life and reveal his links to the wealth generated by trade through the island.

At home in India

Although Patrick made the arduous voyage between India and Britain five times, most of his adult life was spent in India.[15] While on one return visit to Britain in 1774, he married his cousin, Ann Duff (1748–76). She soon died at Madras, however, as he reported to his uncle James Gordon in 1776:

> My last from Madras was giving you the Melancholy account of the death of my wife, I still greatly feel her loss, and I believe no man had ever more reason to regret the death of a wife; for she was possessed of the greatest sweetness of disposition without one

> single fault which I was able to discover in near two years we liv'd together, most of which time she enjoy'd but an indifferent state of health; as my loss is now irretrievable I shall for the future drop the subject.[16]

He was to marry again, in 1794, when as a landed gentleman he married Dorothea, the sister of Andrew Hay, from whom he had purchased his estate. But in between these marriages he lived the life of a bachelor. In July 1785 he wrote concerning rumours of an attachment between himself and a Miss Donaldson that he 'had no more intention of marrying than I have of blowing my brains out'.[17] But he was not without female company, for he had at least three children with Indian women during his stay. Such relationships were common and, as Durba Ghosh points out, we often know little about these women.[18] However, the letters do indicate some concern for these 'bibis' and Duff's bonds of both affection and duty with his children. His children were sent to Britain to acquire an education under the care of his brother John in London.[19] Sending John Kenneth on a Danish ship to join his brother Davie in London, Duff in 1785 wrote, 'I told you before, & I repeat it again that it is my intention should I live, to give them the best education England can afford and to set them out in a proper manner into the world, for tho' they have the misfortune to be illegitimate and of a half cast they are not to blame; the fault is all my own and for that reason I think myself doubly bound to provide for them, and I am as fond of them as if they were of a good cast & had been born according to the rules of Law and Gospel'.[20] Two years later, the eldest boy had been sent to Scotland to visit relatives, much to the initial concern of his father, who 'did not know how he might be treated'. As he continued, 'I know such as he did not meet with much encouragement there sometime ago'. Fortunately, in the event he was well received, leading Patrick to conclude that 'the people in that part are certainly more enlarged in their ideas than they were in my younger day'.[21] In the same letter he confessed that:

> I believe I have got another of the same sort, tho' not so fair as either of the others, I have given him the name of William, you won't see him until I come myself; he is a fine stout good humoured fellow of only eleven months old. I did not intend to have any more of these, but what is to be done, a man more than a woman is not at all times master of his passions don't you show this part of the Letter to Mrs Duff.[22]

Although the last part of the letter conveys a sense of some embarrassment, there is nothing of the deliberate concealment of his Indian children from his extended family that Deborah Cohen has observed from others in the same situation.[23] Indeed, the evidence from the letters and subsequent wills is that Patrick's siblings were fond of these children and sought to provide for them. However, as both Cohen and E. M. Collingham observe, this concern to provide only went so far. As Collingham points out 'a patriarchal concern that Indian families should not undermine the British family unit meant that any children from a legitimate British marriage remained the heirs to their father's estate'.[24] That was true of Patrick, as his estate passed to his legitimate son by his second Scottish wife, Dorothea. While in India, his children did not live with him, but rather at the house of his friend Colonel Deare, where an Indian housekeeper cared for them. Patrick got his brother's wife to commission paintings of his two eldest boys, which were given to this woman 'who took care of them after their Mother's death, and who used them in the kindest manner, and who tho' black possesses a heart that would do no discredit to a white lady'.[25] Duff's letters point to the complexities and contradictions of British racial attitudes in the later eighteenth century, and to the significance of the East India Company's role in bringing these issues 'home' to Scotland and to Britain more broadly.

Patrick himself occupied a country house four miles south of Calcutta and 'a Bungolo or Straw and Matt house at the Practice ground near Dum Dum'.[26] Here he had a piece of ground, and he solicited his brother to send him out seed. He was particularly in search of tomato seed which he had 'from the Sevt at Batchlors Hall Madeira, they throve here remarkably well but I think are now degenerating, they were the first of the sort ever seen in this Country, and I wish to have some more'.[27] He was also in search of hop seed 'or indeed any thing else in that way which could be procured without much trouble; I have now given over hunting, I cant take so much exercise in any way as I was once accustomed to, for that reason I divert myself with my Garden; I succeed very well with vegetables &c for the table'.[28] Already in his period of military service in Bengal, Patrick Duff's practice of domestic life displayed an agrarian bent.

When Patrick started to think about his return to Scotland, gardening and farming formed an important part of his thoughts. 'My farm shall be no larger than will produce Grain and Hay for the horses & a few Cows', he wrote to his brother James, 'with Corn &C sufficient for my Family, which shall not be very large; with this Farm I shall find (at least I think so) full Amusement for my leisure hours, and at the same time not be obliged to attend to it but when I am inclined to do so for pleasure'. We can link this line of agrarian thought through from his childhood on a Speyside farm to his Indian service. In the estimate of a fellow Scot who had returned after Indian military service, Sir Hector Munro of Novar, 'a better practical Mind never was in India' than Duff's.[29] That practical mind was particularly exercised in the management of stock. Patrick's father, John, had farmed the unimproved farm of Pitchaish on the Ballindalloch estate on Speyside before moving in the 1770s to the newly enclosed farm of Newtown of Auchintoul on the outskirts of the planned village of Aberchirder, just five miles away from Carnousie. A feature of farming in the northeast was the widespread use of oxen for draught purposes such as ploughing.[30] That experience would have been invaluable in managing a vital part of artillery operations in India, the use of bullocks to pull the guns. Horses proved to be inadequate to the conditions of eighteenth-century India, with the lack of adequate roads and forage. Obtaining a sufficient supply of bullocks was vital, and these were needed in large numbers. On his arrival from Bengal to come to the aid of the army of Eyre Coote (1726–83) in 1780, Colonel Pearse of the Bengal artillery reported that he had sourced 8,000 bullocks.[31] These animals were for two purposes: draught and carriage. Draught bullocks were trained for pulling gun carriages, while ammunition and other stores were carried on the back of carriage bullocks. In the campaign against Tipu Sultan (1750–99) in 1792 which culminated in the siege of Seringapatam, the regular army officer George Hart noted the arrival of 'Colonel (known by the name of Tiger) Duff, who was appointed to the command of that Fort for the purpose chiefly of getting our artillery and Stores in proper order, and prepared for the arduous siege of the Enemy's Capital: upon the capture of which, perhaps, all must ultimately depend'.[32] Arrangements were put in place to have sufficient provisions available, aided by the decision of the Mahrattas to join in the campaign against Tipu. Patrick was able to put together a siege train of 20 heavy guns. Whereas the heavy guns in the first campaign, reported Major Alexander Dirom – son of Patrick's new neighbour at Muiresk outside Turriff – had slowed down the march, thanks to Patrick's innovations 'this unwieldy department moved with nearly as much ease as any other part of the army'.[33] This success was put down to his yoking bullocks four rather than two abreast and attaching the chain they pulled to the heaviest part of the gun. Buckle records of these preparations:

> During the operations above detailed, convoys of stores and ordnance had been arriving, and every care taken to put the materiel of the army on the best possible footing; everything was collected

> in Bangalore, and the train under Colonel Duff arrived there on the 12th January, 1792, in high order; "the draught cattle were in such high order" (to quote from a letter of that period), "that they literally came in with the heavy guns on a gallop."[34]

This is a reminder of the importance of the logistics that lay behind the more visible aspects of military campaigning in India. British success here has been attributed in part to the quality of their officer corps, to the discipline they instilled and the capacity of the British to pay their troops. It also owed much to skills in the mundane matters of sourcing the right animals, securing their feed and managing them in the best manner.

It was perhaps his early life on a Speyside farm which helped Patrick to develop the understanding and knowledge that were later drawn upon in his correspondence with Sir John Sinclair (1754–1835). Best known as the instigator of the Statistical Accounts, the remarkable series of reports from every parish in Scotland that mobilized the ministers of the Church of Scotland to provide a pioneering account of the country at the end of the eighteenth century, Sinclair was also an indefatigable investigator of the progress of agricultural improvement. It was in this connection that he sought Patrick's opinion on the feeding of cattle. Patrick was able to respond with not only his experience in India, but also observations from his stopping off at the Cape of Good Hope, suggesting he was always keen to learn about such practicalities. He always, he said 'preferred well made Oxen for the Guns in preference to heavy ones tho' much stronger, but generally slow and surly, & who can hardly be made to exert themselves upon any occasion'. He was able to tell Sinclair that:

> I know by experience that if Oxen are hard driven when their Bellys are full, it is very apt to hurt them, and I never permitted the Drivers to feed their Oxen much before a March, or to give them Water while marching in very hot weather; I have known many hundreds of Oxen who were ill fed and hardworked, die in one cold wet night succeeding a Hot Sultry day; they generally lay down and were unable to get on their legs again. This happened on Lord Cornwallis first march against Seringapatam when we had nothing to give our Cattle but roots of Grass and met with exceeding cold rainy weather.[35]

In Patrick Duff's correspondence, we already have a picture of Indian service that is quite different from that of the more spectacular examples of nabobs such as Robert Clive (1725–74). It is one that centred on practical expertise, which maintained a focus on agricultural experience that carried through to the return to Scotland. However, there is another dimension to Patrick's story, one that was central to his ability to use his Indian wealth and experience to return to Scotland. This was the position of his uncles and brothers in Madeira. Just as Patrick's story has helped us to bring to the fore a rather neglected aspect of service in India, so too his connections with Madeira illuminate another important node in the construction of empire.

Madeira

Lying off the coast of Africa and under the rule of Portugal (a longstanding ally of Britain), Madeira was in an ideal position for ships heading either to the Americas or to Asia. It offered opportunities for taking on fresh water and produce. It also lay at the centre of networks of commodity trading, the island's wine being exported to British possessions in both North America and the Caribbean.[36] By the same token, local merchants, many of Scottish origin, drew in timber, cereals and dried fish from the Baltic. One of these merchants was James Gordon, Patrick's uncle. Beginning with a partnership in 1730, James built up a thriving trade in Madeira wine, trading principally with Scottish contacts in the Caribbean.[37] His success may have owed something to his commitment to Roman Catholicism, a handicap in Scotland but a possible source of advantage on the island. His brother, Alexander, fought at Culloden and was forced into exile after defeat there. From France, Alexander made his way to Madeira and learned the trade of a wine merchant. Over time, James returned to Britain to run the London office while first Alexander and then their nephew, James (Patrick's brother) looked after the house's interests in Madeira.

A key part of such operations was providing hospitality to European visitors. In return, they hoped for custom for their wine business. In 1776 James Duff wrote from Madeira to the factor for the Duke of Gordon (1743–1827), reporting on the recent visit of John Duncan from Findlater to the island. He had been intending to continue on to India where he would source porcelain china for the Duke, but he had decided to alter his course and head instead for Jamaica. James was keen to offer the services of Patrick, relatively recently departed for India, to order chinaware from Canton into Bengal and forward it to the Duke from there. The correspondence does not indicate whether this offer was taken up, although the Duke became a customer for the Gordon brothers' wine.[38]

This expansion of the customer base came at a good time, for existing business was badly disrupted by the American War of Independence. Not only did this war close American markets, but it laid the rest of the house's Atlantic trade open to the depredations of American privateers. Patrick's presence in Bengal was of immense value in this context, for he was able to use his contacts to open up a new trade in Madeira to India. The house had long desired to enter this trade, for the seemingly inexhaustible demand from the subcontinent promised good profits. Hard drinking was a feature of the culture of Europeans serving in India.[39] When one of Patrick's friends, the surgeon Kenneth Murchison, fought a duel with Charles Croftes in Lucknow, both had been so drunk on the evening before that they could not remember the cause of their disagreement. Their seconds were in no position to help, for they had been in the same condition.[40] Madeira was one of the drinks of choice of Company men. In 1769 the Council requested that London did not 'send out any more Vidonia Wine as it is not of so wholesome a quality as Madeira & no Body'.[41] Complaints continued about the lack of availability of Madeira wine, laments which are almost comic in their desperation. Thus, in 1785, the Council in Bengal represented to the Court 'the distress to which this settlement has been reduced by being obliged to use very bad wine' occasioned by London refusing to permit any ships from calling at Madeira in the previous season.[42] The merchant Charles Chambers dominated the trade in the early eighteenth century: his business accounted for 34 per cent of the island's wine exports in 1727.[43] His ownership of East India Company stock and the constraints placed by the Company on others carrying wine to India meant that it was hard for the Gordons to win access to the Indian market. It was here that Patrick was invaluable in winning contracts with the Scottish merchant Alexander Colvin to handle the house's wine, as well as providing quality control services by inspecting the newly arrived casks.

Together with the spoils of war and profits made from contracting to the East India Company army, this trade in Madeira enhanced Patrick's fortune and led him to think of investing in a Scottish estate for his eventual return.[44] The challenges posed here were both those of finding a suitable property and of remitting the required funds. As his brother James warned him, 'you should not engage in so capital a purchase without a moral certainty that your remittances will answer, as a failure in them might straiten you very much, as has been the case with some Gentlemen returned from India'.[45] One example of the fate which might befall those who lacked trustworthy allies in India was seen in the case of another of Patrick's Indian friends, Allan Macpherson, who returned from India in 1787 with the money he had made as Quartermaster-General in

Bengal – or rather, the money he thought he had entrusted to the care of his notorious cousin James 'Ossian' Macpherson (1736–96). Best known for the poems which he passed off as the surviving examples of Gaelic epics, Macpherson was a thoroughly unreliable character who managed to reduce his cousin's remittances in such a way as to place him in parlous financial straits on his return to his Blairgowrie estate.[46] Patrick was far more fortunate in his uncles and brothers, who dealt faithfully with the money he remitted. This initially helped his father out of the financial scrapes into which he had fallen, then paid off the debts incurred by his uncles in setting him and his brothers up for military service. Patrick then remitted enough money to purchase his new estate and to carry out the necessary work. How much this was is not clear, but the purchase of Carnousie can be estimated at £22,000. An estimate of some £50,000 in total for Patrick's Indian remittances would seem not so far adrift.

At home in Scotland

By March 1784, Patrick was 'thinking…about buying Land, and if a Man can get a snug spot, with about four per cent for his money, I think it is by much the safest & best way he can lay out his money'.[47] With the help of his brother and uncles, plus other family connections in northeast Scotland, he considered several estates before settling on Carnousie. Patrick's letters generally adopt a down-to-earth tone; there is none of the playing with genre that marks the letters of George Bogle, another Scot in Company service in Calcutta in the 1770s.[48] However, he relaxes a little when writing to his brother, and in one of his letters he enters into a reverie about his potential return:

> I would like above all things to have a place of my own where I could retire to and amuse myself in the fields; I know little of farming tho' fond of that amusement, but above all things I would like to have a good Garden with fruit trees &c and if possible not far from a stream where I could divert myself in fine weather with fishing; to have a hill near where one might go a shooting would make it still more agreeable to my taste and I would like it near the sea if possible. You'll say I want too much and that all these things cannot be had; indeed I don't expect it, but as I was on the topick I mentioned them. I abhor a place entirely without wood and water, and would not like to live where I could not see both. To be in the fields in fine weather, to fish, shoot & hunt; with some Books, and now and then the Company of any friends, are the only pleasures which I can hope to enjoy.[49]

These thoughts prompted him to map out what he hoped to do when he got home, and they are far from the ambitions of a 'nabob'. There were considerable debates at the time about the corrupting influence of Indian wealth on British politics and society.[50] Showy and ostentatious, those who returned with a fortune from India used their wealth, it was alleged, together with the corrupting influences of the 'Orient', to subvert British life. This was far from Patrick's ambitions at that time, as his letter continues:

> I never mean to have any hand in Politicks, nor to gain anything by farming, for after all the Bustle I have lived in all my life, if I get only home, I mean to enjoy myself as much as possible; so I have no idea of being so happy as when in the Country, in the way I mention, with, at same time, having it in my power to go into town in the Winter, or even as far as Edinburgh or London for four months in the Year, without finding it incommode me in the money way, I must also (if I mean to be as I would wish) have a Carriage with four good horses and a couple of saddle horses for myself, & two others for my Servants; all the horses but those I ride shall work in the Cart, plow & harrow. My farm shall be no larger than will produce Grain and Hay for the horses & a few Cows, with Corn &C sufficient for my Family, which shall not be very large; with this Farm I shall find (at least I think so) full Amusement for my leisure hours, and at the same time not be obliged to attend to it but when I am inclined to do so for pleasure. I must have a neat warm house with a few rooms to lodge my friends when they come to see me.[51]

These criteria were eventually to be met by the estate of Carnousie in Banffshire. It was not close to the sea but in the words of the Earl of Fife (whose brother-in-law, George Hay, was seeking to sell the land) 'there is a great deal of good ground and great deal to improve'.[52] Fife confessed that he had little influence over George Hay, leading Patrick to express his concerns:

> altho' I want an estate and particularly in this country, I would not give more for one than my friends thought prudent and reasonable. I know there is an idea that people from India will give more than any person else, but I assure your Lordship this is not the case with me, as I am determined to be guided by the advice of my friends in cases of this kind where I am no judge myself.[53]

However, these scruples were overcome, and Patrick purchased the 3,000 acre estate. It came with a tower house of 1577, with a William Adam addition of 1740. While Patrick had repairs done to this structure, his main work was the building of the impressive courtyard of farm buildings of 1797.[54] As we have seen, the courtyard's design owed much to existing templates, suggesting Duff's desire to manifest through architecture the thirst for agricultural improvement that had come to characterize the area. As Nechtmann points out, a prime critique of Indian wealth was that it did not fit into the accepted model of landed wealth as the foundation of social and political power.[55] It was perhaps easier for Patrick, with his agricultural background, something which had been an important factor in his Indian success, to embrace the role of improving landlord. Probably the finest example of its type in an area known for landlord-led agricultural improvement in the late eighteenth century, his home farm designed in Scottish vernacular was the lasting legacy of Patrick's application of his Indian fortune.

Conclusion

Patrick Duff's letters reveal something of the concerns of those of more middling rank who made fortunes in India and were fortunate enough to return to Britain with this wealth. They present an alternative to the more common narratives of return associated with East India Company nabobs.[56] Although Patrick's wealth undoubtedly had an impact on his locality, and although, despite his earlier resolution, he did dabble in local politics, his horizons were more domestic than those of the nabob elite. His letters give hints as to the material culture which accompanied the life of a successful British military officer, although unfortunately none of the artefacts he might have brought back survived the eventual dispersal of his estate on his son's death in 1828. What is of particular interest is his gift of paintings of his sons to the Indian woman who cared for them, exemplifying a flow of artefacts back from Britain and thereby reversing historians' more common narratives of imperial collecting for their British homes. These gifts are also indicative of bonds of responsibility and affection, tempered of course by assumptions of patriarchal authority, for the children he had with Indian women and, albeit fleetingly, for those women themselves.

Patrick went to India in some measure, as did Thomas Munro (1761–1827), another Scot in the service of the East India Company whose career has been explored by Margot Finn, to restore the family fortunes.[57] As he noted somewhat ruefully in a letter to his uncle about his father's affairs, 'the Old Gentleman is not by any means a good Manager'.[58] Although John Duff appears to have been a competent farmer, his work on behalf of the Grant of Monymusk estate collecting rents for their lands on Speyside had landed him in considerable debt. Between them, Patrick and his brother worked to clear those debts.[59] In this, they were fortunate in their connections with their uncles, the Gordon wine merchants of Madeira. This gave them the ability to settle their father's debts and then to contribute to the expansion of the Madeira wine business. In this way private concerns meshed with the broader economic development of their home country, for their father moved to one of the new farms created by the rage for agricultural improvement in Scotland. George McGilvary has shown how this movement could not have been fuelled by investment from internal sources; the career of Patrick Duff gives an illustration of the process at work for one estate.[60] The magnificence of the surviving farm buildings and the high quality of the farmland that surrounds them testify to the lasting impact of Indian wealth on the Scottish countryside.

Duff's history is also an indication of the important place of Madeira as a key node in the network over which capital and commodities flowed back to Britain from India. It was not just a convenient watering place, but an important centre of trade, one dominated in the late eighteenth century by British, and especially Scottish, merchants. They developed a global trade with British possessions in both the West and East Indies, and so were an important link between those areas and their wealthy customers in Britain. As well as supplying their noble patrons with wines, they also opened up awareness of other goods whose purchase they could facilitate. A gift of preserved lemons for the Duchess of Gordon to accompany an order for wine might build on distant family connections, connections which might also be mobilized to assist in the search for military preferment.[61] In this way, business, family and patronage networks were intimately intertwined.[62] Their lasting memorials are the estate farm buildings which are such a distinctive feature of northeast Scotland.

Section 5
Company families and identities
Writing history today

Thanks to the twenty-first-century efflorescence of family and local history, the proliferation of digital copies of archival materials, the success of the heritage industry in popularizing the country house as a site of belonging and the vibrant contemporary market (both online and at auction houses) for the surviving material objects of empire, writing the history of the East India Company (EIC) is an occupation that extends far beyond the walls of the academy. In this section, each chapter is an exercise in family history inspired by a sense of connection – through lineage, marriage, surviving documents, treasured objects or built environments – with past men and women whose lives were caught up in the Company's imperial networks. Family histories, these chapters remind us, are powerful narratives, animated by emotive recollections and (no less emotive) processes of forgetting, refusal and denial.[1]

Penelope Farmer's chapter on her ancestor, William Gamul Farmer (1746–97), details William's employment as a Company servant in Bombay and the contribution of his wealth to his family at home in Britain. Farmer's efforts to extract a fortune from his labours for the EIC are framed in this chapter by his family's private letters: his mother's laments for her lonely separation from her children and his own complaints to his brother about the Company's treatment provide a backdrop against which we view his struggles to accumulate wealth on the subcontinent. Home and an affluent retirement in Britain proved elusive goals, for William Gamul Farmer (like so many Company men before and after him) died before reaching British shores. In contrast to William, his brother Sam remained in Britain and ran a successful dye manufactory; purchasing Nonsuch Park in Surrey, possibly with the assistance of

William's imperial wealth (which he inherited upon his brother's death), Sam rather than William was elected an MP. The contrasting fortunes of William and Sam Farmer resonate in their descendant's narrative with gendered histories of inclusion and exclusion from the family's private archives (and thus its family histories) in the twentieth century.

David Williams's chapter also examines how Company families engaged with and used the possibilities offered by imperial service to further their fortunes and opportunities. It focuses on the Melvill family, Border Scots who established a Company connection in Bengal in 1777 and expanded this initial base over several succeeding generations. Reconstructing the story of his wife's five-times great grandparents, David Williams uses family letters and Company archives to piece together the chains of association which bound eighteenth- and nineteenth-century Scots to the British empire. Like the other chapters in this section, his study of the Melvills demonstrates the powerful pull of family histories of empire, which continue to capture the historical imaginations of current generations. As twenty-first-century Britons exploit new access to primary materials (whether in public repositories or digitized collections of documents) as part of burgeoning research undertaken by historical communities located outside academia, they dwell on local stories entangled with global and imperial processes. Family history, once synonymous with the personal and the parochial, is increasingly written as connected history, a British history that extends beyond British shores.

Sir John Sykes's chapter delineates a family story that stretches from Britain to Bengal and from the nabob era to the present. Focusing on his ancestor, Sir Francis Sykes (1730–1804), Sir John begins with a familiar narrative in which one man's Company service resulted in the accumulation of a huge fortune which, upon retirement home to Britain, allowed the purchase of country houses and landed estates. Basildon Park in Berkshire, the estate among his many purchases which Sir Francis chose as his family seat, fits easily within the paradigms explored in the third section of this volume. A Palladian stately home financed with Indian capital, it betrays today few external signs of Company commerce as exhibited by the National Trust, but its especially fine collection of Chinese armorial porcelain nestled comfortably in Berkshire's eighteenth-century 'English Hindoostan'. The Sykes chapter, moreover, reminds us that Company fortunes were accrued not only by English officials such as Sir Francis – employed in Bengal as Resident and then Governor of the trading factory at Cossimbazar – but also by Indian merchants such as Sykes's banian (or man of business), Krishna Kanta Nandy (c.1720–94). Nandy's commercial skills were crucial to Sykes's exploitation of the private trading privileges he enjoyed as a Company servant. Working for Sykes also had advantages for Nandy, who was an able trader in his own right and further benefitted from access to Sykes's Company contacts and power. Skill, connections and power allowed both Sykes and Nandy to accumulate wealth. Although Sir Francis's great wealth did not long survive him, and his descendants' excessive expenditure led to the sale of Basildon Park in 1838, Nandy's wealth persisted for generations and ensured the continued growth and prosperity of his family. Told through the biography of a Persian business seal shared by Sir Francis and his banian, this chapter illustrates the ability of objects passed through the generations to connect British and Indian histories in the twenty-first century.

17

The career of William Gamul Farmer (1746–1797) in India, 1763–1795

Penelope Farmer

This chapter originated in a collection of family letters that travelled between England and India from 1763 to 1795. They were generated by the long absence from England of one family member, William Gamul Farmer (1746–98), who was sent to the subcontinent at the age of 16 as an East India Company (EIC) servant. More recently this material has been augmented by the appearance of William's private letter book containing most of the letters he wrote between 1794 and 1796, before leaving India for good.

Family history, in a review of Alison Light's book involving her own family, has been described by Kate Clanchy as 'dabbling' rather than as 'serious' history.[1] But having been accidentally drawn into such history by the discovery of this previously unsuspected cache of material, I see no reason to apologize. The case against Light's family is that they were 'boring' and had little to contribute to Light's thesis. I cannot claim the members of my family, though rather better educated than Light's, had much more of interest to say. On the other hand a mother apologizing to her son – located a six months' journey away – that she is writing at such length because 'I fancy I am talking to you', or the same son telling the supplier of young orange trees that they would have to serve as the children he was never going to have, explains better than any academic analysis the emotional and social costs of eighteenth-century East India Company separations. More generally, the lives and letters of any one family embedded in the wider history of the marauding EIC, though inevitably anecdotal, can help illuminate the private and social workings that underpinned a once mercantile enterprise moving ever faster into the semblance of an imperial government during the latter part of the eighteenth century. On a sociological level, such material demonstrates how families held themselves together despite the vast distances in time and space that separated them, and how crucial sibling relationships could be in helping to provide for a Company servant in India both materially and psychologically. At least one letter (from William) throws new – Indian – light, too, on how one family managed to rise from the merchant class in England into the country gentry. Above all – for me – almost the biggest joy of these letters was their bringing back to life the voice of William Gamul Farmer's mother, a woman who was not the kind of eighteenth-century century lady – literary, intellectual, aristocratic – whose voice and histories are most familiar to us. A very ordinary, decidedly bourgeois woman, she was both deprived by marriage of her family inheritance and deprived by distance of her favourite child. Her undoubted talents and energy thwarted by a society that had no use for them, she seized her chances where she could. The news and gossip she imparted to her far-distant beloved son about life back in his homeland were recounted in the kind of words, many mis-spelt, that have all too rarely survived the years. Her letters may not illuminate the high politics and high finance of the EIC in any direct way. Yet, but for the Company's employment of her son, these letters would never been written and such a lively voice would never have been heard.

The letters in William's letter book, written between 1794 and 1796 at the end of his career, have less to offer on such a private, family level. On the other hand, they are in places as intimate as the earlier individual letters – in some respects even more so. Addressing men to whom after years in India he has often been closer than to members of his family, the writer seems able to admit more freely to his hopes and regrets and his lack of family life – he never married – than he can express to his younger brother. His sometimes affectionate letters to Indian colleagues – with their use of Indian terms, references to Indian festivals and legal processes – suggest, too, how deeply embedded William Gamul Farmer was in an Indian life that could have meant very little to those at home. The survival of such a complete collection of records is unusual. Farmer's comments on financial deals, political events, and political problems in his rich correspondence augment our knowledge of East India Company business and the English men who conducted it.

The letters

The family letters were preserved in a dispatch box held in the family mansion at Nonsuch Park in Surrey (Figure 17.1), passed on to my father

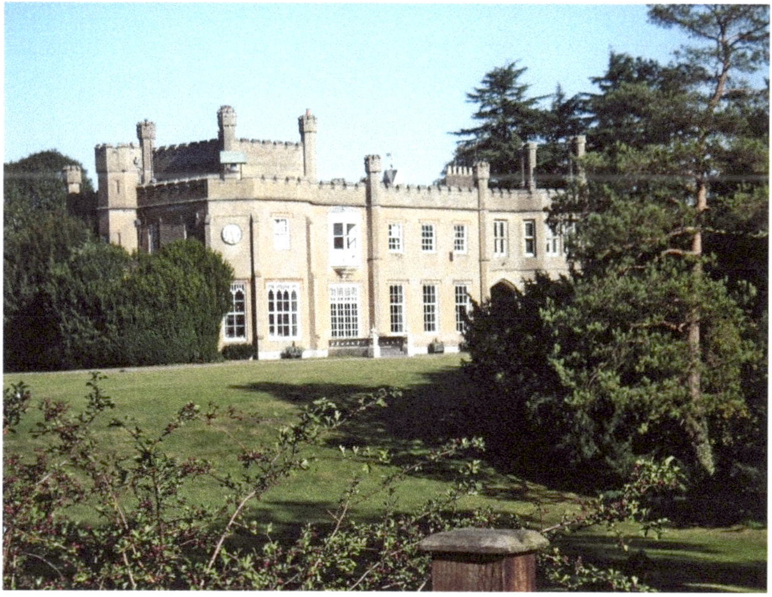

Figure 17.1 Nonsuch Park, Surrey. Image courtesy of Penelope Farmer.

(Hugh R. M. Farmer 1907–2004) at the sale of the house in 1937. After my father's and my brother's deaths, the dispatch box fetched up in a niece's house in Wales; there I encountered it for the first time, eight years or so ago. The collection, still in the private possession of the Farmer family, consists of 36 letters, in all, most of which I have now transcribed, sometimes with difficulty and in need of help.[2]

The writers were the EIC civil servant William Gamul Farmer (1746–97), his younger brother Samuel (1747–1839), a scarlet dye merchant, based in Shoreditch, London, and their mother, Margaret Farmer (c.1725–95). There are also two letters sent to William by two business colleagues in London. Almost all the surviving letters from England were written in the 1770s. Of the 13 sent from India by William himself, two (to his father, George Farmer [1710–84]) were dated 1763 and 1774; the rest were addressed to his brother Sam, between 1789 and 1795. The final group, from Surat, where William ended his career as Chief, are, thankfully – his later writing was hard to read – copies by one of his Indian writers. (This duplication was common practice, as many of the ships carrying mail were lost at sea).

From the beginning William's task in India was to make his fortune, a theme that reverberates throughout both collections of his correspondence. How much money he made in India is still in question. But a letter in his own hand, dated June 1794, states that part of his gains are being sent back anonymously, to avoid suspicion – William was suspected by the Company of dubious transactions in the years he spent down on the Malabar Coast, 1792–4. The sums involved are described in full detail in the letter book and though not enormous compared to some fortunes sent back from Bengal, they do appear substantial enough to indicate that the family's subsequent rise from the merchant class might not have been due simply to Sam's successful dye business, as the family have always assumed: 'the Farmers put the red into redcoats' was the word around Nonsuch Park, the estate where Samuel set himself up as a country gentleman after William's death. I will return to the issue at greater length, later in this chapter.

The 12 letters from Sam to his brother, between 1772 and 1777, detail his life in London, his business, the health and doings of their father, meanwhile complaining about their mother and their disgraceful half-sister in Chelsea, 'withering', as he put it 'on the virgin thorn', adding, still more unkindly, 'tis fortunate for the nation that Heaven has made her plain or she would have introduced the bend sinister into their coat of arms'. He tells of his attempts to get preferment for William, imparts gossip about friends, and outlines his love life. The failure of his first attempt at courtship sends Samuel on an abbreviated Grand Tour, during which he is invited to a private meeting with the then Pope conducted entirely in Italian.[3] This encounter suggests, as does his frequent use of Latin and French tags, that the two brothers were well educated. (In one letter William explains attempts to obtain patronage by Sir Francis Baring (1740–1810), of the banking family, due to their having been school fellows: certainly, Baring's educational record in the *Oxford Dictionary of National Biography* puts him at Mr Fuller's Academy at Lothbury, a well-thought of private school not far from the Farmer family's home and dye works).[4] Sam's command of Italian echoes later evidence of William's own linguistic skills in India, including fluent Marathi, probable Persian, also working knowledge of Portuguese and, possibly of one of the languages of the Malabar coast. There are two further letters from Sam. The first, dated 1784 and addressed to the younger brother of his partner, Goodwin, in Virginia, suggests his involvement in the slave trade; the second dated 1810 to his son, William Meeke Farmer (1778–1836), refuses to advance him the funds he requested following his wife's first pregnancy but does make clear the by now considerable extent of Sam's landed property.

The liveliest of the letters are the five from William and Sam's mother, Margaret Farmer, between 1775 and 1777. She was a difficult woman, evidently, complaining about everything and everyone and obsessed with money (not unreasonably – nominally an heiress, she was entirely dependent on largesse from her male relations, including by this time her two sons). Finally there are four letters, addressed to William between 1776–7, two from Harding Stracey (c.1740– c.1808), a clerk in the House of Commons Committee Office, by the tone of the letters an old friend, and two from William Richardson, (d. 1798), Secretary at the Company headquarters in Leadenhall Street. All touch on politics, East India Company affairs and gossip relating to these topics (Stracey's brother was recently retired from the Company service in Madras).

In comparison to the family letters, the letter book is a much more extensive collection of correspondence. Some letters, again, are to William's brother Sam, in England; others are to London bankers to whom he is intending to transmit his money. There is also one loving and personal letter to Sam's wife, Elizabeth, (c.1755–1805) of whom William is clearly fond. Many more – the majority – are to fellow East India Company servants; with some of these he was clearly on affectionate terms. There are letters too to the Parsi or Portuguese merchants William did business with and to whom he wrote with equal respect and affection, together with several to Murdock Brown (1750–1828) down in Malabar, whose name will feature later. Many letters relate to his worries about sending home his fortune, worries caused by the French Revolution and the fears it aroused in England: 'if the mob has its way we will be "republic of Albion"' he wails, in a letter from Surat dated 23 June 1795. Later that year (29 December 1795) William can be found making arrangements for his sudden departure from India, selling horses and carriages, sending other goods to auction and listing the few things he wants to take with him. Though I have not yet been able to transcribe these letters fully – in numbers they far exceed the original group – I have made a précis of their contents and copied some relevant passages. Even at a glance they make clear just how embedded William Gamul Farmer was within the East India Company hierarchy, and how extensive his acquaintance was with his correspondents, many of them Company hands with a much higher profile than his own. They include Jonathan Duncan (1756–1811), later Governor of Bombay, William Palmer of Delhi (1740–1816, one of William Dalrymple's 'White Mughuls') and Sir Charles Malet (1753–1815), the Resident at Poona (now Pune).[5]

It is the very informality of these letters that makes them interesting; what they leave out is as informative as what they put in. They indicate the kind of forces that drove this Bombay servant during his life in India, how he managed and continued to nurture his family relationships from afar, and how the family managed and fostered their relationship with him, despite the parties being so distant in time and space. In this way, like other such letters, they help humanize our understanding of the effects and experience of Empire at home and abroad. Not least, in the way Sam passes on information about politics in London, and William describes events in India – particularly in the letters from Surat – they show, in informal terms, how 'home' came to seem 'abroad' and 'abroad' became 'home' from the standpoint of the old India hand, no matter how he might continue to regard his original home in theory. Above all they make clear that what made India real for the Farmer family was William's being there; his presence in India was far more significant to them than the nature of India itself. Sarah Pearsall, focusing on trade in the Atlantic world, suggests that it was common for middle-class families of this era to send one member away. She adds that 'strange new locations could force some to cling ever more resolutely to family ties' and that 'these ties could often help to enable imperial and colonial power … . The family … created worlds of trust and allowed for even long distances to be surmounted [helping] forge the tone of familiarity'.[6] William Gamul Farmer's extensive correspondence allows us to trace these linkages between family, trade and empire from the perspective of the later eighteenth-century Indian Ocean world.

The Farmer family

The two brothers, William and Samuel, born 14 months apart in 1746 and 1747, were the sons of George Farmer (1710–84). He and his family lived above the dye-making business in Hogg Lane, just off Shoreditch High Street and half a mile or so from what is now Liverpool Street Station. It was prosperous enough by the time of William and Samuel's birth to employ three or four apprentices and to have premises substantial enough to house a family of eight.[7] The boys' mother, Margaret Shawalter, an heiress from Chester in Cheshire and their father's second wife, gave birth to several other children, none of whom lived beyond early childhood. The marriage was equally unsuccessful. By the time most of these letters were written, in the 1770s, the parents were separated, the father retired and living in the country, the mother back in Cheshire, only spending the odd winter in London lodgings. Unusually, the entire family lived

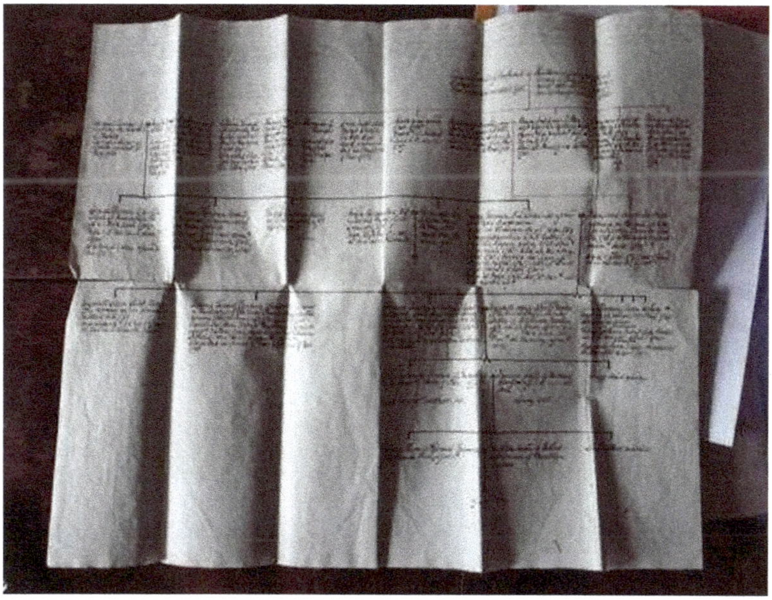

Figure 17.2 The Farmer family tree. Image courtesy of Penelope Farmer.

apart. Sam, having served his dyer's apprenticeship and taken on the dye works alongside his father's partner, Chamberlain Goodwin, remained in Hogg Lane. William was in India, while an elder half-sister, daughter of George's first wife – whose behaviour according to Sam 'would have disgraced an upper servant' – lived by herself in Chelsea.[8] The implied impropriety of such arrangements exercised Sam greatly when courting his future wife, in case it put her family off their marriage.

It was, however, a stolid merchant family in every other respect, and defiantly English (see Figure 17.2). The comments about France made after a sojourn by the brothers' father in Boulogne prefigure attitudes within my family that existed into my own generation. Writing to William on 8 July 1774, Sam asserted that their father:

> left the place as the apostles did when they were not well received, that is he shook the dust from his feet and cursed them, their wine was so thin and fluxed him, add to that the difficulty of procuring pipes and tobacco, you will not wonder at his stay being very uncomfortable, he lost all his belly, the very sight of him convinced that there was not such good beef in France as we have here.

Similarly these letters reflect what was until recently the family's attitude to women – as does the fact that I, a history graduate, was never told that the letters existed. (Sam's statement on his half-sister, 'tis fortunate for the nation that Heaven has made her plain or she would have introduced the bend sinister into our coat of arms', is merely an extreme version of such attitudes).[9] This tone to the family voice leaps out from the letters, not least in the constant complaints of the mother, Margaret Farmer, and in the complaints about her by her younger son, who also referred to the assets brought to him by his wife as his.[10] Such attitudes were then the norm, but you cannot help feeling for querulous Margaret, dependent as she was and even passed over by her own aunts who left the family estate not to her but her eldest son, William. Trailblazers these sons were not in this or any other way, and no more intellectually curious than some, if not all, of their male descendants.

More significant, however, was how close the two brothers obviously remained throughout William's life, despite the geographical distance between them – a closeness that was replicated in other Company families, such as the Russell brothers of Swallowfield Park, also discussed in this volume. Such closeness between siblings was not unusual at this time or in the following century: Jane Austen's life and novels are full of it.[11] My Farmer grandmother's diary between 1877–9, makes clear that apart from husband-trawling seasons in London, her social life too consisted largely of her many siblings, some of whom she continued to support throughout their lives.[12] In Sam and William's case their dysfunctional family may have made them still closer. 'Sam is a good lad', his brother said in his first letter home (October 1763), and so he remained, judging by his willingness to send William what he asked for. Despite the fact that none of Sam's letters to William after 1778 survived, the correspondence that remains makes clear that they kept in continuous contact throughout William's years in India. Not least he depended on Sam to supply his needs: clothing, hats, riding boots, medicines, claret, and, latterly, seeds for his garden. In a letter of 1789 his list of requirements included thin pairs of shoes, thick ones, boots – William is very precise here: 'military boots that is without tops, the same all the way up, waxed leather, buckram will not do'. He also requested bottles of some stuff called 'Dalbrosian' and more of 'Chary', tincture of Bark – i.e., quinine. That Sam is clearly ready to provide everything his brother asks for demonstrates as much as anything how close and how necessary the brothers were to one another.

Their mother's offerings on the other hand would not have been so solicited; on 20 December 1775, she sends jars of her own preserves and the odd Cheshire cheese, all seemingly gratis. Sam's efforts, in contrast, were not. Ever the merchant, on 26 April 1776 he sends full accounts in his letters of what William owed him for these goods, as well as William's share of support for their mother that Sam has advanced her. William for his part (in September 1795) sends home shawls for his half-sister and for his sister-in-law. (These often elaborate and expensive pieces of cloth were a common way of bringing India to the family at home throughout this period).[13]

The closeness between the siblings may have also have been augmented by their geographical separation. In an imperial context, family remained the one constant for the absent member, living in a world barely comprehended by those back at home. It was what the absent one depended on for retaining his sense of identity as an Englishman as well as for more material things they sent him, from clothes to homemade preserves. Similar intimacy between separated siblings in the nineteenth century has been shown elsewhere: in Macaulay's letters from India to his sister Margaret and in Murdoch Stewart's references in his Memoir from Canada to his elder brother back in Scotland, for instance.[14]

Before these letters surfaced, I had only known of the family connection with India via a set of 1789 accounts for a business in Bombay, which appeared after my father's death and set me combing East India Company records for the surprisingly extensive evidence of this unknown ancestor's career in India. William Gamul Farmer's trips to Madras and Calcutta are recorded and the displeasure of his superiors at his belated return to Bombay: so too are his knowledge of Marathi and appointment as Secretary to the Maratha committee in 1777. His year as hostage in the Maratha camp between 1779 and 1780 and his attempts to extricate himself, in particular, are covered in a whole series of letters and documents in the British Library.[15]

With or without the background knowledge, reading the letters themselves has been an affecting experience. Through this correspondence, my eighteenth-century family leapfrogs over the nineteenth and twentieth centuries straight into my hands and feelings in the twenty-first century, colouring the official material in a much more gossipy, personal and recognizable way, not least by demonstrating those enduring family characteristics. The young William's letter written from Bombay shortly after his arrival in 1763, along with another very affectionate letter to his father in 1774, is particularly revealing and touching, as are Sam's accounts of his adventures in love in the 1770s. Sarah Pearsall comments that 'family letters collections demonstrate that familiarity while certainly not the only style was the major note struck'.[16] Such a note, I should add, though invariably present in the letters of Margaret Farmer, was not always apparent in her sons' more political and commercially oriented communications. Yet these letters, too, when they turned to family matters, take quite a different tone: the affection with which William addressed his father on 16 January 1774 makes the point:

> I daresay when I arrive in England again you will be an overmatch for me in walking. The affair of the shot in your arm might have been very serious one and you may thank God for the escape. If I was inclined to be superstitious there is great room to imagine that it was an immediate interposition of providence in favour of the poor partridges for I observe you say that it hindered your sporting about three weeks – in that time ... the young partridges begin to fly strong – and then my dear sir I believe there is no need to tell you – they are fully out of danger from you.

Such letters – and in William's case, too, the more affectionate letter book epistles to friends and colleagues – help soften less kindly aspects of the two Farmer brothers.

William in particular comes across often, both in his letters, and still more in the EIC records, as motivated mostly by making money, and with a far-from endearing tendency to complain and to sound generally hard done by, constantly trying to justify, at length, even the most questionable of activities, his dealings down in the Malabar in particular. Sam's letters generally make him sound more sympathetic – his accounts, of his father, for instance, of his European travels and his subsequent marriage are endearing enough not to say amusing at times, even if in his later history he appears quite curmudgeonly. (The refusal, in 1810, to lend his son money to ease impending fatherhood, is one, private, example; his record as an MP between 1810 and 1818, voting for the suspension of Habeas Corpus and against Catholic Relief another, more public one).[17] It has been suggested to me by Diana Tillman, a Nonsuch historian, that the very openness, not to say intimacy, of some of the private correspondence, by contrast, may have been due, partly, to the distance between the correspondents: feelings, grievances and affections could be more openly revealed and discussed with someone far away than with someone closer at hand.

The two rather touching letters about Sam's courtship and marriage to a Miss Elizabeth Meeke written between 1776 and 1777 reveal the ways in which distance could prompt openness and affection. The union had been embarked on because of his need to make a profitable marriage, and the letters initially evoke a dispassionate description of his intended bride's physical and moral qualities. On 26 April 1776 Sam wrote that 'She is above the middle size and well-made but rather stoops her neck, upon the whole is rather a fine-looking woman, her complexion is fair, fine blue eyes, good nose and fine hair, her face too wide around, her teeth small and even but not of good ivory but not black, her temper all gentleness and love, was never seen in ill humour or in a passion, she is sensible, but it is concealed by her timidity and diffidence.' Less than a year later, on 6 March 1777, Sam reveals he has fallen in love. 'I have been in possession of the best of women since the 16th of last November, it would be doing her an injustice not to say that at the same time she is the best of wives .... I informed you in my last letter that she was tall and genteel, good complexion and hair and very fine eyes, she wants nothing but fine teeth to be judged a very handsome woman indeed.' (He cannot quite forget about the teeth; in a world of much sugar consumption, black English teeth and toothache are perhaps the slaves' revenge). His love is confirmed, by the recent and coincidental appearance, of a harp, now the property of an American harpist, but first bought by Sam for his wife in 1782 for £150, which would have been at the time a very large sum.[18] (According to the present owner, he paid rather more than he needed; business acumen deserted him in this private matter). William, too, appears to have been fond of his sister-in-law; in the later letters he enquires after her tenderly and promises to send her those shawls from India. And the one letter to her that appeared in the letter book, 19 November 1795, more than confirms his affection.

The outpourings of the mother, Margaret Farmer, are still more intimate. They complain of everything: her family, her health, her doctor, her younger son, Sam, his new wife. Of the last, Margaret wrote on 3 March 1777, 'she is only a merchant's daughter but sets up for a woman of quality. She made me a visit of an hour and a half since I came to town and in that time I had enough of her'. In a previous letter of 5 February 1777, she had already decried Sam's over-expensive coach: 'It is quite in taste painted an Apple Green and the armes [*sic.*] in brown. But the liveries are ridiculous, a maroon colour turned up with apple green laced with narrow silver lace at the cape and cuffs with silver tassels on the shoulder'. Above all she complains of her lack of financial independence especially after the family estate owned by her aunts was left over her head to her elder son: 'You are to know I have since found out when he [Sam Farmer] persuaded them to alter their wills I had the house in Barn Lane and £50 a year from the Estate which would not have enabled me to live in any very sumptious [*sic.*] manner but it was too much for a woman who will first and last bring a fortune of ten thousand pounds', she wrote on 15 December 1775.

William's mother bewails his sojourn in India throughout her correspondence with him, attempting to persuade him to come home for good. She promises him his own rooms in her house in cold Chester, and imagines happy tête-à-têtes on winter evenings. On 23 April 1777, Margaret wrote longingly that 'they have got the Chester Playhouse hired but what signify's if there will be no Plays in winter those evenings are dreadful there … . I think if you and I was to gather there we cd pass em away cheerful'. It was a prospect that might well have explained William's failure to return to England permanently until just before his death. Apart from the sadness of women separated from their young by the growth of the Empire, these letters reveal little of the subcontinent and EIC matters. Yet but for the emerging empire in India they would not have been written. They are also exceptionally entertaining, full of contemporary and sometimes scandalous gossip, both private and public, of the kind of which William and his fellows would have been deprived, and might well have looked for. Her description on 23 April 1777 of her successful and intelligent pursuit of the family patron, Lord Sandwich (1718–92), on behalf of a protégé suggests real and frustrated ability with nothing to do and nowhere to go as her main problem, at the same time demonstrating the influence women could have even then when opportunities were rare.

Margaret Farmer's active maintenance of connections with Lord Sandwich demonstrates something else that the letters make clear: the close connection the family had with the East India Company – Lord Sandwich being the patron they looked to for help in advancing William's career with the company, though without a great deal of success. Many of Sam's letters recount meetings with Sandwich, and in one he outlines his lively defence of John Herbert's behaviour in Balambangan, in the EIC council. He is very proud of his oratory here and his presence indicates that he was an EIC proprietor. William's first letter from India, in October 1763, sending thanks to a range of EIC names, from Rous to Manship and the Moffatt brothers (not excluding Lord Clive himself), suggests that the family business was part of a healthy trading network that enabled William's writership in the first place.

The decision to send William abroad would largely have been made by the men involved – not least the boy himself, fired by this prospect of adventure – on commercial and practical grounds. A mother's regret at losing her son appeared to be of no account. Margaret wrote on 5 February 1777: 'Sorry I am from my soul that you ever went to India but I never was considered a person of any consequence. Mr and Mrs Goodwin were the people always consulted, indeed you was so much set upon it that I learned to reconcile to what I cd not prevent in the belief that if young boys were crop'd out of employment they like themselves it hurts their spirits.' Interestingly, one woman was involved in this decision, but not Margaret. Yet if it was George Farmer himself, his partner (Mr Goodwin) and Goodwin's wife who urged the decision – a decision occasioned, possibly, by the bad behaviour for which William apologizes in this first letter – his passage depended on inevitably male EIC servants. The fact of William's having, unusually, been allowed to stay in the captain's cabin during the voyage out and of his being invited to dinner by a member of the Bombay council, shortly after his arrival, also implies good connections within the Honourable Company.

Trade and money

What leaps out from these letters is that India for the two brothers was above all a trading resource: nothing but 'a large warehouse', was how, many years later, William would describe Surat territory to Jonathan Duncan on 8 May 1795. This was an attitude noted, disapprovingly, by contemporaries such as the author William Macintosh, who decried the young men who, he claimed, 'generally set out for [India] with ideas of acquiring wealth, which ideas being nourished not only by example but advice and exhortation soon grew up into the dominant passion of the heart and ruling principal of the mind'.[19] This comment was borne out by the contemporary criticism of 'nabobs', the nickname given to the wealthy merchants who returned to England to throw their financial and political weight about, after making their fortune in India, like those described in other studies here.[20] In reality they were a small minority of the company servants who had headed out to India in the first place, hopeful of such riches – among whom might be numbered William himself.

Money is the letters' chief subject throughout, not unreasonably, given the precariousness of such lives, where fear of bankruptcy stalked even the successful. Bankruptcy had destroyed Margaret Farmer's protégé's father, as it had destroyed some of Sam's fellow businessmen. ('I hope the exaggerated accounts of the bankruptcies here have not alarmed you,' Sam writes on 15 February 1773). Empire builders, bringing civilization to the benighted 'Hindoo' in the way recommended by Thomas Macaulay (1800–59) 75 years later, the Farmers were not, any more than they were evangelical zealots out to convert the heathen like many of their other successors. (Most of the rare appeals to the Almighty are to be found in the letters from Margaret Farmer – and are of the most conventional kind). There is no evidence in the family letters that William fell in love with the subcontinent, adopting its mores and its dress, in the manner of the 'White Mughuls' described by William Dalrymple,[21] even if the letters in the letter book give a more nuanced picture of his life in India. Certainly he complains of much – calling some of his Indian contacts 'thieves and rogues'.

At the same time the more personal letters, particularly the ones to Sir Charles Malet and William Palmer, both of whom had established Indian families, indicate that he wholly accepted their way of life. He asks to be remembered to Palmer's Indian wife, and 'He ends this letter 'Yr faithful and affectionate friend', indicating the strength of the friendship even though till the time of writing the two had not recently been in touch (17 June 1795). This was more evidence of how deeply embedded he was in Indian life in every respect, not surprisingly given how much of it he spent in the Durbars of Indian Rajahs and negotiating with Hindu and Parsi businessmen – not to mention the year he spent as hostage in the Indian army camp. His letters to his chief business colleague, the Parsi merchant Dady Nasserwanjee always begin 'Dear Friend Dady'.[22] In November 1795, he sends Diwali greetings to another Hindu contact and frequently uses Hindi words in this correspondence, in particular the Hindi word for 'fate' whether in relation to his life or theirs. Earlier in his career, according to the letters of April 1776 from his London business colleagues Richardson and Stacey, he had pleaded the cause of another Parsi colleague being fleeced by impecunious English officers. And he also insisted on proper provision for other Indian colleagues and for his 'loyal' servant at his departure for England in 1796. But this did not stop his attitudes hardening over time. In *Trade and Empire in Western India*, Pamela Nightingale quotes Farmer as suggesting, in 1789, that the Company should not leave trade to 'Crew of Parsees in whose welfare the State has no interest and who on every occasion have plucked the Company without mercy'.[23]

Overall, William was what Thomas Macaulay would later call 'one of the young men who came out as Company servants and for whom banishment is their emancipation'.[24] He was one of those who, unlike Macaulay, had become so accustomed to what they saw around them as to regard India as normal if not always to be accepted as it stood. It was a world with which such men had to contend socially and professionally throughout their careers, especially in Bombay where English and Indian lived in much closer contact. One near contemporary, Maria Graham (1785–1842), in her *Journal of a Residence in India*, published in 1812, complained of being much further from Indian life in Madras and Calcutta, places which William also knew.[25] Macaulay, in contrast, retreated thankfully from closer contact with Indian life to a house in Calcutta surrounded by a garden and never ventured into the world beyond without shuddering at the immorality and squalor – 'a dozen half-naked blacks!' – described in an early letter home to his sister Margaret.[26] The much more pragmatic accounts of William himself, let alone the more lyrical, sometimes even dazzled, accounts in James Forbes' (1749–1814) *Oriental Memoirs* of 1813 seem to come from quite different sensibilities, from another world – even if Forbes, in later life did advocate converting the 'Hindoo' to Christianity.[27]

I have a further point to make before detailing William's career more fully. It is a philosophical rather than historical point that would apply to all communication between London and India at this date, given the distance between them and the length of time between letters and reports being written and their arrival in the hands of the intended recipient – not least because ships of that period were only able to sail at certain seasons of the year, in order to utilize more favourable winds and tides. Time has two different faces. On the one hand there is the linear time that the letter-writer is living through and describing. On the other there are the discrete moments in time, the snapshots, read by the recipient. The writer does not know as he or she writes where the recipient is, even if he or she is still alive. Sam around 1775 complains as he writes that he does not know where to send the letters or whether or when they will reach William, currently – he thinks – somewhere between Calcutta and Madras. The contemporary reader likewise does not know exactly how or where the writer is, six months having passed since the letter was written. This leads to various kinds of redundancy: here on 8 July 1774 is Sam, for instance, sending a millstone for William's Biscuit Factory after he has closed it, and Sam again, in the same month in 1774, chiding William for not writing to their father, though a letter had been despatched in January 1774. And here he is being asked to send the seeds for William's garden in a letter that would have arrived after William had left India for good. Finally, late in 1795, Sam asks permission to send his brother a case of claret, just as William was about to leave Surat – permission fortunately was not granted.

I am also conscious of how little those back in England would have known about the real nature of life in India. They would have known about the health problems – William complains in his first letter about having fallen victim to the 'bloody flux' (dysentery) – and they would have known about the malaria he suffered from and which probably killed him in the end. But how much they could have known – or comprehended – about his lodging, his environment, the climate and his travels within India, is harder to gauge. He may have been more open in his earlier letters to Sam; he claims he had told him more about the voyage out than he has time to tell his father. But these letters do not survive and those to his father are determinedly upbeat, even if he complains in the 1774 letter, as throughout his career in India, how difficult it is to make money there. But literary William is not: it seems unlikely that, even to Sam, he would have made the detailed, scholarly, almost thrilled descriptions of the country found in the *Oriental Memoirs* of his near contemporary James Forbes – who mentioned William as an 'intimate acquaintance'.[28] Forbes's memoirs were not published till the 1813 edition – edited, unfortunately, by a pious daughter and at a time when contemporary accounts of India were beginning to flood out – and published descriptions of life in India through the second half of the eighteenth century were much rarer. Many were related to the captive narratives, discussed by Linda Colley, often by women of dubious reputation – Eliza Fay (c.1755–1816) and Elizabeth Marsh (1735–85), for instance.[29] If any of these volumes fell into the hands of the Farmer family, their letters do not say.

The Farmers might have recognized – and been bored by – the stultifying English social life of Bombay, an island only a mile in length and lacking in English women. Sam might have been comfortable with the atmosphere of a place where, according to George Paterson in 1769 'trade and the means of getting money is [men's] principal pursuit'.[30] But could they have imagined the heat of a Bombay summer or the fury of the monsoon, or for that matter the prevalence of various kinds of wildlife indoors and out of which later residents such as Mrs Sherwood (1775–1851) complained?[31] Could they have imagined the 'execrable material effects' of climate described by Macaulay?[32] Could they have understood that Bombay, with a relatively pleasant climate, as noted by James Forbes among others – the malaria inducing marshes by now mostly drained – was quite possibly rather less noisome and dirty than their own filthy and stinking city? William's family lived after all above the dye works, a notoriously smelly business and eighteenth-century London was far from being the 'so clean city' that surprised Indian visitors to my house in the 1980s. (An older man added; 'but your people are so dirty', a statement still more true in the eighteenth century: one of the many complaints made against nabobs when they returned to England was that they had picked up the effete Indian habit of washing daily).[33]

William, on the other hand, would have less difficulty in imagining life in England. He made several home visits (the first in 1768) spending two or three years in England between 1780 and 1784, and both his mother and his brother filled him in on life as it went on. Latterly he even tried to import something more of it than European dress – hence the seeds for his 'English' garden. His mother's gossip about the Duchess of Devonshire's dangerous metal corsets might have seemed very remote from Bombay but at least he could have appreciated the context and maybe been grateful to feel some connection to his family's world. John Gillis's distinction between home as the family we live in and home as the family we live by seems apposite here.[34] William never created a family in India to live in: the family he grew up in, thousands of miles away, was the one he lived by, as these letters suggest.

William Gamul Farmer's career

Nine writers were appointed to the Bombay residency in 1763 according to EIC records.[35] Of five there is no trace later than 1768. One more survived until his return to England in 1780. Two appear in the records till the 1790s. William's death in January 1798, at 51, made him long-lived by these standards, though not by those of his long-lived family – Sam survived till the age of 93. India was a notoriously unhealthy place for Europeans at that time.[36] In part, this high mortality rate was due to tropical diseases, malaria in particular – hence William's request to his brother is for 'bark' otherwise quinine, then the only remedy (December 1789). But it was also in part because of their failure to adapt their habits to the climate. According to one contemporary observer, 'many newcomers shorten their days by a mode of life unsuitable to the climate, eating great quantities of beef and pork and drinking copiously of the strong wines of Portugal in the hottest season. In addition they persisted in wearing European dress which restricted the free circulation of the blood and made the heat more intolerable by confining the limbs'.[37]

William's petition for an EIC writership was standard: it included proof of baptism, of having been educated in writing and accounts ('a regular course of accountancy after the Garton method'), and also the standard promise 'to behave himself with the utmost Diligence and Fidelity and is ready to give such Security as your Honours shall require'.[38]

The man who recommended him, Edward Ward, was an EIC proprietor in 1762, though he is not one of the Company names mentioned in William's first letter from Bombay in October 1763. Having arrived in India, William sounds hopeful of commercial success at first, despite complaining that 'Bombay is not a place for Writers just come out, everything of necessaries is very dear. Our allowance of 30 rupees a month [£3.10] really not enough for subsistence. There never was anyone ever so parsimonious that could make it serve'. He has not much help from his superiors. 'Upon my first landing I was introduced to the governour [*sic.*] and delivered my letters'. He wrote in October 1763. 'He took no notice of them nor as much as mentioned them to me such is the effect of letters of recommendation. The Governour indeed is a very particular man, he has been a Drudge to the Services all his lifetime'.

But William had better welcome from a Mr Spencer, an old India hand and a close ally of Laurence Sulivan (1713–86), later chairman of the East India Company in London:

> Mr Burgess' letter to Mr Spencer I hardly know what to say about. Mr Spencer sent for me and told me I had been very strongly recommended by Mr Burgess, he made no promise of serving me he very seldom does but if he sees a person sober and steady at business that has been recommended to him he always takes notice of that. I had an invitation to dinner, a thing not a very common. (October 1763).

Patronage and connection lay at the heart of Company trade, and here we see William Farmer's first forays into its social and political intricacies at Bombay.

William, of course, like all Company servants at that date, was allowed to conduct his own, private trade whenever he was not put to Company business. (Company business, meant, at the beginning of his career, endlessly copying EIC correspondence within India and to and from London; his title 'writer' meant exactly what it said.) As he points out in this first letter, the Company paid its servants far too little to live on. They had to make money for themselves – or go bankrupt as some in Bombay did, while others returned home without fortunes.[39] This system continued in Bombay till the early nineteenth century; it was the source of the fortunes that were made then – and that had been made in Bengal for many years if among the few rather than the many. It was also the source of the corruption so derided in England in popular descriptions of nabobs, and the reason for the eventual prohibition on private trade first in the Bengal and Madras presidencies and subsequently in the Bombay presidency following the suspect fortunes made, like William's, down the Malabar coast. William himself in the letter book complains that the profits and efficiency of the Company were much undermined by servants' private trade, and is also highly critical of a system which sent many of them to take up office in places where they did not speak the language and had very little idea of local cultural and legal norms – a system the Company did begin to amend at the end of the eighteenth century. Understanding language, law and culture was something that William, on the other hand appears to have sought out for himself, which may partly have explained his friendships with Malet and Palmer, both much closer to Indian life than the norm among Company men.

Company servants were not, of course, allowed to compete with Company trade – which was much less profitable in Bombay than in Bengal. Nor could they trade directly with England, but instead had to send goods east, to China, for example. In particular they were not allowed to compete with Bombay in its chief trade in raw cotton and later pepper. However 'sober and steady at business' William might have tried to be, he had little luck in early years; pickings in Bombay were few, unlike in Bengal. Fortunately his investments were not always so ill advised as the loan the 16-year-old mentions making to the impecunious Mr Waters, without any serious attempt to discover if Mr Waters would ever be in a position to repay him. But the loan, in 'respondentia' – that is, lending money to other merchants to buy ships' cargoes – was one way of making money he continued to use through his career in India, successfully enough, judging by the sums his letters claim that he hopes to bring home. Pamela Nightingale, for example, refers to his lending by responentia in 1789.[40]

Despite managing to stay alive (unlike so many of his fellows), William was not without health problems – in particular chronic malaria to judge from his descriptions of the symptoms that forced him to give up his Chiefship at Surat at very short notice in late 1795 and that probably led to his death in England barely two years later. He was having such problems as early as 1768, judging by the return to England for the sake of his health. His appointment in 1772 was to one of the few posts available to still junior company servants; this post as Assistant to the Marine Storekeeper presumably gave him useful information on matters of ships' cargoes. But in the second letter to his father, on 16 January 1774, while indicating that he is surviving financially, he also complains how much harder it has become in the prevailing political situation to make money: 'When I was in India before I could have lent taking the tune of

£10,000 a year safely on respondentia … now it is difficult to lend one rupee safely insomuch that I think it best to let my money lay at the common interest of 9% which I can lay by and keep corresponding yearly … and with that economy live on the Company allowance … which everything included is only £126 a year and this is little enough let me tell for one who has been in their service now going on 11 years – if had not got the Bakehouse to employment I do not know what I should have done.' The Bakehouse was a factory making hard tack, the staple seaman's diet. Being close to the Marine Storekeeper must have been useful here too. Setting up the bakery appears to have been a piece of typical private initiative on his behalf: throughout his career, the ever-increasing sums he claims he will be able to bring home do suggest that he succeeded in making more money in Bombay than many of his contemporaries, even if not quite the legitimate fortune for which he was hoping. He adds:

> the greatest profit … . is supplying the Company's fighting vessels here with Biscuit I do not know what I should have done – in the last year here between you and me I made one thousand pounds of it but do not expect to make this year more than 500 and shall be content with that for among other reductions the Company have lessened their Marine Force here almost a half, the consequence of which you know must be that there will be fewer biscuits cracked.

His pessimistic assessment was due to the dire financial straits of the Bombay Presidency, always a much less profitable station than Bengal and Madras. William goes on to claim that with all his other financial strategies he should be able to return to England within four years with £8,000, not yet the great fortune that his father might have hoped for, but one he could live on. 'The more I think of it the more I approve of my Plan especially when I consider there is no one depends upon me at present for provision nor I believe ever will be, for unless a man is governed by an unknown destiny in the act of marriage I think I shall die a bachelor'.

It could have been that his warring parents had put him off marriage altogether, or that he did not see himself as making enough to support an English wife, an expensive business in Bombay, and/or he would have preferred to set himself up with an Indian bibi or two like Malet or Palmer or his own first governor, Charles Crommelin (1718–88). Or it could have been for quite another reason. His letter to Palmer many years later says, of Palmer's Indian wife back in 1774, 'she was young and very pretty and I was young, No need to be jealous – of your females

I only troubled the Mattranney,' suggesting that he himself was far from unsusceptible to the charms of Indian women, on a social level at least. (And on that level he certainly did like women, to judge by his fondness for his sister-in-law, Sam's wife). His sexual susceptibilities are less clear. My attempts to chase up the eighteenth-century meaning of 'Maltranny,' have so far been in vain. But the fact that Googling the contemporary word leads to a number of porn sites involving those young men otherwise known as 'ladyboys' may be significant. Could Palmer's household have included a eunuch I wonder? Could it be that William's reluctance to marry was due to his being homosexual? Could it even be that his dabbling in such directions was the bad behaviour that led to him being sent away to India? Who knows? Although he left no will in Bombay providing for any dependents this does not mean he had none, any more than the lack of records in the British Library's IOR series of any unofficial marriage or of any births or christenings resulting from such a union proves that he remained unattached. He would have had the opportunity, both in Bombay and elsewhere to consort with nautch (dancing) girls; in Bombay, parties to which the local Parsi traders invited customers such as William often included nautch girls dancing. To the south in Madras, after parties at the palaces of local Indian nawabs, unmarried Englishmen were reported to go home with the dancers. That said, the Farmers being a conventionally respectable family – the horror evoked by the behaviour of Sam and William's half-sister is significant – it was more than likely he would have kept such attachments – let alone, alternatively, his lack of interest in women – to himself. The one certainty is that he lived, mostly, in a society of bachelors: relatively few wives came out to India before the nineteenth century, and even some of the official ones were Anglo-Indian.[41] Many other bachelors did not marry until they returned to England for good.

The EIC records and, tangentially, the family letters, record William's presence in Madras on private business and thereafter in Calcutta. His senior officer, John Taylor, a Bombay civil servant, had been charged with explaining a recent treaty made by the Bombay Presidency to the government there. In November 1776 Taylor died. Farmer was again in Madras on business. Not only his Bombay masters objected to his long absence: Sam too complained of not knowing where his brother was. Their mother on 15 and 20 December 1775 meanwhile referred to letters coming from 'Calcutter'. Back in England, William had been made heir over his mother's head to her family's run-down estate in Cheshire. Despite her chagrin, her letters thereafter, attempting to entice him home, were full of the orchard she had had planted for him, and

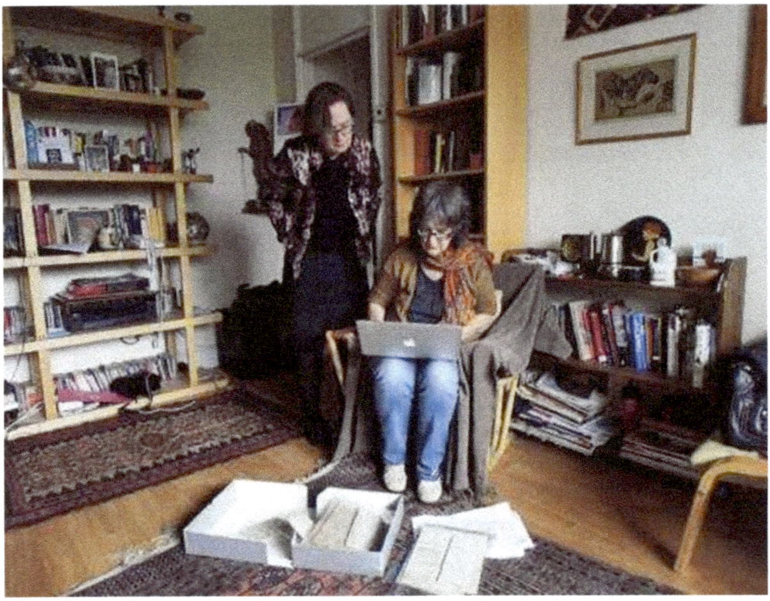

Figure 17.3 Penelope Farmer and Margot Finn with the manuscripts. Image courtesy of Penelope Farmer.

her other attempts to bring the neglected estate up to scratch – another example of an energy and efficiency she was so rarely given the opportunity to use. All this was interwoven with the description of a burglary at her house, probably instigated by a maidservant – 'I got one that let a gang into my house at a celler window and robbed me of more than 30 in cloaths and other things. I heard 'em in the house but would not ring for fear that I should in coming to me be murdered' – and by descriptions of her attempts to find a doctor to cure her of unspecified ailments (15 December 1795). Later, on 3 March 1777, she finds lodgings in London for the winter, only to be forced to move because of the noisy young man downstairs (see Figure 17.3).

Money continued to be a problem throughout this period, as did William's health. In 1777 he was one of the signatories to a letter from all the Company servants to the Council complaining about the inadequacies of the Company salaries.[42] The permission to go to Poona 'for his health' meant that at a time of political crisis he was able to give important intelligence of the Designs of a Monsieur St Lubin, who was endeavouring to conclude an Alliance with the Marathas. (The Marathas were the warlike Indian rulers throughout the territory of the Bombay Presidency, whom the Bombay directorate attempted unsuccessfully during two wars in the 1770s to drive back, while working, more successfully, to keep out the French). It also led to his appointments first as Secretary to the Poona Committee and then as Marathi translator. There was no indication whether he had learned Marathi while in Poona or whether he had acquired the language in Bombay. The language used among themselves by his Parsi colleagues was Persian, a language William may have acquired, as he did others – certainly, according to a letter to Sam in 1789, he encouraged a protégé to learn it. In the diary of his travels sent to the Bombay Council in December 1793 when he was supervisor of the Malabar province, he complains of having to translate some of his dealings into Portuguese, and appears to indicate some knowledge of the local language besides.[43]

William Gamul Farmer's knowledge of Marathi was probably one reason he was, along with a Lieutenant Stuart, left as hostage in the camp of the general, Scindia (c.1730–94) after his defeat of the Company forces in January 1779. The two remained there until March of the following year. No word of this experience to or from William's family survives, though there is a request from Sam Farmer noted in the EIC court records, 27 April 1780, asking for steps to be taken for the release of his brother.[44] A later account of this episode reports William asking if he and Stuart – both young men still – could swim in a river there. They were refused permission on the grounds that the river probably flowed to the sea and that the Englishmen as water people 'might escape that way'.[45] Another reference, this time by James Forbes, has William, his 'intimate acquaintance contriving to send me secretly a few words concealed within the tube of a very small quill, run into the messenger's ear, to inform me of the enemy's determination to recapture Dhuboy; advising me … to make the best terms possible and deliver up the keys to the Maratha sirdar as all resistance would be vain'.[46]

This was not an easy year for William. To summarize a large volume of correspondence in the EIC records, William was continually asking for money for his various expenses in Scindia's camp, was in constant danger because of the Company's immediate failure to keep the terms of the treaty, and was especially at risk because of his supply of secret information to General Goddard commander of the Company army. He was also forced to bribe some of Scindia's men to prevent them roughing him up, and in the end had to pay his own ransom, recouping it from the Bombay Presidency with much difficulty and only with the aid of Warren Hastings himself.[47] It was not surprising that later in his career he so resented his treatment by the Company and expressed his sense that it owed him something for his pains. Certainly William's long and sometimes dangerous sojourn in the Poona area would have deepened his knowledge of an India which he appears – socially, geographically as well as linguistically – to have known as well or better than most. The geographer James Rennell (1742–1830) thanked him for providing information that improved the accuracy of his mapping of the area around Poona.[48] William's close friendship with Charles Malet, long-time resident at Poona, almost certainly stemmed from this time.

Allowed by the Company to go to England after his ordeal, he reported to William Palmer (in a letter of 17 June 1795), that he had returned to India after losing his money investing in 'manufactory'. But the fact he had not resigned his post meantime, suggest that despite taking an adequate fortune home, he had remained ambivalent about leaving India for good. The appointment he then received as Chief at Fort Victoria, a very small settlement, 60 miles from Bombay, was definitely not a lucrative one. The post he really wanted and seemed to think he had earned was as Chief of Surat. But when Ramsay, its Chief, resigned early in 1787, John Griffiths, William's junior, already at Surat as Ramsay's deputy, was appointed to the post, something of which William complained bitterly in a letter from Fort Victoria in February 1787.[49] He protested however in vain.

His posting to Tannah on the Island of Salsette (all now part of the city of Mumbai), if not much more profitable than Fort Victoria, did produce the first surviving family letters for 11 years. There were two from William to Sam (dated 3 July and December), in handwriting by now much deteriorated. Here William shows himself the old India hand, advising newcomers on how to get on in India. Of one boy he says that 'the best thing for him is to leave him some years where he is as that will form him to the habit and knowledge of public business whereas removing a young man from Bombay tho it betters his present income generally renders him indolent and ignorant for ever from the want of sufficient occupation'. Another boy he has taken with him to Tannah, 'which will keep him from bad company and bad habits most of all which prevail in a large and mixed company'. This was also the boy he had taught Persian. William still talks of coming home – if all comes through he hopes to return with £15,000, which together with his inheritance, he considers would be sufficient to live on comfortably.

Sam's continuing support for William in these years was not merely practical. He had, it seems, commiserated with William on being passed over for Surat, for William responds in relatively philosophical mode. 'If it had been my destiny I should have had Surat, as it was your manners were certainly very proper', he wrote in December 1789. Sam's concern is reciprocated in William's affectionate and equally concerned reference to his admirably docile sister-in-law. Elizabeth is no longer living above the business in Hogg Lane or even in Mortimer Street in the West End, where Sam appears to have acquired a house at some point. For by now Sam also possesses a Beckenham country estate, his income from a successful dye business having been added to by his ventures in the slave trade.[50] Elizabeth's only son was now of an age to be off at boarding school, and her husband was still working in London, but she does not seem to be flourishing in the new home. William writes in December 1789 of the fear Sam has given him for 'my sister's health … . I am afraid she keeps too much in the house or perhaps you have now planted Beckenham which precludes proper air or perhaps you are too solitary in the country. I will cure her when I come back again and make her ride out … . I am much younger than when I left England and have much better spirits'.

William Gamul Farmer's fortune

And so, at last, to William's possible acquisition of the fortune he had sought for so long. The climax of his career followed his reluctant departure to the Coromandel Coast after the defeat of Tipu Sultan (1750–99) in 1792. In these years William served first as joint commissioner charged with investigating potential revenue from the pepper trade and a year later, as Supervisor of the Malabar province. Pamela Nightingale's study details the suspicions against him following these appointments.[51] Firstly there was his close collaboration with a disreputable Mahé trader, Murdock Brown, whom he claimed not to have known beforehand, a claim Nightingale disputes.[52] Walter Ewer, an EIC Director from 1792 to 1795 who was sent to report on the province later wrote of Brown, 'I am firmly of opinion that if he had his deserts he ought to be hanged as a traitor to his Country or sent Prisoner of War to Bombay.'[53] Evidently William did not share Ewer's distrust: protesting Brown's virtues many times over, he took Brown with him in his tour round the durbars of the Northern

Province Indian rajahs, as translator for the finer points for which he claimed his own command of the local language was not sufficient. He also took Brown's advice on what he claimed to his superiors in Bombay were the only viable arrangements for the pepper tax.

In William's extensive official diary he recounts in detail his travels in the Malabar and of his difficult dealings with the rajahs.[54] But just how much he – and Murdock Brown – profited from the fiscal arrangements they made is not clear. Though Nightingale acknowledges his relatively astute understanding of local rivalries and the way they could be exploited, she is sure he did profit and not only from the pepper tax. As superintendent, William was also in charge of the mint at Mahé that produced the local coinage, the fanam, in reference to which the critical Walter Ewer noted: 'that [Mr Farmer] had a great advantage from it few people doubt'.[55]

The advantage in either case led almost certainly to the letter written to Sam on 14 June 1794 in which the clandestine nature of his trading activities emerges clearly:

> Not to trust too much to the man who copies for me it is necessary to inform you separately that the reason why I have avoid the appearance of your name or mine in any shape in the bills of exchange to be sent to Europe from China is that it may not be known at the India House to whose accounts these remittances are made. There are certain malicious reports I find prevail here as to the great increase of my fortune by going down the coast. Though not wholly true it would be more expedient to avoid giving weight to them by my combusting circumstances. If it was observed at the India House that such large remittances were making for my account it might give rise to suspicion and perhaps to enquiries which at best are always troublesome.

He appears to rationalize these clandestine transactions, noting the deprivations he had suffered over the course of his long career in India. William Gamul Farmer even here was not going to forego any monies he thought the company owed him:

> You may say this – from my long service and loss of health in the Malabar business I should be entitled to petition the company for some annuity should I be obliged to relinquish Surat which the extent of my fortune if known would prevent me from attaining

> and I shall therefore find it convenient to say I am only worth £25 to 30 000 which at 4% cash is but a poor remittance after 30 years service.

The following year, facing questions in Bombay about the tax arrangements that he had made, William wrote a very lengthy defence of his actions.[56] His defence was not accepted by other observers such as James Stevens, his successor in Malabar.[57] Apart from appealing to Murdock Brown to back him up (in several letters in the letter book between 1794–5), he also sent a copy of his defence to Sam, the one piece of his writing to be found both among the family letters and in the EIC records. This was not merely to justify himself to his brother: according to the letter book it was also so that Sam could use its contents in William's defence if the Council in London showed signs of depriving him of the Surat Chiefship, following suspicions of his activities down on the coast.[58]

Though his arrival in Surat was much delayed, he did at last attain the Chiefship. But William's stay lasted barely nine months and was far from peaceable. He wrote to Sam on 4 September 1795, 'by way of amusement this month we have had an insurrection of the Mahometon mob who rose, plundered and abused the Hindoos and it has occasioned a great deal of writing and a great deal of trouble to me'. Yet he sounds contented enough, even claiming, of the appointment of his friend Jonathan Duncan to the Bombay governorship, 'I am very glad the governorship did not fall on my shoulders as I wish for nothing so much as a quiet retirement somewhere.' (This latter possibility was due to his old school-friend Francis Baring's actions on his behalf, though, given the suspicions against him it seems unlikely that he would have been considered.) He continues in his final letter from Surat in November 1795:

> The truth really is that by the setting in of the cold weather together with an abstinence of wine my stomach and my general health are so much mended that I feel quite comfortable and if it was not for the pleasure of rejoining the family I should feel totally indifferent abut England nor do I think that any part of my life I either have been so comfortable or shall be so comfortable as I am at present with my body in a tolerable state and my mind occupied and gratified … I think at least that your next in answer to this will find me still here, and therefore I must remember for you about the garden seeds that occupation being my principal delight here.

Amid discussions of EIC politics and, Indian politics, of the profits he was proposing to send home, he gives orders for the seeds to be obtained from a Mr Swinton of Brentford, near Isleworth, instructing that they should be packed in a very particular way. He even requests some fruit trees, nectarines. In a letter book missive of 1 July 1795 to his Portuguese agent and friend, Miguel de Lima de Souza (c.1750–1808) he also asks for orange trees from China, here again giving precise instructions as to how they were to be packed. In the letter to his sister-in-law on 19 November, he makes clear that his interest was hands-on in every sense. 'I am frequently up to the elbows in dirt,' he tells her.

This mixture of contentment in his Indian life and nostalgia for home is interesting: William seems as ever in the imperial bind, caught between two worlds. One analysis of his management in Surat suggests it was the start of a greater separation between Indian and white colonial life which became the nineteenth-century norm.[59] If so, maybe his Englishness was reasserting itself, and he wanted to live more as if 'at home', despite having been so close to Indian society and its mores for so long, un-cushioned by family and domestic life. Yet after spending two-thirds of his life in the subcontinent, he did not feel sufficiently English either to engage totally with life in family preferring to recreate this one small part of it in a world by now so much more familiar to him. He could also, in some respects have seen it as his way of creating a family. In a letter to John Forbes in July 1795, referring to his orange trees, he adds that 'planting a tree and getting a child are amongst the cardinal virtues and as I make no attempt at the latter I must compensate in the tree way'. Yet in some respects William's English garden seems as much a myth of family and England as an actuality. I doubt if many peas and cabbages grew behind the family dye works above which William grew up, let alone orange trees.

But William was never to see his peas and cabbages, his orange trees, grow. It was Malabar he always claimed had finally ruined his health. In his official journal there he had reported that illness sometimes prevented his working: this same illness led to his departure from the province. Complaints of ill-health recur throughout the letter book he kept thereafter. His renewed optimism in early December 1795 turned out premature. Due to an injudiciously cold bath after riding, he claimed, he fell ill again. Despite wishing to stay in India till the situation in Europe improved, he was forced to plan his departure. In January 1796, he boarded the Bombay ship, *The Princess Amelia*, hoping the voyage would mend his health. As ambivalent as ever, William did not resign immediately, despite arranging for his local possessions to be auctioned: if he proceeded no further than the Cape, his position at Surat would remain open. He did indeed proceed further; the *Amelia* failed to stop at the Cape, something William claims to have regretted in a shipboard letter to Sam, his health having improved. The ship's log shows him disembarking at Southampton in July 1796.[60] In an ironic, not to say galling coda, it also showed him being accompanied as far as St Helena by his erstwhile junior, John Griffiths. John Griffiths was piped on and off the ship with a 19-gun salute: William's was just 17.

William Gamul Farmer survived less than 18 months in England. His will was proved in February 1798, a month after his death.[61] It is very brief, unlike that of Sam nearly 40 years later,[62] and contains no details of property, making Sam the sole residuary legatee – of how much exactly, I cannot be sure. Letters in the letter book to Dady, Sam and others shift from claiming that he was sending enough money home to be able to live comfortably to claiming he was only bringing back a pittance, not enough, he said, to help out Sam who was having business difficulties of his own. (Sam's venture into the slave trade appears not to have been successful: among the family papers is a copy of a request dated 1 December 1790 for information about one slave ship, indicating almost certain wreck). It is of course true that getting money back from India via Bills of Exchange was an uncertain business at the best of times and particularly in the mid-1790s because of the war with the French and the dangers of attack besides shipwreck. Whether through wreck or attack, the loss of a ship could destroy not only the bills but also the goods – and so the profits – on which merchants depended.

William sent multiple copies of the bills on different ships to avert the first danger and tried to use particularly stable houses like Forbes or Scott to pre-empt the second of these perils. His second set of bills, for instance, was drawn on Scott, and sent to a different bank. One tranche of his money, the 150,000 rupees – approximately £15,000 – sent to China by his Portuguese colleague, Miguel de Lima de Souza in 1795, he claimed reduced to only £2,000 because of the loss of the ship in which the money was invested. On the other hand he also claimed to have insured himself against this possibility, so who knows what the sum did actually come to. Still, adding together the sums of his theoretical assets, £27,000 from the first batch of bills, plus the £28,000 odd from the second and adding to these the £1,000 he had in hand in Bombay, the full amount he could have remitted to England was something between £60,000 and £70,000. Even taking away the £15,000 from de Souza would still have left him with a comfortable £55,000 odd – on which, of course, as it turned out, he did not have to live. On William's death, most of the money would have gone intact to Sam, who did not (unlike his brother) invest it in 'manufactory' but put it straight into that then much safer asset – landed property. This was not, by nabob standards, an enormous fortune: General Richard Smith, for example, was reputed to have returned with £300,000, a huge sum for the time.[63] Even so, it might be fair to suggest that William's fortune from India was one means by which Sam Farmer, the successful but maybe not quite so successful, dye merchant – and slave trader – raised his family to the landed gentry and an entry in Burke's *Landed Gentry*.

Sam had been prosperous enough before his brother died to have acquired one Surrey estate and sent his one son to Harrow and Cambridge. Yet only in 1799 after William's will was proved did he truly spread himself, buying the estates in Cambridgeshire, Huntingdonshire and Surrey that he mentions in an 1810 letter to his son. Above all Sam acquired the Nonsuch estate, along with its Mansion House, which he immediately had remodelled in the Tudor-Gothic style by the future remodeller of Windsor Castle, Sir Jeffrey Wyatt, later known as Wyattville. In 1802 he opened an account at Hoare's Bank with £1,100 – 'a very large and interesting account' according to a letter from the bank to my father. In 1804, for £4,000, he also bought himself the rotten borough of Huntingdon from Lord Sandwich, first putting his son in the seat, then sitting as an MP himself between 1810 and 1818. A nineteenth-century account of MPs listed some as contemporary Dick Whittingtons: men who had made their fortunes in London. Among these figured Samuel Farmer.[64]

Conclusion

Indian fortune or not, William was no nabob in the tradition of the Bengal returnees. Though suspended like them between their English and Indian selves, he did not live long enough to throw his money about, had he been inclined to. Nor did he bring Indian goods and artefacts home with him – his lack of a wife and family might explain this. With him on the *Amelia* he proposed taking only his 'bureau', his papers – among them likely the letter book – cases of wine, and his 'turkies' (that is, carpets). At the sale of the family house in 1937 the sole evidence of India in the sale catalogue was a Benares tray and four 'very large' elephants – carved ones, presumably.[65] And though his heir, Sam, made use of William's money for his acquisitions of property, it was prudent investment judging by his refusal to advance his son more money until his estates had begun earning. His greatest extravagance appears to have been employing Wyatt to work on Nonsuch. Sam's progeny by contrast were country gentry with the tastes and habits of country gentlemen. His eldest grandson had a noted collection of orchids. His eldest great-grandson was Lord Lieutenant of Surrey. Only the younger males of the family continued to seek employment, though not in trade of any kind and none as empire builders, not even the two who emigrated to Canada. Some went into the army or the church, and my own grandfather took up the law, if in a branch of it which provided vacations generous enough to allow him to pursue his preferred activity as a gentleman of leisure: mountaineering.

Nonsuch itself remained in the family until 1937, when it was sold by my father's niece: Sam's intention to pass his house down through the male line had been thwarted by the nineteenth-century clerk who omitted the word 'male' from the entail. (I like to imagine the ghost of William's mother Margaret directing his pen). One subsequent loser, my father, did inherit a little of the family money – perhaps a residue of William's Indian fortune? He used it to put his four children through boarding school. His son being no academic, the last vestiges paid for a daughter, me, to read history at Oxford.

In conclusion I would acknowledge once more that our family story – and that of our EIC ancestor – remains a relative footnote in the history of the Company and its gradual transformation into an imperial government. It did not leave behind a particularly notable story; the fortune brought back was modest by nabob standards and the family mansion the fortune enabled was not imposing enough to have fallen into the hands of the National Trust, let alone to house an astonishing collection of jewellery like those garnered by officials with greater access to Nawab treasuries and the profitable indigo trade. (The haul owned by the Harris family and formerly in Belmont House, Kent is one example). William Gamul Farmer did not come from an aristocratic family – or one that was ennobled because of a career in India – was responsible for no government policy and initiated no military campaigns. He merely went where he was sent and made what he could of it. It was a history, less like that of the famous names of the Imperial story, more like that of the majority of those who went out to eighteenth-century India on behalf of the EIC, and left behind no records other than what remains in the India Office records. William's distinctions, however,

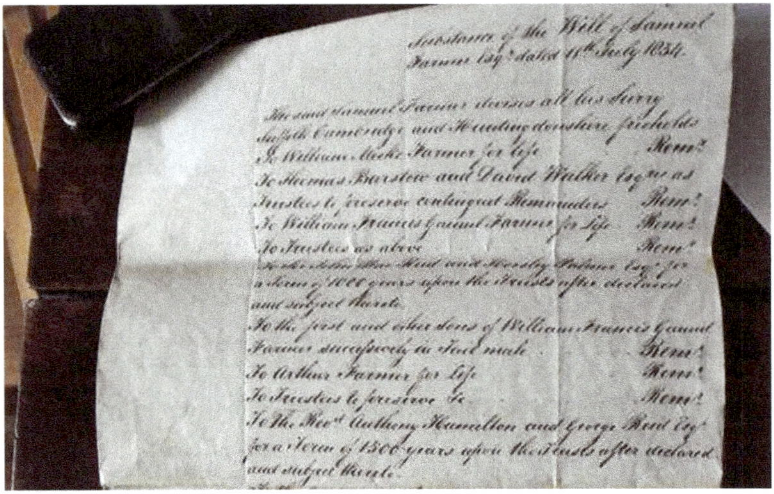

Substance of the Will of Samuel Farmer Esq.r dated 11th July 1834.

The said Samuel Farmer devises all his Surry Suffolk Cambridge and Huntingdonshire freeholds
To William Meeke Farmer for life Rem.r
To Thomas Barstow and David Walker Esq.res as Trustees to preserve contingent Remainders Rem.r
To William Francis Gamul Farmer for Life Rem.r
To Trustees as above Rem.r
To [illegible] and Horsley Palmer Esq.rs for a term of 1000 years upon the Trusts after declared and subject thereto.
To the first and other sons of William Francis Gamul Farmer successively in Tail male Rem.r
To Arthur Farmer for Life Rem.r
To Trustees to preserve &c Rem.r
To the Rev.d Anthony Hamilton and George Reid Esq.r for a term of 1500 years upon the Trusts after declared and subject thereto.

Figure 17.4 Samuel Farmer's will. Image courtesy of Penelope Farmer.

were that he lasted much longer in India than many and managed to make an – in part dubious – profit from the least promising presidency; the more commercial background he came from no doubt helped him in that. But his family's distinction was that he and they not only put themselves on paper in all their ordinariness, but that so much of what they wrote survives. In these writings it is precisely their ordinariness – especially of the female kind – that matters. One woman, Sam Farmer's wife, was smothered by her lack of role in this history, to judge from her brother-in-law's concern in his letter to Sam in December 1789. Another, Sam and William's half-sister, went her own – apparently disreputable – way in Chelsea. A third woman, their mother, also fought back in the only – mostly domestic – ways she knew and documented it for herself in the letters to her eldest son. History may not be made in such insignificant corners, but it can, certainly, in human terms, come to life in them.

Timeline

- Arrived at Bombay 1763 with the appointment of writer.
- October 1764 appointed an assistant in the president's office.
- June 1767 was appointed assistant to the storekeeper.
- In 1768 permitted to return to Europe for the sake of his health. Recommended for leave, to return in 1771.

- 1772 appointed assistant to the marine storekeeper.
- In 1774 obtained permission to proceed to Madras on private affairs.
- In 1775 was sent to Bengal as assistant to Mr Taylor. In 1776 Mr Taylor died. In May 1777 Mr Farmer was censured for not returning from Bengal and on his arrival in Bombay in July 1777 explained the cause of his absence to the satisfaction of the board and the censure was withdrawn.
- Latter end of 1777, permitted to go to Poona (present-day Pune) for his health.
- In 1778 appointed secretary to the Poona committee, in February 1778 he was left as hostage with the Marathas. In March 1779 he was released.
- In 1780 proceeded to Europe on his private affairs and was recommended for leave to return. According to 1794 letter to General William Palmer included in his letter book he had intended to remain, but lost his fortune by investing in 'manufactory' and was forced to return to India.
- December 1784 he was appointed by the court to succeed Mr La Touche as resident at Bussorah (Basra) but to return to Bombay meantime.
- In 1785 he returned to Bombay. On being required to take charge of the residency at Bussora he relinquished this appointment on the grounds of ill-health.
- In November 1795 Mr Farmer was appointed resident at Fort Victoria where he remained until 1787 when he was appointed Chief at Tannah.
- In May 1790 he resigned the Chiefship at Tannah on account of ill-health.
- In 1790 there being a great scarcity of grain provisions for proposals of certain persons for supplying the market were accepted and Mr Farmer was appointed to superintend their conduct.
- In 1791 the scarcity having eased he requested to be released from the appointment which the board granted.
- In April 1991 he was appointed by the court to succeed to the Chiefship at Surat upon the death or resignation of Mr Griffiths.
- In April 1792 he was appointed one of the commissioners for arranging and settling the ceded countries on the Malabar coast.
- In March 1793 he was appointed by General Abercromby Supervisor and Chief Magistrate of the provinces of Malabar which

appointment he accepted on condition that it should not be any bar to the succession the chieftainship of Surat.

- In late 1794 he became chief at Surat on the resignation of John Griffith.
- In January 1796, his ill health recurring he took ship on the *Princess Amelia* arriving in Southampton in July. He died in January 1798. His will was proved in February.

18
The Melvill family and India

David Williams

The Act of Union between England and Scotland in 1707 opened up opportunities for Scots, especially the younger sons of the landed and middle classes, in the British army and overseas in the expanding British empire.[1] This chapter explores the connection, through work and marriage, between one of these Scottish families, the Melvills, and the East India Company (EIC) over several generations in both India and Britain. It concentrates on Philip Melvill (1760–1811) and his descendants. In 1780, Philip was a young British army officer in India, who fought his first battle in the second Mysore War, at Pollilur. Thanks to the actions of a French officer on the opposing side he survived and returned to Britain to marry and have a family. He and his wife had four boys who reached adulthood and they had long and varied careers in the service of the EIC, three in London and one in India. Philip Melvill had 29 grandchildren who survived to adulthood; of the nine boys seven joined the EIC and of the 20 girls, five married husbands with EIC connections.[2] Those who did not follow the EIC/India route were usually successful in other spheres, whether in military or civilian life. While families were shaped by their multi-generational connections to the EIC, the Company also came to be shaped by families who were committed to its continuance and understood its significance over multiple generations. By virtue of their EIC service, the Scottish Melvills became increasingly English by marrying into established English families and, mostly, settling in England.

Philip Melvill

Philip Melvill was born in Dunbar in 1760, the youngest of four sons of Baillie John Melvill and Jean Fall, members of two of the prominent families of the town (see Figure 18.1).[3] Philip and his elder brother John (c.1751–1818) both went to India as young men, but their experiences there could not have been more different. Philip came back to Britain first in 1786, still a young man but severely disabled and penniless, then married, prospered and had nine children. John spent the whole of his working life as a civil servant and judge in India before retiring back to England in 1813 with sufficient funds to purchase an 8,200-acre estate in Sussex. Although he had two sons, neither married and after John's death in 1818, the connection he had built with the EIC went no further. In contrast, Philip's connection to the EIC prospered and expanded through the many generations that followed him.

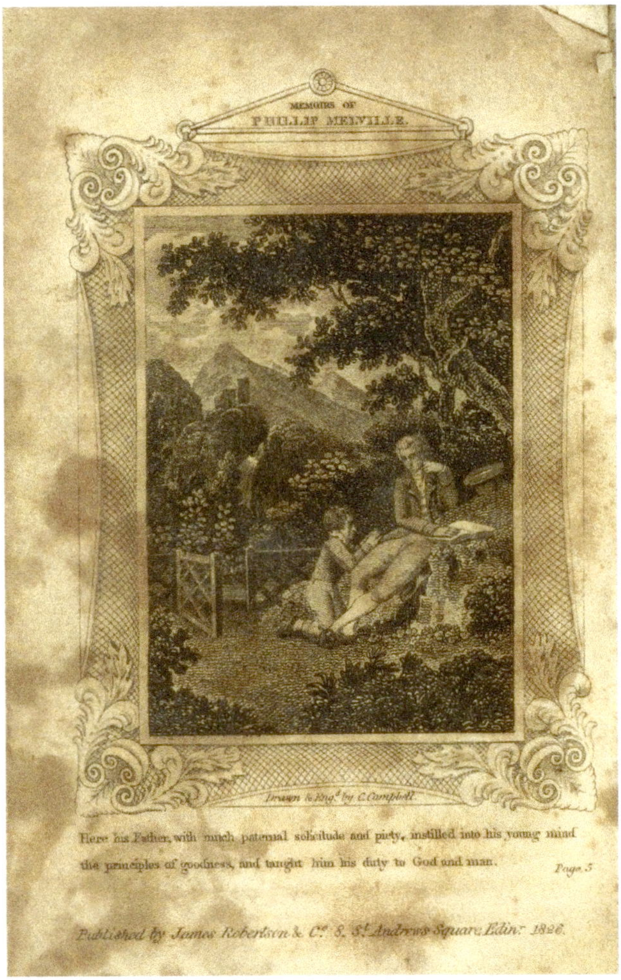

Figure 18.1 Philip and his father at Presmennen (Frontispiece of *Memoirs*). Image courtesy of David Williams.

At the age of 16, Philip's father purchased a commission for him in the 73rd Regiment (Lord Macleod's) Highlanders. He was required to go to the far north of Scotland, where Melvill relatives still lived, to raise a number of men for the regiment before he took up his commission.[4] In 1779 the regiment sailed for India, landing at Madras in January 1780. The Second Anglo-Mysore War (1780–84), between the sultan, Hyder Ali, and the British, broke out soon afterwards and in July, 800 Highlanders together with about 4,000 Indian troops left Madras to rendezvous with a 3,000-strong EIC army under the command of Lt Col William Baillie. The combined armies encountered Hyder Ali's army of 10,000 with French advisors under the command of his son, Tipu Sultan, camped near Conjeveram about 45 miles west of Madras. Historically there had been conflicts between the EIC and British armies over the chain of command. EIC officers tended to be older and more experienced and had gained promotions over a long period, while British army officers usually obtained commissions and promotions by purchase. Although the initial skirmishes went in favour of the British, the mutual antipathy between the officers of the British armies led to disputes, orders being ignored and delays.[5] As a result, on 9 September they found themselves surrounded by the superior Mysorean forces near the village of Pollilur where they were eventually overrun and surrendered (see Figure 18.2). Although quarter was promised, some of Hyder Ali's forces began killing

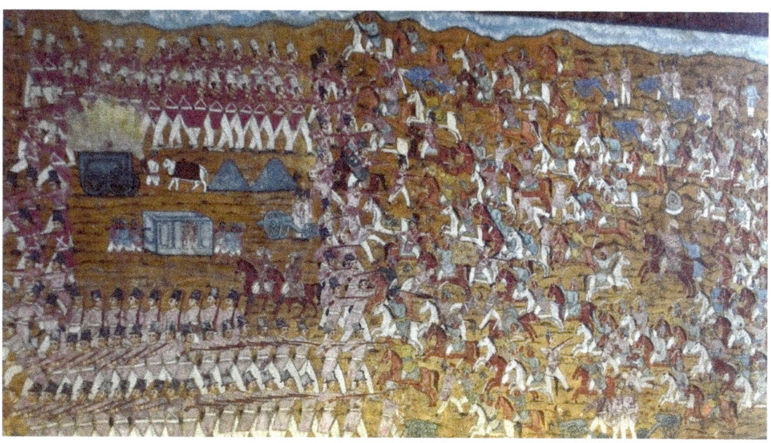

Figure 18.2 The mural at the Summer Palace, Srirangapatna, depicting the Battle of Pollilur. Note the defensive British square, the ammunition cart exploding, Colonel Baillie's palanquin and, somewhere in the centre, Philip Melvill fighting. Image courtesy of David Williams.

the captured and wounded and it was only the intervention of the French officers under Colonel Lally that prevented all the British forces being killed.[6] The Battle of Pollilur was the worst defeat suffered to that date by the British in India.

Philip had suffered terribly during the battle. A musket ball shattered his left arm and a sabre severed the tendons on his right wrist. He suffered over 20 wounds and was left naked on the battlefield for two days.[7] Along with some of the other survivors, he was imprisoned in Bangalore for four years until the end of the war.[8] Upon his release, Philip went to Bengal to stay with his brother John and recuperate; it was not until 1786 that he was well enough to make the journey home.[9] His wounds and treatment in captivity meant that, for a long time, he was unable to cut his own food and needed help dressing and undressing.[10] According to a letter written by his widow, he never regained the full use of his arms.[11]

On his return Philip was offered a promotion to Captain and the command of an invalid garrison in Guernsey where he met his future wife, Elizabeth Dobree (1770–1844) (see Figure 18.3). After five years on Guernsey, the threat of war with France led the Melvills to leave the island in 1793. Following a severe illness, Philip applied to be put on the retired list but in 1796, he was offered the command of an invalid garrison at Pendennis Castle in Cornwall. He took over a run down, ill-disciplined company and there was a running conflict between the invalid garrison and a militia regiment also quartered in Pendennis.[12] Within a year he was promoted to Lieutenant Governor, a post he held until his death in 1811. The castle commanded the entrance to Falmouth harbour and was an important defensive position during the wars with France. Soon after his promotion, Philip established the Pendennis Volunteer Artillery; he helped found a Church girls' school in 1802 and a boys' school in 1805.[13] In 1807 he established the Falmouth Misericordia Society 'for the relief of distressed persons'.[14] The anonymous author of Philip's memoirs emphasized his Christian convictions, an emphasis echoed by other writers. For example, an early history of Cornwall says of Philip that 'he was respected and loved by all who were favoured with his acquaintance. By his death the affluent lost an amiable companion; and the poor, a benefactor who sympathized with them in their distress.'[15]

In 1804 Philip became seriously ill and a change of air was recommended. He took leave of absence and moved, with his family, temporarily to Bristol, but he soon resumed his post at Pendennis while the family remained in Bristol. A number of letters written by him to his wife and children in this period have survived, and illustrate the conscientiousness with which he carried out his duties.[16] Early in 1811 he decided to move

(a)

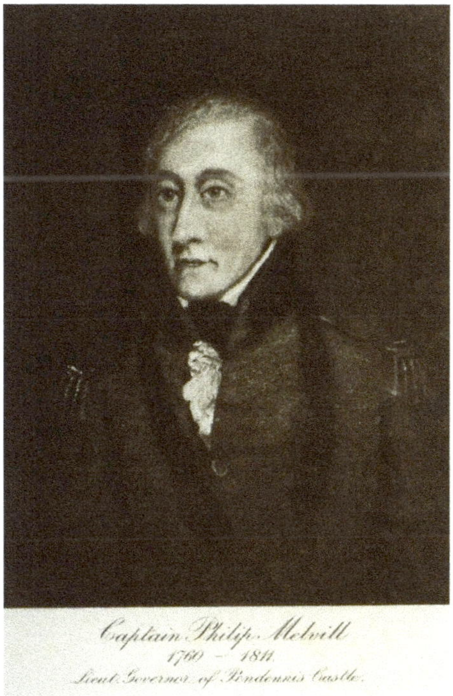

(b)

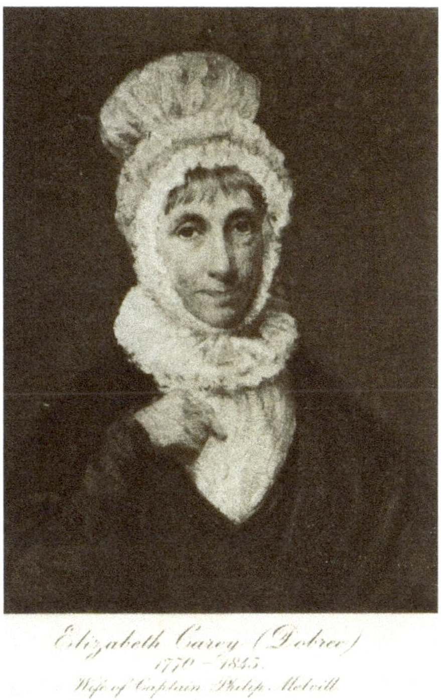

Figure 18.3 Philip and Elizabeth Melvill from *The Melvill Family, Roll of honour.* Image courtesy of David Williams.

his family to London where the children would have better prospects and relocated to Islington.[17] In August 1811 Philip returned to Cornwall to put his affairs in order before returning to London for the winter, but fell ill again.[18] This time he did not recover and died at Pendennis on 27 October 1811 at the comparatively young age of 51 (see Figure 18.4). His contributions to the town of Falmouth were recognized by the road between the town and the castle (now the A39) being named 'Melvill Road'.

After his death, Philip's family continued to live in London but his widow Elizabeth, a woman 'of strong character, piety, and keen intelligence' was left with slender means and five of her children

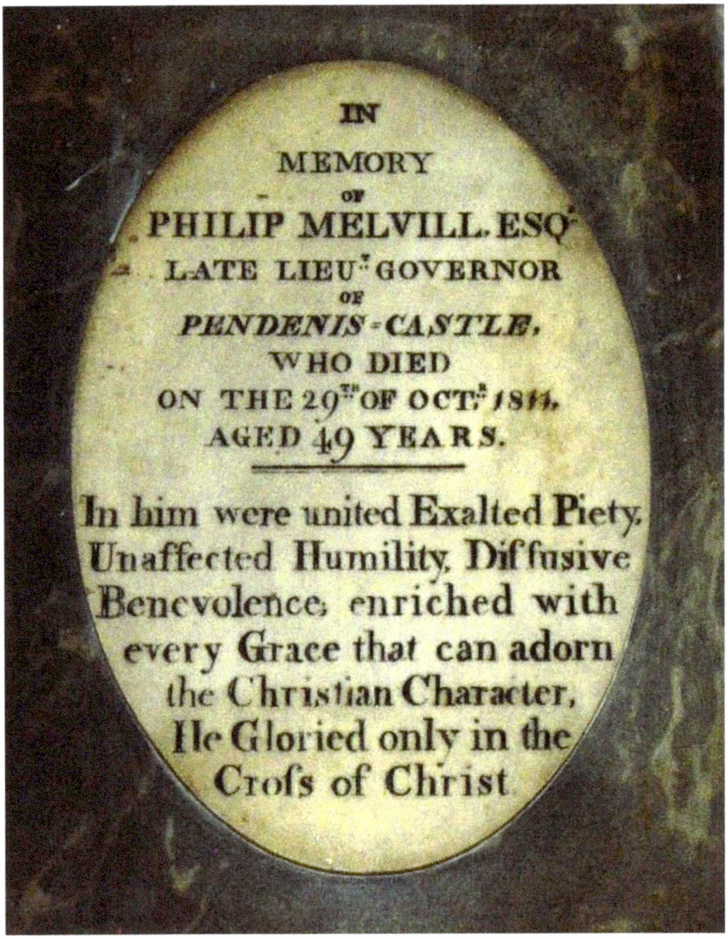

Figure 18.4 The memorial to Philip Melvill in Falmouth Church (with an incorrect age). Image courtesy of David Williams.

unprovided for.[19] Soon after Philip's death she wrote to the governors of Christ's Hospital School asking for financial assistance for her younger sons to allow them to remain at the school.[20] By this time his eldest surviving son was a clerk at the EIC. Elizabeth died in 1844 in Camberwell. On the 1841 census return she had been living in Grove Lane, Camberwell with two of her unmarried daughters and two servants.[21]

Philip Melvill's children

Philip and Elizabeth Melvill had nine children. The two oldest boys did not reach adulthood; the eldest and youngest daughters never married and while the middle one did, she had no children. Philip probably used his family and personal connections to obtain positions in the EIC for the four surviving boys and all went on to have distinguished careers in the service of the Company. The eldest, James Cosmo (1792–1861) ('Cosmo I'), was Chief Secretary from 1836 until the Company's abolition in 1858; the second son, another Philip (1796–1882) ('Philip II'), was Military Secretary in London from 1837 to 1857; the third son, Henry (1798–1871) ('Henry I'), was principal of Haileybury, the EIC training college near London, from 1843 until its closure in 1858; while the youngest son, Peter (1803–95), was the only one who went to India, where he rose to be Secretary to the Government of Bombay from 1840 to 1859 (see Figure 18.5). All four prospered and used their own connections and influence to ensure that many of their children, Philip I's grandchildren, continued to develop and grow the Melvill links with India through their careers and marriages.

James Cosmo Melvill

Cosmo I was born on Guernsey, the third son of Philip I and Elizabeth, but the first to survive to adulthood. In 1811, through a family connection with the Anstruthers – Philip's cousin Sir John Anstruther (1753–1811) had been Chief Justice of Bengal from 1797–1808[22] – his father secured him a position at the EIC office in London.[23] He rose steadily through the organization, becoming auditor of the Indian accounts in 1824, Financial Secretary in 1834 and Chief Secretary in 1836, a post he held until his retirement on 3 September 1858 at the time of the EIC's closure.[24]

(a)

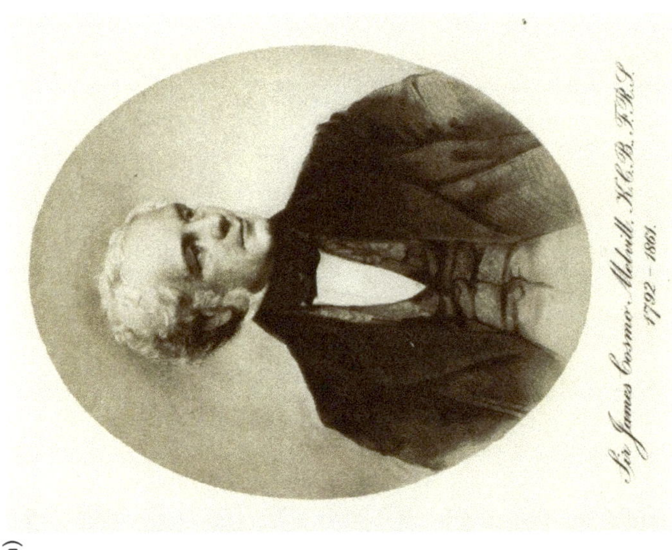
Sir James Cosmo Melvill. K.C.B. F.R.S.
1792 - 1861.

(b)

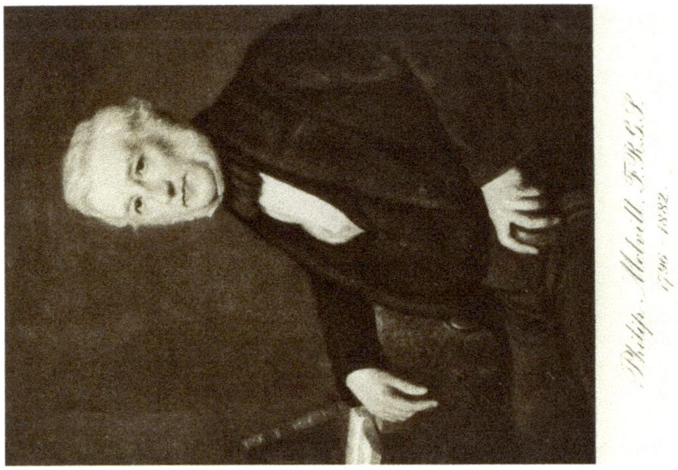
Philip Melvill. F.R.G.S.
1796 - 1882.

(c)

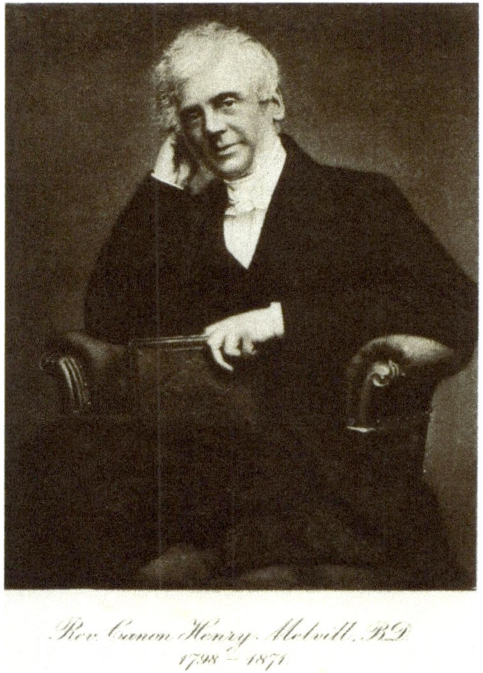

(d)

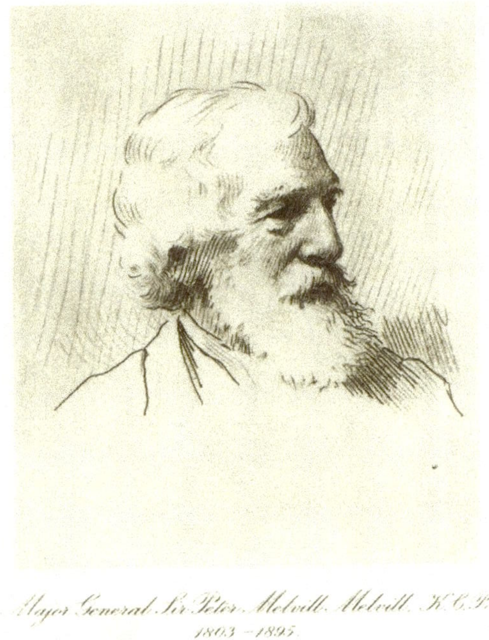

Figure 18.5 Philip I's four sons who had careers in the EIC. From a–d, James Cosmo, Philip, Henry and Peter. From *The Melvill Family, Roll of honour.* Images courtesy of David Williams.

Cosmo spent the whole of his working life at East India House in Leadenhall Street, the London headquarters of the EIC since 1648. Towards the end of the eighteenth century, however, the existing buildings were deemed inadequate and between 1794 and 1797 the EIC purchased parcels of land around its existing site.[25] Based on a design by its surveyor, Richard Jupp, a new 200-foot long and 60-foot high classical-style façade was built and the existing building extended. It included a residence for the Secretary at the west end of the façade and later, a library and museum. One of the highlights of the museum was the mechanical tiger, which had belonged to Tipu Sultan (now in the V&A). In 1858 the India Office briefly used the property, but as the new department wanted to be near the Foreign Office it moved in 1860 to Westminster. In 1861 the building was demolished and replaced by new, multi-purpose offices.[26] The site is now occupied by the Lloyd's Building, built in 1986. At the beginning of the nineteenth century, however, East India House was the location for one of the largest non-government or non-military organizations in London. Large numbers of clerks serviced the continuous correspondence between London and the Indies. It was a prestigious place to work and clerkships were sought after. They were filled by the nomination of directors, to provide for a relative, a friend or a political supporter but there was no evidence of nominations being sold (an 1809 investigation by a Committee of the House of Commons found no ill-practice).[27] Working hours were not onerous, starting with breakfast at 10:00am, time for lunch, and finishing by 4:00pm. John Stuart Mill, of whom more later, found time for his philosophical writings during office hours and often used EIC headed stationery for his non-business correspondence.[28] Pensions for retired employees were generous (See Figure 18.6).

As Chief Secretary, Cosmo held the most important home servant post. It involved a close relationship with the Court of Directors, creating the ability to determine and control the agenda of court meetings. While in office Cosmo appeared before several Parliamentary committees and was regarded as 'one of the shrewdest and most sagacious men whom I have ever met' by a biographer of Indian officers.[29] In 1830, when William Huskisson MP was attacking the perceived privileges of the EIC and accusing them of violating their charter, Cosmo appeared before a Select Committee.[30] Huskisson's plan 'at a stroke was defeated by the clear and convincing statements' made by Cosmo.[31] In another appearance in 1832 he was described as 'an able advocate'.[32]

Cosmo was a traditionalist, believing that economies such as the cutting back of military expenditure were short sighted (this despite his financial background) and opposing the EIC's territorial acquisitions of the 1840s and

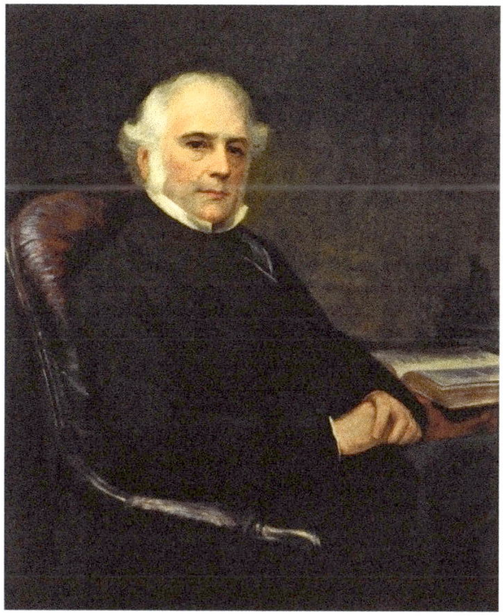

Figure 18.6 Sir James Cosmo Melvill by Eton Upton Ellis c.1853.

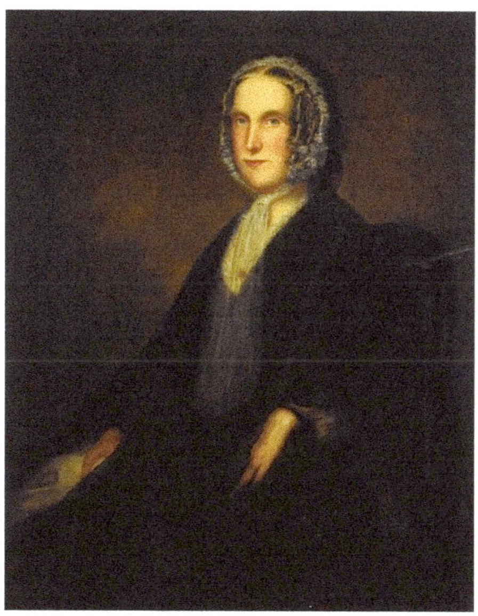

Figure 18.7 Lady Hester Melvill by John James Napier c.1858.

1850s.[33] He was keen to preserve the independence and prestige of India's remaining princes and also observed the simmering resentment among the EIC's Indian troops because of expenditure cutbacks. He corresponded with EIC employees in India and with critics and supporters at home. He was often required to deflect opposition to some of the EIC's difficult decisions.

In the period up to the closure of the EIC, Cosmo and John Stuart Mill, who had risen to be the Examiner of Indian Correspondence – a role which was almost equal in influence to that of the Chief Secretary and possibly had greater responsibilities – were pivotal in the defence of the EIC against Palmerston's attack on its privileges. While their efforts were ultimately in vain, Earl Grey nevertheless pronounced Mill's petition to parliament as one of the ablest state papers he had read. In his autobiography, Mill spoke of 'the folly and mischief of this ill-considered change'.[34] Cosmo had become a member of The Royal Society in 1841, and Commissioner of Lieutenancy of the City of London in 1847. He was awarded a KCB in September 1853.[35]

Some of the letters in the Melvill papers in the British Library include correspondence between Cosmo, the College of Arms and various relations of Cosmo and appear to be an attempt to obtain a grant of arms for the Melvill family.[36] On the cessation of the EIC, Cosmo was appointed Government Director of the Indian Railways but turned down the offer of high office in the new Indian administration because of his advancing years and failing health.[37] His abilities were obviously known at the highest level because when the appointments to the new Indian Office, which took over responsibility for the administration of India from the EIC, were put before Queen Victoria in 1858 she asked how it was that Cosmo's name was not included.[38]

In 1815 Cosmo married Hester Jean Frances Sellon (1789–1854) at St Andrews, Holborn, see Figure 18.7. She was the daughter of William Marmaduke Sellon (1757–1824), who owned a number of properties including several public houses in and around Clerkenwell and was 'for many years a hardworking and exemplary magistrate'.[39] By the time of the 1841 census return Cosmo was living at Cannon Hall in Hampstead with his wife, six daughters, two sons and four servants. The house took its name from the cannons used as bollards outside the house, which were said to have been put there by Cosmo.[40] The Melvills lived at Cannon Hall until they moved to Tandridge Court near Godstone in Surrey in the 1850s, which they leased from the Earls of Cottenham and where Cosmo died in July 1861 (see Figure 18.8).[41]

The church at Tandridge has a pew with Cosmo's name carved into it and he, his wife and three daughters are commemorated in one of the larger graves in the churchyard, which has a prominent stone cross.[42] At All Saints church in Hutton, Essex, there is a window dedicated to Cosmo

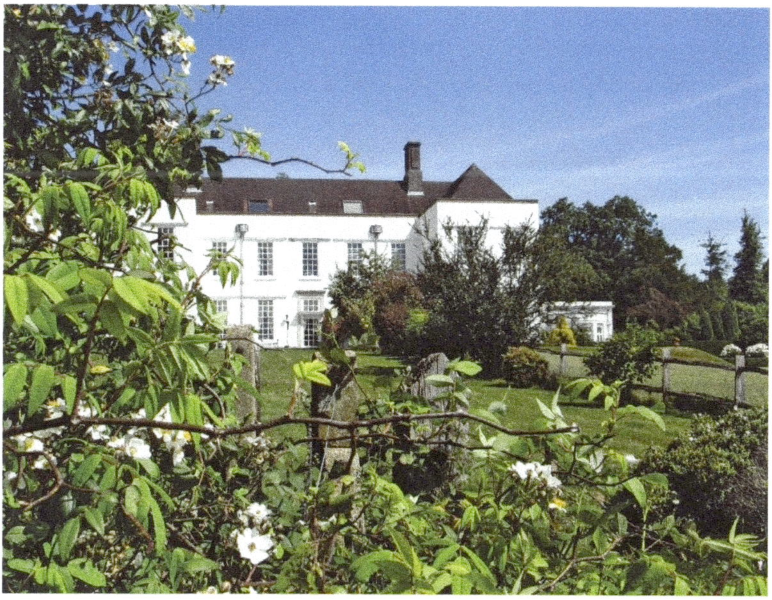

Figure 18.8 Tandridge Court today. Image courtesy of David Williams.

and his wife, put there by their daughter, Fanny (1819–94), who had married the then rector who was instrumental in a major rebuilding of the church in 1873. The Melvill family contributed to the restoration fund.[43]

Philip Melvill

The second of Philip I and Elizabeth's sons to reach adulthood, Philip II, followed a similar career path to his elder brother, Cosmo I. He joined the EIC in London in June 1815 on the military side and rose to be Military Secretary by 1837. He retired in 1857, as the EIC was being wound up. In 1826 he married Eliza Sandys (1805–90) in St Keverne, Cornwall. They had two sons and nine daughters; two of the daughters died in infancy. Their eldest son, Philip Sandys (1828–1906) joined the Bengal civil service and their other son, Teignmouth (1842–79), having gone to Harrow, Cheltenham College and Trinity College, Cambridge, joined the army and was killed at Isandlwana, South Africa, during the Zulu War of 1879. He was awarded a posthumous Victoria Cross 'on account of the gallant effort made by him to save the Queen's Colour of his regiment after the disaster of Isandlwana'.[44] Unlike their brothers, only one of their daughters, Mary Augusta (1833–1917), made an Indian connection, marrying the future Major-General Sweedland Mainwaring

(1819–83) of the Indian Army in 1856. Philip and Eliza retired to her old county of Cornwall and lived at Ethy House, St Winnow, with as many as 11 servants (on the 1871 census return). He died there in 1892, when his estate was valued at almost £44,000 (well over £2 million today).[45]

Henry Melvill

Henry I was the third of Philip I and Elizabeth's sons to reach adulthood. He had an impressive academic record and moved in the highest of social circles. He went up to St John's, Cambridge in 1817 and graduated in 1821 with some distinction.[46] He was awarded an MA in 1824 and from 1822 to 1829 worked as a fellow and tutor at Peterhouse College, Cambridge. In 1836 he became a Doctor of Divinity. He then held various clerical posts before being appointed as principal of the EIC College, Haileybury in 1843, a post he held until the college was closed down on 31 January 1858 (see Figure 18.9).[47] He was appointed chaplain of the Tower of London by the Duke of Wellington in 1840, and was Golden Lecturer at St Margaret's, Lothbury, from 1850 to 1856. From 1853 he was chaplain to Queen Victoria; from 1856 Canon Residentiary of St Paul's; and from 1863 rector of Barnes in Surrey. He was still holding these three posts when he died in 1871.

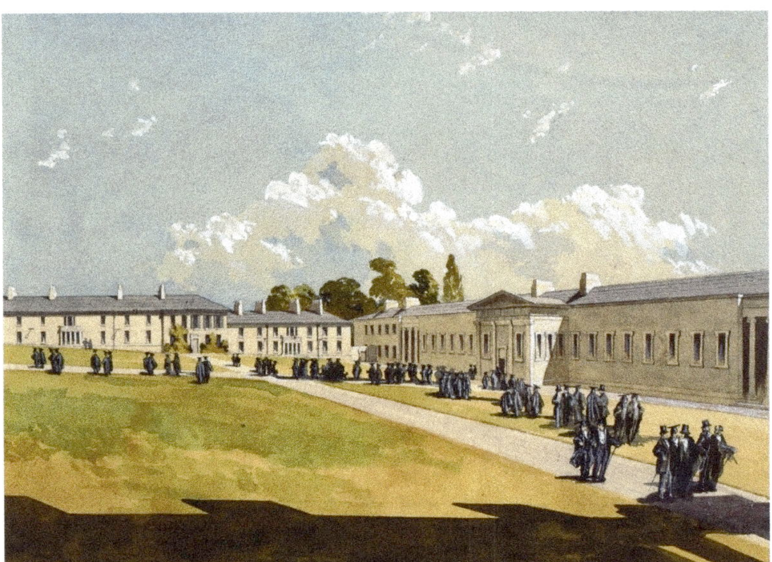

Figure 18.9 Haileybury College, designed by William Wilkins, unknown artist, c.1855. © The British Library Board, WD 541.

Henry had the reputation of being the most popular preacher in London and one of the greatest rhetoricians of his time. First at Camden Chapel, then at St Margaret's, and later on at St Paul's, large crowds of people attended his ministrations. His sermons generally occupied three-quarters of an hour, but such was the rapidity of his utterance that he spoke as much in that time as an ordinary preacher would have done in an hour. His delivery was earnest and animated without distinctive gesticulation; his voice was clear and flexible, while his emphatic pronunciation and his hurried manner of speaking impressed the hearers with a conviction of his sincerity. But his evangelical sermons lacked simplicity and directness of style, and his ornate phraseology, his happy analogies, smoothly balanced sentences, appealed more directly to the literary than to the spiritual sense.[48]

He had many distinguished admirers. John Ruskin described him thus: 'Henry Melvill, afterwards Principal of Haileybury, was the only preacher I ever knew whose sermons were at once sincere, orthodox and oratorical on Ciceronian principles. He wrote them from end to end with polished art, and read them admirably, in his own manner; by which, though the congregation affectionately expected it, they were always deeply impressed … I owe to him all sorts of good help in close analysis, but especially my habit of always looking, in every quotation from the Bible, what goes before it and after'.[49] Similarly, C.E. Buckland's *Dictionary of Indian Biography* records that 'His tenure of the Principalship of Haileybury is estimated to have been successful: of his success as a preacher there can be no doubt: he was noted for his eloquence, earnestness and skilful management of his voice: published numerous sermons and lectures'.[50]

In 1830 he married Margaret Jennings (1805–78) whose own family may have benefitted from her husband's EIC connections. Margaret Jennings' brother, Midgley John Jennings (1806–57), was a Cambridge graduate who was ordained in 1830. He was an EIC chaplain in India from 1832. On 11 May 1857 he and his family were massacred at Delhi, with other members of the Mission, at the outbreak of the Mutiny. A memorial was erected at Cawnpore, on which he is described as 'Priest, Chaplain, and Founder of the S.P.G. Mission to Delhi'.[51] Henry I and Margaret had nine children, four boys and five girls. The four boys all had careers with the EIC in India and later participated in the British governance of India. Of their daughters, the eldest, Clara (1831–1900) married Stewart St John Gordon (1829–66) of the Bengal civil service. Henry I died in 1871 and Margaret in 1878. She left the considerable sum of between £60-70,000 (over £3 million today).[52]

Peter Melvill Melvill

The youngest son of Philip I and Elizabeth, Peter entered the EIC military service in Bombay in 1819 and rose through the administration side, being Adjutant of Bombay and ADC to the Governor and working in Cutch and Sind before becoming Secretary to the Government of Bombay from 1840–59. In 1860 he was knighted for his services, retiring with the rank of Major-General. He was still active in retirement after the demise of the EIC, sitting on Lord Hobhouse's committee on the amalgamation of the Indian and British armies in 1860 and on the Royal Commission to report on memorials of the Indian officers in 1863.[53]

He married Mary Robinson (1814–81) in Bombay in 1836 and they had three daughters in India. Two of them married Bombay-based civil servants, Elizabeth (1836–89) marrying Charles Gonne (1832–95) and Catherine (1840–72), Arthur de Hochepied-Larpent, the 8th Baron, (1832–87) in 1859. The youngest, Rosina, died in infancy. Mary died in early 1881, by which time she and Peter had returned to England. In the 1881 and 1891 census returns, Peter was living at 27 Palmeira Square, Hove in Sussex, one of the most prestigious addresses in the town; in both returns a number of grandchildren, governesses and several servants are registered presumably because the parents were still in India. When he died at the age of 92 in 1895 he left an estate of nearly £60,000 (about £3 million today).

Summary

Philip I's four boys who survived to adulthood had a wide and deep influence on the EIC for nearly 50 years from Cosmo I's first employment in 1811 to its closure in 1858, ranging from developing the special skills needed by boys at Haileybury for their future careers in the EIC or the Indian army to influencing the management and direction of the Company in both India and England. From the evidence we have all four appeared to prosper, retiring to substantial properties in England, educating their children at good schools and universities, and using their connections with India to obtain employment for their some of their sons and to facilitate marriages for several of their daughters to soldiers and civil servants with links to India. As such, in the second generation of the Melvill family's engagement with the EIC the benefits it accrued were wider and deeper than before, suggesting at the mutual and accumulative advantages, which could be derived from approaching the Company as a family project.

Philip Melvill's grandchildren and more

Philip I's four sons who had careers in the EIC had 29 children who survived into adulthood; two of Cosmo I's sons, Philip (1817–54) ('Philip III') and James Cosmo (1821–80) ('Cosmo II'), had careers in the EIC (later the Indian civil service or ICS) and one daughter married a civil servant in India; Philip II's eldest son Philip Sandys had a distinguished career in the Indian civil service and a daughter, Marion (1826–1914), married an India army officer. As principal of Haileybury it is perhaps not surprising that all four of Henry's sons had careers in India, Henry (1832–1908) ('Henry II') in the army; Maxwell (1833–1887) and Richard Gwatkin (1834–1920), as civil servants, while his eldest (of five) daughters, Clara (1831–1900), married an Indian civil servant. Peter had three daughters, two, Elizabeth (1836–89) and Catherine (1840–72) married civil servants in Bombay. The range of the careers of these grandsons and grandsons-in-law of Philip I illustrate the breadth and depth of the Melvill family's involvement and commitment to India, which continued into later generations. They range from some of the highest posts in the ICS through middle-ranking servants to a notorious black sheep who was drummed out of the service. Many of the grandchildren who did not have direct links to India also had high-achieving and varied careers including one of Philip II's sons who was awarded a posthumous VC in 1879.

Philip Melvill

Philip III was the second child and eldest son of Cosmo I and Hester Melvill. Born on 3 October 1817, he was educated at Harrow, Peterhouse College, Cambridge and the EIC College at Haileybury, graduating from the latter in 1839 as a writer.[54] He arrived in India in February 1840; his first posting was as the agent to the Governor General of the North Western Provinces and by 1854 had risen to be secretary to the Punjabi government. He died of cholera in Lahore on 14 July 1854.[55] On 15 July 1845 he married Emily Jane Hogg (1828–64) in Calcutta;[56] they had two daughters and one son, all born in India. Their son, Philip Lawrence Melvill (1850–79) joined the 97th (Earl of Ulster's) Regiment in 1870 as a lieutenant,[57] was promoted to captain in 1878[58] but died shortly afterwards at the young age of 29.

James Cosmo Melvill

Cosmo II was born in London on 8 August 1821. He was educated at Totteridge School and joined the EIC office in Leadenhall Street, aged 16, in 1837. His advancement seems to have owed much to his father.

William Foster relates the story of a clerk, who kept being promoted quickly and unexpectedly and without particular merit or influence. He discovered that the clerk below him was the son of the Secretary who had devised the stratagem of promoting the clerk immediately above him to create a vacancy his son could fill.[59] While the Melvills are not mentioned by name, this anecdote almost certainly relates to them, given Cosmo I's long tenure as Secretary and Cosmo II's advancement during that period.

After the transfer of EIC power to the British Crown in 1858, Cosmo II became Under-Secretary of State for India, a post he held until retirement in 1872. In 1844 he had married Eliza Jane Hardcastle (1822–1904) in Camberwell. After his retirement they went to live in Augusta Road in Folkestone where, judging by the address and the fact that in the 1881 census return they had six servants, they lived in some style. They had four sons, one of whom died in infancy, and five daughters.

Philip Sandys Melvill

Philip II and Eliza's eldest son was educated at Rugby and Haileybury, where he received several prizes for Sanskrit and Persian. He arrived in India in 1846 and entered the Bengal Civil Service as an assistant to Sir Henry Lawrence, the Resident at Lahore as well as Agent to the Governor General for the North West Frontier. Lawrence governed the area with the help of his officers such as Philip, who were known as 'Henry Lawrence's Young Men'. Philip became commissioner of a division of the Punjab after an exceptionally short service of thirteen and a half years, then Financial Commissioner of the Punjab before becoming a Judge of the Chief Court in the Punjab. He established a reputation almost unrivalled for an intimate acquaintance with the peoples and their languages. He was then agent to the Governor General at Baroda until retirement in 1882.[60]

In 1851 he married Eliza Johnstone (1832–1920) in Jullundur. They had two sons and six daughters, some of whom died in infancy in India. Their eldest daughter, Eliza Jane (1853–1942) married Charles Joubert de la Ferté (1846–35) a colonel in the India Medical Service (IMS) in Jullundur. It was Eliza Jane who, under her married name, published *The Melvill Family, A Roll of Honour of the descendants of Philip Melvill* in 1920. The de la Ferté's second son was Air Chief Marshal Sir Philip Bennet Joubert de la Ferté KCB, CMG, DSO (1887–1965), a senior commander in the Royal Air Force during the 1930s and the Second World War.[61]

At least two more of their daughters married in India, Harriot (1854–1937) to William Warburton (1843–1911), another officer in the IMS, and

Helen (1856–96) to Rowland Bateman (1840–1916), a minister of the church. Their eldest son, Philip James Melvill (1858–1935) was educated at Harrow and Sandhurst and returned to India in the Bengal Light Infantry. He married Jessie Ross (1867–1900) in Bushire in what was then Persia and had a long career in the army, including service in the Persian Gulf, until he retired in 1908. During his time in India he had strongly supported the cause of Christian missions with personal support and financial aid and after retirement was involved in the Church Missionary Society in London.

Henry Melvill

Another Henry, the eldest son of Henry I and Margaret, joined the Bengal cavalry, part of the EIC army, in 1849 and retired in 1891 with the rank of Lieutenant-General. He was involved in the mutiny of 1857 and the subsequent fighting. He married Elizabeth Curling (1833–1913) and they had six children, three of them boys who all became army officers, one, yet another Henry (1856–1901), was a staff officer in the Indian army.

Maxwell Melvill

Maxwell was the second son of Henry I and Margaret. He was educated at Tonbridge and Trinity College Cambridge before going to Haileybury College in 1853 where he was a prize-winner in classics, mathematics, law, and history and political economy.[62] He had a brilliant career in the Bombay Civil Service from 1855 to 1887, serving in the Bombay Revenue and Judicial Departments as Assistant Collector and Magistrate, as Assistant Judge at Konkan from 1858 to 1860 and as Assistant Commissioner in Sind from 1862 to 1866. He was admitted to Gray's Inn in 1866. He then rose through the judiciary, becoming a Judge at the High Court at Bombay in 1869 and then a member of the Council of the Bombay Presidency from 1884 until he died, unmarried, of cholera at Garnish Kurd House, near Poona, in August 1887. He was described by one historian as the 'most brilliant member of the Bombay Council'.[63]

Richard Gwatkin Melvill

Henry I and Margaret's third son Richard also had a career in India but with a very different outcome to those of his brothers. His early life was conventional; he was one of the last graduates of Haileybury College before it closed and was a prize winner in Persian. He joined the Bengal

Civil Service in 1855. He married Gertrude van Cortland (1837–1918) in Umballa in 1858 and they had six children in India, two of whom died in infancy. He worked at various stations during the next 15 or 16 years, excluding a three-year furlough from 1867. When he returned in 1870 he was appointed as Deputy Commissioner in Sirsa which is in the Punjab about 150 miles west-north-west from Delhi and about 80 miles from what is now the Pakistan border. His youngest daughter was born in Sirsa in 1871.

However, by 1873, his wife and children were no longer with him and he had some sort of breakdown. The press reported that he had gone 'native', changing his name to Shaik Abdool Rahman and was known as 'The Muslim Melvill'.[64] He was described as a 'pervert' who had 'married a Moslem bride. Unfortunately, he had a Christian wife to start with'. A letter from a J. M. Machan dated 20 October 1873 confirms the report that on 18 September Richard had made a profession of Mohammadism in the Sirsa town hall before witnesses and married according to the rites of the Mohammeden religion Kureshi Brynon, the daughter of Hydari Brynon, the mistress of the female school in Sirsa.[65] In the letter, Machan went on to say that after the marriage Hydari Brynon (aged 30 and her husband being an absentee), her sister (aged about 16) and her brother took up their residence in the Melvill house. The same letter says that 'the girl is said to be 8 years of age', and the marriage was 'designed to cover an intrigue with the mother'. Machan went on to say that Richard invited him to dinner but refused to talk of the marriage saying that he would rather give up the service than his present mode of life and that 'nothing but superior physical force should tear him away from those who were now drawn to him than anything else in this life'. While this kind of behaviour had been condoned in the early days of the EIC in India, by the middle of the nineteenth century it was not approved of and was regarded as a form of insanity.[66]

However, the furor did not last too long. Further press cuttings debated whether he should be prosecuted under British or Muslim law and the consensus was that his Muslim marriage was not recognised under Western law, while a second marriage was not illegal for Muslims. So he was not prosecuted, but was dismissed from the ICS.

The 1891 English census return recorded Richard's first wife Gertrude as a 'widow' living on the Isle of Wight with three of her children. Ten years later, in 1901, Gertrude continued to describe herself as a widow. Nevertheless, in the 1911 census, which asked for more details about marriages than the previous return, she was recorded as boarding with a family, the head of which noted that she was married, with six children, three of whom were still living. Unfortunately, the return does not include her age or the number of years she had been married.

Meanwhile, in India, Richard had seemingly come to his senses and wrote a letter to a newspaper, unfortunately not dated, in which he apologizes for his actions and blames the fact that living in Sirsa is enough to drive anybody mad.[67] The newspaper cutting said

> *Interested in the letter From Mr R. G. Melvill which we published in our correspondence columns on the 14th, we wrote to that gentleman suggesting that he should, if it were possible to do this without too bitterly offending Christian sentiment, furnish our readers with an explanation of the considerations which had induced him to embrace the Mahomedan faith. In reply we have received the following letter:-*
>
> *"Sir, – The only reply I can give to yours of 10th instant is that I never really adopted the Mahomedan faith. The only explanation of my having for a short time professed the faith appears to be that a 3- years' residence at Sirsa had so far acted on my brain that I was ready to do anything for the sake of a little excitement, without reflecting on the consequences. Those who have seen Sirsa will have no difficulty in crediting this.*
>
> *"Of course, I have since repented of my folly, and have long since ceased to profess a faith in which I never believed; but I was hurried out of the service without a chance of retracing my steps.*
>
> *"I should be glad to have it generally known that I am a Christian and not a Mahomedan.*

In 1885 he married, at the age of forty, sixteen-year-old Emily Mathias (1869–1942), the daughter of Bishunbenanth Mathias, in a Christian ceremony in Dehra Dun. There is no sign in any documentation that he had divorced Gertrude and the second marriage register records his status as 'widower'. Richard and Emily had four children and for some years lived in Landour, about 20 miles from Dehra Dun. On the baptism records for his sons Richard's occupation in 1888 was pleader and in 1895 vakil, an Urdu word for a lawyer or representative. His death was recorded in Dehra Dun in 1920.[68]

Summary

Many of Philip I's grandchildren continued the family's commitment to service in the EIC/ICS and the Indian army by following a variety of careers all over the Indian sub-continent or marrying into Indian-based families. There was also a strong commitment to the British armed forces in other parts of the world. Meanwhile, other members of the family pursued successfully professional and academic careers in the UK. In 1900, at least 14 of Philip I's descendants were serving or married to people serving in India while no less than 29 were officers or married to officers in the Army or Royal Navy, a commitment which continued into the twentieth century.

Conclusion

The Melvill family showed a commitment to the EIC (and subsequently to Crown rule in India) from the last years of the eighteenth century until well into the twentieth. They were a good example of those Scots who, after the Act of Union, took opportunities with the British army and in the overseas empire to make their careers. By virtue of their EIC service, this Scottish family became increasingly English by marrying into established English families and settling in England. In the early years of the EIC, few of the employees had received a university education but its increasing bureaucratization in the nineteenth century is illustrated by the number of Melvill men who went to universities, especially Cambridge, as the century progressed. Those who did not follow the EIC/India route were usually successful in other spheres, whether in military or civilian life. Many of their daughters married into other, Indian-orientated families or other military men. Some of their families tended to be large with up to 11 children and had good survival rates.[69]

When the EIC was disbanded in 1858 following the Indian Mutiny of the previous year, of the sons of Philip I there were two (Cosmo I and Philip II) in very senior positions in the London office, a third (Henry I) was principal of the EIC college at Haileybury and the fourth (Peter) had recently retired as Secretary of the Bombay presidency. Seven of the men of the next generation had started (or were about to start) their careers with the EIC and another joined the army and would be awarded a VC; of the women of this generation, five would marry civilians or army officers based in India.

While never achieving the highest offices of state, and without any of them being elevated to the peerage, nevertheless several of the Melvills were knighted and most seemed to live comfortable lives both while working and in retirement. The family's wealth and status, derived from their association with the EIC, in turn enriched diverse aspects of English culture in these and successive generations, including religious life, arts and sciences and architecture. In 1914, on the outbreak of the First World War, the effect of the large families and good survival rates combined with a tendency towards public or military service resulted in over 60 of the first Philip Melvill's descendants being directly involved in the First World War with at least 50 helping as nurses, medical orderlies, in factories or as other volunteers. The chivalrous action of the Frenchman Colonel Lally, who was fighting with Hyder Ali at the Battle of Pollilur in 1780, in saving the life of a badly wounded 20-year-old lieutenant in the 73rd Highlanders was to have wide-ranging and significant effect on the history of the EIC and India and greatly assisted the British war effort from 1914.

19
The Indian seal of Sir Francis Sykes

A tale of two families

Sir John Sykes

This chapter demonstrates how a single object can illuminate the histories of two families, one English (see Figure 19.2), the other Indian (see Figure 19.1), who were originally closely connected with each other through the East India Company (EIC) in the eighteenth century but subsequently diverged until they met again in the twentieth. It shows the long and lasting impact of the influence on the fortunes of both families caused by the British Empire in India and how imperial connections can survive until today in a postcolonial world. Despite wide cultural differences the common denominators of the original partnership (which was designed to achieve financial goals), together with friendship and loyalty

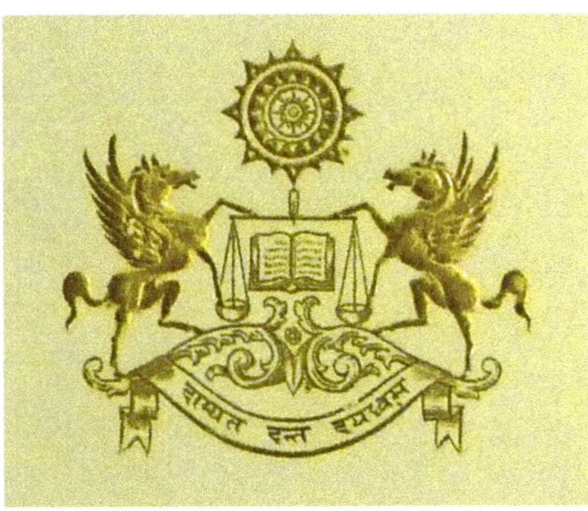

Figure 19.1 Image of coat of arms of the Cossimbazar Raj. Image courtesy of Dr S.C. Nandy.

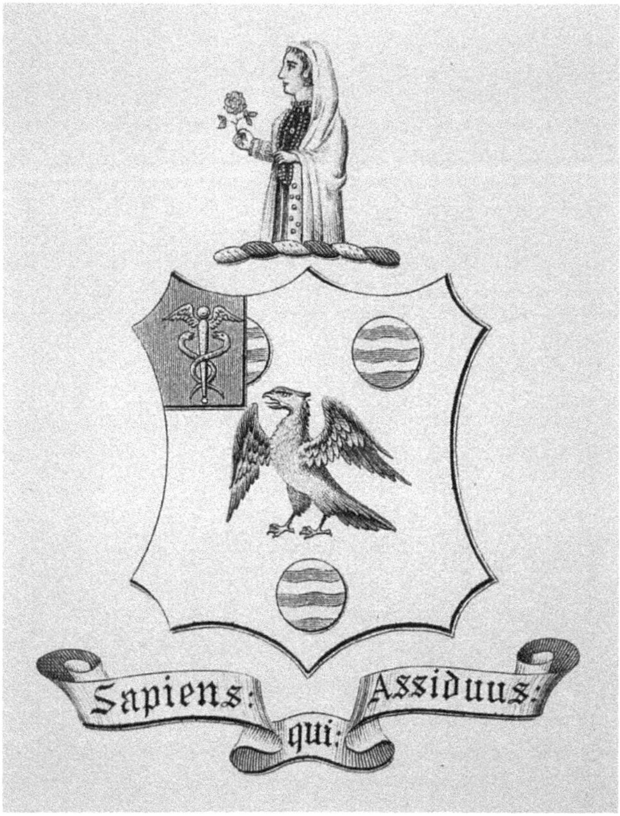

Figure 19.2 Image of coat of arms of Sykes of Basildon. Image courtesy of Sir John Sykes.

on both sides, bound each family together both then and now. The longevity of the relationship is in itself remarkable and worthy of record.

The seal

The seal is small, its total height no more than 40mm, the seal itself only 25mm by 20mm (see Figure 19.3). It is engraved in steel and is set in a holder probably made of gun metal, the holder tapering pyramid-like to a tiny swivel, which might have been used to hold a cord. Although nothing much to look at on first appearance, this seal held the authority of one of the most powerful British men in mid-eighteenth-century Bengal. It is written in a script called *Nastaylick*, the name given to the form of old Persian, which had been used in seals and coins since the latter part of the Emperor Akbar's reign (1556–1605) and continued as the language

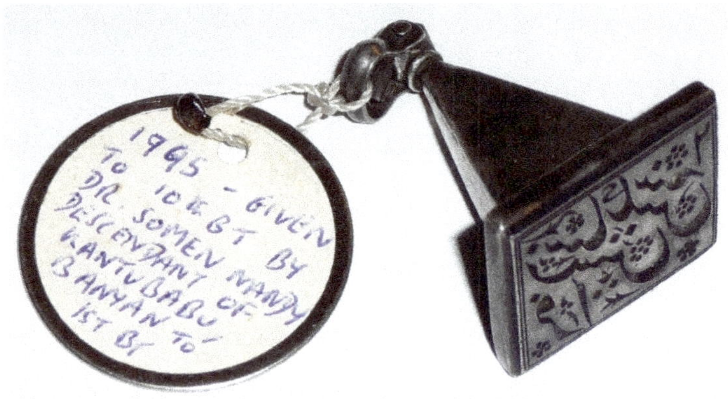

Figure 19.3 Seal, engraved steel and gunmetal holder. Image courtesy of Sir John Sykes.

of administration in eighteenth-century Mughal India. The inscription reads from right to left 'Francis Sykes (written as Sikshi) – 6'. The number '6' refers to its manufacture in the sixth year of the reign of the Mughal Emperor Shah Alam II (reigned 1759–1806), namely 1765.[1] In addition to the lettering three flowers are engraved on the seal. These flowers were important, since under the rules governing the cutting of seals in the Mughal period only elites were permitted to use such decorative elements. Since all official work was completed in Persian it was necessary for all important persons to have a seal in that language for the use in the Nawab's Court and administrative establishments to authorize legal documents, trade and business contracts, administrative directions, formal correspondence and various other official and quasi-official documents and papers. The seals were precious possessions and were only left with the person in whom the principal had total confidence, such as the banian. As in Britain, trust was an important element of official and business relationships in eighteenth-century Bengal as more abstract checks and balances had yet to be established. It is presumed that when he left for England, Francis Sykes left the seal with his banian Krishna Kanta Nandy (known as Cantoo Baboo, c.1720–94) to complete his unfinished business, reference to which can be found in his letters to Warren Hastings.[2] Unfortunately no document has yet come to light where the seal has been used.

The owner

Francis Sykes (1730–1804) arrived in India for the second and last time with Robert Clive on 3 May 1765 after a tedious 11-month voyage

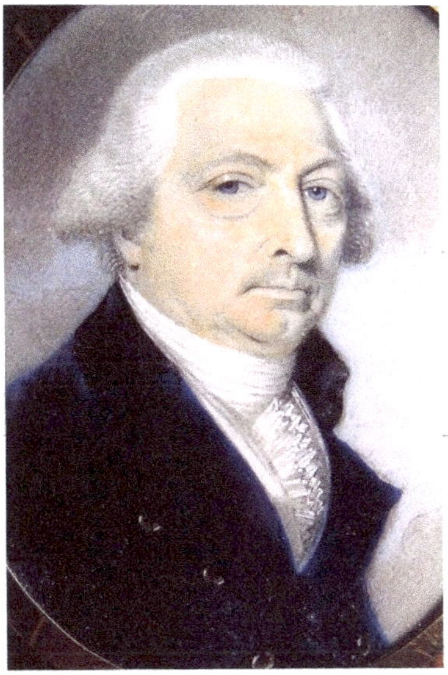 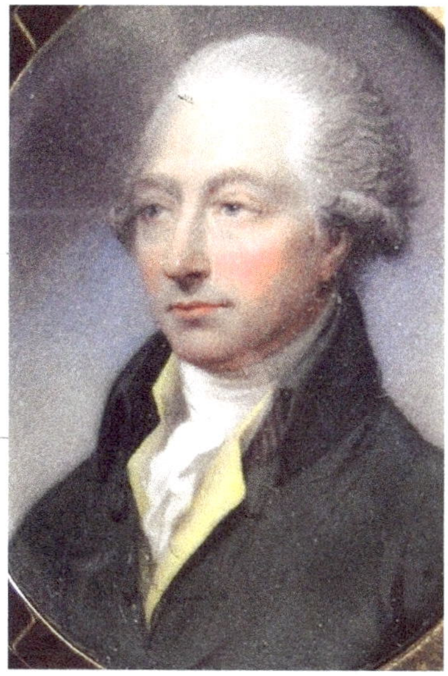

Figure 19.4 Two miniature portraits of Francis Sykes. On the left, as an older man, possibly by Thomas Richmond and on the right as a younger man by Henry Bone, 1804, copied from an earlier portrait by Thomas Gainsborough destroyed by fire in 1874. Images courtesy of Sir John Sykes.

(see Figure 19.4). Clive's Select Committee (only five in number), of which he was a member, had been given extraordinary powers by the East India Company Directors in London to bring an end to the increasingly chaotic state of affairs in Bengal, which had included the outbreak of war between the Company and the Nawab of Bengal, Mir Qasim. Prior to journeying to Calcutta in 1765, Sykes had spent nine years in India from 1751–60 working his way up the ladder of the Company's civil service at the important trading 'factory' of Cossimbazar, sited just outside the Nawab's capital of Murshidabad on the upper reaches of the Hughli River about five days, journey from Calcutta.[3] It was here that his connection with another 'writer', Warren Hastings, began, a friendship that only ended with Sykes's death in 1804. Sykes had survived the upheaval of the Company's war with Suraj-ud-daulah (1733–57) when, following the Nawab's capture of the Cossimbazar factory and of Calcutta itself, the EIC was in danger of being expelled completely from Bengal. He had played a part in the dangerous negotiations with both Suraj-ud-daulah and, secretly, with the man who was destined to succeed him, Mir Jafar (1691–1765), which led to the successful outcome of the Battle of Plassey in 1757, domination by the Company of Bengal and ultimately the foundation of the British Raj. During this time he accumulated sufficient wealth through private trade to purchase an estate, Ackworth Park in Yorkshire, in 1763. In the same year he took out a grant of arms, interestingly taking as his crest 'A demy lady of Bengal, in the compleat dress of that kingdom, holding in the dexter hand a rose' (see Figure 19.5).

At this time, Sykes also came to the notice of Clive who, as a condition of his return to India in 1764, hand-picked the Select Committee. On the day of their arrival in Calcutta, Clive wrote that 'Sykes may be thoroughly relied on'.[4] After Sykes had been sent to the *durbar* of the Nawab at Murshidabad he wrote 'I need only add, that Sykes, for whom we intend the Residentship, is a gentleman whose flexible integrity, and long experience in the country politics, we have reason to expect the most exact performance of every duty in such an important station.'[5] After the Emperor granted the Company the *diwani* (the right to collect the revenues of Bengal, Behar and Orissa) in 1765, Sykes's position as Resident at the Court of the Nawab increased in importance. The changing power structure gave rise to the 'dual system' whereby the Nawab

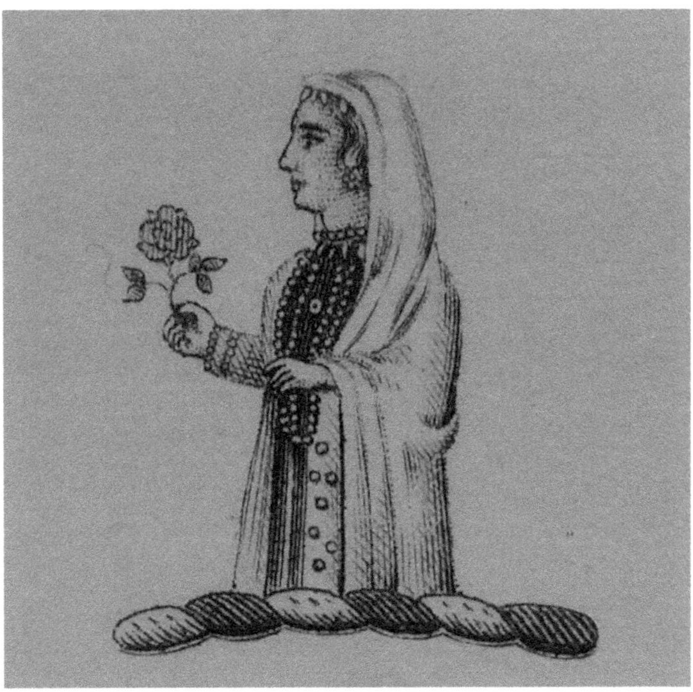

Figure 19.5 Detail of Sykes crest. Image courtesy of Sir John Sykes.

was the *subahdar* (provincial governor) of those provinces under the Emperor, but the real power lay with the Company who held financial jurisdiction (see Figure 19.6). Sykes, as Resident, was set the task of maximizing the revenues (which often involved a rigorous overhaul of the ways in which they were collected and of the 'expenses' deducted by the assigned collectors) and of controlling the Nawab's own expenditure, working in close co-operation with the Nawab's Chief Minister. The Mughal title by which Sykes was known to many of the Indians said it all: *Intizam-ud-daulah* 'The Administration of the State'.

Alongside Sykes's official activities, he carried on very substantial private trade. Together with his expense allowances and the commissions on taxes due to him in his official position, Sykes accumulated extensive wealth over three and a half years. His private trade was in numerous commodities but chiefly in salt, betel nut, tobacco, timber, saltpeter and silk. He appears to have used his position ruthlessly to oust competitors and secure monopolies of some of these items. But none of this would have been possible without the support of a trusted Indian agent or *banian*.

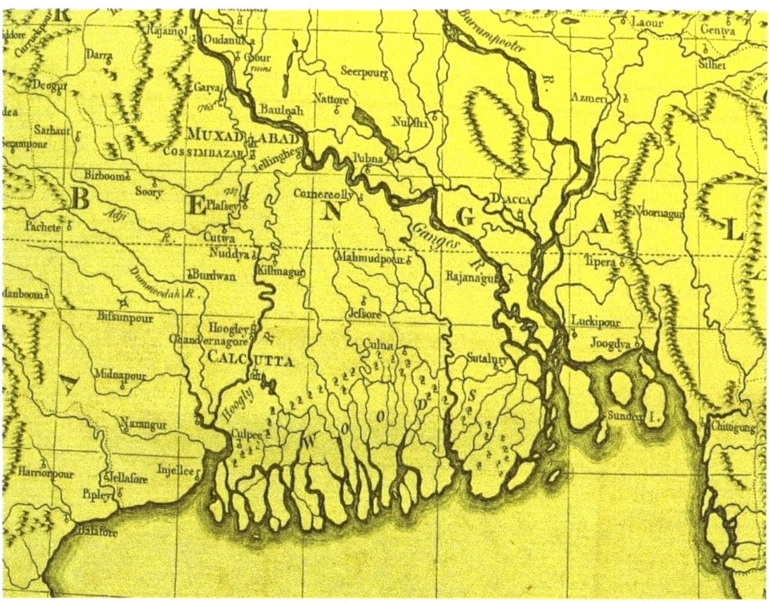

Figure 19.6 Detail from map of 'The Countries of Indostan East of Delhi' by James Rennell published in Robert Orme, *A History of the Military Transactions of the British Nation in Indostan* (London, 1778). Muxadabad was the former name of the Nawab of Bengal's capital of Murshidabad. Image courtesy of Sir John Sykes.

The banian

> A Banyan is a person … by whom the English gentlemen in general conduct all their business. He is interpreter, head book-keeper, head secretary, head broker, the supplier of cash and cash-keeper, and in general also secret-keeper. He puts in the under-clerks, the porter or door-keeper, stewards, bearers of the silver wands, running footmen, torch and branch-light carriers, palanqueen bearers, and all the long tribe of under-servants, for whose honesty he is deemed answerable; and he conducts all the trade of his master, to whom, unless pretty well acquainted with the country languages, it is difficult for any of the natives to obtain access.[6]

William Bolts' contemporary description of the eighteenth-century banian indicates the wide range and importance of these Indian intermediaries' roles in the Company era. As historian Peter Marshall has argued, the banian occupied a crucial place in Company commerce, often exercising significant power and accumulating substantial wealth:

> Nominally their status was servile and they performed some menial tasks, such as managing their master's household and his personal spending. But the banian of a prominent European was a man to be reckoned with … Men like … Cantu Babu, banian to Warren Hastings, were among the richest and most influential members of the Indian community in Calcutta … They might appear to have become their masters' servants, merely managing their trade for them; but the reality was often less that of master and servant than of trading partners. The banian brought his skill and his capital to the partnership; the European contributed his privileges.[7]

Cantoo Baboo, the great-grandson of a farmer who migrated from the Burdwan District of Bengal to Murshidabad to set up business as a cloth weaver, was a successful silk merchant at Cossimbazar when he became banian to Warren Hastings in 1754, serving him until his departure for England in 1764 (see Figure 19.7). It must have been Sykes's previous knowledge of Cantoo and of his services to Hastings, especially after Plassey, coupled with Hastings's recommendation, which determined his choice of Cantoo as his banian.

Sykes's official roles as Resident and subsequently as Governor of the trading factory at Cossimbazar would have occupied most of his time and energy in a climate which was immensely enervating for most of the year. His monthly reports to the Select Committee in Calcutta give detailed accounts of his work, problems, challenges and achievements. He would have had little time to devote to his private trading, important though it was to his financial position. In such circumstances, Cantoo seems to have been the ideal choice. He was an experienced trader, extremely astute, well able to take advantage of trading opportunities, but at the same time very cautious. As a devout Baisnab Hindu, austere and frugal, conservative, religious and conventional, he was above reproach in his private life. The trust which Sykes placed in Cantoo is demonstrated by a letter in which he wrote: 'I need say nothing here regarding my situation as Cantoo can tell you how I stand in every circumstance. I never hided anything from him.'[8] Such trust was clearly well placed: Sykes's fortune undoubtedly owed much to Cantoo's skill.

So what was in it for Cantoo? Sykes's privileges as a Company servant (and thus the freedom he enjoyed from internal customs dues) for a start, but more than that Sykes's power and prestige were undoubtedly assets of which he could take full advantage, and if Sykes became rich his own affairs would prosper. His situation as banian meant that he could branch out from one highly profitable business, silk trading, into others. Moreover it was valuable insurance. At this time of transition Bengal could be a precarious place to carry on business – Cantoo must have realized that his interests were best served by attaching himself to one of the major players in the East India Company who would not only provide support for his own business dealings but also protection should things go wrong. The latter was amply proved after Sykes's return to England when parliamentary committees began enquiries into the manner in which nabob fortunes had been acquired and, by extension, into the activities of their banians. Several letters written by Sykes to Warren Hastings, then in India, asked him to ensure that no harm came to Cantoo. In May 1776, he instructed Hastings to, 'Settle Cantoo privately and if possible peaceably otherwise he will from Party be in much trouble, my respects to him, his holding the lands I have explained till I am tired, they will not see the propriety of having substantial men in the management of the collections.'[9] In March the following year, Sykes again wrote to Hastings, noting that 'I fear Cantoo will suffer much from the spirit of the Party, you must place him somewhere, that he may enjoy what he has, in Peace and Quietness'.[10] Finally, in March 1785 shortly before Hastings' return from India, he wrote again, 'I hope you will leave

Cauntoo *(sic)* in a happy situation'.[11] The friendship that Sykes extended to Cantoo was reciprocated. On 22 February 1785 Cantoo sent what must have been a large amount of mango chutney to Sykes (in the order written Sikshi Shahab) in England at a cost of 54 rupees, a substantial sum for such a commodity.[12]

The Cossimbazar Raj

Cantoo Baboo was 'brought up in a village community amidst Bengal's commonest surroundings' according to his biographer.[13] Yet from his first purchase of property (the produce of a jack fruit tree) in 1742 at the age of 22, he amassed a great fortune through his shrewdness, skill, hard work, persistence, strict economy and, notwithstanding his caution, ability to seize opportunities. Trading in silk was profitable (up to 300 per

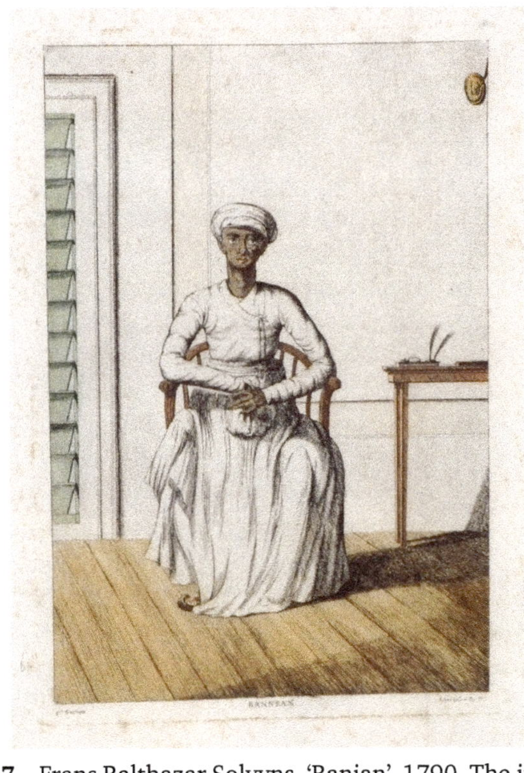

Figure 19.7 Frans Balthazar Solvyns, 'Banian', 1790. The image included here is thought to be of Cantoo Baboo. Image courtesy of Victoria Memorial Hall, Kolkata.

cent on some items) but his later investment in land and *Zemindaris* was even more so.[14] Working with and for powerful Company servants such as Hastings and Sykes did not in itself seem to have increased his wealth – what it did do was increase his power and influence as well as acting as an insurance against attack from his enemies. As his biographer puts it 'He laid the foundation of his house by his own hands and then created the steel frame and the super-structure all by himself.'[15]

Cantoo died in 1794 and was succeeded by his son Lokenath who, weak in health, only survived him by 10 years. He was the first of the family to be styled 'Maharajah'. Although, unlike Cantoo, he lived in a grand style, under his able management the estate thrived. A much-desired son and heir, Harinath, was born only two years before Lokenath died and consequently the management of the estate was taken under the Company's Court of Wards in Calcutta during his minority. In 1809 the annual income of the estate was calculated at approximately 1.42 million rupees, at the then rate of exchange equivalent to about £180,000. By the end of the nineteenth century the estate's income had doubled to about 3 million rupees, because of a falling exchange rate equivalent to about £200,000. Despite the accumulation of such wealth, during the nineteenth century, inefficient management, personal extravagance, prolonged litigation and internecine feuds severely threatened the existence of the Cossimbazar Raj.[16]

The estate was in particularly acute danger during the four years after Cantoo's great-grandson Maharajah Krisnanath (1822–44) attained his majority in 1840. 'He indulged tastes for horses, dogs, wine and the company of predatory European cronies, as well as more high-minded ones for experiments in science, new technology and education'.[17] However Krisnanath killed himself in 1844 and the management of the estate was in due course taken in hand by his 16-year-old widow Maharani Swarnamoyee (1827–97) who had lived and continued to live in *purdah* (strict seclusion). Though initially illiterate she learned four languages in four years and developed sufficient tenacity and shrewdness to cope with immense challenges. After prolonged litigation she secured the estate for herself and her children (who predeceased her) and managed it in an exemplary fashion for the rest of her life. She was very philanthropic, setting a trend, which was followed by her successors for as long as resources would allow. Social reform, education and, paradoxically, emancipation of women were her greatest concerns.[18]

On Maharani Swarnamoyee's death, Cantoo Baboo's extremely distinguished great-great-grandson Maharajah Sir Manindra Chandra

Nandy (1860–1929) inherited the estate and it was in this period that the prestige of the family reached its zenith. He was one of the leading Zemindars in India, a vigorous proponent of industrialisation, a generous philanthropist founding and endowing no fewer than 21 colleges and schools, a moderate member of Congress, a nationalist and friend of Gandhi. In a tribute to him after his death the Governor of Bengal, Sir John Anderson said, 'Though a member of the most conservative class, the landed aristocracy of Bengal, he recognised in the light of a personal obligation the importance of developing the industrial and commercial resources of the Province and devoted much of his great wealth and influence to [furthering] that end'. Anderson continued, 'His was indeed a happy blend of respect for the old world tradition with a very modern appreciation of the needs of the changing times'.[19] Sadly, through excessive philanthropy coupled with mismanagement and fraud by his mainly British agents, in 1928 Manindra had to declare himself insolvent and apply for the Cossimbazar Raj estate to be administered by the Court of Wards.

Manindra's son Srischandra (1897–1952) was the last Maharajah. He inherited an estate that was 30 million rupees in debt and set about paying it off so that the estate could be released to him. He ultimately achieved his aim in 1944. Elected to the Assembly he became Minister of Communications and Works in the Government of Bengal.[20] But Partition and Independence brought insurmountable problems not least the impending abolition of the zemindari system on which so much of the estate depended. In 1951 the Cossimbazar Raj's East Pakistan (now Bangladesh) zemindari estate, which had comprised the bulk of its landholdings was confiscated and this, combined with poor health and the uncertainties of the estate's future, led to Srischandra's death in 1952. In the words of his son 'The death became a landmark, ending the leadership of a special pattern of social, economic and cultural supremacy of Bengal. The idealism nurtured in the aristocratic families came to an end, ushering the age of free for all and selfish pragmatism'.[21]

Maharajkumar Somendra Chandra Nandy (Dr S. C. Nandy) was born in 1928 shortly before his grandfather's death. Aged only 23 when he came into his inheritance, he faced challenges greater than any of those which had gone before. Income tax arrears and estate debts totalled almost 10 million rupees. Confiscation of the estate's zemindaris in five Indian states was not long in coming but before it did swift rearguard action ensured that properties were sold wherever possible so that debts could be paid and retrenchment costs discharged. The surplus was invested in the estate's stone quarries and china clay mines, which had been retained, and Dr Nandy even came to England to learn the china clay business at first hand and acquire much needed machinery.[22]

Dr Nandy is a remarkable man. At a time of radically altered personal circumstances and of profound change in the social system and economy of India, he transformed the Cossimbazar estate from the status of a great landowner to the thriving industrial and commercial enterprise it is today. He is also an academic historian and amongst his wide-ranging interests a lecturer, playwright, essayist and critic, writing in both Bengali and English. Thanks to his substantial family records, persistence and hard work in mastering a complex scenario, his four books on the Nandy family history are a magnificent achievement, a record of its triumphs and tragedies over 250 years.

The Sykes family

The fortune brought back by Francis Sykes was reckoned by his contemporaries to be one of the largest to come out of India (see Figure 19.8).[23] It was sufficient to enable him to buy two more large estates, Basildon Park, Berkshire and the Gillingham Estate, Dorset as well as a seat in Parliament and in 1781 a much-coveted baronetcy. But his wealth was not destined to last. Even during his lifetime losses on his investment in East India stock, court proceedings, the rebuilding and decoration (never completely finished by him) of the house at Basildon Park, a ne'er-do-well elder son who ran up gambling and other debts (not to mention notorious and expensive court proceedings) meant that his estates were heavily mortgaged by the time of his death in 1804.

His son, the 2nd Baronet Francis William Sykes (1767–1804), survived him by only two months leaving three small children, the eldest son being four years of age when he inherited the baronetcy and the estates. The inevitable mismanagement during his lengthy minority, coupled with protracted and presumably expensive court proceedings connected with family trusts, further depleted family resources, not aided by the 3rd Baronet's own expensive tastes and his marriage to a beautiful woman similarly inclined, who was Disraeli's mistress for three years. Disraeli's novel *Henrietta Temple* (1836) was inspired by this love affair and contained many heartfelt personal references, such as 'To violate in her favour every duty of society; this is a lover, and this is love'.[24] In fact the heroine's letters in the novel 'are so like those of the real Henrietta that one is tempted to think that Disraeli transcribed them verbatim'.[25] For the

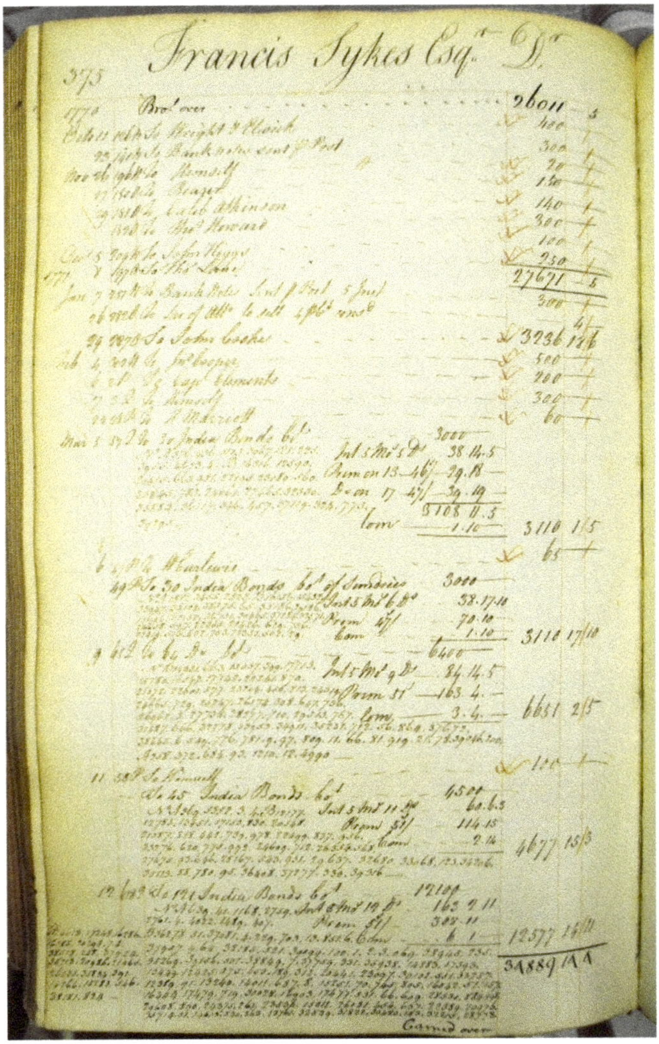

Figure 19.8 Page from Francis Sykes's bank account at Goslings Bank (1770/1771), showing purchases of East India stock. Image courtesy of Barclays Group Archives.

3rd Baronet and his wife (but not for Disraeli) the eventual outcome was social disgrace. The estates were sold off – the last, Basildon Park, in 1838. Henrietta's sons became successively the 4th, 5th and 6th Baronets and at each step the family money diminished. In 1874, the most valuable Sykes chattels (including the largest portrait Gainsborough ever painted) were destroyed in a devastating fire at the London Pantechicon, a supposedly fireproof storage facility, and this again was followed by court proceedings against its owners.[26] The senior branch of the family died out and the descendants of the brother of the 3rd Baronet inherited the Baronetcy but without any of the money which had previously gone with it. The 7th Baronet was a tutor at Cheltenham, the 8th a country parson.[27]

There is a family story that an Indian princess (note the family crest in Figure 19.2) assisted Francis Sykes in his escape from the English factory at Cossimbazar on the understanding that he would marry her. When he did not she cursed him with the words 'From the land you came, to the land you shall return'. Francis's father had been a Yorkshire farmer and the 9th Baronet (1907–90), who worked as a teaplanter in Darjeeling before World War II (and was married in Calcutta Cathedral) and later became an agricultural estate manager, reckoned that the curse had worked itself out with him (see Figure 19.9). The curse, if that is what it was, is nothing if not ambiguous but there is no doubt that the Sykes family was back to square one after only four generations. The contrast with the fortunes of the Nandy family could not have been more spectacular.

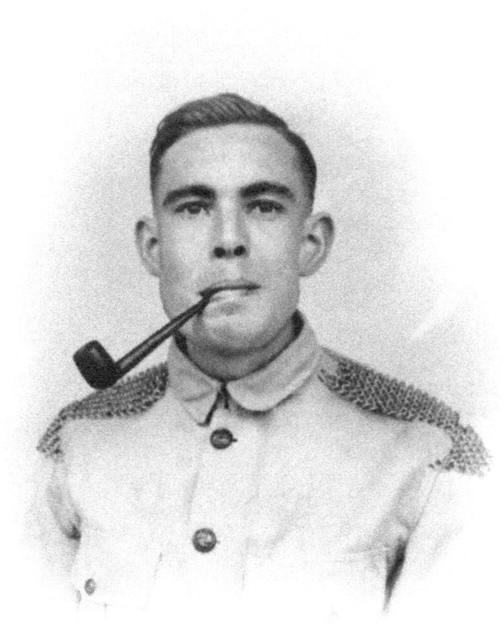

Figure 19.9 Photograph featuring Sir Francis Sykes 9th Baronet in Bengal Mounted Rifles uniform c.1931. Image courtesy of Sir John Sykes.

The reunion

On 7 April 1978 Dr Nandy wrote to the 9th Baronet to introduce himself as the biographer of his ancestor, Cantoo Baboo, and the two families met the following month after a gap of 210 years (see Figure 19.10). After the visit, in a letter dated 10 June 1978, Dr Nandy wrote 'It was a pleasure to meet John again in London. The way we cropped the time together was almost like a romance in terms of reality. We felt so close, so known to each other that an outsider would take us to be friends for ages.'[28] After this point, Dr Nandy has visited the 10th Baronet and his family almost every year since 1978 and has entertained the 10th Baronet at his home in Calcutta and at his palace in Cossimbazar on three separate visits, most notably for the marriage of his son Samit Chandra in Calcutta in 1988 (see Figures 19.11 and 19.12). Fifteen years after the success of the initial meeting and connection in 1978, Dr Nandy wrote 'I am so glad that you reminded me of the seal of Sir Francis Sykes (written Sikshi – as the Persian alphabets are very archaic) which we have decided to present you. This gift to you and your family will complete the circle of friendship that was begun 250 years ago.'[29]

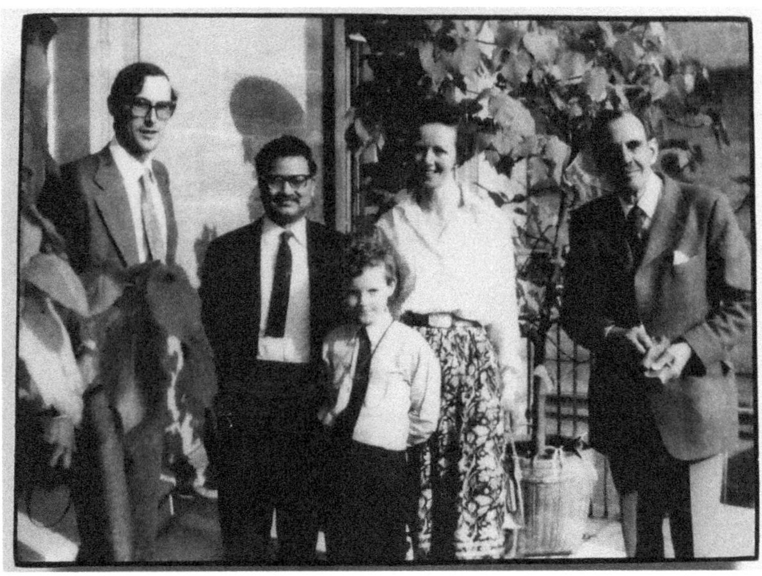

Figure 19.10 Photograph featuring from left to right, Sir John Sykes 10th Baronet, Dr Nandy, Charles Sykes, Lady Susan Sykes and Sir Francis Sykes 9th Baronet at Basildon Park, 1978. Image courtesy of Sir John Sykes.

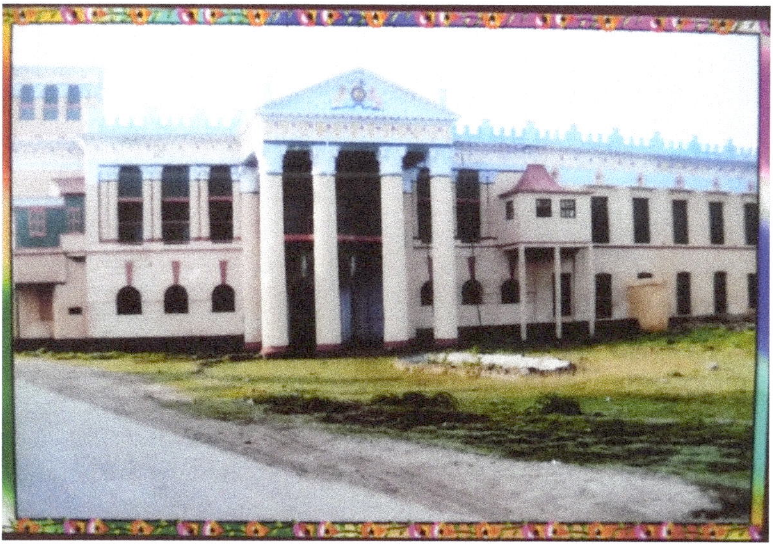

Figure 19.11 Photograph featuring Sripur Palace, Cossimbazar, 2012. Image courtesy of Dr S.C. Nandy.

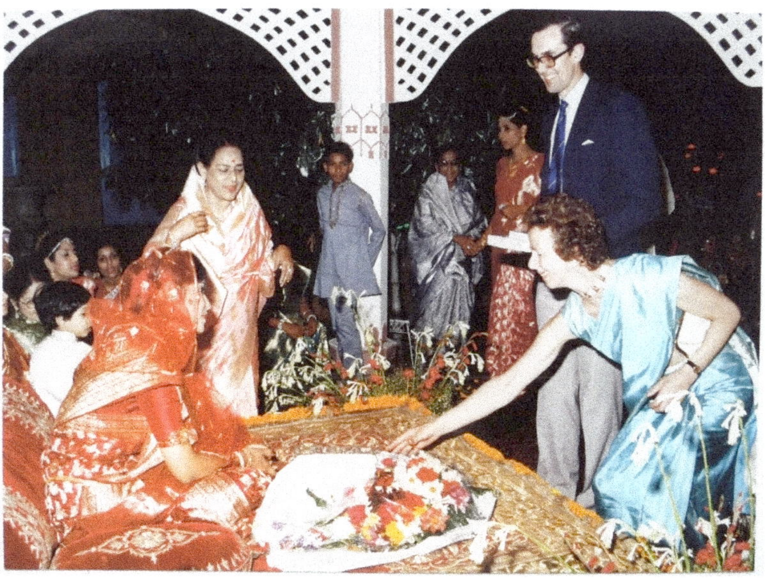

Figure 19.12 Photograph featuring the wedding of Dr Nandy's son Samit Chandra, 1988. Image courtesy of Sir John Sykes.

The seal as witness

The seal thus speaks of power, of common interest, of the meeting of differing cultures, of trust and of friendship. It is a vivid illustration of the way in which the East India Company and its servants operated in the early years of the British Raj: that is nominally as vassals of the Emperor in Delhi while actual power lay with the Company. It witnesses the bond between the English Company servant and the banian, a business arrangement which progressed through shared aims to a friendship which lasted the lifetimes of the original participants. It symbolises the trust Sykes placed in Cantu Babu, a trust which rose above differences of 'race' and the apparent inequalities of status, as evidenced by his leaving the seal with the latter after his departure for England. Paradoxically it reflects the similarity as well as the contrasting fortunes of the Nandy and Sykes families in that wealth of itself brought trial and tribulation as well as the enjoyment and display of position and grandeur, especially in the way both families became mired in litigation and were sometimes brought low by unworthy or ill-starred inheritors. Finally, while not the catalyst for the reunion, this small historic artefact does represent a remarkable connection between two families from two different continents, of two different religions and widely contrasting backgrounds, fortunes and cultures, which has transcended the centuries.

Conclusion

Margot Finn and Kate Smith

Country houses, their elite occupants and luxurious furnishings conventionally figure in twenty-first-century British media as icons of an insular national identity. In Julian Fellowes's film *Gosford Park* (2001), as in his wildly successful *Downton Abbey* (2010–15), stately homes appear to radiate timeless convention, depicting power in material form as tradition and continuity even as their occupants' lives reflect fundamental changes in British society, culture, economics and politics. By treating stately homes and their material culture as active historical agents rather than as passive backdrops against which human agency occurs, the chapters in *The East India Company at Home* have sought to suggest both alternative genealogies of country house power and alternative definitions of British identity. New imperial wealth – an exogenous force in pervasive present-day media representations of the eighteenth-, nineteenth- and twentieth-century country house – emerges from these studies as a vital cog in the machinery that maintained traditional 'British' structures of power and identity. To be sure, the threat of nabob wealth loomed large in Georgian caricature, where its conspicuous presence in elite stately homes represented an affront to established systems of property, privilege and Englishness. By the Victorian era however, this critique and its accompanying stereotype had long lost their force: Berkshire, Essex and Hertfordshire – like myriad British regions outside the Home Counties – proved more than capable of absorbing the material spoils of empire and of accommodating Company men, women and children into the propertied governing elite. Far from undermining the British country house as a bastion of power, East India Company (EIC) fortunes helped to underpin the 'power house' tradition in these decades.

The East India Company at Home has demonstrated the importance not only of imperial wealth, but also of imperial objects and their meanings to Britain's country houses in the eighteenth and nineteenth century. As Jan de Vries has shown, the significance in Europe of Asian luxury goods lay less in the sheer volume of goods traded than in the impacts they exerted on culture and society.[1] By studying the interlinked material histories of 'objects' across a range of scales – in and between country houses, in different types of furniture and fine art and among different family groupings – we have sought to locate local and regional identities into a more productive dialogue with global and cosmopolitan histories of material culture. Adopting this approach helps to illuminate both the interconnections and the differences that marked Georgian and Victorian mobilizations of wealth and goods from Asia in British 'power houses'. Shared cultural systems such as the stereotype of the nabob afforded a common language for contemporary critiques of imperial endeavour in public discourse, but in the private settings of family and home a wider spectrum of interpretation – and validation – was available and repeatedly exploited. Meanings varied across time and space; they were activated by contexts, by individuals and by relationships with other objects. Global material culture studies, we suggest, must give greater attention to how local contexts produced meanings and power relations through imperial goods. More exploration is required of how such understandings then shaped the very systems of political control, exploitation, manufacturing, trade and consumption that produced these material items.

Ultimately, the chapters in this volume scratch only the surface of the EIC's material legacy on Georgian and Victorian stately homes, and the stately home itself affords only a partial view of the wider impact of empire on wealth and power in Britain in this period. While this volume has actively sought to bring into view the women, children and extended family members involved in EIC activities, the Indian servants who toiled in Company country houses are largely absent from our chapters, although archival traces of their journeys from the subcontinent to the country house – charged with the care of Company wives, children and animals – provide fleeting glances of their residence and labour.[2] Further research is needed to locate their lives, and the biographies of Company fathers' mixed-race children, more securely within the histories of the British country house and its material cultures.[3] By identifying EIC wealth, personnel and objects as integral components of Georgian and Victorian stately homes, however, we hope to prompt other family historians (and historians of the family) to uncover these hidden histories, and to encourage heritage sites to incorporate these imperial stories fully into their displays and narratives. Gaining and voicing a clearer understanding of the relationship between the local and the global will prompt historians and the wider public to move beyond the false dichotomy of the imperial 'here and there'. At the same time it will allow for a fuller investigation of the processes of silencing and evasion that have long been underway, hiding histories of empire in plain sight.

Empire fundamentally shaped elite British country houses in the eighteenth and nineteenth century, adding to the constellation of dynamic processes by which British built environments absorbed and reflected global material cultures. Situating EIC objects and their owners within specific country houses and locales and focusing in depth on the practices and identities they animated, the chapters in this volume demonstrate how global tastes and practices were embedded in local contexts. Entangled with fortunes built with Caribbean slave labour, stately homes are domestic sites that embody Britain's global histories. These histories, often painful and often effaced, deserve to be recovered more fully.

Notes

Introduction

1. For an introduction to these themes, see Astrid Swenson, 'The Heritage of Empire', in Astrid Swenson and Peter Mandler (eds), *From Plunder to Preservation: Britain and the Heritage of Empire, c.1800–1940* (Oxford, 2013), 3–28. The 'Rhodes Must Fall' campaign initiated in 2015 demonstrates the force and rapidity with which these landscapes' imperial meanings can be rediscovered and politicized, both locally and globally. See for example Alex von Tunzelmann, 'Rhodes Must Fall? A Question of When Not If', *History Today*, 66:3 (2016), 6–7.
2. Good introductions are provided by Stephanie Barczewski, *Country Houses and the British Empire, 1700–1930* (Manchester, 2014); Adeline Koh, 'Inspecting the Nineteenth-century Literary Digital Archive: Omissions of Empire', *Journal of Victorian Culture*, 19:3 (2014), 385–395; Sarah Longair and John McAleer (eds), *Curating Empire: Museums and the British Imperial Experience* (Manchester, 2012).
3. For Kedleston as 'Rome reborn' and the impress of Adam's neoclassicism, see https://www.nationaltrust.org.uk/kedleston-hall/features/the-history-of-kedleston-hall. The collections of its Eastern Museum can be identified by searching http://www.nationaltrustcollections.org.uk/place/kedleston-hall. For the history of Government House, see Ina Puri (ed.), *Raj Bhavan of Kolkata: Two Hundred Years of Grandeur* (New Delhi, 2003).
4. The function of the stately home as a 'power house' that embodied English or British national identities is underlined, for example, by Mark Girouard, *Life in the English Country House: A Social and Architectural History* (London, 1978); and Roy Strong, Marcus Binney and John Harris (eds), *The Destruction of the Country House 1875–1975* (London, 1974). Historicized analyses of the country house's emergence as a national icon are provided by Ruth Adams, 'The V&A, the Destruction of the Country House and the Creation of "English Heritage"', *Museum & Society*, 11: 1 (2013), 1–18, and Peter Mandler, *The Fall and Rise of the Stately Home* (London, 1997), chap. 9.
5. Edward Said, *Culture and Imperialism* (New York, 1994), 69–70, 73, 100–116.
6. Madge Dresser and Andrew Hann (eds), *Slavery and the British Country House* (Swindon, 2013); Catherine Hall, Keith McClelland, Nick Draper, Kate Donnington and Rachel Lang, *Legacies of British Slave-ownership: Colonial Slavery and the Formation of Victorian Britain* (Cambridge, 2014). For the contested place of empire in British life from the nineteenth century to the present, see the opposing views presented in Catherine Hall and Sonya Rose (eds), *At Home with the Empire* (Cambridge, 2006), and Bernard Porter, *The Absent-minded Imperialists: Empire, Society, and Culture in Britain* (Oxford, 2004).
7. For risks, see Jean Sutton, *Lords of the East: The East India Company and Its Ships 1600–1874* (London, 2000). Company India's excessive mortality rates are discussed by Philip Curtin, *Death by Migration: Europe's Encounter with the Tropical World in the Nineteenth Century* (Cambridge, 2009), chap. 1. For wealth accumulation, see Huw Bowen, *The Business of Empire: The East India Company and Imperial Britain, 1756–1833* (Cambridge, 2006); James M. Holzman, *The Nabobs in England: A Study of the Returned Anglo-Indian, 1760–1785* (New York, 1926); and Tillman Nechtman, *Nabobs: Empire and Identity in Eighteenth-century Britain* (Cambridge, 2010).
8. Romita Ray, 'Going Global, Staying Local: Elihu Yale the Art Collector', *Yale University Art Gallery Bulletin* (December 2012), 34–51, citations 40, 42; Diane Scarisbrick and Benjamin Zucher, *Elihu Yale: Merchant, Collector and Patron* (London, 2014). Plas Grono is now part of Erddig estate, whose stately home boasts eighteenth-century Company connections and

retains Chinese wallpaper dating from the 1770s: Emile de Bruijn, Andrew Bush and Helen Clifford, *Chinese Wallpaper in National Trust Houses* (London, 2014), 23–25.

9. The classic study, still essential reading, is P.J. Marshall, *East India Fortunes: The British in Bengal in the Eighteenth Century* (Oxford, 1976).
10. For Company families and their diasporic households, see William Dalrymple, *White Mughals: Love and Betrayal in Eighteenth-century India* (London, 2002); Margot Finn, 'Anglo-Indian Lives in the Later Eighteenth and Early Nineteenth Centuries', *Journal for Eighteenth-Century Studies*, 3:1 (2010), 49–65; Durba Ghosh, *Sex and the Family in Colonial India: The Making of Empire* (Cambridge, 2006); Christopher Hawes, *Poor Relations: The Making of a Eurasian Community in British India, 1773–1833* (London, 1996); Emma Rothschild, *The Inner Life of Empires: An Eighteenth-century History* (Princeton, 2011).
11. See for example Natasha Eaton, 'Between Mimesis and Alterity: Art, Gift, and Diplomacy in Colonial India, 1770–1800', *Comparative Studies in Society and History*, 46:4 (2004), 816–844;. Natasha Eaton, 'Excess in the City? Consumption of Imported Prints in Colonial Calcutta, c.1780-c.1795', in Martin Jay and Sumathi Ramaswamy (eds), *Empires of Vision: A Reader* (Durham, NC, 2014), 159–188; Maya Jasanoff, *Edge of Empire: Conquest and Collecting in the East 1750–1850* (London, 2005).
12. We elaborate on and illustrate this methodology in Margot Finn and Kate Smith (eds), *New Paths to Public Histories* (Basingstoke, 2015).
13. For a broad overview of country house visiting and decline in this period, see Merlin Waterson, *A Noble Thing: the National Trust and Its Benefactors* (London, 2011). The burgeoning secondary literature of this period includes Girouard, *Life in the English Country House*; Christopher Hussey, *English Country Houses: Mid-Georgian, 1760–1800*, 2nd ed. (London, 1963); Gervase Jackson-Stops and James Pipkin, *The English Country House: A Grand Tour* (London, 1984); Giles Worsley, *England's Lost Houses: From the Archives of Country Life* (London, 2002).
14. Strong, Binney and Harris, *Destruction*, 13.
15. Strong, Binney and Harris, *Destruction*, 12.
16. Gervase Jackson-Stops, Gordon J. Schochet, Lena Cowen Orlin and Elisabeth Blair MacDougall (eds), *The Fashioning and Functioning of the British Country House* (Washington, DC, 1989).
17. For the impact of the Grand Tour, see for example Viccy Coltman, *Classical Sculpture and the Culture of Collecting in Britain since 1760* (Oxford, 2009); David R. Marshall, Susan Russell and Karin Wolfe (eds), *Roma Britannica: Art Patronage and Cultural Exchange in Eighteenth-century Rome* (London, 2011); Maria Dolores Sánchez-Jáuregui and Scott Wilcox, *The English Prize: The Capture of the Westmorland, an Episode of the Grand Tour* (New Haven, 2012). The significant presence of women is highlighted by Rosemary Sweet, *Cities and the Grand Tour: The British in Italy, c.1690–1820* (Cambridge, 2012).
18. Julius Bryant, 'From "Gusto" to "Kentissime": Kent's Designs for Country Houses, Villas and Lodges', in Susan Weber (ed.), *William Kent: Designing Georgian Britain* (New Haven, 2014), 186.
19. Jasanoff, *Edge of Empire* highlights the trans-European character of the community of collectors in Company-era 'British' India.
20. For an overview, see Andrew D. Madsen and Carolyn L. White, *Chinese Export Porcelain* (Walnut Creek, CA, 2011). David Sanctuary Howard, *Chinese Armorial Porcelain* (London, 1974) details British acquisitions and their European context, while Rocío Díaz, *Chinese Armorial Porcelain for Spain* (London, 2010) and Jochem Kroes, *Chinese Armorial Porcelain for the Dutch Market: Chinese Porcelain with Coats of Arms of Dutch Families* (The Hague, 2007) examine continental markets.
21. David Sanctuary Howard, *Chinese Armorial Porcelain: Volume II* (Chippenham, 2003), chap. 3. Howard notes that in the 1770s, perhaps 24 per cent of Chinese armorial services were made for Scottish families, rising to nearly 28 per cent of those made after 1810 (58).
22. Oliver Impey, 'Eastern Trade and the Furnishing of the British Country House', in Jackson-Stops et al., *Fashioning and Functioning*, 177.
23. Impey, 'Eastern Trade and the Furnishing of the British Country House', 189.
24. Examples of this approach include Lawrence Stone and J.C. F. Stone, *An Open Elite? England, 1540–1880* (Oxford, 1984), chap. 6, and Richard Wilson and Alan Mackley, *The Building of the English Country House* (London, 2000), 44–45, 322–333.
25. See esp. Maxine Berg, Felicia Gottman, Hanna Hodacs and Chris Nierstrasz, *Goods from the East, 1600–1800: Trading Eurasia* (Basingstoke, 2015) and Jon Stobart and Mark Rothery, *Consumption and the Country House* (Oxford, 2016).

26. Barczewski, *Country Houses and the British Empire*, 122, 47, 52.
27. See for example, Holzman, *The Nabobs in England*; Nechtman, *Nabobs*; Tillman W. Nechtman, 'Nabobinas: Luxury, Gender, and the Sexual Politics of British Imperialism in India in the Late Eighteenth Century, *Journal of Women's History*, 18:4 (2006), 8–30; Andrew MacKillop, 'The Highlands and the Returning Nabob: Sir Hector Munro of Novar, 1760–1807', in Marjory Harper (ed.), *Emigrant Homecomings: The Return Movement of Emigrants, 1600–2000* (Manchester, 2000), 233–262.
28. See Helen Clifford, 'The Dundas Property Empire and Nabob Taste: Accommodating the East: Sir Lawrence Dundas as Nabob of the North?', *East India Company at Home* (February 2013), 2: http://blogs.ucl.ac.uk/eicah/files/2013/02/Aske-Hall-Final-PDF-19.08.14.pdf.
29. Nechtman, *Nabobs*, 136.
30. For Benfield, see http://www.historyofparliamentonline.org/volume/1790–1820/member/benfield-paul-1741–1810. The caricature is available in the National Portrait Gallery's digital collections: http://www.npg.org.uk/collections/search/portrait/mw62162/Count-Roupee?LinkID=mp61740&search=sas&sText=benfield&role=sit&rNo=0.
31. For perceptions of EIC women see Nechtman, 'Nabobinas'.
32. Nechtman, *Nabobs*, 166.
33. Ellen Filor and Jan Sibthorpe, 'Outside the Public: The Histories of Sezincote and Prestonfield in Private Hands', in Finn and Smith (eds), *New Paths to Public Histories*, chap. 4.
34. Sheryllynne Haggerty and Susanne Seymour, 'Property, Power and Authority: The Implicit and Explicit Slavery Connections of Bolsover Castle and Brodsworth Hall in the 18th century', in Dresser and Hann (eds), *Slavery and the British Country House*, 87.
35. See esp. Hall, McClelland, Draper, Donnington and Lang, *Legacies of British Slave-ownership*.
36. See for example the cosy domestic interior depicted in: https://www.artfund.org/supporting-museums/art-weve-helped-buy/artwork/7086/the-drawing-room-at-whittington-hall-lancashire.
37. Girouard, *Life in the English Country House*, 2.
38. Sven Beckert, *Empire of Cotton: A New History of Global Capitalism* (London, 2014), esp. xv–xvi, 30, chaps 2–3.
39. Adrian Carton, *Mixed-race and Modernity in Colonial India: Changing Concepts of Hybridity across Empires* (London, 2012); Indrani Chatterjee, *Gender, Slavery and Law in Colonial India* (Oxford, 2002); Ghosh, *Sex and the Family*; Hawes, *Poor Relations*; Chandra Mallampalli, *Race, Religion, and Law in Colonial India: Trials of an Interracial Family* (Cambridge, 2011).
40. R. Bin Wong, *China Transformed: Historical Change and the Limits of European Experience* (London, 1997); Kenneth Pomeranz, *The Great Divergence: China, Europe, and the Making of the Modern World Economy* (Princeton, 2000); Berg, Gottmann, Hodacs and Nierstrasz (eds), *Goods from the East*.
41. Berg, Gottmann, Hodacs and Nierstrasz (eds), *Goods from the East*. See also Chris Nierstrasz, *Rivalry for Trade in Tea and Textiles: The English and Dutch East India Companies* (New York, 2015); Hanna Hodacs, *Silk and Tea in the North: Scandinavian Trade and the Market for Asian Goods in Eighteenth-Century Europe* (New York, 2016); Felicia Gottmann, *Global Trade, Smuggling and the Making of Economic Liberalism: Asian Textiles in France 1680–1760* (New York, 2016).
42. Maxine Berg, 'In Pursuit of Luxury: Global History and British Consumer Goods in the Eighteenth Century', *Past & Present*, 182 (2004), 85–142; Maxine Berg, 'From Imitation to Invention: Creating Commodities in Eighteenth-Century Britain', *Economic History Review*, 55:1 (2002), 1–30.
43. Stacey Pierson, 'The Movement of Chinese Ceramics: Appropriation in Global History', *Journal of World History*, 23:1 (2012), 9–39; Giorgio Riello, *Cotton: The Fabric that Made the Modern World* (Cambridge , 2013), 115; Robert S. DuPlessis, *The Material Atlantic: Clothing, Commerce, and Colonization in the Atlantic World, 1650–1800* (Cambridge, 2016), 211.
44. For the 'glocal', see Roland Robertson, 'Globalisation or Glocalisation?', *Journal of International Communication*, 1:1 (1994), 33–52.
45. Jon Stobart, *Sugar and Spice: Grocers and Groceries in Provincial England, 1650–1830* (Oxford, 2013), esp. chaps 2–3.
46. Stobart and Rothery, *Consumption and the Country House*.
47. Stobart and Rothery, *Consumption and the Country House*, 51.
48. The constraints of a three-year grant precluded attention to Ireland, but abundant evidence in other studies suggests the rich potential of analysis of Irish material culture from an imperial

perspective. See for example Toby Barnard, *Making the Grand Figure: Lives and Possessions in Ireland, 1641–1770* (New Haven and London, 2004) and Arthur MacGregor, *The Cobbe Cabinet of Curiosities: An Anglo-Irish Country House Museum* (New Haven and London, 2015).

49. Historians' increasing recognition of the agency of objects has been informed by anthropological approaches to material culture, perhaps most notably Arjun Appadurai, (ed.) *The Social life of Things: Commodities in Cultural Perspective* (Cambridge, 1986) and Bruno Latour, *Reassembling the Social: An Introduction to Actor-network-theory* (Oxford, 2005). For examples of this approach, see esp. Frank Trentmann, 'Materiality in the Future of History: Things, Practices, and Politics', *Journal of British Studies*, 48:2 (2009), 283–307, and Patrick Joyce, *The State of Freedom: A Social History of the British State since 1800* (Cambridge, 2013).
50. Howard, *Chinese Armorial Porcelain*; Amin Jaffer, *Luxury Goods from India: The Art of the Indian Cabinet Maker* (London, 2002); Mildred Archer, Christopher Rowell and Robert Skelton, *Treasures from India: The Clive Collection at Powis Castle* (London, 1987).
51. Stacey Sloboda, *Chinoiserie: Commerce and Critical Ornament in Eighteenth-century Britain* (Manchester, 2014), 3.
52. Stephen McDowall, 'The Shugborough Dinner Service and Its Significance for Sino-British History', *Journal for Eighteenth-Century Studies*, 37:1 (2014), 1–17.
53. The lives of Indian servants, glimpsed only occasionally in these chapters, have been illuminated more fully for example by Michael Fisher, *Counterflows to Colonialism: Indian Travellers and Settlers in Britain, 1600–1857* (Delhi, 2004) and Rozina Visram, *Ayahs, Lascars and Princes: Indians in Britain 1700–1947* (London, 1986).
54. For the wider significance of this topic, see Tony Bennett, Fiona Cameron, Nélia Dias, Ben Dibley, Rodney Harrison, Ira Jacknis and Conal McCarthy, *Collecting, Ordering, Governing: Anthropology, Museums and Liberal Government* (Durham, NC, 2017).
55. See esp. Antoinette Burton, *Archive Stories: Facts, Fictions, and the Writing of History* (Durham, NC, 2005); Miles Ogborn, *Indian Ink: Script and Print in the Making of the English East India Company* (Chicago, 2007); Ann Laura Stoler, *Along the Archival Grain: Epistemic Anxieties and Colonial Common Sense* (Princeton, 2009).
56. Andrew Prescott, 'I'd Rather Be a Librarian: A Response to Tim Hitchcock, "Confronting the Digital"', *Cultural and Social History*, 11:3 (2014), 339.
57. Jan de Vries, 'Understanding Eurasian Trade in the Era of the Trading Companies', in Berg, Gottmann, Hodacs and Nierstrasz (eds), *Goods from the East,* 22.
58. Michael Fisher, *Counterflows to Colonialism*, explores these journeys in greater depth.
59. Deborah Cohen's *Family Secrets: Shame and Privacy in Modern Britain* (Oxford, 2013), chap. 1, provides a wonderful prototype for such research.

Section 1

1. Arjun Appadurai, 'Introduction: Commodities and the Politics of Value', in Arjun Appadurai (ed.), *The Social Life of Things: Commodities in Cultural Perspective* (Cambridge, 1986), 5.
2. John Plotz, 'The First Strawberries in India: Cultural Portability in Victorian Greater Britain', *Victorian Studies*, 49:4 (2008), 659–684; John Plotz, *Portable Property: Victorian Culture on the Move* (Princeton, 2009).

Chapter 1

1. The authors would like to thank Margot Finn, Kate Smith, Sue Stronge, Helen Clifford, Richard Blurton, Sarah Choy, Vesta Curtis, Imma Ramos and Paramdip Khera for their advice and assistance in researching this case study.
2. This gallery will be refurbished and re-opened as the Albukhary Foundation Gallery of the Islamic world, scheduled for October 2018. The casket will then be redisplayed in the South Asia gallery.
3. http://www.britishmuseum.org/research/search_the_collection_database/search_object_details.aspx?objectid=249650&partid=1&searchText=1904%2c1006.1.a&fromADBC=ad&toADBC=ad&numpages=10&orig=%2fresearch%2fsearch_the_collection_

database.aspx&currentPage=1 Accessed 10 May 2013. Only transcripts of the original documents now survive.

4. Accepted spellings include 'Haidar', 'Haider', 'Haydar' and 'Hayder'.
5. Maya Jasanoff, *Edge of Empire: Conquest and Collecting in the East 1750–1850* (London, 2005), 184.
6. In this approach we build on the pioneering work of Kopytoff and Appadurai, Gosden and many others: Igor Kopytoff, 'The Cultural Biography of Things: Commoditization as Process', in Arjun Appadurai (ed.), *The Social Life of Things: Commodities in Cultural Perspective* (Cambridge, 1986), 64–91; Chris Gosden and Yvonne Marshall, 'The Cultural Biography of Objects', *World Archaeology* 31:2 (1999), 169–178.
7. Useful comparisons can be drawn with the gendered treatment of the Koh-I-Noor diamond whose history as a looted object was subsequently shaped, and physically reshaped, in line with changing imperial priorities: Danielle C. Kinsey, 'Koh-I-Noor: Empire, Diamonds, and the Performance of British Material Culture', *Journal of British Studies* 48:2 (2009), 391–419.
8. Pierson notes the care we must take in analyzing the representativeness of individual object histories: Stacey Pierson, 'The Movement of Chinese Ceramics: Appropriation in Global History', *Journal of World History* 23:1 (2012), 13.
9. Mohammad Moienuddin, *Sunset at Srirangapatam: After the Death of Tipu Sultan* (Hyderabad, 2000), xii.
10. Andrew Mackillop gives a useful overview of the characteristics of this earlier group: Andrew Mackillop, 'The Highlands and the Returning Nabob: Sir Hector Munro of Novar, 1760–1807', in Marjory Harper (ed.), *Emigrant Homecomings: The Return Movement of Emigrants, 1600–2000* (Manchester, 2005), 233. For further examples of mobile imperial families, see Elizabeth Buettner, *Empire Families: Britons and Late Imperial India* (Oxford, 2004); David Lambert and Alan Lester, (eds), *Colonial Lives across the British Empire: Imperial Careering in the Long Nineteenth Century* (Cambridge, 2006).
11. For an image of the open casket showing the bottles and ladle, see: http://www.britishmuseum.org/research/collection_online/collection_object_details/collection_image_gallery.aspx?partid=1&assetid=1392153001&objectid=249650. Accessed 16 July 2017.
12. Maria Menshikova and Jet Pijzel-Dommisse, *Silver: Wonders from the East: Filigree of the Tsars* (Amsterdam, 2006).
13. Menshikova and Pijzel-Dommisse, *Silver: Wonders from the East*, 18–28.
14. Susan Stronge, *Tipu's Tigers* (London, 2009), 50, fig 50. See Victoria and Albert Museum collection, IS.4.2013. http://collections.vam.ac.uk/item/O1277970/casket/. Accessed 15 August 2016.
15. Mildred Archer, Christopher Rowell and Robert Skelton, *Treasures from India: The Clive Collection at Powis Castle* (London, 1987).
16. Stronge, personal communication, 3 August 2016.
17. We are grateful to Dr. Vesta Curtis and Paramdip Khera, Coins and Medals department, British Museum, and Susan Stronge, Victoria and Albert Museum for assisting in the reviewing of the stamp's translation.
18. 'Imam' is a title used for Islamic religious leaders and most commonly refers to those who lead prayers in mosques. 'Ali was the cousin and son-in-law of the Prophet Muhammad. Shi'ites, members of the Shi'a branch of Islam, believe that 'Ali was the first Imam of Islam and the heir of Muhammad.
19. Stronge, *Tipu's Tigers,* 36.
20. Another example of this stamp being used on items from Tipu's court can be found in a jewelled Navratna pendant which went to auction at Bonhams on 28 September 2011. http://www.bonhams.com/auctions/19576/lot/163N/. Accessed 13 May 2013.
21. See Kate Brittlebank, 'Sakti and Barakat: The Power of Tipu's Tiger', *Modern Asian Studies*, 29: 2 (1995), 257– 69; Denys Forrest, *Tiger of Mysore* (London, 1970), 315–37.
22. Brittlebank, 'Sakti and Barakat', 257–269; Richard H. Davis, *Lives of Indian Images* (Princeton, 1997), 150–2.
23. Davis, *Lives of Indian Images*, 150–2.
24. Anne Buddle, 'The Tiger and the Thistle', in Anne Buddle (ed.), *The Tiger and the Thistle: Tipu Sultan and the Scots in India, 1760–1800* (Edinburgh, 1999), 10.
25. Forrest, *Tiger of Mysore*, 2.

26. Quoted in Iain Gordon Brown, 'Griffins, Nabobs and a Seasoning of Curry Powder: Walter Scott and the Indian Theme in Life and Literature', in Buddle, (ed.) *The Tiger and the Thistle*, 79.
27. Pauline Rohatgi, 'From Pencil to Panorama: Tipu in Pictorial Perspective', in Buddle, (ed.), *The Tiger and the Thistle*, 48.
28. Rohatgi, 'From Pencil to Panorama', 51–2.
29. Moienuddin, *Sunset at Srirangapatam*, xii.
30. Quoted in Buddle, 'The Tiger and the Thistle', 37.
31. See also Stronge, *Tipu's Tigers*; Sadiah Qureshi, 'Tipu's Tiger and Images of India, 1799–2010', in John McAleer and Sarah Longair (eds.), *Curating Empire: Museums and the British Imperial Experience* (Manchester, 2012), 207–24.
32. Moienuddin, *Sunset at Srirangapatam*, xii. Spectacular pieces included the tent of Tipu Sultan which was installed in Powis Castle, the home of Lord and Lady Clive, the latter travelling to Seringapatam in 1800 where she 'collected obsessively.' Jasanoff, *Edge of Empire*, 187, 186–96.
33. Anne Buddle, 'Myths, Melodrama and the Twentieth Century', in Buddle, (ed.), *The Tiger and the Thistle*, 63.
34. Buddle, 'Myths, Melodrama and the Twentieth Century', 65.
35. Jasanoff, *Edge of Empire*, 182. Forrest wryly recalls a friend remarking that 'the reason why he did not put up a more effective fight on the battlements of his capital might well be that he was carrying thirteen swords at the time'. Forrest, *Tiger of Mysore*, 2. We are grateful to Sue Stronge for alerting us to this reference.
36. Moienuddin, *Sunset at Srirangapatam*, xii.
37. Rina Prentice, *The Authentic Nelson* (London, 2005).
38. See esp. Tillman Nechtmann, *Nabobs: Empire and Identity in Eighteenth-Century Britain* (Cambridge, 2010), chap. 4.
39. Moienuddin, *Sunset at Srirangapatam*, 33.
40. Forrest, *Tiger of Mysore*, 3; Qureshi, 'Tipu's Tiger and Images of India'.
41. 'Celebrities at home: No. VIII. Mr. Lowe at Sherbrooke', *The World: A Journal for Men and Women*, no. 119 (11 October 1876), 4–5.
42. Deborah Cohen, *Household Gods: The British and Their Possessions* (New Haven, 2006); Jacqueline Yallop, *Magpies, Squirrels and Thieves: How the Victorians Collected the World* (London, 2011).
43. A. Patchett Martin, *Life and Letters of the Right Honourable Robert Lowe, Viscount Sherbrooke, with a Memoir of Sir John Coape Sherbrooke* (London, 1893), 596–7.
44. Martin, *Life and Letters*, 539.
45. *Major Allan's Account of his Interview with the Princes in the Palace of Seringapatam, and of Finding the Body of the Late Tippoo Sultaun* in A. Beatson, *A View of the Origin and Conduct of the War with Tippoo Sultaun; Comprising a Narrative of the Operations of the Army under the Command of Lieutenant-General George Harris, and of the Siege of Seringapatam* (London, 1800). Appendix No. XLII, cxxvii–cxxxi.
46. Alexander Mackenzie, *History of the Frasers of Lovat with Genealogies of the Principal Families of the Name: To Which Is Added Those of Dunballoch and Phopachy* (Inverness, 1896), 656.
47. Mackenzie, *History of the Frasers of Lovat*, 656.
48. Mackillop, 'The Highlands and the Returning Nabob', 233.
49. Mackenzie, *History of the Frasers of Lovat*, 657.
50. Julian Cotton, *List of Inscriptions on Tombs or Monuments in Madras Possessing Historical or Archaeological Interest* (Madras, 1946), vol. 2:36.
51. The account by an anonymous officer of the cavalry in *Recollections of the Deccan: With Misscellaneous Sketches and Letters* (Calcutta, 1838), 58 describes the 'chateau' at Mount Capper, 3–4 miles south of Cuddalore, as the former favoured residence of the late General Fraser. Although dismissive of the house, the estate for this writer 'more resembles an English park than any I have seen elsewhere in India'. According to the *Madras District Gazetteer: South Arcot* (Madras, 1962), 3, 'Mount Capper derives its name from Captain (afterwards Colonel) Francis Capper of the "Native Infantry". In 1798 he obtained permission to enclose upon it a piece of land and build a house. In 1805 the property was transferred by him to Captain (afterwards General) Fraser, to whom a grant of it was made by the Government in 1815, and, later on, by the terms of the grants, it reverted to the Government.' This is distinct from Capper House, commissioned by Francis Capper, to be constructed on the beachfront north of St Thomé, Madras, possibly around 1800.

52. Charles was brother of Charlotte Carpenter, who in 1797 married Walter Scott. For details of Scott's interaction with the Carpenter family see Brown, 'Griffins, Nabobs and a Seasoning of Curry Powder', 76–77; *The Edinburgh Annual Register for 1816, Vol. 9* (Edinburgh, 1820), ccccxvi.
53. The National Archives, 'Will of Hugh Fraser, Commander of the Ship Hastings in the Honourable East India Companies Service', PROB 11/1082/388.
54. Hastings Fraser's grave is in Kensal Green cemetery in London. http://www.findagrave.com/cgi-bin/fg.cgi?page=pv&GRid=71385081&PIpi=43951669. Accessed 15 April 2013.
55. Hastings was notable for his service in Hyderabad and his attention to improving living conditions for local people: Mackenzie, *History of the Frasers of Lovat*, 669.
56. Josiah Sr. spent his early years in India and was notable for his attempt to establish iron and steel manufacturing plants in the Madras Presidency: Shyam Rungta, *The Rise of Business Corporations in India, 1851–1900* (Cambridge, 1970), 276. See also Thomas Webster, *The Case of Josiah Marshall Heath, the Inventor and Introducer of the Manufacture of Welding Cast Steel from British Iron* (London, 1856).
57. Such specific bequests were not unusual, particularly with material related to Tipu Sultan, see for example: M.O. Campbell, *Supplement to a Memorial History of the Campbells of Melfont Argyllshire ...* . (1894), p. 23. 'It may be interesting to mention that Captain John Campbell bequeathed to his brother, Captain Archibald Campbell, a handsome silver bowl, of beautiful Indian workmanship, to be kept in the Melfont family as an heirloom. To his brother, general Frederick Campbell, he left a watch found under Tippoo Saib's pillow. It is a large gold repeater, of French make. General F. Campbell wore it for many years; he also left his brother a crimson silk damask coverlet used by Tippoo Saib ... .' Our thanks to Margot Finn for this reference.
58. An attardan now in the National Army Museum was commissioned by the 35th Regiment Bengal Native infantry in 1842 after Afghan war campaigns, which the officers subsequently voted to present to their commander supporting the fluid gender associations of such items. http://www.nam.ac.uk/online-collection/detail.php?acc=1959–04–278–1. Accessed 19 August 2016.
59. British Museum Acquisition Registers, 6 October 1904.
60. Edward Millar, *That Noble Cabinet: A History of the British Museum* (London, 1973), 299–320. https://www.britishmuseum.org/about_us/departments/asia/history_of_the_collection.aspx. Accessed 11 August 2016.
61. See the sword in the Wallace collection http://www.wallacecollection.org/whatson/treasure/10) and the Tipu's tiger organ in the Victoria and Albert Museum (http://collections.vam.ac.uk/item/O61949/tippoos-tiger-mechanical-organ-unknown/ Both accessed 22 August 2016.
62. For discussion of the 'colonial moment' in the lives of objects, see Sarah Longair, 'The Colonial Moment in the Lives of Objects on the Swahili Coast' in P. Meier and A. Purpura (eds), *World on the Horizon: Swahili Arts across the Indian Ocean* (Champaign-Urbana, IL, 2018).
63. Moienuddin, *Sunset at Srirangapatam*, xii.

Chapter 2

1. Emile de Bruijn, Andrew Bush and Helen Clifford, *Chinese Wallpaper in National Trust Houses* (Swindon, 2014), 4.
2. There are very few known examples of European made chinoiserie style wallpaper that look like the Chinese wallpapers made for export. One of these came from Berkeley House, Wotton-under-Edge, Gloucestershire c.1740, now in the V&A: W.93:1–63–1924.
3. Charles Saumarez Smith, *Eighteenth-century Decoration Design and the Domestic Interior in England* (London, 1993), 48.
4. Oliver Impey, 'Eastern Trade and Furnishing of the British Country House', in Gervase Jackson-Stops (ed.), *The Fashioning and Functioning of the British Country House, Studies in the History of Art,* 25 (Washington, DC, 1989), 177.
5. Ian Kelly, *Mr Foote's Other Leg: Comedy, Tragedy and Murder in Georgina London* (London, 2013), 382. As Emile de Bruijn noted in a remark on this contribution, the fewer examples of Chinese wallpaper in town as opposed to country houses may reflect a higher rate of rebuilding, sale and exchange in the latter.
6. These houses contain not just Chinese wallpaper but many other examples of Asian decorative art. For example the dining room at Tregothan, seat of the Boscawen family since the fourteenth century, contains a K'ang vase supposedly brought back by Admiral Boscawen

from Pondicherry in 1749. See Stephanie Barcezewski, 'Is Britishness always British?', in M. Farr and X. Guegan, *The British abroad since the Eighteenth Century*, vol.1, *Travellers and Tourists* (Heidelberg, 2013), 45.

7. This mapping has been made possible by the Chinese Wallpaper Study Group, see de Bruijn et al., *Chinese Wallpaper in National Trust Houses*, 10–11.
8. Of formalized pomegranate design, derived from a contemporary Italian velvet or damask, see: Textile influences on wallpaper: http://www.vam.ac.uk/content/articles/t/textile-influences-on-wallpaper/.
9. For example woodblock print on paper, late seventeenth-century found on an early seventeenth-century box now in the V&A Museum (E.405–1968), showing a scene of a seated figure fishing before a pond, a house in the backgrounds, with trees and flowers and birds, set within a border, measuring 39.5 cm by 49.5 cm.
10. When the tax on paper was lifted in 1861, wood pulp began to replace rags, and new technology enabled the production of continuous sheets of paper which could be printed faster.
11. Henry G. Bohn, *Diary and Correspondence of John Evelyn*, vol. 1 (London, 1859), 402–403.
12. I. Lambert & C. Laroque, 'An Eighteenth-century Chinese Wallpaper: Historical Context and Conservation', in 'Works of art on paper: books, documents and photographs: techniques and conservation: contributions to the Baltimore Congress', 2–6 September 2002,122–128. See: https://www.iiconservation.org/node/2002.
13. Quoted G. L. Hunter, *Decorative Textiles: An Illustrated Book on Coverings for Furniture, Walls and Floors* (Philadelphia, 1918), 363.
14. Craig Clunas, *Chinese Export Watercolours* (London, 1984), 10.
15. Robert Fortune, *A Residence among the Chinese* (London, 1865), chap. 4.
16. Quoted in Margaret Jourdain and Soame Jenyns, 'Chinese Export Art in the Eighteenth Century', *Country Life* (1950), 34.
17. Emily J. Climenson (ed.), *Diaries of Mrs Philip Lybbe Powys of Hardwick House, Oxon* (London, 1899), 146–147, entry for October 1771, quoted by Gill Saunders, *Wallpaper in Interior Decoration*, (London, 1994), 49, note 15.
18. Emile de Bruijn, Chinese Wallpaper in Britain and Ireland (London, 2017), 30.
19. *London Gazette*, 16–20 March, quoted in Jourdain and Jenyns, 'Chinese Export Art', 25.
20. It was 'probably hand painted in the same workshops in Canton since the technique to stain wallpapers was very similar to the preparation of hand painted silks' see Saunders, *Wallpaper*, 50.
21. John Macky, *A Journey through England* (London, 1724) vol.1, 21.
22. See de Bruijn et al., *Chinese Wallpaper in National Trust Houses*, 10–11.
23. de Bruijn, Chinese Wallpaper in Britain and Ireland, 30.
24. Two companies dominate the supply of Chinese wallpaper in Britain today: de Gournay founded 30 years ago by Claud Cecil Gurney and Fromental established by Tim Butcher and Lizzie Deshayes in 2005.
25. Quoted in Andrea Feeser, Maureen Daly Goggin and Beth Fowkes Tobin, *The Materiality of Color: The Production, Circulation, and Application of Dyes and Pigments, 1400–1800* (London, 2012), 86.
26. Lady Anna Miller, *Letters from Italy, Describing the Manners, Customs, Antiquities, Painting*, vol. 2 (London 1776), 358.
27. E. Hargrove, *The History of the Castle, Town and Forest of Knaresborough with Harrogate* (4th ed., York, 1789), 265.
28. A. J. Valpy, 'On the Life and Times of Casimir', *The Classical Journal*, 31 (1825), 308.
29. de Bruijn et al., *Chinese Wallpaper in National Trust Houses*, cat. no. 36, p. 39. This paper was moved from Walcot Hall in North Shropshire, (purchased by Robert Clive in 1764) to Powis in 1936.
30. Quoted in A.V. Sugden, *A History of English Wallpaper 1509–1914* (London, 1914), 56.
31. R. Phillips, *Monthly Magazine and British Register*, 30: 2 (1810), 199.
32. Pauline Webber, 'Chinese Wallpapers in the British Galleries', *V&A Conservation Journal*, 39 (2001), 6.
33. Webber, 'Chinese Wallpapers', and her paper 'The Conservation and Restoration of Chinese Wallpapers: An Overview', given at the 'Chinese Wallpaper: Trade, Technique and Taste International Conference', Coutts Bank and V&A, London 7–8 April 2016.
34. See de Bruijn et al., *Chinese Wallpapers in National Trust Houses*, and Johnson, *Peeling Back the Years*.

35. Although it has been possible to identify repeat motifs, such as the ducks which appear on the paper at Ightham Mote, Belton and Woburn, see de Bruijn et al., *Chinese Wallpaper in National Trust Houses*, 30.
36. J.D. Hooker (ed.), *Journal of the Rt Hon Sir Joseph Banks* (New York, 1896), vol.4, 45.
37. Malachy Postlethwayt, *The Universal Dictionary of Trade and Commerce* (London, 1757), 56.
38. John Cornforth, *Early Georgian Interiors* (New Haven and London, 2004), 265–6.
39. *The Letters and Journals of Lady Mary Coke*, vol.4 (Bath, 1970), 43.
40. Miller, *Letters from Italy*, 23.
41. Liza Picard, *Dr Johnson's London* (London, 2001), 297.
42. Gill Saunders, 'The China Trade: Oriental Painted Panels', in Lesley Hopkins (ed.), *The Papered Wall: History, Pattern Technique* (New York, 1994), 42–55, with thanks to Andrew Bush for this reference.
43. Margaret Ponsonby, *Stories from Home: English Domestic Interiors, 1750–1850* (Aldershot, 2007), 53.
44. A. Fennetaux, A. Junqua and S. Vasset, *The Afterlife of Used Things: Recycling in the Long Eighteenth Century* (London, 2015), 3.
45. There is evidence that other East India Companies did experiment with official as opposed to private trade in Chinese wallpapers, thanks to research undertaken as part of the 'Europe's Asian Centuries' project at the University of Warwick 2010–14, funded by the European Research Council, and led by Maxine Berg. According to Chris Nierstrasz the Dutch East India Company (VOC) imported 200 pieces in 1757 as part of the official trade, although this does not seem to have tempted them to develop the trade further. Information relayed in a private communication to the author in 2014, based on his work for his book *Rivalry for Tea and Textiles: The English and Dutch East India Companies (1700–1800)*, (Basingstoke, 2015). Felicia Gottman's work on the French East India Company for the same project reveals that in a memorandum written in the 1730s a Company ship's captain noted 'there are more than 50 different sorts of paper made in China, the one from Nankin is however the most highly esteemed – it is also from where the best painted ones come', the latter presumably referring to wallpaper, which was also auctioned by the Company in 1768. Private communication from the author, June 2014.
46. See further, 'The Honourable East India Company trading to China' in David S. Howard, *A Tale of Three Cities: Canton, Shanghai & Hong Kong* (London, 1997), xiv.
47. Meike von Brescius, 'Worlds Apart? Merchants, Mariners and the Organisation of the Private Trade in Chinese Export Wares in Eighteenth-Century Europe', in Maxine Berg et al. (eds), *Trading Eurasia: Europe's Asian Centuries 1600–1830* (Farnham: 2015), 71–2.
48. Meike Fellinger (von Brescius), 'The Principal-agent Problem Revisited: Supercargoes and Commanders of the China Trade'. Accessed 2 September 2016. http://studylib.net/doc/13209578/the-principal-agent-problem-revisited–supercargoes.
49. Meike Fellinger (von Brescius), 'Supercargoes and the English East India Company in the China Trade 1700–1760' (PhD thesis, University of Warwick, 2015).
50. Howard, *Tale of Three Cities*, xiv.
51. Jan de Vries, 'Goods from the East', in Berg et al. (eds), *Trading Eurasia*, 30.
52. *The World*, 1:38 (20 September 1753), 242.
53. Based on an ongoing database, part of the National Trust Chinese wallpaper project, which at March 2014 included 149 houses, 30 of which have East India Company connections.
54. He also acquired amongst other things a porcelain 'Palaceware' dessert service, c.1795 which also travelled back with him to Scotland. See Howard, *Tale of Three Cities*, cat. no. 41, 47–8. With thanks to Emile de Bruijn for this reference. The Castle had been in the Drummond family since the thirteenth century. It was sold in 1910 to Sir James Roberts, in whose family it remains today. The Chinese wallpaper was purchased by the Peabody Essex Museum with funds donated in part by The Lee and Juliet Folger Fund, 2006. See further William R. Sargent, 'The Strathallan Castle Wallpaper at the Peabody Essex Museum', *Orientations*, 45: 8 (2014), 22–23.
55. See further The Centre for the Study of the Legacies of British Slave-ownership, http://www.ucl.ac.uk/lbs/.
56. See Yuthika Sharma and Pauline Davies, '"A jaghire without a crime": East India Company and the Indian Ocean Material World at Osterley 1700–1800', in this volume.
57. With many thanks to Emile de Bruijn for his very helpful comments on this wallpaper.

58. See information included in the entry on Sir Edward Turner (1719–66) in L. Namier and J. Brook, *The History of Parliament: the House of Commons 1754–1790* (London, 1964) via online resource: http://www.histparl.ac.uk/volume/1754–1790/member/turner-sir-edward-1719–66.
59. The following taken from Gladys Scott Thomson, *The Russells in Bloomsbury 1669–1771* (London, 1940), 312–338.
60. See Lucy Johnson, *Peeling Back the Years: Chinoiserie at Woburn Abbey* (Bedford, 2014).
61. For example Denys Sutton (ed.), *Treasures from Woburn Abbey from the Collection of the Duke of Bedford*, originally published in *Apollo Magazine* (December 1965).
62. See Hannah Armstrong's case study 'Josiah Child and the Wanstead Estate' at http://blogs.ucl.ac.uk/eicah/josiah-child-and-the-wanstead-estate-case-study/.
63. Thomson, *The Russells*, 316.
64. One of the duties of a supercargo was 'to cause every package in private-trade to be marked with the initial of the name of the person to whom it belongs, register them with these marks, the nature of the package, the contents, and quality of the contents', *Rule CIV (Instructions from the Commanders of The East India Company's Own Ships to Their Officers, &c* (London, 1819), 39.
65. Information kindly supplied by Lucy Johnson, 29 June 2014.
66. Jean Sutton, *Lords of the East: The East India Company and its Ships* (London, 1981), 166.
67. The Chinese paper in this room at Woburn was protected by another layer of paper added 28 years later when the room was redecorated, and was rediscovered in 2014.
68. Johnson, *Peeling Back the Years*, 3.
69. Johnson, *Peeling Back the Years*, 4.
70. Gill Saunders, *Wallpaper in Interior Decoration* (London, 2002), 3.
71. http://howtospendit.ft.com/interior-design/25123-wall-important
72. In 1771 he was appointed physician to the Queen's household; in 1782, physician in ordinary to the Queen, and physician extraordinary to the King; and in 1797, physician in ordinary to the King, and to the Prince of Wales.
73. Extended in the nineteenth century by Alfred Waterhouse, now converted into seven apartments.
74. E. Jordan, 'Chinese Wallpapers in England', *The Star,* Issue 9680 (23 October 1909), 1.
75. Listed 1954, English Heritage Building ID 356912. Also described as 'illustrating the different arts and manufactures of the Celestial empire', in J. Cave-Brown, *History of Brasted, Its Manor, Parish and Church,* vol.II (Westerham, 1874), 284.
76. De Bruijn et al., *Chinese Wallpaper*, 3.
77. Christina Baird, *Liverpool China Traders* (Bern, 2007), 136.
78. See Gordon Lang, 'The Royal Pavilion, Brighton: The Chinoiserie Designs by Frederick Crace', in Megan Aldrich (ed.), *The Craces, Royal Decorators 1768–1899* (Brighton, 1990), 43.
79. The wallpaper noted here in the Saloon was not original to this space, and has now been removed and replaced by another, red silk scheme as at 2016. With many thanks to Emile de Bruijn for this information revealing the complexities related to the mobility of the wallpaper.
80. *The Birds of America* was first published as a series in sections between 1827 and 1838 in Edinburgh and London. The work consists of hand-coloured, life size prints, made from engraved plates. The plates were published unbound and without any text to avoid having to furnish free copies to English libraries. It is estimated that not more than 200 sets were ever completed.
81. Avray Tipping, 'In English Homes: The Internal Character, Furniture & Adornments of Some of the Most Notable Houses of England', *Country Life*, 2 (1908), 150.
82. Helen Fetherstonhaugh, *Three Hundred Years of Private Banking* (London, nd), 21.
83. He acquired the lease of number 59 and designed a premises specifically for banking.
84. Helen Henrietta Macartney Robbins, *Our First Ambassador to China: An Account of the Life of George, Earl of Macartney, with Extracts from His Letters, and the Narrative of His Experiences in China, as Told by Himself, 1737–1806* (Cambridge, 2011), 442.
85. See book of copy letters BL, Add MS 22462 letters between Coutts, Lord Macartney and Lady Macartney, with thanks to Margot Finn for this reference.
86. Maxine Berg, 'Britain, Industry and Perceptions of China: Matthew Boulton, "useful knowledge" and the Macartney Embassy to China 1792–94', *Journal of Global History,* 1 (2006), 268.
87. Berg, 'Britain, Industry and Perceptions of China', 280.

88. Paul Gillingham, 'The Macartney Embassy to China, 1792–94', *History Today*, 43 (1993), 5.
89. G. L. Staunton, *An Authentic Account of an Embassy from the King of Great Britain to the Emperor of China* (London, 1797), 155.
90. Berg, 'Britain, Industry and Perceptions of China', 268.
91. Thanks to Anna Wu for this information.
92. William Marshall, *The Rural Economy of Yorkshire: Comprizing the Management of Landed Estates, and the Present Practice of Husbandry in the Agricultural Districts of that County*, vol. 1 (London, 1788), 282.
93. C. Bruyn Andrews (ed.), *The Torrington Diaries Containing the Tours through England and Wales of the Hon. John Byng (Later Fifth Viscount Torrington) between the Years 1781 and 1794*, vol. 2 (London, 1935), 40.
94. Clive Aslet, *The English House: The Story of a Nation at Home* (London, 2008), 131.
95. Clunas, *Chinese Export Watercolours*, 14.
96. Quoted in Catherine Pagani, *Eastern Magnificence & European Ingenuity: Clocks of Late Imperial China* (Ann Arbor, 2001), 74.
97. Philip Beresford and William D. Rubinstein, *The Richest of the Rich: The Wealthiest 250 People in Britain since 1066* (London, 2011), 302.
98. National Maritime Museum: BHC3664.
99. British Library, Letter dated 23 May 1817, Mss Eur. B376.
100. British Library, Letter dated 23 May 1817, Mss Eur. B376.
101. See manuscript account in the form of an autograph letter from the carpenter on board HMS *Alceste* to his father, [c.1817], details from sale at Christie's, King Street, London, 26–27 September, 2007, lot 507.
102. Henry Ellis, *Journal of the Proceedings of the Late Embassy to China* (London, 1817).
103. Despite being dismissed by the Emperor, Amherst like Macartney, travelled extensively throughout China and did not depart until January of 1817. On the voyage back to England HMS *Alceste,* struck a rock near the Straits of Gaspar in the Java Sea and sank. There was no loss of life and Lord Amherst was taken to Batavia aboard the H.M. *Brig Lyra*.
104. Margot Finn, 'The Homes of England', in James Chandler, (ed.), *The New Cambridge History of English Literature: The Romantic Period* (Cambridge, 2009), 293–313.
105. Henry Carey Baird, *The Interior Decorator, Being the Laws of Harmonious Colourings Applied to Interior Decorations with Observation on the Practice of House Painting* (Philadelphia, 1867).
106. Clive Wainwright, *The Romantic Interior: The British Collector at Home 1750–1850* (New Haven and London, 1989), 154.
107. John Gibson Lockhart, *Memoirs of the Life of Sir Walter Scott*, vol. 3, (Paris, 1838), 142.
108. D.R. Hay, *The Laws of Harmonious Colouring adapted to Interior Decoration*, 6th ed. (Edinburgh, 1847), 181.
109. Hay, *Laws of Harmonious Colouring*,182.
110. Hay, *Laws of Harmonious Colouring*,183.
111. Charles Rogers, *Genealogical Memoirs of the Family of Sir Walter Scott, Bart. of Abbotsford* (London, 1877), 102.
112. See further on Scott and India: http://www.tigerandthistle.net/scots432.htm.
113. Herbert J.C. Grierson (ed.) *The Letters of Walter Scott,* vol.7 (London, 1932–1937), 278–80.
114. David Veddar, *Memoir of Sir Walter Scott, Bart: With Critical Notices of His Writings Compiled from Various Authentic Sources* (Dundee, 1832), 5.
115. Pair of framed Chinese wallpaper fragments, 56 x 49 cm, Christie's 10–11/1/202, sale 2530 Lot 295; Box covered with Chinese wallpaper, 19th c., 28 x 65.5 x 42 cm, sold Christie's 21 October 2003, lot 229; For example 6-fold screen, c.1790s, sold Sotheby's 24 October 2008, lot 174.
116. Allyson McDermott, http://www.allysonmcdermott.com/chinoiserie/.

Chapter 3

1. Amin Jaffer, *Luxury Goods from India: The Art of the Indian Cabinet-Maker* (London, 2002), 125.
2. Kirsten A. Seaver, 'Desirable Teeth: The Medieval Trade in Arctic and African Ivory', *Journal of Global History*, 4:2 (2009), 276.

3. Tillman W. Nechtman, *Nabobs: Empire and Identity in Eighteenth-Century Britain* (Cambridge, 2010), 170.
4. For the importance of being seen to wear Indian goods in public see Tillman W. Nechtman, 'Nabobinas: Luxury, Gender, and the Sexual Politics of British Imperialism in India in the Late Eighteenth Century', *Journal of Women's History*, 18:4 (2006), 8–30.
5. Anne Gerritsen and Stephen McDowall, 'Global China: Material Culture and Connections in World History', *Journal of World History*, 23:1 (2012), 5.
6. For snuffboxes and fans for example see 'lost property' notices in *Post Boy* (London), 8–10 April 1712; *Daily Courant* (London) 18 February 1713; *Daily Courant* (London), 1 April 1713.
7. Jaffer, *Luxury Goods from India*, 82.
8. Jaffer, *Luxury Goods from India*, 85.
9. Amin Jaffer, 'Tipu Sultan, Warren Hastings and Queen Charlotte: The Mythology and Typology of Anglo-Indian Ivory Furniture', *The Burlington Magazine*, 141:1154 (1999), 278; British Library, European Inhabitants of Bengal, IOR/0/5/26.
10. Jaffer, 'Tipu Sultan, Warren Hastings and Queen Charlotte', 277.
11. Amin Jaffer and Karina Corrigan, *Furniture from British India and Ceylon: A Catalogue of the Collections in the Victoria and Albert Museum and the Peabody Essex Museum* (London, 2001), 172.
12. As cited in Mildred Archer, Christopher Rowell and Robert Skelton, *Treasures from India: The Clive Collection at Powis Castle* (London, 1987), 84.
13. The increased interest in the manufacturing of ivory products mirrors a more general and emerging interest on the part of consumers as to how consumer goods were made. See Kate Smith, *Material Goods, Moving Hands: Perceiving Production in England, 1700–1830* (Manchester, 2014).
14. Stacey Sloboda, 'Displaying Materials: Porcelain and Natural History in the Duchess of Portland's Museum', *Eighteenth-Century Studies*, 43:4 (2010), 464.
15. Maxine Berg, 'In Pursuit of Luxury: Global History and British Consumer Goods in the Eighteenth Century', *Past & Present*, 182:1 (2004), 85–142; Maxine Berg, 'From Imitation to Invention: Creating Commodities in Eighteenth-Century Britain', *Economic History Review*, 55:1 (2002), 1–30.
16. Paul Sangster, *Balls Park, Hertford* (Caxton Hill, 1972), 3.
17. See 'The Harrison & Townshend Anglo-Indian Furniture', *The Exceptional Sale*, Christie's, London, 7 July 2011, 60. With many thanks to Sharon Goodman for her original research on the Harrison and Townshend collection, which has greatly enhanced this study, particularly in uncovering the Rainham Hall 1732 inventory and the Lord Lynn 1737 inventory (see below).
18. See Anthony Farrington, *A Biographical Index of East India Company Maritime Service Officers, 1600–1834* (London, 1999), 355; Anthony Farrington, *Catalogue of East India Company Ships' Journals and Logs 1600–1834* (London, 1999), 359 and 515.
19. Sir Charles Lawson, *Memories of Madras* (London, 1905), 54.
20. George K. McGilvary, *East India Patronage and the British State: The Scottish Elite and Politics in the Eighteenth Century* (London and New York, 2008), 5.
21. British Library, 'Order and instructions to Captain Edward Harrison, Edward Herris and John Cooke, Supercargoes of the Kent, bound for Canton', 1 December 1703, IOR/E/3/95, 83–86.
22. Edward Harrison also used his connections to commission an armorial porcelain service from China. See David Sanctuary Howard, *Chinese Armorial Porcelain* (London, 1974), 43.
23. For discussion of use of inventories in historical research see Nancy Cox and Jeff Cox, 'Probate 1500–1800: A System in Transition', in Tom Arkell, Nesta Evans and Nigel Goose (eds), *When Death Do Us Part: Understanding and Interpreting the Probate Records of Early Modern England* (Oxford, 2000), 13–37; Margaret Spufford, 'The Limitations of the Probate Inventory', in John Chartres and David Hey (eds), *English Rural Society, 1500–1800: Essays in Honour of Joan Thirsk* (Cambridge, 1990), 139–74.
24. This is in contrast to ceramic goods, which are often difficult to identify with any clarity in inventories. See Francesca D'Antonio, 'The Willow Pattern: Dunham Massey', East India Company at Home (June, 2014), 3. http://blogs.ucl.ac.uk/eicah/files/2014/06/Willow-Pattern-PDF-Final-19.08.14.pdf.

25. Raynham Hall Archive, 'An Inventory and Appraism', 15 December 1732, RAS H1/4/3. With thanks to the Marquess Townshend's kindness in granting permission for information from the Raynham Hall Archive to be cited. The inventory is also mentioned in 'The Harrison & Townshend Anglo-Indian Furniture', 61.
26. Raynham Hall Archive 'An Inventory and Appraism', 15 December 1732, RAS H1/4/3.
27. Raynham Hall Archive 'An Inventory and Appraism', 15 December 1732, RAS H1/4/3. For images of bookcase see 'The Harrison & Townshend Anglo-Indian Furniture', 64–7.
28. British Library, Townshend Papers, 'An Inventory of the Right Honorable the Lord Lynn's Goods taken at His Lordships House in Littel Grosvenor Street this 11 day of July 1737', Ms. 41656, 209–10. The inventory is mentioned in 'The Harrison & Townshend Anglo-Indian Furniture', 62.
29. Linda Frey and Marsha Frey, 'Townshend, Charles, second Viscount Townshend (1674–1738)', *Oxford Dictionary of National Biography*, (Oxford, 2004). Accessed 6 Jan 2017. http://www.oxforddnb.com/view/article/27617; John Martin, 'Townshend, Etheldreda, Viscountess Townshend (c.1708–1788)', *Oxford Dictionary of National Biography* (Oxford, 2004). Accessed 6 Jan 2017. http://www.oxforddnb.com/view/article/68358.
30. Farrington, *A Biographical Index*, 793. He captained the *Augusta* on the following voyages: 1738/9, 1741/2 and 1744/5.
31. Raynham Hall Archive, Augusta Townshend to Charles Townshend, 24 December 1744, RAS B2/6.
32. Raynham Hall Archive, *A Journal of a Voyage from London to China on Board the Augusta Kept by Roger Townshend Anno Domini 1745*, RAS H4/3.
33. Raynham Hall Archive, Charles Townshend to a brother, 5 December 1747, RAS B2/6.
34. See 'The Harrison & Townshend Anglo-Indian Furniture', 60–77.
35. See Kate Smith, 'Imperial Objects? Country House Interiors in 18th-Century Britain', in Jon Stobart and Andrew Hann (eds), *The Country House: Material Culture and Consumption* (London, 2015), 111–18. See also 'The Harrison & Townshend Anglo-Indian Furniture', 66.
36. See 'The Harrison & Townshend Anglo-Indian Furniture', 60–77. This strong sense of provenance can be seen in the marketing materials produced for the piece during its sale in 2011. Items no longer made available by Christie's. See also catalogue details for Sir Thomas Rumbold's ivory desk, another Madras Governor: http://www.fitzmuseum.cam.ac.uk/collections/furniture/vizagapatamdesk.
37. Many thanks to Elizabeth Jamieson, MA (Freelance furniture historian) for allowing me to include the research she completed for Bonhams.
38. Jonathan Andrews, 'Monro, John (1715–1791)', *Oxford Dictionary of National Biography* (Oxford, 2004). Accessed 21 May 2014. http://www.oxforddnb.com/view/article/18976 .
39. Farrington, *A Biographical Index*, 552.
40. Farrington, *A Biographical Index*, 552.
41. Jaffer and Corrigan, *Furniture from British India and Ceylon*, 172.
42. Elizabeth Jamieson mentions this letter in the research she completed on the cabinet for Bonhams. London Metropolitan Archives, James Monro to Charles Monro, 22 November 1785, Acc/1063/034.
43. This close relationship appears to be the case as a selection of letters between the two brothers survives in the archives of the London Metropolitan Archives. The survival of these letters suggests they were valued, but as it is only them that survive it might also be misleading in terms of the wider network James Monro established and used while working as a captain for the East India Company. See multiple letters in London Metropolitan Archives, James Monro to Charles Monro, ACC/1063/014–043 (1775–1790). Many thanks to Elizabeth Jamieson for the reference to these letters.
44. London Metropolitan Archives, James Monro to Charles Monro, 31 January 1780, ACC/1063/015.
45. London Metropolitan Archives, Charles Monro to Mrs Caroline Monro, 14 January 1811, ACC/1063/121.
46. For more on the inheritance of household goods by women see Laurel Thatcher Ulrich, 'Hannah Barnard's Cupboard: Female Property and Identity in Eighteenth-century New England', in Ronald Hoffman, Mechal Sobel and Fredrika J. Teute, *Through a Glass Darkly: Reflections on Personal Identity in Early America* (Chapel Hill and London, 1997),

238–273; Laurel Thatcher Ulrich, *The Age of Homespun: Objects and Stories in the Creation of an American Myth* (New York, 2002).

47. P. J. Marshall, 'Hastings, Warren (1732–1818)', *Oxford Dictionary of National Biography*, (Oxford, 2004). Accessed 19 May 2014. http://www.oxforddnb.com/view/article/12587.
48. Nechtman, 'Nabobinas', 8–30.
49. Nechtman, *Nabobs*, 197.
50. Nechtman, *Nabobs*, 190.
51. Hastings landed at Plymouth on 13 June 1785.
52. *St James's Chronicle or the British Evening Post* (London), 29 September 1785.
53. *World* (London), 16 July 1792.
54. *Morning Post and Fashionable World* (London), 6 October 1795.
55. *Oxford Journal* (Oxford), 10 September 1853.
56. Cynthia Wall, 'The English Auction: Narratives of Dismantlings', *Eighteenth-Century Studies*, 31:1 (1997), 3.
57. Information regarding Grisewood taken from the *Dundee Courier*, 14 September 1853.
58. *Catalogue of the Valuable Contents of Daylesford House, Worcestershire, the Seat of the Late Right Hon. Warren Hastings* (London, 1853).
59. *Catalogue of the Valuable Contents of Daylesford House*.
60. Barbara Benedict, 'Encounters with the Object: Advertisements, Time, and Literary Discourse in the Early Eighteenth-Century Thing Poem', *Eighteenth-Century Studies*, 40:2 (2007), 196.
61. Peter Betjeman, 'Craft and the Limits of Skill: Handicraft Revivalism and the Problem of Technique', *Journal of Design History*, 21:2 (2008), 189.
62. Benedict, 'Encounters with the Object', 198.
63. Wall, 'The English Auction', 14.
64. Caroline Dakers, *A Genius for Money: Business, Art and the Morrisons* (New Haven and London, 2011), 170.
65. See Lots 769 and 769a in *Antique and Modern English and Continental Furniture, 1920 October 26 – November 3* (London, 1920).
66. Many thanks to Caroline Dakers for her help in ascertaining this.
67. Jan Sibthorpe, 'Sezincote, Gloucestershire', *East India Company at Home* (May 2014), 8. http://blogs.ucl.ac.uk/eicah/files/2013/06/Sezincote-PDF-Final-19.08.14.pdf; Ellen Filor and Jan Sibthorpe, 'Outside the Public: The Histories of Sezincote and Prestonfield in Private Hands', in Margot Finn and Kate Smith, (eds), *New Paths to Public Histories* (London, 2015), 103.
68. Sibthorpe, 'Sezincote', 28.
69. A connection further highlighted in material terms by Sezincote's current owners, the Peake family. Sibthorpe, 'Sezincote', 29; Filor and Sibthorpe, 'Outside the Public', 105–106.
70. In contrast to Bernard Porter's argument that the impact of empire was neither broad nor deep. See Bernard Porter, *The absent-minded Imperialists: Empire, Society, and Culture in Britain* (Oxford, 2004), xv.

Chapter 4

1. Horace Walpole to Lady Ossory, 21 June 1773, in W.S. Lewis (ed.), *Yale Edition of Horace Walpole's Correspondence*, vol. 32 (New Haven, 1937), 125.
2. Tillman Nechtman, *Nabobs: Empire and Identity in Eighteenth-Century Britain* (Cambridge, 2010), 227–230.
3. John Hardy and Maurice Tomlin, *Osterley Park House* (London, 1985).
4. It has been suggested that this painting was bought by Sir Francis Child in Amsterdam in 1697 and was housed in his house in Lincoln's Inn Fields before it was removed to Osterley House. See below.
5. Walpole to Lady Ossory 21 June, 1773. Lewis, (ed.), *Yale Edition*, vol. 32, 127. Lewis has suggested that Mr Banks refers to a person in Walpole's earlier writings (Tale V of the *Hieroglyphic Tales*) who 'was going all over the world in search of he did not know what.' See note 30. It is quite evident that Mr Banks is Joseph Banks (1743–1820), the renowned naturalist and botanist.
6. Maxine Berg, 'In Pursuit of Luxury: Global History and British Consumer Goods in the Eighteenth Century', *Past & Present*, 182, (2004), 85–142.

7. 'Mayors and Lord Mayors of London from 1189 to 1900,' in Sir Walter Besant, *London City*. London Adam & Charles Black, (1910) Appendices, 455–460.
8. Alice Carter, 'Analyses of Public Indebtedness in Eighteenth-Century England', *Bulletin of the Institute of Historical Research*, 24: 70 (1951), 176–181.
9. Numerous references in Court Minutes of the EIC, British Library, IOR/B51–3, B56–62.
10. The National Archives, HCA 26/8/107 & HCA 26/4/86.
11. British Library, Court Minutes of April 1699- April 1702, IOR /B 43, 5 July 1699.
12. David Hayton, E. Cruickshanks and S. Handley (eds), *The House of Commons, 1690–1715* (London, 2002).
13. British Library, Court Minutes, IOR/B53, 336.
14. British Library, Court Minutes (1714–1716), IOR/B53, 458.
15. British Library, Court Minutes (1722–34), IOR/B57–62.
16. Chapman, 'Sans Coronet', 7–8.
17. Philip Beresford and William D. Rubinstein *The Richest of the Rich: The Wealthiest 250 People in Britain since 1066* (Petersfield, 2007).
18. Philip Winterbottom, 'Child, Sir Francis, the Elder (1641/2–1713)', *Oxford Dictionary of National Biography*, Oxford University Press, 2004. Accessed 22 July 2013. http://www.oxforddnb.com/view/article/5286.
19. D. M. Joslin, 'London Private Bankers, 1720–1785', *Economic History Review*, New Series, 7:2 (1954), 167–186. Eventually, Child's involvement with the Old East India Company came into conflict with the interests of the Government, which created a rift between Child and the Whigs.
20. British Library, Court Minutes (1699–1702), IOR/B 43 (27 April 1699).
21. British Library, Court Minutes (1706–1708), IOR/B50a.
22. Edgar R. Samuel, 'Sir Francis Child's Jewellery Business', *The Three Banks Review* (March 1977), 43–54.
23. Lawrence H. Officer and Samuel H. Williamson, 'Purchasing Power of British Pounds from 1270 to Present', MeasuringWorth, 2017: https://www.measuringworth.com/ppoweruk/.
24. *The History of England: During the Reigns of King William and Queen Mary ... By Mr. Oldmixon* (London, 1735); Winterbottom, 'Child, Sir Francis, the Elder'.
25. For an overview of the trade networks in this period, see Tijl Vanneste, *Global Trade and Commercial Networks: Eighteenth-century Diamond Merchants* (London, 2011).
26. Samuel, 'Sir Francis Child's Jewellery Business', 43–54. Also see, Raphaelle Schwarzberg, 'Becoming a London Goldsmith in the Seventeenth Century: Social Capital and Mobility of Apprentices and Masters of the Guild', Working Papers No. 141/10, Department of Economic History, London School of Economics, June 2010. For a larger discussion of the role of precious metals in supporting EIC trade see, Bruce P. Lenman, 'The East India Company and the Trade in Non-metallic Precious Materials from Sir Thomas Roe to Diamond Pitt', in Huw Bowen, M. Lincoln, N. Rigby (eds), *The Worlds of the East India Company* (Woodbridge, 2002), 97–110.
27. Richard Grassby, *The English Gentleman in Trade: The Life and Work of Sir Dudley North 1641–1691* (Oxford, 1994), 68.
28. London Metropolitan Archives, ACC/1128, 177 and 178.
29. London Metropolitan Archives, ACC/1128/177, 14.
30. London Metropolitan Archives, ACC/1128/178.
31. London Metropolitan Archives, ACC/1128/177, 3 (2 June 1697).
32. Winterbottom, 'Child, Sir Francis, the elder (1641/2–1713)', *Oxford Dictionary of National Biography*, Oxford University Press, 2004; online edn, May 2006.
33. Abel Boyer, 'Child, Robert', http://www.historyofparliamentonline.org/volume/1690–1715/member/child-robert-1674–1721.
34. Cited by http://www.historyofparliamentonline.org/volume/1690–1715/member/child-robert-1674–1721.
35. The club's name related to the annual celebration of the festival of St Luke, the patron saint of painters and is understood to have originated from the weekly celebration hosted by the Flemish artist Anthony van Dyke. Martin Myrone, 'Society of the Virtuosi of St Luke (*act.* c.1689–1743)', *Oxford Dictionary of National Biography*, 2013. Also, Bignamini, 'George Vertue, Art Historian, and Art Institutions in London, 1689–1768', *Walpole Society*, 54 (1988), 20–27.

36. D. M. Joslin, 'London Private Bankers, 1720–1785', *Economic History Review*, New Series, 7:2 (1954), 167–186.
37. F.G. Hilton Price, *The Marygold by Temple Bar* (London, 1902), 31.
38. The National Archives, Will of Samuel Child, PBOB 11/797/390.
39. Carter, 'Analyses of Public Indebtedness', 180.
40. British Library, EIC Stock Ledgers A-G, IOR/L/AG.
41. Quoted in William Harrison Ukers, *All about Tea* (London 1935), 40.
42. 'Mr Walsh in a letter to Lord Clive of 14th of Feb 1765 after telling him of Mr Sulivan's having split a number of votes and of Mr Divon (Thomas Devon, a partner of Child's house) having split 30,000l.' Major General Sir John Malcolm, *The Life of Robert, Lord Clive: Collected from the Family Papers Communicated by the Earl of Powis*, vol. 2 (London, 1836), 212.
43. This information is summarized from British Library, IOR/L/MAR/400.
44. British Library, Journal Entry for 13–24 February 1769, IOR/L/MAR/B400A-E.
45. British Library, IOR/R/E/4 868, 465.
46. *The Asiatic Annual Register for 1799*, 1 (London, 1801), 89–90; BL, Osterley Ship's Log, IOR/L/MAR/B/400-O.
47. The National Trust displays the rooms at Osterley in line with the 1782 inventory.
48. Summarized from Marianne Webb, *Lacquer: Technology and Conservation: A Comprehensive Guide to the Technology and Conservation of Asian and European lacquer* (Boston, 2000).
49. 'By the *Princess of Wales* your Honours will have two large lacquered screens with the Company's arms upon them, being made purposely for the Court Room.' British Library, IOR/G/12/30, 10 Dec 1730. One such screen with the EIC coat of arms is known to exist in the collection of the Peabody Essex Museum. Further information on such screens can be found in W DeKesel, and Greet Dhont, *Coromandel Lacquer Screens* (Brussels, 2002).
50. D Stillman, 'Robert Adam and Piranesi', in D Fraser et al., (eds) *Studies in Architecture Presented to Rudolf Wittkower* (London, 1978), 65–80. See also John Wilton-Ely, 'Style and Serendipity: Adam, Walpole and Strawberry Hill', *The British Art Journal*, 11:3 (2011), 3–14.
51. Mark Taylor and Mark Garcia, 'Relentless Patterns: the Immersive Interior', *Architectural Design*, 79:6 (2009), 42–47.
52. Taylor and Garcia, 'Relentless Patterns', 44.
53. Emile de Bruijn, 'Lacquer Lost and Found, NT Treasure Hunt': https://nttreasurehunt.wordpress.com/category/osterley-park/page/2/.
54. For an overview of the China trade system see H B. Morse, 'The Chronicles of the East India Company Trading to China 1635–1834' in Patrick Tuck, *Britain and the China Trade 1635–1842,* vol. I (Reprint, London, 2000). Further discussions about the nature of interaction between EIC supercargoes and Chinese merchants can be gleaned from BL, IOR/R/10/7, 1769.
55. For an overview of armorial porcelain see David Sanctuary Howard, *Chinese Armorial Porcelain* (London, 1974).
56. Patricia Fergusson, personal correspondence, May–July 2013. We are grateful to Patricia Fergusson for her comments and notes, which greatly enriched this section.
57. Summarised from notes prepared by Patricia Fergusson.
58. For an overview of the cotton trade see Beverly Lemire, *Fashion's Favourite: The Cotton Trade and the Consumer in Britain 1660–1800* (London, 1991).
59. For the Calico Acts and their aftermath, see Jonathan P. Eacott, 'Making an Imperial Compromise: The Calico Acts, the Atlantic Colonies, and the Structure of the British Empire', *William & Mary Quarterly*, 69:4 (2012), 731–762.
60. Lemire, *Fashion's Favourite*, 90.
61. We are grateful to Rosemary Crill for this input and for her observations about the Indian embroideries at Osterley. See also Rosemary Crill, *Indian Embroidery* (London, 1999).
62. Ashin Das Gupta, *Indian Merchants and the Decline of Surat c.1700–1750* (Oxford, 2004), 23.
63. John Irwin, 'Origins of the "Oriental Style" in English Decorative Art', *Burlington Magazine*, 97: 625 (1955), 106–114. Also see, John Styles, 'Indian Cottons and European Fashion, 1400–1800', in Glen Adamson, G. Riello, and S. Teaseley (eds), *Global Design History* (London, 2011), 37–46.
64. British Library, Diaries of the Council of China (1732), IOR/G/12/33 (8 July 1732).
65. British Library, Court Minutes, IOR/B76 (1760–61).

66. British Library, Captain Payne to Governor Hodges, IOR/R/10/7, 1769/70, 66.
67. London Metropolitan Archives, Diary of Francis Child, ACC/1128/177, 6.
68. This information is summarized from C. H. de Jonge *Delft Ceramics*, trans. Marie-Christine Hellin (New York, 1970).

Section 2

1. See Frank Trentmann, 'Materiality in the Future of History: Things, Practices, and Politics', *Journal of British Studies*, 48:2 (April 2009), 283–307; Tony Bennett and Patrick Joyce (eds), *Material Powers: Cultural Studies, History and the Material Turn* (London, 2010); Jane Bennett, *Vibrant Matter: A Political Ecology of Things* (Durham, NC, 2010).
2. Maya Jasanoff, *Edge of Empire: Lives, Culture and Conquest in the East, 1750–1850* (New York, 2006); Maya Jasanoff, 'Collectors of Empire: Objects, Conquests and Imperial Self-Fashioning', *Past & Present*, 184 (2004), 109–136.

Chapter 5

1. See for example Elizabeth Kowaleski-Wallace, *Consuming Subjects: Women, Shopping, and Business in the Eighteenth Century* (New York, 1997); David Porter, *The Chinese Taste in Eighteenth-century England* (Cambridge, 2010).
2. For more on European demands for armorial porcelain see Rocío Díaz, *Chinese Armorial Porcelain for Spain* (London, 2010); Jochem Kroes, *Chinese Armorial Porcelain for the Dutch Market: Chinese Porcelain with Coats of Arms of Dutch Families* (The Hague, 2007).
3. David Sanctuary Howard, *Chinese Armorial Porcelain* (London, 1974), 69.
4. David Sanctuary Howard argues that no large armorial services were made before the turn of the eighteenth century. See Howard, *Chinese Armorial Porcelain*, 36.
5. Thanks to Meike Fellinger for alerting me to the importance of country trade in armorial porcelain service commissions.
6. Sarah Richards, *Eighteenth-century Ceramics: Products for a Civilized Society* (Manchester, 1999), 58.
7. Robert Finlay, *The Pilgrim Art: Cultures of Porcelain in World History* (Berkeley, 2010), 28.
8. Finlay, *Pilgrim Art*, 27.
9. David Sanctuary Howard, *Chinese Armorial Porcelain: Volume II* (Chippenham, 2003), 9.
10. Howard, *Chinese Armorial Porcelain*, 70; Howard, *Chinese Armorial Porcelain: Volume II*, 50.
11. Howard, *Chinese Armorial Porcelain*, 75.
12. Howard, *Chinese Armorial Porcelain*, 97.
13. Howard, *Chinese Armorial Porcelain*, 97.
14. Finlay, *Pilgrim Art*, 28; Howard, *Chinese Armorial Porcelain*, 67.
15. For more on the ways in which literary scholars have examined eighteenth-century representations of the relationship between women and porcelain see Kowaleski-Wallace, *Consuming Subjects,* 53; Porter, *Chinese Taste in Eighteenth-Century England,* 141.
16. See Section 1: Chapter 4 '"A jaghire without a crime": East India Company and the Indian Ocean Material World at Osterley 1700–1800'; Section 3: Chapter 11 'Valentines, the Raymonds and Company Material Culture'; Stephen McDowall, 'Shugborough: Seat of the Earl of Lichfield', *The East India Company at Home* (April 2013), 1–16. http://blogs.ucl.ac.uk/eicah/files/2013/02/Shugborough-PDF-Final-19.08.14.pdf
17. Sir John Sykes, 'Sykes, Sir Francis, 1st baronet (bap. 1730, d. 1804)', *Oxford Dictionary of National Biography*, Oxford, 2004. Accessed 8 May 2014. http://www.oxforddnb.com/view/article/64747.
18. Henry French and Mark Rothery, *Man's Estate: Landed Gentry Masculinities, c.1660-c.1900* (Oxford, 2012), 14.
19. French and Rothery, *Man's Estate*, 15.
20. French and Rothery, *Man's Estate*, 3, 37.
21. Kowaleski-Wallace, *Consuming Subjects*, 53. Also see Porter, *Chinese Taste in Eighteenth-century England*, 141.

22. Kowaleski-Wallace, *Consuming Subjects*, 53.
23. Porter, *Chinese Taste in Eighteenth-century England*, 139. Stacey Sloboda has made similar arguments for a wider range of Chinese-style or 'chinoiserie' goods. See Stacey Sloboda, *Chinoiserie: Commerce and Critical Ornament in Eighteenth-Century Britain* (Manchester, 2014), 108–159.
24. Kowaleski-Wallace, *Consuming Subjects*, 56.
25. Elizabeth Hope Chang, *Britain's Chinese Eye: Literature, Empire and Aesthetics in Nineteenth-Century Britain* (Stanford, CA, 2010), 75. See also Jon Stobart and Mark Rothery, *Consumption and the Country House* (Oxford, 2016), 155.
26. Amanda Vickery, *The Gentleman's Daughter: Women's Lives in Georgian England* (New Haven and London, 2003), 169.
27. Hence women of middling or low social status who desired porcelain wares were critiqued for spending precious family money in the pursuit of personal desire. See for example John Gay, 'To a Lady on Her Passion for Old China' (1725).
28. Porter, *Chinese Taste in Eighteenth-century England*, 136.
29. Porter, *Chinese Taste in Eighteenth-century England*, 143.
30. Porter, *Chinese Taste in Eighteenth-century England*, 149.
31. Notwithstanding Amanda Vickery, Karen Harvey and Margot Finn's research into male consumption and use of primarily English goods, little work has investigated specifically male consumption of Asian goods. More broadly, the historiography on consumption has tended towards female consumption, further perpetuating an existing bias and stereotype of women as consumers. See Karen Harvey, 'Barbarity in a Teacup? Punch, Domesticity and Gender in the Eighteenth Century', *Journal of Design History*, 21:3 (2008), 205–21; Karen Harvey, 'Ritual Encounters: Punch Parties and Masculinity in the Eighteenth Century', *Past and Present*, 214 (2012), 166–203; Amanda Vickery, 'His and Hers: Gender, Consumption and Household Accounting in Eighteenth-Century England', Past & Present, Supplement, ns, 1 (2006), 12-38; Margot Finn, 'Men's Things: Masculine Possession in the Consumer Revolution', *Social History*, 25:2 (2000), 133–55.
32. For an interview with Sir Francis Sykes's descendent Sir John Sykes regarding the service, see http://blogs.ucl.ac.uk/eicah/basildon-park-recordings/.
33. Gloucester Record Office, Gerard Gustavus Ducarel to his mother, 18 September 1767, D2091/F11. Many thanks to Sir John Sykes for this reference.
34. British Library, Francis Sykes to Harry Verelst, 21 June MSS Eur/F218/108, 7-8. Francis Sykes marked the letter as being sent from 'Baseldon'.
35. For more on Sykes's work in India see Section 5: Chapter 19 'The Indian Seal of Sir Francis Sykes: A Tale of Two Families'.
36. *Basildon Park, Berkshire* (Warrington, 2002), 19.
37. Claire Walsh, 'Shop Design and the Display of Goods', *Journal of Design History*, 8:2 (1995), 172.
38. James Schofield, *The Scarborough Guide* (2nd ed., Hull, 1796), 63.
39. Charles Bowden Topham, *A Tour through Ireland* (Dublin, 1791), 52. Thanks to Anna Moran for pointing me to this source.
40. Kate Smith, 'Sensing Design and Workmanship: The Haptic Skills of Shoppers in Eighteenth-Century London', *Journal of Design History*, 25:1 (March 2012), 2.
41. For an example of this see Kate Smith, *Material Goods, Moving Hands: Perceiving Production in England, 1700–1830* (Manchester, 2014), 59.
42. During this period there were never more than two ships each year that completed this trade. Many thanks to Meike Fellinger for her notes here.
43. British Library, Francis Sykes to Thomas Pattle, 15 September 1767, Mss Eur G37/47/1, 92.
44. Anthony Farrington, *A Catalogue of East India Company Ships' Journals and Logs 1660–1834* (London, 1999), 616; Anthony Farrington, *A Biographical Index of East India Company Maritime Service Officers, 1600–1834* (London, 1999), 608.
45. Howard, *Chinese Armorial Porcelain*, 43.
46. Amanda Vickery, *Behind Closed Doors: At Home in Georgian England* (New Haven & London, 2009), 277.
47. Finn, 'Men's Things', 142; Vickery, *Behind Closed Doors*, 278.
48. Iain Moncreiffe and Don Pottinger, *Simple Heraldry* (Edinburgh and London, 1978), 10.

49. As cited in John Sykes, 'The Indian Seal of Sir Francis Sykes', *East India Company at Home* (February 2013), 4. http://blogs.ucl.ac.uk/eicah/files/2013/02/THE-INDIAN-SEAL-Final-PDF-19.08.14.pdf.
50. See for example Laurel Thatcher Ulrich, 'Hannah Barnard's Cupboard: Female Property and Identity in Eighteenth-century New England', in Ronald Hoffman, Mechal Sobel and Fredrika J. Teute, *Through a Glass Darkly: Reflections on Personal Identity in Early America* (Chapel Hill and London, 1997), 263.
51. Laurel Thatcher Ulrich, *The Age of Homespun: Objects and Stories in the Creation of an American Myth* (New York, 2002), 141.
52. Although wares such as punch pots challenged this clear distinction. See Harvey, 'Barbarity in a Teacup?', 205–21.
53. Markman Ellis, Richard Coulton and Matthew Mauger, *Empire of Tea: The Asian Leaf that Conquered the World* (London, 2015), 85–86.
54. Kowaleski-Wallace, *Consuming Subjects*, 68.
55. Vickery, *Behind Closed Doors*, 271.
56. Vickery, *Behind Closed Doors*, 272.
57. Vickery, *Behind Closed Doors*, 274.
58. Vickery, *Gentleman's Daughter*, 208.
59. Mark Girouard, *Life in the English Country House: A Social and Architectural History* (New Haven and London, 1978), 203.
60. Girouard, *Life in the English Country House*, 205.
61. Girouard, *Life in the English Country House*, 233.
62. The dining room also emerged as a highly masculine space in middle-class homes during the nineteenth century, but shifted in nature at the turn of the twentieth. See Juliet Kinchin, 'Interiors: Nineteenth-Century Essays on the "Masculine" and the "Feminine" Room', in Pat Kirkham (ed.), *The Gendered Object* (Manchester and New York, 1996), 12.
63. Similarly, Karen Harvey's work on punch pots has shown how middling sort and genteel men adopted certain ceramic wares as part of a distinctly male homo-social culture within domestic spaces. See Harvey, 'Barbarity in a Teacup?', 216.
64. Stephen McDowall, 'The Shugborough Dinner Service and its Significance for Sino-British History', *Journal for Eighteenth-Century Studies*, 37:1 (2014), 1–17.
65. McDowall, 'Shugborough Dinner Service', 1.
66. McDowall, 'Shugborough Dinner Service', 13.
67. McDowall, 'Shugborough Dinner Service', 7.
68. McDowall, 'Shugborough Dinner Service', 13.

Chapter 6

1. Fanny Parkes, *Wanderings of a Pilgrim in Search of the Picturesque during four-and-twenty years in the East; with revelations of life in the Zenana*, 2 vols (London, 1850). The India Museum closed in 1879 and its collection was shared between The South Kensington Museum (later The Victoria and Albert Museum), Kew Gardens and The British Museum. This copy of the book, with its inscription 'Presented by C. Archer, Esq, February 17th 1876 to the India Museum' is now in the British Library collection, 1947b170.
2. J. Coutts Antrobus was married to Fanny Swetenham, daughter of Fanny Parkes' first cousin Edmund Swetenham who lived for many years at Cloud End in the Himalayan hill station Mussoorie, and who died at Dehra Dun in 1863.
3. *Blackwood's Lady's Magazine*, January 1852, 196.
4. Parkes, *Wanderings*, I, vii.
5. David Arnold, *The Tropics and the Travelling Gaze: India, Landscapes and Science, 1800–1856* (Seattle and London, 2006), 23.
6. Parkes, *Wanderings*, II, 496.
7. Maya Jasanoff, *Edge of Empire: Conquest and Collecting in the East 1750–1850* (London, 2005), 7.
8. See, for instance, her comment that: 'A friend has made me a present of the most magnificent cow-tails … They are great curiosities, and shall go with my collection to England.' Parkes, *Wanderings*, I, 238. See also Parkes, *Wanderings*, I, 227, 253.

9. Parkes, *Wanderings,*, II, 496.
10. See Section 1, Chapter 1 'The Attar casket of Tipu Sultan'.
11. See Esther Chawner's invaluable introduction and notes to the reprint of the complete text of *Wanderings of a Pilgrim*, vols. 1 and 2 (Karachi, 1975). See also *Blackwood's Lady's Magazine*, January 1852, 195–9.
12. Parkes, *Wanderings*, I, 59.
13. Parkes, *Wanderings,* I, 209–10.
14. And, she forbore to add, many servants. Parkes, *Wanderings*, II, 191–2.
15. As cited in Janet Dunbar, *Tigers, Durbars and Kings: Fanny Eden's Indian Journals 1837–1838* (London, 1988), 106.
16. 'Nothing is going forward, stupid as possible, shut up all day, languid and weary ... ...', Parkes, *Wanderings*, I, 303. In the absence of the journals themselves, the quotations cited here throughout are from the published version, and the interpretation of the text is based on this version. The extent to which the journals were edited by Fanny is therefore impossible to know. However, self-awareness appears to have been lacking in Fanny as her accounts frequently reflect unflatteringly on her and I suspect any editing was minimal.
17. Parkes, *Wanderings*, I, 238.
18. Parkes, *Wanderings*, I, 247.
19. Dunbar, *Tigers, Durbars and Kings*, 106. Some of the collaborators on the diorama funded by Fanny in 1851 are likely to have been men Fanny befriended while she was in India. Amongst them were Lieutenant Colonel Luard, Mr Louis Haghe, Mr William Prinsep and Mr Knell, all of whom are credited in the pamphlet accompanying the diorama. See Fanny Parkes, *Grand Moving Diorama of Hindostan, displaying the scenery of the Hoogly, the Bhagirathi, and the Ganges, from Fort William, Bengal, to Gangoutri, in the Himalaya* (London, 1851), 2.
20. Parkes, *Wanderings*, II, 57.
21. Parkes, *Wanderings*, II, 124.
22. Dunbar, *Tigers, Durbars and Kings*, 133. Fanny Parkes' account of this episode is rather different: 'I like playing at soldiers, and it gave me an excellent idea of an attack, without the horror of the reality ... The sun was high and very hot, – we rode home as fast as our horses could carry us ...'. See Parkes, *Wanderings*, II, 196.
23. 'There are moments when a feeling of desperation comes over me to think I must dream this dream so distinct from all my past life, for five years' Fanny Eden, as cited in Dunbar, *Tigers, Durbars and Kings*, 4.
24. Emily Eden, *Up the Country: Letters Written to her sister from the Upper Provinces of India by the Hon. Emily Eden* (London, 1866), 70. Also quoted in Arnold, *The Tropics and the Travelling Gaze*, 81.
25. Arnold, *The Tropics and the Travelling Gaze*, 80.
26. For map of 1840 India highlighting places Fanny and Charles lived and visited, see http://www.geographicus.com/P/AntiqueMap/India-black-1840.
27. Parkes, *Wanderings*, II, 330–331.
28. Parkes, *Wanderings*, II, 334.
29. 21 December 1875 at 7 Cornwall Terrace, Marylebone, London, in the presence of Clement R. Archer, first cousin. Death Certificate, General Register of Deaths, England.
30. Grave No 5975, The General Cemetery of All Souls, Kensal Green, London.
31. Parkes, *Wanderings*, II, 496. For seaside British communities of returned 'Indians' later in the century see Chapter 5 of Elizabeth Buettner, *Empire Families: Britons and Late Imperial India* (Oxford, 2004).
32. Parkes, *Wanderings*, II, 496.
33. Jasanoff, *Edge of Empire,* 5.
34. Maya Jasanoff, 'Collections of Empire: Objects, Conquests and Imperial Self-fashioning', *Past and Present*, 184 (2004), 112.
35. As cited in Parkes, *Grand Moving Diorama of Hindostan*, 72.
36. Parkes, *Grand Moving Diorama of Hindostan*, 72.
37. Parkes, *Grand Moving Diorama of Hindostan*, 72.
38. *Blackwood's Lady's Magazine*, January 1852, 195.
39. *Calcutta Review*, 15:30 (1851), 476–77.
40. See, for instance, Sara Suleri, *The Rhetoric of English India* (Chicago, 1992); K.N. Panikkar, 'History as a Site of Struggle', *The Hindu*, 15 August 2007.

41. Susan Stewart, *On Longing: Narratives of the Miniature, the Gigantic, the Souvenir, the Collection* (Durham and London, 1993), 135.
42. Parkes, *Grand Moving Diorama of Hindostan*. This handsome illustrated 64-page booklet was available to purchase, price one shilling, and contained short essays on each scene of the diorama.
43. Lara Kriegel, 'Narrating the Sub-Continent in 1851: India at the Crystal Palace' in Louise Purbrick (ed.), *The Great Exhibition of 1851: New Interdisciplinary Essays* (Manchester, 2001), 149–50.
44. Jasanoff, 'Collections of Empire', 122.
45. Helmut Gernsheim and Alison Gernsheim, *L.J.M. Daguerre: The History of the Diorama and the Daguerreotype* (London, 1956), 21. For an image of Daguerre's Diorama see the 'Dead Media Archive' website: http://cultureandcommunication.org/deadmedia/index.php/Daguerre%27s_Diorama.
46. The booklet accompanying the "Diorama of the Ganges" mounted at the Portland Gallery in 1850 credits a pianist: see Herr Adolph, *An Illustrated Description of the Diorama of the Ganges* (London, 1850).
47. Quoted in Gernsheim and Gernsheim, *L.J.M. Daguerre*, 17.
48. Gernsheim and Gernsheim, *L.J.M. Daguerre*, 41.
49. *London as it is to-day: Where to go and what to see* (London, 1851), 267.
50. *Blackwood's Lady's Magazine*, January 1852, 198–9.
51. *Blackwood's Lady's Magazine*, January 1852,198–9.
52. Parkes, *Grand Moving Diorama*, title page.
53. Quoted in Arthur MacGregor, *Curiosity and Enlightenment: Collectors and Collections from the Sixteenth to the Nineteenth Century* (London, 2007), 11.
54. Tony Bennett, *The Birth of the Museum: History, Theory, Politics* (London, 1995), 2.
55. MacGregor, *Curiosity and Enlightenment*, 17.
56. Arthur MacGregor, 'The Cabinet of Curiosities in Seventeenth-Century Britain' in Oliver Impey and Arthur MacGregor (eds), *The Origins of Museums: The Cabinet of Curiosities in Sixteenth- and Seventeenth-Century Europe* (London, 2001), 201–15.
57. Bennett, *The Birth of the Museum*, 73.
58. Gavin Lucas, 'Fieldwork and Collecting' in Dan Hicks and Mary C. Beaudry (eds), *The Oxford Handbook of Material Culture Studies* (Oxford, 2010), 231–2.
59. Stewart, *On Longing*, 135.
60. Parkes, *Wanderings*, I, 121.
61. Parkes, *Wanderings*, I, 132.
62. The Thugs operated in gangs, strangling their victims. See Parkes, *Wanderings*, I, 151.
63. Parkes, *Wanderings*, II, 487.
64. The 2013 Maha Kumbh Mela attracted 100 million pilgrims to Allahabad over a two-month period, 30 million of whom are reputed to have entered the holy water on one day, 10 February 2013.
65. Parkes, *Wanderings*, I, 227.
66. Parkes, *Wanderings*, I, 227.
67. Parkes, *Wanderings*, I, 253.
68. Parkes, *Wanderings*, I, 254.
69. Parkes, *Wanderings*, I, 261–262.
70. Parkes, *Wanderings*, I, 262.
71. Parkes, *Wanderings*, I, xi.
72. Parkes, *Wanderings*, I, 238.
73. Parkes, *Wanderings*, I , 265.
74. Parkes, *Wanderings*, I, 239–40.
75. Parkes, *Wanderings*, I, 234–5.
76. Stewart, *On Longing*, 136.
77. Parkes, *Wanderings*, I, 271.
78. Parkes, *Wanderings*, I, 26–8.
79. Victoria & Albert Museum, India Museum Donations and Loans 1870–1879 N.F. Part II, item 11993 (original number 366), MA/1/I108.
80. Parkes, *Wanderings*, II, 385.
81. Parkes, *Wanderings*, II, 385.
82. Parkes, *Wanderings*, II, 417–8.

83. Arnold, *Tropics and the Travelling Gaze*, 23
84. Jasanoff, *Edge of Empire*, 7; Stewart, *On Longing*, 135.

Chapter 7

1. For a comprehensive overview, see Theodore Koditschek, *Liberalism, Imperialism and the Historical Imagination: Nineteenth-century Visions of a Greater Britain* (Cambridge, 2011).
2. For the significance of these diverse networks 'at home' in England, see esp. Naomi Tadmor, *Family and Friends in Eighteenth-century England: Household, Kinship, and Patronage* (Cambridge, 2001). In the Company context, key works include Huw Bowen, *The Business of Empire: The East India Company and Imperial Britain, 1756–1833* (Cambridge, 2006), esp. chaps 4–5; Durba Ghosh, *Sex and the Family in Colonial India: The Making of Empire* (Cambridge, 2006); George McGilvary, *East India Patronage and the British State: The Scottish Elite and Politics in the Eighteenth Century* (London, 2008).
3. Maya Jasanoff details the process of imperial self-fashioning of individual Company men in *Edge of Empire: Conquest and Collecting in the East 1750–1850* (London, 2005). For material culture as an integral component of collective identities in this period, see for example Matthew Dziennik, 'Whig Tartan: Material Culture and Its Use in the Scottish Highlands, 1746–1815', *Past & Present*, 217 (2012), 117–147.
4. The prevalence of imperial culture in the metropole is highlighted in Catherine Hall and Sonya Rose (eds), *At Home with the Empire: Metropolitan Culture and the Imperial World* (Cambridge, 2006).
5. Mark Girouard, *Life in the English Country House: A Social and Architectural History* (New Haven and London, 1978), 2.
6. James M. Holzman, *The Nabobs in England: A Study of the Returned Anglo-Indians, 1760–1785* (New York, 1926), 70–80. Tillman W. Nechtman, *Nabobs: Empire and Identity in Eighteenth-Century Britain* (Cambridge, 2010), 165.
7. Richard Wilson and Alan Mackley, *The Building of the English Country House: Creating Paradise* (New York and London, 2000), 66.
8. Judith S. Lewis, 'When a House Is Not a Home: Elite English Women and the Eighteenth-Century Country House', *Journal of British Studies*, 48:2 (2009), 346.
9. The estate's twenty-first century function is detailed on the estate website: http://www.touchestate.co.uk/the-house/. For its architecture embellishment under successive Setons, see: http://www.scotlandsplaces.gov.uk/record/rcahms/46238/touch-house/rcahms?item=786393.
10. John Cornforth, 'Touch, Stirlingshire—I: The Home of Mrs. E.P. Buchanan and Mr. and Mrs. P.B. Buchanan', *Country Life* (19 August 1965), 442–443. Now held by National Museums Scotland, the gold ring with a gilt medallion head of Prince Charles Edward under a crystal can be viewed at https://www.artfund.org/supporting-museums/art-weve-helped-buy/artwork/1510/seton-ring-french.
11. Murray Pittock, *Material Culture and Sedition, 1688–1760: Treacherous Objects, Secret Places* (Houndmills, 2013); Ellen Filor, 'William Rattray of Downie Park', http://blogs.ucl.ac.uk/eicah/case-studies-2/william-rattray-of-downie-park/; Jennifer Novotny, 'Polite War: Material Culture of the Jacobite Era, 1688–1760', in Allan Macinnes, Kieran German and Lesley Graham (eds), *Living with Jacobitism, 1690–1788: The Three Kingdoms and beyond* (London, 2014), 153–172, 245–246.
12. For this broader context, see Andrew MacKillop, *'More fruitful than the soil': Army, Empire and the Scottish Highlands, 1715–1815* (East Linton, 2000).
13. For the family history, see Bruce Gordon Seton, *The House of Seton: A Study of Lost Causes*, vol. 2 (Edinburgh, 1941), 392–496. Hugh Smith's improvements are detailed in John Cornforth, 'Touch, Stirlingshire—II: The Home of Mrs. E.P. Buchanan and Mr. and Mrs. P.B. Buchanan', *Country Life* (26 August 1965), esp. 504–506. Images of the house and its Georgian facade can be accessed from the CANMORE website: https://canmore.org.uk/. See esp. SC 679682.
14. The *Gazetteer from Scotland* (http://www.scottish-places.info/features/featurefirst5253.html) details Touch's architectural history. For Clayton (an associate of Robert Adam), see Geoffrey Beard, *Decorative Plasterwork in Great Britain* (Abingdon, 2015), 85.
15. Cornforth, 'Touch, Stirlingshire, II', 506–507.

16. See the portrait of Hugh Seton as a bearded Arab featured on the Seton family history website: http://www2.thesetonfamily.com:8080/history/Profiles/Hugh_Seton_Baron_of_Touch_and_Tullibody.htm. The image itself is at the British Library: https://imagesonline.bl.uk/assets/thumbnails/133/3/dd7b7dff656720080f361bd9c1e4a272.jpg.
17. McGilvary, *East India Patronage*, esp. chap. 6.
18. *Gentleman's Magazine*, vol. 124 (August 1818), 184–185.
19. National Library of Scotland, Hugh Seton to Archibald Seton, 1 January-19 May 1791, MS 19207, 11, 13.
20. William Dalrymple, *White Mughals: Love and Betrayal in Eighteenth-century India* (London, 2002). Surviving images of Seton in India emphasise his frockcoat and top-hat, rather than depicting him in 'native' dress. See the pencil drawing of the Delhi durbar c.1806–1810 sold at Bonhams for £1,400: http://www.bonhams.com/auctions/16223/lot/413/ and the image of c.1810 at: https://twitter.com/dalrymplewill/status/729757187778744320.
21. National Library of Scotland, Archibald Seton to Hugh Seton, 28 October 1795, MS 19208, 31–31 verso.
22. National Library of Scotland, Archibald Seton to Alexander Anderson, 6 November 1795 and 9 December 1795, MS 19208, 35, 41–42.
23. National Library of Scotland, Archibald Seton to Henry Stewart, 20 September 1808, MS 19208, 97. He later estimated that James's failed business ventures had cost him at least £20,500, a swingeing sum. National Library of Scotland, Archibald Seton to Henry Stewart, 4 January 1811, MS 19208, 122 verso. Cornforth, 'Touch, Stirlingshire—III', 557, gives a sum of £28,000.
24. National Library of Scotland, Archibald Seton to Henry Stewart, 20 September 1808, MS 19208, 96.
25. National Library of Scotland, Archibald Seton to Henry Stewart, 18 December 1808, MS 19208, 100–100 verso.
26. National Library of Scotland, Archibald Seton, 'Sketch of Instructions to Mr. Hamilton', c.1809, MS 19208, 120–121 verso.
27. National Library of Scotland, Archibald Seton to Henry Stewart, 2 September 1812, MS 19208, 154.
28. National Library of Scotland, Archibald Seton to Henry Stewart, 4 January 1811, MS 19208, 123.
29. National Library of Scotland, Henry Stewart to Archibald Seton, 12 February 1814, MS 19208, 176.
30. National Library of Scotland, Henry Stewart to Archibald Seton, 7 April 1809, MS 19208, 108, 112.
31. National Library of Scotland, Archibald Seton to Henry Stewart, 19 October 1812, MS 19208, 139.
32. See for example National Library of Scotland, Archibald Seton to Henry Stewart, 20 March-23 May 1807, MS 19208, 96.
33. National Library of Scotland, Archibald Seton to Henry Stewart, 19 October 1812, National Library of Scotland, MS 19208, 133–139 verso.
34. For Fraser, see Katherine Prior, 'Fraser, William (1784–1835)', *Oxford Dictionary of National Biography* (Oxford, 2004). Accessed 9 October 2016. http://www.oxforddnb.com/view/article/10129.
35. National Library of Scotland, Henry Stewart to Archibald Seton, 26 September 1813, MS 19208, 158 verso-159.
36. National Library of Scotland, Archibald Seton to Henry Stewart, 14 February 1815, and Henry Stewart to Archibald Seton, 28 March 1817, MA 19208, 196 verso, 259–263 verso.
37. National Library of Scotland, Henry Stewart to Archibald Seton, 25 January 1816, MS 19208, 229.
38. National Library of Scotland, Archibald Seton to Henry Stewart, 22 November 1817, MS 19208, 288–288 verso.
39. Douglas M. Peers, 'Amherst, William Pitt, first Earl Amherst of Arracan (1773–1857)', *Oxford Dictionary of National Biography*, (Oxford, 2004); online edn, May 2009. Accessed 19 June 2013. http://www.oxforddnb.com/view/article/445.
40. Amherst's son Jeffrey died in 1826.
41. Kate Teltscher, 'The Sentimental Ambassador: The Letters of George Bogle from Bengal, Bhutan and Tibet, 1770–1781', in Rebecca Earle (ed.), *Epistolary Selves: Letters and Letter-writers,*

1600–1945 (Aldershot, 1999), 79–94; Elizabeth Vibert, 'Writing "Home": Sibling Intimacy and Mobility in a Scottish Colonial Memoir', in Tony Ballantyne and Antoinette Burton (eds), *Moving Subjects: Gender, Mobility and Intimacy in an Age of Global Empire* (Urbana and Chicago, 2009), 67–88; Margot Finn, 'Colonial Gifts: Family Politics and the Exchange of Goods in British India, c.1780–1820', *Modern Asian Studies*, 40:1 (February 2006), 203–232; Sarah M. S. Pearsall, *Atlantic Families: Lives and Letters in the Later Eighteenth Century* (Oxford, 2008), esp. 5; Kate Smith, 'Imperial Families: Women Writing Home in Georgian Britain', *Women's History Review*, 24:6 (2015), 843–860.

42. British Library, Prints and Drawings Collection, 'Drawings of Government House, Calcutta', August 1824, WD4131.
43. For letter reading as a shared practice see Rebecca Earle, 'Introduction: Letters, Writers and the Historian', in Earle (ed.), *Epistolary Selves*, 1–14.
44. Claydon House Trust, Journals of Sarah Amherst, 'Notes on the events of my own time', 10/1082/3.
45. Claydon House Trust, Journals of Sarah Amherst, 'Notes on the events of my own time', 10/1082/3.
46. British Library, Unknown to William Pitt Amherst, 24 November 1822, MSS Eur F140/55.
47. Jeffrey Amherst, *Wandering Abroad: The Autobiography of Jeffrey Amherst* (London, 1976), 19.
48. Claydon House Trust, Journals of Sarah Amherst, 'Notes on the events of my own time, beginning with the year 1820' (1820–1842), 10/1082/3.
49. Claydon House Trust, Journals of Sarah Amherst, 'Notes on the events of my own time, beginning with the year 1820' (1820–1842), 10/1082/3.
50. Girouard, *Life in the English Country House*, 220.
51. Claydon House Trust, Journals of Sarah Amherst, 'Notes on the events of my own time, beginning with the year 1820' (1820–1842), 10/1082/3.
52. Claydon House Trust, Journals of Sarah Amherst, 'Notes on the events of my own time, beginning with the year 1820' (1820–1842), 10/1082/3.
53. Claydon House Trust, Journals of Sarah Amherst, 'Notes on the events of my own time, beginning with the year 1820' (1820–1842), 10/1082/3.

Section 3

1. Stephanie Barczewski, *Country Houses and the British Empire, 1700–1930* (Manchester, 2014), 52.
2. Clive Williams, *The Nabobs of Berkshire* (Purley on Thames, 2010), 12.

Chapter 8

1. National Library of Wales, 'Memoir of Margaret Walsh', FE5. The National Library of Wales catalogue records that Sir John Benn Walsh wrote the memoir between 1852 and 1859.
2. National Library of Wales, 'Memoir of Margaret Walsh', FE5/3, 177.
3. National Library of Wales, 'Memoir of Margaret Walsh', FE5/3, 177–9.
4. See for example, for EIC families, Emma Rothschild, *The Inner Life of Empires* (Princeton, 2011). For a wider discussion of the importance of families to empire see Esme Cleall, Laura Ishiguro, Emily J. Manktelow, 'Imperial Relations: Histories of Family in the British Empire', *Journal of Colonialism and Colonial History*, 14:1 (2013), n.p. Accessed January 3, 2017. https://muse.jhu.edu/.
5. Kate Teltscher, 'The Sentimental Ambassador: The Letters of George Bogel from Bengal, Bhutan and Tibet, 1770–1781', in Rebecca Earle (ed.), *Epistolary Selves: Letters and Letter-writers, 1600–1945* (Aldershot, 1999), 79–94; Margot Finn, 'Colonial Gifts: Family Politics and the Exchange of Goods in British India, *c.*1780–1820', *Modern Asian Studies*, 40:1 (2006), 203–232; Sarah M. S. Pearsall, *Atlantic Families: Lives and Letters in the Later Eighteenth Century* (Oxford, 2008).

6. Kate Smith, 'Imperial Families: Women Writing Home in Georgian Britain', *Women's History Review*, 24:6 (2015), 843–60.
7. For example see the importance of their Berkeley Square house to the Clive family: Smith, 'Imperial Families', 852–55.
8. Stephanie Barczewski has identified 229 landed estates that were purchased by nabobs between 1700 and 1850. Within this, she finds that the period of substantial purchases was brief and principally fell between the 1750s and 1790s. See Stephanie Barczewski, *Country Houses and the British Empire, 1700–1930* (Manchester, 2014), 52.
9. E. I. Carlyle, 'Walsh, John (1726–1795)', rev. Anita McConnell, *Oxford Dictionary of National Biography* (Oxford, 2004). Accessed 16 Aug 2016. http://www.oxforddnb.com/view/article/28609.
10. British Library, John Walsh to Robert Clive, 12 January 1765, Mss Eur G37/33, 24.
11. British Library, John Walsh to Robert Clive, 12 January 1765, Mss Eur G37/33, 24.
12. As cited in Clive Williams, *The Nabobs of Berkshire* (Purley on Thames, 2010), 306.
13. James Hakewill, *The History of Windsor and its Neighbourhood* (London, 1813), 290.
14. British Library, 'Memoir of Margaret Walsh', vol. 3, Photo Eur 32, 117.
15. Walsh did buy several properties, which seemed to have been exclusively retained as investments rather than homes. For instance in 1769 he bought lands in County Cork from the Ogle family, who had them as part of the Anglesey estate. In 1771, Walsh purchased County Kerry lands and in 1774 he bought further lands from the Earl of Kerry.
16. Richard Wilson and Alan Mackley, *Creating Paradise: The Building of the English Country House, 1660–1880* (London and New York, 2000), 294.
17. This is corroborated in Hakewill, *History of Windsor*, 291.
18. National Library of Wales, 'Memoir of Margaret Walsh', FE5/3, 117.
19. For Stuart's country house commissions see Julius Bryant, '"The Purest Taste" – James "Athenian" Stuart's Work in Villas and Country Houses', in Susan Weber Soros (ed.), *James "Athenian" Stuart, 1713–1788: The Rediscovery of Antiquity* (New Haven and London, 2006), 265–315.
20. It seems likely that Joseph and Elizabeth Fowke's first child Arthur (b.1752) died at an early age. For more on their other son Francis Fowke, see T. H. Bowyer, 'Fowke, Joseph (1716–1800)', *Oxford Dictionary of National Biography* (Oxford, 2004). Accessed 12 Sept 2012. http://www.oxforddnb.com/view/article/63560.
21. British Library, 'Memoir of Margaret Walsh', vol. 1, Photo Eur 32, 41.
22. Ian Woodfield, 'The "Hindostannie Air": English Attempts to Understand Indian Music in the Late Eighteenth Century', *Journal of the Royal Musical Association*, 119:2 (1994), 190.
23. British Library, Margaret Fowke to John Walsh, 20 April 1781, MSS Eur D546/11, 37.
24. Transcript of letter from Margaret Fowke to John Walsh, 3 February 1786, included in Margaret Walsh's memoir. See 'Memoir of Margaret Walsh', vol. 1, Photo Eur 32, 92.
25. British Library, 'Memoir of Margaret Walsh', vol. 1, Photo Eur 32, 92.
26. National Library of Wales, 'Letters and Memorandum from 1811 to 1815 of Margaret Benn Walsh', 31 August 1811, FE 4/1, f. 49.
27. National Library of Wales, 'Letters and Memorandum from 1811 to 1815 of Margaret Benn Walsh', 31 August 1811, FE 4/1, f. 49.
28. National Library of Wales, 'Memoir of Margaret Walsh', FE5/2, 65.
29. Bowyer, 'Fowke, Joseph (1716–1800)'. John Benn Walsh, 1st Baron Ormathwaite refers to Francis Fowke's children and partner in deeply disparaging terms, suggesting the nature of the exclusion, see National Library of Wales, 'Memoir of Margaret Walsh', FE5/2, 83. For more details, see Deborah Cohen, *Family Secrets: Living with Shame from the Victorians to the Present Day* (London, 2013), 15–24.
30. http://www.historyofparliamentonline.org/volume/1790–1820/member/benn-walsh-john-1759–1825. Accessed 12 September 2012.
31. British Library, 'Memoir of Margaret Walsh', vol. 1, Photo Eur 32, 67. See also Bowyer, 'Fowke, Joseph (1716–1800)'.
32. http://www.historyofparliamentonline.org/volume/1790–1820/member/benn-walsh-john-1759–1825. Accessed 12 September 2012.
33. British Library, Margaret Fowke to John Walsh, 1787, Mss Eur D546/22, 61.

34. British Library, Margaret Benn to John Walsh, 2 July 1787, Mss Eur D546/22, 65. This letter also tells us that having the wedding at Francis Fowke's house meant that John Walsh did not attend.
35. The National Archives, John Walsh Will, PROB 11/1258. The only major asset John Benn and Margaret did not inherit from John Walsh was his estate in Pontefract, Yorkshire, which he had bought in order to enable him to nominate one MP for the borough. In his will Walsh stipulated that the Pontefract estate should be sold by his executors along with his London house in Chesterfield Street in order to pay off any outstanding debts. Also see Bowyer, 'Fowke, Joseph (1716–1800)'.
36. British Library, 'Memoir of Margaret Walsh', vol. 3, Photo Eur 32, 45.
37. British Library, 'Memoir of Margaret Walsh', vol. 3, Photo Eur 32, 47.
38. British Library, 'Memoir of Margaret Walsh', vol. 3, Photo Eur 32, 47.
39. Tillman W Nechtman, *Nabobs: Empire and Identity in Eighteenth-Century Britain* (Cambridge, 2010), 63.
40. National Library of Wales, 'Letters and Memorandum from 1811 to 1815 of Margaret Walsh', FE4/1, 9.
41. National Library of Wales, 'Letters and Memorandum from 1811 to 1815 of Margaret Walsh', FE4/1, 9.
42. British Library, 'Memoir of Margaret Walsh', vol. 3, Photo Eur 32, 21.
43. British Library, 'Memoir of Margaret Walsh', vol. 3, Photo Eur, 117.
44. British Library, 'Memoir of Margaret Walsh', vol. 3, Photo Eur, 127.
45. British Library, 'Memoir of Margaret Walsh', vol. 3, Photo Eur, 117.
46. National Library of Wales, 'Memoir of Margaret Walsh', FE5/3, 131.
47. National Library of Wales, 'Memoir of Margaret Walsh', FE5/3, 131.
48. National Library of Wales, 'Memoir of Margaret Walsh', FE5/3, 133.
49. National Library of Wales, 'Memoir of Margaret Walsh', FE5/3, 135.
50. National Library of Wales, 'Memoir of Margaret Walsh', FE5/3, 163.
51. National Library of Wales, 'Memoir of Margaret Walsh', FE5/3, 163.
52. National Library of Wales, 'Memoir of Margaret Walsh', FE5/2, 23.
53. National Library of Wales, 'Memoir of Margaret Walsh', FE5/5, 45.
54. National Library of Wales, 'Memoir of Margaret Walsh', FE5/5, 45, 71. In 1870 Cooper's Hill became the Royal Indian Engineering College and it now forms part of the Runnymede Campus of Brunel University.
55. National Library of Wales, 'Memoir of Margaret Walsh', FE5/5, 45, 73.
56. National Library of Wales, 'Memoir of Margaret Walsh', FE5/5, 45, 75.
57. National Library of Wales, 'Memoir of Margaret Walsh', FE5/5, 45, 75.
58. See National Library of Wales, 'Margaret Benn Walsh Diary', 2 April–29 December 1827, FE4/17.
59. National Library of Wales, 'Memoir of Margaret Walsh', FE5/5, 77.
60. National Library of Wales, 'Margaret Benn Walsh Diary', Friday 11 October 1827, FE4/17, 69.
61. National Library of Wales, 'Margaret Benn Walsh Diary', Friday 11 October 1827, FE4/17, 69.
62. National Library of Wales, 'Margaret Benn Walsh Diary', Friday 11 October 1827, FE4/17, 69.
63. National Library of Wales, 'Margaret Benn Walsh Diary', Saturday 12 October 1827, FE4/17, f. 69.
64. For the trials of dependence that unmarried women and wives experienced see Amanda Vickery, *Behind Closed Doors: At Home in Georgian England* (New Haven and London, 2009), 184–206.
65. National Library of Wales, 'Memoir of Margaret Walsh', FE5/5, 29.
66. National Library of Wales, 'Memoir of Margaret Walsh', FE5/5, 127.
67. Viccy Coltman, *Fabricating the Antique: Neoclassicism in Britain, 1760–1800* (Chicago and London, 2006), 17.
68. National Library of Wales, 'Memoir of Margaret Walsh', FE5/5, 129.
69. National Library of Wales, 'Memoir of Margaret Walsh', FE5/5, 131.
70. Amanda Vickery, *The Gentleman's Daughter: Women's Lives in Georgian England* (New Haven and London, 1999), 127–160.
71. National Library of Wales, 'Memoir of Margaret Walsh', FE5/5, 133.
72. National Library of Wales, 'Memoir of Margaret Walsh', FE5/4, 35.
73. National Library of Wales, 'Memoir of Margaret Walsh', FE5/3, 163.

74. National Library of Wales, 'Diary of Sir John Benn Walsh, 1st Lord Ormathwaite', May-November 1836, FG1/9, 162.
75. National Library of Wales, 'Memoir of Margaret Walsh', FE5/4, 115.
76. Rosemary Marangoly George, *The Politics of Home: Postcolonial Relocations and Twentieth-century Fiction* (Cambridge, 1996), 9.

Chapter 9

1. W. Fletcher and Edmund J. Niemann, *A Tour round Reading, a Guide to Its Environs* (Reading and London, 1840), 88–9.
2. Fletcher and Niemann, *A Tour round Reading*, 88–9.
3. Geoffrey Tyack, Simon Bradley and Nikolaus Pevsner, *The Buildings of England: Berkshire* (London and New Haven, 2010), 293.
4. As Madge Dresser and Andrew Hann remind us, although the classical and romantic aesthetics of many country houses are regarded as worlds away from slavery interests, they were in fact related and need to be understood as such. They suggest that in order to read these histories back into country houses it is necessary to read against the grain. See Madge Dresser and Andrew Hann, 'Introduction', in Madge Dresser and Andrew Hann (eds), *Slavery and the British Country House* (Swindon, 2013), 14. For more on Bolsover Castle, Brodsworth Hall, Marble Hill, Northington Grange, Kenwood House and Osborne House see Dresser and Hann (eds), *Slavery and the British Country House*.
5. For the movement of objects into and through Englefield House see Kate Smith, 'Imperial Objects? Country House Interiors in 18th-Century Britain', in Jon Stobart and Andrew Hann (eds), *The Country House: Material Culture and Consumption* (London, 2015), 111–18.
6. Zoë Laidlaw, *Colonial Connections, 1815–45: Patronage, the Information Revolution and Colonial Government* (Manchester, 2005).
7. The Tyssen family papers are in Hackney Archives, see Hackney Archives Department, D/F/AMH. Francis Tyssen (d.1690) had a son, another Francis Tyssen (d.1699) who possibly acted as East India Company Deputy Governor 1693–95. See British Library, IOR/B/40. He bought several manors in Hackney between 1697 and 1699 and before dying in 1699, had a son, another Francis Tyssen (d.1710). This Francis Tyssen also had a son, another Francis Tyssen (d.1712) and it was he who married Rachel Beauvoir in 1712. Francis and Rachel had a son Francis John Tyssen (d. 1717), who inherited, and a daughter Mary Tyssen, who married Powlett Wrighte and then Richard Benyon.
8. The National Archives, PROB 11/708, 106 and 114.
9. Clive Williams, *The Nabobs of Berkshire* (Purley on Thames, 2010), 174.
10. See Constance Russell, *Swallowfield and Its Owners* (London and New York, 1901), 206. http://www.archive.org/stream/swallowfielditso00russ#page/206/mode/2up/search/benyon. Many thanks to John C. (who contacted the East India at Home project via the website) for his notes, which suggest that Lady Russell's claim is supported by Bernard Burke's A *Genealogical and Heraldic Dictionary of the Landed Gentry of Great Britain and Ireland* (London, 1855) and the findings of the De Beauvoir Association. These texts note that Daniel Benyon (1664–c.1709) was Richard Benyon's father.
11. Williams, *Nabobs of Berkshire*, 174.
12. Williams, *Nabobs of Berkshire*, 174.
13. British Library, IOR/N/2/1 f.15, N/2/1, 12.
14. Russell, *Swallowfield and its Owners*, 208.
15. British Library, IOR/N/2/1, 66.
16. British Library, IOR/N/2/1, 66.
17. Lady Russell incorrectly assumed that Fleetwood was the Governor of Fort St George shortly before his death in 1715. See Russell, *Swallowfield and its Owners*, 208. Henry Davison Love notes Edward Fleetwood as supercargo in this period. See Henry Davison Love, *The Vestiges of Old Madras, 1640–1800 Vol. II* (New Delhi, 1913), 55.
18. Williams, *Nabobs of Berkshire*, 175.
19. The catalogue also notes that the painting was lent by Sir C. Russell and describes it as 'A Family Group by HOGARTH (Lady Shelley, Mr and Mrs Richard Shelley, Capt The Hon.

W. Fitzwilliam, Mr Benyon, and Miss Beard)'. Many thanks to Elizabeth Einberg of The Paul Mellon Centre for Studies in British Art for the reference.

20. Williams, *Nabobs of Berkshire*, 173. The original Coptfold Hall was demolished in the 1850s and replaced by a new house, which was demolished in the 1960s, although the stables and chapel remained intact. A new house was built on the site between 2002 and 2005.
21. British Library, IOR/N/2/1, 161.
22. British Library, IOR/N/2/1, 185 and 188.
23. British Library, IOR/N/2/1, 195.
24. For the affective value Richard and Mary Benyon placed on objects see Smith, 'Imperial Objects? Country House Interiors in 18th-Century Britain', 111–18.
25. Thanks to Georgina Green for these references. W. R. Powell (ed.), *Victoria County History of Essex*, vol. V (Oxford, 1966), 208; W. R. Powell (ed.), *Victoria County History of Essex*, vol. VII (Oxford, 1978), 112.
26. Powell, *Victoria County History of Essex*, vol. VII, 112.
27. Gervase Jackson-Stops, 'Englefield House, Berkshire II', *Country Life*, 5 March 1981, 560–61.
28. Jackson-Stops, 'Englefield House, Berkshire II', 561.
29. Jackson-Stops, 'Englefield House, Berkshire II', 562.
30. John Habakkuk, *Marriage, Debt, and the Estates System: English Landownership 1650–1950* (Oxford, 1994), 285–289.
31. For the significance of debt and credit in modern England see Margot Finn, *The Character of Credit: Personal Debt in English Culture, 1740–1914* (Cambridge, 2003).
32. The National Archives, Probate Records, Powlett Wrighte of Englefield (1741), PROB 11/708, 106 and 114.
33. Berkshire Record Office, Benyon Papers, Nathaniel Wrighte to Richard Benyon, 27 September 1779, D/EBy/C1.
34. Berkshire Record Office, Nathaniel Wrighte to Richard Benyon, 27 September 1779, D/EBy/C1.
35. Berkshire Record Office, Nathaniel Wrighte to Richard Benyon, 27 September 1779, D/EBy/C1.
36. Berkshire Record Office, Benyon Papers, Richard Benyon to Nathaniel Wrighte, 29 June 1781, D/EBy/C3.
37. Berkshire Record Office, Benyon Papers, Nathaniel Wrighte to Richard Benyon, 3 July 1781, D/EBy/C3. For Englefield in debt see Jackson-Stops, 'Englefield House, Berkshire – II', 562.
38. Berkshire Record Office, Benyon Papers, Nathaniel Wrighte to Richard Benyon, 21 July 1781, D/EBy/C3.
39. Berkshire Record Office, Nathaniel Wrighte to Richard Benyon, 21 July 1781, D/EBy/C3.
40. This is not Charles D'Oyly (1781–1845) or his father Baron Sir John Hedley D'Oyly as he did not return to England from India with his family until 1785. Nevertheless, there were many D'Oylys in the EIC, thus perhaps suggesting a connection.
41. Berkshire Record Office, Benyon Papers, Mr Southouse to Richard Benyon, 9 August 1781, D/EBy/C3.
42. Berkshire Record Office, Benyon Papers, Nathaniel Wrighte to Richard Benyon, 19 December 1781, D/EBy/C3.
43. Berkshire Record Office, Nathaniel Wrighte to Richard Benyon, 19 December 1781, D/EBy/C3.
44. See Tillman W. Nechtman, 'Nabobinas: Luxury, Gender, and the Sexual Politics of British Imperialism in India in the Late Eighteenth Century, *Journal of Women's History*, 18:4 (2006), 8–30.
45. British Library, Margaret Fowke to John Walsh, 1787, Mss Eur D.546/22, 61.
46. Berkshire Record Office, Benyon Papers, R. Crockford to Mr Benyon, 9 April 1788, D/EBy/C5.
47. Lawrence Stone and Jeanne C. Fawtier Stone. *An Open Elite? England 1540–1880* (Oxford and New York, 1986), 283.
48. His father-in-law Sir Francis Sykes, who had connections to Pontefract both through his upbringing in Yorkshire and his marriage to Elizabeth Monckton, daughter of Viscount Galway, may have helped Benyon into this position.
49. Powell, *Victoria County History of Essex* vol. VII, 67–9.
50. Jackson-Stops, 'Englefield House, Berkshire II', 565. Jackson-Stops notes that two of Sir John Soanes' drawings remain in the family papers.
51. Jackson-Stops, 'Englefield House, Berkshire II', 565.
52. Williams, *The Nabobs of Berkshire*, 173; Jackson-Stops, 'Englefield House, Berkshire II', 565.
53. Jackson-Stops, 'Englefield House, Berkshire II', 565.
54. Jackson-Stops, 'Englefield House, Berkshire II', 565.

55. Jackson-Stops, 'Englefield House, Berkshire II', 565.
56. Powell, *Victoria County History of Essex* vol. VII, 112 and 119.

Chapter 10

1. Lady Constance Russell, *Swallowfield and Its Owners* (London, 1901), esp. chaps 6–12, 34. An electronic facsimile of the text is available at: http://www.archive.org/stream/swallowfield-itsoo0russ#page/n9/mode/2up.
2. http://sunleyheritage.co.uk/swallowfield-park-bucolic-refinement-royal-berkshire/.
3. http://sunleyheritage.co.uk/swallowfield-park-estate-living/.
4. Russell, *Swallowfield and Its Owners*, chaps. 21–4.
5. Russell, *Swallowfield and Its Owners* , 249–251, citation 251. The wider connections of British country houses to Caribbean slavery are explored in Madge Dresser and Andrew Hann (eds), *Slavery and the British Country House* (Swindon, 2013). A free download of this volume is available at: https://content.historicengland.org.uk/images-books/publications/slavery-and-british-country-house/slavery-british-country-house-web.pdf/. The histories of slavery marked (or obscured) by civic monuments and built environments in urban contexts are explored for example by Peter Ashan, *Remembering Slavery and Its Legacy, 1807–2007: The Roots of Diversity in Waltham Forest* (London, 2007) and Madge Dresser, *Slavery Obscured: The Social History of the Slave Trade in an English Provincial Port* (London, 2001).
6. http://www.ucl.ac.uk/lbs/search/: Timothy Hare Altabon Earle.
7. Catherine Hall, Nicholas Draper, Keith McClelland, Katie Donington and Rachel Lang. *Legacies of British Slave-ownership: Colonial Slavery and the Formation of Victorian Britain* (Cambridge, 2014), esp. chap. 5.
8. For the family's role in India, see Stephen Wheeler, 'Russell, Sir Henry, first baronet (1751–1836)', rev. Ainslie T. Embree, *Oxford Dictionary of National Biography*, Oxford University Press, 2004. Accessed 30 Sept 2015. http://www.oxforddnb.com/view/article/24311. Francis Whitworth Russell senior's career is documented in British Library, Asian & African Studies, IOR/J/1/21,155. His son's military service is documented in the British Library, Asian & African Studies, IOR/L/MIL/9/222, 685–689 and IOR/N/1/80, 90. Lady Russell's family connections with Berkshire and the EIC are discussed by Kate Smith in her study of Englefield House in this volume.
9. The broader impact of empire on the country house is surveyed by Stephanie Barczewski, *Country Houses and the British Empire, 1700–1930* (Manchester, 2014).
10. For the role played by elite male consumers in fashioning 'English' interiors of the Georgian period, see Amanda Vickery, *Behind Closed Doors: At Home in Georgian England* (London, 2009).
11. Dresser and Hann (eds), *Slavery and the British Country House.*
12. I borrow here Said's concept of imperial sublimation, developed in his analysis of Jane Austen's *Mansfield Park* (1814). Edward Said, *Culture and Imperialism* (London, 1993), esp. 69–70.
13. See Jennifer Speake, 'Backhouse, William (1593–1662)', *Oxford Dictionary of National Biography*, Oxford University Press, 2004. Accessed 21 Oct 2016. http://www.oxforddnb.com/view/article/985; and W. A. Speck, 'Hyde, Henry, second earl of Clarendon (1638–1709)', *Oxford Dictionary of National Biography*, Oxford University Press, 2004. Accessed 21 Oct 2016. http://www.oxforddnb.com/view/article/14329.
14. Peter Smith, 'Talman, William (*bap*. 1650, *d*. 1719)', *Oxford Dictionary of National Biography*, Oxford University Press, 2004. Accessed 21 October 2016. http://www.oxforddnb.com/view/article/26956.
15. Edward Hyde, third earl Clarendon (1661–1723) sold the house to Pitt in 1719, having earlier suffered imprisonment for debt at the hands of his creditors. For this sale, see Russell, *Swallowfield and Its Owners*, 191–2. For the endemic culture of debt and credit in Georgian and Victorian England, which often underpinned the sale and purchase of country houses, see Margot Finn, *The Character of Credit: Personal Debt in English Culture, 1740–1914* (Cambridge, 2003).

16. For a synopsis of Pitt's career, see Perry Gauci, 'Pitt, Thomas (1653–1726)', *Oxford Dictionary of National Biography*, Oxford University Press, 2004. Accessed 21 October 2016. http://www.oxforddnb.com/view/article/22333.
17. The centrality of diamonds in the Company's trade in this period is explored by Bruce Lenman, 'The East India Company and the Trade in Non-Metallic Precious Materials from Sir Thomas Roe to Diamond Pitt', in Huw V. Bowen, Margarette Lincoln and Nigel Rigby (eds), *The Worlds of the East India Company* (Woodbridge, 2002), 97–109; Edgar Roy Samuel, 'Diamonds and Pieces of Eight: How Stuart England Won the Rough-Diamond Trade', *Jewish Historical Studies*, 38 (2003), 23–40; and Edgar Roy Samuel, 'Gems from the Orient: The Activities of Sir John Chardin (1643–1713) as a Diamond Importer and East India Merchant', *Proceedings of the Huguenot Society of Great Britain and Ireland*, 27: 3 (2000), 351–68.
18. For Pitt, his Indian ventures and his family, see also C.A.N. Dalton, *The Life of Thomas Pitt* (Cambridge, 1915) and Tresham Lever, *The House of Pitt: A Family Chronicle* (London, 1947). For the Pitt Diamond, see Harold Newman, *An Illustrated Dictionary of Jewellery* (London, 1981).
19. Russell, *Swallowfield and Its Owners*, chaps 21–24, esp. 215.
20. Berkshire Record Office, *New Landscapes: Enclosure in Berkshire*: http://www.berkshireenclosure.org.uk/find_via_parish_details.asp?parish=Swallowfield. For the broader context of these changes, see J.M. Neeson, *Commoners: Common Right, Enclosure and Social Change in England, 1700–1820* (Cambridge, 1993).
21. Russell, *Swallowfield*, 226–251; *Gentleman's Magazine*, 127 (1820), 169. For Earle's biography and compensation, see his entry in https://www.ucl.ac.uk/lbs/search/.
22. For this development, see esp. P.J. Marshall, *The Making and Unmaking of Empires: Britain, India, and America c.1750–1783* (Oxford, 2005).
23. The family genealogy is traced in *Swallowfield and Its Owners*, esp. chaps 28–29.
24. For a popular account of this phenomenon, see Ann De Courcy, *The Fishing Fleet: Husband-Hunting in the Raj* (London, 2012).
25. Sir Henry's home was a site of considerable sociability for Calcutta's Anglo-Indian governing classes, as recalled in the memoir of his contemporary, William Hickey. See Alfred Spencer (ed.), *Memoirs of William Hickey*, 4 vols (London: Hurst & Blackett, 1925), esp. 4: 194–6, 211, 220–22.
26. For Lake, see Anthony S. Bennell, 'Lake, Gerard, First Viscount Lake of Delhi (1744–1808)', *Oxford Dictionary of National Biography*, Oxford University Press, 2004. Accessed 22 October 2016. http://www.oxforddnb.com/view/article/15900.
27. For an introduction to the family, see Stephen Wheeler, 'Russell, Sir Henry, first baronet (1751–1836)', rev. Ainslie T. Embree, *Oxford Dictionary of National Biography*, Oxford University Press, 2004. Accessed 22 October 2016. http://www.oxforddnb.com/view/article/24311.
28. 'Nabob' was an Anglicisation of the Persian term 'nawab', or official of the Mughal empire (the Indian empire displaced in this period by the EIC). The word emerged as a term of abuse in England in the 1760s. Key studies of the nabobs include Thomas George Percival Spear, *The Nabobs: A Study of the Social Life of the English in Eighteenth Century India* (London, 1932), Tillman Nechtman, *Nabobs: Empire and Identity in Eighteenth-Century Britain* (Cambridge, 2010), and Christina Smylitopoulos, 'Rewritten and Reused: Imaging the Nabob through "Upstart Iconography"', *Eighteenth-Century Life*, 32:2 (2008), 39–59.
29. Henry's complex love life prior to his second marriage is discussed in William Dalrymple, *White Mughals: Love and Betrayal in Eighteenth-century India* (London, 2002), chap. 9.
30. See for example Amin Jaffer, *Furniture from British India and Ceylon: A Catalogue from the Collections in the Victoria and Albert Museum and the Peabody Essex Museum* (London, 2001).
31. For a contemporary account of Calcutta consumer culture in this period, see Captain Thomas Williamson, *The East India Vade-Mecum; Or, Complete Guide to Gentlemen Intended for the Civil, Military, or Naval Service of the Hon. East India Company*, 2 vols (London, 1810), esp. vol. 2: 165–172. The role of material goods in knitting together the East India Company's far-flung imperial families (including the Russells) is discussed in Margot Finn, 'Colonial Gifts: Family Politics and the Exchange of Goods in British India, c.1780–1820', *Modern Asian Studies*, 40:1 (2006), 203–31.
32. Finn, 'Colonial Gifts', 223.
33. Bodleian Library, Oxford, Sir Henry Russell to Charles Russell, MS. Eng. lett. c. 152, 13–14.

34. For the English experience of marital home-making at this time, see Vickery, *Behind Closed Doors*, esp. chap. 3.
35. Henry Dodwell, *The Nabobs of Madras* (London, 1926), chaps. 11–13; Jaffer, *Furniture from British India and Ceylon*. For marriage and family formation in colonial India at this time, see Margot Finn, 'Family Formation: Anglo-India and the Familial Proto-State', in Jon Lawrence and David Feldman (eds), *Structures and Transformations in Modern British History* (Cambridge, 2011), 100–17.
36. Bodleian Library, Oxford, Henry Russell to Charles Russell, 9 March 1808, MS. Eng. lett. c. 155, 128, and Bodleian, Henry Russell to Charles Russell, MS. Eng. lett. c. 156, 3 verso-4.
37. Finn, 'Colonial Gifts', 213.
38. Emma Rothschild, *The Inner Life of Empires: An Eighteenth Century History* (Princeton, 2011), reminds us of the significance of family in empire at this time.
39. See Zubaida Yazdani, *Hyderabad during the Residency of Henry Russell, 1811–1820: A Case Study in the Subsidiary Alliance System* (Oxford, 1976); Omar Khalidi, *The British Residency in Hyderabad: An Outpost of the Raj, 1779–1948* (London, 2005).
40. Dalrymple, *White Mughals*, xxxii, 327, 118. For the social and gender dynamics of the bungalow in Anglo-India, see E.M. Collingham, *Imperial Bodies: The Physical Experience of the Raj, c.1800–1947* (Cambridge, 2001), 99–102.
41. Dalrymple, *White Mughals*, 125, 369–373. Kirkpatrick was not alone in grandiose construction of dual public-private residences in India at this time: Wellesley's rebuilding of Government House, Calcutta in 1803 used Keddleston Hall, Derbyshire as its model. Dalrymple, *White Mughals*, 346.
42. Dalrymple, *White Mughals*, 417–18.
43. See for example Bodleian Library, Oxford, Henry Russell to Charles Russell, 26 January 1808, MS Eng. lett. c. 155, 219–220 verso.
44. Dalrymple, *White Mughals*, 417, 420–21, 426–62.
45. Bodleian Library, Oxford, Henry Russell to Charles Russell, 27 May 1810, MS. Eng. lett. d. 151, 87 verso-88; Henry to Charles, 31 May 1810, MS Eng. lett. d. 151, 95; Henry to Charles, 29 August 1810, MS. Eng. lett. d. 151, 228 verso-229 verso; Henry to J.H. Casamaijor, 26 June 1812, MS. Eng. lett. d. 163, 119–119 verso; Henry to J.H. Casamaijor, 18 July 1812, MS. Eng. lett. d. 163, 126 verso.
46. The peak period of acquisition of Chinese armorial porcelain for wealthy English homes was 1715–1805. See David Sanctuary Howard, *Chinese Armorial Porcelain* (London, 1974), 67–8.
47. For Jones, see Michael Franklin, *Orientalist Jones: Sir William Jones, Poet, Lawyer, and Linguist, 1746–1794* (Oxford, 2011). Bodleian, Henry Russell to Charles Russell, 26 September 1814, MS. Eng. let. c. 157, 92 verso-93; Henry to Charles, 1812, MS. Eng. lett. d. 152, 252–252 verso; Sir Henry Russell to Lady Russell, 11 February 1813, MS. Eng. lett. c. 153, 28–29. For the deployment of classical statuary in the gentleman's library in Britain, see Viccy Coltman, *Classical Sculpture and the Culture of Collecting in Britain since 1760* (Oxford, 2009), chap. 6.
48. See esp. Kate Retford, *The Art of Domestic Life: Family Portraiture in Eighteenth Century England* (London, 2006).
49. For traditions of Anglo-Indian portraiture in this period, see Mildred Archer, *India and British Portraiture, 1770–1825* (London, 1979). For Henry's commission to Chinnery and his request for portraits of the Russell and Casamaijor women in England, see Bodleian, Henry Russell to J.H. Casamaijor, 13 February 1813, MS. Eng. lett. d. 163, 89 verso-90, Henry to Casamaijor, MS. Eng. lett. d. 164, 164–165, and Henry to Sir Henry, November 1813, MS. Eng. lett. d. 164, fols 90–91. See also Finn, 'Colonial Gifts', 214–217.
50. See for example Robert Grindlay, *Scenery, Costumes and Architecture, Chiefly of the Western Side of India* (London, 1830), vol. 2, plate 19.
51. Bodleian Library, Oxford, Sir Henry Russell to Lady Russell, 11 February 1813, MS. Eng. lett. c. 153, fols 25–26, citation 26,
52. Richard Wilson and Alan Mackley accord little attention to women in *The Building of the English Country House: Creating Paradise* (London, 2000). Gentlewomen figure much more prominently in more recent literature, see Judith S. Lewis, 'When a House is Not a Home: Elite English Women and the Eighteenth-Century Country House', *Journal of British Studies*, 48:2 (2009), 336–363; Kate Smith, 'Imperial Families: Women Writing Home in Georgian Britain', *Women's History Review*, 24:6 (2015), 846–860; Jon Stobart and Mark Rothery, *Consumption and the Country House* (Oxford, 2016).

53. Bodleian Library, Oxford, Lady Russell to Charles Russell, 20 January 1805, MS. Eng. lett. c. 154, 63–63 verso. An *ayah* was an Indian nursemaid or lady's maid. The global lives of women such as these are explored in Michael Fisher, 'Bound for Britain: Changing Conditions of Servitude, 1600–1857', in Indrani Chatterjee and Richard Eaton (eds), *Slavery and South Asian History* (Bloomington, IN, 2006), 187–209.
54. Bodleian Library, Oxford, Lady Russell to Charles Russell, 24 May 1806, MS. Eng. lett. c. 154, 81 verso.
55. Bodleian Library, Oxford, Lady Russell to Henry Russell, 24 May 1806, MS. Eng. lett. c. 154, 78–78 verso, 81 verso; Lady Russell to Charles, 13 August 1807, MS. Eng. lett., c. 154, 112 verso.
56. Bodleian Library, Oxford, Lady Russell to Charles Russell, 9 July 1809, Bodleian, MS. Eng. lett. c. 154, 159–159 verso.
57. Bodleian Library, Oxford, Lady Russell to Charles Russell, 10 August 1809, MS. Eng. lett. c. 154, 1164 verso-166.
58. Bodleian Library, Oxford, Henry Russell to J.H. Casamaijor, 15 November 1811, MS. Eng. lett. d. 163, 60 verso; Lady Russell to Sir Henry Russell, MS. Eng. lett. c. 153, 6–7 verso; Caroline Russell to Charles Russell, 27 April 1814, MS. Eng. lett. c. 177, 122–122 verso.
59. See Clive William, *The Nabobs of Berkshire* (Purley on Thames, 2010), esp. chaps 8–10.
60. Bodleian Library, Oxford, Sir Henry Russell to Charles Russell, 25 January 1816, MS. Eng. lett. c. 152, 232–232 verso.
61. The interpenetration of and distinctions between English and French luxury trades in the Georgian era are detailed by Maxine Berg and Helen Clifford (eds), *Consumer Culture in Europe, 1650–1850* (Manchester, 1999) and Helen Clifford and Maxine Berg, 'Selling Consumption in the Eighteenth Century: Advertising and the Trade Card in Britain and France', *Cultural and Social History*, 4:2 (2007), 145–170.
62. Bodleian Library, Oxford, Sir Henry Russell to Charles Russell, 25 January 1816, MS. Eng. lett. c. 152, 234 verso.
63. See for example Vanessa Alayrae-Fielding, '"Frailty Thy Name is China": Women, Chinoiserie and the Treatment of Low Culture in Eighteenth-Century England', *Women's History Review*, 18: 4 (2009), 659–68; Margot Finn, 'The Homes of England', in James Chandler (ed.), *The Cambridge History of English Romantic Literature* (Cambridge, 2009), 307–10; D.L. Porter, 'Monstrous Beauty: Eighteenth-Century Fashion and the Aesthetics of the Chinese Taste', *Eighteenth-Century Studies*, 35: 3 (2002), 395–412; and Stacey Sloboda, *Chinoiserie: Commerce and Critical Ornament in Eighteenth-Century Britain* (Manchester, 2014).
64. Bodleian Library, Oxford, Sir Henry Russell to Lady Russell, 16 March 1813, MS. Eng. lett. c. 153, 56 verso-57.
65. Bodleian Library, Oxford, Henry Russell to Sir Henry Russell, 20 April 1815, MS. Eng. lett. c. 151, 107–108.
66. Bodleian Library, Oxford, Henry Russell to Sir Henry Russell, 3 October 1816, MS. Eng. lett. c. 151, 176 verso-177.
67. Summer Hill was mentioned, and illustrated with a plate, in Anthony Hamilton's popular *Memoirs of Count Grammont*, of which Sir Walter Scott produced an edition at this time: 2 vols (London, 1811), vol. 2: 210, 213, 226, 332–334. It had earlier been the home of Sir Thomas Walsingham.
68. Bodleian Library, Oxford, Henry Russell to Sir Henry Russell, 22 October 1815, MS. Eng. lett. c. 151, 142 verso-143 verso; Sir Henry Russell to Henry Russell, 13 March 1824, MS. Eng. lett. c. 151, 278–278 verso.
69. Christopher Rowell, 'French Furniture at Uppark: Sir Henry Fetherstonhaugh and His Friends in Post-Revolutionary Paris', *Furniture History*, 43 (2007), 267–92, esp. 277–84.
70. Bodleian Library, Oxford, Henry Russell to Charles Russell, 12 January 1822, MS. Eng. lett., c. 157, 152 and 154.
71. H.M. Chichester, Philip Carter, 'Burgoyne, Sir John, Seventh Baronet (1739–1785)', rev. Philip Cater, *Oxford Dictionary of National Biography*, Oxford University Press, 2004. Accessed 22 October 2016. http://oxforddnb.com/view/article/4012/, Henry leased Sutton Park from the ninth baronet, John Montagu Burgoyne (1796–1856).
72. Bodleian Library, Oxford, Henry Russell to Robert Pitman, 14 September 1822, MS. Eng. lett. c. 169, 80–80 verso, 82, 83.

73. It is not clear whether Charles, as originally intended, was a co-proprietor of the estate with his father an elder brother, or what proportion of the cost of its purchase was met by Sir Henry and Henry Russell.
74. For building and refurbishing country houses in this era, see Macklin and Mackley, *Creating Paradise*.
75. Bodleian Library, Oxford, Charles Russell to Henry Russell, 4 October 1826, MS. Eng. lett. c. 159, 79–79 verso.
76. Bodleian Library, Oxford, Charles Russell to Henry Russell, MS. Eng. lett. c. 159, 85 verso-86.
77. For French influences in Georgian country house furnishing, see esp. Ivan Hall, 'French Influence at Burton Constable', *Furniture History*, 8 (1972), 70–77; Rowell, 'French Furniture at Uppark', 267–292; and Charles Cator, 'French Furniture at Wanstead', *Furniture History*, 43 (2007), 227–236.
78. Bodleian Library, Oxford, Charles Russell to Henry Russell, MS. Eng. lett. c. 159, 139 verso-140. For wallpaper as a signifier of taste, see Vickery, *Behind Closed Doors*, chap. 6.
79. Bodleian Library, Oxford, Charles Russell to Henry Russell, 20 November 1827, MS. Eng. lett. c. 159, 158–158 verso.
80. Bodleian Library, Oxford, Charles Russell to Henry Russell, 22 March 1828, MS. Eng. lett. c. 159, 183–183 verso; Henry Russell to Clotilde Russell, 25 May 1828, MS. Eng. lett. d. 150, 17–17 verso. Tournai had long been a production centre for high-quality draperies and tapestries and was now also known for its carpets.
81. Bodleian Library, Oxford, Charles Russell to Henry Russell, 26 November 1828, MS. Eng. lett. c. 160, 44–44 verso.
82. http://www.historyofparliamentonline.org/volume/1820–1832/member/russell-charles-1786–1856.
83. See for example Bodleian Library, Oxford, Charles Russell to Henry Russell, 11 February 1830, MS. Eng. lett. c. 160, 127–128 verso.
84. For developments in the art market in this period, see James Hamilton, *A Strange Business: Making Art and Money in Nineteenth-century Britain* (London, 2014).
85. Bodleian Library, Oxford, Henry Russell to Charles Russell, 10–11 August 1831, MS. Eng. lett. d. 153, 127–128, 130.
86. Bodleian Library, Oxford, Henry Russell to Charles Russell, 26 October 1834, MS. Eng. lett. d. 155, 146; Henry Russell to Charles Russell, 22 May 1836, MS. Eng. lett. c. 161, 260 verso.
87. Bodleian Library, Oxford, Henry Russell to Charles Russell, 12 July, 6 October, 19 October and 15 December 1840, MS. Eng. lett. d. 156, 9, 111–111 verso, 119–120, 163.
88. For the traditions of travel to which the Russells were accommodating their cultural tastes, see Rosemary Sweet, *Cities and the Grand Tour: The British in Italy, c.1690–1820* (Cambridge, 2012).
89. Bodleian Library, Oxford, Henry Russell to Charles Russell, 14 March 1837, MS. Eng. lett. c. 163, 128–129.
90. Bodleian Library, Oxford, Henry Russell to Charles Russell, 13 February and 6 May 1838, MS. Eng. lett. c. 163, 8, 21–21 verso.
91. Bodleian Library, Oxford, Henry Russell to Charles Russell, 15 August 1838, MS. Eng. lett. c. 163, 60 verso-61.
92. Bodleian Library, Oxford, Henry Russell to Charles Russell, 3 March 1839, MS. Eng. lett. c. 163, 184–184 verso.
93. Bodleian Library, Oxford, Henry Russell to Charles Russell, 7 July 1836, MS. Eng. lett. c. 162, 48–49 verso.
94. Dalrymple, *White Mughals*, 259, 306, 340–342, 388–389, 480. The painting is reproduced opposite 277.
95. Dalrymple, *White Mughals*, 416–417, 445–446, 461, 465–466.
96. Bodleian Library, Oxford, Testimonial of 8 January 1821, MS Eng. let. C. 169, 26–27 verso.
97. See the image and description in the online auction catalogue of 2010: http://www.woolleyandwallis.co.uk/Lot/?sale=SV280410&lot=1015&id=171067.
98. Russell, *Swallowfield and Its Owners*, 268, 271–272.
99. http://www.woolleyandwallis.co.uk/Lot/?sale=SV280410&lot=1015&id=171067.
100. The inherent violence of empire is underlined, for example, by Richard Gott, *Britain's Empire: Resistance, Repression and Revolt* (London, 2011).

101. The case is delineated in British Library, IOR/F/4/626/16088. The use of the men to inform on their comrades in return for a reduced sentence mirrored Company officials' strategies for dealing with 'thugs'. See for example Tom Lloyd, 'Thuggee, Marginality and the State Effect in Colonial India, circa 1770–1840', *Indian Economic and* Social *History Review*, 45:2 (2008), 201–37.
102. British Library, Henry Russell to John Adam, 7 August 1818 and William Currie to Henry Russell, 8 August 1818, IOR/F/4/588/14274, 8,22, 23–24.
103. Testimony of assistant surgeon Guard, in William Currie to Henry Russell, 8 August 1818, British Library, IOR/F/4/588/14274, p. 25.
104. British Library, Undated letter, IOR/F/4/588/14274, 31–2.
105. British Library, Charles Metcalfe (secretary) to Henry Russell, 16 September 1820, IOR/F/4/796/21426, 6–7.
106. See for example Bodleian Library, Oxford, Charles Russell to Henry Russell, May [1824], MS Eng. lett. C. 158, 72–72 verso; Henry Russell to Charles Russell, 28 May 1826, MS Eng. lett. C. 159, 40–41.
107. For men's roles in Georgian consumer culture, see Margot Finn, 'Men's Things: Masculine Consumption in the Consumer Revolution', *Social History*, 25:2 (2000), 133–155, and Vickery, *Behind Closed Doors*, esp. chaps 2, 4.
108. The next generations of Russells had predominantly literary, rather than Company, circles of friends to visit, although this did not preclude Indian themes from shaping Swallowfield sociability. Family tradition held that Wilkie Collins' novel *The Moonstone* (1868) was inspired by tales of Pitt's diamond heard at Swallowfield. Russell, *Swallowfield and Its Owners*, 211, 303.
109. Bodleian Library, Oxford, Henry Russell to Pitman, 9 October 1839, MS Eng. lett. c. 170, 51. For the broader context of such exclusions, see Durba Ghosh, *Sex and the Family in Colonial India: The Making of Empire* (Cambridge, 2006).

Chapter 11

1. Georgina Green, 'Sir Charles Raymond of Valentines', *Essex Journal*, 43:2 (2008), 38–43.
2. John Carswell, *The South Sea Bubble* (Stroud, 2001), 188, 228, 254; John Biddulph Martin, *The Grasshopper in Lombard Street* (London, 1892), 87; F. G. H. Price, *A Handbook of London Bankers* (London, 1890), 172; Anthony Farrington, *A Catalogue of East India Company Ships' Journals and Logs 1660–1834* (London, 1999); Essex Record Office, 'Abstract of the title of Charles Thomas Holcombe Esq to the Freehold Estate called Valentines situate in the Parish of Barking in the County of Essex', DDU/539, 24, 26.
3. British Library, East India Company Court Book 1738–1740, IOR/B/65, 403, 467, 607; British Library, Ledger for *Wager* 1737/8, L/MAR/B/592H(1).
4. Basil Cozens-Hardy (ed.), *The Diary of Sylas Neville, 1767–1788* (London, 1950), 325.
5. Guildhall Library, Sun Fire Office policy registers, Volume 109, Policy Number 145324, 7 March 1755, MS 11936, 614; GL, Sun Fire Office policy registers, Volume 188, Policy Number 269293, 21 April 1769, MS 11936, 504. In spite of the restoration and refurbishment, the actual building insurance remained the same.
6. David Sanctuary Howard, *Chinese Armorial Porcelain* (London, 1974), 69; Robert Finlay, *The Pilgrim Art: Cultures of Porcelain in World History* (Berkeley, 2010), 27–8.
7. Gifts of European goods and of exotic 'Oriental' luxuries, exchanged between relations and between patrons and their clients, were vital means by which the East India Company's servants and families established and maintained their ties of affection and obligation across vast distances over time. See Margot Finn, 'Colonial Gifts: Family Politics and the Exchange of Goods in British India, c.1780–1820', *Modern Asian Studies*, 40 (2006), 203–31.
8. The book is around 86 x 34 cm. The book now resides in the Royal College of Physicians Library in London.
9. *A New and Complete History of Essex by a Gentleman* vol. 4 (Chelmsford, 1771), 276.
10. *Essex Review*, January 1927, No. 141, vol. XXXVI, 16.
11. *A New and Complete History of Essex by a Gentleman*, 276–79.
12. William Gilpin, *Remarks on Forest Scenery, and Other Woodland Views* (London, 1791) 149–51; George Tasker, *Ilford Past and Present* (Ilford, 1901), 86.

13. Andrea Wulf, *The Brother Gardeners: Botany, Empire and the Birth of an Obsession* (London, 2008); Finn, 'Colonial Gifts', 203–31.
14. 'Letter to the Royal Society from George Edwards', *Philosophical Transactions (1683–1775)*, LXI (1771), 55–6.
15. The National Archives, Will of Sir Charles Raymond, 29 August 1788, PROB 11/1169.
16. See John H. Farrant, 'Burrell, Sir William, second baronet (1732–1796)', *Oxford Dictionary of National Biography*, (Oxford, 2004). Accessed 5 Jan 2017. http://www.oxforddnb.com/view/article/4102; Details of the *Wager* can be found, EIC Court Book, 18 Dec 1734, IOR/B/63, 226.
17. See Thomas Newte tablet, situated on the wall inside St. Margaret's Church, Barking. See also Anthony Farrington, *A Biographical Index of East India Company Maritime Service Officers, 1600–1834* (London, 1999), 580.
18. J. R. Clube, 'The Boulton Family of Thorncroft Manor, 1763–1828', *Leatherhead & District Local History Society Proceedings*, 6:1 (1997), 10–13. See also Farrington, *Biographical Index*, 181.
19. Essex Record Office, Parish Register for St Mary the Virgin, Woodford, 12 July 1763, D/P 167/1/7; Price, *A Handbook of London Bankers*, 79, 177–8; Farrington, *Catalogue of East India Company Ships' Journals*, 767; Essex Record Office, 'Abstract of the title of Charles Thomas Holcombe Esq to the Freehold Estate called Valentines situate in the Parish of Barking in the County of Essex', DDU/539, 36–7, 53.
20. *St James's Chronicle or the British Evening Post* (London), 7 September 1797.
21. J. G. Parker, 'The Directors of the East India Company, 1754–1790', (PhD thesis, Univ. of Edinburgh, 1977). See also Local Studies & Archives, Valence House, Dagenham, Barking Parish Poor Rate Books, 2/3/1.
22. For more on high death rates of Company men in India, see Philip D. Curtin, *Death by Migration: Europe's Encounter with the Tropical World in the Nineteenth Century* (Cambridge, 1989). For more on the risks experienced by Company servants in the Georgian era see P. J. Marshall, *East India Fortunes: The British in Bengal in the Eighteenth Century* (Oxford, 1976).
23. For a full account of the voyage and the discovery of the wreck in 1986, see Charles Daggett and Christopher Shaffer, *Diving for the Griffin* (London, 1990).
24. Farrington, *Catalogue of East India Company Ships' Journals*, 673.
25. Discussed, for example, in Margot Finn, 'Family Formations: Anglo India and the Familial Proto-State', in David Feldman and Jon Lawrence, (eds), *Structures and Transformations in Modern British History* (Cambridge, 2011), 100–17.
26. British Library, 'Journal of Valentine (2) 1776/7', IOR/L/MAR/B/452F.
27. British Library, 'Journal of Valentine (2) 1776/7', IOR/L/MAR/B/452F.
28. British Library, East India Company Court Book, 22 December 1779, IOR/B/95, 380–1.
29. East India Company Court Book, 22 December 1779, IOR/B/95, 380–1.
30. See Aletha Hayter, *The Wreck of the Abergavenny* (London, 2002).
31. As cited in Hayter, *The Wreck of the Abergavenny*, 192.
32. Georgina Green, *Sir Charles Raymond of Valentines and the East India Company* (Ilford, 2015), 29, 52.
33. Green, *Sir Charles Raymond of Valentines*, 29 and 52.
34. Daggett and Shaffer, *Diving for the Griffin*, 107.
35. British Library, East India Company Commercial Ledger, August 1739, IOR/L/AG/1/6/11, 178.
36. http://www.museums.gov.gg/romanship.
37. http://www.priaulxlibrary.co.uk/.
38. It was a topographical map of the islands of Guernsey, Sark, Herm & Jethou likewise all the adjacent rocks, shoals and passages with the tides, soundings, anchorages etc. The map had been surveyed and drawn by Andrew Gray Esq, a Dept. Quartermaster General and Captain Nova Scotia Fenabler, assisted by M. P. Goodwin in 1808. The map was dedicated to Lt. General Sir John Doyle who was responsible for the reclamation of the Braye du Valle.
39. British Library, Miscellaneous Letters received by EIC, 22 January 1777, IOR/E/1/61, 35–37.
40. David Hancock, 'Commerce and Conversation in the Eighteenth-Century Atlantic: The Invention of Madeira Wine', *The Journal of Interdisciplinary History*, 29:2 (1998), 210.
41. For more detailed information see Green, *Sir Charles Raymond of Valentines*.

Chapter 12

1. *Hertfordshire Life*, 7 April 2011: http://www.hertfordshirelife.co.uk/homes-gardens/property-market/why_it_39_s_time_to_move_to_brookmans_park_1_1644000.
2. Historically spelt North Mimms, but changed by the County Council in 1933. To avoid confusion, I use the current spelling unless quoting directly.
3. Peter Kingsford, *A Modern History of Brookmans Park 1700–1950* (London, 1983), 34–8. From the mid-1970s until 2015, the parish had a vibrant local history society. Much of its research is available on the village website: http://www.brookmans.com/history/.
4. Kingsford, *Brookmans Park*, 46–50.
5. The parish's principal manor and namesake, North Mymms, lies slightly west of Brookmans Park. North Mymms Park is now a conference centre, whilst the adjacent parish church served all the local estates. See 'Parishes: North Mimms', in William Page (ed.), *A History of the County of Hertford*, vol. 2 (London, 1908), 251–261: http://www.british-history.ac.uk/vch/herts/vol2/pp251-261.
6. Dorothy Colville, *North Mymms – Parish and People* (Letchworth, 1972).
7. On this charged debate see Stuart Ward, 'Echoes of Empire', *History Workshop Journal*, 62:1 (2006), 264–78; J. M. MacKenzie, 'The British Empire: Ramshackle or Rampaging? A Historiographical Reflection', *Journal of Imperial and Commonwealth History*, 43:1 (2015), 99–124; c.f. Bernard Porter, *The Absent-minded Imperialists: How the British Really Saw Their Empire* (Oxford, 2004).
8. Madge Dresser and Andrew Hann (eds), *Slavery and the British Country House* (Swindon, 2013); Stephanie Barczewski, *Country Houses and the British Empire 1700–1930* (Manchester, 2014); *East India Company at Home, 1757–1857*: http://blogs.ucl.ac.uk/eicah/case-studies-2/.
9. Caroline Bressey, 'Contesting the Political Legacy of Slavery in England's Country Houses: A Case Study of Kenwood House and Osborne House', in Dresser and Hann, *Slavery and the British Country House*, 114–22, esp. 114–16.
10. Dominik Geppert and Frank Lorenz Müller (eds), *Sites of Imperial Memory: Commemorating Colonial Rule in the Nineteenth and Twentieth Centuries* (Manchester, 2015).
11. See for example Amia Srinivasan, 'Under Rhodes', *London Review of Books*, 38:7 (31 March 2016), 32; David Anderson, 'Guilty Secrets: Deceit, Denial, and the Discovery of Kenya's "Migrated Archive"', *History Workshop Journal*, 80:1 (2015), 142–60; Hilary Beckles, *Britain's Black Debt: Reparations for Caribbean Slavery and Native Genocide* (Mona, 2012).
12. Geoffrey Cubitt, 'Bringing it Home: Making Local Meaning in 2007 Bicentenary Exhibitions', *Slavery & Abolition*, 30:2 (2009), 259–75.
13. Catherine Hall and Sonya Rose (eds), *At Home with the Empire: Metropolitan Culture and the Imperial World* (Cambridge, 2006).
14. Catherine Hall, 'Troubling Memories: Nineteenth–century Histories of the Slave Trade and Slavery', *Transactions of the Royal Historical Society*, 6:21 (2011), 147–69.
15. Katie Donington, 'Local Roots/Global Routes': Slavery Memory and Identity in Hackney', in Katie Donington, Ryan Hanley, and Jessica Moody (eds), *Britain's History and Memory of Transatlantic Slavery: Local Nuances of a 'National Sin'* (Liverpool, 2016), 172.
16. See for example, Maxine Berg, *Luxury and Pleasure in Eighteenth–century Britain* (Oxford, 2005); Tillman Nechtman, *Nabobs: Empire and Identity in Eighteenth–century Britain* (Cambridge, 2010); Catherine Hall, Keith McClelland, Nick Draper, Katie Donington and Rachel Lang, *Legacies of British Slave–ownership: Colonial Slavery and the Formation of Victorian Britain* (Cambridge, 2014).
17. For example, Sarah Pearsall, *Atlantic Families: Lives and Letters in the Later Eighteenth Century* (Oxford, 2008); Margot Finn, 'Family Formations: Anglo India and the Familial Proto–state', in David Feldman and Jon Lawrence (eds), *Structures and Transformations in Modern British History* (Cambridge, 2011), 100–17; Perry Gauci, *William Beckford: First Prime Minister of the London Empire* (New Haven, CT, 2013).
18. For an outstanding recent work that uses a local, family history approach to illuminate wider processes of historical change see Alison Light, *Common People: The History of an English Family* (London, 2014).
19. Boyd Hilton, *A Mad, Bad and Dangerous People: England 1783–1846* (Oxford, 2008), 124–87.
20. Nechtman, *Nabobs*, passim.

21. Donington, Hanley and Moody (eds), *Britain's History and Memory of Transatlantic Slavery*, 6–8.
22. Quoted in Lawrence & Jeanne Stone, 'Country Houses and Their Owners in Hertfordshire, 1540–1879', in William O. Aydelotte (ed.), *The Dimensions of Quantitative Research in History* (Oxford, 1972), 56–123, 59.
23. In her *Country Houses,* Barczewski identifies 35 Herts estates owned by EIC employees and/or Directors, colonial merchants, West India planters and military officers who served in empire, 247–85; Lawrence and Jeanne Stone, *An Open Elite: England 1540–1880* (Oxford, 1984), 125–6.
24. Legacies of British Slave-ownership Report, 'Hertfordshire in the Compensation Notes': http://www.cnmd.ac.uk/lbs/project/hertfordshirenotes.
25. Hertfordshire has numerous county histories dating from the eighteenth to the twentieth centuries. Amongst the most notable are Sir Henry Chauncy, *The Historical Antiquities of Hertfordshire* (London, 1700); Robert Clutterbuck, *The History and Antiquities of the County of Hertford*, 3 vols (London, 1815–27); John Edwin Cussans, *History of Hertfordshire*, 3 vols (London, 1870–81); William Page (ed.), *The Victoria History of the County of Hertford*, 4 vols (London, 1902–12); Richard Lydekker, *Hertfordshire* (Cambridge, 1909).
26. Stone and Stone, 'Country Houses and Their Owners', 58–63.
27. Hugh Prince, *Parks in Hertfordshire since 1500* (Hatfield, 2008), 2–5. See also enclosed lists on changing size of estates.
28. Kate Harwood, 'Some Hertfordshire Nabobs', in Anne Rowe (ed.), *Hertfordshire Garden History: A Miscellany* (Hatfield, 2007), 49–77.
29. H. V. Bowen, *The Business of Empire: The East India Company and Imperial Britain, 1756–1833* (Cambridge, 2005), 119–50.
30. Anthony Farrington, *The Records of the East Indian College Haileybury and Other Institutions* (London, 1976).
31. Peter Marshall, *East India Fortunes: The British in Bengal in the Eighteenth Century* (Oxford, 1976), 106–28. Pagodas were gold coins issued by Mughal emperors and retained in use by the EIC.
32. This reflected national patterns, see J. A. Habakkuk, *Marriage, Debt and the Estates System* (Oxford, 1994), 448–53.
33. Marshall, *East India Fortunes*, 238; Harwood, 'Some Hertfordshire Nabobs', 58–9.
34. George Alexander Cooke, *Topographical and Statistical Description of the County of Hertford* (London, 1817), 71; Stone and Stone, *An Open Elite*, 103–4.
35. Peter Marshall, 'Paul Benfield', *Oxford Dictionary of National Biography*.
36. Perry Gauci, *Emporium of the World: The Merchants of London 1660–1800* (London, 2007), 205–10.
37. George McGilvary, *Guardian of the East India Company: The Life of Laurence Sulivan* (London, 2006), 109–11.
38. Stone and Stone, 'Country Houses in Hertfordshire', 108–09.
39. Nechtman, *Nabobs*, 167–70; Harwood, 'Some Hertfordshire Nabobs', 71.
40. Clutterbuck, *History and Antiquities*, vol. I (London, 1815), 277.
41. David Lambert and Alan Lester (eds), *Colonial Lives across the British Empire: Imperial Careering in the Long Nineteenth Century* (Cambridge, 2006), 8–13.
42. Arthur Collins, *The English Baronetage*, vol. 4 (London, 1741), 89–90.
43. The National Archives, Will of Jeremy Sambrooke, 9 October 1754, PROB/11/811/173.
44. Geoffrey Tyack, 'The Freemans of Fawley and Their Buildings', *Records of Buckinghamshire*, vol. 24 (1982), 130–43.
45. 'The Late Mr Hunter', *The Times*, 12 February 1803, 3.
46. *The Monthly Magazine or British Register*, vol. 15 (1803), 198.
47. Pembrokeshire Record Office, Tasker Papers (henceforth TP), John Tasker to John Hunter, 10 January 1795, DE/TE/5.
48. On the various strategies for remitting wealth back from India see Anthony Webster, *The Twilight of the East India Company: The Evolution of Anglo-Asian Commerce and Politics, 1790–1860* (Woodbridge, 2013).
49. 'Daniel Carpenter', Legacies of British Slave-ownership database: https://www.ucl.ac.uk/lbs/person/view/2146634736.
50. Margaret Bellasis, *Honourable Company* (London, 1952), pp. 218–19. On the challenges of finding care for returning children see Margot Finn, 'The Female World of Love &

Empire: Women, Family & East India Company Politics at the End of the Eighteenth Century', *Gender and History* (forthcoming).

51. A. P. Baggs, Diane K. Bolton, Eileen P. Scarff and G. C. Tyack, 'South Mimms: Other estates', in T. F. T. Baker and R. B. Pugh (eds.), *A History of the County of Middlesex*, vol. 5. (London, 1976), 290.
52. The National Archives, John Hunter and Ann Dick marriage agreement (1763), C/111/210
53. The National Archives, Will of Ann Hunter, 8 March 1786, PROB/11/1140/66.
54. J. Gordon Parker, 'The Directors of the East India Company' (Unpublished PhD, University of Edinburgh, 1977), 137–8.
55. The National Archives, Will of John Hunter, 11 January 1803, PROB/11/1385/108.
56. Harford Jones, *An Account of the Transactions of His Majesty's Mission to the Court of Persia 1807–1811*, vol. 1 (London, 1834), 13–16.
57. Pembrokeshire Record Office, TP, Tasker to Hunter, 24 September 1794, DE/TE/5.
58. *Report of the Cause between Hugh Doherty, Esq., Plaintiff, and Philip Wm. Wyatt, Esq., Defendant, for Criminal Conversation with the Plaintiff's Wife* (London, 1811).
59. Hertfordshire County Record Office, 'Law v Hunter', Chancery Case (1826), DGE/34174; 'Hornby v Hunter', *Reports of Cases Decided in the High Court of Chancery*, vol. 46 (London, 1871), 77–87.
60. The National Archives, Will of Thomas Hunter formerly Holmes, 29 November 1827, PROB 11/1732/420.
61. W. D. Rubinstein, *Who Were the Rich: A Biographical Directory of British Wealth Holders*, vol. 1 (London, 2009), 374.
62. Fire Insurance Policy Registers, 1777- 1786, available through London Lives 1690–1800: https://www.londonlives.org/browse.jsp?id=persName7fire_1775_1780_404_40464&div=fire_1775_1780_404_40464#highlight.
63. Offering a richly detailed excavation of Glenesk's own intricate empire connections, J. M. MacKenzie, 'The Intersection of the Local and the Global: Edzell, Glenesk and District and the British Empire', paper given at Festschrift Conference in honour of Professor John M. MacKenzie, Edzell, 6 August 2016. I am extremely grateful to Professor MacKenzie for sharing an unpublished version of this paper with me.
64. *London Gazette*, 13 May 1755.
65. *London Gazette*, 20 December 1760.
66. See for example *Lloyd's Evening Post*, 29 February 1764–2 March 1764. Michie is listed along with his business partners, George Rogers, John Kennion and James Dickson of Crutched Friars, London as agents responsible for the distribution of loot to members of the Royal Navy who served there under Pocock.
67. Lucy Sutherland, *A London Merchant: 1695–1774* (Oxford, 1962), 81–109.
68. *Morning Chronicle and London Advertiser*, 11 August 1787.
69. *World and Fashionable Advertiser*, 29 September 1787; Kingsford, *Brookmans Park*, 12.
70. David Carnegie and Andrew Agnew, *Protestant Exiles from France in the Reign of Louis XIV* (London, 1871), 251–52.
71. Hertfordshire County Record Office, DEGA/36494; The National Archives, Will of Peter Gaussen, 28/11/1788, PROB/11/1171/338.
72. Hertfordshire County Record Office, DEGA/36498.
73. Hertfordshire County Record Office, DEGA/36500.
74. John Brewer, *The Sinews of Power: War, Money and the English State* (London, 1989).
75. The National Archives, Will of Samuel Robert Gaussen Sr, 21 August 1812, PROB/11/1536/307.
76. Rubinstein, *Who Were the Rich*, 58.
77. Stone and Stone, *An Open Elite*, 99–101.
78. Hertfordshire County Record Office, R. W. Gaussen Notebook, DEGA/36522.
79. The family's surname was predominantly spelled Casamaijor in the eighteenth century and Casamajor in the nineteenth century.
80. Anonymous, *Descent of the Family of Casamayorga, or Casamayor, from the Royal Houses of Castille and Leon* (London, 1871).
81. The National Archives, Will of Justinian Casamajor, 29 August 1820, PROB/11/1633/366.
82. Finn, 'Family Formations', 105–11; Finn, Chapter 10 of this volume.
83. Stone and Stone, *An Open Elite*, 101.

84. Mary M. Drummond, 'John Hunter', History of Parliament: http://www.historyofparliamentonline.org/volume/1754–1790/member/hunter-john-1724–1802.
85. R. G. Thorne, 'Samuel Robert Bosanquet', History of Parliament: http://www.historyofparliamentonline.org/volume/1790–1820/member/gaussen-samuel-robert-1759–1812.
86. On the importance of women in sustaining global networks see Kate Smith, 'Imperial Families: Women Writing Home in Georgian Britain', *Women's History Review*, 24:6 (2015), 843–60.
87. The National Archives, Will of Caroline Lydia Casamajor, 10 September 1853, PROB/11/2178/164.
88. Harwood, 'Some Hertfordshire Nabobs', 53–7.
89. Clutterbuck, *History of Hertford*, 441.
90. *Farmer's Magazine*, vol. 3 (1802), 476.
91. John Brushe, 'Potterells', *Hertfordshire Past*, 21 (Autumn, 1986): http://www.brookmans.com/history/potterells/potterells.shtml.
92. *The Morning Post*, 13 June 1814.
93. Pembrokeshire Record Office, TP, Hunter to Tasker, 5/4/1792, DE/TE/4; the mango request is quoted in Barczewski, *Country Houses*, 226.
94. The National Archives, PROB/11/1140/66; TNA, PROB/11/1385/108.
95. Caroline Bressey, 'Invisible Presence: The Whitening of the Black Community in the Historical Imagination of British Archives', *Archivaria*, 61 (2006), 47–61.
96. Antoinette Burton and Dane Kennedy (eds), *How Empire Shaped Us* (London, 2016), 4–5.
97. David Lowenthal, *The Past is a Foreign Country* (Cambridge, 1985), 3–18.

Section 4

1. For Bengal's instrumental role in this period, see P. J. Marshall, *Bengal—the British Bridgehead: Eastern India, 1740–1828* (Cambridge, 1987).

Chapter 13

1. V. C. P. Hodson, *List of the Officers of the Bengal Army 1758–1834*, vol. 4:4 (London, 1947), 133; Raymond Head, *Redcliffe & Colonel Robert Smith: A History of the Redcliffe Hotel and its Original Designer* (Torquay, 1997), n.p.
2. Raymond Head, *Redcliffe & Colonel Robert Smith*; Bideford Parish Register as cited in Hodson, *List of the Officers*, 133.
3. Raymond Head, *Colonel Robert Smith (1787–1873) and Redcliffe* (The Torbay Civic Society, n.d.).
4. Head, *Redcliffe & Colonel Robert Smith*.
5. Hodson, *List of the Officers*, 133; British Library, 'Cadet Papers for Robert Smith', 1802–3, IOR/MIL/9/112.
6. British Library, 'Cadet Papers for Robert Smith', 1802–3, IOR/MIL/9/112; Reginald Henry Phillimore, *Historical Records of the Survey of India*, 4:2 (Dehra Dun, 1950), 442. Smith transferred from Infantry to Engineers in June 1805.
7. Hodson, *List of the Officers*, 133.
8. *Torquay Herald Express* (12 September 2001), 19.
9. Mildred Archer, 'An Artist Engineer: Colonel Robert Smith in India (1805–1830)', *The Connoisseur* (February 1972), 79.
10. Luke Herrmann, 'Delamotte, William (1775–1863)', *Oxford Dictionary of National Biography* (Oxford, 2004), 705–706; Richard Garnett, 'Alexander, William (1767–1816)', rev. Heather M. MacLennan, *Oxford Dictionary of National Biography* (Oxford, 2004), 695–6.
11. See Rosie Dias, 'Memory and the Aesthetics of Military Experience: Viewing the Landscape of the Anglo-Mysore Wars', *Tate Papers*, 19. Accessed 16 October 2013. http://www.tate.org.uk/research/publications/tate-papers/memory-and-aesthetics-military-experience-viewing-landscape-anglo. See also Jennifer Howes, *Illustrating India: the Early Colonial Investigations of Colin Mackenzie (1784–1821)* (Oxford, 2010), 14.

12. Head, *Redcliffe & Colonel Robert Smith*; A. W. Skempton (ed.), *A Biographical Dictionary of Civil Engineers in Great Britain and Ireland* (London, 2002), 637.
13. Skempton, *Dictionary of Civil Engineers*, 637.
14. *Survey of India Records*, transferred from Dehra Dūn to NAI., New Delhi, 1947, 126 (134); 9 April 1812 by Surveyor General, quoted in Phillimore, *Historical Records*, 442.
15. Lady Maria Nugent, *A Journal from the Year 1811 Till the Year 1815, Including a Voyage to and Residence in India with a Tour to the North-Western Parts of the British Possessions in that Country under the Bengal Government*, 2, 1 (London, 1839), 395.
16. Hodson, *List of the Officers,* 133.
17. He was first appointed to the post on 11 November 1814. However, his posting was postponed due to his military tour with Lord Moira, and his involvement in the Nepal War. Bombay General Orders (BGO) 11 November 1814, quoted in Hodson, *List of the Officers*, 133; Phillimore, *Historical Records*, 442.
18. Archer, 'An Artist Engineer', 81. It must also be noted that Smith was not alone in publishing his art, several East India Company Officers published engravings of their watercolour landscapes as an aspect of their private trading, for instance Captain R. H. Colebrooke, an East India Company surveyor, published *Twelve Views of Places in the Kingdom of Mysore, with Descriptions, and a Brief Detail of the Operations of the Army under Marquis Cornwallis* (1794), engraved by the English artist John William Edy. For more on this see Thomas Egerton, *A Catalogue of an Extensive Collection of Books: in all Languages and Every Branch of Science and Literature* (London, 1796), 396.
19. Skempton, *Dictionary of Civil Engineers*, 637.
20. Sir Thomas Metcalfe, *Reminiscences of Imperial Dehlie* Album, RP 3041 (microfilm). Facsimile published as M. M. Kaye (ed.), *The Golden Calm and English Lady's Life in Moghul India* (Exeter, 1980), 84–5.
21. See Charles Cramer-Roberts, 'Notes on *The Taj Mahal and Its Garden*, 1884', British Library online gallery. Accessed 19 September 2013 http://www.bl.uk/onlinegallery/onlineex/apac/other/019wdz000002131u00000000.html.
22. Aleck and William Fraser's letters in the Moniack House archive, quoted in William Dalrymple, *City of Djinns: a Year in Delhi* (London, 2005), 100–9.
23. Major Edward Archer, *Tours in Upper India and in Parts of the Himalaya Mountains*, 2, 1 (London, 1833), 107–9.
24. Archer, *Tours in Upper India*, 107–8.
25. Sylvia Shorto, 'Public Lives, Private Spaces: British Houses in Delhi, 1803–1853', Ph.D. thesis (Institute of Fine Arts, New York University, 2003), 132.
26. Shorto, 'Public Lives', 133.
27. Shorto, 'Public Lives', 131.
28. Skempton, *Dictionary of Civil Engineers*, 637.
29. Skempton, *Dictionary of Civil Engineers*, 637.
30. Skempton, *Dictionary of Civil Engineers*, 637.
31. Hodson, *List of the Officers*, 133. It was reported that Robert Smith, Captain: Sappers and Miners, was awarded a clasp to his India Medal, 'Dispatches', *London Gazette*, 10 June 1826.
32. Hodson, *List of the Officers*, 133.
33. Archer, *Tours in Upper India*, 107.
34. Hodson, *List of the Officers*, 133; Phillimore, *Historical Records*, 442. See Mildred Archer, *The Tranquil Eye: The Watercolours of Colonel Robert Smith [of] a Journey Down the Ganges 1830* (London, 1982).
35. Skempton, *Dictionary of Civil Engineers*, 637.
36. Hodson, *List of the Officers,* 133; Phillimore, *Historical Records*, 442; British Library, 'Smith, Lieutenant Colonel Robert Smith, Bombay Infantry created C.B', IOR/Z/E.4/43/S464; Robert Smith's medals, including the Order of the Bath, were sold for £5200 in Lot 1036, 22 September 2006 by Dix Noonan Webb. Accessed 19 September 2013. www.dnw.co.uk.
37. Raymond Head, *The Indian Style*, (London, 1986) 19.
38. Raymond Head, 'Indian Fantasy in Devon', *Country Life*, 28 May 1981, 1524. Smith's wife's last name was likely to be Vitton and her maiden name Claude. See British Library, 'Cadet Papers for Robert Claude Smith', 1859–60, IOR/MIL/9/252/287–94.
39. Charles Mills died in 1846, so Smith would have purchased the villa between 1846 and 1856 when the house was acquired by the Sisters of the Visitation.

40. Samuel Ball Platner and Thomas Ashby, *A Topographical Dictionary of Ancient Rome* (London, 1929), 1.
41. Alba della Fazia Amoia and Enrico Iruschini, *Stendhal's Rome: Then and Now* (Rome, 1997), 67–68. Charles Mills' mother was said to claim ancestry from Governor Hamilton of the Leeward Islands, see H. V. Morton, *A Traveller in Rome* (New York, 1957), 359–362.
42. H. V. Morton, *A Traveller in Rome* (London, 2002), 419. Peruzzi was one of the leading artists in Rome c.1520. *Collections of the Metropolitan Museum of Art*. Accessed 9 September 2013. http://www.metmuseum.org/collections/search-the-collections/437274.
43. Morton, *A Traveller in Rome*, 419.
44. Amoia and Iruschini, *Stendahl's Rome*, 67–68. Rodolfo Lanciani, *New Tales of Old Rome* (London, c.1901), 325–326.
45. Morton, *A Traveller in* Rome, 420.
46. Lanciani, *New Tales*, 325–236.
47. James Balfour Paul (Lyon King of Arms), *An Ordinary of Arms: Contained in the Public Register of all Arms and Bearings in Scotland* (Edinburgh, 1895), 70.
48. The Hon. F. Leveson-Gower (ed.), *Letters of Harriet Countess Granville 1810–1845*, 2, 2 (London and New York, 1894), 340.
49. It has not been possible to identify the site of this house in Nice. Principal Probate Registry, Somerset House, London, Prerogative Court of Canterbury, 'Will of Proby Thomas Cautley', March 1871; see also Joyce Brown, 'A Memoir of Colonel Sir Proby Cautley, F.R.S., 1802–1871, Engineer and Palaeontologist', *Notes and Records of the Royal Society of London*, 34:2 (March 1980), fn. 85.
50. Didier Gayraud 'Le Château Smith: di Château de l'Anglais ou Château de Mont Boron', *Nice Historique*, 113:1 (2011), 53.
51. Gayraud, 'Le Château Smith', 53; Registre des demandes des visas, ADAM 1Z273; Shorto, 'Public Lives', 135.
52. Translation from Élisée Reclus, *Les villes d'hiver de la Méditerranée et Les Alpes-Maritimes* (Paris, 1864), 243, quoted in Véronquie Thuin-Chaudron, 'Le mont Boron autour des années 1860. Une colline en pleine mutation,' *Nice Historique*, 113:1 (2011), 21.
53. 'Nice à vol d'oisseau', *Nouvelle revue européenne* (1895). As cited in Gayraud, 'Le Château Smith', 56.
54. Gayraud, 'Le Château Smith', 54.
55. This was after Savoy and Nice were annexed by plebiscite under the Treaty of Turin which transferred Nice from Italy to France. See Samuel B. Crandall, *Treaties: Their Making and Enforcement* (New Jersey, 2005), 226, 306, 322 and 435.
56. Gayraud, 'Le Château Smith', 55.
57. Shorto, 'Public Lives', 136.
58. Lise Didier-Moulonguet published a small survey taken from an 1872 local property register, 'Nice: le château de l'Anglais', *Monuments historiques de la France*, I (1778), 31–33. As cited in Shorto, 'Public Lives', 136, fn 88.
59. Gayraud, 'Le Château Smith', 59.
60. Terry Leaman, 'Description, Residents and Tradesman List', extracted from, *Kelly's Post Office Directory of Devonshire*, 1856. Accessed 18 September 2013. 'Torquay Gentry Listings' extracted from *Kelly's Post Office Directory of Devonshire 1856*. http://myweb.tiscali.co.uk/terryleaman/Tiscali/1856-Kellys-gentry.html.
61. Royal Institute of British Architects, Archive Collection, *Memoranda of a Journey through Devon and Wales*, 23 July 1806, COC/9, COC/10 (Box 9–10), cited in David Watkin, *The Life and Work of C.R. Cockerell* (London, 1974), 5. Although Ilfracombe is 90 miles away in North Devon, the climate of Paignton is equally mild. William Hodges, known for his Picturesque paintings of India settled on his return to England in the nearby resort of Brixham.
62. Four drawings including An *Elevation of the East or Sea Front*, signed by Robert Smith came to light in Messrs. Cooksleys estate agents in the early 1970s, Archer, 'An Artist Engineer', 88. However, this cannot be verified as the drawings have since disappeared, but the date concurs roughly with that of a map drawn up by Smith and submitted in 1854 to the Admiralty to gain assent to build a seawall around Redcliffe. The National Archives, *Redcliffe, Tor Bay, Devon; Construction of Seawall by Lieutenant Colonel R Smith*, BT 356/10656.
63. In the Paignton rate books it was identified as Redcliffe Castle. Head, *Redcliffe & Colonel Robert Smith*.

64. R. Sercombe and Raymond Head, 'Redcliffe Paignton and Its Builder, Col Robert Smith', *Devon Life*, [n.d], 24. Conversation with Mr Stephen Twigger, owner of the Redcliffe Hotel, 14 March 2013. Mr Twigger pointed out the hotel's copy of the Paignton vignette, see figure 10.
65. Unsigned and undated, it is a copy of an earlier map. It is unknown whether all features were copied from the original map, or whether the features marked were introduced at a later date. *Nelumbo nucifera* or the sacred lotus, has divine associations in Asian religions.
66. For full architectural details see English Heritage, 'List entry for Redcliffe Hotel, No: 1195234'. Accessed 10 July 2013. www.english-heritage.org.uk.
67. 'List entry for Redcliffe Hotel, No: 1195234'.
68. Smith's comments were found on the reverse of one of the original architectural drawings, found in the 1970s. Head, *Redcliffe & Robert Smith*.
69. Head, *Redcliffe & Robert Smith*.
70. Many books were published in the late seventeenth and early eighteenth centuries advocating ways to increase life expectancy, see John Floyer, *An Enquiry into the Right Use and Abuses of the Hot, Cold and Temperate Baths in England* (London, 1697); John Locke, *Some Thoughts Concerning Education* (London, 1703).
71. E. M. Collingham, *Imperial Bodies: The Physical Experience of the Raj, c.1800–1947* (Oxford, 2001), 44–49.
72. Jane Austen, *Sanditon* (Unfinished, 1817), Chapter Two, University of Virginia Library. Accessed 30 October 2013. www.onread.com.
73. Head, *Redcliffe & Colonel Robert Smith.*
74. Head, *Redcliffe & Colonel Robert Smith.*
75. England and Wales, National Probate Calendar (Index of Wills and Administrations), 1858–1966 for Rober [sic] Smith (1874), 59.
76. Raymond Head, 'From Obsession to Obscurity: Colonel Robert Smith: Artist, Architect and Engineer – I', *Country Life* (21 May 1981), 1434.

Chapter 14

1. Post-1996, these counties are known as Ynys Môn and Gwynedd respectively.
2. Linda Hall, *Period House Fixtures and Fittings 1300–1900* (Newbury, 2005); Rachael Barnwell and Richard Suggett, *Y Tu Mewn i Gartrefi Cymru/Inside Welsh Homes* (Aberystwyth, 2012), 55–99.
3. National Monument Record of Wales Site Files: Caernarvonshire Domestic SH57SE (Tan-yr-Allt); Anglesey Domestic SH67NW (Bishopsgate House); Anglesey Domestic SH47SW (Trefeilir).
4. See for example H. V. Bowen (ed.), *Wales and the British Overseas Empire: Interactions and Influences, 1650–1830* (Manchester, 2011). Similarly, Lowri Ann Rees is currently working on her monograph, provisionally entitled *Welsh Nabobs: Wales and the British East India Company, 1757–1857*.
5. http://www.bangorcivicsociety.org.uk/files/Tanrallt_report.pdf. Accessed 17 June 2013.
6. *An Inventory on the Ancient Monuments in Caernarvonshire: II Central: the Cantref of Arfon and the Commote of Eifionydd* (Aberystwyth, 1958), 61.
7. National Monument Record of Wales Site Files: Anglesey Domestic SH67NW (Bishopsgate House).
8. *An Inventory on the Ancient Monuments in Caernarvonshire: II Central.*
9. *An Inventory on the Ancient Monuments in Caernarvonshire: II Central,* 61.
10. *An Inventory of the Ancient Monuments in Anglesey* (Aberystwyth, 1937) 156.
11. *An Inventory of the Ancient Monuments in Anglesey,* 244.
12. Oliver Garrett, *Plas Newydd: Isle of Anglesey* (London, 2010).
13. By Royal Licence on 29 January 1770, Henry Bayly took the surname Paget in place of his birth name.
14. Hall, *Period House Fixtures and Fittings*; Margaret Jourdain, *English Furniture: The Georgian Period (1750–1830)* (London, 1953), 26–27.
15. http://www.historyofparliamentonline.org/volume/1690–1715/member/paget-hon-henry-1663–1743. Accessed 4 May 2013.

16. Peter D. G. Thomas, 'The Rise of Plas Newydd', *Welsh History Review,* 16:2 (1992), 160–76.
17. Jourdain, *English Furniture*, 26.
18. Charles Saumarez Smith, *Eighteenth-Century Decoration: Design and the Domestic Interior in England* (New York, 1993), 132.
19. Saumarez Smith, *Eighteenth-Century Decoration*, 132.
20. Saumarez Smith, *Eighteenth-Century Decoration*, 132.
21. *The World,* 22 March 1753, as cited in Jourdain, *English Furniture*, 27.
22. *An Inventory on the Ancient Monuments in Caernarvonshire: I East: the Cantref of Arllechwedd and the Commote of Creuddyn* (Aberystwyth, 1956), 252.
23. *An Inventory on the Ancient Monuments in Caernarvonshire: II Central,* 286.
24. Thomas Chippendale, *The Gentleman and Cabinet Maker's Director* (London, 1754).
25. Saumarez Smith, *Eighteenth-Century Decoration*, 132.
26. Aldous Bertram, 'Cantonese Models for the Great Pagoda at Kew', *The Georgian Group Journal*, 21 (2013), 47–57.
27. Saumarez Smith, *Eighteenth-Century Decoration*, 143.
28. Jeanne K. Pirtle, *Sotterley Plantation* (Charleston, SC, 2013), 27.

Chapter 15

1. Thanks to my occasional research assistant Viccy Coltman and Lucy Dow for her help deciphering Hall's eating habits. Also to Sally Wilson, Deborah Kirk and the editors who provided valuable feedback on the original case study.
2. National Archives of Scotland, Alexander Hall to Isabella Hall, 4 December 1755, GD206/504/1/6.
3. John Riddy, 'Warren Hastings: Scotland's Benefactor?', in Geoffrey Carnall and Colin Nicholson (eds), *The Impeachment of Warren Hastings* (Edinburgh, 1989), 30–57; B.R. Tomlinson, 'From Campsie to Kedgeree: Scottish Enterprise, Asian Trade and the Company Raj', *Modern Asian Studies*, 36 (2002), 769–91; Thomas Devine, 'Scottish Élites and the Indian Empire, 1700–1815', in T.C. Smout (ed.), *Anglo-Scottish Relations from 1603 to 1900* (Oxford, 2005), 213–29.
4. Miles Ogborn, *Indian Ink: Script and Print in the Making of the English East India Company* (London, 2007), 58.
5. Dianne Lewis, 'The Dutch East India Company and the Straits of Malacca, 1700–1784: Trade and Politics in the Eighteenth Century', unpublished PhD thesis, Australian National University, 1970.
6. John Sturgus Bastin, 'Introduction', *The British in West Sumatra, 1685–1825* (Kuala Lumpur, 1965), xii-xiii.
7. Anne Lindsey Reber, 'The Private Trade of the British in West Sumatra 1735–1770', unpublished PhD thesis, University of Hull, 1977, 4.
8. J. Kathirithamby-Wells, *The British West Sumatran Presidency, 1760–1785: Problems of Early Colonial Enterprise* (Kuala Lumpur, 1977), 198.
9. P.J. Marshall, *East Indian Fortunes: The British in Bengal in the Eighteenth Century* (Oxford, 1976); George McGilvary, *East India Patronage and the British State* (London, 2008), 184–202; Tillman W. Nechtman, 'A Jewel in the Crown? Indian Wealth in Domestic Britain in the Late Eighteenth Century', *Eighteenth Century Studies*, 41 (2007), 71–86.
10. K. N. Chaudhuri, *The Trading World of Asia and the English East India Company: 1660–1760* (Cambridge, 1978), 65.
11. Prasannajit de Silva, 'Representing Home Life Abroad: British Domestic Life in Early-Nineteenth-Century India', *Visual Culture in Britain*, 12 (2011), 313–31; Swati Chattopadhyay, '"Goods, Chattels and Sundry Items": Constructing 19th-Century Anglo-Indian Domestic Life', *Journal of Material Culture*, 10 (2005), 197–214.
12. A. G. Harfield, *Bencoolen: A History of the Honourable East India Company's Garrison on the West Coast of Sumatra, 1685–1825* (Barton-on-Sea, 1995), 49–98.
13. Frenise A. Logan, 'The British East India Company and African Slavery in Benkulen, Sumatra, 1687–1792', *Journal of Negro History*, 41 (1956), 339–48.
14. Cited in Logan, 'The British East India Company', 340–41.

15. Philip J. Stern, *The Company-State: Corporate Sovereignty and the Early Modern Foundations of the British Empire in India* (Oxford, 2011), 29.
16. 'Bencoolen Slaves', *Bengal Hakuru,* 25 January 1825.
17. Kate Teltscher, 'Writing Home and Crossing Cultures: George Bogle in Bengal and Tibet, 1770–1775', in Kathleen Wilson (ed.), *A New Imperial History: Culture, Identity and Modernity in Britain and the Empire 1660–1840* (Cambridge, 2004), 282.
18. Harfield, *Bencoolen*; Robert J. Young, 'The English East India Company and Trade on the West Coast of Sumatra, 1730–1760', unpublished PhD thesis, University of Pennsylvania, 1970.
19. Daniel Defoe, *A Tour thro' the Whole Island of Great Britain* (originally published 1724–1727; New Haven, 1991), 302.
20. Christopher A. Whatley, *Scottish Society, 1707–1830: Beyond Jacobitism, Towards Industrialisation* (Manchester, 2000), 185.
21. National Archives of Scotland, Alexander Hall to John Hall, 9 November 1749, GD206/499/1.
22. National Archives of Scotland, John Hall to Alexander Hall, 15 February 1764, GD206/2/294.
23. See my case study on Downie Park for an example of a Jacobite family securing Army positions in India: http://blogs.ucl.ac.uk/eicah/case-studies-2/william-rattray-of-downie-park/.
24. National Archives of Scotland, Alexander Hall to John Hall, 9 November 1749, GD206/499/1.
25. National Archives of Scotland, Alexander Hall to John Hall, 9 November 1749, GD206/499/1.
26. National Archives of Scotland, Alexander Hall to Margaret Hall, [c. November 1850], GD206/4/2.
27. British Library, James Swinton to David Anderson, 23 March 1770, Add. 45429/41–42.
28. National Archives of Scotland, Alexander Hall to John Hall, 15 November 1750, GD206/499/9.
29. National Archives of Scotland, Alexander Hall to Margaret Hall, [c. November 1850], GD206/4/2.
30. National Archives of Scotland, Alexander Hall to John Hall, 29 November 1750, GD206/2/499/11.
31. National Archives of Scotland, Alexander Hall to John Hall, 13 December 1750, GD206/2/499/13.
32. National Archives of Scotland, Alexander Hall to John Pringle, 15 December 1751, GD206/2/503.
33. National Archives of Scotland, Alexander Hall to Margaret Hall, 17 December 1751, GD206/500/2.
34. National Archives of Scotland, List of Persons serving in the East India Company on West Coast of Sumatra, 1760–64, GD206/2/502.
35. National Archives of Scotland, Robert Hay, to [William?] Hall, 15 April 1775, GD206/4/33.
36. See, Donald F. Lach and Edwin J. Van Kley, *Asia in the Making of Europe, Volume III: A Century of Advance* (London, 1993), 1362–66.
37. National Archives of Scotland, Alexander Hall to John Pringle, 15 December 1751, GD206/2/503.
38. National Archives of Scotland, Alexander Hall to Margaret Hall, 1 January 1753, GD206/4/2.
39. National Archives of Scotland, Alexander Hall to John Pringle, 24 December 1753, GD206/4/30.
40. National Archives of Scotland, Claud Russell to Alexander Hall, no date, GD206/2/503.
41. National Archives of Scotland, Alexander Hall to John Hall, 24 February 1756, GD206/499/17.
42. National Archives of Scotland, Alexander Hall to Margaret Hall, 17 December 1751, GD206/500/2.
43. See, for example, Syed Hussein Alatas, *The Myth of the Lazy Native* (London, 1977), 35–42.
44. National Archives of Scotland, Alexander Hall to Isabella Hall, 9 December 1755, GD206/2/504.
45. National Archives of Scotland, Alexander Hall to George Pigott [copy], 12 July 1761, GD206/2/502.
46. National Archives of Scotland, Alexander Hall to East India Company Directors, 10 March 1762, GD206/2/502.
47. National Archives of Scotland, Alexander Hall and Richard Wyatt to Christian Ludowick Senff and Frederick Van de Wall, 16 June 1760, GD206/2/502.

48. National Archives of Scotland, Alexander Hall to East India Company Directors, 10 March 1762, GD206/2/502.
49. Linda Colley, *Captives: Britain, Empire and the World 1600–1850* (London, 2003).
50. National Archives of Scotland, Alexander Hall to John Hall, 17 April 1762, GD206/2/499/19.
51. National Archives of Scotland, Alexander Hall to East India Company Directors, 10 March 1762, GD206/2/502.
52. National Archives of Scotland, Alexander Hall to John Hall, 17 April 1762, GD206/2/499/19.
53. L. Stuart Sutherland, 'Lord Shelburne and East India Company Politics, 1766–9', *English Historical Review*, 49 (1934), 450–86.
54. National Archives of Scotland, Alexander Hall to John Hall, 2 December 1762, GD206/2499/22. See also, George K. McGilvary, *Guardian of the East India Company: The Life of Laurence Sulivan* (London, 2006), 80.
55. National Archives of Scotland, Alexander Hall to John Hall, 3 September 1763, GD206/500/24.
56. National Archives of Scotland, John Hall to Alexander Hall, 15 February 1764, GD206/2/294.
57. National Archives of Scotland, Extracts from Madras Letters, 7 March 1761, GD206/2/502.
58. National Archives of Scotland, Duncan Clerk to Alexander Hall, 4 January 1764, GD206/2/502.
59. National Archives of Scotland, Alexander Hall to John Hall, 3 September 1763, GD206/2/499/24.
60. National Archives of Scotland, Alexander Hall to sister [Isabella?], 9 December 1755, GD206/2/504.
61. National Archives of Scotland, Alexander Hall to John Hall, 3 September 1763, GD206/2/499/24; National Archives of Scotland, Alexander Hall to John Hall, 15 October 1764, GD206/2/499/25.
62. National Archives of Scotland, Alexander Hall to John Hall, 26 March 1751, GD206/499/15.
63. National Archives of Scotland, Alexander Hall to Margaret Hall, 5 June 1754, GD206/4/2.
64. National Archives of Scotland, Alexander Hall to Margaret Hall, 15 November 1757, GD206/2/500/3.
65. National Archives of Scotland, Alexander Hall to John Hall, 15 October 1764, GD206/499/25.
66. National Archives of Scotland, Alexander Hall to John Hall, 30 November 1755, GD206/499/16.
67. Benedict Anderson, *Imagined Communities: Reflections on the Origin and Spread of Nationalism* (London, 1983), 37.
68. Anderson, *Imagined Communities*, 37.
69. National Archives of Scotland, Alexander Hall to William Hall, 4 December 1755, GD206/501/6.
70. National Archives of Scotland, Alexander Hall to William Hall, 4 December 1755, GD206/501/6.
71. National Archives of Scotland, Alexander Hall to John Hall, 8 January 1763, GD206/499/23.
72. National Archives of Scotland, Alexander Hall to John Hall, 3 September 1763, GD206/499/24.
73. For the shipping of food between colony and metropole during this period, see Elizabeth M. Collingham, *Imperial Bodies: The Physical Experience of the Raj, c.1800–1947* (Cambridge, 2001), 68–71; Troy Bickham, 'Eating the Empire: Intersections of Food, Cookery and Imperialism in Eighteenth-century Britain', *Past & Present*, 198 (2008), 71–109.
74. Durba Ghosh, *Sex and the Family in Colonial India: The Making of Empire* (Cambridge, 2006).
75. National Archives of Scotland, Isabella Hall to Robert Hay and Henry Nell, nd, GD206/4/38.
76. National Archives of Scotland, John Hall to Robert Hay, 16 December 1765, GD206/2/295.
77. National Archives of Scotland, Robert Hay to Isabella Hall, 5 March 1767, GD206/4/40.
78. Michael Fisher, *Counterflows to Colonialism: Indian Travellers and Settlers in Britain, 1600–1857* (Delhi, 2004). See also, Ghosh, *Sex and the Family in Colonial India*.
79. National Archives of Scotland, Henry Idell to Isabella Hall, 5 August 1767, GD206/4/33.
80. National Archives of Scotland, Robert Hay to Isabella Hall, 5 March 1767, GD206/4/40.
81. National Archives of Scotland, Isabella Hall to Robert Hay, 13 January 1770, GD206/4/38; Isabella Hall to Robert Hay, 9 January 1771, NAS, GD206/4/38.

82. National Archives of Scotland, Isabella Hall to Robert Hay, 18 November 1773, GD206/4/38.
83. National Archives of Scotland, London signed Thomas Neilson, 26 August 1767, GD206/4/33.
84. National Archives of Scotland, Henry Idell to Isabella Hall, 5 August 1767, GD206/4/33.
85. Emma Rothschild, *The Inner Life of Empires: An Eighteenth-Century History* (Princeton, 2011), 91–96; Margot Finn, 'Slaves out of Context: Domestic Slavery and the Anglo-Indian Family, c.1780–1840', *Transactions of the Royal Historical Society*, 19 (2009), 193–6.
86. National Archives of Scotland, John Hall to Neilson, 7 Sep 1768, GD206/4/30//13; National Archives of Scotland, John Hall to Mr Braham, 7 September 1768, NAS, GD206/4/30/10.
87. National Archives of Scotland, Isabella Hall to Robert Hay, 29 October 1768, GD206/4/38.
88. National Archives of Scotland, Isabella Hall to Robert Hay, 9 January 1771, GD206/4/38.
89. National Archives of Scotland, Isabella Hall to Robert Hay, 4 January 1776, GD206/4/38.
90. Sally Wilson, *Lady Helen Hall Lang-heidit Ledy of Dunglass 1762–1837* (Dunglass, 2013), p. 65.
91. National Archives of Scotland, Sederunt book for Pringle of Torwoodlee, 1820, CS96/323.
92. See Royal Commission on the Ancient and Historical Monuments of Scotland, 'Photograph of Dunglass Drawing Room', 1925, G90479PO.
93. Tillman W. Nechtman, *Nabobs: Empire and Identity in Eighteenth-Century Britain* (Cambridge, 2010), 146.

Chapter 16

1. Miles Glendinning, and Susanna Wade Martins, *Buildings of the Land: Scotland's Farms 1750–2000* (Edinburgh, 2008) feature the farm complex as an exemplary example of 'high' farming.
2. H. Gordon Slade, 'Carnousie-Banffshire', *Archaeological Journal*, 136 (1979), 229–39.
3. On the development of home farm steadings in the north east, see Alistair Mutch, 'Agriculture and Empire: General Patrick "Tiger" Duff and the Shaping of North-east Scotland', *Review of Scottish Culture*, 22 (2010), 85–98.
4. See for example the discussion of Sezincote in Ellen Filor and Jan Sibthorpe, 'Outside the Public: The Histories of Sezincote and Prestonfield in Private Hands', in Margot Finn and Kate Smith (eds), *New Paths to Public Histories* (Basingstoke, 2015).
5. Joseph Sharples, David Walker and Matthew Woodworth, *Aberdeenshire: South and Aberdeen* (New Haven, 2015), 519.
6. Charles McKean, *The Scottish Chateau: The Country House of Renaissance Scotland* (Stroud, 2004).
7. David Walker and Matthew Woodworth, *Aberdeenshire: North and Moray* (New Haven, CT, 2015), 161.
8. Mutch, 'Agriculture and Empire', 91.
9. Eric Grant and Alistair Mutch, 'Indian Wealth and Agricultural Improvement in Northern Scotland', *Journal of Scottish Historical Studies*, 35 (2015), 25–44.
10. Alistair Mutch, 'A Contested Eighteenth Century Election: Banffshire 1795', *Northern Scotland*, 2 (2011), 22–35.
11. Kate Teltscher, 'The Sentimental Ambassador: The Letters of George Bogle from Bengal, Bhutan and Tibet, 1770–1781', in Rebecca Earle (ed.), *Epistolary Selves: Letters and Letter-Writers, 1600–1945* (Aldershot, 1999), 80.
12. Aberdeen University Special Libraries and Collections, Patrick Duff to James Duff, from Fort William, Bengal, 15 July 1785, Gordon of Letterfourie papers, Letters of Patrick 'Tiger' Duff, Bundle 2.
13. Elizabeth Vibert, 'Writing "Home": Sibling Intimacy and Mobility in a Scottish Colonial Memoir', in Tony Ballantyne and Antoinette Burton (eds), *Moving Subjects: Gender, Mobility and Intimacy in an Age of Global Empire* (Urbana and Chicago, 2009), 69.
14. David Hancock, 'Commerce and Conversation in the Eighteenth-Century Atlantic: The Invention of Madeira Wine', *Journal of Interdisciplinary History*, 29:2 (1998), 197–219; David Hancock, *Oceans of Wine: Madeira and the Emergence of American Trade and Taste* (New Haven, 2009).
15. Arriving in India in 1761, Patrick served until his involvement in the mutiny of European officers in 1766. He was dismissed from the service and sent back to Britain, but he lobbied

successfully to return, which he did in 1769. In 1772 he had an encounter with a tiger when out hunting, which gave him the nickname 'Tiger' Duff throughout the army. It also caused him to return to Britain for health reasons in 1774. Here he married his cousin, returning with her in 1775. This was his longest tour of duty, finishing with his return to Britain in 1789 to visit his new estate. He returned to India in 1790 to fight in the campaign for Seringapatam, returning to Britain on its successful completion in 1792. In 1796, having secured the rank of major-general, he returned to India for the final time, leaving again in late 1797.

16. Aberdeen University Special Libraries and Collections, Patrick Duff to James Gordon, from Calcutta, 24 November 1776, Gordon of Letterfourie papers, Bundle 4.
17. Aberdeen University Special Libraries and Collections, Patrick Duff to James Duff, from Fort William, Bengal, 15 July 1785, Gordon of Letterfourie papers, Bundle 2.
18. Durba Ghosh, *Sex and Family in Colonial India: The Making of Empire* (Cambridge, 2006), 17.
19. Christopher J. Hawes, *Poor Relations: The Making of a Eurasian Community in British India, 1773–1833* (London, 1996), 79.
20. Aberdeen University Special Libraries and Collections, Patrick Duff to James Duff, 15 September 1785, Gordon of Letterfourie papers, Bundle 2.
21. Aberdeen University Special Libraries and Collections, Patrick Duff to James Duff, from Cawnpore, 2 March 1787, Gordon of Letterfourie papers, Bundle 3.
22. Aberdeen University Special Libraries and Collections, Patrick Duff to James Duff, from Cawnpore, 2 March 1787, Gordon of Letterfourie papers, Bundle 3.
23. Deborah Cohen, *Family Secrets: Shame and Privacy in Modern Britain* (New York, 2013), 16.
24. E. M. Collingham, *Imperial Bodies: The Physical Experience of the Raj, c.1800–1947*, (Cambridge, 2001), 76.
25. Aberdeen University Special Libraries and Collections, Patrick Duff to James Duff, from Cawnpore, 22 June 1787, Gordon of Letterfourie papers, Bundle 3.
26. Aberdeen University Special Libraries and Collections, Patrick Duff to James Duff, from Fort William, Bengal, 15 July 1785, Gordon of Letterfourie papers, Bundle 2.
27. Aberdeen University Special Libraries and Collections, Patrick Duff to James Duff, from Fort William, Bengal, 15 July 1785, Gordon of Letterfourie papers, Bundle 2.
28. Aberdeen University Special Libraries and Collections, Patrick Duff to James Duff, from Fort William, Bengal, 15 July 1785, Gordon of Letterfourie papers, Bundle 2.
29. National Library of Scotland, Hector Munro to Henry Dundas 26 April 1791, MSS 1073. For Munro, see Andrew MacKillop, 'The Highlands and the Returning Nabob: Sir Hector Munro of Novar, 1760–1807' in Marjory Harper (ed.) *Emigrant Homecomings: The Return Movement of Migrants, 1600–2000* (Manchester, 2005), 233–61.
30. Ian Carter, *Farm Life in Northeast Scotland 1840–1914: The Poor Man's Country* (Edinburgh, 1979), 15.
31. Samuel Parlby, 'Memoir of Colonel Thomas Deane Pearse', *The British Military Repository*, 2 (Calcutta, 1823), 36.
32. National Register of Archives of Scotland, George Hurt, camp at Lanambaddy about five miles above Serringapatam, to James Grant, London, 25 May 1791, Macpherson-Grant, NRAS771, bundle 426.
33. Alexander Dirom, *A Narrative of the Campaign in India Which Terminated the War with Tippoo Sultan in 1792* (London, 1793), 112.
34. J.W. Kaye (ed.), E. Buckle, *Memoir of the Services of the Bengal Artillery, from the Formation of the Corps to the Present Time, With Some Account of Its Internal Organization* (London, 1852), 146.
35. West Sussex Record Office, Copy letter from Patrick Duff to Sir John Sinclair c. March 1802, PHA9336.
36. Hancock, *Oceans of Wine*, 107–32.
37. Alistair Mutch, 'Europe, the British Empire and the Madeira Trade: Catholicism, Commerce and the Gordon of Letterfourie Network c.1730-c.1800', *Northern Scotland*, 7 (2016), 21–42.
38. National Records of Scotland, James Duff, Madeira to James Ross, Gordon Castle, 18 April 1776, Duke of Gordon muniments, GD44/43/160/5.
39. This aspect of British life in India is rather neglected by Collingham, whose discussion of consumption practices only mentions alcohol in passing, and Madeira wine not at all: Collingham, *Imperial Bodies*, 29, 30.
40. Alfred Spencer (ed.), *Memoirs of William Hickey Vol. 1 (1749–1775)* (London, 1948), 291.

41. Narendra Krishna Sinha (ed.), *Fort William – India House Correspondence: And Other Contemporary Papers Relating Thereto (Public Series). Vol.5 1767–69,* (Delhi, 1949), 526 (2 February 1769).
42. B. A. Saletore (ed.), *Fort William - India House Correspondence: And Other Contemporary Papers Relating Thereto (Public Series). Vol.9 1782–85,* (Delhi, 1959), 540 (22 February 1785).
43. Hancock, *Oceans of Wine*, 136.
44. Grant and Mutch, 'Indian Wealth'.
45. Aberdeen University Special Libraries and Collections, James Duff, London to Patrick Duff, Bengal, 3 October 1784, Gordon of Letterfourie Papers, Tiger box, Bundle two.
46. Stephen Foster, *A Private Empire* (Millers Point, NSW, 2010), 89–98.
47. Aberdeen University Special Libraries and Collections Patrick Duff to James Gordon, from Fort William, Bengal, 17 March 1784, Bundle two.
48. Teltscher, 'Sentimental Ambassador', 83.
49. Aberdeen University Special Libraries and Collections, Patrick Duff to James Gordon, from Fort William, Bengal, 16 March, 1784, Gordon of Letterfourie papers, Bundle two.
50. Tillman Nechtman, *Nabobs: Empire and Identity in Eighteenth-century Britain* (Cambridge, 2010), 133.
51. Aberdeen University Special Libraries and Collections, Patrick Duff to James Gordon, from Fort William, Bengal, 16 March, 1784, Gordon of Letterfourie papers, Bundle 2.
52. A. Tayler and H. Tayler, *The Book of the Duffs*, 2 vols (Edinburgh, 1914), 2:479.
53. Tayler and Tayler, *The Book of the Duffs*, 2:478–9.
54. Slade, 'Carnousie-Banffshire', 238.
55. Tillman Nechtman, 'A Jewel in the Crown? Indian Wealth in Domestic Britain in the Late Eighteenth Century', *Eighteenth-century Studies*, 41:1 (2007), 75.
56. Andrew Mackillop, 'Locality, Nation, and Empire: Scots in Asia, c.1695 – c.1813' in John MacKenzie and T. M. Devine (eds), *Scotland and the British Empire* (Oxford, 2011), 70.
57. Margot Finn, 'Anglo-Indian Lives in the Later Eighteenth and Early Nineteenth Century', *Journal for Eighteenth-Century Studies*, 33:1 (2010), 55.
58. Aberdeen University Special Libraries and Collections, Patrick Duff to James Gordon, 14 September 1780, Gordon of Letterfourie papers, Bundle four.
59. National Records of Scotland, Mr Jas Duff of Madeira & his father Mr Duff of Pitchaish, James Duff to Archibald Grant, 8 November 1775, Grant of Monymusk, GD345/943.
60. George McGilvary, *East India Patronage and the British State: The Scottish Elite and Politics in the Eighteenth Century* (London, 2008), 185.
61. National Records of Scotland, James Gordon to James Ross, 22 July 1777, Duke of Gordon muniments, GD44/43/185/20.
62. Margot Finn, 'Colonial Gifts: Family Politics and the Exchange of Goods in British India, c.1780–1820', *Modern Asian Studies*, 40:1 (2006), 203–31.

Section 5

1. These themes are explored eloquently by Deborah Cohen, *Family Secrets: Shame and Privacy in Modern Britain* (Oxford, 2013) and Alison Light, *Common People: The History of an English Family* (London, 2015).

Chapter 17

1. Kate Clanchy, 'Common People: The History of an English Family (Review)', *Guardian*, 18 October 2014: https://www.theguardian.com/books/2014/oct/18/common-people-the-history-of-an-english-family-review-alison-light.
2. Thank you to Margaret Woodall, archivist at Belmont House, Kent.
3. Samuel Farmer to William Gamul Farmer, 29 March 1795. Letters in the private possession of the family, if not footnoted, are identified in the body of the text by date of composition.
4. Samuel Farmer to William Gamul Farmer, 16 September 1795. For Baring, see John Orbell, 'Baring, Sir Francis, 1st baronet (1740–1810', *Oxford Dictionary of National Biography*, Oxford University Press, 2004. http://www.oxforddnb.com/view/article/1382.

5. For Duncan, see Pamela Nightingale, 'Duncan, Jonathan (bap. 1756, d. 1811)', *Oxford Dictionary of National Biography*, Oxford University Press, 2004.http://www.oxforddnb.com/view/article/8224; for Palmer, see William Dalrymple, *White Mughals: Love and Betrayal in Eighteenth-Century India* (London, 2002); for Malet, see David J. Howlett, 'Malet, Sir Charles Warre, first baronet (1753–1815)', *Oxford Dictionary of National Biography*, Oxford University Press, 2004. http://www.oxforddnb.com/view/article/17876.
6. Sarah Pearsall, *Atlantic Families: Lives and Letters in the Later Eighteenth Century* (Oxford, 2010), 13.
7. Thanks to Diana Tillman for her very helpful work on the Farmer family.
8. Samuel Farmer to William Gamul Farmer, 26 April 1796.
9. Samuel Farmer to William Gamul Farmer, 8 July 1777.
10. Samuel Farmer to William Gamul Farmer, 6 March 1777.
11. This phenomenon and its significance are discussed at length in Leonore Davidoff, *Thicker than Water: Siblings and Their Relations, 1780–1920* (Oxford, 2012).
12. Penelope Farmer, *Sisters: An Anthology* (London, 1999), xvii ff.
13. Gifting of shawls by Company men and women is discussed in Margot C. Finn, 'Colonial Gifts: Family Politics and the Exchange of Goods in British India, c.1780–1820', *Modern Asian Studies*, 40:1 (2006), 203–231.
14. See Catherine Hall, *Macaulay and Son: Architects of Imperial Britain* (London, 2012), and Elizabeth Vibert, 'Writing "Home": Sibling Intimacy and Mobility in a Scottish Colonial Memoir', in Tony Ballantyne and Antoinette Burton (eds), *Moving Subjects: Gender, Mobility, and Intimacy in an Age of Global Empire* (Urbana, 2009), 67–88.
15. British Library, IOR/P/D/62–65.
16. Pearsall, *Atlantic Families*, 13.
17. R.G Thorne, History of Parliament online, Record for Samuel Farmer MP (1748–1839): http://www.historyofparliamentonline.org/volume/1790–1820/member/farmer-samuel-1748–1839.
18. Using the 'Measuring Worth' calculator to determine a real price equivalent for 2015 yields a value today for the piano of £16,630. https://www.measuringworth.com/ukcompare/relativevalue.php.
19. William Macintosh, *Travels in Europe Asia and Africa* (London, 1782), 250–3.
20. For the stereotype of the nabob, see Tillman Nechtman, *Nabobs: Empire and Identity in Eighteenth-Century Britain* (Cambridge, 2010).
21. Dalrymple, *White Mughals*.
22. For this distinguished family of Parsi merchants and shipbuilders, who also boasted strong trade ties with the French and the Americans, see Paula Bradstreet Richter, 'Fabrics and Fashion of the India Trade at a Salem Sea Captain's Wedding', in Patricia Johnston and Caroline Frank (eds), *Global Trade and the Visual Arts in Federal New England* (Durham, NH, 2014), 198–199.
23. Pamela Nightingale, *Trade and Empire in Western India, 1784–1806* (London, 1970).
24. Cited by Hall, *Macaulay and Son*, 239.
25. Maria Graham, *Journal of a Residence in India* (Edinburgh, 1812), 136.
26. Cited by Hall, *Macaulay and Son*, 216.
27. James Forbes, *Oriental Memoirs: Selected and Abridged from a Series of Familiar Letters Written during Seventeen Years' Residence in India* (London, 1813).
28. Forbes, *Oriental Memoirs*, vol. I, 548.
29. Linda Colley, *Captives: Britain, Empire and the World, 1600–1850* (London, 2002); *The Ordeal of Elizabeth Marsh: A Woman in World History* (London, 2007).
30. Pamela Nightingale, *Fortune and Integrity: A Study of the Moral Attitudes in the Indian Diary of George Paterson, 1769–1774* (Oxford, 1985), 39.
31. Sophia Kelly, (ed.), *The Life of Mrs. Sherwood, Chiefly Autobiographical; With Extracts from Mr. Sherwood's Journal during His Imprisonment in France and Residence in India* (London, 1854).
32. Hall, *Macaulay and Son*, 238.
33. William Dalrymple, quoted by Nechtman, *Nabobs*, 171.
34. John Gillis, *A World of Their Own Making: Myth, Ritual and a Quest for Family Values* (New York, 1996).
35. British Library, General letter to Bombay, 1762, IOR/E/4/33.

36. Even in the nineteenth century, European death rates remained high. See Philip Curtin, *Death by Migration: Europe's Encounter with the Tropical World in the Nineteenth Century* (Cambridge, 1989).
37. Carsten Niebuhr, *Travels through Arabia and Other Countries in the East* (London, 1763), vol. 2, 375.
38. British Library, IOR/ J/1/432, 367.
39. See Peter Marshall, *East Indian Fortunes: The British in Bengal in the Eighteenth Century* (Oxford, 1976). For trade and risk in this period, see Holden Furber, *John Company at Work: A Study of European Expansion in India in the Late Eighteenth Century* (Cambridge, MA, 1948), and Huw Bowen, *The Business of Empire: The East India Company and Imperial Britain, 1765–1833* (Cambridge, 2006).
40. Nightingale, *Trade in Western India*, 79.
41. See esp. Durba Ghosh, *Sex and the Family in Colonial India: The Making of Empire* (Cambridge, 2006).
42. *Selections from the Letters, Despatches and Other State Papers Preserved in the Bombay Secretariat: Home Series* (Bombay, 1887), 197.
43. British Library, IOR/P/E/6, 58–66.
44. British Library, IOR/L/L/2/21.
45. Edward Moor, *The Hindu Pantheon* (London, 1810), 359.
46. Forbes, *Oriental Memoirs*, vol. 2, 548.
47. British Library, IOR/P/D/65, 342.
48. James Rennell, *Memoir of a Map of Hindoostan: Or, the Mogul Empire* (London, 1788), 148.
49. Nightingale, *Trade and Empire*, 74.
50. For his slaving interests, see *An Account of the Number of Vessels, with the Amount of their Tonnage, their Names, the Port to which They Belong, and the Names of the Respective Owners of Each, that Have Cleared out from the Ports of London, Bristol and Liverpool, to the Coast of Africa, for the Purpose of Purchasing Slaves, in the Three Years Preceding the 5th of January 1792*, House of Commons Sessional Papers of the Eighteenth Century, 82: 329–37.
51. Nightingale, *Trade in Western India*, 73–110. Nightingale gives a detailed description and critique of the arrangements WGF made for the collection of the pepper tax in the Malabar and for the organization of the mint at Mahé.
52. Nightingale, *Trade in Western India*, 79.
53. British Library, Home Miscellany CDXXXVIII, Walter Ewer to Henry Dundas 17 July 1797.
54. British Library, IOR P/E/6 1793, 58–66.
55. Quoted in Nightingale, *Trade in Western India*, 99.
56. British Library, 11 January 1795 letter to Sam enclosing copy of the defence of his tax arrangements, IOR/P/366/16.
57. British Library, James Stevens to Bombay 20 December 1794, IOR/P/366/17, 28–9.
58. Letter book in Farmer family possession, two letters of 17 June 1795 by William Gamul Farmer to Jonathan Duncan defending himself.
59. Michelguglielmo Tori, 'Trapped inside the Colonial Order: The Hindu Bankers of Surat and Their Business World during the Second Half of the Eighteenth Century', *Modern Asian Studies*, 25:2 (1991), 367–401.
60. British Library, *Princess Amelia*: Journal, IOR/L/MAR/B/36J: 23 February 1795–10 September 1796.
61. The National Archives, Kew, Will of 28 February 1798, PROB 11/1301/252.
62. The National Archives, Will of 9 June 1839, PROB 11/1912/56.
63. James M. Holzman, *The Nabobs in England: A Study of the Returned Anglo-Indian, 1760–1785* (New York, 1926).
64. R.G. Thorne, *The House of Commons, 1790–1820* (London, 1986), vol. I, 291.
65. Nonsuch Sale Catalogue in the collection of Bourne Hall Museum. Ewell Surrey.

Chapter 18

1. Alan Tritton, *When the Tiger Fought the Thistle: The Tragedy of Colonel William Baillie of the Madras Army* (London, 2013), 7–8.
2. In this the history of the Melvills over several generations complements the family biography of the Stracheys. See for example Barbara Caine, *Bombay to Bloomsbury: A Biography of the Strachey Family* (Oxford, 2005) 17–22.

3. The same Christian names are frequently used in the family. If there is a common Christian name and the context is unclear, names are numbered in order of birth dates, so Philip Melvill will be referred to as Philip I.
4. *Memoirs of the Late Philip Melvill, Esq. Lieut. Gov. of Pendennis Castle, Cornwall: With an Appendix Containing Extracts From His Diaries and Letters Selected by a Friend* (London, 1812), 9–11. Soon after Philip's death an evangelical friend or relation published this memoir anonymously. An abridged version of this was published in Edinburgh in 1825.
5. Tritton, *When the Tiger Fought the Thistle*, 149–55.
6. *Memoirs of the Late Philip Melvill*, 44–5.
7. *Memoirs of the Late Philip Melvill*, 46.
8. For more on being taking captive in this period see Linda Colley, *Captives: Britain, Empire and the World 1600–1850* (London, 2002).
9. *Memoirs of the Late Philip Melvill*, 62.
10. *Memoirs of the Late Philip Melvill*, 66.
11. British Library, Sir James Cosmo Melvill papers, 1811–1957, Mss Eur Photo 071, 122.
12. *Memoirs of the Late Philip Melvill*, 87.
13. Bob Dunstan, *The Book of Falmouth & Penryn* (Chesham, 1975), 34–35.
14. *Memoirs of the Late Philip Melvill*, 122.
15. S. Pasfield Oliver, *Pendennis and St Mawes: An Historical Sketch of Two Cornish Castles* (London, 1875), 77–8. Oliver is quoting from Fortescue Hitchens, *The History of Cornwall*, vol. 2, Samuel Drew (ed) (London, 1824), 257–8.
16. British Library, Philip Melvill (1760–1811), 1804–5, Add MS 58438.
17. *Memoirs of the Late Philip Melvill*, 129.
18. *Memoirs of the Late Philip Melvill*, 133.
19. E.J. Joubert de la Ferté, *The Melvill Family, A Roll of Honour of the Descendants of Philip Melvill and their Immediate Connections by Marriage in the Years of the World War 1914–18* (London, 1920), 6.
20. British Library, Sir James Cosmo Melvill papers, 1811–1957, Mss Eur Photo 071, 122.
21. The National Archives, 1841 census return HO107/1050/3, 4.
22. J. S. Cotton, 'Anstruther, Sir John, fourth baronet and first baronet (1753–1811)', rev. T. H. Bowyer, *Oxford Dictionary of National Biography*, Oxford, 2004; online edn, Jan 2008. Accessed August 2013. http://www.oxforddnb.com/view/article/587.
23. *Memoirs of the Late Philip Melvill*, 123. However, according to his entry in the *Oxford Dictionary of National Biography* he started with the EIC in 1808. See E. I. Carlyle, 'Melvill, Sir James Cosmo (1792–1861)', rev. Katherine Prior, *Oxford Dictionary of National Biography*, Oxford, 2004. Accessed August 2013. http://www.oxforddnb.com/view/article/18541.
24. de la Ferté, *Melvill Family*, 9.
25. William Foster, *The East India House: Its History and Associations* (London, 1924), 136.
26. Foster, *East India House*, 154.
27. Foster, *East India House*, 226.
28. John M. Robson, Martin Moir and Zawahir Moir (eds), John Stuart Mill, *Writings on India* vol. 33 (London, 1990), xx.
29. John William Kaye, *Lives of Indian Officers*, vol. 1 (London, 1867), 434.
30. http://www.historyofparliamentonline.org/volume/1820–1832/member/huskisson-william-1770–1830. Accessed 30 March 2014.
31. Edward Thornton, *The History of the British Empire in India*, vol. 5 (London, 1843), 285–86.
32. Thornton, *History of the British Empire in India,* 304.
33. These and the following observations are from Carlyle, 'Melvill, Sir James Cosmo (1792–1861)', n.p.
34. Robson, Moir and Moir, *Writings on India*, xxvi.
35. Carlyle, 'Melvill, Sir James Cosmo (1792–1861)', n.p.
36. British Library, Sir James Cosmo Melvill papers, 1811–1957, Mss Eur Photo 071, 60–61. This was later followed up in the 1920s by Lt Col P.J. Melvill in correspondence with E.J. Joubert de la Ferté. See British Library, Sir James Cosmo Melvill papers, 1811–1957, Mss Eur Photo 071, 62–65.
37. de la Ferté, *The Melvill Family*, 9.
38. Arthur Christopher Benson and Viscount Reginald Baliol Brett Esher (eds), *The Letters of Queen Victoria* vol. 3 1854–61 (London, 1908), 229.
39. *Gentleman's Magazine* (1824), 572.

40. http://www.hampsteadheath.net/cannon-hall.html. Accessed 26 March 2014.
41. Gerald Walkden, *Tandridge Parish News*, February 2010, n.p.
42. Walkden, *Tandridge Parish News,* n.p.
43. Mary Kenyon, *A History of All Saints Church Hutton* (Essex County Council, 1999), n.p.
44. Cambridge Alumni database, http://venn.lib.cam.ac.uk/Documents/acad/search.html, accessed August 2013; *London Gazette*, 15 March 1879.
45. England & Wales, National Probate Calendar (Index of Wills and Administrations) for 1882, 184.
46. Cambridge Alumni database; 1st Smith's prize and 2nd Wrangler.
47. Imogen Thomas, *Haileybury 1805–1987* (Hertford, 1987), 24.
48. Much of the information about Henry Melvill comes from G. C. Boase, 'Melvill, Henry (1798–1871)', rev. H. C. G. Matthew, *Oxford Dictionary of National Biography*, Oxford, 2004. Accessed August 2013. http://www.oxforddnb.com/view/article/18540.
49. E. T. Cook and Alexander Wedderburn (eds), *Works of John Ruskin*, vol. 35 (London, 1908), 386.
50. C. E. Buckland, *Dictionary of Indian Biography* (London, 1906), 285.
51. Cambridge Alumni database.
52. Probate Calendar, 1878, 183.
53. Buckland, *Dictionary of Indian Biography*, 285.
54. Cambridge Alumni database.
55. *The Times*, 22 September 1854.
56. *Allen's India Mail* on FIBIS database, http://search.fibis.org/frontis/bin/, accessed at various times.
57. *London Gazette*, 2 September 1870.
58. *London Gazette*, 28 July 1878.
59. Foster, *East India House*, 228.
60. Buckland, *Dictionary of Indian Biography*, 285.
61. Edward Chilton, 'Joubert de la Ferté, Sir Philip Bennet (1887–1965)', rev. Christina J. M. Goulter, *Oxford Dictionary of National Biography*, Oxford, 2004; online edn, Jan 2011. Accessed August 2013. http://www.oxforddnb.com/view/article/34244.
62. Cambridge Alumni database.
63. William Wilson Hunter, *Bombay, 1885 to 1890: a Study in Indian Administration* (Oxford, 1892), 64.
64. British Library, Sir James Cosmo Melvill papers, 1811–1957, Mss Eur Photo 071, 177–86. Contains newspaper cuttings and letters on the subject of the Muslim Melvill. Unfortunately, the cuttings are not dated nor does it say which newspapers they are from. It is not clear as to which Melvill some of the letters are addressed and the signatures on the letters are not clear.
65. British Library, Sir James Cosmo Melvill papers, 1811–1957, Mss Eur Photo 071, 179–81.
66. See William Dalrymple, *White Mughals: Love and Betrayal in Eighteenth-Century India* (New York and London, 2003); Durba Ghosh, *Sex and the Family in Colonial India: the Making of Empire* (Cambridge, 2006).
67. British Library, Sir James Cosmo Melvill papers, 1811–1957, Mss Eur Photo 071, 178.
68. British Library, British India Office Ecclesiastic Returns, parish register transcripts from the Presidency of Bengal 1713–1948, N-1-192, 78; N-1-205, 25; N-1-242, 279; N-1-243, 247.
69. For more on the importance of sibling relationships see Leonore Davidoff, *Thicker Than Water: Siblings and Their Relations, 1780–1920* (Oxford, 2012).

Chapter 19

1. Information obtained from Professor A. M. K. Masumi, William Jones Professor at the Persian Department of the Asiatic Society of Calcutta, who studied the seal on 28 July 1995.
2. See for example, British Library, Francis Sykes to Warren Hastings, 28 Jan 1773, Add Ms 29133, 347.
3. The term 'factory' was used to describe a trading post, which was often, as in the case of Cossimbazar, fortified.

4. As cited in John Malcolm, *The Life of Robert, Lord Clive: Collected from the Family Papers Communicated by the Earl of Powis*, vol. 2 (London, 1836), 318–20.
5. As cited in C. S. Srinivasachari (ed.), *Fort William India House Correspondence and Other Contemporary Papers Relating Thereto*, vol. 4 (Delhi, 1962), 339.
6. William Bolts, *Considerations on Indian Affairs*, vol. 1 (London, 1772–5), 84.
7. P. J. Marshall, *East Indian Fortunes: The British in Bengal in the Eighteenth Century* (Oxford, 1976), 45.
8. British Library, Francis Sykes to Warren Hastings, 28 January 1773, Add Ms 29133, 347.
9. British Library, Francis Sykes to Warren Hastings, 13 May 1776, Add Ms 29137, 189.
10. British Library, Francis Sykes to Warren Hastings, 29 March 1777, Add Ms 29138, 280–281.
11. British Library, Francis Sykes to Warren Hastings, 8 March 1785, Add Ms 29168, 166.
12. S. C. Nandy, *Life and Times of Cantoo Baboo*, vol. 2 (Calcutta, 1981), 275.
13. S. C. Nandy, *Life and Times of Cantoo Baboo*, vol. 1 (Calcutta, 1978).
14. The Zemindari system was one whereby the Zemindar or landholder was responsible for collecting revenues on behalf of the rulers from land held by a number of cultivators while retaining a percentage (usually 10 per cent) for himself.
15. Nandy, *Life and Times of Cantoo Baboo*, vol. 2, 407.
16. S.C. Nandy, *History of the Cossimbazar Raj in the Nineteenth Century* (Calcutta, 1986).
17. Nandy, *History of the Cossimbazar Raj in the Nineteenth Century,* Chapter 8. See also foreword to publication, written by P. J. Marshall: Nandy, *History of the Cossimbazar Raj in the Nineteenth Century,* vii.
18. Nandy, *History of the Cossimbazar Raj in the Nineteenth Century,* 286.
19. As cited in S. C. Nandy, *History of the Cossimbazar Raj in the Twentieth Century* (Calcutta, 1995), 348.
20. Nandy, *History of the Cossimbazar Raj in the Twentieth Century*, 473.
21. Nandy, *History of the Cossimbazar Raj in the Twentieth Century*, 603.
22. S. C. Nandy in discussions with Sir John Sykes.
23. Marshall, *East Indian Fortunes*, 238.
24. As cited in in Robert Blake, *Disraeli* (London, 1966), 143.
25. Blake, *Disraeli*, 143.
26. 'Great Fire. The Pantechnicon Destroyed', *The Times*, 14 February 1874.
27. In discussions between Sir John Sykes 10th Baronet and Sir Francis Sykes 9th Baronet.
28. Private Collection, S. C. Nandy to J. Sykes, 10 June 1978.
29. Private Collection, S. C. Nandy to J. Sykes, 25 June 1993.

Conclusion

1. Jan de Vries, 'Understanding Eurasian Trade in the Era of the Trading Companies', in Maxine Berg, Felicia Gottmann, Hanna Hodacs and Chris Nierstrasz (eds), *Goods from the East, 1600–1800: Trading Eurasia* (Basingstoke: 2015), 22.
2. Michael Fisher, *Counterflows to Colonialism: Indian Travellers and Settlers in Britain, 1600–1857* (Delhi, 2004) explores these journeys in greater depth.
3. Deborah Cohen's *Family Secrets: Shame and Privacy in Modern Britain* (Oxford, 2013), chap. 1 provides a wonderful prototype for such research.

Bibliography

Archives

Aberdeen University Special Libraries and Collections, Aberdeen
Berkshire Record Office, Reading
British Library, London
Bodleian Library, Oxford
Essex Record Office, Chelmsford
Gloucester Record Office, Gloucester
Guildhall Library, London
Hackney Archives, London
Kent Library and History Centre, Maidstone
London Metropolitan Archives, London
National Library of Scotland, Edinburgh
National Library of Wales, Aberystwyth
National Monument Record of Wales, Aberystwyth
National Records of Scotland, Edinburgh
National Register of Archives of Scotland, Edinburgh
Royal Astronomical Society, London
Raynham Hall Archive
West Sussex Record Office, Chichester

Published Primary Sources

Periodicals

The Asiatic Annual Register for 1799 Vol I (London, 1801)
Blackwood's Lady's Magazine (London)
Calcutta Review (Calcutta)
Daily Courant (London)
Dundee Courier (Dundee)
The Edinburgh Annual Register for 1816 Vol IX (Edinburgh, 1820)
Essex Review (London)
Farmer's Magazine (Edinburgh)
Gentleman's Magazine (London)
The Hindu (Chennai)
Lloyd's Evening Post (London)
London Gazette (London)
Madras District Gazetteer (Madras)
Morning Chronicle and London Advertiser (London)
Morning Post and Fashionable World (London)
Oxford Journal (Oxford)

Post Boy (London)
St James's Chronicle or the British Evening Post (London)
Tandridge Parish News (Tandridge, East Surrey)
The World (London)
World and Fashionable Advertiser (London)

Printed

An Account of the Number of Vessels, with the Amount of their Tonnage, their Names, the Port to which They Belong, and the Names of the Respective Owners of Each, that Have Cleared out from the Ports of London, Bristol and Liverpool, to the Coast of Africa, for the Purpose of Purchasing Slaves, in the Three Years Preceding the 5th of January 1792, House of Commons Sessional Papers of the Eighteenth Century, 82: 329–37.
A New and Complete History of Essex by a Gentleman, vol. 4 (Chelmsford, 1771).
Catalogue of the Valuable Contents of Daylesford House, Worcestershire, the Seat of the Late Right Hon. Warren Hastings (London, 1853).
'Celebrities at home: No. VIII. Mr. Lowe at Sherbrooke', *The World: A Journal for Men and Women*, 119 (11 October 1876), 4–5.
Descent of the Family of Casamayorga, or Casamayor, from the Royal Houses of Castille and Leon (London, 1871).
'Hornby v Hunter', in *Reports of Cases Decided in the High Court of Chancery* Vol XLVI (London, 1871), 77–87.
'Letter to the Royal Society from George Edwards', *Philosophical Transactions (1683–1775)* 61 (1771), 55–6.
London as it is to-day: Where to go and what to see (London, 1851).
Memoirs of the Late Philip Melvill, Esq. Lieut. Gov. of Pendennis Castle, Cornwall: With an Appendix Containing Extracts From His Diaries and Letters Selected by a Friend ... together with Two Letters and a Sermon, Occasioned by His Death (London, 1812).
Recollections of the Deccan: With Miscellaneous Sketches and Letters (Calcutta, 1838).
Report of the Cause between Hugh Doherty, Esq., Plaintiff, and Philip Wm. Wyatt, Esq., Defendant, for Criminal Conversation with the Plaintiff's Wife (London, 1811).
Rule CIV (Instructions from the Commanders of The East India Company's Own Ships to Their Officers, &c) (London, 1819).
The History of England: During the Reigns of King William and Queen Mary ... By Mr. Oldmixon (London, 1735).
The Letters and Journals of Lady Mary Coke, vol. 4 (Bath, 1970).
Adolph, Herr, *An Illustrated description of the Diorama of the Ganges* (London, 1850).
Amherst, Jeffrey, *Wandering Abroad: The Autobiography of Jeffrey Amherst* (London, 1976).
Andrews, C. Bruyn (ed.), *The Torrington Diaries Containing the Tours through England and Wales of the Hon. John Byng (Later Fifth Viscount Torrington) between the Years 1781 and 1794 Vol II* (London, 1935).
Austen, Jane, *Mansfield Park* (London, 1814).
Baird, Henry Carey, *The Interior Decorator, Being the Laws of Harmonious Colourings Applied to Interior Decorations with Observation on the Practice of House Painting* (Philadelphia, 1867).
Beatson, A., *A View of the Origin and Conduct of the War with Tippoo Sultaun; Comprising a Narrative of the Operations of the Army under the Command of Lieutenant-General George Harris, and of the Siege of Seringapatam* (London, 1800).
Benson, Arthur Christopher and Viscount Reginald Baliol Brett Esher (eds), *The Letters of Queen Victoria*, vol. 3 1854–61 (London, 1908).
Bohn, Henry G., *Diary and Correspondence of John Evelyn* vol. 1 (London, 1859).
Bolts, William, *Considerations on Indian Affairs*, vol. 1 (London, 1772–5).
Buckle, E., *Memoir of the Services of the Bengal Artillery, from the Formation of the Corps to the Present Time, With Some Account of Its Internal Organization*, J. W. Kaye (ed.) (London, 1852).
Burke, Bernard, A., *Genealogical and Heraldic Dictionary of the Landed Gentry of Great Britain and Ireland* (London, 1855).

Campbell, M. O., *Supplement to a Memorial History of the Campbells of Melfort Argyllshire, and of Other Highland Families with Whom They Have Intermarried* (London, 1894).
Carnegie, David, and Andrew Agnew, *Protestant Exiles from France in the Reign of Louis XIV* (London, 1871).
Cave-Brown, J., *History of Brasted, Its Manor, Parish and Church*, vol. 2 (Westerham, 1874).
Chauncy, Sir Henry, *The Historical Antiquities of Hertfordshire* (London, 1700).
Chippendale, Thomas, *The Gentleman and Cabinet Maker's Director* (London, 1754).
Climenson, Emily J. (ed.), *Diaries of Mrs Philip Lybbe Powys of Hardwick House, Oxon* (London, 1899).
Clutterbuck, Robert, *The History and Antiquities of the County of Hertford*, 3 vols (London, 1815–27).
Collins, Athur, *The English Baronetage*, vol. 4 (London, 1741).
Collins, Wilkie, *The Moonstone* (1868).
Cook, E. T. and Alexander Wedderburn (eds), *Works of John Ruskin* vol. 35 (London, 1908).
Cooke, George Alexander, *Topographical and Statistical Description of the County of Hertford* (London, 1817).
Cozens-Hardy, Basil (ed.), *The Diary of Sylas Neville, 1767–1788* (London, 1950).
Cussans, John Edwin, *History of Hertfordshire*, 3 vols (London, 1870–81).
Dirom, Alexander, *A Narrative of the Campaign in India Which Terminated the War with Tippoo Sultan in 1792* (London, 1793).
Eden, Emily, *Up the Country: Letters Written to her sister from the Upper Provinces of India by the Hon. Emily Eden* (London, 1866).
Ellis, Henry, *Journal of the Proceedings of the Late Embassy to China* (London, 1817).
Fletcher, W. and Edmund J. Niemann, *A Tour round Reading, a Guide to Its Environs* (Reading and London, 1840).
Forbes, James, *Oriental Memoirs: Selected and Abridged from a Series of Familiar Letters Written during Seventeen Years' Residence in India* (London, 1813).
Fortune, Robert, *A Residence among the Chinese* (London, 1865).
Gay, John, *To a Lady on Her Passion for Old China* (London, 1725).
Gilpin, William, *Remarks on Forest Scenery, and Other Woodland Views* (London, 1791).
Graham, Maria, *Journal of a Residence in India* (Edinburgh, 1812).
Grierson, Herbert J. C. (ed.), *The Letters of Walter Scott*, vol. VII (London, 1932–1937).
Grindlay, Robert, *Scenery, Costumes and Architecture, Chiefly of the Western Side of India* (London, 1830).
Hakewill, James, *The History of Windsor and its Neighbourhood* (London, 1813).
Hamilton, Anthony, *Memoirs of Count Grammont*, 2 vols (London, 1811).
Hargrove, E., *The History of the Castle, Town and Forest of Knaresborough with Harrogate* (4th ed, York, 1789).
Hay, D. R., *The Laws of Harmonious Colouring adapted to Interior Decoration* (6th ed., Edinburgh, 1847).
Hitchens, Fortescue, *The History of Cornwall*, vol. 2, Samuel Drew (ed.) (London, 1824).
Hooker, J. D. (ed.), *Journal of the Rt Hon Sir Joseph Banks* vol. 4 (New York, 1896).
Hunter, William Wilson, *Bombay, 1885 to 1890: a Study in Indian Administration* (Oxford, 1892).
Jones, Harford, *An Account of the Transactions of His Majesty's Mission to the Court of Persia 1807–1811* vol. 1 (London, 1834).
Kaye, John William, *Lives of Indian Officers*, vol. 1 (London, 1867).
Kelly, Sophia (ed.), *The Life of Mrs. Sherwood, Chiefly Autobiographical; With Extracts from Mr. Sherwood's Journal during His Imprisonment in France and Residence in India* (London, 1854).
Lewis, W. S. (ed.), *Yale Edition of Horace Walpole's Correspondence* (New Haven, 1937).
Lockhart, John Gibson, *Memoirs of the Life of Sir Walter Scott*, vol. 3 (Paris, 1838).
Love, Henry Davidson, *The Vestiges of Old Madras, 1640–1800*, vol. 2 (New Delhi, 1913).
Macintosh, William, *Travels in Europe Asia and Africa* (London, 1782).
Mackenzie, Alexander, *History of the Frasers of Lovat with Genealogies of the Principal Families of the Name: To Which Is Added Those of Dunballoch and Phopachy* (Inverness, 1896).
Macky, John, *A Journey through England*, vol. 1 (London, 1724).
Malcolm, Major General Sir John, *The Life of Robert, Lord Clive: Collected from the Family Papers Communicated by the Earl of Powis*, vol. 2 (London, 1836).
Marshall, William, *The Rural Economy of Yorkshire: Comprizing the Management of Landed Estates, and the Present Practice of Husbandry in the Agricultural Districts of that County*, vol. 1 (London, 1788).

Martin, A. Patchett, *Life and Letters of the Right Honourable Robert Lowe, Viscount Sherbrooke, with a Memoir of Sir John Coape Sherbrooke* (London, 1893).
Martin, John Biddulph, *The Grasshopper in Lombard Street* (London, 1892).
Miller, Lady Anna, *Letters from Italy, Describing the Manners, Customs, Antiquities, Painting*, vol. 2 (London, 1776).
Moor, Edward, *The Hindu Pantheon* (London, 1810).
Niebuhr, Carsten, *Travels through Arabia and Other Countries in the East*, vol. 2 (London, 1763).
Oliver, S. Pasfield, *Pendennis and St Mawes: An Historical Sketch of Two Cornish Castles* (London, 1875).
Parkes, Fanny, *Grand Moving Diorama of Hindostan, displaying the scenery of the Hoogly, the Bhagirathi, and the Ganges, from Fort William, Bengal, to Gangoutri, in the Himalaya* (London, 1851).
Parkes, Fanny, *Wanderings of a Pilgrim in Search of the Picturesque during Four-and-twenty Years in the East; with Revelations of Life in the Zenana*, 2 vols (London, 1850).
Parkes, Fanny, *Wanderings of a Pilgrim*, 2 vols (Karachi, 1975).
Parlby, Samuel, 'Memoir of Colonel Thomas Deane Pearse', *The British Military Repository*, 2 (Calcutta, 1823), 1–89.
Phillips, R., *Monthly Magazine and British Register*, 30:2 (1810), 199.
Postlethwayt, Malachy, *The Universal Dictionary of Trade and Commerce* (London, 1757).
Price, F. G. H., *A Handbook of London Bankers* (London, 1890).
Rennell, James, *Memoir of a Map of Hindoostan: Or, the Mogul Empire* (London, 1788).
Rogers, Charles, *Genealogical Memoirs of the Family of Sir Walter Scott, Bart. of Abbotsford* (London, 1877).
Saletore, B. A. (ed.), *Fort William - India House Correspondence: And Other Contemporary Papers Relating Thereto (Public Series)*, vol. 9 1782–85 (Delhi, 1959).
Schofield, James, *The Scarborough Guide* (2nd ed., Hull, 1796).
Selections from the Letters, Despatches and Other State Papers Preserved in the Bombay Secretariat: Home Series (Bombay, 1887).
Sinha, Narendra Krishna (ed.), *Fort William - India House Correspondence: And Other Contemporary Papers Relating Thereto (Public Series)*, vol. 5 1767–69 (Delhi, 1949).
Srinivasachari, C. S. (ed.), *Fort William India House Correspondence and Other Contemporary Papers Relating Thereto*, vol. 4 (Delhi, 1962).
Staunton, G. L., *An Authentic Account of an Embassy from the King of Great Britain to the Emperor of China* (London, 1797).
Thornton, Edward, *The History of the British Empire in India*, vol. 5 (London, 1843).
Topham, Charles Bowden, *A Tour through Ireland* (Dublin, 1791).
Valpy, A. J., 'On the Life and Times of Casimir', *The Classical Journal*, 31 (1825).
Veddar, David, *Memoir of Sir Walter Scott, Bart: With Critical Notices of His Writings Compiled from Various Authentic Sources* (Dundee, 1832).
Webster, Thomas, *The Case of Josiah Marshall Heath, the Inventor and Introducer of the Manufacture of Welding Cast Steel from British Iron* (London, 1856).
Williamson, Captain Thomas, *The East India Vade-Mecum; Or, Complete Guide to Gentlemen Intended for the Civil, Military, or Naval Service of the Hon. East India Company*, 2 vols (London, 1810).

Secondary Sources

An Inventory of the Ancient Monuments in Anglesey (Aberystwyth, 1937).
An Inventory on the Ancient Monuments in Caernarvonshire: I East: the Cantref of Arllechwedd and the Commote of Creuddyn (Aberystwyth, 1956).
An Inventory on the Ancient Monuments in Caernarvonshire: II Central: the Cantref of Arfon and the Commote of Eifionydd (Aberystwyth, 1958).
Antique and Modern English and Continental Furniture, 1920 October 26 – November 3 (London, 1920).
Basildon Park, Berkshire (Warrington, 2002).
'The Harrison & Townshend Anglo-Indian Furniture', *The Exceptional Sale*, Christie's, London, 7 July 2011.

The Exceptional Sale, Christie's, London, 7 July 2011.
Adams, Ruth, 'The V&A, the Destruction of the Country House and the Creation of 'English Heritage', *Museum & Society*, 11:1 (2013), 1–18.
Adamson, Glenn, G. Riello, and S. Teaseley (eds), *Global Design History* (London, 2011).
Alayrae-Fielding, Vanessa, '"Frailty Thy Name is China": Women, Chinoiserie and the Treatment of Low Culture in Eighteenth-Century England', *Women's History Review*, 18:4 (2009), 659–68.
Aldrich, Megan (ed.), *The Craces: Royal Decorators 1768–1899* (Brighton, 1990).
Anderson, David, 'Guilty Secrets: Deceit, Denial, and the Discovery of Kenya's "Migrated Archive"', *History Workshop Journal*, 80:1 (2015), 142–60.
Andrews, Jonathan, 'Monro, John (1715–1791)', *Oxford Dictionary of National Biography* (Oxford, 2004). [http://www.oxforddnb.com/view/article/18976, accessed 21 May 2014].
Appadurai, Arjun (ed.) *The Social life of Things: Commodities in Cultural Perspective* (Cambridge, 1986).
Archer, Mildred, *India and British Portraiture, 1770–1825* (London, 1979).
Archer, Mildred, Christopher Rowell and Robert Skelton, *Treasures from India: The Clive Collection at Powis Castle* (London, 1987).
Arkell, T., N. Evans and N. Goose (eds), *When Death Do Us Part: Understanding and Interpreting the Probate Records of Early Modern England* (Oxford, 2000).
Arnold, David, *The Tropics and the Travelling Gaze: India, Landscapes and Science, 1800–1856* (Seattle and London, 2006).
Ashan, Peter, *Remembering Slavery and Its Legacy, 1807–2007: The Roots of Diversity in Waltham Forest* (London, 2007).
Aslet, Clive, *The English House. The Story of a Nation at Home* (London, 2008).
Aydelotte, William O. (ed.), *The Dimensions of Quantitative Research in History* (Oxford, 1972).
Baird, Christina, *Liverpool China Traders* (Bern, 2007).
Ballantyne, Tony, and Antoinette Burton (eds), *Moving Subjects: Gender, Mobility and Intimacy in an Age of Global Empire* (Urbana and Chicago, 2009).
Barczewski, Stephanie, *Country Houses and the British Empire 1700–1930* (Manchester, 2014).
Barcezewski, Stephanie, 'Is Britishness always British?', in M. Farr and X. Guegan (eds), *The British abroad since the Eighteenth Century* Vol I, *Travellers and Tourists* (Heidelberg, 2013), 38–55.
Barnard, Toby, *Making the Grand Figure: Lives and Possessions in Ireland, 1641–1770* (New Haven and London, 2004).
Barnwell, Rachael and Richard Suggett, *Y Tu Mewn i Gartrefi Cymru/Inside Welsh Homes* (Aberystwyth, 2012).
Beard, Geoffrey, *Decorative Plasterwork in Great Britain* (Abingdon, 2015).
Beckert, Sven, *Empire of Cotton: A New History of Global Capitalism* (London, 2014).
Beckles, Hilary, *Britain's Black Debt: Reparations for Caribbean Slavery and Native Genocide* (Mona, 2012).
Benedict, Barbara, 'Encounters with the Object: Advertisements, Time, and Literary Discourse in the Early Eighteenth-Century Thing Poem', *Eighteenth-Century Studies*, 40:2 (2007), 193–207.
Bennell, Anthony S., 'Lake, Gerard, First Viscount Lake of Delhi (1744–1808)', *Oxford Dictionary of National Biography* (Oxford, 2004). [http://www.oxforddnb.com/view/article/15900, accessed 22 October 2016].
Bennett, Tony, *The Birth of the Museum: History, Theory, Politics* (London, 1995).
Bennett, Tony, Fiona Cameron, Nélia Dias, Ben Dibley, Rodney Harrison, Ira Jacknis and Conal McCarthy, *Collecting, Ordering, Governing: Anthropology, Museums and Liberal Government* (Durham, NC, 2017).
Bennett, Tony and Patrick Joyce (eds), Material Powers: Cultural Studies, History and the Material Turn (London, 2010).
Beresford, Philip and William D. Rubinstein, *The Richest of the Rich: The Wealthiest 250 People in Britain since 1066* (Petersfield, 2007).
Berg, Maxine, 'Britain, Industry and Perceptions of China: Matthew Boulton, "useful knowledge" and the Macartney Embassy to China 1792–94', *Journal of Global History*, 1 (2006), 269–88.
Berg, Maxine and Helen Clifford (eds), *Consumer Culture in Europe, 1650–1850* (Manchester, 1999).
Berg, Maxine, 'From Imitation to Invention: Creating Commodities in Eighteenth-Century Britain', *Economic History Review*, 55:1 (2002), 1–30.

Berg, Maxine, 'In Pursuit of Luxury: Global History and British Consumer Goods in the Eighteenth Century', *Past & Present*, 182:1 (2004), 85–142.
Berg, Maxine, Felicia Gottmann, Hanna Hodacs and Chris Nierstrasz (eds), *Goods from the East, 1600–1800: Trading Eurasia* (Basingstoke, 2015).
Berg, Maxine, *Luxury and Pleasure in Eighteenth-century Britain* (Oxford, 2005).
Berg, Maxine and Helen Clifford, 'Selling Consumption in the Eighteenth Century: Advertising and the Trade Card in Britain and France', *Cultural and Social History*, 4:2 (2007), 145–70.
Bertram, Aldous, 'Cantonese Models for the Great Pagoda at Kew', *The Georgian Group Journal*, 21 (2013), 47–57.
Betjeman, Peter, 'Craft and the Limits of Skill: Handicraft Revivalism and the Problem of Technique', *Journal of Design History*, 21:2 (2008), 183–93.
Bignamini, Ilaria, 'George Vertue, Art Historian, and Art Institutions in London, 1689–1768', *Walpole Society*, 54 (1988), 20–7.
Bin Wong, R., *China Transformed: Historical Change and the Limits of European Experience* (Ithaca and London, 1997).
Blake, Robert, *Disraeli* (London, 1966).
Boase, G. C., 'Melvill, Henry (1798–1871)', rev. H. C. G. Matthew, *Oxford Dictionary of National Biography* (Oxford, 2004). [http://www.oxforddnb.com/view/article/18540, accessed August 2013].
Bowen, H. V., *The Business of Empire: The East India Company and Imperial Britain, 1756–1833* (Cambridge, 2005).
Bowen, H. V. (ed.), *Wales and the British Overseas Empire: Interactions and Influences, 1650–1830* (Manchester, 2011).
Bowen, H. V., M. Lincoln and N. Rigby (eds.), *The Worlds of the East India Company* (Woodbridge, 2002).
Bowyer, T. H., 'Fowke, Joseph (1716–1800)', *Oxford Dictionary of National Biography* (Oxford, 2004). [http://www.oxforddnb.com/view/article/63560, accessed 12 Sept 2012].
Bressey, Caroline, 'Contesting the Political Legacy of Slavery in England's Country Houses: A Case Study of Kenwood House and Osborne House', in Madge Dresser and Andrew Hann (eds), *Slavery and the British Country House* (Swindon, 2013), 114–22.
Bressey, Caroline, 'Invisible Presence: The Whitening of the Black Community in the Historical Imagination of British Archives', *Archivaria*, 61 (2006), 47–61.
Brewer, John, *The Sinews of Power: War, Money and the English State* (London, 1989).
Brittlebank, Kate, 'Sakti and Barakat: The Power of Tipu's Tiger', *Modern Asian Studies*, 29:2 (1995), 257–69.
Brown, Iain Gordon, 'Griffins, Nabobs and a Seasoning of Curry Powder: Walter Scott and the Indian Theme in Life and Literature', in Anne Buddle (ed.), *The Tiger and the Thistle: Tipu Sultan and the Scots in India, 1760–1800* (Edinburgh, 1999), 71–9.
Brushe, John, 'Potterells', *Hertfordshire Past*, 21 (Autumn, 1986), [http://www.brookmans.com/history/potterells/potterells.shtml, accessed 2 February 2017].
Bryant, Julius, '"The Purest Taste" – James "Athenian" Stuart's Work in Villas and Country Houses', in Susan Weber Soros (ed.), *James "Athenian" Stuart, 1713–1788: The Rediscovery of Antiquity* (New Haven and London, 2006), 265–315.
Buckland, C. E., *Dictionary of Indian Biography* (London, 1906).
Buddle, Anne, *The Tiger and the Thistle: Tipu Sultan and the Scots in India, 1760–1800* (Edinburgh, 1999).
Buettner, Elizabeth, *Empire Families: Britons and Late Imperial India* (Oxford, 2004).
Burton, Antoinette, *Archive Stories: Facts, Fictions, and the Writing of History* (Durham, NC, 2005).
Burton, Antoinette and Dane Kennedy (eds), *How Empire Shaped Us* (London, 2016).
Caine, Barbara, *Bombay to Bloomsbury: A Biography of the Strachey Family* (Oxford, 2005).
Carlyle, E. I., 'Melvill, Sir James Cosmo (1792–1861)', rev. Katherine Prior, *Oxford Dictionary of National Biography* (Oxford, 2004). [http://www.oxforddnb.com/view/article/18541, accessed August 2013].
Carswell, John, *The South Sea Bubble* (Stroud, 2001).
Carter, Alice, 'Analyses of Public Indebtedness in Eighteenth-Century England', *Bulletin of the Institute of Historical Research*, 24:70 (1951), 176–81.
Carter, Ian, *Farm Life in Northeast Scotland 1840–1914: The Poor Man's Country* (Edinburgh, 1979).
Carton, Adrian, *Mixed-race and Modernity in Colonial India: Changing Concepts of Hybridity across Empires* (London, 2012).

Cator, Charles, 'French Furniture at Wanstead', *Furniture History*, 43 (2007), 227–36.
Chang, Elizabeth Hope, *Britain's Chinese Eye: Literature, Empire and Aesthetics in Nineteenth-Century Britain* (Stanford, CA, 2010).
Chartres, J., and D. Hey (eds), *English Rural Society, 1500–1800. Essays in Honour of Joan Thirsk* (Cambridge, 1990).
Chatterjee, Indrani, *Gender, Slavery and Law in Colonial India* (Oxford, 2002).
Chatterjee, Indrani, and Richard Eaton (eds), *Slavery and South Asian History* (Bloomington, IN, 2006).
Chichester, H. M. and Philip Carter, 'Burgoyne, Sir John, Seventh Baronet (1739–1785)', rev. Philip Cater, *Oxford Dictionary of National Biography* (Oxford, 2004). [http://oxforddnb.com/view/article/4012/, accessed 22 October 2016].
Clanchy, Kate, 'Common People: The History of an English Family (Review)', *Guardian*, 18 October 2014, [https://www.theguardian.com/books/2014/oct/18/common-people- the-history-of-an-english-family-review-alison-light].
Cleall, Esme, Laura Ishiguro, Emily J. Manktelow, 'Imperial Relations: Histories of Family in the British Empire', *Journal of Colonialism and Colonial History*, 14:1 (2013), n.p.
Clifford, Helen, 'The Dundas Property Empire and Nabob Taste: Accommodating the East: Sir Lawrence Dundas as Nabob of the North?', *East India Company at Home* (February 2013), 1–27: [http://blogs.ucl.ac.uk/eicah/files/2013/02/Aske-Hall-Final-PDF-19.08.14.pdf.]
Clube, J. R., 'The Boulton Family of Thorncroft Manor, 1763–1828', *Leatherhead & District Local History Society Proceedings*, 6:1 (1997), 10–13.
Clunas, Craig, *Chinese Export Watercolours* (London, 1984).
Cohen, Deborah, *Family Secrets: Living with Shame from the Victorians to the Present Day* (Oxford, 2013).
Colley, Linda, *Captives: Britain, Empire and the World 1600–1850* (London, 2002).
Colley, Linda, *The Ordeal of Elizabeth Marsh: A Woman in World History* (London, 2007).
Collingham, E. M., *Imperial Bodies: The Physical Experience of the Raj, c.1800–1947* (Cambridge, 2001).
Coltman, Viccy, *Classical Sculpture and the Culture of Collecting in Britain since 1760* (Oxford, 2009).
Coltman, Viccy, *Fabricating the Antique: Neoclassicism in Britain, 1760–1800* (Chicago and London, 2006).
Colville, Dorothy, *North Mymms – Parish and People* (Letchworth, 1972).
Cornforth, John, *Early Georgian Interiors* (New Haven and London, 2004).
Cotton, J. S., 'Anstruther, Sir John, fourth baronet and first baronet (1753–1811)', rev. T. H. Bowyer, *Oxford Dictionary of National Biography* (Oxford, 2004). [http://www.oxforddnb.com/view/article/587, accessed August 2013].
Cotton, Julian, *List of Inscriptions on Tombs or Monuments in Madras Possessing Historical or Archaeological interest* vol. 2 (Madras, 1946).
Cox, N. and J. Cox, 'Probate 1500–1800: A System in Transition', in T. Arkell, N. Evans and N. Goose (eds), *When Death Do Us Part: Understanding and Interpreting the Probate Records of Early Modern England* (Oxford, 2000), 13–37.
Crill, Rosemary, *Indian Embroidery* (London, 1999).
Cubitt, Geoffrey, 'Bringing It Home: Making Local Meaning in 2007 Bicentenary Exhibitions', *Slavery & Abolition*, 30:2 (2009), 259–75.
Curtin, Philip D., *Death by Migration: Europe's Encounter with the Tropical World in the Nineteenth Century* (Cambridge, 1989).
D'Antonio, Francesca, 'The Willow Pattern: Dunham Massey', *East India Company at Home* (June 2014), 1–21. [http://blogs.ucl.ac.uk/eicah/files/2014/06/Willow-Pattern-PDF-Final-19.08.14.pdf].
Daggett, Charles and Christopher Shaffer, *Diving for the Griffin* (London, 1990).
Dakers, Caroline, *A Genius for Money: Business, Art and the Morrisons* (New Haven and London, 2011).
Dalrymple, William, *White Mughals: Love and Betrayal in Eighteenth-Century India* (London, 2002).
Dalton, C. A. N., *The Life of Thomas Pitt* (Cambridge, 1915).
Das Gupta, Ashin, *Indian Merchants and the Decline of Surat c.1700–1750* (Oxford, 2004).
Davidoff, Leonore, *Thicker Than Water: Siblings and Their Relations, 1780–1920* (Oxford, 2012).
Davis, Richard H., *Lives of Indian Images* (Princeton, 1997).
de Bruijn, Emile, Andrew Bush and Helen Clifford, *Chinese Wallpaper in National Trust Houses* (Swindon, 2014).

De Courcy, Ann, *The Fishing Fleet: Husband-Hunting in the Raj* (London, 2012).

de Jonge, C. H., *Delft Ceramics*, trans. Marie-Christine Hellin (New York, 1970).

de Kesel, W. and Greet Dhont, *Coromandel Lacquer Screens* (Brussels, 2002).

de la Ferté, E. J., *The Melvill Family, A Roll of Honour of the Descendants of Philip Melvill and Their Immediate Connections by Marriage in the Years of the World War 1914–18* (London, 1920).

de Vries, Jan, 'Understanding Eurasian Trade in the Era of the Trading Companies', in Maxine Berg, Felicia Gottmann, Hanna Hodacs and Chris Nierstrasz (eds), *Goods from the East, 1600–1800: Trading Eurasia* (Basingstoke, 2015).

Díaz, Rocío, *Chinese Armorial Porcelain for Spain* (London, 2010).

Dodwell, Henry, *The Nabobs of Madras* (London, 1926).

Donington, Katie, Ryan Hanley, and Jessica Moody (eds), *Britain's History and Memory of Transatlantic Slavery: Local Nuances of a 'National Sin'* (Liverpool, 2016).

Donington, Katie, 'Local Roots/Global Routes': Slavery Memory and Identity in Hackney', in Katie Donington, Ryan Hanley, and Jessica Moody (eds), *Britain's History and Memory of Transatlantic Slavery: Local Nuances of a 'National Sin'* (Liverpool, 2016), 172–94.

Dresser, Madge and Andrew Hann (eds), *Slavery and the British Country House* (Swindon, 2013) [https://content.historicengland.org.uk/images-books/publications/slavery-and-british-country-house/slavery-british-country-house-web.pdf/].

Dresser, Madge and Andrew Hann, 'Introduction', in Madge Dresser and Andrew Hann (eds), *Slavery and the British Country House* (Swindon, 2013), 13–16.

Dresser, Madge, *Slavery Obscured: The Social History of the Slave Trade in an English Provincial Port* (London, 2001).

Dunbar, Janet, *Tigers, Durbars and Kings: Fanny Eden's Indian Journals 1837–1838* (London, 1988).

Dunstan, Bob, *The Book of Falmouth & Penryn* (Chesham, 1975).

DuPlessis, Robert S., *The Material Atlantic: Clothing, Commerce, and Colonization in the Atlantic World, 1650–1800* (Cambridge, 2016).

Dziennik, Matthew, 'Whig Tartan: Material Culture and Its Use in the Scottish Highlands, 1746–1815', *Past & Present*, 217 (2012), 117–47.

Eacott, Jonathan, 'Making an Imperial Compromise: The Calico Acts, the Atlantic Colonies, and the Structure of the British Empire', *William & Mary Quarterly*, 69:4 (2012), 731–62.

Earle, Rebecca, 'Introduction: Letters, Writers and the Historian', in Rebecca Earle (ed.), *Epistolary Selves: Letters and Letter-Writers, 1600–1945* (Abingdon, 1999), 1–14.

Eaton, Natasha, 'Between Mimesis and Alterity: Art, Gift, and Diplomacy in Colonial India, 1770–1800', *Comparative Studies in Society and History*, 46:4 (2004), 816–44.

Eaton, Natasha, 'Excess in the City? Consumption of Imported Prints in Colonial Calcutta, c. 1780–c. 1795', in Martin Jay and Sumathi Ramaswamy (eds), *Empires of Vision: A Reader* (Durham, NC, 2014), 159–88.

Ellis, Markman, Richard Coulton and Matthew Mauger, *Empire of Tea: The Asian Leaf that Conquered the World* (London, 2015).

Farmer, Penelope, *Sisters: An Anthology* (London, 1999).

Farr, M., and X. Guegan (eds), *The British abroad since the Eighteenth Century* vol. 1, *Travellers and Tourists* (Heidelberg, 2013).

Farrant, John H., 'Burrell, Sir William, second baronet (1732–1796)', *Oxford Dictionary of National Biography* (Oxford, 2004). [http://www.oxforddnb.com/view/article/4102, accessed 5 January 2017].

Farrington, Anthony, *A Biographical Index of East India Company Maritime Service Officers, 1600–1834* (London, 1999).

Farrington, Anthony, *Catalogue of East India Company Ships' Journals and Logs 1600–1834* (London, 1999).

Farrington, Anthony, *The Records of the East Indian College Haileybury and Other Institutions* (London, 1976).

Feeser, Andrea, Maureen Daly Goggin and Beth Fowkes Tobin, *The Materiality of Color. The Production, Circulation, and Application of Dyes and Pigments, 1400–1800* (London, 2012).

Fennetaux, Ariane, Amélie Junqua and Sophie Vasset, *The Afterlife of Used Things: Recycling in the Long Eighteenth Century* (London, 2015).

Fetherstonhaugh, Helen, *Three Hundred Years of Private Banking* (London, 1992).

Filor, Ellen and Jan Sibthorpe, 'Outside the Public: The Histories of Sezincote and Prestonfield in Private Hands', in Margot Finn and Kate Smith (eds), *New Paths to Public Histories:* (Basingstoke, 2015), 100–23.

Filor, Ellen, 'William Rattray of Downie Park', *East India Company at Home*, n.p. [http://blogs.ucl.ac.uk/eicah/case-studies-2/william-rattray-of-downie-park/].

Finlay, Robert, *The Pilgrim Art: Cultures of Porcelain in World History* (Berkeley, 2010).

Finn, Margot, 'Anglo-Indian Lives in the Later Eighteenth and Early Nineteenth Century', *Journal for Eighteenth-Century Studies*, 33:1 (2010), 49–65.

Finn, Margot, *The Character of Credit: Personal Debt in English Culture, 1740–1914* (Cambridge, 2003).

Finn, Margot, 'Colonial Gifts: Family Politics and the Exchange of Goods in British India, *c.*1780–1820', *Modern Asian Studies*, 40:1 (2006), 203–32.

Finn, Margot, 'Family Formation: Anglo-India and the Familial Proto-State', in Jon Lawrence and David Feldman (eds), *Structures and Transformations in Modern British History* (Cambridge, 2011), 100–17.

Finn, Margot, 'Men's Things: Masculine Possession in the Consumer Revolution', *Social History*, 25:2 (2000), 133–55.

Finn, Margot, and Kate Smith (eds), *New Paths to Public Histories* (Basingstoke, 2015).

Finn, Margot, 'The Homes of England', in James Chandler (ed.), *The New Cambridge History of English Literature: The Romantic Period* (Cambridge, 2009), 293–313.

Fisher, Michael, 'Bound for Britain: Changing Conditions of Servitude, 1600–1857', in Indrani Chatterjee and Richard Eaton (eds), *Slavery and South Asian History* (Bloomington, IN, 2006), 187–209.

Fisher, Michael, *Counterflows to Colonialism: Indian Travellers and Settlers in Britain, 1600–1857* (Delhi, 2004).

Forrest, Denys, *Tiger Of Mysore* (London, 1970).

Foster, Stephen, *A Private Empire* (Millers Point, NSW, 2010).

Franklin, Michael, *Orientalist Jones: Sir William Jones, Poet, Lawyer, and Linguist, 1746–1794* (Oxford, 2011).

Fraser, D., H. Hibbard and M. J. Lewine (eds), *Essays in the History of Architecture Presented to Rudolf Wittkower* (London, 1978).

French, Henry and Mark Rothery, *Man's Estate: Landed Gentry Masculinities, c.1660-c.1900* (Oxford, 2012).

Frey, Lina, and Marsha Frey, 'Townshend, Charles, second Viscount Townshend (1674–1738)', *Oxford Dictionary of National Biography* (Oxford, 2004). [http://www.oxforddnb.com/view/article/27617, accessed 6 January 2017]

Furber, Holden, *John Company at Work: A Study of European Expansion in India in the Late Eighteenth Century* (Cambridge, MA, 1948).

Garrett, Oliver, *Plas Newydd: Isle of Anglesey* (London, 2010).

Gauci, Perry, *Emporium of the World: The Merchants of London 1660–1800* (London, 2007).

Gauci, Perry, 'Pitt, Thomas (1653–1726)', *Oxford Dictionary of National Biography* (Oxford, 2004). [http://www.oxforddnb.com/view/article/22333, accessed 21 October 2016].

Gauci, Perry, *William Beckford: First Prime Minister of the London Empire* (New Haven, 2013).

George, Rosemary Marangoly, *The Politics of Home: Postcolonial Relocations and Twentieth-century Fiction* (Cambridge, 1996).

Geppert, Dominik and Frank Lorenz Müller (eds), *Sites of Imperial Memory: Commemorating Colonial Rule in the Nineteenth and Twentieth Centuries* (Manchester, 2015).

Gernsheim, Helmut and Alison Gernsheim, *L.J.M. Daguerre: The History of the Diorama and the Daguerreotype* (London, 1956).

Gerritsen, Anne and Stephen McDowall, 'Global China: Material Culture and Connections in World History', *Journal of World History*, 23:1 (2012), 3–8.

Ghosh, Durba, *Sex and Family in Colonial India: The Making of Empire* (Cambridge, 2006).

Gillingham, Paul, 'The Macartney Embassy to China, 1792–94', *History Today,* 43 (1993).

Gillis, John, *A World of Their Own Making: Myth, Ritual and a Quest for Family Values* (New York, 1996).

Girouard, Mark, *Life in the English Country House: A Social and Architectural History* (New Haven and London, 1978).

Glendinning, Miles and Susanna Wade Martins, *Buildings of the Land: Scotland's Farms 1750–2000* (Edinburgh, 2008).

Gosden, Chris and Yvonne Marshall, 'The Cultural Biography of Objects', *World Archaeology,* 31:2 (1999), 169–78.

Gott, Richard, *Britain's Empire: Resistance, Repression and Revolt* (London, 2011).

Gottmann, Felicia, *Global Trade, Smuggling and the Making of Economic Liberalism: Asian Textiles in France 1680–1760* (New York, 2016).

Grant, Eric and Alistair Mutch, 'Indian Wealth and Agricultural Improvement in Northern Scotland', *Journal of Scottish Historical Studies*, 35 (2015), 25–44.

Grassby, Richard, *The English Gentleman in Trade: The Life and Work of Sir Dudley North 1641–1691* (Oxford, 1994).

Green, Georgina, 'Sir Charles Raymond of Valentines', *Essex Journal*, 43:2 (2008), 38–43.

Green, Georgina, *Sir Charles Raymond of Valentines and the East India Company* (Ilford, 2015).

Habakkuk, John, *Marriage, Debt, and the Estates System: English Landownership 1650–1950* (Oxford, 1994).

Haggerty, Sheryllynne, and Susanne Seymour, 'Property, Power and Authority: The Implicit and Explicit Slavery Connections of Bolsover Castle and Brodsworth Hall in the 18th Century', in Dresser and Hann (eds), *Slavery and the British Country House*, 78–88.

Hall, Catherine, Keith McClelland, Nick Draper, Katie Donington and Rachel Lang, *Legacies of British Slave-ownership: Colonial Slavery and the Formation of Victorian Britain* (Cambridge, 2014).

Hall, Catherine, *Macaulay and Son: Architects of Imperial Britain* (London, 2012).

Hall, Catherine and Sonya Rose (eds), *At Home with the Empire: Metropolitan Culture and the Imperial World* (Cambridge, 2006).

Hall, Catherine, 'Troubling Memories: Nineteenth-century Histories of the Slave Trade and Slavery', *Transactions of the Royal Historical Society*, 6:21 (2011), 147–69.

Hall, Ivan, 'French Influence at Burton Constable', *Furniture History*, 8 (1972), 70–7.

Hall, Linda, *Period House Fixtures and Fittings 1300–1900* (Newbury, 2005).

Hamilton, James, *A Strange Business: Making Art and Money in Nineteenth-century Britain* (London, 2014).

Hancock, David, 'Commerce and Conversation in the Eighteenth-Century Atlantic: The Invention of Madeira Wine', *Journal of Interdisciplinary History*, 29:2 (1998), 197–219.

Hancock, David, *Oceans of Wine: Madeira and the Emergence of American Trade and Taste* (New Haven, 2009).

Hardy, John and Maurice Tomlin, *Osterley Park House* (London, 1985).

Harper, Marjory (ed.), *Emigrant Homecomings: The Return Movement of Migrants, 1600–2000* (Manchester, 2005).

Harvey, Karen, 'Barbarity in a Teacup? Punch, Domesticity and Gender in the Eighteenth Century', *Journal of Design History*, 21:3 (2008), 205–21.

Harvey, Karen, 'Ritual Encounters: Punch Parties and Masculinity in the Eighteenth Century', *Past and Present*, 214 (2012), 166–203.

Harwood, Kate, 'Some Hertfordshire Nabobs', in Anne Rowe (ed.), *Hertfordshire Garden History: A Miscellany* (Hatfield, 2007), 49–77.

Hawes, Christopher J., *Poor Relations: The Making of a Eurasian Community in British India, 1773–1833* (London, 1996).

Hayter, Alethea, *The Wreck of the Abergavenny* (London, 2002).

Hayton, David, E. Cruickshanks and S. Handley (eds), *The House of Commons, 1690–1715* (London, 2002).

Hayton, D., E. Cruickshanks, S. Handley (eds), 'Child, Robert (1674–1721), *The History of Parliament: the House of Commons 1690–1715*, (London, 2002). [http://www.historyofparliamentonline.org/volume/1690–1715/member/child-robert-1674–1721, accessed 2 February 2017].

Hicks, Dan, and Mary C. Beaudry (eds), *The Oxford Handbook of Material Culture Studies* (Oxford, 2010).

Hodacs, Hanna, *Silk and Tea in the North: Scandinavian Trade and the Market for Asian Goods in Eighteenth-Century Europe* (New York, 2016).

Hoffman, Ronald, Mechal Sobel and Fredrika J. Teute, *Through a Glass Darkly: Reflections on Personal Identity in Early America* (Chapel Hill and London, 1997).

Holzman, James M., *The Nabobs in England: A Study of the Returned Anglo-Indians, 1760–1785* (New York, 1926).

Hopkins, Lesley (ed.), *The Papered Wall: History, Pattern Technique* (New York, 1994).

Howard, David Sanctuary, *Chinese Armorial Porcelain* (London, 1974).

Howard, David Sanctuary, *Chinese Armorial Porcelain: Volume II* (Chippenham, 2003).

Howard, David Sanctuary, *A Tale of Three Cities: Canton, Shanghai & Hong Kong* (London, 1997).

Howlett, David J., 'Malet, Sir Charles Warre, first baronet (1753–1815)', *Oxford Dictionary of National Biography* (Oxford, 2004). [http://www.oxforddnb.com/view/article/17876].

Hunter, G. L., *Decorative Textiles: An Illustrated Book on Coverings for Furniture, Walls and Floors* (Philadelphia, 1918).
Hussey, Christopher, *English Country Houses: Mid-Georgian, 1760–1800* (2nd ed., London, 1963).
Impey, Oliver, 'Eastern Trade and Furnishing of the British Country House', in Gervase Jackson-Stops (ed.), *The Fashioning and Functioning of the British Country House, Studies in the History of Art,* 25 (Washington, DC, 1989), 117–92.
Impey, Oliver, and Arthur MacGregor (eds), *The Origins of Museums: The Cabinet of Curosities in Sixteenth- and Seventeenth-Century Europe* (London, 2001).
Irwin, John, 'Origins of the "Oriental Style" in English Decorative Art', *Burlington Magazine*, 97:625 (1955), 106–14.
Jackson-Stops, Gervase, 'Englefield House, Berkshire II', *Country Life* (1981), 560–2.
Jackson-Stops, Gervase, and James Pipkin, *The English Country House: A Grand Tour* (London, 1984).
Jackson-Stops, Gervase, Gordon J. Schochet, Lena Cowen Orlin and Elisabeth Blair MacDougall (eds), *The Fashioning and Functioning of the British Country House* (Washington, DC, 1989).
Jaffer, Amin and Karina Corrigan, *Furniture from British India and Ceylon: A Catalogue of the Collections in the Victoria and Albert Museum and the Peabody Essex Museum* (London, 2001).
Jaffer, Amin, *Luxury Goods from India: The Art of the Indian Cabinet-Maker* (London, 2002).
Jaffer, Amin, 'Tipu Sultan, Warren Hastings and Queen Charlotte: The Mythology and Typology of Anglo-Indian Ivory Furniture', *The Burlington Magazine*, 141:1154 (1999), 271–81.
Jasanoff, Maya, 'Collections of Empire: Objects, Conquests and Imperial Self-fashioning', *Past and Present*, 184 (2004), 109–135.
Jasanoff, Maya, *Edge of Empire: Conquest and Collecting in the East 1750–1850* (London, 2005).
Jay, Martin, and Sumathi Ramaswamy (eds), *Empires of Vision: A Reader* (Durham, NC, 2014).
Johnson, Lucy, *Peeling Back the Years: Chinoiserie at Woburn Abbey* (Bedford, 2014).
Johnston, Patricia, and Caroline Frank (eds), *Global Trade and the Visual Arts in Federal New England* (Durham, NH, 2014).
Jordan, E., 'Chinese Wallpapers in England', *The Star,* 9680 (1909), n.p.
Joslin, D. M., 'London Private Bankers, 1720–1785', *Economic History Review*, New Series, 7:2 (1954), 167–86.
Jourdain, Margaret, and Soame Jenyns, 'Chinese Export Art in the Eighteenth Century', *Country Life* (1950), n.p.
Jourdain, Margaret, *English Furniture: The Georgian Period (1750–1830)* (London, 1953).
Joyce, Patrick, *The State of Freedom: A Social History of the British State since 1800* (Cambridge, 2013).
Kelly, Ian, *Mr Foote's Other Leg: Comedy, Tragedy and Murder in Georgian London* (London, 2013).
Kenyon, Mary, *A History of All Saints Church Hutton* (Essex, 1999).
Khalidi, Omar, *The British Residency in Hyderabad: An Outpost of the Raj, 1779–1948* (London, 2005).
Kinchin, Juliet, 'Interiors: Nineteenth-Century Essays on the "Masculine" and the "Feminine" Room', in Pat Kirkham (ed.), *The Gendered Object* (Manchester and New York, 1996), 18–20.
Kingsford, Peter, *A Modern History of Brookmans Park 1700–1950* (London, 1983).
Kinsey, Danielle C., 'Koh-I-Noor: Empire, Diamonds, and the Performance of British Material Culture', *Journal of British Studies* 48:2 (2009), 391–419.
Kirkham, Pat (ed.), *The Gendered Object* (Manchester and New York, 1996).
Koditschek, Theodore, *Liberalism, Imperialism and the Historical Imagination: Nineteenth-century Visions of a Greater Britain* (Cambridge, 2011).
Koh, Adeline, 'Inspecting the Nineteenth-century Literary Digital Archive: Omissions of Empire', *Journal of Victorian Culture*, 19:3 (2014), 385–95.
Kopytoff, Igor, 'The Cultural Biography of Things: Commoditization as Process', in Arjun Appadurai (ed.), *The Social Life of Things: Commodities in Cultural Perspective* (Cambridge, 1986), 64–91.
Kowaleski-Wallace, Elizabeth, *Consuming Subjects: Women, Shopping, and Business in the Eighteenth Century* (New York, 1997).
Kriegel, Lara, 'Narrating the Sub-continent in 1851: India at the Crystal Palace', in Louise Purbrick (ed.), *The Great Exhibition of 1851: New Interdisciplinary Essays* (Manchester, 2001), 146–78.
Kroes, Jochem, *Chinese Armorial Porcelain for the Dutch Market: Chinese Porcelain with Coats of Arms of Dutch Families* (The Hague, 2007).
Laidlaw, Zoë, *Colonial Connections, 1815–45: Patronage, the Information Revolution and Colonial Government* (Manchester, 2005).

Lambert, David and Alan Lester (eds), *Colonial Lives Across the British Empire: Imperial Careering in the Long Nineteenth Century* (Cambridge, 2006).
Lambert, I. and C. Laroque, 'An Eighteenth-century Chinese Wallpaper: Historical Context and Conservation', *Works of art on paper: books, documents and photographs: techniques and conservation: contributions to the Baltimore Congress*, (2–6 September 2002), 122–8.
Lang, Gordon, 'The Royal Pavilion, Brighton: The Chinoiserie Designs by Frederick Crace', in Megan Aldrich (ed.), *The Craces: Royal Decorators 1768–1899* (Brighton, 1990), 42–50.
Latour, Bruno, *Reassembling the Social: An Introduction to Actor-network-theory* (Oxford, 2005).
Lawrence, Jon, and David Feldman (eds), *Structures and Transformations in Modern British History* (Cambridge, 2011).
Lawson, Sir Charles, *Memories of Madras* (London, 1905).
Lemire, Beverly, *Fashion's Favourite: The Cotton Trade and the Consumer in Britain 1660–1800* (London, 1991).
Lenman, Bruce P., 'The East India Company and the Trade in Non-metallic Precious Materials from Sir Thomas Roe to Diamond Pitt', in H. V. Bowen, M. Lincoln and N. Rigby (eds.), *The Worlds of the East India Company* (Woodbridge, 2002), 97–110.
Lever, Tresham, *The House of Pitt: A Family Chronicle* (London, 1947).
Lewis, Judith S., 'When a House is Not a Home: Elite English Women and the Eighteenth-Century Country House', *Journal of British Studies*, 48:2 (2009), 336–63.
Light, Alison, *Common People: The History of an English Family* (London, 2014).
Lloyd, Tom, 'Thuggee, Marginality and the State Effect in Colonial India, circa 1770–1840', *Indian Economic and Social History Review*, 45:2 (2008), 201–37.
Longair, Sarah, 'The Colonial Moment in the Lives of Objects on the Swahili Coast', in P. Meier and A. Purpura (eds), *World on the Horizon: Swahili Arts across the Indian Ocean* (Champaign-Urbana, IL, 2017), n.p.
Longair, Sarah and John McAleer (eds), *Curating Empire: Museums and the British Imperial Experience* (Manchester, 2012).
Lowenthal, David, *The Past is a Foreign Country* (Cambridge, 1985).
Lucas, Gavin, 'Fieldwork and Collecting', in Dan Hicks and Mary C. Beaudry (eds), *The Oxford Handbook of Material Culture Studies* (Oxford, 2010), 229–45.
Lydekker, Richard, *Hertfordshire* (Cambridge, 1909).
MacGregor, Arthur, 'The cabinet of curiosities in seventeenth-century Britain', in Oliver Impey and Arthur MacGregor (eds), *The Origins of Museums: The Cabinet of Curosities in Sixteenth- and Seventeenth-century Europe* (London, 2001), 201–15.
MacGregor, Arthur, *Curiosity and Enlightenment: Collectors and Collections from the Sixteenth to the Nineteenth Century* (London, 2007).
MacGregor, Arthur, *The Cobbe Cabinet of Curiosities: An Anglo-Irish Country House Museum* (New Haven and London, 2015).
Macinnes, Allan, Kieran German and Lesley Graham (eds), *Living with Jacobitism, 1690–1788: The Three Kingdoms and beyond* (London, 2014).
MacKenzie, J. M., 'The British Empire: Ramshackle or Rampaging? A Historiographical Reflection', *Journal of Imperial and Commonwealth History*, 43:1 (2015), 99–124.
MacKenzie, John, and T. M. Devine (eds), *Scotland and the British Empire* (Oxford, 2011).
MacKillop, Andrew, 'The Highlands and the Returning Nabob: Sir Hector Munro of Novar, 1760–1807', in Marjory Harper (ed.) *Emigrant Homecomings: The Return Movement of Migrants, 1600–2000* (Manchester, 2005), 233–61.
Mackillop, Andrew, 'Locality, Nation, and Empire: Scots in Asia, c.1695–c.1813', in John MacKenzie and T. M. Devine (eds), *Scotland and the British Empire* (Oxford, 2011), 4–83.
MacKillop, Andrew, *'More fruitful than the soil': Army, Empire and the Scottish Highlands, 1715–1815* (East Linton, 2000).
Madsen, Andrew D., and Carolyn L. White, *Chinese Export Porcelain* (Walnut Creek, CA, 2011).
Mallampalli, Chandra, *Race, Religion, and Law in Colonial India: Trials of an Interracial Family* (Cambridge, 2011).
Mandler, Peter, *The Fall and Rise of the Stately Home* (London, 1997).
Marshall, David R., Susan Russell and Karin Wolfe (eds), *Roma Britannica: Art Patronage and Cultural Exchange in Eighteenth-century Rome* (London, 2011).
Marshall, P. J., *Bengal–The British Bridgehead: Eastern India, 1740–1828* (Cambridge, 1987).
Marshall, P. J., *East India Fortunes: The British in Bengal in the Eighteenth Century* (Oxford, 1976).

Marshall, P. J., 'Hastings, Warren (1732–1818)', *Oxford Dictionary of National Biography* (Oxford, 2004). [http://www.oxforddnb.com/view/article/12587, accessed 19 May 2014]

Marshall, P. J., *The Making and Unmaking of Empires: Britain, India, and America c.1750–1783* (Oxford, 2005).

Martin, John, 'Townshend, Etheldreda, Viscountess Townshend (*c.*1708–1788)', *Oxford Dictionary of National Biography* (Oxford, 2004). [http://www.oxforddnb.com/view/article/68358, accessed 6 January 2017].

McDowall, Stephen, 'The Shugborough Dinner Service and its Significance for Sino-British History', *Journal for Eighteenth-Century Studies*, 37:1 (2014), 1–17.

McDowall, Stephen, 'Shugborough: Seat of the Earl of Lichfield', *The East India Company at Home* (April 2013), 1–16 [http://blogs.ucl.ac.uk/eicah/files/2013/02/Shugborough-PDF-Final-19.08.14.pdf].

McGilvary, George K., *East India Patronage and the British State: The Scottish Elite and Politics in the Eighteenth Century* (London and New York, 2008).

McGilvary, George, *Guardian of the East India Company: The Life of Laurence Sulivan* (London, 2006).

McKean, Charles, *The Scottish Chateau: The Country House of Renaissance Scotland* (Stroud, 2004).

Meier, P., and A. Purpura (eds), *World on the Horizon: Swahili Arts across the Indian Ocean* (Champaign-Urbana, IL, 2017).

Menshikova, Maria and Jet Pijzel-Dommisse, *Silver Wonders from the East: Filigree of the Tsars* (Amsterdam, 2006).

Millar, Edward, *That Noble Cabinet: A History of the British Museum* (London, 1973).

Moienuddin, Mohammad, *Sunset at Srirangapatam: After the Death of Tipu Sultan* (Hyderabad, 2000).

Moncreiffe, Iain and Don Pottinger, *Simple Heraldry* (Edinburgh and London, 1978).

Morse, H. B., 'The Chronicles of the East India Company Trading to China 1635–1834', as reprinted in entirety in Patrick Tuck, *Britain and the China Trade 1635–1842* vol. 1 (London, 2000).

Mutch, Alistair, 'Agriculture and Empire: General Patrick "Tiger" Duff and the Shaping of North-east Scotland', *Review of Scottish Culture*, 22 (2010), 85–98.

Mutch, Alistair, 'A Contested Eighteenth-Century Election: Banffshire 1795', *Northern Scotland*, 2 (2011), 22–35.

Mutch, Alistair, 'Europe, the British Empire and the Madeira Trade: Catholicism, Commerce and the Gordon of Letterfourie Network c.1730-c.1800', *Northern Scotland*, 7 (2016), 21–42.

Myrone, Martin, 'Society of the Virtuosi of St Luke (*act. c.*1689–1743)', *Oxford Dictionary of National Biography* (Oxford, 2004). [http://www.oxforddnb.com/view/theme/96316, accessed 9 February 2017].

Namier, L. and J. Brook, *The History of Parliament: the House of Commons 1754–1790* (London, 1964) [http://www.histparl.ac.uk/volume/1754–1790/member/turner-sir-edward-1719–66, accessed 2 February 2017].

Nandy, S. C., *History of the Cossimbazar Raj in the Nineteenth Century* (Calcutta, 1986).

Nandy, S. C., *History of the Cossimbazar Raj in the Twentieth Century* (Calcutta, 1995).

Nandy, S. C., *Life and Times of Cantoo Baboo* vol. 1 (Calcutta, 1978).

Nandy, S. C., *Life and Times of Cantoo Baboo* vol. 2 (Calcutta, 1981).

Nechtman, Tillman W. 'Nabobinas: Luxury, Gender, and the Sexual Politics of British Imperialism in India in the Late Eighteenth Century', *Journal of Women's History*, 18:4 (2006), 8–30.

Nechtman, Tillman W. *Nabobs: Empire and Identity in Eighteenth-century Britain* (Cambridge, 2010).

Nechtman, Tillman, 'A Jewel in the Crown? Indian Wealth in Domestic Britain in the Late Eighteenth Century', *Eighteenth-century Studies*, 41:1 (2007), 71–86.

Neeson, J. M., *Commoners: Common Right, Enclosure and Social Change in England, 1700–1820* (Cambridge, 1993).

Newman, Harold, *An Illustrated Dictionary of Jewellery* (London, 1981).

Niertstrasz, Chris, *Rivalry for Tea and Textiles: The English and Dutch East India Companies (1700–1800)* (Basingstoke, 2015).

Nightingale, Pamela, 'Duncan, Jonathan (bap. 1756, d. 1811)', *Oxford Dictionary of National Biography* (Oxford, 2004). [http://www.oxforddnb.com/view/article/8224, accessed 2 February 2017].

Nightingale, Pamela, *Fortune and Integrity: A Study of the Moral Attitudes in the Indian Diary of George Paterson, 1769–1774* (Oxford, 1985).

Nightingale, Pamela, *Trade and Empire in Western India, 1784–1806* (London, 1970).

Novotny, Jennifer, 'Polite War: Material Culture of the Jacobite Era, 1688–1760', in Allan Macinnes, Kieran German and Lesley Graham (eds), *Living with Jacobitism, 1690–1788: The Three Kingdoms and beyond* (London, 2014), 153–72.

Ogborn, Miles, *Indian Ink: Script and Print in the Making of the English East India Company* (Chicago, 2007).

Orbell, John, 'Baring, Sir Francis, first baronet (1740–1810)', *Oxford Dictionary of National Biography* (Oxford, 2004) [http://www.oxforddnb.com/view/article/1382, accessed 2 February 2017].

Pagani, Catherine, *Eastern Magnificence & European Ingenuity: Clocks of Late Imperial China* (Ann Arbor, 2001).

Page, William (ed.), *A History of the County of Hertford* vol. 2 (London, 1908) [http://www.british-history.ac.uk/vch/herts/vol2/].

Page, William (ed.), *The Victoria History of the County of Hertford*, 4 vols (London, 1902–12).

Pearsall, Sarah M. S., *Atlantic Families: Lives and Letters in the Later Eighteenth Century* (Oxford, 2008).

Peers, Douglas M., 'Amherst, William Pitt, first Earl Amherst of Arracan (1773–1857)', *Oxford Dictionary of National Biography* (Oxford, 2004). [http://www.oxforddnb.com/view/article/445, accessed 19 June 2013].

Picard, Liza, *Dr Johnson's London* (London, 2001).

Pierson, Stacey, 'The Movement of Chinese Ceramics: Appropriation in Global History', *Journal of World History*, 23:1 (2012), 9–39.

Pirtle, Jeanne K., *Sotterley Plantation* (South Carolina, 2013).

Pittock, Murray, *Material Culture and Sedition, 1688–1760: Treacherous Objects, Secret Places* (Houndmills, 2013).

Pomeranz, Kenneth, *The Great Divergence: China, Europe and the Making of the Modern World Economy* (Princeton, 2000).

Ponsonby, Margaret, *Stories from Home: English Domestic Interiors, 1750–1850* (Aldershot, 2007).

Porter, Bernard, *The Absent-Minded Imperialists: Empire, Society, and Culture in Britain* (Oxford, 2004).

Porter, D. L., 'Monstrous Beauty: Eighteenth-Century Fashion and the Aesthetics of the Chinese Taste', *Eighteenth-Century Studies*, 35:3 (2002), 395–412.

Porter, David, *The Chinese Taste in Eighteenth-Century England* (Cambridge, 2010).

Powell, W. R. (ed.), *Victoria County History of Essex* vol. 5 (Oxford, 1966).

Powell, W. R. (ed.), *Victoria County History of Essex* vol. 7 (Oxford, 1978).

Prescott, Andrew, 'I'd Rather Be a Librarian: A Response to Tim Hitchcock, "Confronting the Digital"', *Cultural and Social History*, 11:3 (2014), 335–341.

Prentice, Rina, *The Authentic Nelson* (London, 2005).

Price, F. G. Hilton, *The Marygold by Temple Bar* (London, 1902).

Prince, Hugh, *Parks in Hertfordshire since 1500* (Hatfield, 2008).

Prior, Katherine, 'Fraser, William (1784–1835)', *Oxford Dictionary of National Biography* (Oxford, 2004). [http://www.oxforddnb.com/view/article/10129, accessed 9 October 2016].

Purbrick, Louise (ed.), *The Great Exhibition of 1851: New Interdisciplinary Essays* (Manchester, 2001),

Puri, Ina (ed.), *Raj Bhavan of Kolkata: Two Hundred Years of Grandeur* (New Delhi, 2003).

Qureshi, Sadiah, 'Tipu's Tiger and Images of India, 1799–2010', in John McAleer and Sarah Longair (eds), *Curating Empire: Museums and the British Imperial Experience* (Manchester, 2012), 207–24.

Ray, Romita, 'Going Global, Staying Local: Elihu Yale the Art Collector', *Yale University Art Gallery Bulletin* (December 2012), 34–51.

Retford, Kate, *The Art of Domestic Life: Family Portraiture in Eighteenth Century England* (London, 2006).

Richards, Sarah, *Eighteenth-Century Ceramics: Products for a Civilized Society* (Manchester, 1999).

Richter, Paula Bradstreet, 'Fabrics and Fashion of the India Trade at a Salem Sea Captain's Wedding', in Patricia Johnston and Caroline Frank (eds), *Global Trade and the Visual Arts in Federal New England* (Durham, NH, 2014), 195–206.

Riello, Giorgio, *Cotton: The Fabric that Made the Modern World* (Cambridge and New York, 2013).

Robbins, Helen and Henrietta Macartney, *Our First Ambassador to China: An Account of the Life of George, Earl of Macartney, with Extracts from His Letters, and the Narrative of His Experiences in China, as Told by Himself, 1737–1806* (Cambridge, 2011).

Robertson, Roland, 'Globalisation or Glocalisation?', *Journal of International Communication*, 1:1 (1994), 33–52.

Robson, John M., Martin Moir and Zawahir Moir (eds), *John Stuart Mill, Writings on India*, vol. 33 (London, 1990).

Rohatgi, Pauline, 'From Pencil to Panorama: Tipu in Pictorial Perspective', in Anne Buddle (ed.), *The Tiger and the Thistle: Tipu Sultan and the Scots in India, 1760–1800* (Edinburgh, 1999), 39–52.

Rothschild, Emma, *The Inner Life of Empires: An Eighteenth-Century History* (Princeton, 2011).

Rowe, Anne (ed.), *Hertfordshire Garden History: A Miscellany* (Hatfield, 2007).

Rowell, Christopher, 'French Furniture at Uppark: Sir Harry Featherstonhaugh and His Friends in Post-Revolutionary Paris', *Furniture History*, 43 (2007), 267–92.

Rubinstein, W. D., *Who Were the Rich? A Biographical Directory of British Wealth Holders*, vol. 1 (London, 2009).

Rungta, Shyam, *The Rise of Business Corporations in India, 1851–1900* (Cambridge, 1970).

Russell, Lady Constance, *Swallowfield and Its Owners* (London, 1901) [http://www.archive.org/stream/swallowfielditso00russ#page/n9/mode/2up].

Said, Edward, *Culture and Imperialism* (New York, 1994).

Samuel, Edgar R., 'Sir Francis Child's Jewellery Business', *The Three Banks Review* (1977), 43–54.

Samuel, Edgar Roy, 'Diamonds and Pieces of Eight: How Stuart England Won the Rough-Diamond Trade', *Jewish Historical Studies*, 38 (2003), 23–40.

Samuel, Edgar Roy, 'Gems from the Orient: The Activities of Sir John Chardin (1643–1713) as a Diamond Importer and East India Merchant', *Proceedings of the Huguenot Society of Great Britain and Ireland*, 27:3 (2000), 351–68.

Sánchez-Jáuregui, Maria Dolores, and Scott Wilcox, *The English Prize: The Capture of the Westmorland, an Episode of the Grand Tour* (New Haven, 2012).

Sangster, Paul, *Balls Park, Hertford* (Caxton Hill, 1972).

Sargent, William R., 'The Strathallan Castle Wallpaper at the Peabody Essex Museum', *Orientations*, 45:8 (2014), 22–3.

Saunders, Gill, 'The China Trade: Oriental Painted Panels', in Lesley Hopkins (ed.), *The Papered Wall: History, Pattern Technique* (New York, 1994), 42–55.

Saunders, Gill, *Wallpaper in Interior Decoration* (London, 1994).

Scarisbrick, Diane, and Benjamin Zucher, *Elihu Yale: Merchant, Collector and Patron* (London, 2014).

Schwarzberg, Raphaelle, 'Becoming a London Goldsmith in the Seventeenth Century: Social Capital and Mobility of Apprentices and Masters of the Guild', *Working Papers No. 141/10*, Department of Economic History, London School of Economics (June 2010), 1–55.

Seaver, Kirsten A., 'Desirable Teeth: The Medieval Trade in Artic and African Ivory', *Journal of Global History*, 4:2 (2009), 271–92.

Seton, Bruce Gordon, *The House of Seton: A Study of Lost Causes* (Edinburgh, 1941).

Sharples, Joseph, David Walker and Matthew Woodworth, *Aberdeenshire: South and Aberdeen* (New Haven, 2015).

Sibthorpe, Jan, 'Sezincote, Gloucestershire', *East India Company at Home* (May 2014), 1–30. [http://blogs.ucl.ac.uk/eicah/files/2013/06/Sezincote-PDF-Final-19.08.14.pdf].

Slade, H. Gordon, 'Carnousie-Banffshire', *Archaeological Journal*, 136 (1979), 229–39.

Sloboda, Stacey, *Chinoiserie: Commerce and Critical Ornament in Eighteenth-century Britain* (Manchester, 2014).

Sloboda, Stacey, 'Displaying Materials: Porcelain and Natural History in the Duchess of Portland's Museum', *Eighteenth-Century Studies*, 43:4 (2010), 455–72.

Smith, Charles Saumarez, *Eighteenth-Century Decoration: Design and the Domestic Interior in England* (New York, 1993).

Smith, Kate, 'Imperial Objects? Country House Interiors in 18th-Century Britain', in Jon Stobart and Andrew Hann (eds), *The Country House: Material Culture and Consumption* (London, 2015), 111–18.

Smith, Kate, 'Imperial Families: Women Writing Home in Georgian Britain', *Women's History Review*, 24:6 (2015), 843–60.

Smith, Kate, *Moving Hands, Material Goods: Perceiving Production in England, 1700–1830* (Manchester, 2014).

Smith, Kate, 'Sensing Design and Workmanship: The Haptic Skills of Shoppers in Eighteenth-Century London', *Journal of Design History*, 25:1 (2012), 1–10.

Smith, Peter, 'Talman, William (*bap.* 1650, *d.* 1719)', *Oxford Dictionary of National Biography* (Oxford, 2004) [http://www.oxforddnb.com/view/article/26956, accessed 21 October 2016].

Smylitopoulos, Christina, 'Rewritten and Reused: Imaging the Nabob through "Upstart Iconography"', *Eighteenth-century Life*, 32:2 (2008), 39–59.
Soros, Susan Weber (ed.), *James "Athenian" Stuart, 1713–1788: The Rediscovery of Antiquity* (New Haven and London, 2006).
Spear, Thomas George Percival, *The Nabobs: A Study of the Social Life of the English in Eighteenth Century India* (London, 1932).
Speake, Jennifer, 'Backhouse, William (1593–1662)', *Oxford Dictionary of National Biography* (Oxford, 2004). [http://www.oxforddnb.com/view/article/985, accessed 21 October 2016].
Speck, W. A., 'Hyde, Henry, second earl of Clarendon (1638–1709)', *Oxford Dictionary of National Biography* (Oxford, 2004) [http://www.oxforddnb.com/view/article/14329, accessed 21 October 2016].
Spencer, Alfred (ed.), *Memoirs of William Hickey*, 4 vols (London, 1925).
Spufford, M., 'The Limitations of the Probate Inventory', in J. Chartres and D. Hey (eds), *English Rural Society, 1500–1800. Essays in Honour of Joan Thirsk* (Cambridge, 1990), 139–74.
Srinivasan, Amia, 'Under Rhodes', *London Review of Books*, 38:7 (2016) 32.
Stewart, Susan, *On Longing: Narrative of the Miniature, the Gigantic, the Souvenir, the Collection* (Durham and London, 1993).
Stillman, D., 'Robert Adam and Piranesi', in D. Fraser, H. Hibbard and M. J. Lewine (eds), *Essays in the History of Architecture Presented to Rudolf Wittkower* (London, 1978), 65–80.
Stobart, Jon and Andrew Hann (eds), *The Country House: Material Culture and Consumption* (London, 2015).
Stobart, Jon and Mark Rothery, *Consumption and the Country House* (Oxford, 2016).
Stobart, Jon, *Sugar and Spice: Grocers and Groceries in Provincial England, 1650–1830* (Oxford, 2013).
Stoler, Ann Laura, *Along the Archival Grain: Epistemic Anxieties and Colonial Common Sense* (Princeton, 2009).
Stone, Lawrence, and Jeanne Stone, 'Country Houses and Their Owners in Hertfordshire, 1540–1879', in William O. Aydelotte (ed.), *The Dimensions of Quantitative Research in History* (Oxford, 1972), 56–123.
Stone, Lawrence and Jeanne C. Fawtier Stone, *An Open Elite? England 1540–1880* (Oxford and New York, 1986).
Strong, Roy, Marcus Binney and John Harris (eds), *The Destruction of the Country House 1875–1975* (London, 1974).
Stronge, Susan, *Tipu's Tigers* (London, 2009).
Styles, John, 'Indian Cottons and European Fashion, 1400–1800', in Glenn Adamson, Giorgio Riello, and Sarah. Teaseley (eds), *Global Design History* (London, 2011), 37–46.
Sugden, A. V., *A History of English Wallpaper 1509–1914* (London, 1914).
Suleri, Sara, *The Rhetoric of English India* (Chicago, 1992).
Sutherland, Lucy, *A London Merchant: 1695–1774* (Oxford, 1962).
Sutton, Denys (ed.), *Treasures from Woburn Abbey from the Collection of the Duke of Bedford* (1965).
Sutton, Jean, *Lords of the East: the East India Company and its Ships* (London, 1981).
Sweet, Rosemary, *Cities and the Grand Tour: The British in Italy, c.1690–1820* (Cambridge, 2012).
Swenson, Astrid and Peter Mandler (eds), *From Plunder to Preservation: Britain and the Heritage of Empire, c.1800–1940* (Oxford, 2013).
Sykes, John, 'The Indian Seal of Sir Francis Sykes', *East India Company at Home* (February 2013), 1–17. [http://blogs.ucl.ac.uk/eicah/files/2013/02/THE-INDIAN-SEAL-Final-PDF-19.08.14.pdf].
Tadmor, Naomi, *Family and Friends in Eighteenth-century England: Household, Kinship, and Patronage* (Cambridge, 2001).
Tasker, George, *Ilford Past and Present* (Ilford, 1901).
Tayler, A. and H. Tayler, *The Book of the Duffs*, 2 vols (Edinburgh, 1914).
Taylor, Mark and Mark Garcia, 'Relentless Patterns: the Immersive Interior', *Architectural Design*, 79:6 (2009), 42–7.
Teltscher, Kate, 'The Sentimental Ambassador: The Letters of George Bogel from Bengal, Bhutan and Tibet, 1770–1781', in Rebecca Earle (ed.), *Epistolary Selves: Letters and Letter-Writers, 1600–1945* (Aldershot, 1999), 79–94.Thomas, Imogen, *Haileybury 1805–1987* (Hertford, 1987).
Thomas, Peter D. G., 'The rise of Plas Newydd', *Welsh History Review*, 16:2 (1992), 160–76.
Thomson, Gladys Scott, *The Russells in Bloomsbury 1669–1771* (London, 1940).

Thorne, R. (ed.), 'Benn Walsh, John (1759–1825)', *The History of Parliament: The House of Commons 1790–1820* (London, 1986). [http://www.historyofparliamentonline.org/volume/1790–1820/member/benn-walsh-john-1759–1825, accessed 2 February 2017].

Thorne, R. (ed.), 'Farmer, Samuel (1748–1839)', *The History of Parliament: The House of Commons 1790–1820* (London, 1986). [http://www.historyofparliamentonline.org/volume/1790–1820/member/farmer-samuel-1748–1839, accessed 2 February 2017].

Thorne, R. (ed.), 'Gaussen, Samuel Robert (1759–1812)', *The History of Parliament: The House of Commons 1790–1820* (London, 1986). [http://www.historyofparliamentonline.org/volume/1790–1820/member/gaussen-samuel-robert-1759–1812, accessed 2 February 2017].

Thorne, R. (ed.), 'Hunter, John (?1724–1802)', *The History of Parliament: The House of Commons 1790–1820* (London, 1986). [http://www.historyofparliamentonline.org/volume/1754–1790/member/hunter-john-1724–1802, accessed 2 February 2017].

Thorne, R. (ed.), 'Huskisson, William (1770–1830)', *The History of Parliament: The House of Commons 1790–1820* (London, 1986). [http://www.historyofparliamentonline.org/volume/1820–1832/member/huskisson-william-1770–1830, accessed 30 March 2014].

Thorne, R. (ed.), 'Paget, Henry William (1768–1854)', *The History of Parliament: The House of Commons 1790–1820* (London, 1986). [http://www.historyofparliamentonline.org/volume/1690–1715/member/paget-hon-henry-1663–1743, accessed 4 May 2013].

Tipping, Avray, 'In English Homes: The Internal Character, Furniture & Adornments of Some of the Most Notable Houses of England', *Country Life*, 2 (1908).

Tori, Michelguglielmo, 'Trapped inside the Colonial Order: The Hindu Bankers of Surat and Their Business World during the Second Half of the Eighteenth Century', *Modern Asian Studies*, 25:2 (1991), 367–401.

Trentmann, Frank, 'Materiality in the Future of History: Things, Practices, and Politics', *Journal of British Studies*, 48:2 (2009), 283–307.

Tritton, Alan, *When the Tiger Fought the Thistle: The Tragedy of Colonel William Baillie of the Madras Army* (London, 2013).

Tyack, Geoffrey, 'The Freemans of Fawley and Their Buildings', *Records of Buckinghamshire* 24 (1982), 130–43.

Tyack, Geoffrey, Simon Bradley and Nikolaus Pevsner, *The Buildings of England: Berkshire* (London and New Haven, 2010).

Ukers, William Harrison, *All about Tea* (London, 1935).

Ulrich, Laurel Thatcher, 'Hannah Barnard's Cupboard: Female Property and Identity in Eighteenth-century New England', in Ronald Hoffman, Mechal Sobel and Fredrika J. Teute, *Through a Glass Darkly: Reflections on Personal Identity in Early America* (Chapel Hill and London, 1997), 238–73.

Ulrich, Laurel Thatcher, *The Age of Homespun: Objects and Stories in the Creation of An American Myth* (New York, 2002).

Vanneste, Tiil, *Global Trade and Commercial Networks: Eighteenth-century Diamond Merchants* (London, 2011).

Vibert, Elizabeth, 'Writing "Home": Sibling Intimacy and Mobility in a Scottish Colonial Memoir', in Tony Ballantyne and Antoinette Burton (eds), *Moving Subjects: Gender, Mobility and Intimacy in an Age of Global Empire* (Urbana and Chicago, 2009), 67–88.

Vickery, Amanda, *The Gentleman's Daughter: Women's Lives in Georgian England* (New Haven and London, 2003).

Vickery, Amanda, *Behind Closed Doors: At Home in Georgian England* (New Haven and London, 2009).

Vickery, Amanda, 'His and Hers: Gender, Consumption and Household Accounting in Eighteenth-Century England', *Past and Present*, 2006:1 (2006), 12–38.

Visram, Rozina, *Ayahs, Lascars and Princes: Indians in Britain 1700–1947* (London, 1986).

von Brescius, Meike, 'The Principal-agent Problem Revisited: Supercargoes and Commanders of the China Trade' [http://studylib.net/doc/13209578/the-principal-agent-problem-revisited—supercargoes, accessed 2 September 2016].

von Brescius, Meike, 'Worlds Apart? Merchants, Mariners and the Organisation of the Private Trade in Chinese Export Wares in Eighteenth-Century Europe', in Maxine Berg, Felicia Gottmann, Hanna Hodacs and Chris Nierstrasz (eds), *Goods from the East: 1600–1800 Trading Eurasia* (Basingstoke, 2015), 168–82.

von Tunzelmann, Alex, 'Rhodes Must Fall? A Question of When Not If', *History Today*, 66: 3 (2016), 6–7.

Wainwright, Clive, *The Romantic Interior, The British Collector at Home 1750–1850* (New Haven and London, 1989).
Walker, David, and Matthew Woodworth, *Aberdeenshire: North and Moray* (New Haven, 2015).
Wall, Cynthia, 'The English Auction: Narratives of Dismantlings', *Eighteenth-Century Studies*, 31:1 (1997), 1–25.
Walsh, Claire, 'Shop Design and the Display of Goods', *Journal of Design History*, 8:2 (1995), 157–76.
Ward, Stuart, 'Echoes of Empire', *History Workshop Journal*, 62:1 (2006), 264–78.
Waterson, Merlin, *A Noble Thing: the National Trust and Its Benefactors* (London, 2011).
Webb, Marianne, *Lacquer: Technology and Conservation: A Comprehensive Guide to the Technology and Conservation of Asian and European Lacquer* (Boston, 2000).
Webber, Pauline, 'Chinese Wallpapers in the British Galleries', *V&A Conservation Journal*, 39 (2001).
Wheeler, Stephen, 'Russell, Sir Henry, first baronet (1751–1836)', rev. Ainslie T. Embree, *Oxford Dictionary of National Biography* (Oxford, 2004). [http://www.oxforddnb.com/view/article/24311, accessed 30 September 2015].
Williams, Clive, *The Nabobs of Berkshire* (Purley on Thames, 2010).
Wilson, Richard and Alan Mackley, *Creating Paradise: The Building of the English Country House, 1660–1880* (London and New York, 2000).
Wilton-Ely, John, 'Style and Serendipidy: Adam, Walpole and Strawberry Hill', *The British Art Journal*, 11:3 (2011), 3–14.
Winterbottom, Philip, 'Child, Sir Francis, the Elder (1641/2–1713)', *Oxford Dictionary of National Biography* (Oxford, 2004). [http://www.oxforddnb.com/view/article/5286, accessed 22 July 2013].
Woodfield, Ian, 'The "Hindostannie Air": English Attempts to Understand Indian Music in the Late Eighteenth Century', *Journal of the Royal Musical Association*, 119:2 (1994), 189–211.
Worsley, Giles, *England's Lost Houses: From the Archives of Country Life* (London, 2002).
Wulf, Andrea, *The Brother Gardeners: Botany, Empire and the Birth of an Obsession* (London, 2008).
Yallop, Jacqueline, *Magpies, Squirrels and Thieves: How the Victorians Collected the World* (London, 2011).
Yazdani, Zubaida, *Hyderabad during the Residency of Henry Russell, 1811–1820: A Case Study in the Subsidiary Alliance System* (Oxford, 1976).

Unpublished Theses

Parker, J. G., 'The Directors of the East India Company, 1754–1790' (PhD thesis, University of Edinburgh, 1977).
von Brescius, Meike, 'Supercargoes and the English East India Company in the China Trade 1700–1760' (PhD thesis, University of Warwick, 2015).

Websites

Allyson McDermott: [http://www.allysonmcdermott.com/chinoiserie/].
Art Fund: Seton Ring by French: [https://www.artfund.org/supporting-museums/art-weve-helped-buy/artwork/1510/seton-ring-french].
Bangor Civic Society: [http://www.bangorcivicsociety.org.uk/].
Berkshire Record Office: New Landscapes—Enclosure in Berkshire: [http://www.berkshireenclosure.org.uk/find_via_parish_details.asp?parish=Swallowfield].
The British Library: Hugh Seton Portrait: [https://artuk.org/discover/artworks/hugh- seton-191194]
British Museum: Casket: [http://www.britishmuseum.org/research/search_the_collection_database/search_object_details.aspx?objectid=249650&partid=1&searchText=1904%2c1006.1.a&fromADBC=ad&toADBC=ad&numpages=10&orig=%2fresearch%2fsearch_the_collection_database.aspx&currentPage=1, accessed 10 May 2013].

British Museum: History of the Asian Collection: [https://www.britishmuseum.org/about_us/departments/asia/history_of_the_collection.aspx, accessed 11 August 2016].
Brookmans Park Newsletter: History: [http://www.brookmans.com/history/].
Cambridge Alumni Database: [http://venn.lib.cam.ac.uk/Documents/acad/search.html].
The Centre for the Study of the Legacies of British Slave-ownership: [http://www.ucl.ac.uk/lbs/].
Christie's: Anglo Indian Ivory Inlaid Teak Ebony and Tortoiseshell Desk: [http://www.christies.com/lotfinder/furniture-lighting/an-anglo-indian-ivory-inlaid-teak-ebony-and-tortoiseshell-5461627-details.aspx].
Culture and Communication: Dead Media Archive: [http://cultureandcommunication.org/deadmedia/index.php/Daguerre%27s_Diorama, accessed 12 October 2017.].
de Bruijn, Emile, NT Treasure Hunt: Lacquer Lost and Found: [https://nttreasurehunt.wordpress.com/category/osterley-park/page/2/].
FIBIS Database: [http://search.fibis.org/frontis/bin/].
Find a Grave: Catherine Mary Fraser: [http://www.findagrave.com/cgi-bin/fg.cgi?page=pv&GRid=71385081&PIpi=43951669, accessed 15 April 2013].
Fitzwilliam Museum, Cambridge: Vizagapatam Desk: [http://www.fitzmuseum.cam.ac.uk/collections/furniture/vizagapatamdesk].
Geographicus: 1840 Black Map of India: [http://www.geographicus.com/P/AntiqueMap/India-black-1840].
Guernsey Museums: [http://www.museums.gov.gg/].
Hampstead Heath: [http://www.hampsteadheath.net].
Hampstead Heath: Cannon Hall: [http://www.hampsteadheath.net/cannon-hall.html, accessed 26 March 2014].
History of Parliament Online: [http://www.historyofparliamentonline.org].
London Lives: Fire Insurance Policy Registers, 1777- 1786: [https://www.londonlives.org/browse.jsp?id=persName7fire_1775_1780_404_40464&div=fire_1775_1780_404_40464#highlight].
Measuring Worth: Purchasing Power of British Pounds from 1270 to Present: [https://www.measuringworth.com/ppoweruk/].
National Army Museum: Attar Dan: [http://www.nam.ac.uk/online-collection/detail.php?acc=1959–04–278–1, accessed 19 August 2016].
Priaulx Library: [http://www.priaulxlibrary.co.uk/].
Queen Square Centre for Neuromuscular Diseases: Legacies of British Slave-ownership Report, 'Hertfordshire in the Compensation Notes': [http://www.cnmd.ac.uk/lbs/project/hertfordshirenotes].
Royal Collection: Two Armchairs: [http://www.royalcollection.org.uk/eGallery/object.asp?category=279&object=11197_1&row=70&detail=about].
Scotland's Places: Touch House: [http://www.scotlandsplaces.gov.uk/record/rcahms/46238/touch-house/rcahms?item=786393].
The Seton Family: Hugh Seton Baron of Touch Profile: [http://www2.thesetonfamily.com:8080/history/Profiles/Hugh_Seton_Baron_of_Touch_and_Tullibody.htm].
Sunley Heritage: [http://www.sunleyheritage.co.uk/].
Touch Estate: [http://www.touchestate.co.uk/the-house/].
Twitter: Portrait of Archibald Seton: [https://twitter.com/dalrymplewill/status/729757187778744320].
University College London: [http://www.ucl.ac.uk/].
University College London Blog: Basildon Park Recordings [http://blogs.ucl.ac.uk/eicah/basildon-park-recordings/].
University College London Blog: East India Company at Home, 1757–1857: [http://blogs.ucl.ac.uk/eicah/case-studies-2/].
V&A Collection: Tippoos Tiger Mechanical Organ: [http://collections.vam.ac.uk/item/O61949/tippoos-tiger-mechanical-organ-unknown].
V&A: Textile Influences on Wallpaper: [http://www.vam.ac.uk/content/articles/t/textile-influences-on-wallpaper/].
The Wallace Collection: Treasure of the Month, 2006: [http://www.wallacecollection.org/whatson/treasure/10, accessed 22 August 2016].
Woolley and Wallis, Salisbury Salerooms: [http://www.woolleyandwallis.co.uk].

Index

Page numbers in italics are figures; with 't' are tables.

Abbotsford (Roxburgh) 63–5
Abergavenny (ship) 242–3
Adam, Robert 1, 22, 58, 89, 90, 99, 101, 103
Amherst family 163
Jeffrey, 1st Baron Amherst 163
Sarah Elizabeth 163–5, 167–9
William Pitt, 1st Earl Amherst of Arracan 62, 163, 165, 167
Archer, Frances Susanna *see* Parkes, Fanny
armorial porcelain 6, 15, 50, 51, 109, 113–17, *114*, 121
Basildon Park 119–27, 122–3, *125*
Osterley House 90, 103–4, *104*, 107
Shugborough Estate 128, *129*
Austen, Jane 293, 362
Avebury Manor (Wilts) 64, 66

Balls Park (Herts) 74–5, 256
banians 352, 414, 417–20
see also Nandy, Krishna Kanta (Cantoo Baboo)
bankruptcy 257, 367–8, 372
Banks, Sir Joseph 50, 57
Basildon Park (Berks) 84–6, *85*, 352–3, 423
armorial service 119–27, 122–3, *125*
Bayly family 305–8
Belton House (Lincs) *46*, 50
Benfield, Paul 8, 257
Benn, John (later Benn Walsh) 182–3
Benn Walsh family 172
John, 1st Baron Ormathwaite (1798–1881) 175–176, 178, 180, 186–9
John (1759–1847) 182–6
Margaret (1758–1836) 10, 175–6, 180–90, 200
Benyon family
Richard (1698–1774) 76, 172, 193, 194, 195–6, 238
Richard (1770–1854) (later Benyon Powlett Wright) (later
Benyon de Beauvoir) 173, 201–3, 203
Richard the Younger (1746–97) 197, 198, 201
Betty (nurse to Peggy Hall) 330–2
Bishopsgate House (Anglesey) 299, 301–2, *301*, 305, 311, 315, 316
Blair Castle (Perthshire) 40, 63
Blickling (Norfolk) 49–50
Bonham, Pinson 174, 237–8
Bosanquet family 258, 264–5, 267
Brasted Place (Kent) 58
Brighton Pavilion 59–60
Brookmans Manor (Herts) 251, 264, 265, 270
Broughton Castle (Oxon) 54
Bulkeley family 301–2, 307–8

cabinets of curiosities 143–52, 234
Cameron, Donald 174, 232, 236–7, 239
Cantoo Baboo/Cantu Babu *see* Nandy, Krishna Kanta
Capper, Colonel Francis 33
Casamajors family 185, 264, 266, 267, 269
casket of Tipu Sultan 21–2, 25–38, *27*
Chambers, Sir William 316
Designs for Chinese Buildings 313–14, *314*
Chateau Smith (Le Château de l'Anglais) 287–8, *289*
Child family 22, 88–9, 107
businesses of 90–6
Francis III 96, 98
Osterley Park 7, 54, 66, 99–106, *99*, 101–2, 104–5
Osterley ships 97–8, 97t
Sir Francis the Elder (1642–1713) 90–4, 91t, *92*, 103, 104, 107
Sir Francis the Younger, II (1684–1740) 91t, 95, 100
Sir Robert 91t, 94–5, 103
'Chinese' style 14, 106, 308–15, *309*, *311*, 313–14
staircases 274, 298–317, 300–1, *303*
Chinnery, George 216, 225–6, 230
chintzes 40, 48, 54, 75, 214, 222
Chippendale, Thomas 60, 316
Gentleman and Cabinet Maker's Director, The 71, 102, 274, 311–12, *311*, *313*
Churchill, Sarah, Duchess of Marlborough 154
Clive, Henrietta, Countess of Powis 72, 74
Clive, Margaret, Lady Clive of Plassey 10–11, 36, 172, 181–2, 193, 199–201, *199*
Clive, Robert, Baron 96, 153, 172, 178, 416
coats of arms 124–6
Cossimbazar Raj 412, *412*
Sykes 124, 412, *413*, *416*
see also armorial porcelain
Cockerell, Charles 8, 86, 259
Cockerell, Samuel Pepys 86
Coke, Lady Mary 50–1
collecting 133–4, 140, 143–52

colonialism 1–2, 12, 37, 253
  see also slavery
connections, maintaining 74, 163–4, 166, 176–7, 230, 326–9, 327–8, 355–6
  see also gifts
Constable, John 203
correspondence, maintaining connections 163, 176–7, 230, 327, 355–6, 369
Cossimbazar Raj 412, *412*, 420–3
Coutts, Thomas 60, 62, 65, 66
Crace, John and Frederick 57, 59
Croome Court (Worcs) 51

Daguerre, Louis 141–2
Dalrymple, William 157, 225, 268
Daylesford House (Glos) 70, 80–4
Defoe, Daniel, *Secret History of the White Stuff, The* 95
Delft earthenware 94, 106–7
Delgaty Home Farm 336, *339*
dioramas 140–3
disease 293, 323, 371
  malaria 148, 370, 371, 373
Drummond, James, 8th Viscount Strathallan 52–3
Du Halde, Jean-Baptiste, *General History of China, The* 309
Duccarel, Gerard Gustavus 119
Duff, General Patrick 10, 274–5, 333–50, *333*, 335–6
Dunglass (East Lothian) 63, 331–2

Eden, Fanny 135–6
Ellis, John 299, 307
Endsleigh Cottage (Devon) 56–7
Englefield family 194
Englefield House (Berks) 8, 10, 172, 191–204, *192*
'English Hindoostan' 171, 193, 203–4
Erdigg (Wrexham) *44*, *47*, 49, 53–4
estates, ownership of 7

failure 9
  bankruptcy 257, 367–8, 372
  taken prisoner 324–5, 332, 363, 368, 377, 392
famille rose 59, 123–4
Farmer family 360–7, *361*, *376*
  acquisition of fortune 379–84
  correspondence 355–60, 363–4
  Margaret (mother of William and Sam) 358, 359, 360, 362–3, 364, 365–7, 375–6, 385
  Sam 11, 351–2, 360–71, 378, 383, 384, 385, 386
  William Gamul 9, 11, 351–2, 360–7, 371–9, 385–8
Felbrigg (Norfolk) 42, *43*, 49
Fletcher, Henry 174, 238, 239
Fowke, Francis 182, 183, 190
Fraser family 22, 33–6, *35*, 37, 38
  Colonel Henry 25, 32, *35*
  General Hastings 25, 31, 33–4, 34, *35*, 38
  James Stuart 34, *35*, 36
Fraser, William 161–2, 282–3
Freeman family 260
furniture *see* ivory, furniture

Gaussen family 264–6, 267
gender
  and porcelain 117–19, 124, 126–7, 129
  and refashioning of houses 154–5
  and space 127
Gidea Hall (Greater London) 196, 238
gifts
  Farmer family 363
  flora and fauna 235
  ivory furniture 87
  and maintaining connections 166
  preserved lemons 350
  silver-gily presentation vase 226–7
  wallpaper 57–65
Gobions (Gubbins) (Herts) 251, 260–3, 269–70
Government House (now Raj Bhavan, Kolkata) 1–2
'Grand Moving Diorama of Hindostan' 140–3, 152
Great Pagoda (Kew) 315
Gresham, Sir Thomas 88–9

Haider Ali 25, 29, 30, 31, 34, 36, 38
Halfpenny, William 316
  Rural Architecture in the Chinese Taste 312–13, *314*
Hall, Alexander 9, 11, 275, 318–32
Hall, Peggy (daughter of Alexander Hall) 275, 329–31
Hampden House (Bucks) 50
Harewood House (near Leeds) 48, 53
Harrison, Edward 70, 74–5, 76, 256
Harrison, Etheldreda (Audrey) 75–6
Harthill Castle (Aberdeenshire) 336, *337*
Hastings, Marian 78, 79–80
Hastings, Warren 70, 78–84, *79*, 153, 257, 415, 419
Hay, D.R., *Laws of Harmonious Colouring adapted to Interior Decoration* 64
Heath family 26, 32, 33, 36
Heppelwhite, George, *Cabinet Maker and Upholsterer's Guide, The* 71
Hertfordshire 251–71, *255*
Holland, Henry 56, 57
Holmes, Thomas (later Holmes-Hunter) 262–3
Howard, Edward, 9th Duke of Norfolk 54
Hunter, Ann 263, 268–9, *268*, 270
Hunter, John 260–3, *261*, 267, *268*, 269–70

Ickworth (Norfolk) 40, *48*, 49
identity
  national/imperial 5, 19, 69, 107, 429
  and objects 14, 17, 27, 89–90, 109–11
  see also porcelain; refashioning houses; Smith, Colonel Robert
Iliffe, Edward, 1st Baron Iliffe 85
India paper *see* wallpaper, Chinese
Indian families, of EIC men 368
Ingram, Frances, Lady Irwin 59
Isabella, Marchioness of Hertford 59
ivory (furniture) 22, 68–71
  and dispossession 78–84
  production 71–4
  purchase 74–8
  recirculation of 84–6, 87

japanning techniques 74

Keen, Richard *244*, 245
Khair un-Nissa 225–6
Kirkpatrick, James Achilles 214–15, 225–6
Kleinwort, Sir Cyril and Lady 84, 86

lacquerware 100–3, 101–2
see also japanning
Lancaster, Nancy 66
Lascelles family 53, 115
Legacies of British Slave-ownership project 253, 255–6
Lockhart, John Gibson, *Memoirs of the Life of Sir Walter Scott* 65
Lowe, Robert, Viscount Sherbrooke 32–3

Macartney, George 60, 61–2, 66
Macaulay, Thomas 368–9, 370
Marshall, William, *Rural Economy of Yorkshire* 61
Melvill family 352, 389–411, 390–1, 393–4, 396–7, *399*, 401–2
Elizabeth (wife of Philip) 392, 393–4, 395
Henry (1798–1871) 395, *397*, 402–3, *402*
Henry II (1832–1908) 405, 407
Hester (wife of James Cosmo) *399*, 400
James Cosmo (1792–1861) 395, *396*, 398, *399*, 400–1, 404
James Cosmo II (1821–80) 405–6, 410
Maxwell 405, 407
Peter 395, *397*, 404
Philip (1760–1811) 12, 389–95
Philip II (1796–1882) 395, *396*, 401–2, 410
Philip III (1817–54) 405
Philip Sandys 406–7
Richard Gwatkin 405, 407–9
Michie, John 263–4, 267
Mill, John Stuart 400
Minto, Lord (Elliot-Murray-Kynynmound, Gilbert, 1st Earl of Minto) 62, 221, 266
mixed-race children 12, 20, 225–6, 229–30, 230, 275, 430
and Alexander Hall 329–31
and Patrick Duff 341–2
Moffat, Andrew 174, 238, 239
Moffats House (Herts) 251, 252, 263, 264, 266, 269, 270
Monro family 77–8
Montreal Park (Kent) 154, 163–9, 165–8
Morrison family 84–6
Mottet, Clotilde (wife of 2nd Baronet Russell) 129, 220, 222, 223
Mount Capper (Cuddalore) 25, 33–4
Murshidabad (India) 71–2, 80, 83, 84

nabobs 7–8, 228, 254, 262, 367
Nandy, Krishna Kanta (Cantoo Baboo) 15–16, 352–3, 418–21, *420*, 426, 428
see also Cossimbazar Raj
Nandy, Maharajkumar Somendra (Dr S. C. Nandy) 422, 423, 426, 426–7
native, going 283, 408
Newby Hall (N Yorkshire) 48
newspapers 327–8
Niemann, Edmund J. 191
Nieuhof, Johan, *Embassy* 308, *309*
Nonsuch Park (Surrey) 11, 356–7, *357*, 384, 385
North Mymms parish (Herts) 174, 259–71, *259*

Oakley House (Beds) 56
Ogilvie, James 241–2
Osterley Park and House (Hounslow) 7, 99–106, *99*, 101–2, 104–5
Chinese wallpaper 54, 66
Osterley ships 97–8, 97t

Paget family 307, 316, 307, 316
Palace of the Eleven Courtyards (Peking) 60–1
Parkes, Charles Crawford 135–7, *138*, 152
Parkes, Fanny 131–7, *138*
collections *132*, 143–52, *149*
'Grand Moving Diorama of Hindostan' 140–3
Wanderings of a Pilgrim 131, *132*, 133–4, 137–40, *139*, 144–5, *147*, 150–1
Pattle, Thomas, Sr. 122
Penrhyn Castle (Gwynedd) 40, 51
Pitt, Thomas 'Diamond' 173, 194, 206, 209–10
Plas Newydd (Anglesey) 305–6, 309–10, 316
Pollilur, Battle of 391–2, *391*, 411
porcelain 6, 15, 103, 107
from shipwreck *Valentine 246*
Osterley Park 103–4, *104*
Valentines 233, *234*
and women 117–19
see also Delft earthenware
portraits 216
Benyon family 195
of Patrick Duff's children 342, 349
Robert Smith *279*
Russell family 216, 218, 223–6, 230
Postlethwayt, Malachy 50
Universal Dictionary of Trade and Commerce 48
Potterells (Herts) 251, 266–7, 269, 270
Powis Castle (Powys) 28, 49, *73*
prisoner/hostage
taken 324–5, 332, 363, 368, 377, 392
see also slavery

race 254, 428
see also mixed-race children; slavery
Raymond, Sir Charles, 1st Baronet (1713–88) 174, 232–4, 235–6, 240–1, 243, 244, 249–50
armorial porcelain *114*, *234*
Redcliffe Towers (Devon) 12, 277, *277*, 287, 290–6, 291–5, *297*
Rees, Lowri Ann 299
refashioning houses 153–5
regionality, and taste 13–14
rented stately homes 11, 187, 192, 197–8, 198, 201
and the Russell family 212, 217–18
Repton, Humphrey 57
Russell family 228–9
Anne Barbara Whitworth (wife of 1st Baronet) (1764–1814) 10, 207, 211, 212, 217–18, 230

Charles (1786–1856) 173, 207, 211, 213–17, 219, 220, 229
Constance Charlotte Elisa, Lady Russell 210
Swallowfield and its Owners 194, 205–6, 208
in Hyderabad 215–17, 221, 226–8, 230
in India 210–17
Sir Henry, 1st Baronet (1751–1836) 195, 207, 208, 211–13, 217, 218–19, 223, 224
Sir Henry, 2nd Baronet (1783–1852) 173, 207, 208, 212, 213–17, 219–20, 221, *221*, 222, 223–5, 226–8, 229, 266
Russell family (Dukes of Bedford) 54–7

Saltram (Devon) *45*
Sambrooke family 260
Sandwich, John Montagu, 4th Earl of 366
scent holders 29, 36
Scots
and the EIC 321–2, 326–7, 332
see also Melvill family
Scott family
Captain Hugh 64
Sir Walter (1771–1832) 63–5
Walter (1801–47) 65
Scott, Walter (1807–76) 65
Scott, Walter, laird of Raeburn 64
seals 15–16, 413–14, *414*, 428
Seringapatam, battle of 25–6, 30–3, 37–8, 343–4
Seton family 155–6
Archibald 11, 156–63
Hugh 156, 157–8, 162
Sezincote (Glos) 8, 84, 86, 259
ships 74, 96, 97–8, 97t, 231, 239–50, *240*, 242–50, 244–9
shopping 120–1
Shugborough Estate (Staffs) 128, *129*
silk 105–6, *105*
slavery 2, 9, 115, 192, 253, 431
Betty (nurse to Peggy Hall) 330–2
and Sam Farmer 383
and Sumatra 318, 320, 323
and Swallowfield 206–7, 208
Smith, Colonel Robert 12, 273–4, 277–8, *279*
early life 278–9
European projects 286–9, *286*, *289*
in India 280–6, 280–3, *285*
Redcliffe Towers (Devon) 12, 277, *277*, 287, 290–6, 291–5, *297*
Song Yingxing, *Tiangongkaiwu* 61
South Sea Company 55, 95
staircases, 'Chinese' style 274, 298–311, 300–1, *303*
status 10, 27, 111
and Fanny Parkes 134, 139, 152
and furniture 69, 87, 213
and gifts 57–8, 65
and houses 153, 154, 164, 172, 190, 256
and porcelain 115, 118, 127, 130
Staunton, George 60–1
Stewart, Henry (1759–1836) 158
Strathallan Castle, Chinese wallpaper 53
Stuart, James 'Athenian' 180
Sulivan, Laurence 96, 257, 258, 260, 372
Sumatra 318–32
supercargoes 114–15, 121, 315
Surman, Robert 232, 235
Sutton Park (Beds) 220–1
Swallowfield Park (Berks) 10, 173, 194, 205–30, *206*
renovations 222–5
Sykes family 423–5
coat of arms 124, 412, *413*, *416*
Elizabeth 172–3, 203
Sir Francis, 1st Baronet 15–16, 84, 116, *116*, 119–20, 124, 125–6, 352–3, 413–20, 414–15, 423, *424*
Sir Francis, 3rd Baronet 85
Sir Francis, 9th Baronet 425–6, 425–6

Tan-yr-Allt (Caernarvonshire) 299–301, *300*, 302, 305, 310, 311, 312, 315, 316
Tandridge Court (Surrey) 400, *401*
tea wares 126–7
Temple Newsam (Leeds) 59
textiles 77, 105–6
at Osterley Park 104–5, *105*
at Swallowfield 222
calico 75, 104–5, 244
chintzes 40, 48, 54, 75, 214, 222, 244
and Fanny Parkes 146
silk 105–6, *105*, 244
Thellusson, Charles 9
Thellusson, George Woodford 257
tiger motif 29–30
Tipu Sultan 21, 25, 26, 29–33, 31, 36, 343, 379, 391
Touch House (Stirlingshire) 11, 154, 155–63, 169
Townshend family
August 75–6
Charles, 3rd Viscount Townshend 75–6
Roger 76
trade 11–13, 97, 254, *417*
Chinese wallpaper 41–2, 51–7, 60
and ivory 69
private 51–7, *247*, 285, 372–3, 417, 419
slave 2, 9, 115, 192
and Sumatra 324
and textiles 104–5
Tradescant, John and John 143
Trefeilir (Anglesey) 299, 302–4, *303*, 305, 311, 315, 316
Turner, Sir Edward and Elizabeth 54
Turton, Dr John 58
Twistleton, Frederick, 16th Lord Saye and Sele 54
tykhanas 283–4
Tyntesfield (Somerset) *72*

Valentines Mansion (London) 174, 231–50, *231*, *235*
vase, silver-gilt presentation 226–7
veneer (ivory) 68, 71, 72–3, *73*, 77, 83, 86
Villa Mills (Rome) 286–7, *286*
Vizagapatam (India) 72, *72*, *73*, 76, 77, 78

Wales, and 'Chinese' style staircases 273
wallpaper 41
Chinese 22, 39–41, *43*, *48*
characteristics 47–50
as gifts 57–65

private trade in 51–7
types 44–7, *44–7*
Walpole, Horace 88, 89, 269
Walsh family 172
John (1726–95) 177–80, 181, 182, 200
Warfield Park (Berks) 10, 172, 175, 177–90, *179*
Webber, William 174, 237, 238–9, 239
Whittington Hall (Lancs) 9
Williams, John 174, 237, 239
Windham, William II *43*
Windsor, Lady Maria 167–8
'withdrawing' 127
wives/women, Company 10
Woburn Abbey (Beds) 50, 55–7
women, and porcelain 117–19, 126–7, 129
Woodhall Park (Herts) 8, 257
Wordsworth, William 243
Wrighte family
Nathaniel 172, 197–8, 199–200, 201
Powlett (d.1741) 194
Powlett, the Younger 194, 196–7
Wyatt, James, Doddington (Glos) 167

Yale, Elihu 3
Yorke, Philip and Elizabeth 53–4

Lightning Source UK Ltd.
Milton Keynes UK
UKHW051325200121
377385UK00017B/266

9 781787 350298